Non-Western responses to terrorism

MANCHESTER 1824
Manchester University Press

NEW DIRECTIONS IN TERRORISM STUDIES

A series edited by

Max Taylor
Professor in International Relations (retired), University of St Andrews, Scotland, where he was formerly Director of the Centre for the Study of Terrorism and Political Violence

P. M. Currie
Senior Visiting Fellow at the School of International Relations at the University of St Andrews, Scotland

John Horgan
Distinguished University Professor, Department of Psychology, Georgia State University, USA

New Directions in Terrorism Studies aims to introduce new and innovative approaches to understanding terrorism and the terrorist. It does this by bringing forward innovative ideas and concepts to assist the practitioner, analyst and academic to better understand and respond to the threat of terrorism, challenging existing assumptions and moving the debate forward into new areas. The approach is characterized by an emphasis on intellectual quality and rigor, interdisciplinary perspectives, and a drawing together of theory and practice. The key qualities of the series are contemporary relevance, accessibility and innovation.

Previously published

The role of terrorism in twenty-first-century warfare
Susanne Martin and Leonard Weinberg

Non-Western responses to terrorism

Edited by MICHAEL J. BOYLE

Manchester University Press

Published by Manchester University Press
Altrincham Street, Manchester M1 7JA

www.manchesteruniversitypress.co.uk

British Library Cataloguing-in-Publication Data
A catalogue record for this book is available from the British Library

ISBN 978 1 5261 0581 3 hardback

ISBN 978 1 5261 0582 0 paperback

First published 2019

Typeset
by Toppan Best-set Premedia Limited
Printed in Great Britain
by TJ International Ltd, Padstow

Contents

Figures

Tables

Notes on contributors

Ridzuan Abdul Aziz is a superintendent in the Royal Malaysia Police. He graduated from the Royal Military Defence College, and obtained his master's in defence studies from the Universiti Kebangsaan Malaysia. As a senior police officer, he has years of experience in managing the counterterrorism desk in the force. He has been tasked to monitor movements of various foreign-based terrorist groups in the country.

Kamarulnizam Abdullah is professor in national security at the Department of International Affairs, School of International Studies-COLGIS, Universiti Utara Malaysia. He obtained his PhD in politics from Lancaster University, United Kingdom; MA in international relations from the Australian National University, Canberra, Australia; and BSc in political science and certificate in international relations from the University of Utah. His main research areas are political violence, religious militancy, and national security issues pertinent to Malaysia and the Southeast Asia region.

Dina Al Raffie is a German-Egyptian PhD candidate on the University of Navarra's Law of Global Society programme, and returning adjunct professor on the George C. Marshall Center's Program on Terrorism and Security Studies. She has held various teaching positions related to the study of terrorism and political violence, as well as international relations with the Middle East and the Maghreb. Her research explores the impact of non-violent radical Islamist narratives on religious identity in Western diaspora contexts, and questions common standards for assessing de-radicalization. She has published on a variety of terrorism-related topics including identity dynamics of radicalization, terrorist leadership, terrorist motivations and countering violent extremism, and was previously research fellow at the Program on Extremism at George Washington University. She is fluent in Arabic, English, and German.

Ali M. Ansari is professor of Iranian history and Founding Director of the Institute for Iranian Studies at the University of St Andrews, a senior associate fellow at the Royal United Services Institute and president of the British Institute for Persian Studies. He is the author of *Iran: A Very Short Introduction* (Oxford University Press, 2014); *The Politics of Nationalism in Modern Iran*

(Cambridge University Press, 2012); *Crisis of Authority: Iran's 2009 Presidential Election* (Chatham House, 2010); *Iran under Ahmadinejad: The Politics of Confrontation*, Adelphi Paper 393 (International Institute for Strategic Studies, 2007); *Confronting Iran: The Failure of US Policy and the Roots of Mistrust* (Hurst, 2006); *Modern Iran since 1921: The Pahlavis and After* (Longman, 2nd edn, 2007); and *Iran, Islam and Democracy: The Politics of Managing Change* (Royal Institute of International Affairs, 2nd edn, 2006).

Chiyuki Aoi is professor of international security at the Graduate School of Public Policy, University of Tokyo. She gained a BA from Sophia University, an MSc from the Massachusetts Institute of Technology, and a PhD from Columbia University. From 2008 to 2009, she was a visiting fellow at the Department of War Studies, King's College London. Her main research interest is the history and theory of counterinsurgency (British and American), the use of force in the era after the Cold War and the transformation of warfare. For five years she held professional positions at the United Nations High Commissioner for Refugees and the United Nations University. Her main publications include *Legitimacy and the Use of Armed Force: Stability Missions in the Post-Cold War Era* (Routledge, 2011); *Asia-Pacific Nations in International Peace Support and Stability Missions* (Palgrave, 2014, as co-editor with Yee-Kuang Heng); *UN Peacekeeping Doctrine towards the Post-Brahimi Era?: Adapting to Stabilization, Protection and New Threats* (Routledge, 2017, as co-editor with Cedric de Coning and John Karlsrud); and 'Japanese strategic communication: Its signifcance as a political tool', *Defence Strategic Communications: The Official Journal of the NATO Strategic Centre of Excellence* 3 (Autumn 2017): 69–98.

Michael J. Boyle is associate professor of political science at La Salle University in Philadelphia and a senior fellow with the Foreign Policy Research Institute. He holds a PhD in international relations from the University of Cambridge and has held fellowships at Harvard, Stanford and the Australian National University. Previously, he was a lecturer in international relations and research fellow of the Centre for the Study of Terrorism and Political Violence at the University of St Andrews. He has published widely on political violence, terrorism, drone warfare and American foreign policy. His previous books include *Violence after War: Explaining Instability in Post-Conflict States* (Johns Hopkins Press, 2014) and the edited volume *Legal and Ethical Implications of Drone Warfare* (Routledge, 2017).

Irene Chan is a senior research analyst with the China Programme in the S. Rajaratnam School of International Studies (RSIS). She received her BA in history from the Nanyang Technological University's National Institute of Education, and her MSc in Asian studies from RSIS. She has given a keynote lecture on China's role in regional cooperative security in tandem with the US Pacific Command China Desk Director at the 2012 Pacific Rim Air Power Symposium in Hokkaido, Japan, jointly organized by the US Pacific Air Force and the Japan Air Self Defense Force. She has also given presentations on political will and energy exploitation in the South China Sea at the National Institute of South China Sea Studies and at Shandong University. She has written commentaries for the *Straits Times* and RSIS. Her research interests are Chinese foreign policy, China–ASEAN (Association of Southeast Asian Nations) and China–US relations, regional maritime security and China's territorial disputes in East Asia.

Muhammad Feyyaz, a soldier turned academic, joined the Pakistan Army in 1980 and, among several other assignments, including overseas as United Nations peacekeeper and command of a brigade in tribal areas of Pakistan, has remained instructor at the army's Command and Staff College, Quetta, National Defence University (NDU), Islamabad, and National School of Public Policy, Lahore. He has also headed the Centre of Excellence for Peacekeeping Studies at NDU. He holds an MPhil in peace and conflict studies (PCS) from NDU and is currently a doctoral candidate at Queen's University, Belfast, in Northern Ireland. He teaches in the School of Governance and Society at the University of Management and Technology in Lahore, and also acts as country coordinator for the Pakistan chapter of the Terrorism Research Initiative. His main areas of interest are PCS and terrorism studies.

Jennifer Giroux currently works with ReD Associates, a management consultancy that works with the top companies in the world. Prior to this, she was a senior researcher with the Risk and Resilience Team at the Center for Security Studies (CSS) at ETH Zürich in Switzerland, where she specialized in research on (societal) resilience, business in conflict zones and critical infrastructure protection. She led a multi-year project that examined the targeting behaviours of non-state actors and conflict in energy-producing and transit regions – becoming a notable expert on energy infrastructure vulnerability and non-technical risk management. She oversaw the development of the Energy Infrastructure Attack Database to analyse global trends in energy infrastructure targeting; managed the *Tracking Energy Attacks* blog; carried out field research in Colombia, Liberia and Nigeria as well as case/site visits to other countries and regions of interest; and managed collaborations with the United States Institute of Peace, the Fund for Peace and the Paul Scherrer Institute. In addition to CSS, she has worked with various other notable organizations such as the United Nations Al-Qaida and Taliban (1267) Sanctions Committee, the Center for Nonproliferation Studies, and the Center for Terrorism and Intelligence Studies.

Yee-Kuang Heng is associate professor of international relations and assistant dean for research at the Lee Kuan Yew School of Public Policy, National University of Singapore. He obtained a BSc and PhD in international relations from the London School of Economics and Political Science, where he studied on a British Government research scholarship. He has previously held faculty positions as assistant professor (lecturer) at Trinity College Dublin (2004–7) and at the University of St Andrews (2007–11). His research interests include the globalization of risk in strategic studies and counterterrorism strategies. He has written several books – namely, *War as Risk Management* (Routledge, 2006); *Risk, Global Governance, and Security* (Routledge, 2009); and *Asia-Pacific Nations in International Peace Support and Stability Missions* (Palgrave, 2014, as co-editor with Chiyuki Aoi) – and published in peer-reviewed journals such as *Security Dialogue* and the *Review of International Studies*.

George Joffé teaches the international relations of the Middle East and North Africa to graduate students at the Department of Politics and International Studies in the University of Cambridge, where he is the director of the Centre for North African Studies, now part of the Centre for the Study of the International Relations of the Middle East. He is also the founder and co-editor of the *Journal of North African Studies*, the official journal of the American Institute for Maghrib Studies. Previously, he was deputy director of the Royal Institute of International Affairs (Chatham House).

Evan A. Laksmana is a political science PhD candidate at the Maxwell School of Citizenship and Public Affairs, Syracuse University, where he has been a Fulbright presidential scholar (2011–13). He is also a researcher with the Centre for Strategic and International Studies, Jakarta, and a non-resident fellow of the German Marshall Fund of the United States. He has published in *Asian Security*, *Contemporary Southeast Asia*, *Defence Studies*, the *Journal of the Indian Ocean Region*, *Harvard Asia Quarterly*, the *Journal of Strategic Studies*, *Political Studies Review*, and others. He is currently working on research projects pertaining to comparative civil–military relations, military change and effectiveness, and the spread of innovative military doctrines.

Jorge M. Lasmar is professor of international relations at the Department of International Relations, Pontifical Catholic University of Minas Gerais, Brazil, as well as dean of graduate studies at Milton Campos Law School, Brazil. He holds a PhD in international relations from the London School of Economics and Political Science. He is also the country coordinator (Brazil) of the Terrorism Research Initiative Collaboration Network. He is the author of three books, the editor/co-editor of a further three, and has published more than thirty articles and book chapters in both English and Portuguese, including his most recent *Passporte para Terror: Os Voluntarios do Estado Islamico* (Passport to Terror: Volunteers of the Islamic State; Appris, 2017). He is a frequent media commentator on terrorism and political violence and has been awarded several professional and academic awards.

Emma Leonard Boyle is assistant professor of political science at La Salle University in Philadelphia. She received her PhD in political science and African studies from Pennsylvania State University in 2016, and has previously studied at St Andrews University and the University of Oxford. She has held research positions at the Centre for the Study of Terrorism and Political Violence at St Andrews and at the International Center for the Study of Terrorism at Penn State. She is the co-editor of *Globalizing Somalia: Multilateral, International, and Transnational Repercussions of Conflict* (Bloomsbury, 2013) and her recent research has appeared in *Terrorism and Political Violence* and *Security Studies*.

Roel Meijer is lecturer in Middle East history in the Department of Religious Studies at the Radboud University, Nijmegen, Netherlands. He has edited seven volumes, including *Global Salafism: Islam's New Religious Movement* (Hurst/Columbia University Press, 2009; translated into Arabic and Chinese) and, more recently, *The Muslim Brotherhood in Europe* (Hurst/Columbia University Press, 2012). He has published widely on social movements, the Islamist movement and the political situation in Egypt, Saudi Arabia, Iraq and Bahrain. His latest interest is in concepts of citizenship in the Middle East. A new anthology, edited together with Nils Butenschøn, *The Crisis of Citizenship in the Arab World*, was published by Brill in 2017; a sequel (also co-edited with Nils Butenschøn), *The Middle East in Transition: The Centrality of Citizenship*, will appear in 2018 with Edward Elgar. He is currently working on a general history of state–citizen relations in the Middle East.

Michael Newell received his PhD in political science from the Maxwell School of Citizenship and Public Affairs at Syracuse University in 2017, a master's in political science from Syracuse University in 2013, and a master's from the Committee on International Relations at the University of Chicago in 2010. His research interests are international security, international humanitarian law, international norms, and terrorism and counterterrorism. He has published on interstitial rules in international law, and his doctoral dissertation investigated the significance of historical context for security policy through a case study of American counterterrorism from early responses to the Ku Klux Klan, Irish-American Fenians and anarchists in the late 1800s through the 'War on Terror'.

Michael Nwankpa is director for the Centre for African Conflict and Development. He holds a PhD in sociology from the University of Roehampton, London. His main research area is the nexus between conflict and development, including the concept of a human-rights-based approach to development. His other research interests are counterinsurgency and counterterrorism. He has published several articles on Boko Haram and conflict in Nigeria generally. He has held two prestigious fellowships at the Baker Institute for Public Policy, Rice University, and at the National Consortium for the Study of Terrorism and Responses to Terrorism, University of Maryland. He has worked for the Royal United Services Institute for Defence and Security Studies as a consultant on behalf of the Global Community Engagement Resilience Fund.

Oscar Palma is assistant professor (profesor principal) at the Department of Political Science, Government and International Relations, and former director of the Observatory on Illicit Drugs and Weapons, both at Universidad del Rosario. He has a PhD in international relations from the London School of Economics and a master's in international security from the University of Leicester. Previously, he was a visiting research fellow at the Department of War Studies, King's College London; visiting lecturer at the George C. Marshall Center for European Security Studies in Germany; and scholar of the William J. Perry Center for Hemispheric Security Studies in Washington DC for several courses. He has also been a visiting professor at the Joint War College of Colombia and the Schools of Intelligence of the Colombian Navy and Army. He is a former professional officer of the Colombian Army, commissioned to the Joint Intelligence Department; a former researcher at the Centre for Strategic Studies in National Security and Defense at the Joint War College in Bogotá; coordinator in Colombia for the International Federation of Committees for the Liberation of Hostages in Colombia; and an analyst for several national and international media outlets.

Jeremy Prestholdt is professor of African and global history at the University of California, San Diego. He specializes in eastern Africa with emphases on politics and consumer culture. He is the author of a forthcoming book, *Icons of Dissent: The Global Resonances of Che, Marley, Tupac and Bin Laden* (Oxford University Press/Hurst), and also of *Domesticating the World: African Consumerism and the Genealogies of Globalization* (University of California

Press, 2008). His current research addresses the politicization of ethnic, racial and religious identities in coastal Kenya from decolonization to the 'Global War on Terrorism'.

Bashir Saade is interdisciplinary lecturer in politics and religion at the University of Stirling and an affiliated researcher at the Arab Council for the Social Science Critical Security Studies Group. He holds a PhD in war studies from King's College, London, and has previously taught at the University of Edinburgh and the American University of Beirut. He has published on themes related to political Islam, nationalism, postcolonialism, and premodern non-Western political thought. He is the author of *Hizbullah and the Politics of Remembrance: Writing the Lebanese Nation* (Cambridge University Press, 2016).

Alex P. Schmid is professor emeritus at the University of St Andrews, editor-in-chief of *Perspectives on Terrorism* and former co-editor of *Terrorism and Political Violence*. Until 2009 he was director of the Centre for the Study of Political Violence at the University of St Andrews, where he also held a chair in international relations. Currently he is a research fellow at the International Centre for Counter-Terrorism in the Hague, and director of the Terrorism Research Initiative, an international network of scholars who seek to enhance human security through collaborative research. His previous positions include officer in charge of the Terrorism Prevention Branch at the United Nations Office on Drugs and Crime in Vienna.

Rashmi Singh is associate professor in international relations at the Department of International Relations, Pontifical Catholic University of Minas Gerais, Brazil. She has regional expertise in both South Asia and the Middle East and works on issues related to terrorism, political violence, counterterrorism and national security. She is the author of *Hamas and Suicide Terrorism: Multi-Casual and Multi-Level Approaches* (Routledge, 2012).

Hussein Solomon is senior professor in the Department of Political Science, University of Free State. His previous appointments include executive director of the International Institute of Islamic Studies (2009–10); professor and director of the Centre for International Political Studies, University of Pretoria (2000–10); research manager at the African Centre for the Constructive Resolution of Disputes (1998–2000); senior researcher at the Institute for Security Studies (1996–98); and research fellow at the Centre for Southern African Studies, University of the Western Cape (1993–95). In 2011 he was a visiting professor at the Osaka School for International Public Policy, in 2007 and 2010 a visiting professor at the Global Collaboration Centre at Osaka University in Japan, and in 2008 he held the Nelson Mandela Chair of African Studies at Jawahrlal Nehru University in New Delhi. In 1994, he was a senior visiting fellow at the Department of War Studies, King's College London. Currently he is a visiting fellow at the MacKinder Programme for the Study of Long-Wave Events at the London School of Economics and Political Science, a senior associate for the Israeli-based think tank Research on Islam and Muslims in Africa, and a senior analyst for WikiStrat. For the past sixteen years, he has been writing about terrorism and counterterrorism in Africa.

Ekaterina Stepanova is a lead researcher and head of the Peace and Conflict Studies Unit at the Primakov Institute of the World Economy and International Relations (IMEMO), Moscow. In 2007–9, she directed the Armed Conflicts and Conflict Management Programme at the Stockholm International Peace Research Institute. She is the author of several books, including *Terrorism in Asymmetrical Conflict: Ideological and Structural Aspects* (Oxford University Press, 2008), and over 180 other publications in ten languages. Her latest edited volume is *Addressing Terrorism, Violent Extremism and Radicalization: Perspectives from Russia and the United States* (IMEMO, 2017). She serves on the editorial boards of *Global Governance*, *Terrorism and Political Violence* and *Global Responsibility to Protect*, and edits the IMEMO journal *Pathways to Peace and Security*. She is a member of the expert panel of the Global Peace Index, the International Panel of Social Progress, and the Joint US–Russia Expert Group on Afghanistan. She is also a contact point for the Global Research Network, hosted by the UN Counterterrorism Committee's Executive Directorate. For more detail, see www.estepanova.net.

Foreword

Alex P. Schmid

Twenty-five years ago, I edited, together with Ronald D. Crelinsten, the volume *Western Responses to Terrorism*. It was first published as a special issue of the journal *Terrorism and Political Violence* (vol. 4, no. 2, winter 1992) and subsequently as a hardcover volume by Frank Cass (Abingdon and New York, 1993). I could not have imagined that it would take a quarter of a century before someone would finally come up with a volume on *Non-Western responses to terrorism*. Maybe that volume – which is now in your hands – would still not have seen the light of the day were it not that Michael Boyle and I met in Scotland when we were both at the University of St Andrews, where I pointed that lacuna out to him.

That 1992 volume derived from the proceedings of a conference held at Leiden University in March 1989, three months after the Lockerbie bombing. It contained a number of case studies covering the national experiences of the Netherlands, Spain, France, Germany, Italy, the United Kingdom, Switzerland and Austria. In addition, there were some overarching themes covered, like 'terrorism and democracy', 'European response to terrorism' and 'West's counterterrorist strategy'. My co-editor and I concluded the volume with a chapter entitled 'Western responses to terrorism: A twenty-five year balance sheet'. Since then, another twenty-five years have passed, and after half a century of Western counterterrorist operations, the problem has only become worse. Many national responses have been inadequate, if not at times downright counterproductive. While some of the terrorist threats – for example, those from secessionist movements like the Irish Republican Army (IRA) and the Basque separatist movement ETA – have disappeared, a new terrorist threat of much larger dimensions has arisen in the form of jihadist terrorism, affecting Western countries as well as non-Western ones.

In our concluding chapter, Ron Crelinsten and I lamented that, while law enforcement and military responses to terrorism were prominent, the propaganda dimension of terrorism was insufficiently addressed. We suggested that 'By considering the communicative aspects of different control models, repressive or conciliatory, short term or long term, political or coercive, domestic or international, governments can perhaps discover more innovative ways to deal with the problem of terrorism that are both effective and acceptable to our democratic way of life.'[1] While it is now – twenty-five years later – widely acknowledged that terrorism is a form of media-oriented coercive political discourse based on the instrumental killing of civilians and other non-combatants, most governments still fail to make the battle for the 'hearts and minds' the centre of gravity in counterterrorist campaigns – despite the fact that terrorist organizations like the Islamic State have carried much of their fight into cyberspace, from which they also convert and recruit young people to their cause.

Ironically, terrorists have managed to utilize both traditional and Internet-based media – themselves largely products of Western technology – and turn these against the West. The same has taken place with some of Western democracies' non-material values: respect for freedom of expression and the toleration of religious intolerance in Western democracies have allowed religious fanatics to thrive among immigrant diaspora subcultures, and provide them with operational bases for further subversion of Western values like gender equality, separation of state and religion, and man-made laws based on the will of the majority of the people.

Have non-Western responses a better chance to counter terrorism? The reader will find in the chapters of this volume that some non-Western, often non-democratic, responses to terrorist violence also offer no lasting solutions. Russia, for instance, after repressing ethno-secessionist and religious terrorists in the Caucasus with an iron fist, finds itself confronting Chechen fighters on the Syrian battlefield. China, which claims that terrorism, separatism and religious extremism form one package of 'three evils', has also seen an exodus of Uyghur terrorists to the Middle East and before long might also encounter them abroad. Many other non-Western states – especially former colonies – have used some of the same laws and repressive instruments originally introduced in response to national liberation struggles for the suppression of terrorist groups. This makes any strict dichotomy of Western versus non-Western responses to terrorism problematic.

The reader can learn much from the eighteen case studies in this volume – it allows the development of a broader perspective not just of counterterrorism but also of local causes of terrorism. While terrorism has become a global phenomenon in the last fifty years, solutions must ultimately be found in resolving local conflicts.

Note

1 Alex P. Schmid and Ronald D. Crelinsten, *Western Responses to Terrorism* (Abingdon, UK, and New York: Frank Cass, 1993), p. 337.

Acknowledgements

This project was conceived of during my time teaching courses on terrorism and political violence at the University of St Andrews and has been under development for about four years (2013–17). I am grateful to my authors for volunteering to write these chapters and to the many anonymous referees who reviewed each chapter and provided a written report to aid the authors' revisions. I am also grateful to the editors and staff of Manchester University Press for their help in shepherding this volume to publication.

Some parts of Roel Meijer's chapter were previously published in Roel Meijer, 'Saudi Arabia's war on terrorism: Combating passions, ignorance and deviation,' in Jeevan Deol and Zaheer Kazmi (eds), *Contextualizing Jihadi Thought* (London/New York: Hurst/Columbia University Press, 2012), pp. 165–90. I am very grateful to Jeevan Deol, Zaheer Kazmi and Michael Dwyer from Hurst for kind permission to republish some parts of this material.

On a personal note, I would like to thank Emma, George, Millie and Pob for their love and patience as I finished this project. This edited volume is dedicated with love to my grandfather, John Vincent McArdle (1899–1982).

Introduction

Michael J. Boyle

Introduction

Since 2001, the world has witnessed an unprecedented expansion of counterterrorism activity, effectively transforming what was once largely a domestic policy issue into one of vast international significance.[1] The September 11th attacks on New York and Washington marked an inflection point in history in many ways, but perhaps their greatest impact was in the practice of counterterrorism. While nearly all governments had acknowledged the reality of terrorist violence and had institutions and laws in place to punish its perpetrators, counterterrorism was considered a residual issue for many governments in the pre-September 11th era, rarely surfacing in public consciousness except in moments of profound national crisis. The US declaration of a 'war on terror' in 2001 changed all of this. It placed counterterrorism as the central priority on the agendas of governments, international organizations and even some businesses and civil society actors. In practice, this meant different things to different actors. For many states, it was immediately obvious that the scope, pace and intensity of the counterterrorism response would dramatically change.[2] But it was also obvious that adopting a reactive approach or primarily relying on law enforcement to handle terrorist threats would no longer be sufficient. A counterterrorism response to a global threat like al Qaeda would have to transcend borders and go beyond the narrow limits that a purely law-enforcement approach implied. In essence, counterterrorism would have to be effectively globalized to be successful in the post-September 11th era.

This globalization of counterterrorism could be seen first in the demands that the United States made of its allies. As part of its efforts to build a coalition against al Qaeda, the US insisted on international cooperation in information gathering, transfer, extradition and the prosecution of terrorist suspects, and even collusion in controversial policies such as extraordinary rendition and torture.[3] Governments that had previously devoted relatively little attention to counterterrorism found that they needed new legislation and coordinating offices to satisfy the demands of the US for counterterrorism cooperation. With American assistance, many governments rapidly expanded their police and internal security forces and boosted the capacity of their intelligence services to monitor domestic and foreign threats. A number of governments also produced new national legislation which specified substantial criminal penalties for aiding and assisting terrorist activity. Counterterrorism – long a province of law enforcement and intelligence services – became militarized, with some governments folding their long-running secessionist conflicts into the fight against terrorism to draw more American aid.[4] At the international level, the United Nations and leading regional organizations like the European Union developed new task forces and coordinating bodies to harmonize cooperation around counterterrorism issues.[5]

More than fifteen years later, these changes have permanently altered the political landscape. Despite turnover in US administrations and the gradual abandonment of the 'war on terror' language, counterterrorism remains at the centre of the global agenda, with states continuing to develop new policies to come to grips with the threat posed by al Qaeda and its successor, the Islamic State. By most measures, terrorism has not faded as a threat, but rather has become more amorphous, with Islamic State cells waging attacks on civilians in urban areas; 'terror wars' emerging in Syria and elsewhere; and rising ethnic and nationalist extremism in the US, Europe and elsewhere.[6] The processes through which counterterrorism became globalized are now almost complete; many European governments have drifted closer to a paramilitary response to al Qaeda's and the Islamic State's activities, which would have been unthinkable with previous nationalist–separatist terrorist threats. Counterterrorism has also been transformed by technological change, specifically the ability of police and other law-enforcement officials to conduct electronic surveillance of phone, Internet and other forms of communication. The revelations of former National Security Agency (NSA) contractor Edward Snowden show the extent to which counterterrorism has fostered the growth of a deep surveillance state in the United States and many European countries. This surveillance state has not appeared in exactly the same form in all cases, but even those without sweeping or intrusive powers of surveillance have begun to experiment with electronic eavesdropping and social media monitoring to anticipate real and potential threats. Neither terrorism nor counterterrorism has the same face that it did in the early years of the war on terror, but the threat itself has not receded in importance at the national and international level.

The globalization of counterterrorism policy illustrates an important point: that many governments have tackled counterterrorism in ways very different to that of the United States, the United Kingdom and other European governments. While much has been made of the differences in the 'culture of counterterrorism' between the US and Europe, a much greater array of differences marks the approaches of the US, UK, Europe and other Western countries from those of governments in the non-Western world.[7] Perhaps the most crucial difference concerns the conceptualization of terrorism as a threat. It is well known that terrorism lacks a single agreed-upon definition, and that the academic literature boasts hundreds of different definitions proposed by scholars and governments.[8] Even within the US Government, the various bureaucratic agencies have presented varying definitions of terrorism. After the September 11th attacks, the administration of George W. Bush set aside this conceptual complexity and presented terrorism as something incorrigible, exceptional and fundamentally driven by the cultural and religious antipathies of Islamist groups like al Qaeda to American values. In other words, it presented the problem of terrorism as an intolerable ideological threat, akin to the threat that global communism posed during the Cold War.[9] While the Obama administration attempted to reframe the debate over terrorism by focusing on specific groups (like al Qaeda) rather than Islamist ideology per se, this framing of terrorism as a global threat with an ideological dimension remains a key element of American thinking. It has recently resurfaced with calls by President Donald J. Trump to condemn 'radical Islamic terrorism' and to pursue Islamist terrorists until they and the ideology itself are destroyed.

What many American policymakers failed to notice was how culturally distinct this particular framing of the threat of terrorism was. It is part of the American way of war to cast conflicts in Manichean ideological terms, to assume conspiracies to destroy the American way of life and to justify extreme measures on that basis.[10] But that was not how much of the rest of the world thought about counterterrorism. Throughout the George W. Bush administration (2001–8), a number of European governments objected to the American interpretation of terrorism, highlighting how their domestic experience of terrorism as a tactic deployed by groups on the margins of society did not correspond with the American view of terrorism as something which threatens the fabric of civilization itself. For many European states, terrorism was a tactical, rather than ideological, threat. This explains some of the political divisions around counterterrorism between the US and Europe that emerged during the debate over the Iraq war. Yet, gradually, some elements of convergence between US and European counterterrorism policy began to appear as bargaining over discrete issues (such as transferring data and extraditing suspects) proceeded over time. By the point that Barack Obama had assumed the presidency in 2009, the US and many European countries had ironed out many of the differences in their respective counterterrorism approaches, thus providing a rough foundation for what might be considered a Western approach to counterterrorism. Although there has been a deterioration in relations between the US and European countries since the election of Donald J. Trump, this foundation has survived and been adapted to a world where nationalism and anti-immigrant sentiment is on the rise across the Western world.

But this was not the case for the rest of the world. Even more so than European states, many non-Western states rejected the American portrayal of terrorism as an incorrigible ideology. Some governments in the Middle East and North Africa saw an implied Islamophobia in that American portrayal of the 'evil ideology' of terrorism. Instead, they argued that the Salafi interpretation to Islam underlying al Qaeda's ideology should not be confused with the diversity of thought and practice of millions of Muslims worldwide. Even more, this conceptualization of an 'ideology' of terrorism was foreign to their experience of terrorism. For some governments, al Qaeda's style of spectacular terrorism posed a lesser threat to the security of their populations than insurgent or ethno-nationalist groups that regularly used violence against their populations. Only a relatively small percentage of terrorist groups worldwide embrace the Salafi ideology that motivated al Qaeda and alarmed American officials. Governments like India and Colombia had been dealing with their own violent insurgencies for decades, and saw terrorism as a small but routine part of these long-running conflicts. The death tolls that they faced were from traditional insurgent attacks rather than the spectacular terrorist violence that al Qaeda specialized in. Others in Africa and Asia found the American emphasis on terrorism as a threat to be misplaced relative to other threats they faced from disease, poverty and other ills. Finally, some non-Western governments were also sceptical about the American contention that terrorists are actors with whom no negotiation is possible. This was particularly the case among governments composed of parties once described as terrorists during decolonization struggles, such as the African National Congress (ANC) in South Africa and the Front de Libération Nationale (FLN) in Algeria. These bitter memories led some leaders to point out that the definition of who was a 'terrorist' was notoriously changeable as the political winds blow.

Although it took some time for the US to acknowledge this fact, the globalization of counterterrorism yielded a harsh lesson: that there was no single conceptualization of terrorism as a threat that would motivate the world to action, but rather a multiplicity of conceptions of terrorism rooted in the historical, political and cultural experiences of those in power. These different conceptualizations of terrorism have shaped how states respond to the emergence of the 'war on terror' across the non-Western world. For example, some governments, like Brazil and South Africa, have underplayed the threat posed by terrorism and denied some US demands or 'slow rolled' them in order to extract more concessions. Others, like China, have reacted opportunistically, taking the war on terror as a chance to enact repressive legislation that restricts the civil liberties of citizens or boosts the capacity of the intelligence and security services. Still others, like Egypt, have linked their own long-running secessionist conflicts to the global struggle against terrorism and used the cover of 'fighting terrorism' to legitimize a series of increasingly repressive measures to destroy their opponents. Finally, some states like Pakistan have used the priority placed by the United States on counterterrorism to their own advantage by exploiting American fears to gain additional aid and military resources. Rather than simply accepting the conceptualization and counterterrorism approach favoured by the United States and its allies, non-Western governments have naturally recast the threat to their own ends. In doing so, many non-Western governments have refused to accept the priority accorded to counterterrorism and denied that states like the US should be able to act across borders without sanction by the United Nations. Some powerful non-Western governments like China and Japan have struggled to find a middle path between respecting other important political and cultural norms (such as non-intervention) with the need to respond to the threat posed by terrorism.[11] As the US discovered when it attempted to strike counterterrorism partnerships with non-Western societies, many governments advance very different visions of counterterrorism practice from what the United States has in mind.

Gaps in the literature

Despite this diversity in conceptualization and responses to terrorism, the academic literature on counterterrorism has been remarkably silent on the response of non-Western governments to the threat of terrorism. The vast majority of empirical studies of counterterrorism have focused on countries in the Western world, such as the United States, United Kingdom, France, Germany and Italy.[12] To a lesser degree, there is also case study literature on countries with long-standing terrorism problems, such as Ireland, Israel and Sri Lanka. What literature exists on counterterrorism in Asia, Africa, South Africa and the Middle East consists largely of studies of regions, with few detailed country case studies available. Many of the available country case studies are conducted through a specific Western lens, evaluating the response of non-Western governments in complying with the demands and priorities of the United States or other Western governments. The typical identifying feature of these studies is that they offer some concluding observations for how such countries may adjust to fight the 'war on terror' in the way that the United States prefers. Only a small number of edited volumes in English have included non-Western cases, generally either to contrast them with predominant Western approaches or to criticize them from the vantage point of the security priorities of Western states.[13]

To some extent, this gap in coverage is due to data availability and poor coverage of global counterterrorism threats in English-language newspapers. As a general matter, terrorism has been under-reported in much of the non-Western and developing world. For example, many of the most important cross-national data sets on terrorism (such as the *Global Terrorism Database*, managed by the University of Maryland's Study of Terrorism and Responses to Terrorism (START) programme) have problems with under-reporting, especially in the developing world during the pre-2001 era.[14] Also, attacks outside the Western world are less likely to attract the label 'terrorism' and instead be called acts of insurgency or criminality. This introduces an inevitable bias into much of the terrorism and counterterrorism literature, and makes researchers more inclined to use data-rich Western cases (for example, the Irish Republican Army (IRA) and the Basque separatist group ETA in Spain) than under-reported non-Western cases. The problem of under-reporting terrorist threats and counterterrorism responses in the non-Western world may be more severe with autocracies, which tend to suppress or fail to record terrorist events and to cloak many of their counterterrorism policies in secrecy.[15] This problem is remarkably persistent despite the vast increase in the number of counterterrorism studies since the September 11th attacks.[16] Even after the arrival of the Internet and automatic translation services made access to information from non-English sources easier, these cases remain systematically understudied in the counterterrorism literature.

Another reason why this gap in the literature persists is that writing about counterterrorism can be dangerous. While democratic societies generally allow free inquiry into counterterrorism policies, some authoritarian governments often do not, especially when writing about terrorism touches on sensitive ethnic, nationalist or religious fault lines. A critique of counterterrorism policy, in some authoritarian countries, is effectively a critique of the military and intelligence establishment, which may be the most powerful actor in that society. In a few cases, scholars have been subject to censorship or more severe forms of pressure for criticizing the government's response to terrorism; in others, scholars have engaged in a form of self-censorship and do not write about counterterrorism for fear of what may follow. In other cases, there is a strong personal and professional incentive not to be critical of counterterrorism policies or to raise issues about severe or repressive counterterrorism responses in countries where scholars will continually need to seek a visa. This authoritarian censoring of counterterrorism literature is obviously not uniformly present across the non-Western world – for example, academics in liberal democracies like India, Brazil and South Africa would not find writing about terrorism dangerous – but in authoritarian or illiberal democracies among the non-Western states the risks may be considerably higher.[17]

What affects counterterrorism policies?

The purpose of this volume is to offer the first comprehensive account of the varied counterterrorism policies that exist across the non-Western world. As such, it provides a series of structured case studies on how different governments understood and responded to the threat of terrorism in the post-9/11 world. The theoretical argument of this volume is simply that counterterrorism responses are, to greater and lesser degrees, mediated and influenced by four factors: (1) historical experience of war, occupation and colonialism; (2) local politics and the distribution of power among domestic stakeholders; (3) internal religious divisions or debates among key sectarian communities; and (4) cultural traditions and experience. This book sees each of these factors as an input into counterterrorism policy and hypothesizes that the response offered by each government will be consistent with and reflective of its country's historical, political, religious and cultural traditions. In other words, these contextual factors will shape the contours of the counterterrorism policy and affect the discourse surrounding it in meaningful, empirically measurable ways.

It is important to stress what is, and is not, argued here. Each of these factors is an input into counterterrorism policy, but not necessarily a determinative one. This book does not hold that counterterrorism policies are wholly socially constructed, or that they are wholly derivative of one or more of these factors. In some cases, the perception of an internal or external threat from a terrorist organization or pressure from other states (like the United States) may be a bigger factor in shaping policy choices than any domestic factor. In other cases, contextual, case-specific factors will act like a thin filter, shaping how certain types of counterterrorism policies are implemented or presented, but not fundamentally altering the decisions themselves. The bottom line is that the causal weight of these factors will vary across cases. The claim here is relatively modest: either as drivers of policy or as filters for expressing policy choice, these factors can play an important role in explaining non-Western responses to terrorism.

It is also important to stress that the influence of historical, political, religious and cultural factors will be present in different ways across different cases. This volume does not claim that counterterrorism policy is wholly socially constructed or that factors like history and culture are always determinative of the way that counterterrorism policies are conducted in the non-Western world (or the Western world, for that matter). Such an argument would be reductionist and would not do justice to the complex intentions that lay behind most governments' counterterrorism policies. This volume also does not suggest that non-Western states are somehow different in the way that these factors matter, or that historical, political, religious and cultural factors are irrelevant in Western cases. No one could sensibly look at America's response to terrorism without seeing an obvious connection to its own crusading historical mission and cultural 'way of war'.[18] All states construct their counterterrorism approaches based on their own distinct historical, political, cultural and religious foundations. The issue here is merely one of coverage: that, by comparison, the drivers behind non-Western approaches to terrorism have been less studied than Western cases.

Identifying and analysing these factors has a clear policy impact because the perception of the threat shapes the government's response to it. How policymakers see and respond to the threat of terrorism is based on their society's experience of it and these historical, political, cultural and religious drivers. Requests for bilateral and multilateral counterterrorism cooperation will also be filtered through and interpreted on the basis of these drivers. Understanding why some societies prioritize terrorism in different ways, and offer varying levels of cooperation on areas of joint concern, requires understanding how the problem looks from 'inside' the society. Each case study is designed to provide contextual detail, as well as a view from 'inside' the society, for the benefit of those who are not experts of that particular case. The case studies will tie together an analysis of the perception of the threat of terrorism and the counterterrorism response in each country to provide a holistic account of how that society understands terrorism as a social and political problem. Together, the diverse practices showcased in the case studies are designed to challenge the unspoken assumption that the Western practices of counterterrorism are universal by showing how differently non-Western societies have conceptualized, recast and responded to the terrorist threat.

Finally, it is important to stress that this account of the role of culture as an input into counterterrorism is not an orientalist one. As Edward Said pointed out, many representations of the non-Western world are 'othered' – that is, defined by their opposition to the Western world and assumed in a variety of ways to be inferior.[19] Although this volume groups a diverse range of countries as 'non-Western' as a shorthand, it makes no such assumptions. A true orientalist account of counterterrorism would assume that the non-Western world would be anti-rational, inflexible and underdeveloped relative to the Western alternatives. A true orientalist approach to counterterrorism would assume that non-Western policymakers are dragging their heels on responding to terrorism because they are irrational, mendacious or sympathetic to the terrorists themselves. There is simply no evidence that any of this is true. The diversity of practice in counterterrorism does not suggest in any way that non-Western governments are being irrational, inflexible or slow. Similarly, close adherence to a US-recommended formula for counterterrorism does not suggest that Western governments are being more rational and effective. The grouping of 'Western' and 'non-Western' is a shorthand for grouping countries based on the degree of their coverage in the existing literature and does not imply a normative judgement about which is better or worse. Moreover, while this volume posits that culture is an input in shaping counterterrorism practices, there is nothing generalizable about the cultural practices of non-Western states that makes counterterrorism any easier or harder there than it is in the United States or Europe.

Defining the non-Western world

Who belongs in the non-Western world? The boundaries of the 'non-Western' world are obviously not set in stone. To some extent, it is defined by its geographical opposite, the Western world, which is conventionally assumed to include North America and Europe. In this volume, the non-Western world is defined as every region outside those two distinct continents. Given this broad definition of 'non-Western', it is obvious that the non-Western world is not united by any single cultural heritage. The degree of diversity in cultural and political practices across the regions of the non-Western world is immense and no conclusions can be drawn about the counterterrorism practices of the non-Western world as a single political unit. This volume aims to demonstrate the diversity of counterterrorism practices across the non-Western world, not to flatten them down into some caricature of 'non-Western' approaches to terrorism. The non-Western world is also not hermetically sealed from influences of the Western world; each government in the non-Western world has had to wrestle with an array of political, religious and cultural influences from the West and specific demands from the US and others which have had a decisive impact on its society and government. This was especially true during the colonial era, where European governments often directly occupied non-Western societies and in some cases dramatically reordered their politics and society. Especially in these cases, the tension between the Western and non-Western worlds is inextricably a part of the latter's politics and would naturally bleed over into discussions over their counterterrorism policies. In the end, there is no inevitable 'clash of cultures' between Western and non-Western approaches to counterterrorism; upon closer inspection, the practices of some non-Western governments are deeply influenced by, or even emulative of, Western practice.

Given this broad definition of non-Western world, there is inevitably a degree of subjective judgement in the definitions of regions and case selection. This volume gathers a number of cases and groups them under broadly defined regions. For example, it defines the Middle East and North Africa as a single region and Latin and South America as a single region despite the cultural and political differences among the countries there. Some regions – for example, South Asia – group together two countries (India and Pakistan) with politically salient religious and cultural differences. Other regions, such as Latin and South America, are included even though they could arguably be considered part of the Western world. The book is ordered into regions, but this should not be as read as saying that counterterrorism practices are uniform, or even much alike, within regions. For example, only Russia is included here under the region for Russia and Central Asia, but Central Asian states, long dominated by Russia and marked by a complex relationship with the Government of Russia, would likely deny that their counterterrorism policies are wholly derived from Russian practice.

For space considerations, it was not possible to include an equal number of cases from every region of the world. Choices had to be made about what countries to include as representative of a region. In general, this volume focuses on countries with a significant terrorism problem, but obviously it was not possible to include every case where terrorism had become a serious problem. For example, there is no chapter on Peru, which dealt with terrorism from the Shining Path in the 1970s and 1980s, or South Korea, which has experienced terrorism from North Korea, such as the 1987 bombing of Korean Air Flight 858. Some regions are more comprehensively covered than others. For example, only two South American cases (Brazil and Colombia) are included in the Latin and South America section. Only Russia is covered in the section which ideally should cover Russia and Central Asia. In the Middle East and

North Africa, countries in the midst of armed conflicts – Syria, Iraq and Libya – were excluded because their political situation was too fluid to allow for a separate analysis of how they conceived of counterterrorism apart from the wars that they currently face. In other regions, more prosaic reasons governed why some cases were included. For example, some case selection was limited due to problems finding experts and to space considerations for a volume aiming for a global scope.

It was also necessary to make judgements about the borderline cases for inclusion. Some decisions to include or exclude were made on the basis of the degree of academic and journalistic coverage that the case received. For example, one could arguably locate Israel in the Western world due to the degree of European influence in its founding and elements of its political, religious and cultural heritage, or in the Middle East due to its geographic location. Ultimately, Israel was excluded from the volume because its counterterrorism policies have been extensively covered in the academic literature elsewhere.[20] Similarly, Sri Lanka's long struggle against the Liberation Tigers of Tamil Eelam (LTTE) has been covered extensively elsewhere and a chapter on this case is not included here. By contrast, Russia, also arguably culturally Western and part of Europe, was included because its counterterrorism policies have received less coverage in the English-language academic literature but play an important role in its relationships with the United States, the European Union and its neighbours in Central Asia. On balance, case selection was done with an eye towards covering understudied cases while whenever possible being broadly representative of regions, but this inevitably involved judgement calls and unfortunate omissions.

Key questions

The case studies in this volume are designed to address (1) how terrorism is conceptualized in each society; (2) how case-specific historical, political, cultural and religious factors shape that conceptualization; and, finally, (3) how that conceptualization affects the government's response to terrorism. To ensure comparability, each case study addresses some or all of the following questions:

- How is terrorism understood within that society?
- How does that conceptualization relate to those advanced by the US, UK and other European societies?
- What are seen as the chief security threats facing that society? What priority is accorded to terrorism relative to other security threats?

- What are the sources – historical, political, cultural and religious – that affect how terrorism is viewed and responded to within that society?
- How do these sources affect how the threat of terrorism is conveyed publicly to domestic audiences? How does this contrast with how the threat is presented or conveyed in international fora?
- How do norms or discursive practices within that country shape its conceptualization and practice of counterterrorism?
- How does this conceptualization shape the practice of counterterrorism in that case? How is this manifested in the specific policies of the government with respect to the internal security services, police, intelligence apparatus and legal framework in which terrorism is prosecuted?
- In what ways, if any, do the counterterrorism policies and practices in that society significantly differ from those advanced by the US, UK and other European governments? Has the government actively opposed or criticized the US approach to counterterrorism?
- How has the US-led campaign against terrorist organizations been addressed within that society? Has this campaign forced the government to recast or reformulate its counterterrorism policies, or to change its approach to existing military campaigns against secessionist movements? More broadly, what has been the consequence of this change?
- How has the experience of counterterrorism practice over the last ten years shaped and influenced the conceptualization of terrorism within that society today?

The authors were asked to address the most relevant of these questions with respect to their own case studies. As a result, the case studies will vary considerably in their emphasis and scope. Some of the chapters focus more on the threat of terrorism and less on the response, while others have the opposite emphasis. This is due to the fact that the threat and the response to it are obviously interdependent and cannot be considered in isolation.

Finally, there has been no attempt to impose a single theoretical or empirical viewpoint on the authors. Any such effort would be contrary to the purpose of this volume, which is to illustrate the diversity of approaches in conceptions of and responses to terrorism among non-Western states. The empirical strategies of the chapters also vary. Some case studies present data on incidents of terrorism, while others are less focused on the events than on the discursive construction of the threat. Some chapters focus on the legal definition of and response to terrorism, while others see the problem as political or religious in nature. The volume is deliberately interdisciplinary, with some chapters adopting theoretical approaches common in the study of terrorism, while others draw inspiration from other fields, such as history, sociology and criminology.

Summary

Each of the case studies of counterterrorism policies presented here casts a new light on the diversity of the conceptualizations of terrorism and shows how these conceptualizations can feed into different policy responses. In her chapter on Russia, Ekaterina Stepanova acknowledges the distinct inputs to the Russian perspective on terrorism, noting that it is based on a contextual reading of the threat and 'the general functionality of the state; type of political and governance system; and degree of social, ethnic and other diversity' (see p. 24). As a country with a hybrid identity, partially tied to the West but also separated from it in many ways, Russia's conception of terrorism has gradually expanded. While it has traditionally been focused on terrorist threats emerging from the wars in the North Caucasus, Russia today sees serious threats from Salafi Islamists and ISIS-inspired groups, as well as right-wing extremists. Accordingly, Russia's counterterrorism approach has evolved from a short-term, reactive approach based on collective punishment to a forward-leaning combination of what Stepanova describes as 'smarter suppression'– that is, targeted strikes to kill enemy operatives – and efforts to divide and rule and buy off local insurgent forces. One crucial conceptual distinction that emerges from this analysis is between counterterrorism (i.e., narrowly construed as the actions taken by the security services to address terrorist threats) and anti-terrorism, which is broader and includes preventive measures taken by the state and civil society organizations to head off terrorist threats. Seen in this light, Russia's strategy of anti-terrorism combines elements of counterinsurgency with a determined effort to contain the problem of Islamist forces and others who might threaten the state. Russia's intervention in Syria in 2015 can indeed be seen as an attempt to sow division in local forces but also contain a growing ISIS-inspired threat which may eventually move to Russian territory.

In some ways, China has some similarities to Russia in its approach, in that its conceptualization of terrorism is drawn heavily from its experience in suppressing the Uyghur independence movement in Xinjiang. But rather than rely heavily on a model of counterterrorism influenced by counterinsurgency practice, China has built a corpus of law designed to identify and criminalize subversive actions which may lead to dissent or terrorism. As Irene Chan has noted in her chapter, this practice has worked in part because the Communist Party of China (CPC) has struck a bargain with the population which offers security and stability for cooperation on these measures, even if the cost is a more repressive government. This bargain can be seen clearly in China's depiction of terrorism as one of the 'three evil forces', along with separatism and religious extremism, that must be countered by the state.

In Japan, the situation is quite different, but culture continues to play a role and shape the government's counterterrorism policy. As Chiyuki Aoi and Yee-Kuang Heng document, Japan has a long but often unacknowledged experience of terrorism, both domestic and international, which has threatened the harmony and stability of its society. Japan tends to underplay the political rationales of terrorists, treating them as aberrations or circumstantial statements, and therefore denying them their symbolic power. For Japan this is crucial, because refusing to acknowledge them also allows the government and society more generally to deny the existence of social divisions. As the authors argue, Japanese counterterrorism policies are driven by a concern for *meiwaku* – that is, causing trouble for others – which produces some behaviours not seen elsewhere. For example, Japanese Government officials have apologized for the involvement in terrorism by Japanese nationals and have, from time to time, offered themselves in trade for hostages. Unlike those in China, Japan's counterterrorism policies have been informal and rely less on legal measures than on mobilizing the community to head off and redirect potential recruits to terrorist organizations.

In Malaysia, the historical legacy of experience with British colonialism and counterinsurgency in the 1950s has deeply influenced its practice of counterterrorism. This can be seen in the use of pre-emptive legal measures designed to prevent terrorist attacks and rehabilitate those who might be considering them. This allows the law-enforcement authorities to arrest individuals without a warrant, and even to hold them for thirty-eight days until charges can be filed. Malaysia also draws from its history of counterinsurgency to use specialized police units to deal with potential terrorist threats. Conceptually, Malaysia supports moderation in all things – the concept known as *wasatiyyah* – to insist that its citizens balance their commitments to the real world and not err too much on the side of supernatural punishments and rewards. In this way it offers an ideology, as well as a corpus of law and police forces, which is designed to swim against the tide of extremism that so often motivates terrorist organizations. In Indonesia, Evan A. Laksmana and Michael Newell offer a different interpretation of the legacy of colonialism, emphasizing the country's special status as a 'disputed postcolonial state'. They note that Indonesian counterterrorism is deeply tied up with the state's history of dealing with internal security challenges and cannot be separated neatly from that. The New Order regime (1966–98) has produced a central government with a strong authoritarian bent, which sees violent unrest in its periphery as a serious threat to the legitimacy of its rule. For this reason, Indonesian counterterrorism is intertwined with counterinsurgency, as the government vacillates between repressive (hard) and population-centred (soft) approaches to deal with potential threats.

A similar dynamic exists in the case studies in South Asia. As Rashmi Singh documents, India's long postcolonial experience of terrorism from a wide variety of different ethnic, cultural and religious groups shapes in a fundamental way how the government sees the problem of terrorism. Violent challenges to the state in India 'interact and intersect' with the key markers of identity, such as ethnicity, caste, religion and socio-economic concerns, producing a hybrid threat which combines elements of terrorism and insurgency. In response, the government tries to manipulate some of the violent challengers, while isolating and fighting others at different times. The result is a counterterrorism policy that is at best uneven and contradictory. In Pakistan, the situation is even more complex. As Muhammad Feyyaz discusses, the government's approach towards terrorist groups is particularly ambiguous, as elements within the state's security and intelligence establishment may sustain and protect terrorist groups while destroying others. This is in part due to the legacy of insecurity that emerges from Pakistan's founding as a state – specifically, its fear of India, its fight for Kashmir and the homogenizing tendency of its central government which has produced resentment among ethnic minorities and others along the periphery of the state. These factors, combined with a diffuse security and intelligence establishment and a failure of leadership at points in Pakistan's history, have allowed its problem of domestic terrorist groups to get worse over time.

In Brazil, the situation is quite different. As Jorge M. Lasmar argues, Brazil has a deep problem with political violence – particularly assassinations and other forms of criminal activity – but this is often not seen as 'terrorism' per se. In fact, many Brazilian elites are convinced that the country is not at risk of terrorism because Brazil's foreign policy is pacifist and leans towards not confronting violent non-state actors in its midst. Having successfully insulated the country from the risk of terrorism, the movement towards criminalizing terrorist activities has historically been slow, though recent progress in criminalizing acts in support of terrorism are a sign that things may be changing. Brazil's hesitancy around terrorism is also attributable to the presence of former leftist guerrilla fighters in the government, most of whom are suspicious of the term 'terrorism' and reluctant to get close to the United States. In Colombia, the role of the US also looms large, though for different reasons. Oscar Palma argues that the discourse of terrorism has radically changed over time in Colombia, with terms like 'narcoterrorism' being applied to the activities of different groups of traffickers, guerrillas and paramilitary organizations over time. In particular, the shift towards describing insurgents as terrorists was part of the post-9/11 approach to terrorism and was particularly influenced by the aid and political support offered by the United States.

In four of the Middle East case studies, the central theme that emerges is that the state itself is a violent actor that often uses repression for its own ends while also negotiating with non-state actors with sporadic violence. For example, as George Joffé notes in Algeria, violent extremism has always been engaged in dialectic with the state itself. Violence is so enmeshed with the nature of state power that it has developed 'the informal status of being the ultimate mechanism of legitimization for the acquisition of material assets and cultural capital' (see p. 274). This is in part derivative from Algeria's painful colonial legacy but also from its long experience in dealing with violent or revolutionary non-state actors on its periphery. In Egypt, Dina Al Raffie notes a similar trend, but argues that the common view of Egypt's counterterrorism approach – that it is uniformly repressive for fear of Islamist groups – simplifies the complex relationship that the government has had with its Islamist challengers. The government selectively punishes some Islamist groups while tolerating others, in part because the bogeyman of an Islamist takeover is useful to the government as a way of retaining and legitimating its own hold on power. Al-Raffie points out that the Egyptian Government also skilfully deploys anti-Semitic conspiracy theories to tarnish jihadist groups and to strengthen its grip on power. This is in defence of what Al Raffie calls Egypt's 'securitocracy', a constellation of elites from the intelligence, military and security agencies that exercise disproportionate control over the state's policies. Similarly, as Bashir Saade shows, in the case of Lebanon, violence is embedded within the nature of the state's politics, with some groups punished for it and others like Hizbullah given semi-official status due to their opposition to Israel. As he demonstrates, Lebanon's approach to counterterrorism cannot be understood outside of the regional dynamics, specifically the degree to which actors like Syria endorse and support violent politics. Even Hizbullah offers its own interpretation of terrorism within Lebanese politics. In Iran, Ali M. Ansari argues that the government has deployed terror against the population, including torture and political assassinations, but has remained uneasy with the 'tidy distinctions' that the West imposes with its definition of the concept. The Iranian Government denies the label of 'terrorism' to its own violent actions and those of its proxies, while eagerly casting US actions in the Middle East as terrorism in their own right.

By contrast, in his case study, Roel Meijer points out that the kingdom of Saudi Arabia defines terrorism in Islamic terms as the 'corruption of the earth', as essentially a personal deviation from good religious behaviour rather than flowing from political, social or economic conditions. In the Saudi conception of terrorism, the behaviour flows from personal ignorance, an imbalance of the passions, deviation from doctrine and finally political extremism. The Saudi conception of terrorism assumes that Wahhabi Islam and terrorism are mutually exclusive and therefore attacks are the result of a 'miscreant minority'. It is hardly surprising that Saudi Arabia conceives of extremism and deviation from accepted religious practice in individual and personal terms, apart from the government or the wider social and political life of the state. Its focus is then naturally on re-education and rehabilitation of terrorists rather than negotiating and repressing violent non-state actors, as many other governments in the region do.

The final four studies, on African countries, show that even when governments adopt Western conceptions of terrorism this does not lead to a coherent counterterrorism policy. In the Kenya case study, Jeremy Prestholdt points out that the response to terrorism from al Shabaab and other actors has reflected and aggravated communal divisions and tensions within Kenyan society. As a result of adhering close to US positions, Kenya now faces two counterterrorism fronts: one within its own borders and another across the border with Somalia. Similarly, in Nigeria, terrorism from Boko Haram is only one part of the violent conflicts that have divided and wracked the state and undermined its political and economic development. Yet, as Jennifer Giroux and Michael Nwankpa show, it has enabled the Nigerian Government to engage in ever-more repressive measures under the guise of counterterrorism, often with the support of the United States and other powerful actors. In the Uganda case study, Emma Leonard Boyle shows how the Government of Yoweri Museveni skilfully exploited an alliance with the United States for counterterrorism aid as a way of boosting his regional ambitions. While Uganda has always struggled with terrorism, especially from groups like the Lord's Resistance Army (LRA), it remains unclear whether the threat to Uganda will diminish as a result of his aggressive actions and courting of the West. In contrast, in South Africa, Hussein Solomon points out that the government has been in deep denial about the scale of the threat that it faces from terrorism, believing, as Brazil does, that its politically correct foreign policy would immunize it against more serious threats. This has clearly not been the case, and groups like Hizbullah and al Qaeda have been able to exploit South Africa as neutral ground for planning attacks. The result of this denial has been policy incoherence between the various government agencies responsible for dealing with the threat.

Conclusion

Together, these chapters show that non-Western accounts of terrorism are diverse and hardly monolithic. This volume uncovers no single 'non-Western' response to terrorism. Rather, it shows the true diversity in the conceptions and responses to terrorism that have become evident since the 'war on terror' began. Seen together, the case studies that follow present an alternative perspective to the rigid, ideological depiction of the threat of terrorism typically offered by the United States, the United Kingdom and other Western states. They also show that the concept of terrorism and the ensuing counterterrorism response are both heavily contested across the non-Western world. While the concept of terrorism may have first arisen in the West, these case studies show that it has been translated and reshaped in different ways based on the historical, political, cultural and religious conditions of other societies. Counterterrorism may have been globalized, but it has not arrived in every society in the same guise or with the same assumptions. Understanding this crucial fact, and developing a sensitivity to how other states may 'see' terrorism, is crucial to developing the kind of robust international cooperation needed to address this growing threat.

Notes

1 This statement means something very different from the conventional notion that a backlash against globalization has spread terrorism and requires a new kind of response. This argument is best expressed by Benjamin Barber, 'Jihad vs. McWorld,' *Atlantic*, March 1992, available at: www.theatlantic.com/magazine/archive/1992/03/jihad-vs-mcworld/303882/ (accessed 7 June 2018); Audrey Kurth Cronin, 'Behind the curve: Globalization and international terrorism,' *International Security* 27:3 (2002–3): 30–58; and Fathali Moghaddem, *How Globalization Spurs Terrorism: The Lopsided Benefits of 'One World' and How That Fuels Violence* (London: Praeger, 2008).

2 On counterterrorism generally, see Alex P. Schmid (ed.), *The Routledge Handbook of Terrorism Research* (London: Routledge, 2013); Ronald Crelinsten, *Counterterrorism* (Cambridge: Polity, 2009); and Daniel Byman, *The Five Front War: The Better Way to Fight Global Jihad* (New York: Wiley, 2007).

3 Jane Mayer, *The Dark Side: The Inside Story of How the War on Terror Turned Into a War on American Ideals* (New York: Anchor, 2009). On managing US demands, see Michael J. Boyle, 'The war on terror in American grand strategy,' *International Affairs* 84:2 (2008): 191–209.

4 On the militarization of counterterrorism, see Michael J. Boyle, 'Do counterterrorism and counterinsurgency go together?' *International Affairs* 86:2 (2010): 333–53.

5 See Jane Boulden and Thomas Weiss, *Terrorism and the UN: Before and after September 11th* (Bloomington, IN: University of Indiana Press, 2004); Daniel Keohane, 'The absent friend: EU foreign policy and counterterrorism,' *Journal of Common Market Studies* 46:1 (2008): 126–46; Javier Argomaniz, 'Post 9/11 institutionalization of European Union counterterrorism: Emergence, acceleration and inertia,' *European Security* 18:2 (2009): 151–72.

6 The term 'terror war' comes from Paul Wilkinson, *Terrorism vs. Democracy: The Liberal State Response* (London: Frank Cass, 2001).

7 See Wyn Rees and Richard J. Aldrich, 'Contending cultures of counterterrorism: Transatlantic divergence or convergence?' *International Affairs* 81:5 (2005): 905–23, and Jon Stevenson, 'How Europe and America defend themselves,' *Foreign Affairs* 82:2 (2003): 75–90.

8 See particularly Schmid, *Handbook of Terrorism Research.*

9 See particularly Boyle, 'War on Terror.'

10 See particularly Russell Weigley, *The American Way of War* (Bloomington, IN: University of Indiana Press, 1977); Robert Kagan, *Dangerous Nation: America's Foreign Policy from Its Earliest Days to the Dawn of the Twentieth Century* (New York: Vintage, 2007); William Appleman Williams, *The Tragedy of American Diplomacy* (New York: W.W. Norton, 2009); Richard Hofstadter, *The Paranoid Style in American Politics* (New York: Vintage, 2008).

11 This is nicely summarized in Asia in Jonathan T. Chow, 'ASEAN counterterrorism cooperation since 9/11,' *Asian Survey* 45:2 (2005): 302–21.

12 See particularly Alex P. Schmid and Ronald Crelinsen, *Western Responses to Terrorism* (London: Frank Cass, 1993), and Yonah Alexander, *Counterterrorism Strategies: Successes and Failures of Six Nations* (Washington, DC: Potomac Books, 2006).

13 For an example, see Alexander, *Counterterrorism Strategies.*

14 Michael Jensen, 'Discussion point: The benefits and drawbacks of methodological advancements in data collection and coding: Insights from the Global Terrorism Database (GTD),' GTD website, 25 November 2013, available at: www.start.umd.edu/news/discussion-point-benefits-and-drawbacks-methodological-advancements-data-collection-and-coding (accessed 6 March 2017).

15 See Konstantinos Drakos and Andreas Gofas, 'The devil you know but are afraid to face: Underreporting bias and its distorting effect on the study of terrorism,' *Journal of Conflict Resolution* 50:5 (2006): 714–35; Erica Chenoweth, 'Terrorism and democracy,' *Annual Review of Political Science* 16 (2013): 355–78.

16 On this, see Schmid, *Handbook of Terrorism Research.*

17 One author pulled out of this project under threat of violence. Another pulled out due to a fear of being denied a visa for future research.

18 On America's way of war, see Weigley, *American Way of War.*

19 Edward Said, *Orientalism* (New York: Vintage, 1979).

20 See particularly Daniel Byman, *A High Price: The Triumph and Failures of Israeli Counterterrorism* (Oxford: Oxford University Press, 2013).

PART I

Russia and Central Asia

1

Russia's response to terrorism in the twenty-first century

Ekaterina Stepanova

Introduction

The definition of terrorism used in this chapter interprets it as *premeditated use or threat to use violence against civilian and other non-combatant targets intended to create broader intimidation and destabilization effects in order to achieve political goals by exercising pressure on the state and society.*[1] This definition of terrorism excludes both the use of force by insurgent–militant actors against military targets and the repressive use of violence by the state itself against its own or foreign civilians. This author's definition predates and is more narrow and concise than the 2011 so-called 'academic consensus definition' of terrorism.[2] It is also close to the list of criteria that are employed, for the purpose of data collection, by the world's largest database on terrorism – the US-based *Global Terrorism Database*.[3]

An emerging degree of consensus in academia on the definition of terrorism does not, however, question – and, further, even underscores – the fact that terrorism displays a wide variety of forms and manifestations and is a highly *contextual* phenomenon. Terrorism's main hallmark is its unique ability to disproportionately affect politics and its asymmetrical communicative, intimidation and destabilization effect, intended to far exceed the immediate, direct human and physical damage caused by a terrorist attack. This broader destabilizing effect largely depends on how well terrorist activity is tailored to a specific political context. For instance, a single or rare Islamist–jihadist terrorist attack with a limited number of fatalities anywhere in an otherwise peaceful, developed and democratic Europe may produce a much larger political resonance than either hundreds of minor non-lethal terrorist incidents by local separatists, or a series of mass-casualty terrorist bombings in the midst of ongoing hostilities in the world's major conflict spots, such as Iraq, Syria or Afghanistan.

Along with other systemic factors and more concrete specifics of counterterrorism as a security function, it is the highly contextualized nature of terrorism itself that partly explains why the main centre of gravity of *anti-terrorism* remains at the national (state) level. The national dimension in countering and preventing terrorism remains critical, even as terrorism itself is increasingly transnationalized and international cooperation on countering terrorism has significantly intensified in the early twenty-first century, especially following the attacks of September 11th, 2001, in the United States. All international agreements on anti-terrorism notwithstanding, an individual nation's response to terrorism is highly *contextual* and is shaped not only by the dominant type and level of terrorist threat (which varies significantly from one state and society to another), but also by the general functionality of the state; type of political and governance system; and degree of social, ethnic and other diversity and integration, etc. This is true for Western and non-Western nations alike, as well as for such a 'special-case' country with a hybrid identity as Russia, with strong historical and cultural ties to the West, but firmly and, perhaps, irreversibly outside the West as a political and security space and value system.

In the 2010s, the main context and source of terrorism in post-Soviet Russia – the protracted armed conflict in the North Caucasus – has largely faded away from the world's attention as a hotbed of high-profile terrorism and a major jihadist battleground. This is only partly explained by the shift of global attention to other or new major centres of terrorism activity of the Islamist bent, such as Iraq, Afghanistan, the Maghreb, or West and East Africa, and to growing manifestations of Islamist–jihadist terrorism in Western countries. The main explanation draws upon a set of major changes that occurred domestically in the Russian/North Caucasian context over the decade following the mid-2000s.

First, Russian perceptions of the centrality of terrorism and other violence linked to the North Caucasus and its impact on Russian national politics have changed significantly. Through the mid-2000s, two bitter wars in Chechnya (the first one 1994–96, and the second one lasting from late 1999 to the late 2000s) and terrorism generated by that on-and-off armed conflict had dominated domestic violence and the security agenda in Russia. Violence in and from the North Caucasus had been the first-order issue in national politics. In contrast, from the late 2000s to the early 2010s, the North Caucasus case no longer dominated national politics, as the situation there started to stabilize and the violence started to decline. It was also effectively overshadowed both by other domestic developments (e.g., a wave of mass non-violent civil/pro-democracy protests in 2011–12) and by select crises in the neighbouring states with major domestic implications for Russia (the 2008 conflict in South Ossetia/Georgia, the accession of the Crimea to Russia following an unconstitutional change of government in Ukraine in early 2014, and the separatist armed conflict in Donbass that started in late spring of 2014).

Second, even in terms of domestic sources of *violent* threats, the North Caucasus no longer poses the single largest, overwhelming problem. Instead, it has become just one of at least three main domestic security issues, along with two other, closely interrelated processes:

- The rise of right-wing extremism and nationalism in the late 2000s, directed especially against migrants, mostly from Central Asia and the Caucasus (with violent manifestations mostly taking forms other than terrorism: i.e. provoking violent scuffles, public beatings, ethno-confessional vandalism, and even pogroms and mass disturbances)
- Mass, uncontrolled and largely illegal labour migration and the growing problems of integration of migrants.

By the early 2010s, a combination of these two issues had arguably become more problematic on a national scale than any terrorism/militancy of North Caucasian origin.

Third, the main form of violent extremism in the North Caucasus – the insurgency that combined guerrilla-style combat with terrorist tactics – has itself undergone some major shifts in the early twenty-first century. The critical ones have been the gradual disintegration of what was a more consolidated ethno-separatist insurgency in Chechnya and a shift to a fragmented, less intensive violence of a more explicit Islamist–jihadist bent that spread across the wider region, while its original hotbed – Chechnya – became relatively pacified.

While the North Caucasus at large remains one of the most problematic regions in the Russian Federation and low-level violence resurfaces in different spots across the region, terrorism of North Caucasian origin ceased to be the most destabilizing domestic security threat in Russia. How did Russia arrive at this stage, following two bitter wars in Chechnya – wars of the type that, in principle, cannot be won – and despite major past failures and deficiencies in confronting terrorism? How did Russia's response to terrorism evolve over time, especially in the twenty-first century? What are the main specifics of Russia's response to the problem that allowed it to significantly diminish the threat in the 2010s, as compared with the previous decade? Why does this response fall short of a long-term solution? What new sources of terrorist threats, beyond the North Caucasus, have emerged for Russia, domestically and transnationally, and how are they managed? And finally, what broader lessons, if any, may be learnt from Russia's response to its main type of terrorist threat? Before addressing these questions, it is useful to have a look at where Russia stands, in terms of the scale, intensity, level and dominant type of terrorism threat, compared with the rest of the world.

Terrorism in Russia in the global context

A useful starting point is to acknowledge the fact that, in the first decade and a half of the twenty-first century, global terrorism dynamics were heavily and increasingly dominated by regions other than Eastern Europe or post-Soviet Eurasia. The most explicit global pattern of terrorism during this period involves a combination of two trends. The first trend is a sharp general increase in terrorism (with 2013 and 2014 as peak years not only for the period since 2001, but also for the entire period since 1970 that is covered by the best available terrorism statistics).[4] The second trend is a sharp increase in and disproportionately high concentration of terrorist activity in two regions – the Middle East and South Asia (figure 1.1) – with all other regions lagging far

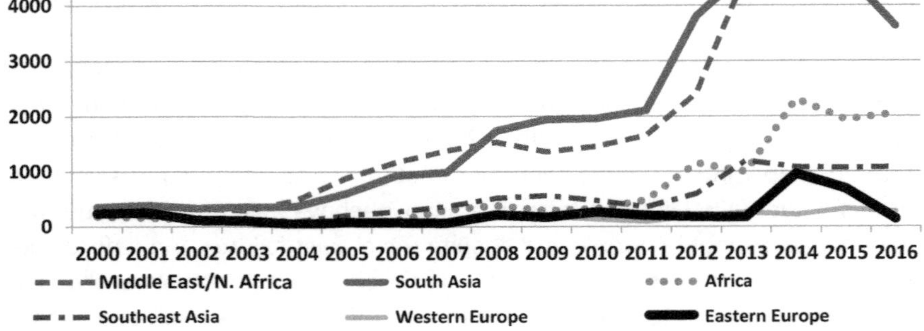

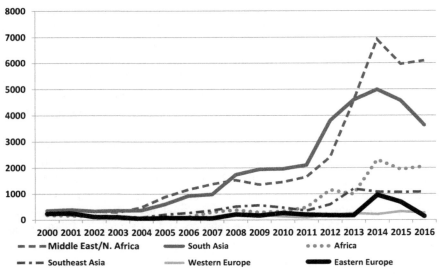

Figure 1.1 Terrorist attacks, by select region, 2000–16.

behind (including Eastern Europe, where terrorism statistics were heavily dominated by Russia until 2014).[5]

This sharp increase of terrorism in the Middle East and South Asia in the 2000s was primarily driven by a spike in terrorist activity in Iraq and Afghanistan, and occurred not before but after both countries had become central targets for the US-led 'war on terrorism'. The military involvement led by the United States was the key factor that set forth the dynamics of escalating armed resistance in these two Muslim countries that was directed against US/Western troops backing weak proxy governments, and gradually morphed into and overlapped with internal sectarian, communal and other violence by a host of actors, including through terrorist means. In 2002–11, Iraq alone accounted for *more than one third* of all terrorism fatalities worldwide (well before the rise of Islamic State in Iraq and al-Sham (Levant), or IS/ISIS, in the mid-2010s), while in 2004–16 Iraq, Afghanistan and Pakistan together accounted for almost half – 47.2 per cent – of all terrorist incidents (see figure 1.2).[6]

Overall, Iraq and Afghanistan had a stronger effect on global terrorism dynamics and statistics in the 2000s than all of the other top twenty terrorism-affected states in the world put together. Other top twenty terrorism-affected states can be linked to two broad types of context. First, there is terrorism in the context of transnationalized conflicts in very weak, failed and dysfunctional states, often involving or following declared or undeclared external military/security involvement (Somalia, Yemen, Libya, Syria, Pakistan). In contrast,

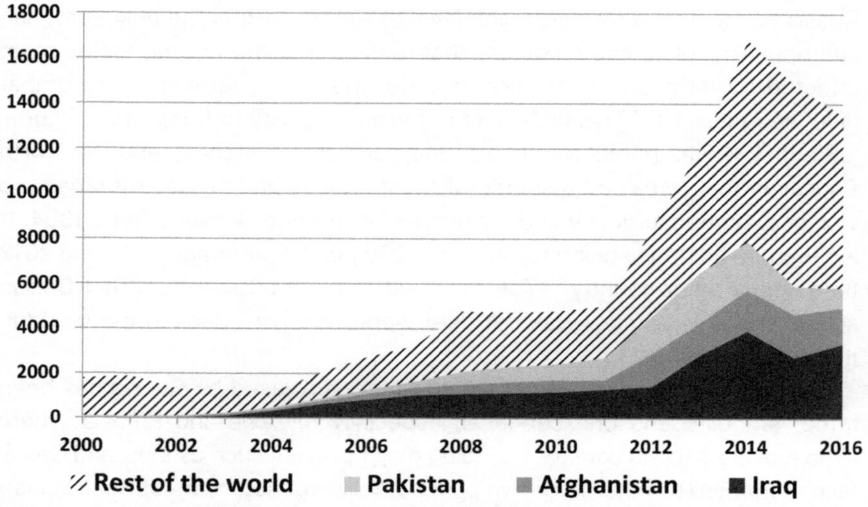

Figure 1.2 Terrorist incidents in Iraq, Afghanistan, Pakistan and the rest of the world, 2001–16.

the second category refers to non-internationalized armed conflicts on the periphery of functional states, including some major regional powers (India, Russia, China, Thailand, the Philippines, Nigeria, etc.). It is to this second category that Russia belongs. While this type of context is the more common among the world's top twenty terrorism-affected states, terrorism as a tactic employed by insurgencies on the periphery of functional states hardly poses a terrorist challenge on a global scale today, nor does it dominate in the world's main centres of terrorist activity.

These distinctions are important, as different types of terrorism (by prevailing motivation/ideology, degree of transnationalization or relation to broader armed conflict) may require significantly nuanced anti-terrorism strategies to deal with. In particular, the range of resources, actors and strategies to address conflict-related terrorism may vary significantly, depending on which of the following two broad categories a certain case in point falls under:

- International security and peace-building operations in failed, weak, seriously fractured or emerging states (Afghanistan, Iraq, Somalia, Libya or Mali)
- Security ('stabilization', counterinsurgency) operations carried out by functional national governments in (the periphery of) their own territory, with – or, in the Russia/Chechnya case, without – a formal peace process.

The overall picture and dynamics of terrorist activity in Russia in the early twenty-first century have been mixed and uneven. On the one hand, post-Soviet Russia has shown a relatively high level of terrorism. It is the only European and upper-middle-income country that made it into the top ten states most affected by terrorism in the first decade after 9/11, coming in at number nine (see table 1.1).[7] This high level of terrorist activity in Russia (see figures 1.3 and 1.4) was primarily linked to the conflict in Chechnya and the North Caucasus that remained a source of most intense and protracted organized violence, both insurgency and terrorism, for the two decades from 1994. It led to more hostages being taken (over 7200 people) between 1992 and 2012 than in any other country.[8] (The deadliest terrorist crisis – the 2004 Beslan school hostage-taking – was the third worst terrorist attack in the world in the decade after 9/11.)[9]

On the other hand, typologically, the terrorism faced by Russia has been rather standard and unexceptional, especially for Asia and Eurasia where almost every second country, including major powers such as India and China, faces terrorism by a home-grown peripheral insurgency, often of the Islamist/separatist type. The scale of threat to Russia in the 2000s was closest to that of Thailand or the Philippines, with all three primarily threatened by

Table 1.1 Countries ranked by level of terrorist activity

	GTI 2012[a] (2002–11)	GTI 2014[b] (2000–13)	GTI 2015[c] (2000–14)	GTI 2016[d] (2000–15)	GTI 2017[e] (2000–16)
1	Iraq	Iraq	Iraq	Iraq	Iraq
2	Pakistan	Afghanistan	Afghanistan	Afghanistan	Afghanistan
3	Afghanistan	Pakistan	Nigeria	Nigeria	Nigeria
4	India	Nigeria	Pakistan	Pakistan	Syria
5	Yemen	Syria	Syria	Syria	Pakistan
6	Somalia	India	India	India	Yemen
7	Nigeria	Somalia	Yemen	Somalia	Somalia
8	Thailand	Yemen	Somalia	India	India
9	**Russia**	Philippines	Libya	Egypt	Turkey
10	Philippines	Thailand	Thailand	Libya	Libya
11		**Russia**			
23			**Russia**		France
27		UK			
28	UK		UK		
29				France	
30		USA		**Russia**	
32					USA
33					**Russia**

a Institute for Economics and Peace, *Global Terrorism Index: Capturing the Impact of Terrorism in 2002–2011* (Sydney: Institute for Economics and Peace, 2012).

b Institute for Economics and Peace, *Global Terrorism Index 2014: Measuring and Understanding the Impact of Terrorism* (Sydney: Institute for Economics and Peace, 2014).

c Institute for Economics and Peace, *Global Terrorism Index 2015: Measuring and Understanding the Impact of Terrorism* (Sydney: Institute for Economics and Peace, 2015).

d Institute for Economics and Peace, *Global Terrorism Index 2016: Measuring and Understanding the Impact of Terrorism* (Sydney: Institute for Economics and Peace, 2016).

e Institute for Economics and Peace, *Global Terrorism Index 2017: Measuring and Understanding the Impact of Terrorism* (Sydney: Institute for Economics and Peace, 2017).

Islamist/separatist terrorism. Terrorism linked to the conflict in the North Caucasus has also remained an overwhelmingly subnational phenomenon: out of 1,500 terrorist attacks by North Caucasian militants, all but 5 took place within Russia, mostly inside the region itself. Furthermore, by the late 2000s, the intensity of the conflict between Russia's federal government and the rebel 'Chechen Republic of Ichkeria' had declined to the point that, after 2007, it no longer appeared in the Uppsala Conflict Data Program/International Peace

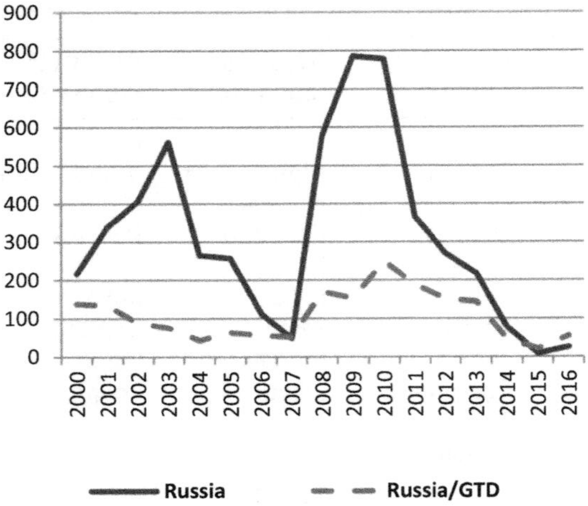

Figure 1.3 Terrorist attacks in Russia, 2000–16.

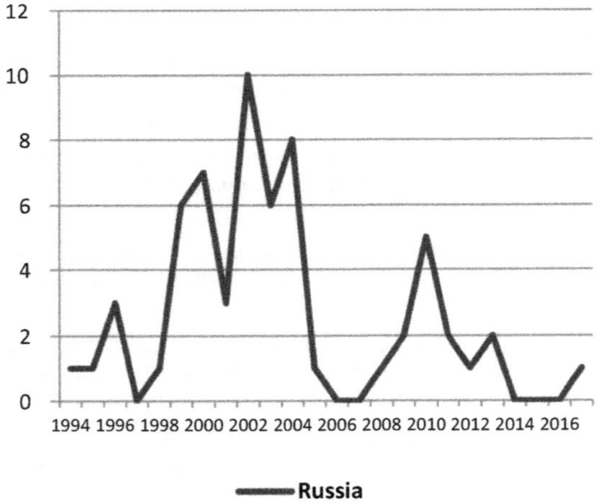

Figure 1.4 Terrorist attacks with over ten fatalities in Russia, 1994–2017.

Research Institute (UCDP/PRIO) data set – the world's leading data set of armed conflicts.[10]

Also, Russia's comparative standing has actually improved. Terrorism in Russia has been *steadily in decline* since 2010 (see figures 1.3 and 1.4). Depending on the source of data and definition of terrorism, the decline in terrorist incidents in Russia is estimated as a tenfold drop (from 779 in 2010 to 78 in 2014, according to Russian Government data) or a fivefold decrease (from 250 in 2010 to 46 in

2014, according to the *Global Terrorism Database*). Even a short spike in terrorist activity before the 2014 Sochi Winter Olympic Games neither spoiled the Olympics, nor reversed the overall downward trend in terrorist activity. In the *Global Terrorism Index* (GTI) 2014, Russia fell out of the top ten, even though it remained at number eleven (see table 1.1).[11] It then fell to 23rd place in GTI 2015, to 30th place in GTI 2016 and to 33rd in GTI 2017. By this measure, Russia was faring better in 2017 than either the United States or France. As shown by GTI 2015, which encompasses the period 2000–14, after 2014 Russia even left the top twenty states most heavily affected by terrorism.[12]

How much of this decline has resulted from Russia's conscious strategy and measures to fight and prevent terrorism of North Caucasian origin? To what extent could this have been an outcome of developments beyond Russia's direct control, including those internal to the Chechen insurgency movement and the North Caucasian region – or, in other words, a side effect of *the problem taking care of itself*? How, following Russia's major counterterrorism failures of the late 1990s to early 2000s, was some form of security solution found at the domestic level? While this 'solution' (perhaps too strong a term in itself) has been imperfect, incomplete and interim (short to mid-term), and has hardly removed the terrorism problem altogether, how did it manage to degrade the threat to a manageable and relatively peripheral issue – a fragmented, low-intensity conflict that no longer dominates national politics?

Confronting domestic terrorism of North Caucasian origin: the 'solution' and the costs

Origins of the threat and problems with the initial response

Chechnya proclaimed its independence in 1991, as part of the general turmoil and disintegration at the time of collapse of the Soviet Union, and has been increasingly taking a separatist course, but was largely neglected by Moscow until late 1994. Russia's shift from neglect to intervention needs to be placed in its domestic political context, especially the 1993 conflict between President Boris Yeltsin and the Russian Parliament that ended in unconstitutional violent suppression of the democratically elected parliament by the democratically elected president (the closest Russia has come to internal civil conflict since the civil war of 1917–21). It is since the 1993 coup that an authoritarian tendency has started to gain ground in post-Soviet Russia. The Yeltsin Government that lacked full legitimacy had to demonstrate strength, reinforce its domestic position and direct any public discontent elsewhere. It is in this spirit that Yeltsin, in urgent need of a 'small victorious war', launched the first military campaign in Chechnya in December 1994 – officially, to 'restore constitutional order'. In sum, the war started more as a sign of state (regime) weakness than of its strength. As usual, what was meant to be a 'small victorious war' led to a sequence of two major armed conflicts of the type that are unlikely ever to be decisively won.

The first war involved fierce fighting and several high-profile and relatively successful terrorist operations by Chechen separatists (especially the June 1995 Budennovsk and the January 1996 Kizlyar attacks, with over 2,000 hostages taken in each case). Poorly managed by the federal centre, the war ended in the Khasav-Yurt ceasefire agreement (August 1996) on terms of if not outright defeat than hands-off retreat of the federal centre, with the Russian troops to be withdrawn from Chechnya. However, the ceasefire did not solve anything or address any of the underlying incompatibilities and dilemmas, ranging from issues of autonomy/self-determination/territorial integrity to those of painful and distorted modernization of a society with significant traditionalist elements. Furthermore, whereas in Russia from the late 1990s the ruling regime consolidated and basic state functionality improved, Chechnya's self-governance experiment during the short quasi-independence period between two wars (1996–99) did not succeed; it failed to provide basic security, order or public services and instead led to more chaos and instability.

The conflict in and around Chechnya became the main generator of the surge of terrorism in Russia for the next decade. Certain conditions on both sides made this conflict particularly conducive for the use of terrorist means as one of the insurgents' main modes of operation. Terrorism tends to be more effective when it is employed against a type of state that is neither a consolidated democracy nor an overly rigid autocracy, neither too weak nor too strong –characteristics that fully applied to Russia's 'semi-democratic' regime of the 1990s. Also, the state can only be systematically threatened by conflict-related terrorism if faced with a determined and sufficiently capable opponent. Such a high level of determination and motivation is usually catalysed and mobilized by an extremist ideology – in Chechnya, this was a combination of ethnic nationalism with growing religious radicalism, supported by such local norms and traditions as blood feud. A militant–terrorist actor's asymmetrical structural capability (type of organization) may be more important than even its access to arms and money – the Chechen insurgents fully benefited from their dynamic hybrid structure, which combined network, clan and loose hierarchy elements.

As the conflict became protracted, terrorist acts dramatically increased in number and lethality, although not linearly: according to official data, going from 18 terrorist attacks in 1994 to 561 in 2003, amounting to a thirtyfold increase over the course of a decade. The federal response was harsh and brutal but ineffective, poorly tailored to counterterrorist needs and, at times, counterproductive. While the Chechen terrorism became a serious challenge after, not before, the Russian military operation had started in December 1994, 'counterterrorism' became the main official rationale and post hoc justification for the first war. And, inversely, use of force in a massive but poorly conducted counterinsurgency operation became Russia's primary strategy to fight terrorism throughout the first war and into the second one.

In terms of counterterrorism as such,[13] the short-term reactive approach initially prevailed in federal strategy both inside and outside Chechnya. It prioritized coercion, retaliation, and post hoc investigation and punishment, was based on limited or poor (counter)intelligence and involved weak decision-making capacity. The frequent use of the so-called *zachistka* operations by federal forces in Chechnya (a cordon and search operation to carry out a total identity check, often involving arbitrary arrests, by special forces in a given populated area, after it had been completely blocked by internal troops or army units) amounted to collective punishment and stimulated more violence than it was meant to quell. In a highly insecure environment, with a capable opponent and amidst an unfriendly local population, the use of this tactic was often a substitute for other security operations (such as patrolling or operating checkpoints), and was dictated more by an inability to effectively conduct such operations than by genuine counterterrorist needs.[14] Outside Chechnya, especially in Moscow (and, to a lesser extent, other cities), this approach also involved some upgrade of defensive measures of physical protection following every large-scale terrorist attack (partly fading away later, if only until the next mass-casualty attack). Subject to domestic political and security pressures to respond rapidly and decisively to a terrorist threat, the Russian Government seemed to have little time, will and resources to explore other options for responding to a terrorist threat than those suggested by the dominant short-term reactive approach.

In broader anti-terrorism terms, while the first war was waged in an almost complete legal vacuum, the second one was squeezed into the framework of a 'counterterrorist operation', in line with Russia's first 1998 federal law 'On the Fight against Terrorism', which also legalized the use of armed forces in domestic counterterrorism and was strongly oriented towards suppression of terrorism, with minimal attention to prevention.[15] The militarized notion of a 'counterterrorist operation' was stretched beyond limits to apply to the entire territory of a federal republic. The same applied to Russia's broad and vague definition of terrorism, which, among other things, refused to explicitly acknowledge that terrorist actors pursue political goals or to distinguish between terrorist acts against non-combatants and attacks against military targets. Not surprisingly, Russia's first list of terrorist organizations, adopted by its supreme court in 2003,[16] was even less targeted and specific in identifying Chechen terrorist groups than the respective US lists. The political, social and other underlying sources of Chechen terrorism and the Chechnya problem as a whole were also either ignored or insufficiently addressed at this stage.

The government of Vladimir Putin (premier 1999–2000, and president 2000–8 and since 2012) made the task of ensuring security in general and countering terrorism in particular its top declared priority. As Russia's main response to terrorism from the 1990s – the 'war' option (i.e., what primarily generated terrorism in the first place) – had not worked, the federal centre had to search for new strategies and approaches. Ultimately, relatively unorthodox approaches had to be devised that went far beyond military strategy, or counterterrorism in the narrow sense, or even broadly interpreted anti-terrorism. However, these strategies did not materialize until a certain window of opportunity opened in the Chechnya context –one that was hardly of the federal centre's own making or design. Paradoxically, this opportunity emerged in the context of the highly controversial impact of the rise of radical Islamism/jihadism on the insurgency itself.

Jihadization of the Chechen insurgency: the beginning of the end

The Chechen insurgents gradually shifted from an originally predominantly ethno-separatist movement largely confined to Chechnya to an increasingly Islamist/jihadist one in the broader North Caucasian context. This radicalization of the insurgents along the Islamist–jihadist lines is noteworthy not only as the most important ideological/motivational trend, but also because it set forth the dynamics that ultimately created the conditions for the beginning of the end of the consolidated Chechen resistance, and catalysed a semblance of a national solution to the Chechnya problem.

The jihadization of the insurgency became more salient gradually, as the conflict became protracted and required additional mobilization drivers, and prompted the insurgents to increasingly resort to more asymmetrical and extreme tactics. The main conditions for jihadization of the insurgency were created by the increasing intensity and bitterness of the war itself (in a way, Russia had 'bombed' Chechnya into radical Islam') and by the vacuum of governance, with the absence of central government power inside Chechnya and the failure of the rebels' own civil governance experiment during the quasi-independence period between the two Chechen wars (1996–99). While external ideological and financial influences, including the inflow of foreign jihadists (especially Arabs and diaspora Chechens from the Middle East) did have a role to play in the jihadization process, they were hardly decisive for the rebels' combat or even terrorist activity.[17] The jihadization of insurgency first culminated in 1999 when two commanders – Shamil Basayev and the Jordanian Khattab – launched an incursion to support Salafi enclaves in neighbouring Dagestan, with an explicitly Islamist goal of establishing an Islamic republic of Ichkeria (Chechnya) and Dagestan.

Overall, however, the role of radical or jihadi Islamism was highly controversial for the insurgents. On the one hand, it increased the resolve of the more radical elements and definitely encouraged the use of more extreme tactics. In addition to typical terrorist tactics of the first war (hostage-taking and the use of remotely detonated bombs), the second war was strongly associated with the rise of suicide terrorism and a unique phenomenon of suicidal mass barricade hostage-taking (that culminated in the 2002 Nord-Ost and the 2004 Beslan hostage crises). Jihadization of the insurgency also helped to cross the multiple ethnic barriers across the region and facilitated the overspill of violence from Chechnya to other parts of the North Caucasus. Finally, it helped bring in some foreign funding from other radical Islamist organizations, foundations and charities.

On the other hand, the timing of the jihadization of the insurgency, of the second Chechen war and, especially, of the related high-profile Islamist terrorist attacks proved to be extremely unfavourable for the rebel movement, in view of the international implications of the 9/11 attacks by al Qaeda in the United States, and the unfolding global 'war on terrorism'. Nothing facilitated the Kremlin's efforts to politically integrate the war in Chechnya into the post-9/11 'war on terrorism' more than jihadization of the Chechen insurgency. A series of particularly outrageous mass-casualty attacks against civilians – for example, the taking of hostages in a theatre in Moscow in October 2002 (the 'Nord-Ost' crisis, by the name of the performance) and at a school in Beslan, North Ossetia, in September 2004, and the blowing up of two outbound passenger planes from Moscow in mid-air by female Chechen suicide bombers in August 2004 – were undertaken explicitly under an Islamist–jihadist banner, with some of the slogans borrowed word for word from al Qaeda. Such attacks were particularly counterproductive to the rebels' original separatist cause, in more ways than one.

Most importantly, the rise of jihadism catalysed the beginning – and one of the three main pillars – of a solution to the major armed conflict in Chechnya and of large-scale terrorism related to that conflict (the term 'solution' is used in this chapter as a euphemism for degrading the problem to a peripheral one, rather than eliminating it). The growing role of jihadists inside the resistance catalysed a series of major splits within it – an unorchestrated process, endemic to the movement. In brief, the more traditionalist and nationalist forces within the movement, led by the chief mufti of Chechnya (a traditionalist Islamic cleric) and the head of one of the two largest Sufi orders (the Qadiriyya), Akhmad Kadyrov, increasingly fell out with the Salafi–jihadist radicals for reasons ranging from religious and cultural tensions to the competition for territory and power. The followers of Kadyrov and many other Chechen fighters opted for leaving the insurgency, thus depriving it of some of its key clans, manpower, clout and territory, and ultimately chose to switch loyalty to and join forces with the federal side. Once their main opponents had left, the radical Islamists of the Salafi–jihadist type within the movement (led by commanders such as Yandarbiyev, Basayev and Khattab) won control over the insurgency from the remaining relative moderates (such as elected Chechen President Maskhadov), but lost Chechnya instead. Figuratively speaking, they won the battle, but lost the war.

Federal response: Chechenization, smarter suppression and financial aid

On the political/security side, the federal centre seized upon this split by shifting towards a new strategy dubbed 'Chechenization'. This strategy involved (1) outsourcing stabilization and a significant part of governance tasks primarily to the Chechen forces who had left the resistance and switched sides in exchange for staying in control, while (2) stepping up Moscow's security and, especially, financial support. The combination of the major split within the insurgents and Russia's Chechenization policy produced the rise of formally pro-federal Chechen militias (*kadyrovtsy*). In June 2000, a new Chechen administration headed by Mufti Akhmad Kadyrov was established and, in 2001, the loyalist Chechen Government was formed and moved to the republican capital of Grozny.

Chechenization was coupled with, and reinforced by, the shift in federal security strategy from the brutal suppression of the first and the early second wars to what could be called *smarter suppression*. This implied a move away from controversial collective punishment operations in favour of more targeted, surgical special operations, focused especially on locating and exterminating militant leaders (a tactic which was found to be a relatively effective way to counter and manage, if not entirely eliminate, militant networks). Also, after the Beslan tragedy, the human and technical (counter)intelligence capacity had been significantly improved, including measures ranging from creation of special Federal Security Service (FSB) units to collect intelligence on insurgent groups to the use of drones for reconnaissance purposes, especially in the mountains.

In contrast to many other cases around the world of a limited outsourcing of counterinsurgency and counterterrorism tasks to loyal local forces (e.g., by the US forces to the some Sunni tribes in the Anbar province of Iraq in the late 2000s), Russia's Chechenization strategy has been *literal*. The burden of keeping order inside Chechnya was gradually, but ultimately fully, shifted to the Kadyrov militias, who gained a virtual monopoly on the use of force – which also explains the heavy human losses borne by the *kadyrovtsy*, especially police and special and other security forces, in countering the remaining anti-government militants. Ramzan Kadyrov (who succeeded his father Akhmad following the latter's assassination in a terrorist bombing on 9 May 2004) has become the only republican head in the North Caucasus (and in Russia) who controls security services on his territory and personally supervises anti-terrorist operations. While heavily enforcement-centred, the *kadyrovtsy*' response to terrorism and militancy was not confined to brutal suppression alone. It also included reintegration of ex-combatants through formal amnesties (such as the ones timed to coincide with the adoption of the Chechen Constitution in 2003 and the targeted killing of Shamil Basayev in 2006) and informal (clan, kin and other) ties and leverages.

The third, economic, element of the solution – disbursement of massive reconstruction and development aid from the federal budget to Chechnya (without repayment requirements) – has been no less essential than the other two. In 2000–10, Russia allocated a huge sum of federal funds to the North Caucasus (up to US$30 billion), with the bulk of it destined to the Kadyrov regime in exchange for formal loyalty and suppression of major violence (the funding increased tenfold from US$0.6 billion in 2000 to US$6 billion in 2010, or US$600–700 per capita – i.e., four times Russia's average). By 2025, an additional US$80 billion of federal funds are to be allocated.[18] These expenses were facilitated for Russia by the upward economic trend and favourable oil and gas prices throughout almost all of the 2000s. Even as this massive economic support has had an inevitable downside of 'privatization' and siphoning off of state funds, reinforcing patronage–clientele relationships and resource distribution, and stimulating corruption, it actually did result in visible and remarkable signs of reconstruction in Chechnya. The formerly completely destroyed downtown area of Grozny is now crowded with brand new skyscrapers, much of the destroyed infrastructure – and even some industrial potential – has been rebuilt, and the educational system and public services are functioning.

A combination of Chechenization, 'smarter suppression' and large-scale economic assistance predetermined the outcome of the second Chechen war – disintegration of consolidated Chechen insurgency, decline in more intense combat-style violence and in terrorist activity by Chechens, general stabilization and pacification of Chechnya, and the rise of a formally pro-Moscow Chechen Government enjoying a very broad autonomy. In 2009, the ten-year 'counterterrorist operation' regime in Chechnya was officially lifted.

The costs

However imperfect, this three-pillar pacification strategy for Chechnya holds. Even as occasional larger terrorist attacks in, or related to, Chechnya, cannot be excluded (such as the attack on a press house and a school in Grozny in December 2014), overall, the Kadyrov regime has remained firmly in control and, in the 2010s, Chechnya has stood out as an island of relative stability amidst constantly emerging flashpoints of low-level violence and insecurity across the North Caucasus. In sum, Chechenization is working for the time being, albeit at a very high security, political, economic and human cost.

The main security cost has been borne by the Chechen security and police forces. The Kadyrov regime's overall response remains harsh and security focused, and involves promotion of traditional Sufi/Sunni Islam and rigid suppression of all forms of Salafism. While it has provided stabilization in the short to mid-term, it is hardly a substitute for long-term stability or applicable to different contextual conditions in other North Caucasian republics.

The main financial costs have been paid from Russia's federal budget – i.e., by the entire society (in a situation of economic slowdown in the 2010s, this cost has increasingly appeared to be excessively high, especially in view of concerns about local ruling elites siphoning off budget funds, most actively voiced by Russian nationalists).

Political, civil and human costs and repercussions have also been grave. They include authoritarianism: if Russia is a hybrid regime, combining some formally democratic institutions with more autocratic elements, Chechnya is a very rigid autocracy (a dictator fighting extremists). This is aggravated by serious problems with human rights: the policy of Chechenization implied outsourcing not only of combat, law enforcement and counterterrorism, but also 'dirty work' (which has included forced disappearances, and de facto retributive punishment of the militants' families).

The ultimate political cost, however, concerns governance issues and involved ceding (outsourcing) an extensive amount of sovereignty to the Chechen Government – in fact, almost everything short of formal sovereignty. As a result, Chechnya under Kadyrov has largely pursued an autonomous state-building project that appears to aim at something closer to an emirate in the style of the United Arab Emirates than to the rest of Russia (even as Kadyrov himself has been playing an increasingly high-profile role in Russian politics and, among other things, in a show-off of loyalty, even started sending conscripts to the Russian armed forces). While this might have been the single heaviest price to pay, it could also be seen as Russia's specific 'undeclared' way of addressing the main political incompatibility over which the conflict was fought in the first place.

In sum, Russia's 'solution' to its main terrorist threat since 1994 – terrorism of Chechen origin – was found at the domestic (national) level. It was partly made possible by a problem 'taking care of itself', through involvement of an indigenous Chechen element, and partly resulted from a significant shift in Russia's federal-centre policies (Chechenization, smarter suppression and massive economic support). No matter how incomplete and imperfect that solution has been and how dearly it has cost the entire nation (Russia *including* Chechnya), this cost has still been much lower than the cost of war.

Responding to domestic and transnational terrorism beyond Chechnya

Unsurprisingly, Russia has developed a very genuine interest in making sure that the overall stabilization in Chechnya and decline in Chechen terrorism are not disturbed by any new destabilizing factors, domestic or transnational. There are various sources of *extremism*, including violent extremism, in Russia: the roughly 2,600 groups on Russia's federal list of extremist organizations range from the right wing (radical nationalist, anti-migrant) and the radical left to religious sects. However, *terrorist* threats to Russia are strongly dominated by radical Islamist terrorism and related transnational connections (as of June 2017, out of twenty-seven groups on Russia's list of terrorist organizations, all but four were violent Islamist organizations).[19] There have been two main trends concerning domestic Islamist terrorism and militancy in Russia beyond Chechnya: one that has evolved since the 2000s and is confined to the North Caucasus region, and a more recent one manifesting itself in different places across Russia.

Domestic Islamist militancy and terrorism in and beyond the North Caucasus

Since 2009–10, following the 'pacification' of Chechnya, militant and terrorist activity in the region has not disappeared – rather, it has adapted and changed its form. A major, fully manifested trend has been the general fragmentation of violence in the broader North Caucasus, hovering at the stage of lower-level, low-intensity conflict (that can still, however, result in up to several hundred fatalities per year). Its centre of gravity has decisively shifted from Chechnya to other North Caucasian republics. The most heavily affected republic has been Dagestan: of 144 terrorist attacks in 2013, 120 took place in Dagestan. Second has been Ingushetia, followed by Kabardino-Balkaria, Karachai-Cherkessia and even majority-Russian Stavropol Krai. Several high-profile, deadly terrorist attacks of North Caucasian origin conducted in Russia in the 2010s (such as nearly simultaneous blasts in the two central underground stations in Moscow on 29 March 2010, or the Moscow Domodedovo airport attack on 24 January 2011), while increasingly rare, were also prepared and carried out primarily by perpetrators of North Caucasian origin other than Chechens.

On the one hand, this low-scale insurgency/terrorist activity in the North Caucasus attracted younger people with a more explicit Islamist orientation, compared with the past wars – even as militancy and terrorism are only the most extreme manifestations of the broader process of the spread of a non-traditionalist/fundamentalist form of Islam.[20] On the other hand, violence in the region often involves a mix of motivations, actors, contexts and forms, including elements of communal/clan-based strife (for land, access to financial resources, etc.); blood revenge; and ethnic, predatory and vigilante/self-defence militia violence. Militant and terrorist actors with a clear Salafist–jihadist imperative display increasingly fragmented structures such as mini-*jamaats*. While these underground factions and cells have been proclaimed to act under the umbrella-network framework of the self-declared Islamic Emirate of the Caucasus ('Imarat Kavkaz'), they appeared to represent more the same type of actor than the same organizational framework and tended to operate largely on their own, not taking direct orders from anyone, with Imarat claiming responsibility for larger attacks only. Imarat Kavkaz was founded in 2007 by Doku Umarov, the first militant leader to call for an Islamic state across the entire region. The high degree of fragmentation of radical Islamist violence in the region is well illustrated by the fact that the largest number of terrorist attacks in 1992–2011 for which a clear perpetrator could be identified were attributed to the loose network of Imarat Kavkaz (with even such major groups active in the context of the Chechen wars as Armed Forces of Ichkeria and Basayev's 'Riyadus Salihin' battalion lagging behind). The short-lived increase in the number of terrorist incidents in the late 2000s, prior to their subsequent decline (see figure 1.3), also primarily revealed fragmentation of terrorism in the North Caucasus and not an increase in its intensity: the bulk of these more numerous attacks were low-scale ones, and only few of them were deadly, with no analogues of such high-profile mass-casualty attacks as those of Nord-Ost and Beslan of the early 2000s (see figure 1.4).

While such fragmented militant–terrorist violence is less deadly and intense than a more structured full-scale conflict, it is too elusive and non-linear (may fade away but frequently recur) and, thus, not easy to manage and even harder to decisively quell. Russia's main approach to addressing such violence has become *containment* – that is, keeping it at a low level. This strategy does not solve the problem, but is a preferred and more 'economical' option to any more decisive 'wipe out'. The latter would have be extremely costly and inefficient for the state, given that the underlying causes of instability and violence (the region's deeply entrenched governance problems linked to a still predominantly patronage–clientele system, corruption, lack of integration into the rest of Russia and of socio-economic development) persist and may take decades to reach meaningful progress on.

On the ground, various measures and strategies were tried: in such a diverse and complex region, what works in one republic may not work in another. For Dagestan in particular (the most ethnically diverse republic, with a larger percentage of (non-violent) Salafists than anywhere else in the region), the Chechnya-style rigid dictatorship, heavy-handed law enforcement and brutal suppression of all forms of Salafism may not be appropriate. 'Smarter' law enforcement, more pluralistic power-sharing, more inclusive religious policy, and the use of formal and informal (clan, kin) reconciliation mechanisms were all tried by republican authorities in Dagestan (and Ingushetia), with some limited success, especially under the presidency of Dmitri Medvedev (2008–12). Since Putin was back as president in 2012 and especially in view of security preparations for the Olympics, a greater emphasis appeared to be placed on the harsher, security-first model. In this sense, the North Caucasus surprisingly well reflects the change of emphasis at the federal-centre level; at least in this respect, the region seems to closely mirror, and be integrated into, the Russian political space.

The second, more recent, phenomenon has been increasingly disturbing and deserves particular attention in view of new transnational influences on, and connections of, Russia-based radical Islamists. It is the emergence of very small autonomous Islamist cells in cities across Russia, with members increasingly drawn from Muslims outside of the North Caucasus and even ethnic Russian converts to Islam. Such violent extremists were, for instance, already involved in the preparation of the October and December 2013 bombings in Volgograd, a city 600 miles north of the Olympic Sochi. New radicalization trends and radical elements could be traced in small segments of Russia's large native Muslim community beyond the North Caucasus, with no direct link to the North Caucasian context or agenda (e.g., several hundred Hizb-ut-Tahrir followers in the Urals).[21] While such signs may even emerge in rural areas (e.g., in the predominantly Salafist village of Belozerje in the upper Volga region of Mordovia),[22] the phenomenon tends to appeal to urban, relatively well educated youth, including young women. In many respects, such cells more closely resemble self-generating jihadist cells – as seen, for example, in Europe – than the North Caucasian underground (the 'forest people'). Remarkably, these types of cells, not mired in the North Caucasian contextual dynamics, have developed a greater interest in the ideology and agenda of the 'global' versions of Islamist jihadism. They also appear to have a better grasp of transnational jihadist propaganda, increasingly spread through modern information and communication means and channels and involving more markedly transnationally minded popularizers and preachers. One early example is the case of a native Siberian convert to Islam, Said Buryatski (killed in 2010) who made a point of reaching out to new audiences, such as educated urban youth, including females and non-Muslims, across Russia. Since the mid-2010s, this type of cell has been heavily inspired by, and susceptible to, propaganda from and the example of ISIS or IS.

This new type of radical Islamist cell has mostly involved Russian citizens (both native Muslims and converts). There have already been, however, attempts to manipulate the issue of mass formal and informal migration, especially from Muslim regions, for Islamist radicalization purposes in connection with the IS phenomenon (e.g., the May 2015 call by a Tajik member of ISIS, ex-Colonel Khalimov, for Tajik migrants in Russia to join IS). Some of Russia's fledgling home-grown jihadist micro-cells have involved Muslim migrants, mostly Central Asians (who generally dominate Russia's migrant labour market). The perpetrators and planners of the 3 April 2017 terrorist bombing in Saint Petersburg's metro that killed sixteen and injured dozens (the first successful attack in Russia by ISIS adepts beyond the North Caucasus, and the first one that involved migrants) were of Central Asian origin. However, that should not obscure the fact that the immediate perpetrator of that attack was a naturalized Russian citizen, and that radicalization usually occurs not before but after migrants from Central Asia arrive in Russia, and has not (yet) become a widespread phenomenon. This pattern is typical for the first generation of labour migrants, overwhelmed by elementary economic survival and the need to support families left behind, while the problem of radicalization of Muslim migrants may increase at the second-generation stage.

Countering new transnational links and influences: The case of ISIS

In the mid-2010s, the North Caucasian/Russian context reappeared in relation to Islamist terrorism and militancy due to new connections with – and influence from – the world's main centre of terrorist and militant activity in the Middle East (especially the Iraq–Syria context). These actual and potential links became a major concern to Moscow. Prior to that, foreign radical Islamist influences appeared to decline in Russia's domestic context: most foreign jihadists shifted to other hotspots, the North Caucasus has not attracted many new outsiders or financing, and no more than 10 per cent of funding for the militancy and terrorism in the region has been officially estimated to come from foreign sources. Against this background, it has been in Russia's very genuine interest to ensure that this trend is not reversed by new destabilizing transnational links. As of the mid-2010s, the most destabilizing transnational connections were those actualized by the Syria–Iraq context. ISIS, or IS, as an ideology and a catalyst for Islamist violent extremism, has posed several challenges to Russia.[23]

The immediate concern has been the actual back-and-forth movement of Islamist militants and the direct implications of the actual and potential return of some of them for the state of militant/terrorist activity in Russia. While a sizeable share of militants 'of North Caucasian origin' came to the Middle East not directly from Russia, but were émigré militants (who had had to flee the North Caucasus due to growing security pressures on them), the majority of Russian citizens who ended up fighting on behalf of radical Sunni Islamist opposition in Syria and Iraq were from the North Caucasus. Some also came from the Volga Muslim regions, the Urals, etc.[24] Most were spotted in the ranks of Jabhat al-Nusrah and ISIS, often in formations that changed loyalty from the former to the latter (such as Katiba al-Muhajireen, or 'battalion of migrants', in Syria, later upgraded to Jaish al-Muhajireen wal'Ansar – 'army of migrants and followers'). According to Russian officials, overall numbers of militants from Russia stood at 300–400 in Syria in 2013,[25] increased to 800 in both Syria and Iraq in 2014, and had jumped to 2,900 by December 2015.[26] This was fewer than the approximately 5,000 jihadists from the EU states at the same time,[27] and much fewer than the foreign militants from other Middle Eastern states fighting on behalf of jihadist groups in Syria and Iraq. The outflow of Islamist radicals to Syria and Iraq has led Russia, among other things, to introduce criminal punishment for joining and acting with armed groups abroad (with 250 such criminal cases in 2014 alone),[28] and to include both ISIS and Jabhat al-Nusrah in its list of terrorist organizations. As of February 2017, President Putin estimated the number of foreign fighters in Syria originating from Russia at approximately 4,000,[29] while the FSB assessed the number of North Caucasians alone among Russian jihadists in Syria and Iraq at 2,700.[30]

Domestically, a major phenomenon in the mid-2010s related to ISIS was a series of pledges of support for that group in the North Caucasus by many local insurgent commanders and mini-*jamaats*, in the hope of gaining additional legitimization by association with ISIS successes (at least until 2016) and influence, and perhaps some help from violent Islamist groups in the Near Eastern context. This trend, however, has had controversial implications for the violent underground. In the short term, it stimulated struggles for influence between figures and groups claiming loyalty to IS and those sticking to the old loose umbrella framework of Imarat Kavkaz (remarkably, the Imarat leadership expressed reservations about fighters' departure for the Near East, which, however, they said they had no right to stop). The Imarat leaders claimed the outflow of fighters to Syria and Iraq diverted manpower from the local insurgency (and, it should be added, diminished their own influence). In the end, the internal struggles weakened the new leadership of Imarat (that had succeeded Imarat's first leader Doku Umarov after the latter's death in early 2014), and for the authorities have facilitated the task of eliminating it.

Despite being a major country of origin of jihadist fighters in Syria and Iraq, Russia, mostly due to harsh security constraints at home, displayed quite low rates of return of such fighters from the Near East: from 7.4 per cent as of December 2015 to 10 per cent by February 2017 (while comparable to rates of return to Central Asian states, this stands in contrast with, for instance, a 50 per cent return rate of ISIS fighters to the UK, as of mid-2016).[31] However, the problem of the spread and return of ISIS fighters posed a serious concern for Russia in three main ways. First, as the international – including military – pressure on ISIS in Syria and Iraq intensified and its situation deteriorated, the overall flow-back of foreign fighters increased, and return rates to Russia have also been slowly growing.

Second, the risk of some of the undetained returnees engaging in violence and their potential role in radicalization at home cannot be discounted. While it is commonly expected that a natural place for such fighters to come back to would be the North Caucasus (where they could try to reactivate and upgrade the heavily fragmented underground of mini-*jamaats*), the federal containment strategy and security pressures inside the region impose serious limits on such flow-back. As a result, the latter amounts at most to another complicating factor for the state. In fact, there might be as much demand for jihadist returnees elsewhere in the country, in view of the new phenomenon noted above: the emergence of small autonomous Islamist cells with no direct connection to the North Caucasus in cities and towns across the country, with members increasingly drawn from Muslims from outside the North Caucasus and ethnic Russians. While these cells are few, compared with home-grown jihadism in Europe, much like their Western counterparts, they tend to display a mismatch between ideological ambition and limited capacity or qualification to launch terrorist attacks (in contrast to the North Caucasian militants). The returning jihadists from the Middle East, with an explicitly transnational agenda, may well help bridge that gap by upgrading their capacity to engage in destabilizing violent activity through training, experience-sharing, etc.

Third, the fact that many of the surving ISIS fighters from Russia preferred to move from Syria and Iraq to other countries (in the Middle East, Europe and South Asia) has involved its own risks for Russia. They include both a general impact on transnational terrorism (with seasoned foreign fighters aiding the generation of and providing a new lifeline for transnational and cross-regional jihadist networks) and more specific risks for Russia. These range from a growing threat of terrorist attacks against Russian civilians abroad to the emergence and potential accumulation of returning jihadists of Eurasian (especially Central Asian) origin in northern Afghanistan (a grey area populated by their ethnic kin), which could further destabilize the situation in the south 'soft underbelly' of Russia and the Russian-led Collective Security Treaty Organization (CSTO), and pose a threat to Russia's Central Asian allies.

Russia's concern about terrorism and extremism has not been the only impulse driving its actions abroad undertaken in the name of countering the ISIS challenge, including its activities in Syria and Iraq. Other drivers may be both genuine foreign policy considerations – such as Moscow's general interest in international cooperation on anti-terrorism and concerns about the stability of the Middle Eastern region next to its main region of concern (Eurasia) – and more instrumental goals, such as the need to build upon the ISIS challenge as a rare shared concern with the West at the time of the major deterioration in Russia's relations with the West that has occurred since 2014 (over Ukraine).

Nevertheless, Russia has made a major contribution to international anti-terrorist efforts centred on the ISIS challenge as the new leading force of 'global jihad', primarily in relation to ISIS's main area of control and operations – the Iraq–Syria context. This contribution has been threefold:

1. *Reducing transnational flows of jihadist fighters and money to fund militant/terrorist activity in Syria and Iraq.* This has included Russia's support of the adoption and implementation of the UN Security Council (UNSC) 2014 resolution (2178) on foreign militants and terrorist threats to international peace and security, and Russia's role in initiating UNSC Resolution 2199 on preventing terrorism financing from illegal oil trade in the region, unanimously adopted by the Council in February 2015.
2. *Launching its own military air operation in Syria in late September 2015* (with an active combat phase lasting from September 2015 to December

2017), officially – and, indeed, partly – in pursuit of anti-terrorism goals[32] – Russia's first security operation at least typologically similar to the US dominant pattern of 'fighting terrorists overseas'. This strategic direction also involved a '*careful solidarity*' approach to the US-led anti-ISIS coalition operation (despite major disagreements with coalition members, both Western and Arab, on many other issues) and cooperation with and support to states whose forces fight ISIS on the ground (Iraq and Syria) and, increasingly, with key regional stakeholders. While Russian military involvement 'corrected' the military balance by helping Bashar al-Assad's Government survive and even expand areas under its control, in anti-terrorism terms it also helped to stave off the possible 'Somalization' of Syria or its takeover by jihadist groups.

3. *Trying to balance anti-terrorism with the political settlement imperative*, within the broader UN framework. For Russia, these efforts included both dialogue with the United States as the leading extra-regional player (to revive and co-broker the UN Geneva process on Syria, especially under the outgoing Obama administration in 2016) and, increasingly, cooperation with regional powers (with Turkey and Iran, as co-brokers of the Astana ceasefire process since 2017, and with other key regional players, such as Egypt, the Arab Gulf states, and Israel). On Syria, anti-terrorism and peacemaking may follow parallel tracks, but it is the overlap that is critical for both, as demonstrated by the US-Russian on-and-off attempts to revive and co-broker Geneva talks and ceasefire in Syria throughout 2016. On a tactical level, the overlap boils down to how to get reconcilable home-grown armed opposition (mostly Islamist) involved in the peace process, while helping suppress and destroy irreconcilable transnational militants and terrorists such as ISIS. On a strategic level, the limited ability of both Russia and the United States to adequately address this issue not only reflects the limits of any 'grand deals' by external (extraregional) powers to manage such fragmented, heavily transnationalized and regionalized cross-border civil wars as those in Syria and Iraq, but also boils down to the more fundamental disagreements between Russia and the US/West on conflict management and post-conflict transitions. While the US emphasizes democracy promotion and democratic transitions, including from war to peace, regardless of the context and feasibility, Russia insists on the centrality of retaining basic state functionality during the transition, regardless of the nature of the political regime. Nevertheless, while requiring both a substantive intra-Syrian dialogue and some form of underlying regional compact, any peacemaking/anti-terrorism solution for Syria may not be practical without the United

States and Russia arriving at some lowest common denominator on how to move towards a more pluralistic, inclusive, representative, multi-level political solution while also preserving basic functionality of key state institutions during the transition.

Conclusions: Lessons to be learnt from the Russian case

All transnational terrorist links, implications, anti-terrorism operations abroad and international anti-terrorism cooperation notwithstanding, both the main source of terrorist threat to post-Soviet Russia and the ultimately devised 'solution' to address this threat have been domestic. Above all, this solution was not 'war' (neither the first, nor the second Chechen war). Not only had war not worked as a solution, but it had also served as the primary context and driver of terrorist activity. No matter how imperfect Russia's gradually evolving 'solution other than war' has been and how dearly it has cost the nation, that cost is much lower than that of war – which is, perhaps, the single most critical general lesson to be gleaned from Russia's response to terrorism.

No anti-terrorism strategy is effective unless it challenges two key asymmetrical advantages of militant actors that employ terrorist means – their extremist ideologies and organizational systems. When it comes to radical Islamist (Salafist) networks – the ideological and structural form of the largest terrorist threat to Russia in the early twenty-first century – a variety of methods could be employed. Following initial failures, Russia ultimately opted for a relatively non-trivial solution (and was partly 'pushed into' it by the conflict dynamics and related events largely beyond its control). Russia's recourse to the policy of Chechnization was made possible by a genuine split within the radicalizing Chechen insurgency and has been an attempt to take the local ground away from Salafist–jihadist terrorism and extremism by betting on the more traditionalist ethno-confessional forces and inducing them to develop a pragmatic stake in administrative power, autonomous self-governance and economic reconstruction. While having to tolerate their autocratic tendencies and elements of an (ethno)nationalist and re-Islamicization agenda, the federal centre has used them as a hedge against, and a more manageable alternative to, violent jihadism. All the multiple downsides and political, economic and human costs of this strategy notwithstanding, it has worked out at least as an interim solution, in terms of decreasing the level of terrorist and other militant activity and downgrading the problem to a relatively peripheral one.

Clearly, the lessons that can be learnt from Russia's case do not directly apply to everyone. They are certainly worth consideration by those non-Western states who are faced with terrorism of a similar type and scale (e.g., by functional, and predominantly non-Muslim, states facing terrorism employed by domestic insurgencies in the context of peripheral conflicts). This means some direct lessons could partly apply to Asian states faced with a similar or comparable type of problem (ranging from India and China to Thailand and the Philippines) and perhaps to some African states (such as Nigeria). For Western states and non-Western Muslim states, the lessons that could be gleaned from Russia's unorthodox 'solution' are less directly applicable, and not only because these states are not primarily targeted by the type of terrorism that mainly threatens Russia.

Even as Western democracies generally create fewer conditions and pretexts for domestic terrorism and socio-political violence, they also have lower tolerance for – and are thus more politically vulnerable to – attacks involving civilian casualties. They are more constrained in their domestic counterterrorist options and strategies, compared with anocratic or autocratic regimes, and at the same time have a low level of tolerance for the 'dictators-fighting-extremists' types of solutions abroad. Furthermore, as shown by Western interventions in Iraq, Afghanistan and Libya, the removal or disintegration of autocratic regimes (the secular dictatorships of Saddam Hussein or Muammar Gaddafi, the Taliban Islamist de facto government, etc.) resulting from such interventions and the ensuing state collapse have tended to set forth the asymmetrical conflict dynamics that breed more, not less, terrorism.

Overall, Muslim states suffer far more heavily from terrorism than all Western states combined (in 2000–14, all Western states together accounted for only 2.6 per cent of all terrorist fatalities and 4.4 per cent of terrorist attacks worldwide).[33] The world's main centres of terrorist activity are also in Muslim or predominantly Muslim states (Iraq, Afghanistan, Pakistan, Syria). Apart from the dominance in these areas of types of terrorism that differ from the peripheral Islamist–separatist terrorism that has primarily threatened Russia, in most such contexts the essential condition that made Russia's type of 'solution' possible at all – sufficient functionality of the state at the national level – is absent or severely undermined by either post-intervention state-building failures or bloody civil strife. Consequently, in failed states destabilizing transnational influences are stronger, security meddling by external actors is an unavoidable reality, and no solution is possible unless a degree of basic state functionality and domestic legitimacy (rather than some unfeasible and artificial calque of a Western-style liberal democracy) is achieved first.

This does not mean that no broader lessons can be learnt from Russia's response to terrorism, in terms of both counterterrorism as a specific task, function and segment of the state's security sector and anti-terrorism (and broader sphere of countering and preventing violent extremism) as a broad combination of different types of measures and policies, including legal, political, socio-economic and other tools and strategies that go beyond security as such.

The main *counterterrorism* lesson highlighted by Russia's case stems from its earlier counterterrorist failures of the 1990s to early 2000s, and points at a major problem intrinsic to many national counterterrorist strategies and to the post-9/11 global 'war on terrorism' alike. It is the failure to account for the highly specific nature of counterterrorism as a security activity distinct from traditional military or policing tasks, even if it has to be conducted in the context of an ongoing armed conflict and is combined with, and integrated into, a counterinsurgency campaign. In contrast to military operations, the primary goals of counterterrorism *are not* post hoc coercion, enforcement or retaliation. The tasks central and most specific to counterterrorism are prevention, pre-emption and pre-emptive disruption. The bulk of this work should be conducted before, not after, an actual terrorist attack occurs (which is already a counterterrorism failure in itself). By the late 2000s, this lesson had largely been learnt by Russia, albeit at a very high price, prompting a shift from brutal suppression to a combination of 'smarter suppression', better intelligence and prevention.

At the same time, it has to be acknowledged that parts of the state security sector most closely specializing in counterterrorism (in Russia, the domestic counterintelligence service (FSB) and other security services, the Ministry of Interior, and respective regional security bodies) cannot be held primarily responsible for the persisting underlying socio-political causes and conditions that continue to produce terrorism, along with other types of violence and instability (such as the continuing low-level violence in Russia's North Caucasus and sporadic, although increasingly rare, terrorist attacks in and beyond the region). Counterterrorism in a narrow sense is not about removing the deeper political, socio-economic and other causes of terrorism. That is a long-term task which requires the combined efforts of both state and society, but for which the ultimate responsibility lies with a country's political leadership. Effective counterterrorism is about minimizing terrorist manifestations under given conditions, even while certain basic socio-political and other causes of terrorism persist and cannot be removed in the foreseeable future.

As noted above, the critical role of counterterrorism as a security strategy to manage and address the problem *under given conditions* centres on prevention; pre-emption; and the pre-emptive disruption of terrorist networks, operations and incidents. That requires sophisticated and solid state-counterintelligence capacity tailored to counterterrorism specifics, and better knowledge not only of the general nature and type of terrorist threats, but of the motivations, ideologies, organizational systems, methods and 'routes' of terrorist actors. Such capacity involves, and is completely dependent on, not only accurate and robust intelligence of a strategic, psychological and tactical nature, collected on a permanent, rather than case-file basis through all available human and technical means, but also the analytical capacity to interpret this intelligence in a timely manner and, above all, the resolute capacity to take decisions promptly based on such intelligence and to conduct, as required, targeted 'special operations' (such as Russia's routine surgical liquidation of a several militant/terrorist leaders, which had some effect in countering these networks). Some balance should also be found between, in declining order of importance, specialized counterterrorist tasks performed by the (counter-) intelligence community, the more general law-enforcement tasks centred on broad prophylactic and preventive measures (physical protection of the population and critical infrastructure), and the support role that the military can play in counterterrorism.

A broader *anti-terrorism* lesson, hardly unique for Russia, is that short-term responses to and pre-emption of terrorism do not have a lasting effect if they are not part of a comprehensive approach that also includes mid-term and long-term strategies and goes beyond security as such. While in the early twenty-first century reactive and preventive security strategies to address direct manifestations of terrorism were upgraded at the national to the global level, the critical 'meso-level' of anti-terrorism – the need to undermine main comparative strategic advantages of militant actors employing terrorist means (i.e., their extremist ideologies and organizational structures) remains inadequately addressed. Russia has gradually developed its own way of countering terrorism at this critical meso-level, by trying to weaken and undermine the Islamist–jihadist extremist ideology and violent networks by relying on, accommodating and financially supporting the more traditionalist nationalist/Islamic forces and elites in Chechnya. However, in the long term, the success of an integrated strategy aimed at undermining ideological and organizational pillars of terrorism in a post-conflict environment hinges on progress towards a more general demilitarization (and even significant de-securitization) of politics – and that does not seem to be a near prospect in the North Caucasus.

Efforts to prevent and mitigate the effects of terrorism in the long run require addressing the underlying causes of terrorism – which often demands political, governance and development solutions far beyond anti-terrorism as such. In the case of conflict-related terrorism, the basic political incompatibilities about which the armed conflict was first fought need to be addressed in one way or another. While this could be part of a formal peace process, in some cases (such as peripheral insurgencies in fully functional anocracies, especially large non-Western regional powers in Asia and Eurasia) this is more likely to be done de facto, if at all, even in the absence of a formal negotiated settlement. This is well illustrated by the Russian case, with Chechnya under the loyalist autocratic Kadyrov regime having arguably acquired an even higher de facto level of autonomy and development assistance than the original rebel leadership had initially dreamt of.

Finally, as shown by Russia's experience, the more general efforts aimed at increasing both basic functionality of the state and its legitimacy *for its own population* themselves have a long-term anti-terrorism effect, even though they hardly suffice to foster socio-political integration of marginalized segments of an ethnically, religiously, culturally and socially diverse society.

Notes

1 Ekaterina Stepanova, *Terrorism in Asymmetrical Conflict: Ideological and Structural Aspects* (Oxford: Oxford University Press, 2008), pp. 13–20.

2 Alex P. Schmid (ed.), *The Routledge Handbook of Terrorism Research* (London: Routledge, 2011), pp. 86–7.

3 This is also the primary database used in this chapter. National Consortium for the Study of Terrorism and Responses to Terrorism (START), *Global Terrorism Database (GTD)*, University of Maryland, available at: www.start.umd.edu/data/gtd (accessed 25 May 2018).

4 *Ibid.*

5 In 2014–15, Russia was outmatched by Ukraine as the Eastern European country most heavily affected by terrorism; *ibid.*

6 *Ibid.*

7 Institute for Economics and Peace, *Global Terrorism Index: Capturing the Impact of Terrorism in 2002–2011* (Sydney: Institute for Economics and Peace, 2012), p. 7, available at: http://reliefweb.int/sites/reliefweb.int/files/resources/2012-Global-Terrorism-Index-Report.pdf (accessed 16 January 2018).

8 START, *Terrorism and the Olympics: Sochi, Russia 2014*, START Backgrounder Report (College Park, MD: START, 2014), p. 4, available at: www.start.umd.edu/pubs/STARTBackgroundReport_TerrorisminOlympicsSochiRussia_Jan2014_0.pdf (accessed 24 May 2018).

9 Institute for Economics and Peace, *Global Terrorism Index* (2012), p. 14.

10 Uppsala Conflict Data Program (UCDP) and International Peace Research Institute in Oslo (PRIO), *UCDP/PRIO Armed Conflict Dataset v.4–2009*, conflict table, available at: www.prio.org/Global/upload/CSCW/Data/UCDP/2009/Main%20Conflict%20Table.xls; see also www.prio.org/Data/Armed-Conflict/UCDP-PRIO/Armed-Conflicts-Version-X-2009/ (both accessed 25 May 2018).

11 Institute for Economics and Peace, *Global Terrorism Index 2014: Measuring and Understanding the Impact of Terrorism* (Sydney: Institute for Economics and Peace, 2014), p. 8.

12 Institute for Economics and Peace, *Global Terrorism Index 2015: Measuring and Understanding the Impact of Terrorism* (Sydney: Institute for Economics and Peace, 2015).

13 'Counterterrorism' is a more narrow term that refers to a range of specialized functions undertaken by the state security sector. 'Anti-terrorism' is both an umbrella term to encompass all activity to prevent and manage terrorism and a special term for political, legal, civil-society and other measures against terrorism beyond security functions.

14 Ekaterina Stepanova, 'Russia and the combat against terrorism in local/regional conflicts,' in *Russia: Arms Control, Disarmament and International Security*, IMEMO Contribution to the Russian Edition of the SIPRI Yearbook 2001 (Moscow: Nauka, 2002), pp. 42–58; Ekaterina Stepanova, 'Russia's approach to the fight against terrorism,' in Jakob Hedenskog, Vilhelm Konnander, et al. (eds), *Russia as a Great Power: Dimensions of Security under Putin* (London: Routledge-Curzon, 2005), pp. 301–22.

15 'Federal law "On the fight against terrorism",' *Rossiiskaya Gazeta*, 4 August 1998.

16 'List of organizations recognized as terrorist groups in the Russian Federation,' *Rosbusinessconsulting*, 14 February 2003 [in Russian].

17 Cerwyn Moore and Paul Tumelty, 'Foreign fighters and the case of Chechnya,' *Studies in Conflict and Terrorism* 31:5 (2008): 412–33.

18 Ben Judah, 'Putin's medieval peace pact in Chechnya,' Bloomberg, 26 April 2013, available at www.bloomberg.com/view/articles/2013-04-25/putin-s-medieval-peace-pact-in-chechnya (accessed 25 May 2018).

19 Federal Security Service (FSB), 'Federal list of organizations, including foreign and international, recognized as terrorist organizations by the Russian Federation' [as of 2 June 2017], FSB official website [in Russian], available at: www.fsb.ru/fsb/npd/terror.htm (accessed 25 May 2018).

20 Alexei Malashenko and Akhmed Yarlykapov, *Radicalization of Russia's Muslim Community*, Microcon Policy Working Paper no. 9 (Brighton: Microcon, 2009); International Crisis Group (ICG), *The North Caucasus: The Challenges of Integration (II), Islam, the Insurgency and Counter-Insurgency*, ICG Europe Report no. 221 (Brussels: ICG, 2012).

21 TASS Information Agency, 'FSB: since 2010, 600 new followers of radical Islam identified in the Urals,' *Nezavisimaya Gazeta*, 14 April 2015, available at: www.ng.ru/news/500309.html (accessed 25 May 2018).

22 Vladislav Maltsev, 'Mordovan chaliphate,' *NG-Religion*, 1 April 2015.

23 For more detail see Ekaterina Stepanova, *The 'Islamic State' as a Security Problem for Russia: The Nature and Scale of the Threat*, Program on New Approaches to Research and Security in Eurasia (PONARS Eurasia) Policy Memo no. 393, October 2015 (Washington, DC: Institute for European, Russian and Eurasian Studies (IERES), Elliott School of International Affairs, George Washington University, 2015), available at: www.ponarseurasia.org/sites/default/files/policy-memos-pdf/Pepm393_Stepanova_Oct2015_2.pdf (accessed 25 May 2018).

24 Joanna Paraszczuk, 'Three years, 10 months for Tatar from Kazan who fought in Syria,' Radio Free Europe/Radio Liberty, 18 December 2014.

25 According to First Deputy Director of the Federal Security Service (FSB) Sergei Smirnov, speaking at the meeting of the Shanghai Cooperation Organization; quoted in 'FSB: 300–400 mercenaries from Russia are fighting in Syria,' *Kavkazski Uzel* (Caucasian knot), 20 September 2013, available at: www.kavkaz-uzel.eu/articles/230365/ (accessed 25 May 2018).

26 According to Director of Russia's FSB Aleksandr Bortnikov, speaking at the meeting of the National Antiterrorism Committee, 25 December 2015; quoted in Maxim Solopov, 'Russian security services identifies hundreds of fighters returning from Syria and Iraq,' *Rosbisnessconsulting*, 25 December 2015, available at: www.rbc.ru/politics/25/12/2015/567bfdfd9a7947a3b3bc7387 (accessed 25 May 2018).

27 Soufan Group, *Foreign Fighters: An Updated Assessment of the Flow of Foreign Fighters into Syria and Iraq* (New York: Soufan Group, 2015), pp. 7–10, available at: http://soufangroup.com/wp-content/uploads/2015/12/TSG_ForeignFightersUpdate1.pdf (accessed 16 January 2018).

28 According to Russia's Prosecutor General Yuri Chaika, quoted in: Velimir Razuvayev, 'Putin calls the security bloc to order,' *Nezavisimaya Gazeta*, 25 March 2015.

29 This would make Russia the largest single country of origin of foreign fighters in Syria. 'Vladimir Putin: There are up to 9000 of militants from the former USSR in Syria,' *Kommersant*, 23 February 2017, available at: www.kommersant.ru/doc/3227219 (accessed 25 May 2018).

30 'Patrushev provided the number of North Caucasians fighting in Syria and Iraq,' Lenta.ru, 19 April 2017, available at: https://lenta.ru/news/2017/04/19/nortcaucasus/ (accessed 25 May 2018).

31 FSB director Alexandr Bortnikov, quoted in TASS News Agency, 'FSB head called for increasing penalty for participation in terrorism,' TASS News Agency website, 15 December 2015, available at: http://tass.ru/politika/2528411 (accessed 25 May 2018); Soufan Group, *Beyond the Caliphate: Foreign Fighters and the Threat of Returnees* (New York: Soufan Group, 2017), pp. 10, 12–13; UK Government, *CONTEST: The United Kingdom's Strategy for Countering Terrorism: Annual Report for 2015*, CM9310 (London: Her Majesty's Stationery Office, 2016), p. 7.

32 For more detail, see Ekaterina Stepanova, *Russia's Policy on Syria after the Start of Military Engagement*, PONARS Eurasia Policy Memo no. 421, February 2016 (Washington, DC: IERES, Elliott School of International Affairs, George Washington University, 2016), available at: www.ponarseurasia.org/sites/default/files/policy-memos-pdf/Pepm421_Stepanova_Feb2016.pdf (accessed 25 May 2018).

33 Institute for Economics and Peace, *Global Terrorism Index 2015*, p. 49.

PART II

Asia

2

Xi Jinping, China's legal reform and counterterrorism

Irene Chan

Introduction

China's phenomenal economic development and rapid social changes have brought about increased pressure on the courts to handle complex socio-economic issues that government agencies have failed to resolve. Beijing faces thousands of mass incidents annually from people who have lost confidence in government officials due to corruption and incompetence.[1] Although China has tried to strengthen its judicial system through a rush of procedural, substantive and organizational legislation over the three decades, the legal system remains painfully inadequate to handle certain sensitive issues, particularly counterterrorism. A closer examination of China's counterterrorism policy shows a pattern of knee-jerk reactions to violent incidents, followed by preventive measures characterized by repression of religious expression and cultural practices. Little has been discussed about China's counterterrorism legislation in the international media. The approach to counterterrorism in China has been seen by many as an attempt to jump on the bandwagon to justify Beijing's long-term religious, cultural and political suppression of the Uyghur community, both internationally and domestically. Critics have pointed out that terrorism is a rhetorical tool to secure and legitimize Chinese rule over restive autonomous regions such as Tibet and Xinjiang.[2]

Terrorism in China has been closely related to separatist movements in ethnic autonomous regions, particularly the Xinjiang Uyghur Autonomous

Region (henceforth 'Xinjiang'). An examination of the spike in violent incidents in Xinjiang and mainland China since 2008 shows that the potential of social unrest in Xinjiang is real. Therefore, the threat of terrorism that China faces should not be discounted.[3] There is evidence that militant groups in China from ethnically linked independence movements have connected with international terrorist organizations such as the Turkistan Islamic Party (TIP) and the Islamic State. For instance, the TIP claimed responsibility for a suicide car-bombing attack in Beijing's famed Tiananmen Square in October 2013.[4] In March 2014, a group of extremists carried out another high-profile attack at a train station in Kunming, the capital of Yunnan Province, after failing to leave China for Syria.[5] Months later, both al Qaeda and the Islamic State announced China as a target because of its alleged occupation of Xinjiang.[6] These organizations framed Chinese rule in Xinjiang as an occupation in an effort to delegitimize Chinese sovereignty. Lessons from terror attacks abroad and at home have taught the Chinese authorities that there is a need to expand their repertoire of legal instruments and to establish a new, well-coordinated counterterrorism structure within China to handle and prevent future terror attacks. Therefore, on 27 December 2015, after two rounds of public consultation, Beijing passed the first comprehensive counterterror legislation in the history of the People's Republic of China.

This chapter focuses on China's efforts in dealing with the rising threat of terrorism through new legal initiatives. Given the extensive nature of the new counterterrorism legislation, it is crucial to examine how the concept of terrorism within China evolved from revolutionary terrorism to the 'three evils' and the contemporary interpretation focused on jihadi groups. The reader may ask – why is it important to examine China's legal initiatives for counterterrorism? The reason is simple: to gain a better understanding of how China views terrorism and the evolution of its counterterrorism legislation. Despite China's judicial weaknesses, it is making efforts to deal with the rising threat of terrorism by strengthening its counterterrorism legislation. This chapter will also attempt to unpack the complex factors behind the accelerated promulgation of legal measures, and the extent to which this acceleration derives from Xi's overall policy approach, which attempts to accumulate and recentralize power in the governing party.

The first section of the chapter outlines China's general approach to counterterrorism. It also provides a brief explanation of why counterterrorism in Xinjiang and the maintenance of stability are playing an increasingly crucial role in the survival of the Communist Party of China (CPC). The second section discusses how this restive province has shaped China's counterterrorism approaches. The third section examines the evolution of China's legal approach towards counterterrorism and how the Xi regime has accelerated the institution of legal measures that his predecessors had deemed premature for China.

China's existing counterterrorism strategy

Although there is no global consensus on a single definition of terrorism, observers have often singled out China's ambiguous legal definition of terrorism as being inconsistent with international norms.[7] This led scholars such as Rohan Gunaratna et al. and Kent Roach to suggest that China should create its own concept, with reference to counterterrorism legislation from abroad, and adopt that according to the Chinese context.[8] More on China's counterterrorism legislation will be discussed in the next section. In addition to this legislation, China has traditionally used a supplementary 'strike-hard' (严打, *yanda*) strategy to quell the increasing militancy in Xinjiang since the 1990s. It should be pointed out that this strategy was not originally designed as a counterterrorism tool, but its use in Xinjiang was effective in achieving short-term success from the late 1990s until 2008. However, this heavy-handed approach also resulted in serious human rights violations and has received wide international condemnation.

China's strike-hard strategy originated in the 1981 National Work Forum on Public Security in Five Major Chinese Cities.[9] Crime rates across the major Chinese cities of Beijing, Tianjin, Wuhan, Shanghai and Guangzhou soared following China's reform and opening up in the late 1970s. The severe lack of public security affected quality of life and industrial productivity. Due to domestic calls for greater justice, the forum decided the CPC had a moral obligation to devise a new strategy to clamp down swiftly and decisively on violent crime, rather than to rely on criminal prosecution procedures. Chinese legal scholars have since questioned the legality of the strike-hard strategy for its overemphasis on substantive justice and subsequent neglect of procedural justice.[10]

As mentioned earlier, the CPC felt morally obliged to uphold substantive justice during the early years of China's reform and opening up. Having lived through the turbulent post-war years and the social upheaval caused by the 1966–76 Cultural Revolution, Chinese citizens craved stability and security. However, the lawlessness brought about by the Cultural Revolution had left the courts in a shambles. In order to maintain the legitimacy of its control over the country, the CPC made an unwritten social contract with the Chinese citizens to be the sole provider of social stability and security. This, rather than the Chinese Constitution, forms the basis for China's seemingly infinite political will to ensure its ability to manage unrest in peripheral regions such as Xinjiang and Tibet. Insurgency in Xinjiang and the spillover into Beijing and neighbouring provinces since 2013 increasingly demonstrates the state's inability both to manage unrest and to provide social stability as demanded by the core provinces. According to Martin Wayne, 'If the state is perceived as weak, challenges and challengers will rise. Because of these socio-structural and political historic factors, the state must strongly confront the insurgency in Xinjiang if it is to survive. Failing this, not only would the periphery rupture but the core would rebel.'[11]

The CPC-led central government also worked to repair its image and ensure its legitimacy by liberalizing social control in China at the same time as the implementation of the strike-hard strategy. Amid this general liberalization of control was greater freedom of religious expression and cultural practices in ethnic minority autonomous regions such as Xinjiang and Tibet. Reopened borders, relaxed policies on the use of Arabic language and private Islamic schools (*madrasahs*), and increasing contact with the greater Muslim world brought about the spread of Salafism and political Islam from the Middle East in Xinjiang during the 1980s.[12] Violent separatist protests erupted in Xinjiang during the 1980s following the implementation of China's reform and opening-up policies. Scholars have pointed to the clash between Salafism and the Chinese state's more accommodative practices as a leading cause for the first wave of violence in the early 1990s, which saw local imams and government officials falling victim to political assassination.[13]

Scholars have pointed out that there is a vicious cycle of violent contention in Xinjiang.[14] The violent 1990 Baren Town riot and the 1997 Ghulja/Yining riot were part of the first wave of contention in Xinjiang.[15] After the Chinese authorities reacted forcefully with the strike-hard campaigns, there was a marked decline in civil unrest and separatist movements during the early 2000s.[16] In June 2001, China applied its doctrine of 'three evil forces' (三股势力, *sangu shili*) of separatism, terrorism and religious extremism for international cooperation on counterterrorism with the Russian Federation and Central Asian states of Kazakhstan, Tajikistan, Kyrgyzstan and Uzbekistan under the auspices of the Shanghai Cooperation Organization (SCO).[17] In August 2001, the Chinese military undertook large-scale exercises in Xinjiang, reportedly involving 50,000 troops. The month-long exercises were among the largest ever staged in the region. This also included an imposing military parade in the southern Xinjiang city of Kashgar, presided over by General Fu Quanyou, then chief of general staff of the People's Liberation Army (PLA) and a member of the Central Military Commission.

However, the fragile peace was torn when protests erupted in Urumqi and Khotan in March 2008, and spread to Kashgar and other parts of Xinjiang in the following months. There were also reports of a series of attacks on police stations and bombings in Xinjiang. It has been argued that such protests and attacks were premeditated by Uyghur terrorists to coincide with the 2008 Olympic Games in Beijing.[18] Ethnic tensions continued unabated in 2009, culminating in violent clashes between Uyghurs and Han Chinese in the provincial capital of Urumqi in July. According to officials, the unrest claimed the lives of nearly 200 people, mostly Han Chinese. This prompted the Chinese Government to send large numbers of troops to patrol the streets.

Scholars have argued that extremist elements in the Uyghur separatist movement began transforming into terrorists in 2014, citing factors such as the failure of the Chinese state's ethnic policies, its increasing repression in the name of stability and the recent trend of increasing Arabization of Uyghur society.[19] There was an alarming increase in 2014 in the death toll of incidents of extremist violence (as compared with the period 2009–13) and also a change in the nature of the violence (see table 2.1). It has been pointed out that, prior to 2014, anti-state acts of violence in Xinjiang usually targeted security and other state apparatus. However, the 2014 attacks targeted ordinary citizens regardless of ethnicity, and without establishing their direct connection with the Chinese state.[20] In September 2015, at least fifty people, mostly Han Chinese, were killed in an attack on the residential quarters of a coalmine by Uyghur extremists. It was the highest ever number of casualties in a single terror attack within Xinjiang.[21]

The incidents of extremist violence also spilled out of the confines of Xinjiang into China proper, beginning with the suicide car-bombing attack at

Table 2.1 Death toll from Xinjiang-related violence, 2013–15

Year	Total deaths (Xinjiang)	Total deaths (outside Xinjiang)	Remarks
2013	114	5	Golden Waters Bridge incident, Tiananmen Square – 5 killed, 40 injured
2014	256	29	Kunming Railway Station attack, Yunnan Province – 29 killed, 143 injured Guangzhou Railway Station attack, Guangdong Province – 6 injured
2015	78	20	Bangkok bombing, Thailand – 20 killed, suspects are Uighur PRC nationals; suspected revenge attack against Thailand for deporting 109 ethnic Uighurs to China

PRC, People's Republic of China.

Data analysis based on Chinese and overseas media reports. The reported death tolls for Xinjiang-related violence in China are conflicting and unverifiable. A report from the Agence France-Presse estimated the total deaths in 2014 to be more than 450, and in 2013 more than 220, based on data from the Uyghur Human Rights Project.

Tiananmen Square in 2013, and the railway station attacks in Kunming and Guangzhou in 2014. China's terrorism is also threatening to spill over into Southeast Asian countries, which are a transit point for Uyghurs who have fled from China in the hope of travelling to Turkey. There has also been speculation that a criminal gang which trafficked Uyghurs from China to Turkey via Thailand was behind the 2015 Bangkok bombing after Thai authorities deported 109 Uyghurs to China, causing international outcry and anger in the Uyghur community.[22]

In response to the recent developments in Xinjiang, there have been many changes in China's approaches to dealing with counterterrorism. Chinese political will to adopt and implement new such approaches was given a significant boost under the new leadership of Xi Jinping in 2013. This will be discussed in greater detail in the next section.

Has Xinjiang transformed China's counterterrorism policies?

Fear of the 'three evils' – ethnic separatism, religious extremism and violent terrorism – in Xinjiang over the recent years has changed the CPC's perception of threat. Some scholars have warned that this reflects a gradual 'Xinjiang-ization' of China, where hardline approaches 'paradoxically expand the scope and scale of terrorist threats throughout the country.'[23] However, an accurate analysis of contemporary China must acknowledge the country's turbulent past and how it made stability *the* obsession for its government and its people.[24] This explains China's tendency to use force, not just in Xinjiang but also throughout the country. In addition to strike-hard campaigns, the Chinese Government implemented draconian measures such as blanket surveillance of cities and highways, normalization of militarized policing, and increased censorship and repression of dissent throughout China.[25] Although there is domestic concern over the increasing censorship and surveillance throughout China, the average Chinese citizen accepts and appreciates such hardline approaches to safeguard stability. In fact, the Chinese population expects and demands that the CPC deliver on its promise to provide stability and ensure national security at all costs.

Furthermore, the label 'terrorism' seems to be applied almost exclusively to acts carried out by disgruntled ethnic minorities such as the Uyghurs and Tibetans, rather than attacks perpetrated by the Han majority. For instance, the Chinese authorities were quick to rule that the perpetrator of seventeen parcel bomb explosions in Liucheng County of the Guangxi Province on 30 September 2015 was not a terrorist. In spite of the scale of the attack, which killed seven and injured fifty-one people, the authorities classified it as a 'criminal case', rather than a terrorist act.[26] Neither was the Shanghai Pudong Airport bomb attack on 13 June 2016 classified as a terrorist act. In fact, the authorities identified the bomber as a gambler with heavy debts, rather than a terrorist.[27] The incident was not widely covered by the mainstream Chinese media. The online community's comments on the *Global Times*' online report of the bombing showed a strong concern over the lack of security checks and surveillance at the airport. In fact, they accused the authorities of being too complacent.[28]

Returning to the question of whether Xinjiang has changed China's overall counterterrorism strategy, evidence has shown that there are indeed ways in which Xinjiang has done this, particularly in grass-roots participation in surveillance and intelligence gathering, and in the building of a national framework to combat terrorism.

Grass-roots awareness and participation

The Chinese authorities have blanketed Xinjiang with video surveillance cameras following the incidents of unrest in 2008 and 2009.[29] According to guidelines on improving social management, released by the National Development and Reform Commission and eight other departments, there will be blanket electronic surveillance of all key public areas in China by 2020 in order to maintain national security and social stability while preventing and combating violent terrorist crimes.[30] It bears highlighting that, although terror attacks have spilled out of the confines of Xinjiang, China is a country that faces hundreds of large-scale non-terrorism-related incidents annually.[31] The decision to expand surveillance measures throughout China also helps in keeping the lid on non-terror-related incidents and contributes towards maintaining law and order across China.

Although Xi's dominance, combined with the increasing normalization of military policing, persecution of activist lawyers and harsher repression of ethnic minorities in the name of counterterrorism, has unnerved some Chinese, he retains popular support from the Chinese population in general.[32] Xi's influence and popularity outmatch those of his predecessors of recent decades. As a result, the strict measures undertaken by the central government under Xi's leadership seem to be gaining acceptance in China in a way that outsiders cannot fathom. A report claimed that as many as 850,000 volunteers joined the professional enforcement forces in patrolling the streets of Beijing after the central government heightened security measures in the Chinese capital in May 2014.[33]

In addition to the increasing use of electronic surveillance, the Chinese authorities have also taken steps to legalize grass-roots surveillance to supplement the electronic form and strengthen intelligence collection. There has been a gradual strengthening of this grass-roots surveillance network, which was implemented before the outbreak of mass protests in Xinjiang in 2008.[34] Positive feedback from practical experiences in Xinjiang has highlighted the importance of public support in providing information on would-be terrorists and suspects following an attack. For instance, more than seventy locals reported relevant information about suspected perpetrators of a violent terror attack that killed dozens of people in Xinjiang's Shache County in July 2014.[35] In a newly announced provincial counterterrorism law, which took effect on 1 August 2016, the Xinjiang authorities have emphasized the importance of a public reporting mechanism for terrorist activity. The law stipulates that public security bureaus and state security organizations will be ready to receive information from the public.

Building a national counterterror framework

The changes that Xi has brought about represent a late realization of the necessity for concrete and coordinated measures on counterterrorism, following the 2013 Tiananmen suicide car-bombing attack.[36] Besides supporting increased efforts to stabilize Xinjiang, the Xi regime also extended a wide range of directives and policies to ensure stability across the whole of China. The new leadership also created a new National Anti-Terror Work Leading Group in August 2013, to replace the previous anti-terrorism coordination group. Headed by Guo Shengkun, minister of public security, the upgraded group has a stronger leading role and wider responsibilities to better direct and mobilize resources in counterterrorism efforts throughout the country.[37] In January 2014, Xi established a National Security Commission (NSC) to coordinate strategic issues of preserving stability and safeguarding territorial rights (统筹维稳和维权两个大局, *tongchou weiwen he weiquan liangge daju*). The NSC's four main functions are to:

1. develop an all-encompassing national security strategy instead of a military strategy
2. construct a legal system for national security by introducing new laws and enhancing existing ones in areas of the military, foreign policy, economics, technology and intelligence, among others
3. define and adopt national security policies which focus on issues such as sovereignty, terrorism, and maritime and cyber concerns
4. address specific national security threats and incidents, particularly those involving Xinjiang, Tibet and Hong Kong.[38]

More than two decades since China enacted its first national security legislation with the 1993 State Security Law, it adopted a new all-encompassing National Security Law, which gave the NSC a statutory definition and outlined its responsibilities, on 1 July 2015.[39] It was drafted jointly by the Chinese domestic security, military and diplomatic authorities in December 2014. At the inaugural meeting of the NSC, Xi announced a new comprehensive national security concept covering varied aspects of security, including human, economic, cultural and social, and military security.

Chinese counterterrorism experts have argued that while the Ministry of Public Security and its National Anti-Terror Work Leading Group may be able to counter terror plots, they are unable to solve the fundamental causes of terrorism.[40] Therefore, Chinese counterterrorism experts claimed that this new overall security concept would serve to guide China's counterterrorism efforts and to tackle the issue of terrorism at its roots.[41] However, apart from establishing state authority over the national security apparatus, it is currently unclear how the NSC will function and how the National Security Law will ultimately enhance China's counterterrorism efforts as claimed. It is also unclear how the National Anti-Terror Work Leading Group will be effective in managing the plethora of leading groups handling internal security operations under the Ministries of Public Security and State Security, such as the Political-Legal Affairs Committee, the Leading Small Group for Preventing and Handling the Problem of Heretical Organizations and the Leading Small Group for Preserving Stability, in terms of overlapping responsibilities.[42]

Evolution of China's legal approaches towards counterterrorism

This section examines the evolution of the Chinese understanding of the concept of terrorism, China's legal approaches towards counterterrorism since the 1950s and the changes brought about by the current Chinese leadership. This examination of the evolution seeks to highlight two important facts: (1) like the West, China struggled with its understanding of terrorism and response to terrorism-related incidents, and (2) regardless of China's failure to uphold its own laws with its harsh response to separatism and terrorism in Xinjiang, it has an existing set of counterterrorism laws under the umbrella of the Chinese Criminal Law. There are also many robust debates among Chinese law professionals regarding the enforcement of such laws and their failure to protect human rights; however, the scope of this chapter does not include an evaluation of enforcement.

Instead, it attempts to draw attention to the fact that the new counterterrorism law is in fact not a new creation but a reinvention, or reinterpretation, of existing laws, intended to streamline China's counterterrorism efforts. The current Chinese leadership began to take a different approach towards counterterrorism by attempting to use legislation to justify counterterrorism as a national security priority. It has also taken bold strides in streamlining the counterterrorism legal framework, in comparison with its predecessors.

Chinese academics have put forth various opinions on the definition of terrorism since 2001, without reaching a consensus on this issue.[43] One opinion considers terrorism as a crime, while other opinions consider terrorism as an ideological concept, or a system of terrorist activities.[44] Chinese scholars have pointed out that the problem in defining terrorism lies not only in theoretical definitions but also in setting the practical boundaries of what constitutes a terrorist activity or group. A Chinese law expert, Du Miao, noted that China's counterterrorism legislation has undergone three critical phases – the embryonic stage (1950–90), the generation stage (1991–2001) and the development stage (2002–present).[45]

Embryonic stage (1950–90)

During the embryonic stage, terrorism was first mentioned in China's draft penal code as part of the description of counter-revolutionary activities in 1950. Scholars have pointed out that China's first criminal legislation, adopted in 1951 and entitled 'Regulations for the Suppression of Counterrevolution', was in essence counterterrorism legislation.[46] However, due to China's revolutionary legacy, the definitions of insurgency and sabotage fell under the category of counter-revolutionary offences listed in the first legislation and the subsequent Criminal Law of the People's Republic of China that was promulgated in 1979, even though such premeditated acts of anti-state violence are commonly referred to as terrorist activities by the international community. Terrorism was later redefined as a politically motivated crime against the Chinese state in the 1998 revision of the Chinese Criminal Law. Du claims that this redefinition marked China's earliest understanding of terrorism, and that it conformed to the international community's early cognition of terrorism.[47]

Generation stage (1991–2001)

During the generation stage, the external influences of political Islam, Pan-Turkism and the dissolution of the Soviet Union brought about the creation of the East Turkestan Independence Movement (ETIM) in the early 1990s.[48] This resulted in a spate of terror attacks within China that necessitated the counterterrorism legislation. According to Chinese scholar Li Zhe, the first legal provision in China to mention 'terrorist acts' was Article 8 of the Implementing Rules of the National Security Law of the People's Republic of China (PRC), which was effective from 4 June 1994.[49] While it listed the 'organizing, planning or implementing a terrorist act as one of the other acts endangering the national security', it did not include any definition of terrorism, terror acts or terrorist organizations.[50]

In 1996, the issue of separatism and social stability in Xinjiang was given particular prominence at a Politburo Standing Committee (PSC) meeting. The meeting outcomes, summarized in the *Central Document No. 7 (1996)*, identified separatism and illegal religious activity as major threats to stability in Xinjiang and the nation.[51] What began as an attempt to assert control over Islam 'marked a watershed moment in Xinjiang's ethnic conflict'.[52] It should be noted that the SCO term 'three evils' originated from this document. However, it did not provide a definition of terrorism, but provided the basis for China's conflation of ethnic, religious and violent activities. It has been noted that while Article 120 of the 1997 PRC Penal Code prohibits the commission of 'terrorist activities' and the financing of a 'terrorist organization', at the same time it makes no attempt to define such terms.[53] There was little urgency to push for the legal definitions of terms at this point in time, as regular nationwide strike-hard anti-crime campaigns, which began in 1996, were having success in rounding up thousands of terrorists, murderers and criminals across China.

Developmental stage (2001–present)

The stage that China is currently in – the developmental stage – began after the attacks of 11 September 2001 (hereafter referred to as 9/11 attacks) in the US. The attacks reinforced Beijing's fears of links between separatism and political Islam.[54] The impact that the 9/11 attacks had on national security also created a strong sense of urgency in the Chinese Government to accelerate its search for a definition of terrorism. Most of the Chinese literature on terrorism agrees that China's attempts to define its home-grown terror threat and put forward a credible and internationally palatable definition began in earnest after the 9/11 attacks.[55] China's international cooperative efforts on counterterrorism suffered from its lack of a clear and precise definition of terrorist activities, organizations and personnel. In response to Resolution 1373 adopted by the United Nations Security Council on 28 September 2001, China began to undertake a series of criminal law amendments and promulgated new legislation on counterterrorism (see table 2.2).

Looking at table 2.2, one can sense that China's old legal framework on counterterrorism was piecemeal, a product mostly of reactions from individual

Table 2.2 Evolution of China's counterterrorism legislation framework, 2001–15

Year	Amendment/Legislation	Counterterrorism Measures
2001	Amendment (III) of the Criminal Law of the PRC (commonly referred to as the 2001 Anti-Terror Amendment)	• Introduction of new offences and revision of existing provisions, such as criminalization of the financing of terror activities and handling of dangerous substances (e.g., anthrax powder), as well as intensifying the suppression of money laundering
2006	Anti-Money-Laundering (AML) Law	• People's Bank of China (PBC) issued two new rules in conjunction with the AML Law: the *Rules for Anti-Money-Laundering by Financial Institutions* (the AML Rules) and the *Administrative Rules for the Reporting of Large-Value and Suspicious Transaction by Financial Institutions* • The AML Law and the two PBC rules constituted a new legal framework which applied a uniform set of measures, including those combating the financing of terrorism, to the entire financial system[1]
2007	Amendments to the 2006 AML Law – Administrative Measures for Financial Institutions' Report of Transactions Suspected of Financing for Terrorist Purposes	• All financial institutions within China are required to report suspicious transactions – particularly those related to terrorist organizations and activists listed by Chinese organizations and the United Nations Security Council –to the financial authorities, regardless of monetary value[2] • Penalties for failure to report suspicious transactions include business suspension and license revocation; staff members involved in terrorism financing activities will have their professional licenses revoked and be barred from working in the industry

2009	Law on the People's Armed Police Force (PAPF) of the PRC (Presidential Order No. 17)	• Originally proposed in 1995; draft law submitted for first reading in April 2009 • Promulgated on 27 August 2009 (a month after the 2009 Urumqi Riots) with immediate effect, following heightened concerns for the sixtieth anniversary of the PRC's founding • Provides a legal framework for activities that the PAPF has long engaged in • Clarifies how and when the PAPF may be deployed; authority to mobilize and deploy troops strictly limited to the State Council, the Cabinet and Central Military Commission • Significant change: restriction for county-level governments to summon the PAPF to handle disorders to prevent abuse of authority[3] • The army given authority to handle rebellion, riots, serious violent crimes, terror attacks and other emergencies
2011	Amendment (VIII) of the Criminal Law of the PRC Decision on Issues Related to Strengthening Anti-Terrorism Work	• Provided China's first legal definition of terrorism • Establishment of the National Anti-Terrorism Leading Group • Maintenance of terrorist watch lists • Introduction of procedure for freezing terrorist assets
2012	Decision of the National People's Congress on Revising the Criminal Law of the PRC	• Designation of courts for trying terrorism cases (previously, there were no distinctions) • Limitation of suspects' access to counsel in terrorism cases • Provision of special protection for witnesses in terrorism cases • Authorization of residential surveillance for terror suspects • Limitation on the right to notification in terrorism cases • Legalization of the use of technical investigation measures • Introduction of procedure for confiscating illegal earnings in terrorism cases

Continued

Table 2.2 Evolution of China's counterterrorism legislation framework, 2001–15 (Continued)

Year	Amendment/Legislation	Counterterrorism Measures
2014	Proposal for Amendment (IX) of the Criminal Law of the PRC Counterterrorism Law of the PRC (Draft)	• Amendment (IX): 1. Fines and confiscation of property belonging to suspects convicted of organizing, leading or participating in terrorist activities 2. Expansion of list of terrorist activities to include financing and recruitment for terrorist training, preparation of weapons and other hazardous substances for terrorist attacks in the existing list of terrorist activities, disseminating terrorism-related materials, etc. 3. Inclusion of illegal immigration for terrorist training/to join terrorist organizations/to carry out terrorist activities abroad as an offence under illegal border-crossing crimes • Counterterrorism Law: 1. China's first comprehensive counterterrorism legal framework 2. Different legal definition of terrorism from the existing definition from the 2011 Decision 3. Setting up of counterterrorism working bodies in the national, provincial and prefecture-level governments under the leadership of the National Anti-Terror Work Leading Group 4. Improving counterterrorism information collection, and intra-agency and trans-regional information sharing through a national intelligence-gathering centre 5. Restriction of media coverage on terrorism-related news 6. Prohibition of dissemination of terrorism-related information via social media 7. Expanded scope for China to seek international cooperation in its counterterrorism efforts – enforcement cooperation, international financial monitoring, extradition and judiciary assistance, etc. 8. Provision for Chinese armed forces to take part in counterterrorism operations abroad, with approval of the foreign country in question
2015	Amendment (IX) of Criminal Law of the PRC Counterterrorism Law of the PRC	

Compiled by the author from official sources and secondary literature.

[1] Financial Action Task Force (FATF), *First Mutual Evaluation Report On Anti-Money Laundering and Combating the Financing of Terrorism – People's Republic of China* (Paris: FATF, 2007), available at: www.fatf-gafi.org/media/fatf/documents/reports/mer/MER%20China%20full.pdf (accessed 12 June 2018).

[2] Xin Zhiming, 'New measures to fight terror-financing,' *China Daily*, 12 June 2007, available at: http://www.chinadaily.com.cn/china/2007-06/12/content_891900.htm (accessed 1 June 2017).

[3] Global Legal Monitor, Library of Congress, 'China: New law on People's Armed Police passed,' Library of Congress website, 3 September 2009, available at: www.loc.gov/law/foreign-news/article/china-new-law-on-peoples-armed-police-passed/ (accessed 12 June 2018).

law-enforcement stakeholders to policy shifts. In fact, Chinese scholars have made critical analyses of China's lack of a systemic legal framework since the early 2000s.[56] For instance, they see the frequent amendments to the Criminal Law to address counterterrorism needs as confusing and thus detrimental to the stability of the Chinese legal system. They have also pointed out that the old Chinese legal framework did not make provision for law-enforcement agencies to differentiate between terrorist-related investigations and normal criminal investigations.

As such, Chinese law enforcers are not well equipped to handle the specialized investigations and surveillance needed in terrorist-related activities. Another oversight that scholars have noted relates to the assets and money belonging to terrorist organizations or terrorists.[57] The Anti-Money Laundering Law and the Criminal Law did not address the issue of asset seizure in terrorism-related cases until 2011. A Fudan University scholar commented that the problem is that the old framework (before the promulgation of the new counterterrorism law) was the sum of emergency legislation made after the 9/11 attacks, without proper scientific or rational planning.[58]

In order to address the increasing instability of the Xinjiang issue, the National People's Congress (NPC) Standing Committee passed a *Decision on Issues Related to Strengthening Anti-Terrorism Work*, at the 11th NPC in October 2011. It marked a significant milestone in Chinese legal history.[59] The definition of terrorism from the Decision was China's first formal legal definition of terrorism.[60] According to the Decision, terrorist activities are defined as:

> activities aimed at creating terror in the society, endangering public security or threatening state or international organizations. Such activities, carried out by the use of violence, sabotage, intimidation and other methods seeks to cause human casualties, loss of private property, damage to public facilities and disrupt social order, also includes activities that incite, finance or assist the afore-mentioned activities through any other means.[61]

It also defined terrorist organizations as criminal organizations established for the purpose of executing terrorist activities, and terrorists as those who organize, plan and carry out terrorist activities or who are members of terrorist organizations. The Decision also stated that the state's leading working group on counterterrorism will decide on and adjust China's official lists of terrorist organizations and terrorists, to be published by the Ministry of Public Security. The Decision was made with the consideration that it was premature at that time to pass a comprehensive counterterrorism law.

Why did China accelerate the promulgation of the new counterterrorism law when the previous Hu Jintao/Wen Jiabao Government had deemed it premature for a comprehensive legislation only three years earlier? This chapter posits that the answer lies in the current leader, Xi Jinping. Xi's campaign to ensure the security of the state provided the impetus for the counterterrorism legal framework which many scholars had been proposing since the early 2000s. China's first ever draft law on counterterrorism was published for public review on 3 November 2014 by the NPC.[62] The draft counterterrorism law, consisting of 106 articles in ten chapters, drew sharp international criticism not only for human rights concerns, but also for fears that it constitutes unfair regulatory practices.[63]

The first controversy was that the draft law's initial definition of terrorism differed from the existing definition of terrorism as provided in the 2011 Decision. As pointed out earlier, the 2011 Decision focused predominantly on defining terrorist activities. However, the draft law broadly defined terrorism as 'any thoughts, speech or activity that – through violence, sabotage or intimidation – aims to cause social panic, impact national decision-making, sow ethnic hatred, overthrow the state or split the country'.[64] This narrow definition sparked concerns of over-criminalization and abuse as people could potentially be punished for having opinions, even when they did not participate in terrorist activities.[65] This was subsequently changed to 'advocacy' (主张, *zhuzhang*) in the final version of the law, which was passed on 27 December 2015.[66] Therefore, scholars have pointed out that China's counterterrorism law – and, to a greater extent, its rhetoric on terrorism – is more about eliminating dissent so as to secure and legitimize its rule over the restive regions of Tibet and Xinjiang, rather than conforming with new developments in the global campaign against terrorism and maintaining global security.[67]

The second controversy that sparked fears of unfair regulatory practices under the guise of counterterrorism was the draft law's requirement for technology firms, both foreign and domestic, to create software backdoors and share encryption keys with the government upon demand.[68] Such companies were also required to locate their servers and store user data within China, provide law-enforcement authorities with communications records, and censor terrorism-related Internet content. The final bill did not include the controversial backdoor requirement when the counterterrorism law was formally adopted. Nevertheless, it requires Internet providers to give technical assistance and hand over information, including encryption keys, to the government during counterterror operations.[69]

In order to streamline counterterrorism efforts, the law made provisions for the establishment of a national counterterrorism intelligence centre and called for prompt reporting and sharing of vital information and intelligence on terrorism-related cases across relevant departments.[70] While this ensures better information sharing, it underlies the fact that there has been an increase in public surveillance throughout China since 2005.[71]

In comparison with the new counterterror legislation, the existing counterterrorism provisions under the Chinese Criminal Law were scattered and promulgated on an ad hoc basis. Observers have noted that the new law included far-reaching, multifaceted measures that seek to reshape Chinese counterterrorism policy and operations.[72] It also underscored the shift towards an increased role of law in politics and governance, following a landmark decision made in 2014, during the Fourth Plenary Session of the 18th Central Committee of the CPC, to improve governance by strengthening the rule of law.[73] More importantly, the drafting of the new counterterrorism law, and Amendment #9 to the Chinese Criminal Law in 2015, was also in line with the domestic angle of President Xi Jinping's 'overall national security outlook'.[74] Under Xi's directive, Beijing began streamlining coordination within the massive state bureaucracy by 'comprehensively advancing the rule of law' in the country.

The new counterterrorism legislation is truly extensive in its coverage. It is made up of ninety-seven articles in ten chapters. General and supplementary provisions are laid out in the first and last chapters. The remaining chapters deal with major counterterror issues:

- Chapter 2 – Designation of terrorist organizations and personnel
- Chapter 3 – Security and prevention
- Chapter 4 – Intelligence information
- Chapter 5 – Investigation
- Chapter 6 – Response and handling
- Chapter 7 – International cooperation
- Chapter 8 – Safeguard measures
- Chapter 9 – Legal responsibilities.

Although the new counterterrorism law stipulates the authorities responsible for emergency response to terrorist incidents (chapter 6) and provides due procedure for designating terrorist groups and individuals (chapter 2), its combination with existing legislation may result in a confusing set of hardline policies that limit local autonomy in managing local affairs. For instance, the 2009 Law on the People's Armed Police Force (PAPF) strictly limits the authority to mobilize and deploy troops to the State Council, the Cabinet and Central Military Commission. Provincial and county-level authorities are not allowed to summon the PAPF to handle disorder. Under the new counterterrorism law, efforts are underway to establish counterterrorism working bodies in the national, provincial and prefecture-level governments under the leadership of the National Anti-Terror Work Leading Group.

It has been argued that China's new legislation seeks to recentralize control over provincial governments and judiciary so that the current leadership can consolidate power. 'Xi has intensified the uses of legislation and judicial practice as instruments of party ideology and policy in order to impose a more repressive regime than China has witnessed since the June 4 era.'[75] Legal observers have also argued that the reduction of provincial government's role in the policymaking process has brought about a paradoxical increase in the potential scope and scale of terrorist threats across China.[76]

However, the mainstream view in China is that the first counterterrorism law is an unambiguous legal document which clearly defines terrorism.[77] Some scholars applaud the law for formalizing counterterrorism as a top priority for Chinese national security, undergirded by the new leadership's dedication to domestic stability. However, some doubtful voices have also emerged with regard to the differences and duality between the new counterterrorism law and Criminal Law and how these will work together to form a comprehensive legal framework. A Chinese legal expert pointed out that the new law comprises a comprehensive set of 'administrative prevention measures', rather than criminal sanctions.[78] He attributed this to the fact that these laws were drafted by different departments – the Criminal Law amendment by the NPC Law Committee and the counterterrorism law by the Ministry of Public Security. Another expert commented that, in comparison with Amendment (IX) of the Criminal Law of the PRC, the counterterrorism law seems to be 'immature' in handling counterterrorism cases.[79]

One of the criticisms has highlighted institutional weakness as the root cause of current challenges in maintaining stability (维稳, *weiwen*). Chinese scholar Xi Chen argues against the assumption that strengthening of the mechanism to maintain stability addresses China's structural problems. While it may be effective in managing short-term challenges, the overemphasis on maintaining stability without addressing institutional weaknesses has created grave long-term problems for the regime. Xi Chen's interviews with judges and police officers in Hunan and Hubei revealed a blunter assessment of Xi Jinping's efforts: 'The more effort in *weiwen*, the more instability.'[80]

Conclusion

On 5 August 2016, around the time of writing this chapter, the Xinjiang provincial government unveiled China's first local counterterrorism law.[81] It was reported that the chairman of the Standing Committee of the National People's Congress and concurrent deputy head of China's NSC, Zhu Dejiang, personally endorsed this new local counterterrorism law.[82] Xinjiang scholars and provincial government officials commented that since Xinjiang is the frontrunner in China's counterterrorism strategy, this was a major acknowledgement of the efforts that the local authorities have made toward combating terrorism in recent years. They also claim that this new law reinforces and supplements the national counterterrorism law that was passed in December 2015.[83]

The current leadership has indeed made much advancement in passing its series of legislation on counterterrorism and national security. Although China's new counterterrorism laws do not follow all the new trends from around the world, it has been observed that Beijing has taken a few leaves out of the counterterrorism books of many democracies around the world.[84]

Notes

Every effort has been made to provide valid URLs where appropriate in the references below. Unfortunately, that has not always been possible, and for some of the references the URL consulted is no longer valid but no alternative was available.

1 Tong Yanqi and Lei Shaohua, 'Large-scale mass incidents in China,' *East Asian Policy* 2:2 (2010): 23–33.

2 See Gardner Bovingdon, *Autonomy in Xinjiang: Han Nationalist Imperatives and Uyghur Discontent*, Policy Studies 11 (Washington, DC: East-West Center, 2004); Martin I. Wayne, 'Inside China's war on terrorism,' *Journal of Contemporary China* 18:59 (2009): 249–61.

3 See Christopher P. Cunningham, 'Counterterrorism in Xinjiang: The ETIM, China, and the Uyghurs,' *International Journal on World Peace* 29:3 (2012): 7–50; Collin Mackerras, 'Xinjiang in 2013: Problems and prospects,' *Asian Ethnicity* 15:2 (2014): 247–50; Julia Famularo, 'How Xinjiang has transformed China's counterterrorism policies,' *National Interest*, 26 August 2015, available at: http://nationalinterest.org/feature/how-xinjiang-has-transformed-china%E2%80%99s-counterterrorism-13699?page=5 (accessed 18 January 2018).

4 Jonathan Kaiman, 'Islamist group claims responsibility for attack on China's Tiananmen Square,' *Guardian*, 25 November 2013, available at: www.theguardian.com/world/2013/nov/25/islamist-china-tiananmen-beijing-attack (accessed 16 January 2018).

5 Yunnan Party Secretary, 'Kunming station attackers wanted to participate in "Jihad,"' *BBC*, 5 March 2014 [in Chinese], available at: http://www.bbc.com/zhongwen/simp/china/2014/03/140305_yunnan_party_scretary (accessed 8 June 2018).

6 Zachary Keck, 'Al-Qaeda declares war on China, too,' *Diplomat*, 22 October 2014, available at: https://thediplomat.com/2014/10/al-qaeda-declares-war-on-china-too (accessed 16 January 2018).

7 Fu Hualing, 'Responses to terrorism in China,' in Victor V. Ramraj, Michael Hor, et al. (eds), *Global Anti-Terrorism Law and Policy* (Cambridge, UK: Cambridge University Press, 2012), p. 345; Kendrick Kuo, 'New rules for

China's war on terror?' *East Asia Forum*, 25 October 2014, available at: www.eastasiaforum.org/2014/10/25/new-rules-for-chinas-war-on-terror (accessed 16 January 2018); Zhou Zunyou, 'How China defines terrorism,' *Diplomat*, 13 February 2015, available at: http://thediplomat.com/2015/02/how-china-defines-terrorism (accessed 15 May 2016).

8 Rohan Gunaratna, Arabinda Acharya and Wang Pengxin, *Ethnic Identity and National Conflict in China* (New York: Palgrave MacMillian, 2010), p. 145; Kent Roach, 'China's anti-terror law takes its cues from democracies,' *Ottawa Citizen*, 31 December 2015, available at: http://ottawacitizen.com/opinion/columnists/kent-roach-chinas-anti-terror-law-takes-its-cues-from-democracies (accessed 15 May 2016).

9 People.com.cn, 'Chinese Communist 80 years memorabilia,' www.people.com.cn [in Chinese], available at: www.people.com.cn/GB/shizheng/252/5580/5581/20010612/487184.html (accessed 15 May 2016).

10 Zhang Xin, 'On the legitimacy and rationality of the "strike hard" approach', *System and Society* 3:1 (2015): 279–80 [张芯，论'严打'的合法性与合理性，《法制与社会》2015，3(上)].

11 Martin I. Wayne, *China's War on Terrorism: Counter-Insurgency, Politics and Internal Security* (New York: Routledge, 2008), p. 132.

12 Avinash Godbole and Gunjan Singh, 'Terrorism and unrest in Xinjiang: Drivers, policies and external linkages,' in S.D. Muni and Vivek Chadha (eds), *Asian Strategic Review 2016 – Terrorism: Emerging Trends* (New Delhi: Pentagon, 2016), pp. 313–30.

13 *Ibid.* Also see Kendrick Kuo, 'Revisiting the Salafi-jihadist threat in Xinjiang,' *Journal of Muslim Minority Affairs* 32:4 (2012): 528–44; M. Ehsan Ahrari, 'China, Pakistan, and the "Taliban Syndrome,"' *Asian Survey* 40:4 (2000): 658–71; Yan Sun, 'The roots of China's ethnic conflict,' *Current History* 113:764 (2014): 231–7.

14 Brent Hierman, 'The pacification of Xinjiang: Uighur protest and the Chinese State, 1988–2002,' *Problems of Post-Communism* 54:3 (2007): 48–62.

15 The Baren Town riot took place in a small town located south-west of Kashgar, when police tried to suppress a protest about the closure of a mosque. The protest allegedly included calls for jihad. The ensuing violence claimed between twenty and fifty lives. It was quelled by the Public Security Bureau and 1,000 regular army troops. The Ghulja/Yining riot was allegedly sparked off by a fight between police and worshippers on the final day of Ramadan. Between 300 and 500 protesters were arrested before the fighting began. Official reports cited 9 deaths, while unofficial sources cited 300–400. The city was sealed off for two weeks, and the railway and airport were closed.

16 Dru Gladney, 'Responses to Chinese rule: Patterns of cooperation and opposition,' in Starr (ed.), *Xinjiang*, cited in Hierman, 'Pacification of Xinjiang,' p. 50.

17 Sam Dupont, 'China's war on the "Three Evil Forces,"' *Foreign Policy*, 25 July 2007, available at http://foreignpolicy.com/2007/07/25/chinas-war-on-the-three-evil-forces/ (accessed 8 June 2018).

18 Kristen E. Boon, Aziz Huq and Douglas C. Lovelace (eds), *Terrorism: Commentary on Security Documents*, vol, 103, *Global Issues* (New York: Oxford University Press, 2009), pp. 320–4.

19 Godbole and Singh, 'Terrorism and unrest in Xinjiang.'

20 *Ibid.*

21 Ben Blanchard, 'At least 50 said killed in September Xinjiang attack as China warns on security,' *Reuters*, 1 October 2015, available at: www.reuters.com/article/us-china-xinjiang-idUSKCN0RV38020151001 (accessed 16 January 2018).

22 Oliver Holmes, 'Thai police say Uighur trafficking ring behind Bangkok bombing,' *Guardian*, 15 September 2015.

23 *Ibid.*

24 See Wayne, *China's War on Terrorism*; You Ji, *China's Military Transformation* (Cambridge, UK: Polity, 2016).

25 Peter Humphreys, 'China's crackdown on human rights lawyers has ancient roots,' *Financial Times*, 23 August 2016.

26 Jeremy Koh, 'Seven killed by multiple China letter bombs,' *Channel NewsAsia*, 30 September 2015, available at: www.channelnewsasia.com/news/asiapacific/seven-killed-by-multiple/2160846.html (accessed 16 January 2018).

27 *Straits Times*, 'China police say Shanghai airport bomber was gambler with heavy debts,' *Straits Times*, 13 June 2016, available at: www.straitstimes.com/asia/east-asia/china-police-say-shanghai-airport-bomber-was-gambler-with-heavy-debts (accessed 16 January 2018).

28 China.huanqiu.com, 'Shanghai Pudong Airport exploded firecrackers 4 injured were in hospital for treatment (video),' http://china.huanqiu.com, 12 June 2016 [in Chinese], available at: http://china.huanqiu.com/article/2016–06/9029594.html (accessed 16 January 2018).

29 Famularo, 'How Xinjiang has transformed.'

30 State Council of the People's Republic of China, 'China to fully cover key public areas with video surveillance by 2020,' State Council of the People's Republic of China website, 13 May 2015, available at: http://english.gov.cn/state_council/ministries/2015/05/13/content_281475106818300.htm (accessed 16 January 2018).

31 Hou Liqiang, 'Report identifies sources of mass protests,' *China Daily*, 9 April 2014, available at: www.chinadaily.com.cn/china/2014–04/09/content_17415767.htm (accessed 16 January 2018).

32 *Economist*, 'Xi who must be obeyed,' *Economist*, 18 September 2014, available at: www.economist.com/news/leaders/21618780-most-powerful-and-popular-leader-china-has-had-decades-must-use-these-assets-wisely-xi (accessed 16 January 2018).

33 Edward Wong, 'China moves to calm restive Xinjiang region,' *New York Times*, 30 May 2014, available at: www.nytimes.com/2014/05/31/world/asia/chinas-leader-lays-out-plan-to-pacify-restive-region.html (accessed 17 July 2016).

34 Personal communication from a grass-roots community worker in Urumqi, interviewed by the author in June 2014.

35 Xinhuanet.com, 'Xinjiang issues China's first local counterterrorism law,' xinhuanet.com, 9 August 2016, available at: http://news.xinhuanet.com/english/2016–08/06/c_135567634.htm (accessed 16 January 2018).

36 A family of Uyghurs attempted an attack by crashing their explosive-laden car at the Golden Water Bridge situated within Tiananmen Square in 2013.

37 Zhou Zunyou, 'China's draft counter-terrorism law,' *China Brief* 15:14 (17 July 2015), available at: www.jamestown.org/programs/chinabrief/single/?tx_ttnews%5Btt_news%5D=44173&cHash=dc00eedd4c61b21c691b9700b1468049#.Vs6Z1o9OKas (accessed 15 November 2015).

38 Yiqin Fu, 'What will China's National Security Commission actually do?: The four functions of China's top national security body,' *Foreign Policy*, 8 May 2014, available at: http://foreignpolicy.com/2014/05/08/what-will-chinas-national-security-commission-actually-do (accessed 8 June 2018).

39 See David M. Lampton, 'Xi Jinping and the National Security Commission: Policy coordination and political power,' *Journal of Contemporary China* 24:95 (2015): 759–77.

40 Xie Wei Zhang Lujing, 'How to fight terrorism?' available at: http://paper.people.com.cn/zgjjzk/html/2014–06/09/content_1439745.htm (accessed 16 January 2018).

41 *Ibid.*

42 Samantha Hoffman and Peter Mattis, 'Inside China's new security council', *National Interest*, 21 November 2013, available at: http://nationalinterest.org/commentary/inside-chinas-new-security-council-9439 (accessed 16 January 2018).

43 Li Zhe, 'China,' in Kent Roach (ed.), *Comparative Counter-Terrorism Law* (New York: Cambridge University Press, 2015), p. 582.

44 Mo Hongxian and Ye Xiaoqin, 'A literature review of the research on definition of terrorism in China,' *Journal of China National School of Administration* 5 (2005): 72–7 [莫洪宪、叶小琴，我国恐怖主义定义研究综述，《北京行政学院学报》2005年第5期].

45 Du Miao, 'Retrospect and prospect of China 's anti-terrorism legislation,' *Western Law Review* 6:20 (2012): 40–7 [杜邈，中国反恐立法的回顾与展望，《西部法学评论》2012年06期].

46 *Ibid.*

47 *Ibid.*

48 *Ibid.*

49 Zhe, 'China,' p. 582.

50 *Ibid.*

51 Pitman B. Potter, *Law, Policy, and Practice on China's Periphery: Selective Adaption and Institutional Capacity* (London: Routledge, 2010), p. 86.

52 Ilham Tohti, 'Present-day ethnic problems in Xinjiang Uighur Autonomous Region: Overview and recommendations,' transl. Cindy Carter, *China Change*, 22 April 2015, available at: https://chinachange.org/2015/04/22/present-day-ethnic-problems-in-xinjiang-uighur-autonomous-region-overview-and-recommendations-1/ (accessed 6 May 2015).

53 Kent Roach, 'Comparative Counter-Terrorism Law Comes of Age,' in *Comparative Counter-Terrorism Law*, p. 41.

54 Michael Dillon, *China: A Modern History* (London: I.B. Tauris, 2012), p. 381.

55 Liu Renwen, 'Assessment of terrorism and criminal regulations from the lens of the Ninth Amendment,' *China Law Review* 2 (2015): 168–74 [恐怖主义与刑法规范 – 以《刑法修正案九》(草案) 为视角,《中国法律评论》2015年第2期].

56 Bai Li, 'Improve China's anti-terrorist legislation and punish violent criminals in Xinjiang according to law,' *Social Sciences in Xinjiang* 4 (2009): 70–7 [白莉, 完善国内反恐立法 依法惩治新疆暴力恐怖犯罪,《新疆社会科学》, 2009年04期]; Gu Huaxiang, 'Legislation on the fight against the "three forces" of crime,' *Urumqi Vocational University Press* 3 (2009): 17–35 [顾华详，打击 '三股势力' 犯罪的立法完善论,《乌鲁木齐职业大学学报》, 2009年 03期].

57 *Ibid.*; Mei Chuanqiang, 'The review and improvement of the anti-terrorism criminal legislation in China: Comments on the terrorism-related articles of the Ninth Amendment to the Criminal Law of PRC,' *Modern Law Science* 38:1 (2016): 37–47 [梅传强，我国反恐刑事立法的检讨与完善 – 兼评《刑法修正案(九)》相关涉恐条款,《现代法学》, 2016年1月第38卷第1期].

58 Gao Xuemin, 'China's counterterror legislation: Problems and counter measures' *Journal of Administration and Law* 7 (2014): 126–9 [高学敏，中国反恐立法的形势、问题与对策,《行政与法》, 2014年07期].

59 *People Web*, 'Decision of the Standing Committee of the National People's Congress on Strengthening Issues Related to Counter-Terrorism Work,' *People Web*, 29 October 2011, available at http://politics.people.com.cn/GB/70731/16066603.html (accessed 8 June 2018).

60 Zhou Zunyou, *Balancing Security and Liberty: Counter-Terrorism Legislation in Germany and China* (Berlin: Duncker and Humblot, 2014).

61 *Decision on Issues Related to Strengthening Anti-Terrorism Work*, Article 2.

62 *China Law Translate*, 'Counter-terrorism Law (initial draft),' *China Law Translate*, 8 November 2014, available at: http://chinalawtranslate.com/ctldraft/?lang=en#_Toc414451629 (accessed 8 June 2018).

63 See Human Rights Watch, 'China: Draft counterterrorism law a recipe for abuses,' Human Rights Watch, 20 January 2015, available at: www.hrw.org/news/2015/01/20/china-draft-counterterrorism-law-recipe-abuses (accessed 8 June 2018); Brittany Felder, 'China continuing to review draft counter-terrorism law,' *Jurist*, 16 March 2015, available at http://jurist.org/paperchase/2015/03/china-continuing-to-review-draft-counter-terrorism-law.php (accessed 16 January 2018); *BBC News*, 'China and US clash over software backdoor proposals,' *BBC News*, 4 March 2015, available at: www.bbc.com/news/technology-31729305 (accessed 16 January 2018).

64 *Counter-Terrorism Law of the PRC (Draft)*, ch. 10, art. 104, 3 November 2014, available at: www.npc.gov.cn/npc/xinwen/lfgz/flca/2014–11/03/content_1885027.htm (accessed 8 June 2018).

65 Zunyou, 'China's draft counter-terrorism law.'

66 *Counter-Terrorism Law of the PRC*, ch. 1, art. 3.

67 Michael Clarke, 'The Xinjiang calculus,' *Policy Forum*, 8 January 2016, available at: www.policyforum.net/the-xinjiang-calculus (accessed 16 January 2018); James Leibold, 'How China sees ISIS is not how it sees "terrorism,"' *National Interest*, 7 December 2015, available at: http://nationalinterest.org/feature/how-china-sees-isis-not-how-it-sees-%E2%80%98terrorism%E2%80%99–14523?page=2 (accessed 16 January 2018).

68 *Reuters*, 'Controversial China anti-terror law looks set to pass this month,' *Reuters*, 21 December 2015, available at: www.reuters.com/article/us-china-security-lawmaking-idUSKBN0U40VE20151221 (accessed 16 January 2018).

69 Clarke, 'Xinjiang calculus.'

70 Xinhua.net, 'China to set up counter-terrorism intelligence center: law,' xinhua.net, 27 December 2015, available at: http://news.xinhuanet.com/english/2015–12/27/c_134956027.htm (accessed 16 January 2018).

71 The Hu Jintao administration began constructing a nationwide surveillance system, dubbed 'Skynet' by officials, in 2005.

72 See Zunyou Zhou, 'China Comprehensive Counter-Terrorism Law,' *Diplomat*, 23 January 2016, available at: http://thediplomat.com/2016/01/chinas-comprehensive-counter-terrorism-law (accessed 16 January 2018); Peter Mattis, 'New law reshapes Chinese counterterrorism policy and operations,' *China Brief* 16:2 (2016), available at: https://jamestown.org/program/new-law-reshapes-chinese-counterterrorism-policy-and-operations (accessed 16

January 2018); Institute for Defence Studies and Analyses, 'China's first anti-terrorism law: An analysis', Institute for Defence Studies and Analyses, 29 March 2016, available at: www.idsa.in/idsacomments/china-first-anti-terrorism-law_apsingh_290316 (accessed 16 January 2018).

73 See Zachary Keck, '4th Plenum: Rule of law with Chinese characteristics,' *Diplomat*, 20 October 2014, available at: https://thediplomat.com/2014/10/4th-plenum-rule-of-law-with-chinese-characteristics/ (accessed 8 June 2018).

74 This security outlook is seen as Xi's security strategy for China's domestic and international security challenges. It was put forward in a 2014 speech which marked the establishment of China's first National Security Committee (NSC), overseeing a security system covering eleven fields, including politics, the economy, the military, culture, society, science and technology, and information. The construction of a 'rule of law' system for state security is one of the main responsibilities of the NSC.

75 Famularo, 'How Xinjiang has transformed.'

76 *Ibid.*

77 Niu Dongjie, 'Implementing the anti-terror law,' *Social Sciences in China Press*, 15 January 2015, available at http://sscp.cssn.cn/xkpd/xszx/gn/201601/t20160115_2828024.html (accessed 6 May 2016).

78 Mei, 'Review and improvement of the anti-terrorism criminal legislation.'

79 Renwen, 'Assessment of terrorism,' p. 172.

80 Xi Chen, 'The rising cost of stability,' *Journal of Democracy* 24:1 (2013): 57–64.

81 *Radio Free Asia*, 'Xinjiang regional government passes new counterterrorism law,' *Radio Free Asia*, 5 August 2016, available at: www.rfa.org/english/news/uyghur/xinjiang-regional-government-passes-new-counterterrorism-law-08052016160441.html (accessed 5 August 2016).

82 *Paper*, 'Behind the scenes of anti-terrorism measures in Xinjiang: Personal instructions of Zhang Dejiang,' *Paper*, 7 August 2016, available at www.thepaper.cn/newsDetail_forward_1510052 (accessed 7 August 2016).

83 *Ibid.*

84 Roach, 'China's anti-terror law.'

3

Terrorism and counterterrorism in Japan

Chiyuki Aoi and Yee-Kuang Heng

Introduction

Since around 2010, the prevailing perception of threat in Japanese public opinion and official policy circles has been centred on the possible dangers posed by a rising China. Specific incidents such as repeated Chinese maritime and aerial incursions into the Senkaku Islands, which are also claimed by Beijing, certainly reinforce these perceptions. The angst and anxiety of a declining Japan being eclipsed by its giant neighbour undoubtedly marked the so-called *zeitgeist*. In this sense, one might argue that traditional geopolitical concerns topped the priorities of security in Japan, with terrorism coming in way down the list of concerns. However, in January 2015, news of a hostage crisis involving Japanese nationals held captive by the Islamic State (IS) in Syria was greeted by shock and bewildered surprise. Rolling media blanket coverage ensured that terrorism instantly rocketed up the security and public agenda. A typical news report suggested the brutal nature of the beheadings and videos provided a 'shock to a country that can feel insulated from distant geopolitical problems' and that Japan was 'one of the safest places in the world'.[1] The newspaper *Mainichi Shimbun* concluded in an editorial that 'We no longer live in a time when we can feel safe, just because we are Japanese.'[2]

The underlying tone of media debates is that terrorism definitely exists 'somewhere out there' but not so much 'here' in Japan. Yet, contrary to the widespread common perceptions of Japan as a peaceful and law-abiding land that stresses harmony over conflict, the country has in fact a rather chequered history not only of exporting terrorism but also of experiencing terrorism that is far more frequent and bloody than is often assumed. The term 'terrorism' is one of the most difficult to precisely define in the political science literature, but for the purposes of this chapter, the interpretation of 'terrorism' is drawn from the United Kingdom's Terrorism Act 2000, where 'terrorism' refers to the use of threat of action 'designed to influence the government [or an international governmental organization] or to intimidate the public or a section of the public, and ... the use or threat is made for the purpose of advancing a political, religious, racial or ideological cause.'[3] Japan constitutes an important and interesting case for this book, for it is a major non-Western power that underwent traumatic political transitions in its break-neck quest to modernize and, indeed, 'Westernize' in the late nineteenth century. Its experiences with terrorism interestingly mirror the bouts of political violence Europeans and Americans experienced at the turn of the twentieth century, as well as the left-wing ideological groups of the 1970s to the millenarian apocalyptic cults of the 2000s. Yet, in terms of how it has responded to terrorist incidents, the country has not always paralleled Western practices. Japan's pacifism following World War Two and public concerns over a police state have further shaped the way it has implemented its domestic counterterrorism policies. According to the seminal work by Katzenstein and Tsujinaka, the Japanese Government's management of domestic security has been normatively driven, and can only be understood in the context of social and cultural norms in Japanese society.[4] As such, in this chapter, we build on this argument as an explanatory framework underpinning our analysis.

This chapter begins by surveying the history of Japan's experiences with noteworthy terrorist incidents from the late Edo period (1603–1868) to the twenty-first century, particularly focusing on the extent to which such 'incidents' adhere to or depart from pre-existing (and contested) ideas of what terrorism means. It will also demonstrate the prevailing political, ideological and economic contexts of these incidents. The second part of the chapter analyses Japan's responses to terrorism, highlighting the cultural, political and military factors Tokyo has faced since the Second World War.

Japan's historical experiences with terrorism

If the late nineteenth century was a period of 'anarchist' terrorism in the West, usually characterized by assassinations of leading political figures such as French President Sadi Carnot in 1894, Empress Elisabeth of Austria–Hungary in 1898, and US President William McKinley in 1901, Japan too had its fair share of such terror, particularly in the chaotic transition from its late Edo to early Meiji period. In the Sakuradomon incident of 1860, leading Tokugawa Shogunate official Naosuke Ii was assassinated by a group of disgruntled samurai who hated him for negotiating treaties with foreign powers that opened Japan up to trade and commerce, ending centuries of isolation. Unfortunately, 'The successful assassination of Naosuke Ii marked the beginnings of assassination which was to be the common currency of Japanese politics.'[5] The British legation in Edo (modern-day Tokyo) was also attacked by what authors have described as Japanese 'terrorists' in 1861,[6] and indeed such violence was viewed by foreigners as 'terrorism'.[7]

These incidents clearly reflected the contemporary political and economic context of that period, which was marked by Western encroachment into Japan accompanied by anti-foreigner sentiments. Several secret societies were formed by samurai unhappy with what they perceived as feeble and weak government responses to Western governments, and these societies adopted methods of violence that could be described as 'terroristic' in nature. These included the Genyōsha (Black Ocean Society) led by two prominent figures, Kōtarō Hiraoka and Mitsuru Tōyama. The newly established Meiji Government had its fair share of 'terrorist' incidents, for instance when Tōyama organized a group of ex-samurai who threw a bomb at Shigenobu Ōkuma, minister of foreign affairs, in 1889. The Genyōsha has been described as the 'forefather' of numerous organizations which believed in Samurai-derived nationalism, transforming the ideological underpinnings to political practice with the aid of terror.[8] The rise of these groups has to be understood once again as a reflection of contemporary political and economic issues, such as the desire to protect the purity and divinity of the imperial family and restore Japan's lost pride and honour in the face of Western incursions.

If the issues that drove terrorist incidents in the early Meiji period were related to 'external forces' or *gaiatsu* (pressure from the outside) in the form of unequal treaties and commerce with Western powers, the context had changed rather dramatically by the 1920s to 1940s. This was a period marked by radical anarchists, nationalists and young military officers. In the Toranomon Incident of December 1923, a shot was fired by Daisuke Namba at Regent Hirohito. Namba was inspired by writings of French and Russian anarchists, and upset by the atrocities committed against Koreans and socialists during the Great Kantō Earthquake of 1923. Hirohito was unhurt, but Prime Minister Hamaguchi became the first victim of numerous assassination attempts made in the 1930s by right-wing nationalists and radical young officers in the army and navy; he was shot and injured in November 1930. Naval officers who felt betrayed that the London Naval Treaty limited the size of Japan's navy sought to destroy the existing order by means of terror and punish those they felt had betrayed the country internationally. In the *Goichigo Jiken* (or 5–1–5 Incident) on May 15 1932, eleven naval officers shot and killed Prime Minister Inukai. The assassination of Inukai marked a milestone in the rise of militarists and right-wing radicals, and put an end to party government.[9] These incidents could be defined as 'terrorist' in that they were intended to sow terror with a political motivation, but at the same time the targets, usually political leaders, were specifically chosen with discrimination. The general public at large was not harmed physically, although there was certainly fear and anxiety generated over the future of Japan's political order. The Japanese experience of 'terrorism' in the form of predominantly political assassinations during this period therefore differs from those definitions that emphasize *indiscriminate mass targeting of civilians* and the general public with the intention to maximize the number of casualties.

However, Japan's experience with terrorism had turned another corner by the 1960s to 1980s. Instead of the radical anarchists and militarists that had dominated the inter-war period, this was a time of terrorist incidents marked by left-wing socialistic goals. The most prominent was the Japanese Red Army (JRA), which had goals that transcended Japan itself, both geographically and ideologically. The JRA pledged to end global imperialism and overthrow the Japanese Government. It had a worldwide revolution objective, seeking to liberate men and women everywhere and unite the world under communism. Its first committed act of domestic terrorism was on 30 March 1970: the hijacking of a Japan Airlines plane, *the Yodo*, which was en route from the Japanese city of Fukuoka to Tokyo.[10] The subsequent hijacking of the Japan Airlines flight 404 from Amsterdam to Alaska on 20 July 1973 cost one life (a JRA hijacker) and wounded another (a flight attendant). Increasingly, the JRA took its activities overseas. On 4 August 1974, five JRA terrorists invaded the American consulate and Swedish embassy in Kuala Lumpur, which led to the release of five JRA members who were detained in Japan. On 12 September 1974, the JRA stormed the French embassy in the Hague, and escaped to Syria with a ransom of US$300,000. In the 1970s, Japanese nationals were unfortunately implicated in conducting quite a few terrorist attacks. Like many terror groups of that period, these Japanese groups supported ideological goals, and most of them were left-wing radicals involved in the most archetypically defining terrorist method: attacks on aviation infrastructure. For instance, on 30 May 1972, three members of the JRA recruited by the Popular Front for Liberation of Palestinian (PFLP) killed twenty-six people at Tel Aviv's Lod Airport in Israel. They dressed conservatively and hid their guns in slim violin cases. Kōzō Okamoto, who was captured, declared that 'I had no option but to shoot for the sake of armed struggle.'[11] The JRA demonstrated its operational reach by collaborating transnationally once again with the PLFP to launch attacks on Singapore's Pulau Bukom oil refinery on 31 January 1974, with the intention of disrupting oil supplies to the US war effort in Vietnam. These terrorist incidents, however, differed from the political assassinations of the inter-war period, being more aimed at 'soft' targets, such as civilians and critical infrastructure, rather than political leaders.

By the 1990s, Japan's experience with terrorism once again underwent a dramatic shift, this time towards millenarian apocalyptic attacks perpetrated by cults. Most notable of these was the Aum Shinrikyo, a mixed doctrinal cult influenced by Hinayana Buddhism, Mahayana Buddhism, Tibetan Buddhism and yoga philosophy. In Japan, Aum Shinrikyo has about 2,000 ordained members and 10,000 believers. It was founded in 1987 by Shōkō Asahara, who believed that it was his task to build the kingdom of Shambala which is an ideal society consisting of people with psychic powers.[12] On 20 March 1995, Aum Shinrikyo was instructed by its leader Shōkō Asahara to release the nerve gas sarin on the Tokyo subway system. Sarin was a lethal chemical weapon developed by Nazi Germany in World War Two. This incident was the second sarin nerve gas attack in Japan; an earlier one in the city of Matsumoto in Japan had killed 7 people and injured 144 others. At the Tokyo subway system gas attack, 12 people were killed and 5,500 people became ill, some of whom are still suffering from after-effects to this day. The motive was allegedly to bring down the government and hasten the apocalypse.

By 2001, however, Japan's focus on terrorism moved away from the apocalyptically inspired visions of Aum, and shifted towards the Islamic extremism of al Qaeda, particularly after the attacks on New York on 11 September 11 2001 (hereafter called 9/11). Japan itself was not directly attacked but lost around two dozen citizens, many of them working at Fuji Bank, which had offices in the South Tower of the World Trade Centre. Tokyo soon decided to support the resultant US-led 'war on terror' by deploying military forces to the Indian Ocean as well as Iraq, which will be analysed in the second section of this chapter. Several Japanese civilians were taken captive in Iraq and beheaded. While the country has not yet experienced an attack inspired by Islamic extremism on its territory, Japan and its nationals have felt distinctly the fear associated with terrorist incidents. In 2015, the greatest source of threat from terrorism evolved and morphed into Islamic State, which had since February of that year become more targeted at Japan and Japanese nationals. Indeed, the video message posted by IS on beheading journalist Kenji Gotō highlighted the indiscriminate nature of terrorism, which causes anxiety and fear amongst innocent Japanese civilians going about their business, whether as tourists or businessmen or journalists in the Middle East or elsewhere. The IS message read, as addressed to Prime Minister Shinzō Abe, 'Because of your reckless decision to take part in an unwinnable war, this knife will not only slaughter Kenji, but will also carry on and cause carnage wherever your people are found. So let the nightmare for Japan begin.'[13] As former diplomat Kunihiko Miyake, who has experience of the Middle East, noted: 'The Japanese are no exception to terrorist targets. We really should open our eyes to see this reality.'[14] In response, an anti-terror task force was set up at Prime Minister Abe's office, comprising Chief Cabinet Secretary Yoshihide Suga and the foreign and justice ministers.

Japan's response to terrorism: Cultural and normative context

The Japanese public's response to terrorist incidents is interesting to dissect, for it reflects certain cultural norms within the country as well as certain characteristics of the long-running debates about defining terrorism. This is in line with the normatively shaped analytical framework proposed by Katzenstein and Tsujinaka. Despite the long history of political violence, the Japanese authorities and the public in general have tended not to generalize these incidents as 'terrorism' in generic terms. Until recently, the authorities and the public generally failed to equate such incidents with politically motivated attempts at bringing about radical change in the established order or achieving other political, religious or ideological goals through the fear terror generates, even if the political motives of the perpetrators were not altogether missed. The Japanese tended not to emphasize or relate to the political messaging or rationalizations given by terrorists, instead preferring to treat such rationales as aberrations or circumstantial. As Naofumi Miyasaka argues, more often than not the Japanese have tended to equate terrorism with assassination, given major historical precedents such as the aforementioned assassination of Naosuke Ii in 1860 by disgruntled samurai.[15] Japan has to date no anti-terrorism law containing a generic definition of terrorism which could serve as a basis of comprehensive- anti- and counterterrorist strategy, unlike most Western governments such as the UK and even China that recently has embarked on drafting one.

The Japanese before the last World War tended also to accept and at times were even sympathetic towards especially right-wing-inclined radicals – including those who committed the 5–1–5 and 2–2–6 incidents in the first half of the last century.[16] Varying degrees of sympathy for, or at least understanding of, right-wing radicals and their activities continued to be expressed by some nationalist members of society in the post-war era as well, even if such sympathy was not as prevalent as in the pre-war era. As a result, right-wing terrorism as such is not usually viewed by nationalists as a form of radicalization, but as something that is understandable given certain political views and perceptions of given circumstances (of foreign repression). To a varying degree, various branches of nationalists tend to associate with the dislike of foreign influences held by right-wing radicals, although many would disavow the use of violence to vent such frustrations.

The Japanese have also rarely understood the left-wing unrest during the 1970s, or radical student and labour movements that at times escalated into sieges and the use of hand-made grenades and other firebombs, as 'terrorism', referring to those as 'radicals' (*kageki-ha*). Most likely the reasons for this disassociation are perceptual, reflecting a reluctance to admit social divisions based upon political motivations. In a culture and society that value harmony and consensus, such 'radicals' are viewed as outliers and exceptions, with the implication that they are in a minority. Indeed, the term 'terrorism' implies a conceptual division between 'us' (the normal) and 'them' (the radical or fanatic) to justify such naming, and the Japanese public in general have not associated with that sort of division within society, however deplorable some of the incidents have been. The JRA critically alienated itself from the Japanese public through high-profile hijacks and murders, but especially when the brutal 'lynch' murder of thirteen JRA members at its base in Gunma prefecture, as a result of internal power struggles, became widely reported and seen to have gone beyond acceptable limits.

The government reaction to some of the left-wing terrorist incidents during the 1970s was also partially culturally driven. A stark example that implied a communal approach to terrorism was the reaction by the Japanese Government to the 1972 Lod Airport massacre, in which three JRA operatives shot and killed twenty-six people. Two of the three guerrillas involved committed suicide on the spot and the third was captured by Israeli authorities.[17] The subsequent reaction of the Japanese Government was probably hard for Western observers to understand. The Japanese Government formally apologized to families of the victims killed by the Japanese terrorists and offered them compensation, an action indicating that the government felt responsible for the incident caused by Japanese nationals, even if those Japanese nationals committed terrorist acts and were criminally inclined.

Another example of culturally driven practice in response to terrorism by Japan is the willingness of the Japanese Government to negotiate with terrorists and pay ransom, or release prisoners. To form a rather peculiar practice, further, the payment of ransom has often followed negotiations by the Japanese authorities to 'replace' hostages with government officials. When, for example, in 1970, a Japan Airlines aeroplane was hijacked by the Japanese Communist League/Red Army Faction (Sekigun ha, 赤軍派) who demanded to go to North Korea (the *Yodo* incident mentioned earlier), a Transport Ministry official replaced the passengers taken hostage, before being released with ransom. Also, Japan's policy of not only paying ransom but also releasing members of radical organizations from prison has often been criticized by Western nations. For example, at the time of the 1977 Dhaka Incident, when JRA operatives hijacked a Japan Airlines flight, Prime Minister Takeo Fukuda famously declared 'Human life is heavier than the world,'[18] and agreed to the JRA demands, including ransom and release of several imprisoned members of radical movements. Although the Japanese had tended to accept such government policy prior to this, at this time, Fukuda's decision – particularly the extrajudicial release of prisoners – attracted criticism and questions from the public. In an ironic development, the operatives who conducted the Dhaka operation included those who had been released from prison by the Japanese Government in the earlier 1975 Kuala Lumpur incident.

In the January 2015 hostage crisis where Islamic State abducted two Japanese citizens, the Abe Government relied on Jordan as an intermediary with IS. In this incident, however, the Abe Government's official line was to reject IS demands for ransom (of a sum as high as US$200 million) as that would equate to being 'defeated by terrorism', while at the same time promising to do its best to resolve the crisis.[19] Although exactly what went on behind the scenes is hard to gauge, this stance may indicate a change in the long-held policy to pay ransom to terrorists. Also, during this incident, the Abe Government made apparent its intention to prepare a legal basis to send the Japan Self-Defense Forces (JSDF) abroad to conduct hostage-rescue operations, rather than other options such as sending the police for this purpose. This suggests a trend emerging towards the potential use of the JSDF for counterterrorism efforts, although this trend may reflect more the particular leadership style and nationalist motivations of Abe rather than a general cultural shift. Nor is it clear whether there is US pressure behind this particular issue. In fact, the ongoing overhaul of security-related legislation includes legislation covering this contingency, paving the way towards using the JSDF for such a purpose.

Japanese cultural norms still tend to value conformity and to avoid *meiwaku* – causing trouble for others. If terrorism is to be defined by the indiscriminate targeting of civilians, then the Japanese notion of *meiwaku* would tend to suggest a departure from such assumptions about indiscrimination and a tip towards deeply conformist, collectivist value assumptions. In 2015, the Japanese civilians who were victims of terrorist groups in Iraq and Syria were viewed in parts of Japan as 'trouble-makers' who brought misfortune upon themselves through their own actions. When it emerged that Kenji Gotō had ignored three warnings from the Foreign Ministry not to journey to Syria, despite sympathy for his horrific death, senior politicians such as Masahiko Koumura, vice-president of the ruling Liberal Democracy Party, described his actions as 'reckless courage, not true courage, no matter how high his aspirations might have been'.[20]

Indeed, the families of Japanese victims of terrorism in Iraq and Syria have repeatedly apologized for the trouble caused. Some critics have even gone to the extent of saying that 'In the old days, their [the victims'] parents would have had to commit hara-kiri [ritual suicide] to apologize.'[21] Not only is there an unwritten code of honour and ritual that shapes perception of terrorism, this also suggests that terrorism in such cases is likely to be seen in Japan as a misfortune that one brings upon oneself. Japanese hostages later released from Iraq in 2004 were widely criticized, and had to foot the cost of their medical examinations and chartered flights home.

Such reactions are, however, very different from those to the Japanese fatalities suffered in New York, which had an element of being beyond one's control. Japanese public perceptions, it seems, tend to be more discriminate when it comes to assigning blame for terrorist outrages inflicted on Japanese citizens. Of course, this discrimination is not boundless. There is no moral equivalence, in this frame of mind, between the sarin gas attacks where innocent daily commuters were caught up in terrorist attacks, and the Japanese hostages seized and decapitated in the Middle East. Both incidents definitely cause terror – if this is to be a core component of defining terrorism. If terrorism is to be defined according to the nature of the targets and how indiscriminately they were selected, then there is a huge gulf between perceptions of hostages who voluntarily entered conflict zones and commuters going about their daily lives who inadvertently found themselves in a terrorist attack like the sarin gas incident. The understanding of terrorism in this chapter, as mentioned earlier, emphasizes the political motivations of violence to create fear and terror, more than targeting.

Japan's counterterrorism: Reactive incrementalism and domestic orientation

The aforementioned work by Katzenstein and Tsujinaka on cultural norms in Japanese domestic security argues that maintenance of domestic security in Japan has been informal, rather than formal–legalistic, relying on 'operationalization' (*un'yō*, 運用), particularly given that the Japanese have tended to rely less on legal remedies to resolve disputes than Western societies have. Japanese domestic security maintenance has also been communal, with the understanding that crime is a 'community phenomenon' which can only be dealt with by community involvement.[22] The intermingling and interwoven social and soft-legal norms have thus generated the political and policing context for action. For example, in dealing with leftist radical movements, the police have relied on informal operationalization of basic legal instruments and extensive networks that build on close relations with the public, as represented by collaboration from the public with its 'rolling' operations – visits by the police to apartments one by one, searching for radical suspects. One downside of such normatively and culturally embedded practice by the Japanese authorities has been a slow and incremental approach to countering terrorism and terrorist risks. Legal responses have likewise proved slow, as Japan has a tradition of relying on 'operationalization' of existing rules and laws to tackle newer problems. Also, the counterterrorist response has remained largely domestic, despite the international reach of some Japanese terror groups.

In post-war Japan, in responding to threats and risks of terrorism, as a result of the weakening of other security actors – such as the Public Security Intelligence Agency (Kōan Chōsa Chō), the Defense Agency and JSDF – the police have played a central role.[23] In domestic public security, the central government in Tokyo held increased power though the command and personnel and financial control of the public security branches of both the federal and municipal police.[24] The Metropolitan Police Department (MPD), with its Public Security Bureau, and the municipal police provide the necessary operational capabilities.

Since the 1960s, in response to increasingly radical left- and right-wing movements, the National Police Agency (NPA, Keisatsu chō) has established specialized sections. In 1978, it created a special section to deal specifically with the JRA.[25] Intelligence gathering and investigation regarding radical elements were strengthened in 1969 through the creation of a public security special unit (Keishi chō Kōan Tokka Tai, 警視庁公安特科隊) within the MPD. Further, following the 1977 hijacking by the JRA of a Japan Airlines flight in Mumbai (the Dhaka incident), the NPA secretly created counterterrorist Special Assault Teams (SATs) in Tokyo and Osaka. In 1996, the NPA publicly announced the establishment of SATs in five other prefectures,[26] and in Okinawa in 2006. SATs now comprise about 300 personnel.[27] SATs are mandated to deal with domestic hostage, siege and hijack incidents.[28]

There are also, since 2000, specialized units in nine prefectures to counter nuclear, biological and chemical (NBC) terrorism, of about 200 personnel, as well as specialized units in each prefecture to deal with explosive ordinance, totalling about 1,200 personnel under the control of prefectural municipal authorities. Further, in 1998 the NPA established a Terrorism Response Team following a hostage incident in 1996 in the Japanese consulate in Lima. This team has conducted activities outside of Japan, usually in cases of incidents involving Japanese nationals and interests. For example, in the Bali bombing incident in 2002, the team provided assistance to the local authorities in the investigation, following a request from the Indonesian authorities for technical assistance with regard to DNA testing. The Terrorist Response Team was upgraded in 2004 with the creation of a Tactical Wing for Overseas (TRT-2) to enable it to provide broader support to host countries' security actors, and for information collection and coordination purposes. In February 2015, a TRT-2 team was sent to Jordan at the time of an IS hostage incident. Although these teams have been used rather infrequently, possibly due to political and normative sensitivities about security-related deployment abroad, the fact that these police teams have been deployed with relatively little public scrutiny contrasts with the situation surrounding the deployment of JSDF abroad, including for counterterrorism purposes. (In the 2015 IS incident, however, Prime Minister Abe did try to find ways to send a JSDF specialized unit, rather than the police.)

Hence, Japanese counterterrorism efforts are both reactive and incremental, based on the persistent perception that each radical incident is an individual occurrence, without reference to terrorism in a broader generic sense. For example, Aum Shinrikyo's use of sarin gas on two occasions – in Matsumoto and the Tokyo subway – was met with no sense of urgency in preparing a relevant policy and legal framework.[29] The government did pass the Act on the Prevention of Harmful Use of Sarin and Other Agents to ban the making, possession and use of sarin and other agents (Sarin Nado ni Yoru Jinshin Higai Bōshi ni Kansuru Hōritsu), as well as the Act on the Prohibition of Chemical Weapons and the Regulation of Specific Chemicals in 1995, in response to the sarin gas attack by Aum Shinrikyo in Tokyo. But the move came too late to prevent the sarin gas attack on the Tokyo subway, despite the fact that the organization had already used sarin once at Matsumoto and that the authorities – the relevant sections of both JSDF and the police – knew of the group's possession of sarin and its interest in producing not only that but other materials for the purpose of mass destruction. Indeed, the sarin gas attack was carried out by the Aum leadership in the knowledge that a police raid of suspected Aum facilities was planned to take place across the country two days later.

The government also revised the Religious Juridical Persons Law (Shukyō Hōjin hō), to strip the group's legality as a religious association. However, the group itself has remained active under a different identity. Critically, it was rendered problematic to apply the Anti-Subversive Activities Act (Hakai Katsudō Bōshi Hō, 破壊活動防止法) to dissolve and ban the group; the official reason given by the Public Security Examination Commission (Kōan Shinsa Iinkai, 公安審査委員会) for not doing so was that there was not sufficient evidence that the organization posed a threat to public security to justify the application of the law.[30] However, opposition to applying the law (or to the law itself) was strong from those concerned about abuse of governmental power (reminiscent of the pre-war period), particularly given that the law was legislated in 1952 implicitly with the Japan Communist Party (which at that time endorsed violent revolution) in mind. Only in 1999 did the government pass legislation specifically targeting Aum – the Act on the Control of Organizations Which Have Committed Acts of Indiscriminate Mass Murder – putting the organization under surveillance by the authorities.

It was only the 9/11 attacks and the anthrax attacks in the US that made the Japanese Government tackle the possibility of NBC terrorism in a more coordinated manner.[31] Earlier efforts had included the 1998 launch of a government-wide investigation into how to respond to grave incidents of terrorism, and the production of a manual covering responses to terrorism involving mass murder and destruction in 1999. In 2000, the Cabinet Office created a committee on NBC terrorism (NBC Tero Taisaku Kaigi, NBCテロ対策会議). But it was only after 9/11 that a whole-government approach was taken to streamlining and effectuating responses to large-scale terrorism. In October 2001, the government installed an Emergency Anti-Terrorism Headquarters (Kinkyū Tero Taisaku Honbu, 緊急テロ対策本部) headed by the prime minister, which in its first meeting discussed responses to and preparedness for facing weapons of mass destruction (WMDs). In 2004, the Cabinet Office's International Criminal Organization and International Terrorism Response Headquarters (国際組織犯罪等・国際テロ対策推進本部) compiled Japan's first comprehensive plan to prevent biological, nuclear and chemical terrorism, including regulations for managing biological agents, reinforcing defence of airports and nuclear facilities, and strengthening protection of nuclear materials.

Japan's response to terrorism, somewhat surprisingly given the international reach of some core Japanese terror groups, remained largely domestically oriented, in part due to the limitations – perceptional, cultural or legal – of the purview of the main counterterrorist actors in Japan. As Katzenstein and Tsujinaka noted, Japan's response to terrorism was largely internal until well into the 1980s. The Japanese police's international cooperation remained more marginal than that of other advanced nations, although it did start to collaborate with foreign police and investigations much more extensively from the 1980s. As noted, the NPA did not have a specialized unit to deal with the JRA, despite that group's international activities, until 1978.[32] In 1981 and 1984, the NPA reinforced its international sections. It was only in 1988 that the NPA created a counter-international-terrorism section, with thirty-two staff, and a foreign affairs section (*gaiji nika*, 外事二課) in the Security Bureau (Keibi kyoku, 警備局). At the same time the Japanese ministries that deal with international terrorism created international criminal sections to focus on the JRA. Both the Ministry of Foreign Affairs (MOFA) and the Ministry of Justice also created or strengthened relevant sections to more effectively deal with terrorism. (MOFA created the Department for Prevention of Terrorism, a section devoted to counterterrorism, enabling the ministry to better deal with summit discussions on terrorism.)[33] In the Police Law reform of 2004, the Foreign Affairs and Intelligence Department (Gaiji Jōhōbu, 外事情報部) was created under the NPA Security Bureau, as well as the Counter-International-Terrorism Division (Kokusai Terorismu Taisaku ka, 国際テロリズム対策課) under that department.[34]

Japan has ratified all thirteen international treaties relating to terrorism, but three of them only after the 9/11 incidents. These are the International Convention for the Suppression of Terrorist Bombings (November 2001), the Convention for the Suppression of the Financing of Terrorism (June 2002) and the International Convention for the Suppression of Acts of Nuclear Terrorism (2005). In particular, the preparation of domestic laws to ratify the International Convention for the Suppression of Terrorist Bombings after 9/11 was a significant move for Japan as it had not been able to do so prior to this, even amid international criticism that Japan was not moving fast enough in cooperating internationally to tackle terrorism.[35] Japan also moved to legislate against and outlaw terrorist financing after 9/11.

In this case, it is international and external events that prompted Japanese action, rather than domestic drivers of change. As required by United Nations Security Council Resolution (UNSCR) 1373, Japan has frozen the funds and assets of individuals and entities with terrorist ties as designated by the UN. It has also frozen funds of Taliban and al Qaeda members and organizations under UNSCR 1267, 1333 and 1390. Tokyo has also passed legislation to criminalize the financing of terrorism and amended laws to facilitate greater information exchange between government agencies.[36] As of January 2005, 442 individuals and entities have been blacklisted by the decision of the UN Sanctions Committee on al Qaeda members, and 28 individuals and entities have been targeted by the decision of the UN Security Council (UNSC) Counter-Terrorism Committee (CTC). Cooperation with Association of Southeast Asian Nations (ASEAN) countries and capacity-building in the prohibition of terrorist financing have also been launched in the form of training programmes for ASEAN officials and joint information-sharing seminars. Japan annually reports its implementation of domestic measures to combat the financing of terrorism to the UNSC CTC (established by UNSCR 1373). The Act on Punishment of Financing to Offences of Public Intimidation (Law no. 67 of 2002) was enacted against supporters of terrorism. The Law for Customer Identification (Law no. 32 of 2002) was also passed, which requires financial institutions to bar access to anybody whose identity is dubious or suspicious.

In 2014, however, the intergovernmental organization the Financial Action Task Force (FATF) noted that Japan still had incomplete criminalization of financing for terrorists, lack of customer due diligence and an insufficient mechanism for freezing terrorists' assets. Such problems remained unresolved six years after a 2008 FATF mutual evaluation report first highlighted these weaknesses in Japan's counter-terrorist-financing regime. The current system only limits overseas money transfers with terrorists designated by the UNSC. This loophole means that domestic transfers of funds by terrorists remain legally possible. Additionally, the freezing system in Japan is limited to 'funds' and does not cover every kind of asset.

The war model: Japan's response to the 'war on terror' since 9/11

Globally, as the post-9/11 world witnessed the 'war model' of counterterrorism in response to al Qaeda and its affiliates' use of terror tactics, Japan at first seemed to cooperate with this. The US–UK attack on Afghanistan was supported by the Japanese Government, based upon the view that international terrorism is a threat to international peace and security. Further, the then government under the conservative politician Jun'ichirō Koizumi was interested in strengthening the US–Japan alliance in order to allow Japan to better support the United States in addressing the changing security environment in the Far East.

After less than a month of debate in the diet, the Koizumi Government passed legislation – the Anti-Terrorism Special Measures Law (ATSML) – that empowered the Japan Maritime Self-Defense Force (JMSDF) to deploy to the Indian Ocean for refuelling missions. Although the UNSC's and the US's interpretation that the 9/11 attacks warranted the United States to resort to its right of self-defence put Japan in a sensitive position (as Japan could not exercise the right of collective defence under the then interpretation of the Constitution of Japan), based upon the ATSML, the JMSDF – in an unprecedented move – engaged in logistical support, providing fuel to eleven countries in the Indian Ocean. JMSDF activities were justified on the basis of UNSCR 1368 (2001) that linked international terrorism and international peace, as well as other UNSC resolutions that called upon member states to take appropriate measures to prevent international terrorism.[37]

Somewhat surprisingly given the post-war history of pacifism in Japan, Koizumi's swift decision to respond to the 9/11 attacks by sending the JMSDF on a logistical mission was generally supported by the Japanese public, shocked by the scale of the terrorist attacks in the US, which had also claimed the lives of some Japanese nationals. The reasoning the Koizumi Government provided – the need for Japan to respond to the threat of international terrorism proactively and to support its closest ally as visibly as possible – seems to have gained the understanding of the Japanese public. According to public opinion polls conducted by the *Japan Economic Journal* (*Nihon Keizai Shimbun*) on 21 and 22 September 2001, support for the Koizumi cabinet increased from 69 to 79 per cent after Koizumi's visit to the US and the promise he made personally to US President Bush of Japan's support.[38]

Debates at the diet also indicate that international terrorism was understood by both the ruling coalition (of the Liberal Democratic Party (LDP), the Clean Government Party and the Conservative Party) and opposition parties as an attack on freedom and democratic values. Parties also agreed that international terrorism needed to be curtailed.[39] Political parties, however, disagreed over whether, and to what extent, the role of the JSDF would be both to respond independently to the threat of international terrorism and to strengthen the US–Japan alliance. The latter goal was understood to be particularly relevant by conservatives, still deeply traumatized by the failure a decade before of the then Kaifu Government to live up to US expectations of Japan to support the Gulf War. It was Koizumi's leadership, however, that made possible the unprecedentedly swift decision to send the JMSDF to the Indian Ocean. Koizumi, a maverick figure within the LDP, understood that speed in decision-making was important in this case and accordingly took the extraordinary measure to skip time-consuming intra-party coordination to decide the details of the policy, in favour of inter-party collaboration (among the ruling coalition).[40]

Further, when the US-led coalition escalated the 'war on terror' as the G.W. Bush administration prepared to use force against Saddam Hussein in Iraq in 2003, the Japanese Government again supported the United States, amid widespread international discontent with US policy. The Japanese Government argued that although another UNSC resolution would be desirable to legitimate the war, Iraq had still violated the terms of UNSC demands to disarm. When the coalition finally unilaterally resorted to force against Iraq, Japan supported the intervention, justifying the allied use of force on the basis of UNSCR 678, 687 and 1441. Japan also argued for bringing democracy and prosperity to Iraq.

In Iraq, Japan chose to send the JSDF to provide humanitarian and reconstruction assistance on the ground, and logistical support from the air. The Koizumi Government, again, quickly passed the Law Concerning Special Measures on Humanitarian and Reconstruction Assistance in Iraq in July 2003.

The law was again based upon a UNSC resolution (UNSCR 1483, 2003), which recognized the duties of the occupying powers (the Authority) in Iraq and the humanitarian role to be played by the UN, and called upon member states to provide humanitarian and reconstruction assistance to Iraq.

The Japanese Government dispatched the Japan Ground Self-Defense Force (JGSDF) to Al Muthanna Province in Iraq, where Dutch forces under the Multinational Division-South-East (MND-SE), commanded by the British, were responsible for security (later, British and then Australian forces took on the security role in the province). The JGSDF came unprecedentedly under the tactical control of the MND-SE, although the command was kept separate. In January 2004–July 2006, it focused on humanitarian and reconstruction missions, providing primarily medical, water clearing and reconstruction assistance without engaging in broader security tasks beyond immediate force protection. At the same time, the Japan Air Self-Defense Force (JASDF) was deployed on a logistical support mission, providing air transport (first of JSDF personnel and coalition troops, and humanitarian provisions and reconstruction materials, and later including UN humanitarian provisions and personnel) between Kuwait and Erbil between December 2003 and February 2009.

The deployment of the JSDF in Iraq was controversial, particularly given the initial difficulty of legitimating the Iraq war, which divided public opinion in Japan. It was also difficult to clearly distinguish 'combat areas' (*sentō chiiki*) and 'non-combat areas' (*hi-sentō chiiki*) in Iraq, as required by relevant laws as a key condition for JSDF deployment abroad. The decision to send the JSDF to Iraq reflected Koizumi's desire to 'show the flag', again exhibiting his strong motivation and leadership style. The prevailing interest as recognized by the LDP leadership was to support the US and strengthen the US–Japan alliance, particularly against the background of heightening tension in the Far East, caused especially by an increasingly belligerent North Korea. Hence, it would seem that the outrage over international terrorism receded somewhat into background at the time of the Iraq deployment, and the Japanese Government justified Japan's support of the war on the basis of Iraq's violation of the terms of UNSC resolutions pertaining to the ban on Iraq's weapons programmes. JSDF deployment was in turn justified on the basis of the UN resolution that called for humanitarian and reconstruction assistance to post-war Iraq.

The Japanese public was divided on this decision to send the JSDF to Iraq. In April 2004, 42 per cent of those surveyed by *Nihon Keizai Shimbun* supported the JSDF assisting the coalition in Iraq, while 40 per cent opposed it.[41] Those who opposed it increased in May 2004 to 44 per cent, while 43 per cent supported it.[42] However, support for the Koizumi Government was still at a level that allowed Koizumi to exert strong leadership in decision-making. An opinion poll showed that the Koizumi Government maintained an approval rate of 49 per cent (and 38 per cent disapproval rate) even after the adoption of the Iraq Special Measures Law.[43]

The unprecedented nature of JSDF deployments in the Indian Ocean and Iraq notwithstanding, the details of Japan's involvement in both cases speak rather to complex bases for deploying the JSDF, somewhat defying the simple logic that the Bush administration put forward to 'fight' a 'global war on terror'.

Japan recognized strong interests in supporting the US at a time when it was engaged in 'war on terror' for a variety of reasons, but it is obvious that even that strong interest, as well as Japan's own counterterrorist policy, had to be balanced with concerns for risk and political costs, especially those that deployment of the JSDF would entail. For example, the dispatch of the JMSDF to the Indian Ocean was within existing constitutional limits, as the Japanese Government refrained from reinterpreting the ban on resort to collective defence. Unlike the United States' NATO allies, who declared the applicability of Article 5 of the North Atlantic Treaty the day after the attack, Japan never presented the deployment of the JMSDF in the Indian Ocean legally as an exercise of collective defence.[44]

Further, the fact that the JSDF and Japan Ministry Of Defense refrained from sending forces to Afghanistan to take part in or assist the international stabilization mission there, which would last for over ten years, is indicative of Japanese scepticism of the 'war model' of international counterterrorism. This abstention illustrates the country's pragmatic response to events since 9/11. A close investigation also reveals a relatively small scale of civilian assistance to unstable regions in Afghanistan, even though Japan remained one of the largest international donors to that country.[45] Afghanistan did not qualify by Japanese standards for large-scale yen loans (which were provided to Iraq), although smaller grants and technical assistance were provided, and Japan sent only four civilian officials to support NATO Provincial Reconstruction Teams (PRTs) on the ground, embedding four MOFA officials with a Lithuanian PRT.

Likewise in Iraq, at such a small scale, the deployment of the JGSDF was largely symbolic. As had always been the case with JGSDF deployment abroad, political conditions dictated that the role of (JGSDF) infantry was kept to the minimum necessary for the purpose of force protection, although in Iraq force protection comprised a larger unit than in previous deployments. Rules concerning the use of weapons were also kept extremely restrictive. The JGSDF mandate was kept quite separate from those of the MND-SE, and focused exclusively on humanitarian and reconstruction operations, without JGSDF involvement in any security maintenance operations in Samawah or broader Al Muthanna Province. The MND-SE faced quite a different security situation from that faced by the US around Baghdad; in general, hence, the

JGSDF had very little to do with coalition or MND counterterrorism efforts, although its humanitarian and reconstruction work was in theory to contribute to the stability of Samawah in Al Muthanna Province, hence assisting the overall MND-SE mission.

Overall, Japan's purpose for deploying the JSDF in the 'war on terror' context was to 'show the flag' without taking too much risk to itself, and without overstepping the boundaries of prevailing constitutional interpretation. Although the JSDF did contribute logistically, and was efficient within its self-imposed limits, the deployments were more a public relations exercise, as the country's political and bureaucratic leadership needed to legitimize the role of the JSDF in international security, beyond self-defence, as the international environment evolved following the end of the Cold War. Since failure (most symbolically, casualties) would have been extremely costly politically, risk-averse, face-saving calculations over mandate and authority-setting took on additional importance once decisions to send the JSDF were made.

Hence, countering al Qaeda and global terrorism in general was not the single overarching justification for Japan in determining the modality of assistance to affected countries, particularly in determining JSDF involvement. The tendency for Japanese counterterrorist measures to be focused more on domestic aspects remains true in the post-9/11 world as well. This tendency applies both to the Japanese police and the JSDF, although the latter's international activities have expanded unprecedentedly since 1992. Somewhat like the police, the JSDF has to date taken a role, in terms of responding to terrorism, mostly limited to the domestic context, where the JSDF plays a complementary role (when no civilian agencies are able to deal with the situation of concern) by providing special capabilities, such as dealing with after-effects of chemical, biological or nuclear attacks on the mainland. Incidentally, the JSDF's ability to deal with radiation was utilized at the time of the Fukushima nuclear disaster in the aftermath of the Great Eastern Japan Earthquake of 2011, when the JSDF saw its single largest deployment (in Fukushima) in its history. The fallout of that experience for the JSDF is complex, ranging from rapid deployment to issues of coordination and intelligence/information sharing, but the event resulted in a renewed focus on how to protect nuclear facilities not only from natural disasters but also from (foreign instigated) terrorist attacks.[46]

Conclusion

This chapter has demonstrated that despite public perceptions of Japan as a pacifist and peaceful, stable country, in fact it has had long and bitter experiences with political violence and terrorism. The motivations driving such incidents have evolved and changed over the years, from samurai-inspired nationalism in the mid-1860s to right-wing militarists in the 1930s and left-wing revolutionaries in the 1960s. With the use of sarin gas and apocalyptic terrorism by Aum Shinrikyo in 1995 and then the trauma of beheadings inflicted by Islamic State in 2015, it is fair to say that Japan has indeed experienced the full gamut of terrorist motivations and methods of violence.

However, such exposure to terrorist incidents did not trigger a concerted attempt at understanding the broader concept of 'terrorism' in its different manifestations. This perhaps was a result of a communal conformist society and political system built on the idealized notion of harmony, where dissensus leading to violence was not widely acknowledged by society as a whole. As Katzenstein and Tsujinaka might recognize, this cultural and political frame, in turn, has shaped the way Japan has responded to terrorism in its myriad forms. One should also not forget the legacy of militarism during the Second World War in Japan. A consequence of that bitter memory was the weakening of security actors such as the defence forces and security apparatus in order to minimize the chances of a recurrence. The lead agency on counterterrorism has been the police agency, with its own domestic network of intelligence sources, but given how globalized terrorism has become, greater input from international information sources, whether from the MOFA or the JSDF, regardless of their deficiencies, is necessary. By and large, Japan's response to terrorism remains largely incremental and reactive. Japan lacks to date an overall comprehensive strategy to prevent and respond to terrorism, particularly in the international sphere. Tokyo's moves have instead been driven by events and initiatives of other states such as the US, particularly in the case of Iraq. Similarly, the legislation against terrorist financing was finally passed only after the impetus of the 9/11 attacks and UNSCR 1373. Also noteworthy is how other countries such as the UK and US have devoted considerable efforts to define terrorism in order to legislate against it. China too has drafted broad anti-terrorism legislation, although one may object to Beijing's particular definition of terrorism. Japan by contrast does not seem to have similar plans in place. If Japan is to become a more proactive security actor as Prime Minister Shinzo Abe has declared, a significant starting point could be in developing a more comprehensive understanding and approach to the global terrorist threat.

Notes

1 Ken Moritsugu, 'The world's problems enters Japan's psyche, again,' *Japan Today*, 2 February 2015.

2 'Japanese hostage situation utterly brutal,' *Mainichi Shimbun*, editorial, 26 January 2015.

3 UK Terrorism Act 2000, available at: www.legislation.gov.uk/ukpga/2000/11/section/1 (accessed 14 February 2016).

4 Peter J. Katzenstein and Yutaka Tsujinaka, *Defending the Japanese State: Structure, Norms and the Political Responses to Terrorism and Violent Social Protest in the 1970s and 1980s* (Ithaca, NY: Cornell University, 1991). See also Peter Katzenstein and Yutaka Tsujinaka, 'Nihon no Kokunai Anzen Hosho Seisaku-1970•1980 Nendai ni okeru Terorizumu to Bouryoku [bōryoku]teki Shakai Kogi [kōgi] Undo [undo] e no Seijiteki Taiou [taiō]' (Japan's policy on domestic security maintenance: political responses to terroism and violent social protest movements during the 1970s and 80s), *Leviathan* 8 (spring 1991): 145–64.

5 W.G. Beasley, *The Rise of Modern Japan* (London: Weidenfeld and Nicolson, 1990), pp. 37–9.

6 Ian Hill Nish and Yōichi Kibata, *The History of Anglo-Japanese Relations 1600–2000*, vol. I (London: Palgrave, 2000), p. 54.

7 Eiko Maruko Siniawer, *Ruffians, Yakuza, Nationalists: The Violent Politics of Modern Japan 1860–1960* (Ithaca, NY: Cornell University Press, 2008), p. 14.

8 O. Tanin and E. Yohan, *Militarism and Fascism in Japan*, reprint edition (Westport, CT: Greenwood, 1974; originally published by International Publishers, 1934), p. 33.

9 Mikiso Hane, *Modern Japan: A Historical Survey* (Boulder, CO: Westview, 1986), pp. 252–3.

10 National Police Agency (Japan), 'Movements of the Japanese Red Army and the Yodo-go group,' National Police Agency website, n.d., available at: www.npa.go.jp/archive/keibi/syouten/syouten271/english/0301.html, (accessed 14 February 2016).

11 Quoted in *Japan Times*, '70s-era terrorist who killed dozens wants to come home, go to college,' *Japan Times*, 8 May 2003.

12 Manabu Watanabe, 'Religion and violence in Japan today: A chronological and doctrinal analysis of Aum Shinrikyo,' in Brenda J. Lutz and James M. Lutz (eds), *Global Terrorism*, vol. II (Los Angeles: SAGE, 2008), p. 146.

13 Rob Crilly, David Millward and Nicola Harley, 'ISIL murder Japanese hostage Kenji Goto,' *Daily Telegraph*, 1 February 2015.

14 Elaine Kurtenbach and Mari Yamaguchi, 'Japan faces limited options in response to terrorism, killing of hostages,' *CTV News*, 2 February 2015, available at: www.ctvnews.ca/world/japan-faces-limited-options-in-response-to-terrorism-killing-of-hostages-1.2217822 (accessed 5 June 2018).

15 Miyasaka Naofumi, *Nihon ha Terro wo Fusegeru ka* (Can Japan prevent terrorism?) (Tokyo: Chikuma Shinsho 510, 2004), pp. 64–6.

16 *Ibid.*, p. 66.

17 Extensive interview materials for the surviving JRA guerrilla are available in Patricia Steinhoff, *Nihon Sekigunha: Sono Shakaigakuteki Monogatari*, translated into Japanese by Yumiko Kimura (Tokyo: Kawade Shobo Shinsha, 1991).

18 Quoted in Makoto Iokibe, 'Fukuda Takeo,' in Akio Watanabe (ed.), *The Prime Ministers of Postwar Japan, 1945–1995: Their Lives and Times*, Kindle edition (Lanham, MD: Lexington Books, 2016; supervisory translation by Robert D. Eldridge, Sengo Nihon no Saisho tachi; original in Japanese).

19 *Reuters*, 'Kigen Semaru Hojin Hitojichi Jiken: Seifu wa Fukusuu Channeru de Kosho' (Little time remains for hostage incident: the government pursues negotiation through several channels), *Reuters*, 23 January 2015 [in Japanese], available at: http://jp.reuters.com/article/topNews/idJPKBN0KW06L20150123?pageNumber=1&virtualBrandChannel=0 (accessed 27 April 2015).
20 Quoted in Mari Yamaguchi, 'Some Japanese see slain hostages, Abe as troublemakers,' *Miami Herald*, 5 February 2015, available at: http://amp.miamiherald.com/news/nation-world/world/article9386024.html (accessed 9 June 2018).
21 A 64-year-old part-time Japanese worker quoted in Yamaguchi, 'Some Japanese see slain hostages.'
22 Katzenstein and Tsujinaka, *Defending the Japanese State,* p. 115, quoting William Clifford, *Crime Control in Japan* (Lexington, MA: Lexington Books, 1976), p. 97.
23 Katzenstein and Tsujinaka, 'Nihon no Kokunai Anzen Hosho Seisaku,' p. 146.
24 *Ibid.*, p. 147.
25 *Ibid.*
26 Keisatsu chō (National Police Agency, NPA), *Keisatsu Hakusho* (White paper on police) (Tokyo: Keisatsu chō, Heisei 9 [1997]), available at: www.npa.go.jp/hakusyo/h09/h090102.html (accessed 26 May 2015).
27 Keisatsu chō, *Keisatu Hakusho* (Tokyo: Keisatsu chō, Heisei 26 [2014]), available at: www.npa.go.jp/hakusyo/h26/honbun/pdf/11_dai6sho.pdf (accessed 26 May 2015), p. 173.
28 'Keisatu no Jōhō Tokushu Butai "TRT-2" no Jitsuzō' (the realities of TRT-2), *Sankei News*, 9 February 2015.
29 Tero Taisaku wo Kangaeru Kai (Counterterrorism Study Group), *Tero Taisaku Nyūmon: Henzai suru Kiki e no Taisho Hō* (Introduction to counterterrorism: responding to ubiquitous crises) (Tokyo: Aki Shobō, 2006), p. 227.
30 Miyasaka, *Nihon ha Terro wo*, pp. 106–7.
31 Tero Taisaku wo Kangaeru Kai, *Tero Taisaku Nyūmon*, p. 227.
32 Katzenstein and Tsujinaka, 'Nihon no Kokunai Anzen Hosho Seisaku,' p. 153.
33 *Ibid.*
34 Keisatsu chō, 'Keisatsu no Kokusai Tero Taisaku' (Police response to international terrorism) (Tokyo: Keisatsu chō, September 2011), available at: www.npa.go.jp/keibi/biki2/10nennokiseki.pdf (accessed 30 April 2015).
35 Miyasaka, *Nihon ha Terro wo*, p. 40.
36 Hideaki Mizukoshi, 'Terrorists, terrorism, and Japan's counter-terrorism policy', *Gaiko Forum* 53 (summer 2003): 53–63.
37 Boei shō (Japan Ministry of Defense), *Bōei Handbook* (Defense handbook) (Tokyo: Boei shō, Heisei 19 [2007]), p. 778.
38 *Nihon Keizai Shimbun*, 25 September 2001, cited in Tomohito Shinoda, *Reisengo no Nihon Gaiko: Anzen Hosho Seisaku no Kokunai Seiji Katei* (Japanese diplomacy in the post-cold war era: domestic political process of security policy making) (Tokyo: Minerva, 2006), p. 90.
39 Shugiin (Lower House), 'Dai 153 Kai Kokkai, Shugiin Kaigiroku' (Record of Lower House debates in the 153rd National Diet Debate) (Tokyo, Heisei 13 [9 October 2001]); 'Dai 153 Kai Kokkai, Shugiin Kaigiroku' (Record of Lower House debates in the 153rd National Diet Debate) (Tokyo, Heisei 13 [2 October 2001]).
40 Shinoda, *Reisengo no Nihon Gaiko*, pp. 90–1.

41 *Nihon Keizai Shimbun*, 5 July 2004.

42 *Ibid.*

43 Shinoda, *Reisengo no Nihon Gaiko*, p. 58.

44 Akio Watanabe, 'Nihon wa Rubicon wo watatta noka? Higuchi Report igo no Nihon no bouei seisaku o kento suru' (Did Japan cross the Rubicon? Reexamining Japanese defense policy since the Higuchi Report), *Kokusai Anzen hosho* (International Security) 31:2 (2003): 73–85.

45 For an evaluation of Japan's stance regarding stabilization in both Afghansitan and Iraq, see Chiyuki Aoi, 'Japan and stabilisation: Contributions and preparedness,' *RUSI Journal*, 156:1 (2011): 52–7. On Japan's ODA to Afghanistan and Iraq, see Dennis T. Yasutomo, *Japan's Civil-Military Diplomacy: The Banks of the Rubicon* (London: Routledge, 2014).

46 Naikaku Kanbō (Cabinet Secretariat), 'Omona Tero no Mizen Bōshi Taisaku no Genjō' (Actualities of main terrorism-prevention measures),' available at: www.cas.go.jp/jp/siryou/pdf/bousitaisaku_h261126.pdf (accessed 23 April 2015).

4

Adapting to the dynamic changes of terrorist threats

Kamarulnizam Abdullah and Ridzuan Abdul Aziz

Introduction

Terrorism has changed the world security environment and the way that states respond to threat. Alan Dershowitz believes that states can reduce the frequency and severity of terrorist acts by taking significant steps to preserve national security through tougher laws.[1] His reasoning was echoed by Samydorai, who argues that national security laws give the government special powers to stifle dissent, supposedly for dealing with emergency situations.[2] These counterterrorism laws are among the most significant approaches to deal with terrorism. In Southeast Asia, a specific kind of counterterrorism law had been in place long before the 9/11 incidents. Countries that practise these measures view the laws as critical in ensuring socio-political stability. Such counterterrorism laws include Singapore's Internal Security Act (1960); Thailand's Anti-Communist Activities Act (1952); Indonesia's Anti-Subversive Law (1963); Myanmar's Anti-Subversive Law (1975); and the Philippines' Arrest, Search and Seizure Order (1970). Thailand, Indonesia and the Philippines have further tightened their counterterrorism measures since the 9/11 incidents.[3] Indonesia, for instance, adopted several mechanisms, such as the establishment of a special counterterrorism squad called Special Detachment Unit 88, in the aftermath of the 2002 Bali bombings. Furthermore, in 2015, the Tantera Nasional Indonesia (TNI) launched a new counterterrorism squad called the TNI Joint Special Operations Command, or Koopsusgab, to increase the country's effort in combating terrorist threats, especially that from the Islamic State (IS).[4] Yet the Indonesian Government is still grappling with revising its 2003 Anti-Terrorism Law due to the public's fear of possible abuse of power.[5]

Malaysia's management of counterterrorism since independence has been determined by two key factors – the role played by the police's usually hidden Special Branch (SB) unit, and the existence of preventive laws. The function and contribution of Malaysia's SB is crucial in facing current terrorist movements such as the Islamic State of Iraq and Syria (ISIS; later known only as the Islamic State (IS)), al Qaeda and Jemaah Islamiyah (JI). In fact, Malaysia is one of the few Commonwealth countries that has a dedicated unit in the police force that focuses on various forms of intelligence gathering. Another approach to tackle terror threats in the country has been through pre-emptive legal measures. The use of the Emergency (Public Order and Crime Prevention) Ordinance, 1969 (commonly known as the Emergency Ordinance),[6] and the Internal Security Act of 1960 (ISA) has proved effective for the government in wiping out terrorism. Other laws that have been used in Malaysia's counterterror approaches include the Penal Code, Anti-Money Laundering and Anti-Terrorism Financing Act 2001 (AMLAFTA), Criminal Procedure Code (CPC) and the Sedition Act 1948 (revised 1969).

But the use of preventive laws has been criticized by local as well as international civil society for its human rights abuse. After decades of lobbying, the 1969 Emergency Ordinance and ISA were finally repealed by the government in 2011. The two laws were subsequently replaced by the Security Offences (Special Measures) Act 2012 (SOSMA). This replacement appears to be in keeping with the dynamism of the country's democracy and political climate. Yet, the major issue for the security enforcement agencies, and particularly for the Royal Malaysian Police (RMP), is that SOSMA has been perceived as a 'toothless tiger'. To address the issue, the Malaysian Government introduced a new preventive law, the Prevention of Terrorism Act 2015 (POTA), whose major function is to strengthen the country's counterterrorist measures. Unlike ISA, POTA specifically deals with possible terrorist threats. At the same time, the government has decided to reintroduce the Prevention of Crime Act 1959 (revised 1983), as another stop-gap measure for preventing terrorist attacks. Yet, local civil society was not happy with the reintroduction and adaptation of these preventive laws.[7] Critics argued that POTA was reminiscent of ISA, which gave the authorities far-reaching powers to detain suspected terrorists without trial. Questions can then be raised as to why Malaysia needs another preventive law to replace ISA. Were Malaysia's agility and preparedness in counterterrorism weakened by the abolishment of the Emergency Ordinance and ISA, given the changing scenario of counterterrorism approaches? What strategies have been adopted post-ISA to deal with religiously inspired terrorist threats? How has the RMP's SB adapted to the new approaches in managing counterterrorism? What alternatives are available? The aims of this chapter are, therefore, to discuss and analyse those questions.

Counterterrorism in Malaysia: A historical context

Malaysia has a long history of terrorist threats. The counterinsurgency campaign against the communist threat has been recorded as one of the major operations in the country's counterterrorism history.[8] The insurgency was a guerrilla war fought between the British colonial government and the Chinese-dominated Malayan National Liberation Army (MNLA), the armed wing of the Communist Party of Malaya (CPM). It is interesting to note that the MNLA was an offshoot of the Malayan People's Anti-Japanese Army (MPAJ), a CPM-led guerrilla force that was set up as a resistance group against the Japanese occupation during World War Two. The British, in fact, assisted the establishment of the force by secretly providing training and supplying weapons. The force was officially disbanded by the British Government at the end of the war in 1945. Members of the force were persuaded to surrender their weapons in return for economic opportunities and political incentives such as Malayan citizenship. Not all members, however, voluntarily abandoned their weapons.[9]

The guerrilla campaign continued when the British failed to fulfil their promises.[10] The colonial government was in fact struggling not only to rebuild Malaya but also to assist British economic development. The rich Malayan natural resources had been one of the main contributors to the rapid development of the British economy since its occupation of the land in 1864. However, the Malayan economy, which was heavily dependent on tin and rubber, was in a dire state. Malayan post-war economic growth was suppressed by not only high rates of inflation and unemployment, but also a series of CPM-instigated labour protests and strikes.[11] The colonial government's harsh response – through arrests and deportation – in handling the labour protests eventually led to more anti-government rallies. The assassination of three British plantation managers by CPM members in July 1948 was the culmination of conflicts between the labour movements and the government.[12] The British reacted swiftly by outlawing the CPM and other major labour and leftist movements. The Emergency Regulations Ordinance 1948 (no. 17 of 1948), generally referred as the 1948 Emergency Ordinance, was promulgated, marking the beginning of the first counterinsurgency period, which lasted for 12 years. The Ordinance was a preventive mechanism, giving the security authorities sweeping powers to detain subversive elements deemed to be a threat to national security. The Ordinance, in fact, 'allowed for detention without trial, in which the civil legal code took second place to military necessity'.[13]

In this first counterinsurgency period (1948–60),[14] the CPM retreated to the jungle and launched guerrilla attacks on strategic government resources such as tin mines and rubber plantations. The aim was to cripple the Malayan economy and to destabilize the British colonial government. The CPM also instigated a spate of terror acts against the Malayan people, especially the Chinese population. Villages that were situated on the fringe of the jungle were often forced to supply food and intelligence to the CPM.

In can be argued that despite having several thousand members, the CPM was mostly only able to garner support from disaffected Chinese Malayans. The CPM failed to galvanize support from the Malay-Muslim majority population. This failure was due to the fact that the CPM's struggle was viewed as Chinese-centric, since the majority of CPM members were from the Chinese ethnic population. The communists' rejection of religion had also distanced Muslim Malayans from the insurgency. Attempts were made to bridge this ethno-religious gap. In order to encourage Malay-Muslim participation in the party, the CPM leadership created a special regiment consisting only of Malay leftists who shared the CPM's anti-colonial inspiration. Among the Malay leftist leaders were Rashid Maiden, Abdullah CD, Abu Samah Mohamad Kassim and Shamsiah Fakeh; these were the key rebel leaders who led the Malay-based anti-colonial movements, and subsequently joined the tenth regiment, the Malay wing of the CPM.

The British colonial government's counterinsurgency approaches can be divided into two main broad strategies: multilayered security offensive operations and the multifaceted 'hearts and minds' strategy. The first strategy was aimed at safeguarding the country's valuable economic and strategic assets, such as mines and rubber plantation estates. At the same time, the security campaign placed severe pressure on and disrupted the CPM's guerrilla tactics. In this campaign, the colonial British received military support from other Commonwealth countries such as Australia, Fiji and New Zealand. The Australians, for instance, provided a combination of air and ground assaults against the CPM's major hideouts.[15]

An important aspect of this multilayered security offensive operation was the role played by the Malayan Federation Police Force (MFP). Under the Briggs' Plan, discussed further below, the strength and function of the MFP were expanded. Two units were established and revived, respectively, to address the insurgency threats – the Jungle Squad Force and the Special Branch (SB) unit. The MFP's Jungle Squad, also known as Pasukan Polis Hutan (PPH), acted as a paramilitary operational force to suppress and launch attacks on insurgent areas. At the same, the PPH was also tasked with assisting the Malayan Armed Forces (MAF) in the insurgency war. A salient feature of the PPH, furthermore, was the existence of the Senoi Praaq (war) unit, which consisted mainly of the Orang Asli (aboriginal people) of the Malay Peninsula. The setting up of the unit in 1956 had a two-pronged objective. First was to exploit the aborigines' endurance, jungle skills and covertness. Members of the unit were a critical in providing information and tracking the enemy's position and movements. Secondly, the unit was used to neutralize communist influence among the aboriginal community.[16]

The Senoi Praaq remains an important component of the current PPH force, which has been restructured and renamed the Pasukan Gerakan Am (PGA), or the General Operational Force. Under its current structure, the Senoi Praaq unit has become the Third Battalion of the PGA.[17] Although the strength of the force has been reduced, its functions have expanded, including providing protection to strategic government installations such as seaports and airports from terrorist attacks and armed rebels, managing border security, and providing assistance in search and rescue operations.

Another important component of the MFP's counterinsurgency campaign was its intelligence-gathering system, undertaken by Cawangan Khas, or the SB. Daljit Singh argues that Malaya's effectiveness in managing subversive threats was for years greatly attributable to the capability of the SB.[18] The expanded SB unit, established in 1919 as a British Straits Settlement Civil Security Service (CSS), gained importance when General Gerald Templer, the British High Commissioner to Malaya (1952–54), prioritized intelligence gathering as key to the military approach in the counterinsurgency war. Subsequently, the strength of the unit was increased dramatically.[19] This special intelligence unit appointed officers from various racial backgrounds, especially the Chinese. According to Brian Stewart, who served as a young police officer during the first Malayan Emergency period, penetration and infiltration into enemy ground was the major strategy used to cripple the Malayan communism movements.[20] SB officers infiltrated the insurgents' circle of command through covert tactics. They also disguised themselves as local villagers, teachers, students or farmers to gather intelligence. The information and intelligence so gathered were then channelled to the relevant branches of the police force or security agencies for further action.[21]

Nonetheless, it was the multifaceted 'hearts and minds' strategy that has been credited as the crucial element to the British colonial government's success in defeating the insurgency. The strategy was also one of the foundations of the Briggs' Plan. This plan was devised by General Sir Harold Briggs, the British Army's Director of Operations in Malaya. The British colonial government identified that the support for and threat from the insurgents came from various sources. The government also identified that the Chinese population, especially in rural areas, either voluntarily or under coercion supported the CPM by providing essential goods like rice and sugar. In some cases, the CPM's terror tactics of interrogating and killing suspected British supporters, burning whole villages that had failed to provide goods demanded by insurgents, and kidnapping villagers to force them to join the movement, eventually reduced the Chinese population's support for the CPM.[22]

The Briggs' Plan aimed to cut those sources of support or threat through massive forced resettlement of more than half a million people into a guarded camp. The major concern for General Briggs was to gain the cooperation of the Chinese population; the majority of (non-Chinese) Malays were already behind the government. The plan therefore consisted of a psychological warfare approach to win the hearts and minds of the people, particularly the Chinese community. The government began to provide materials for house building and a five-month supply of food and medicine to each resettled family. To prevent possible smuggling of any food excess to the insurgents, the government imposed the Starvation Operation as a control measure, and introduced a national registration programme which required everyone over twelve years old to have an identity card with photograph, fingerprints and personal data.

The resettlement plan, however, caused hardship not only for the Chinese but also the Malays. The Chinese became prisoners in their own villages, with barbed wired, curfews and daily security operations. For the Malays, the resettlement trampled over their rights by allowing 'Chinese squatters to be moved from jungle fringes to "new villages" to be built on Malay state lands ... [where they] enjoyed better facilities such as electricity and water supplies than Malay villages [had].'[23] The resettlement, which physically divided the two ethnic groups, contributed to the socio-political ramifications of the nation-building process in post-independence Malaya.

Terror threats in the post-independence period

The Briggs' plan was a successful British counterterrorism strategy. Popular support for the communists was greatly reduced. The CPM certainly felt the pinch. The British, through the Baling Talks in December 1955, offered amnesty to the CPM, but this was rejected. The failure of the talks led to the CPM's retreat deep into the jungle, mainly at the Malaysia–Thailand border. Hence, the insurgency war was shifted away from populated areas.

Yet the CPM resurrected armed struggle in 1968, marking the Second Emergency period, which lasted for twenty-one years (1968–89). The CPM launched a series of bombing and ambush attacks on government installations, such as military bases and police stations. It can be said that the CPM was highly successful in the first two years of its military campaign against the Malaysian security forces. Government forces suffered considerable losses. In his memoir, Chin Peng, the CPM's revered leader, wrote that once the CPM managed to establish the group's base in the Malaysia–Thailand border area, it reconstituted itself into a 2,500-strong force and developed new techniques of guerrilla warfare.[24] The group, furthermore, became one of the key players instigating the 1969 race riots.[25] The riots killed more than 200 people, mostly Chinese, with a few hundred injured. It was the bloodiest ethnic conflict in Malaysian history.

The Second Emergency had also forced the newly independent Malaysia to adopt several socio-political countermeasures.[26] Elements of the Briggs' Plan were further incorporated into the government's counterinsurgency (COIN) strategies. The RMP introduced a special forces or commando unit called VAT 69 (Very Able Para Trooper 69) to counter the tactics and technique of the communist insurgents.[27] This special forces unit was in fact modelled after the British 22nd Air Services Regiment. In addition to this, the military became an important backbone of the government's COIN strategies. The military was involved in the government's Programme Keselamatan dan Pembangunan (KESBAN), or Security and Development Programme.[28] This programme was part of the government's psychological warfare to win the heart and minds of the population by establishing cordial civil-military and civil-police relations through various local community development programmes, such as the involvement of the military and police in the construction of roads and bridges in rural areas.

Another important aspect of KESBAN was the involvement of communities through the establishment of Rukun Tetangga (neighbourhood watches) and Pasukan Relawan (RELA), or People's Volunteer Groups, to help maintain local public order and security.[29] The Rukun Tetangga programme was a local voluntary service that was set up to bring together people from various ethnic groups from a village or housing complex to look after their community's safety. It is similar to Indonesia's local neighbourhood programme, which also acts as intelligence support on the ground for the government. RELA, on the other hand, is paramilitary civil volunteer corps that was established under the 1964 Emergency Law (Special Power). It has a supporting role to the security agencies in ensuring social order and safety. Members of RELA can be absorbed into the normal military services during times of war.

The post-independence period also witnessed another new terror threat to the country that mainly originated from religiously inspired militant Islamic groups. Since the early 1960s, these groups' ideological contestation was framed in a form of righteous Islamic interpretation. They fought for a pristine Islamic law or *sharia* to be implemented in the country. They averred that

Malaysia needs to become an Islamic state, regardless of the fact that the country is multi-religious and Muslims constitute only two-thirds of the population.

In the 1960s and 1970s, these local religiously inspired militant groups[30] – such as Tentera Sabibullah (1966), or the Army of Sabibullah; Golongan Rohaniah (Rohaniah Group); Koperasi Angkatan Revolusi Islam Malaysia (KARIM), or Malaysia's Islamic Revolutionary Cooperative Force; Kumpulan Crypto (Crypto Group); and Kumpulan Jundullah (Jundullah Group) – had only one objective: to turn Malaysia into a theocratic state through the use of force. Their influence, however, was not widespread. The only group recorded as having a substantial number of members was the Jundullah group. Members of this group underwent military training in southern Thailand, but their grand design to launch military attacks was foiled by the SB and its leaders were detained. Subsequently, more than 100 its paramilitary members were arrested in the RMP's special operations.[31] Leaders of the group were subsequently arrested under ISA.

Yet, interestingly, none of them was labelled as terrorist. The government was inclined to treat them as deviant or radical Islamic movements. Even some radical groups that emerged later in the 1990s and 2000s – such as Kumpulan Mujahidin Kedah (KMK); Kumpulan Perjuangan Islam Perak (KPIK), or Perak Islamic Struggle Group; Kumpulan Revolusi Islam Ibrahim Libya (KRIIL), or the Ibrahim Libya's Islamic Revolutionary Group; Kumpulan Mujahidin Malaysia (KMM), or Malaysia's Mujahidin Group; and Al-Maunah – were instead labelled either as Muslim deviant, fundamental or militant groups. It can be argued that government's perception of those groups was influenced by a conceptualization of terrorism as what Malaysia had experienced for decades: a form of communist insurgency. Secondly, labelling those militant groups as terrorist could produce a political backlash from major Islamic parties, particularly the Pan-Islamic Party (PAS). PAS could capitalize on the issue for its political gain. Furthermore, it can also be argued that the conceptualization of terrorism in Malaysia has to be understood in terms of the structural fragility of society. Terrorism in Malaysia is not only conceptualized in terms of its political motives, violence, or possible mass casualties, but more in terms of its inter- and intra-ethno-religious dimension.[32] The ethnic- and non-ethnic-based political parties, such the ruling coalition party – which consists of, among others, the United Malay National Organization (UMNO) and the Malaysian Chinese Association (MCA) – and the leading opposition parties such PAS and the Chinese-dominated Democratic Action Party (DAP), continue to politicize race and religion as political means to remain in or take power.

Thirdly, the security impact and the magnitude of threat of these groups' 'terror' acts were limited compared with those of communist insurgent groups.

Their planned or staged attacks did not produce large-scale causalities or death among innocent people, and were easily curtailed by the security agencies. Their ideological influences were confined to specific segments of society or geographical areas.[33] KMK and KPIK, for instance, concentrated their activities only in the northern region of peninsular Malaysia.

The legal approach and enforcement mechanism

The Malaysian legal system is largely inherited from the British, especially where it deals with subversive elements and terrorist threats. One example is the 1948 Emergency Ordinance, discussed earlier, which provided the authorities with extensive powers to detain suspected terrorists. Elements of preventive measures, according to Cheah Boon Kheng, were later incorporated into various laws in post-independence Malaya (later Malaysia), such as the 1969 Emergency Ordinance, ISA (1960), the Sedition Act (revised in 1969), the Societies Act (amended in 1981), the Official Secrets Act (amended in 1986), the Essential (Security Case) Regulations (1975), and the Printing Presses and Publication Act 1948 (amended 1984 and 2012).[34]

ISA enabled the post-independence government to swiftly act against suspected terrorists deemed to be threats to national security. The Act was a method of crushing a threat early on, in which the authorities would have an early warning mechanism before the threat spread. The government always argued that ISA was warranted since it would provide a buffer to any attempts to derail religious and racial harmony in the country. Religious and ethnic radicalism were not tolerated at that time in the Malaysian multi-religious and multiracial society. Furthermore, the 9/11 incidents and the United States' global war on terrorism (GWOT) gave the Malaysian Government more rationales to retain the two laws. It was through ISA mechanisms that Malaysia managed to put a brake on possible terror attacks by arresting key al Qaeda and JI leaders.

Rehabilitation was actually the key component of ISA. The idea of the Act was not to punish but to re-educate and to provide opportunities for detainees to prepare themselves to be reintegrated into society.[35] Basically, the objectives of the ISA rehabilitation programmes were to ensure that all the detainees would by the end express their remorse, repent and recant their radical ideologies. Detainees were held at the Kemunting prison complex in the state of Perak. Rehabilitation programmes included religious classes, intellectual discourse with invited experts on various issues and vocational training. Detainees also engaged with individual and religious counsellors who had voluntarily offered their services. They were not treated as ordinary prisoners and were allowed to move around in the prison complex. At the same time, the Social Welfare Department also provided emotional support and individual counselling to the families of detainees. Family involvement in the rehabilitation process, however, was not a successful idea, partly because the families often supported the ISA detainees' 'ideological struggle'. Some families of detainees were even inclined towards getting support from non-governmental organizations rather than cooperating with the authorities.[36]

Yet, both preventive laws – the 1969 Emergency Ordinance and ISA – were most often viewed in terms of their harsh measures. ISA, in particular, was criticized as a governmental tool to stifle peaceful political dissent, since the Act gave the government far-reaching powers to detain suspected subversive elements without due process of law. Under the Act, suspected terrorists can be detained for a maximum of sixty days without trial. Furthermore, the Act empowered the Home Minister to issue a two-year detention decree after the sixty-day detention order had lapsed, and the government could extend the detention period indefinitely, until the Home Minister was satisfied that the suspected person was no longer 'prejudicial to the security of Malaysia'.[37] ISA was probably similar in its nature and objectives to the US McCarran Internal Security Act of 1947. The McCarran Act was intended to protect the country against certain 'un-American' and subversive activities. The 1969 Emergency Ordinance placed restrictions on freedom of assembly, association, expression, movement, residence and employment. Both preventive laws, the 1969 Emergency Ordinance and ISA, allowed for the closing of schools and educational institutions if they were used as meeting places for unlawful organizations or for any other reason deemed to be detrimental to the interests of Malaysia.

The Malaysian Government later decided to introduce a new law to replace ISA – the Security Offences (Special Measures) Act 747 (SOSMA). SOSMA was announced in June 2012 after intense debate in parliament. The Act provides new mechanisms to detain, investigate and prosecute terrorist suspects. It is a measure relating to security offences for the purpose of maintaining public order and security. In addition, it provides procedural and evidential rules pertaining to subversive offences. The Act also includes special powers for the Malaysian police regarding security offences, and special procedures relating to electronic monitoring devices, sensitive information, witness protection and matters related to evidence. Any action considered detrimental to national security would be deemed an offence. In the same vein, security enforcement could take action against any person whose actions 'cause a substantial number of citizens to fear organized violence against persons or property' or 'excite disaffection against the Yang DiPertuan Agong' which is prejudicial to public order in, or the security of, the Federation or any part thereof; or [are intended] to procure the alteration, otherwise than by lawful means, of anything by law established'.[38]

The arrest of al Qaeda operative Yazid Sufaat along with alleged accomplices Halimah Hussein and Muhammad Hilmi Hasim on 3 February 2013 was the first test case of suspected terrorists being charged with terrorism offenses in Malaysia's High Court under SOSMA. The case is viewed as an important barometer for the application of this Act to successfully prosecute suspected terrorists. On 20 May 2013, the Malaysian High Court dismissed the charges on constitutional grounds and released all three defendants. One week after the judicial dismissal, the authorities rearrested Yazid Sufaat and Hilmi Hasim on new charges relating to the same criminal conduct. Halimah Hussein fled, and remains at large in spite of multiple Malaysian operations to rearrest her. On 18 June 2013, an appellate court overturned the original High Court dismissal, and reinstated the original charges. In January 2015 Yazid Sufaat and Hilmi Hasim were each sentenced to seven years for 'for intentionally omitting information on terrorist activities in 2012'.[39]

When ISA and the 1969 Emergency Ordinance were repealed in 2011, the perspective of combating terrorism shifted from preventive to punitive. In other words, ISA 1960, which was used as a preventive law, has been shifted to SOSMA 2012, which is a public law that demands public prosecution and punishment upon conviction. The approach to combating terrorism no longer hinges upon 'prevention and rehabilitation' but rather 'prosecution and judgment'. SOSMA 2012 is a procedural law which is based on investigation and prosecution. The law furthermore has to be read together with other substantive acts such as the Penal Code or the Sedition Act. The process requires collection of concrete evidence to convict the suspects.[40] The prosecutors have had difficulties in gathering sufficient evidence to prove the details of the charges at prima facie level. Thus, in the case of thirty-nine Malaysian jihadists who were arrested while attempting to join IS in Syria, the prosecutors failed to convince the court due to difficulty in proving their acts constituted terrorism, as to prove this in court requires *mens rea* (intention or guilty mind) and *actus rea* (action). In this case, the prosecutor was only to prove an intention to engage in violence in Syria and Iraq, but not the action. The only proof that the prosecutors had was communication in social media.

Furthermore, the abolition of ISA has produced great challenges for the government, and particularly the RMP. ISA was an effective tool in handling subversive elements perceived to be a threat to national security. Yet, threat to national security did not necessarily mean a terrorist threat. The scope and definition of threats were in fact quite wide, which also explains the accusations of political abuse in use of the law, as discussed earlier. At the operational level, the law lessened the burden on the RMP to produce ample evidence in order to detain a suspect. Suspected terrorists could be placed in police custody for an indefinite term with the approval of the Home Minister. The longest detention period was eight years.[41]

Realizing that SOSMA alone could not provide an effective mechanism to manage the growing threat of globally linked terrorist groups like IS and Abu Sayaff, the Malaysian Government decided to enact a new preventive law: the Prevention of Terrorism Act 2015. This empowered the security forces to prevent the 'support for acts of violence involving listed terrorist organizations of a foreign country or in any part of [a] foreign country'.[42] At the same time, the Prevention of Crime Act 1959 (revised 1983), or POCA, is one of the enforcement laws used in dealing with suspected terrorists. It is interesting to note that the purpose of POCA is stated to be to 'provide for the more effectual prevention of crime … and for the control of criminals, members of secret societies and other undesirable persons, and for matters incidental thereto'.[43] How, then, are the two preventive laws enforced?

Suspected terrorists would be arrested by either POTA or POCA, depending on police surveillance data, intelligence reports and existing physical evidence. The police, furthermore, have the power to arrest without a warrant any suspected terrorist, if the investigative police officer has reason to believe there is justification for an inquiry be held into the case of that suspect. But, under POCA, the police need to get a magistrate's approval within twenty-four hours of the detention. The police are also required to consult the public prosecutor for further instruction within seven days of the arrest. The police, with approval from a magistrate, can detain a suspected terrorist for a maximum period of thirty-eight days.[44] Any charge would be based on the evidence that the RMP could gather from the suspected terrorist. A suspect who has direct involvement in terror activities but has been monitored by the SB's Counter Terrorism Unit would be arrested under POTA.

According to an anonymous source from the Counter-Terrorism Department, POTA serves two functions for the police. Firstly, it gives room for further investigation of a suspected terrorist. In most cases, POTA is used when the police have initial strong evidence to implicate the suspected terrorist, but in some cases the police have been able to obtain sufficient evidence but believe that making such evidence public could lead to public disorder. Therefore, the police would present such a case before an inquiry board, seeking permission to arrest and detain a suspected terrorist for a maximum of two years without trial. Secondly, it can be said that POTA has been used as a delaying tactic for the police before a suspected terrorist is officially charged under SOSMA or released. POCA, furthermore, is used as an alternative preventive measure where the police want to initiate an investigation of a person believed to be a supporter of or indirectly involved in terrorist activities, such as fund raising and dissemination of terrorist ideology. Under POCA, however, the investigative police officer has only twenty-eight days to place a suspected terrorist in custody.

In addition to having specific laws, specialized counterterrorism units do play a significant role Malaysia's counterterrorism. In the wake of the growing threat from IS, the Malaysian Government established an integrated National Special Operations Force (NSOF) on 27 October 2016. The force, which consists of RMP, the army and the Malaysian Maritime Enforcement Agency (MMEA), is the Malaysian security forces' rapid first responder to any terror attacks. The structure and command of NSOF, however, are still in question. The RMP SB's Counter-Terrorism Unit has been sceptical about the establishment of the new force, and questions have been raised about its command structure.[45] Who will lead the force remains unanswered.

Nonetheless, the government agency most experienced in this area, which has long dealt with counterterrorism, is the RMP's SB. As mentioned earlier, this intelligence unit was used during the British colonial period as part of the strategy to weaken the communist movement. During the Second Emergency period, the SB managed to gain access the innermost sanctum of the CPM's leadership structure. These covert actions resulted in a leadership split within the CPM.[46]

The SB unit has since been upgraded to become one of the major departments under the RMP in the post-independence period. The roles and functions of the SB department are based on three legal provisions. Firstly, to focus on the collection of security intelligence; secondly, to preserve the country's peace and security as well as to prevent and detect crimes; and, finally, to collect security intelligence that might threaten national security and pass it on to the relevant authorities or bodies.[47] Structurally, the SB is headed by a commissioner of police (CP), assisted by two deputies with the rank of deputy commissioner of police (DCP). The department is divided into eight specialized units, E1–E8. The tasks of these units are summarized in table 4.1.

For terror-related matters, the SB department manages the intelligence gathering itself, since it involves highly covert operations. Normally, counterterrorism operations are carried out by the SB E8 unit, except for complex cases where it may involve multiagency cooperation and action. In the case of the 2013 Lahad Datu incursion, for instance, the intelligence operations involved not only the SB but also numerous other RMP departments and other law-enforcement agencies such the navy and air force. In the case of Mas Selamat Kastari, a JI terrorist wanted by Singapore, the SB department worked closely with the RMP Rapid Action Unit. In the first quarter of 2003, nearly seventy suspected terrorists were caught based on SB intelligence gathering, and the

Table 4.1 Malaysia's Special Branch Units

Unit	Function
E1	Technical assistance
E2	Dealing with social threats
E3	Dealing with external threats
E4	Analysis of domestic political situation
E5	Dealing with economic threats
E6	Providing protection and security to state and visiting dignitaries and officials
E7	Administration
E8	Counterterrorism

This information came from an SB police officer who, for security reasons, cannot be named.

RMP uncovered three tons of ammonium nitrate, a substance used for making bombs. It has also been claimed that Malaysia's SB department warned the Indonesian security authorities of the possibility of Bali being a hard target for internationally linked terrorist groups.[48] The relayed information, however, was brushed aside by the Indonesian authorities for lack of concrete evidence.

Counterterrorism approaches: Changes and adaptability

While the signing of the 1989 Hat Yai Peace Accord marked the end of the insurgency, Malaysia continues to face intermittent terror acts. In recent years, religiously inspired global and regional terrorist groups, such as al Qaeda, JI, and IS or Daesh,[49] have created new challenges for the country's counterterrorism approaches. Such terrorism creates a dilemma for a Muslim-majority country like Malaysia. These terror groups' radical ideological ideas have attracted many individuals and local radical groups to join them – Malaysia needs to ensure that the country is not a breeding ground for terror activities or a safe haven for terrorists.

Terrorism has been defined in various ways, as 'premeditated, politically motivated violence against non-combatants by subnational groups or clandestine agents',[50] or as the 'unlawful use of threats or the use of force or terror or any other attack by person, group or state regardless of objective ... with intention of creating fear [and] intimidation'.[51] Lutz and Lutz moreover, argue that terrorism consists of six vital components: 'Terrorism encompasses ... political aims and motives. It is violent or threatens violence. It is designed to generate fear in a target audience that extends beyond the immediate victim of the violence. The violence is conducted by an identifiable organization. The violence involves a non-state actor or actors as either the perpetrator, the victim of the violence, or both. Finally, the acts of violence are designed to create power in situations in which power previously had been lacking.'[52]

For Malaysia, the act of terror has been defined, under the Penal Code 574 (chapter VI A: 'Offences Relating to Terrorism'), as:

> an act or threat of action within and beyond Malaysia where ... the act is done or the threat is made with the intention of advancing a political, religious or ideological cause, ... or the act or threat is intended ... [firstly, to] intimidate the public or a section of the public; ... [or, secondly, to] influence or compel the Government of Malaysia or the Government of any State in Malaysia, any other government, or any international organization to do or refrain from doing any act.[53]

Furthermore, an act of terror has been committed:

> if it (a) involves serious bodily injury to a person; (b) endangers a person's life; (c) causes a person's death; (d) creates a serious risk to the health or the safety of the public ...; (e) involves serious damage to property; (f) involves the use of firearms, explosives or other lethal devices ... [including any] hazardous, radioactive or harmful substance.[54]

In recent years Malaysia, like other countries, has been faced with a more dangerous threat from terrorist groups inspired to commit acts of extreme violence. In terms of structure, the new terrorism has demonstrated its adaptive capabilities, with a loosely connected decentralized network which is difficult to penetrate and fight against. In terms of motivation, this wave of radical religious extremists continues to fight its 'holy war' as its long-term strategy to achieve its political goals. In terms of resources, the modern world has enabled these religiously motivated terrorists easier access to what they need to attain their objectives; in terms of networking, the terrorist groups have capitalized on advanced technology to disseminate their ideas. Popular social media applications like Facebook, WhatsApp, WeChat and Telegram have been used as a recruitment base for prospective jihadists. The emergence and existence of this kind of terrorism in the post-9/11 era indicates a need to re-evaluate and reassess current counterterrorism policy and rethink the future of terrorism.

Although the Malaysian Government had previously faced intermittent threats from either locally militant movements or externally based terrorist groups such as Darul Islam and the Japanese Red Army,[55] these terror acts did not produce a prolonged threat that could jeopardize the socio-political stability of the nations. The whole scenario, however, has changed since the September 11th incidents. Internationally linked terrorist groups such as al Qaeda, JI and IS have challenged the way the security forces, especially the RMP, strategize their counterterrorism. Although some of these groups, such as al Qaeda and JI, have not launched any direct attacks on Malaysian soil, the country has been implicated as a meeting or transit point for the two groups to launch attacks in Southeast Asia. In fact, Malaysia has been identified as a source of funding for JI's regional activities. In 2000, for instance, al Qaeda and JI leaders like Khalid al-Mihdhar, Tawfiq bin Attash, Nawaf al-Hazmi, Hambali and Ramzi bin al-Shibh held several meetings in Malaysia to allegedly plan future attacks, including the September 11th incidents. The JI became a major concern to the Malaysian Government when, along with the Singaporean authorities, it discovered plots to attack several targets in Singapore.[56] The JI cell in Singapore planned to attack Western strategic assets and establishments such as the American, Australian and Israeli embassies based in the republic.

The emerging threat from IS has become a mirror image to the threat posed by al Qaeda years earlier. But it can be argued that the IS threat has gone beyond human and religious rationales. The 'sex jihad', suicide bombings, and the killing and burning alive in cages of hostages and innocent people illustrate an inhuman side of this group that claims to act in the name of *Allah*. The extent to which the group has posed a threat to Malaysia is highly significant and has been reiterated many times by the Malaysian Government. IS has managed to set up cells with various names – such as Al-Qubro Generation, Kumpulan Gagak Hitam, Kumpulan Fisabilillah and Kumpulan Daulah Islamiah Malizia. The Gagak Hitam cell, for instance, has thirty-eight people who are ready to commit jihad in Malaysia.[57] IS also managed to recruit for the first time several Malaysian jihadists as suicide bombers. Ahmad Tarmimi Maliki, aged twenty-six years, was the first Malaysian suicide bomber, one of nine Malaysians who have blown themselves up in Syria for IS. In 2015, the RMP discovered attempts by Malaysian IS members to launch a high-profile bombing campaign in tourist areas in Kuala Lumpur.[58] One of their strategies was to use a suicide bomber.

The ability of IS to lure teenage girls as young as fourteen or fifteen to their ranks for 'sex jihad' has become a security concern for the Malaysian authorities.[59] IS's cruel image nonetheless has not deterred Malaysian Muslims from joining its war against the Syrian and Iraqi regimes.[60] The man behind IS's Malaysia operation is said to be Muhammad Wanndy Mohamad Jedi, also known as Abu Hamzah al-Fateh or Wandi among the Malaysian members. Assisted by two other Malaysians – Mohd Rafi Udin and Zainuri Kamarudddin (also known as Abu Thalma Malizi), Muhammad Wanndy has been identified as the mastermind behind local funding and recruitment of Malaysian IS members. He has been accused of ordering local IS members to kidnap rich businessmen and rob banks in Malaysia to finance his life and activities in Syria.[61]. He was also responsible for coordinated bomb attacks at the Puchong night club, in a suburban area of Kuala Lumpur, in June 2016. Six people were injured in the incident. It is believed that with the recapturing of Aleppo by Syrian Government forces, more coordinated attacks will be focused in Southeast Asia, especially in Malaysia, the Philippines and Indonesia.[62] In fact, the arrest of a female would-be suicide bomber by the Indonesian Dansus 88 on 11 December 2016, for her plan to attack the presidential palace in Jakarta, shows that IS has already started to focus on the region for its future plans.[63] The Malaysian SB confirmed that it had uncovered fourteen planned attacks on Malaysian soil between November 2016 and January 2017.[64]

In another disturbing development, IS is believed to have lured members of government and security agencies to join the group. According to Assistant Senior Commissioner Ayob Khan, the principle assistant director of the Counter Terrorism Division of the SB, fourteen Malaysian soldiers, including four commandos, were arrested for their involvement in IS in 2016. The authorities have also discovered the involvement of Malaysian and Indonesian JI ex-jihadists in IS, and continue to monitor the release and movements of 200–300 JI members from Indonesian prisons. Out of these, a total of 59 Malaysians have been found to have been involved in terrorist activities in Syria, and 7 have reportedly been killed. So far, more than 250 Malaysian jihadists have been detained, either before they could join their confederates or after they came back from IS-controlled areas in Syria.

It can be argued that Malaysia has no choice but to adapt to the changing nature of the terrorist threat. Not only has this threat has become more global in networking and influence, but also the use of Islam as the major political tool for recruitment produces great challenges for the state and its security-enforcement apparatus. Malaysia, nonetheless, continues with its multifaceted and multilayered approaches in counterterrorism in the areas of policy and legal and enforcement mechanisms.

The campaign of winning hearts and minds continues to be an essential strategy for the post-independence government. The growing demands for Islamization, especially after the Iranian revolution, force the Malaysian Government to re-strategize its approach in order to placate Muslim militant or zealot groups. The government has had to become more adaptive by implementing Islamic-based policies and activities. The Mahathir administration (1981–2003), for instance, introduced an inculcation of Islamic values programme in government agencies. All these approaches can be seen as part of a political strategy to win over *ulama* (Muslim scholars) and vocal Islamic leaders in the country. Some of these *ulama* and Islamic leaders have even been co-opted into the Mahathir administration to strengthen the government's Islamization policy. One of them is Anwar Ibrahim. The strategy can be seen as a way to further pacify would-be militant groups that might otherwise argue that the government has done nothing to raise the status of Islam in the country. The policy, furthermore, was intended to promote the idea of moderate and progressive Islam as practised in Malaysia. Even the current Najib administration (since 2009) continues to promote the idea of moderate Islam – an approach to counter current Muslim terror groups' hardline ideology.

Given that religiously inclined terror groups are the main feature of today's terrorism, Malaysia has adapted an inclusive strategy in dealing the growing phenomenon. Championing the moderation approach in politics and governance is among the inclusive strategies adopted. This is a two-pronged strategy. On the one hand, it shows the moderate position of Malaysia as a Muslim-majority country, and on the other hand, it is another strategy to show that Malaysia neither condones nor supports religiously inclined terrorism. This moderation approach has been expressed through the concept of *wasatiyah*. *Wasatiyah* refers to 'the chosen, the best, being fair, moderate, *istiqamah* [righteous], follow the teaching of Islam, not extreme [in] matters ... pertaining [to the world] or the after-life, spiritual or corporeal, but should be balanced between the two ends.'[65] It can be argued that this concept, promoted by the current Najib administration, is an extension of Mahathir's Islamization programmes. The moderation approach is not only meant for Muslims but more importantly for an international audience. It is a 'showcase' of Malaysia's foreign policy to depict itself as a moderate Muslim country.

At the global level, Malaysia continues to be active in rejecting the unilateral approach, as shown by its critical stance against US policy in the aftermath ofthe 9/11 incidents, in dealing with the growing threat of terrorism. When Malaysia chaired the Association of Southeast Asian Nations (ASEAN), Organization of Islamic Cooperation (OIC) and the Non-Aligned Movement (NAM), multilateralism was seen as the most appropriate approach to handle international security issues. Henceforth, Kuala Lumpur argues that efforts to curb terror threats must be jointly organized by all countries affected, since unilateral action can be seen not only to have failed to solve but also to have exacerbated the situation. This commitment was also demonstrated when Malaysia was one of the promoters for the 2001 ASEAN Declaration on Joint Action to Counter Terrorism.

The introduction of SOSMA poses, nonetheless, great challenges to the SB department, especially in its modus operandi of intelligence gathering.[66] Firstly, officers in the department have to be equipped with greater legal knowledge since the new law requires reasonable evidence to be presented during a trial, the failure of which could result in dismissal of the charges. The intricacies of SOSMA require sound knowledge on the provisions of the law. This also relates to the gathering and collecting of evidence on suspected terrorist activities. The case of Yazid Sufaat, who was jailed for seven years under SOSMA, is a good indicator of how the SB department was unprepared with the new legal method of dealing with terrorist activities. It can be argued that SB personnel do not really have the competence to exercise SOSMA and other related laws. The complexity of the law requires them to dissect and gain a thorough understanding of every provision so that convictions can be secured. In order to comply with such a requirement, ongoing training and exposure are required for those involved. Secondly, the SB department also lacks the necessary logistical and infrastructure capability, such as special detainment centres with particular specifications. These requirements have hampered SB's capability to detain suspected terrorists. The law also requires detainees to be separated from other criminals. However, improvements were made in 2016 when the Malaysian Prisoners Department began to provide separate cells and buildings to house detained members of terrorist groups.[67]

Finally, the skills and knowledge of SB personnel in counterterrorism operations are still lacking in many areas. In fact, it is estimated that 60 per cent of SB's manpower are still relatively new in the force, with an estimated length of service of three to seven years.[68] There is an urgent need to improve skills and technological training for personnel in the department as the complexity of terrorists' advanced tactics requires the most sophisticated search and surveillance technology. Equipment such as Global Positioning System (GPS) satellite tracking has been used by most counterterrorism operators around the world to track suspected terrorist movements, bringing the possibility of stopping them before they can carry out their violence or acts of terror.[69] Despite Malaysia having a porous border, especially at the east coast of Sabah, such equipment is still unavailable to the intelligence agencies. Such high-tech equipment could greatly enhance SB's capability and efficiency in tracking terrorist movements, for instance from the southern part of the Philippines to the rest of the region.

It can be argued that the RMP was ill prepared when SOSMA was introduced. The law does not allow for detaining suspected terrorists unless acts of terror have been carried out, and only provides the normal process of fair trials through the fundamental principles of evidence and due process. Allowing terror acts to happen first before the perpetrators can be arrested does not augur well for a counterterrorism strategy. In fact, it allows more innocent lives to be taken.

Conclusion

Malaysia's effectiveness in managing terror acts in the aftermath of the 9/11 incidents can be attributed into several factors.[70] Firstly, Malaysia has considerable experience of fighting against terrorism, compared with its neighbouring countries. The emergency period during the British colonial administration enriched Malaysia's experiences in managing terrorism. Secondly, the political stability in Malaysia also helps in determining and strategizing the necessary policies to address terrorism. Finally, the combination of psychological approaches and preventive measures has contributed immensely to the ability of the state to contain the spread of terrorism. ISA as a preventive law, in particular, despite being criticized by human rights groups, has served as a good deterrent and helped ensure Malaysia's national security.[71] Furthermore, we can also conclude that the current fast-changing landscape of terrorist threats contributes to the challenging environment for Malaysia in its counterterrorism strategies. Since the end of communist terror threats, Malaysia has encountered several small-scale locally grown religious militant movements. But the real source of its terror threat is in fact outside its borders. Foreign-based terrorist groups have attempted to use the country as a strategic base either to recruit or to launch terror attacks in other countries. But recent developments show that Malaysia itself has become a target for globally linked terror groups. Despite societal resilience to the radical ideology propounded by various foreign-based terrorist groups, there have been cases where Malaysian Muslims have fallen prey to the terrorist groups' propaganda, and been influenced or duped into becoming jihadists or suicide bombers.

The introduction of new laws like SOSMA and POTA, which replace ISA and the Emergency Ordinance law, has placed great strain on security agencies like the RMP. The SB department of the RMP has to quickly adapt to the new legal procedures in dealing with suspected terrorists. It needs not only to re-equip its manpower with advanced legal knowledge and skills, but more importantly to re-strategize its modus operandi of intelligence gathering in order to contain terrorism in the country.

Notes

1 A.M. Dershowitz, *Why Terrorism Works: Understanding the Threat, Responding to the Challenge* (New Haven, CT: Yale University Press, 2002), pp. 2–3.

2 S. Samydorai, '9/11 anti-terrorist measures and their impact on human rights in Asia,' in Uwe Johannen, Alan Smith and James Gomez (eds), *September*

11 and Political Freedom: Asian Perspectives (Singapore: Select Publishing, 2003), p. 223.

3 *Ibid.*

4 Prashanth Parameswaran, 'The trouble with Indonesia's new counterterrorism command,' *Diplomat*, 11 June 2015, available at: http://thediplomat.com/2015/06/the-trouble-with-indonesias-new-counterterrorism-command (accessed 3 December 2016).

5 Bilveer Singh, *Revising Indonesia Anti-terrorism Laws*, RSIS Commentary no. 57 (Singapore: Rajaratnam School of International Studies, 2016), p. 2.

6 During British colonial rule, the Emergency Regulations Ordinance 1948 (no. 17 of 1948) was promulgated to address the communist insurgency. In 1960, the Ordinance was replaced with the Internal Security Act (ISA) by the Malayan Federation Government. Furthermore, a new emergency ordinance, the Emergency (Public Order and Crime Prevention) Ordinance was introduced in 1969 following the outbreak of the 13 May race riots.

7 MalaysiaKini, *POTA*, 12 July 2016, available at: www.malaysiakini.com/tags/en/pota (accessed 8 November 2016).

8 Mohd Sail Hassan and Kamarulnizam Abdullah, 'Ancaman Terorisme Serantau dan Respons Malaysia' (Regional terrorist threats and Malaysian response), in Kamarulnizam Abdullah (ed.), *Malaysia dalam Hubungan Antarabangsa Serantau* (Malaysia in regional international relations) (Sintok, Malaysia: Penerbit Universiti Utara Malaysia, 2010), pp. 64–83.

9 *Jackson Robert, The Malayan Emergency* (London: Pen and Sword Aviation, 2008), p. 10.

10 Malaysia was known as Malaya during the British colonial period (1824–1956) and in the first six years of its independence (1957–63). The name was changed to Malaysia when Singapore, Sabah and Sarawak joined the federation in 1963. Singapore, however, left in 1965.

11 See Eric Stahl, 'Doomed from the start: A new perspective on the Malayan insurgency' (Master's thesis, Tufts University, Medford, MA, 2003).

12 Barbara Watson Andaya and Leonard Y. Andaya, A History of Malaysia (New York: Palgrave, 2001), p. 271.

13 Mohd Rizal Yaakop, *The Emergency Law in Malaysia: Political Security or Liability?* Social Science Research Network (SSRN) paper (Rochester, NY: Elsevier, 2010), p. 4.

14 The country's experiences in counterinsurgency can be divided into two periods. The First Emergency (1948–60) was during the British colonial period. It was at base a British-led counterinsurgency campaign, and led to unprecedented levels surrender among members of the CPM. The Second Emergency (1968–89) was declared when the CPM relaunched its attacks against Malaysia. For further analysis of the Malayan (First) Emergency, see Kumar Ramakrishna's works such as *Emergency Propaganda: The Winning of Malayan Hearts and Minds 1948–1958* (London: Routledge, 2002).

15 For more information on the Australian contribution during the Malayan Emergency period, see the official website of the Australian War Memorial, available at www.awm.gov.au/atwar/malayan-emergency (accessed 16 October 2016).

16 For an excellent analysis of the role and contribution of the Senoi Praaq, see Roy Jumper, *Death Waits in the Dark: The Senoi Praaq, Malaysia's Killer Elite* (Santa Barbara, CA: Greenwood, 2001).

17 There are twenty battalions and five squadrons under the current PGA structure. The regional command centre is divided into five brigades: North, Central, Southeast, Sabah and Sarawak. The number of battalions in each brigade varies, depending on the strategic location and necessities of each regional command centre.

18 Daljit Singh, 'ASEAN counter-terror strategies and cooperation: How effective?' in Kumar Ramakrishna and Seng Seng Tan (eds), *After Bali: The Threat of Terrorism in Southeast Asia* (Singapore: Institute of Defense and Security Studies, 2003), pp. 201–20.

19 Leon Comber has written several articles and books on the SB, including *Malaya's Secret Police 1945–1960: The Role of the Special Branch in the Malaya Emergency* (Singapore: Institute of Southeast Asian Studies, 2008), and 'The Malayan Security Service (1945–1948),' Intelligence and National Security 18:3 (2003): 128–53.

20 Brian Stewart, *Smashing Terrorism in the Malayan Emergency: The Vital Contribution of the Police* (Kuala Lumpur: Pelanduk, 2004).

21 Hassan and Abdullah, 'Ancaman Terorisme Serantau dan Respons Malaysia.'

22 Marhaini Kamaruddin, 'Dosa Yang Tidak Terampun' (The unforgiving sin), Utusan Malaysia website, 22 September 2013, available at: http://utusan.com.my/utusan/Polis…/te_01/Dosa-yang-tak-terampun (accessed 11 October 2016).

23 Cheah Boon Kheng, 'The communist insurgency in Malaysia, 1948–90: Contesting the nation-state and social change,' *New Zealand Journal of Asian Studies* 11:1 (2009): 140.

24 Chin Peng, *My Side of History, as told to Ian Ward and Norma Miraflor* (Singapore: Media Masters, 2003).

25 *Ibid.*

26 For a comprehensive analysis of the Second Emergency, see Ong Weichong, *Malaysia's Defeat of Armed Communism: The Second Emergency, 1968–1989* (London: Routledge, 2014).

27 Another special forces unit established later was the Unit Tindakan Khas (UTK), or the Special Force Unit. The UTK has two major functions – undertaking undercover missions and high-level national special weapons and tactics (SWAT) activities. The VAT 69 and UTK were reorganized under the Pasukan Gerak Khas (PGK), or Special Operations Command, in 1997, but their function and identity remain separate and distinct.

28 Ministry of Defence (Malaysia), *Pamphlet No. 1: The Fundamentals of KESBAN, Malaysian Army Manual of Land Warfare*, pt. 1, *The Conduct of Operations*, vol. 3 (Kuala Lumpur: Ministry of Defence (Malaysia), 1984).

29 *Nazar Talib, Malaysia's Experience in War against Communist Insurgency and Its Relevance to the Present Situation in Iraq* (Quantico, VA: Marine Corps University, 2005), p. 20, available at: www.dtic.mil/dtic/tr/fulltext/u2/a505882.pdf (accessed 6 November 2016).

30 Militant in this chapter refers to the inclination of these groups to use physical force and weapons to achieve ideological goals.

31 Government of Malaysia, Ministry of Home Affairs (KDN), *Kertas Putih: Ancaman Kepada Perpaduan Umat Islam dan Keselamatan Negara* (White paper: Threats to Muslim unity and national security) (Kuala Lumpur: KDN, 1984).

32 Malaysia is an ethnically and religiously diverse country. The presence of several major ethnic groups like the Malays, Chinese, Indians, and the indigenous people of Sabah and Sarawak has created an ethnically based political system. The Malays and the indigenous people of Sabah and Sarawak form the 60 per cent majority of the country. This group is referred to as *bumiputeras*, or the sons of the soil. The Malays, by constitutional definitions, are Muslim, whereas the Chinese practise Buddhism and Christianity, and the Indians are mostly Hindus. Islam is the official religion of the country, but freedom of religion is guaranteed under the Constitution. Islamic matters, moreover, come under individual-state not federal-government jurisdiction.

33 Muhd Haniff Hanudin, interviewed by the author, 22 September 2014.

34 Cheah Boon Kheng, 'From the end of slavery to the ISA: Human rights history in Malaysia,' in K.S. Jomo (ed.), *Reinventing Malaysia: Reflections on Its Past and Future* (Bangi, Malaysia: Penerbit Universiti Kebangsaan Malaysia, 2001), p. 78.

35 Ayob Khan Mydin Pitchay, interviewed by the author, 15 March 2015.

36 For a comparative understanding of the rehabilitation process, see Lawrence Rubin, Rohan Gunaratna and Jolene Anne R. Jerard (eds), *Terrorist Rehabilitation and Counter-Radicalisation: New Approaches to Counter Terrorism* (London: Routledge, 2011).

37 Laws of Malaysia, Act 82, *Internal Security Act 1960*, pt. II, ch. II (*Powers of Preventive Detention*), p. 17.

38 Laws of Malaysia, Act 747, *Security Offences (Special Measures) Act 2012*, p. 7.

39 *New Straits Times Online*, 'Ex-ISA detainee, canteen helper get seven years jail,' *New Straits Times Online*, 27 January 2016, available at: www.nst.com.my/news/2016/01/124257/ex-isa-detainee-canteen-helper-get-seven-years-jail (accessed 2 December 2016).

40 Hanudin, interview; Mohamed Farid Hassan, interviewed by the author, 10 September 2014.

41 Hanudin, interview.

42 Laws of Malaysia, Act 769, *Prevention of Terrorism Act 2015*, p. 5.

43 Laws of Malaysia, Act 297, *Prevention Of Crime Act 1959*.

44 *Prevention of Terrorism Act 2015*, p. 8.

45 From the author's personal communications with several SB officers.

46 See Chin, *My Side of History*.

47 Akhil Bulat, interviewed by the author, 13 October 2014. See also Comber, *Malaya's Secret Police*, for the historical development of the Royal Malaysia Police's Special Branch Unit.

48 Ayob Khan Mydin, interviewed by the author, 15 March 2015.

49 Daesh is an Arabic acronym for the Islamic state of Iraq and Syria (ISIS). This terrorist group has rebranded itself over the years from ISIL (Islamic State of Iraq and the Levant), IS (Islamic State) and ISIS. The Arabic acronym is popularly used in the Malaysian context.

50 This was an official definition by the US State Department in 2008 under Section 140(d) (2) of the Foreign Relations Authorization Act, Fiscal Years 1988 and 1989.

51 This is part of the official definition of the Government of Malaysia under National Security Council Directive no. 18, 2003.

52 James Lutz and Brenda J. Lutz, *Global Terrorism*, 2nd ed. (London: Routledge, 2008), p. 9.

53 Laws of Malaysia, Act 574, *Penal Code as at 1st January 2015*, p. 89.

54 *Ibid.*, p. 90.

55 The Japanese Red Army was involved in the hostage crisis at the American Insurance Associates Building, which also housed the American and Swedish embassies, in Kuala Lumpur in 1975. Several American and Swedish diplomats were taken hostage. The group demanded the release of its jailed members in Japan, and safe passage to Libya. The terror incident ended when the Japanese and Malaysian governments assented to the group's demands.

56 Kamarulnizam Abdullah, 'Malaysia and Singapore: Managing the threats of Muslim radicalism in the post September 11 incidents,' in Takashi Shiraishi (ed.), *Across the Causeway: A Multidimensional Study of Malaysia–Singapore Relations* (Singapore: Institute of Southeast Asian Studies, 2009), pp. 187–99.

57 Aliza Shah, 'New extremist groups uncovered,' *New Straits Times*, 17 December 2016, p. 7.

58 See Government of Malaysia, *Towards Managing the Threats of Islamic State*, government white paper, 26 November 2014; *Star (Malaysia)*, 'Zahid: Terror threat at new level,' *Star (Malaysia)*, 25 November 2015, available at: www.thestar.com.my/News/Nation/2014/11/25/Zahid-Terror-threat-at-new-level (accessed 1 December 2014); *Malaysian Insider*, 'Rekrut rakyat Malaysia "berjihad" di Syria ancaman buat negara, kata Panglima Tentera,' *Malaysian Insider*, 16 October 2014, available at: www.themalaysianinsider.com/bahasa/article/rekrut-rakyat-malaysia-berjihad-di-syria-ancaman-buat-negara-kata-panglima#sthash.KSGtmToo.dpuf (accessed 25 October 2014).

59 It is interesting to note that many Malaysian women have responded to JI's jihadi call. Some of them voluntarily offered themselves as wives or companions to foreign jihadists in Syria and Iraq. They believed that they were contributing to jihad by offering such sacrifice. This information is based on classified materials from SB's interrogation files on returning IS/Daesh members in Malaysia.

60 *Sun (Malaysia)*, 'IS girl held,' *Sun (Malaysia)*, 19 February 2015, front page; *Star (Malaysia)*, 'IS luring young girls for sex jihad,' *Star (Malaysia)*, 23 February 2015, available at: www.thestar.com.my/News/Nation/2015/02/23/IS-luring-young-girls-for-sex-jihad-Bukit-Aman-on-high-alert-for-militant-groups-new-tactic (accessed 23 February 2015).

61 *Star (Malaysia)*, 'Militants may abduct tycoons and target banks in Malaysia, says minister,' *Star (Malaysia)*, 14 February 2015, available at: www.thestar.com.my/News/Nation/2015/02/14/Zahid-IS-plans-kidnap-and-robbery (accessed 14 February 2015).

62 Personal correspondence with Senior Assistant Commissioner Ayob Khan of the Counter Terrorism Division of the RMP's Special Branch Unit, 12 December 2016.

63 Haeril Halim, Arya Dipa, Ganug Nugroho Adi and Nurul Fitri Ramadhani, 'IS shifts focus to female suicide bombers,' *Jakarta Post*, 13 December 2016, available at: www.thejakartapost.com/news/2016/12/13/is-shifts-focus-to-female-suicide-bombers.html (accessed 14 December 2016).

64 Personal correspondence with Senior Assistant Commissioner Ayob Khan of the Counter Terrorism Division of the RMP's Special Branch Unit, 12 December 2016.

65 Mohd Shukri Hanapi, 'The wasatiyyah (moderation) concept in Islamic epistemology: A case study on its implementation in Malaysia,' *International Journal of Humanities and Social Sciences* 4:9 (1) (2014): 54.

66 Bulat, interview.

67 This is based on the author's observations during a special visit, as a de-radicalization member of the RMP, to the Bidor Correctional and Prison Centre.

68 *Ibid.*

69 See Leroy Thompson, *The Counterterrorist Manual* (London: Frontline Books, 2009).

70 Hassan and Abdullah, 'Ancaman Terorisme Serantau dan Respons Malaysia.'

71 For further analysis see Kamarulnizam Abdullah, *The Politics of Islam in Contemporary Malaysia* (Bangi, Malaysia: Penerbit UKM, 2003), p. 210; Amitav Acharya, *The Age of Fear: Power versus Principle in the War on Terror* (Singapore/New Delhi: Marshall Cavendish/Rupa, 2004), p. 9; Samydorai, '9/11 anti-terrorist measures,' p. 224; Elina Noor, 'Terrorism in Malaysia: Situation and response,' in Rohan Gunaratna (ed.), *Terrorism in the Asia-Pacific: Threat and Response* (Singapore: Eastern University Press, 2003), pp. 161–77.

5

Political violence and counterterrorism: Disputed boundaries of a postcolonial state

Evan A. Laksmana and Michael Newell

This chapter seeks to describe how Indonesia has dealt with the threat of terrorism in the post-9/11 era. However, beyond merely identifying the country's counterterror policies, the analysis is placed within the broader context of how the state has historically dealt with internal security threats. This chapter argues that, contrary to the rhetoric of the 'war on terror', Indonesia's counterterrorism policies are neither a specific response to transnational terror networks, nor simply a by-product of the post-9/11 era. Instead, Indonesia's counterterrorism policies are entangled with historical state reactions to internal security challenges – ranging from social violence to terrorism and secessionism – since the country's independence in 1945. While these different conflicts had diverse political, ideological, religious and territorial characteristics, disputes over the basic institutions and boundaries of the state run as a common thread.

As such, the Indonesian state's response to contemporary political violence – including the separatist movement in Aceh and the threat of transnational terrorism, allegedly centred on the Jemaah Islamiyah (JI) group – should be re-examined as part of these broader historical trends in state responses to internal political violence.[1] The chapter further argues that while the state, in seeking to maintain its territorial integrity and defend its institutions, has responded in a variety of ways to these conflicts, the particular tools of coercion and repression used in President Suharto's New Order have contributed to the rise of JI and its splinter groups and left a legacy of mixed responses to terror. The New Order (1966–98) was a military-backed authoritarian regime that emerged through opposition to President Sukarno and the Communist Party (Partai Komunis Indonesia, or PKI). The examination of the evolution of internal political violence and state responses demonstrates that terrorism and counterterrorism in Indonesia are rooted within this context of the disputed postcolonial state. The New Order's repression of domestic challengers and initial covert encouragement of Islamic extremism and the military's historically dominant role within the state have conditioned both contemporary political violence and the state's response to it. While regime change, security-sector reform, and the terrorist attacks of September 11th 2001 (9/11) and the 2002 Bali bombings have substantially altered the political and security landscape for Indonesia, the legacy of the New Order nonetheless exerts significant influence today.

These arguments are substantiated in the four parts of this chapter. The first part describes the evolution of and connection between organized political violence and the state in Indonesia. This overview of the threat environment allows us to place our discussion of post-9/11 terrorism within a broader historical context. The second part examines Indonesia's post-authoritarian environment, where the evolution of JI and the Free Aceh Movement (GAM) are juxtaposed as the state's most significant internal threats. This allows a description of how the evolution of these groups and the threat they posed is tied to how the state has managed past instances of political violence. The third part discusses recent developments in Indonesia's counterterrorism policies. Here, the analysis finds that the historical context of internal political violence competes with the contemporary concerns of the democratic regime to lead to a delicate balance between a repressive (hard) and population-focused (soft) approach in state counterterrorism. Finally, the chapter concludes with a broader take on Indonesia's responses to terror by placing it within the context of the global war on terror.

Violence and the state in Indonesia

Indonesia's internal threat environment has historically been multifaceted and ever-evolving. On the one hand, the diversity of violence in a country of over 17,000 islands inhabited by over 240 million people from hundreds of ethnic groups makes it difficult to identify a single pattern. One scholar has argued, for instance, that there are at least five different types of organized violence in Indonesia: secessionist conflicts, urban riots, ethnic purges, religious wars and terrorist bombings.[2] But, despite this diversity, the state has tended to adopt a coercive strategy to address each form of violence. This is partly because the majority of these threats have been directed against or provoked by discriminatory or repressive actions of the state,[3] but also partly because of the historically prominent role of the military in tackling domestic political violence. One study shows that 67 per cent of 249 military operations between 1945 and 2004 were meant to tackle internal security threats.[4] While the New Order generally managed to keep a lid on major internal challenges, threats of separatism, low-level terrorism, and sporadic violence persisted. Furthermore, the regime's abrupt end sparked these latent tensions and opened the floodgates to a whole host of organized violence.[5]

Taken as a whole, there were at least 215 acts of political violence aimed against the state between 1945 and 2009 (more than half involving acts of terror such as bombings).[6] Approximately half of these acts of political violence involved disputes and contestations over the state's authority, legitimacy or use of repressive measures – which partially explains why around 40 per cent of those attacks occurred in Java (often considered the 'centre' of the state, and thus a legitimate target for grievances against the government).[7] These figures illustrate how violent contestation over the institutions and boundaries of the state has historically dominated the country's threat environment. Notably, violent internal conflicts in Indonesia have often reflected hostilities between the central and local governments and between the state and (political) Islam.[8]

We argue that, given the historical prominence of the Indonesian military (Tentara Nasional Indonesia, TNI), the way the Indonesian state has responded to internal threats has been significantly shaped by how that organization assesses and addresses threats.[9] We further argue that this dynamic often prolonged internal security threats, as we elaborate in the next section. Furthermore, we suggest that the TNI's perspective on threats to and within Indonesian society has been shaped by its colonial legacy. In particular, while Dutch colonialism united the disparate islands that now form its territory, Indonesia's postcolonial history has been fraught with violent conflicts over the character and geography of the state. Therefore, as a postcolonial state, Indonesia inherited from its predecessors an intense distrust towards its own subjects, as well as a strong concentration of power in the centre because of the fear that the delegation of power could lead to disloyalty and separatism.[10]

To 'hold the centre', so the argument goes, Indonesia needed a source of authority or legitimacy to unite its disparate territorial and ideological elements. The military has, more often than not, filled that role through its dispersed command structure designed to exploit the territory and control the people. This mindset of course exacerbates the assumption that the biggest threats to the state, and thus the military, would come from its own people – as its history seems to suggest. The Indonesian military's experience in this regard is in some ways similar to the experience of many third-world states undergoing decolonization in the 1950s and 1960s. The need to manage internal security threats with underdeveloped state capacity and political institutions is similar, but the manner and rationale in which the Indonesian military did so – through its 'dual function' doctrine – came from its unique guerrilla warfare experience during the revolutionary war (1945–49).[11]

Upon declaring independence in 1945, Indonesia's ability to withstand military assaults by colonial powers seeking to re-occupy Indonesia after World War Two depended on the close relationship between the political and military leaders as much as the economic, political and moral support given by the local population for the guerrilla war. As such, the military's doctrine of 'Total People's Warfare' (*Perang Semesta*) was initially designed in the 1940s to align the people with the military in the face of common threats (i.e., foreign forces).[12] This revolutionary experience has since been seared into the military's education and training system and constitutionally codified as the country's national defence doctrine.

Over time this worldview, ironically, has been used to justify a pervasive intervention by the military in all aspects of political life. Under the New Order in particular, military ideology has celebrated the pursuit of economic development as a means to save the nation from the catastrophe of Sukarno's Old Order (1945–67), even portraying and rationalizing political stability as a precondition for development.[13] In somewhat circular fashion, such developmentalist logic was then frequently reasserted and revised to ensure that the military's political intervention was perpetually required by any new evidence of national instability.[14] This evidence often included challenges posed by Islamist and secessionist groups, which jointly served to bolster the perceived necessity of military intervention and the centralization of state power. In turn, the repression of these groups then fuelled the context of political violence that gave rise to JI and GAM.

These imperatives are further guided, and were officially proclaimed in 1973, by the idea of 'national resilience'.[15] The notion of national resilience continued the inward-looking direction of the Indonesian state and its security apparatus which was first present in General Abdul Nasution's 'Middle Way' doctrine.[16] In his initial conception, the military had to stand in the middle of two political polarizing ends – the left (communism) and the right (religious extremism). But as the idea developed, it became increasingly codified as a middle or dual role that combined the military's influence in security and defence with socio-economic and political influence.[17] This logic underpinned the military's doctrine of *dwifungsi*, or 'dual function', and its vision of itself as a 'total social institution.'[18] The doctrine then justified the military's pervasive influence, which further served three functions under the New Order: (1) to monitor the population, including through domestic intelligence gathering; (2) to provide a deterrent to rebellions; and (3) to respond to potential outbreaks of communal political violence.

The domestic influence of the military and the ideology of the New Order regime, by justifying violent and repressive responses to internal threats, perpetuated a cycle of violence. This is particularly the case as Suharto justified state-sponsored violence as a reflection of his intense fear of the wayward proclivities of the Indonesian people and of their consequent social and political eccentricities.[19] As a consequence, one of the many ironies of the New Order was that the security of its citizenry was thought to require 'appropriate, and appropriately timed and calibrated, doses of violence against certain sections of that citizenry'.[20] One scholar argued that the regime's reliance on the military to handle internal security problems reinforced the view that it was the only actor that could secure a unified Indonesia, a view that continues to impact Indonesian security policy today.[21]

Taken as a whole, the evolution of organized domestic political violence and the state's response to it suggests that internal security threats, whether they were armed rebellions or acts of terrorism, have often been viewed by the state as one and the same – as threats to itself. As such, repressive actions, particularly under Suharto's tenure, were perceived to be an 'acceptable' and 'normal' response. The advent of democratization in 1998, however, was supposed to change this basic calculus. But as we hope to show in the next section, the legacy of the Indonesian insecurity state continues to linger.

Threats to the state? Juxtaposing Jemaah Islamiyah and the Free Aceh Movement

The abrupt manner in which Suharto's authoritarian rule ended unleashed a host of centrifugal forces threatening the violent breakup of Indonesia.[22] Once debates over the dissolution of the central state died down, the threat of transnational terrorism and secessionist conflict loomed large among the myriad remaining internal security challenges in the 2000s, particularly JI's terrorist attacks and the independence movement in Aceh as embodied by the Free Aceh Movement (Gerakan Aceh Merdeka, or GAM).[23] Indonesia launched the largest military operation in its history when it went on a full-scale war against GAM in 2003. The conflict ended after the 2004 tsunami led to the signing of the Helsinki peace agreement in 2005, followed by local elections. Meanwhile, since the 2002 Bali bombings, JI – both as a group and as a 'role model' for splinter cells – has topped the country's terror threat list; even more so as nearly all major bombings up to 2009 have been associated with the group's active or former members.

The evolution of these two groups and the threats they posed to Indonesian society can be understood within the broader context of how the state has responded to internal security threats. Both JI and GAM shared a common history as ideological descendants of the Darul Islam movement, which sought to establish an Islamic state in Indonesia during the struggle for independence.[24] Originally loyal to the Republic, S.M. Kartosoewirjo proclaimed an Islamic state – Darul Islam – in 1947 following the Republic's concession of West Java to the Dutch in the Renville Treaty. Thereafter, Kartosoewirjo's forces fought against both the Dutch and the army of the Republic. Parallel movements developed in South Sulawesi and Aceh, and formally joined the Darul Islam revolt against Jakarta in 1953. However, in 1962, Kartosoewirjo was captured and executed by the army, leaving Darul Islam leaderless. Throughout the Old and New Orders, separatists desiring Islamic rule in Aceh and other Islamic groups continued to draw on the ideas of the Darul Islam movement and to clash with the secular and centralized Indonesian state. This included JI, which sought to fulfil the promise of Darul Islam by establishing a region-wide Islamic state in Southeast Asia while also developing solidarity with other Islamist groups, including al Qaeda and GAM.

Not only do these groups share these common ideological origins, both also represent the cyclical pattern of domestic political violence in Indonesia, with the control over the boundaries and institutions of the state at their centre. While religious ideas motivated their fight against the state, they were also fuelled by the repressive, heavy-handed tactics of the state. Indeed, while Darul Islam and its 'satellite rebellions' in Aceh and Sulawesi were effectively defeated by the late 1960s, the Indonesian state under Suharto's authoritarian New Order had a hand in 'reviving' these groups.[25] When it comes to JI, it was under Suharto that two key factors came together in a way that ultimately produced the Bali bombers.[26] First, the Indonesian intelligence apparatus, particularly Suharto's Special Operations (Opsus), helped resuscitate Darul Islam in the 1970s in the hope that it would become an asset to Golkar, Suharto's political party. General Ali Moertopo, the head of Opsus, believed he could fund and co-opt Darul Islam to promote the New Order's anti-communist stance and to help ensure the electoral dominance of Golkar by uniting with Muslims against leftist groups.[27] While the new representatives of Darul Islam were seen as political assets, the group's splinters – including Komando Jihad – usefully served as an internal threat to justify military excursions and weaken Islamic political parties when they resorted to violence.[28] However, unforeseen by Suharto and Moertopo, a revived Darul Islam also became the precursor of JI inside Indonesia.

The second factor that contributed to the establishment of JI in Indonesia was the suppression of Islamic political parties in a way that not only denied Indonesian Islamists any role in the government but made them the target of active repression. All political parties were forced to amalgamate into a small number of closely supervised organizations in 1973, leading the Muslim parties to fuse into the United Development Party (PPP). Further into the 1970s and 1980s, Suharto sought to neutralize any potential Islamic opposition by developing a range of corporatist initiatives for the capture of target segments of the Muslim constituency, such as mosques, preachers, intellectuals, religious scholars and women's organizations, into non-party organizations.[29] This was coupled with other forms of political repression, including restrictions on political expression and Islamic gatherings.[30]

This repression was exacerbated by the fact that internal security agencies, primarily under the Operational Command to Restore Order and Security (*Kopkamtib*), were given extrajudicial authority to root out communist sympathizers while muffling any dissenting voices against the regime.[31] For more than twenty years, the army-dominated *Kopkamtib* arrested those it considered 'subversive elements', including student activists, journalists, Muslim leaders and even dissenting politicians. Among those who fell victim to this strategy were the founders of JI, Abdullah Sungkar and Abu Bakar Ba'asyir.

Sungkar and Ba'asyir were targets of Suharto's crackdown following the bombings of the 1970s, and were jailed from 1978 to 1982 after they began their rise within the radical Islamic community in Central Java.[32] They left Indonesia after their release. While the details of their travels and activities abroad are not well established, including how and to what extent they were connected to al Qaeda,[33] they appeared to have set up a base in Southeast Asia in the early 1990s and eventually returned to Indonesia after Suharto's downfall in 1998. While there have been disagreements over who in the JI organization orchestrated the Bali bombings,[34] Suharto's repression gave the group's leaders their formative ideological experience of fighting the state. The banning of independent Islamic parties also meant the removal of any meaningful political role for youth organizations that shared their goals, opening the door for young disenfranchised youths to a militant, clandestine movement such as JI.[35]

In short, Suharto's policies towards Islamic political parties and non-state groups set the stage for tensions between the state and the Muslim community and for JI's rise. Further, tied to the narrative of national resilience and the role of the security apparatus in maintaining the New Order, state agents set their perceived enemies against each other. The co-option of Darul Islam to counter domestic communists, followed by the restrictions on Muslim political parties and Islamic practices, were illustrative of the Suharto regime's confrontational stance towards its domestic competitors. This consequently intensified the opposition to the state by extreme supporters of Darul Islam. Arguably, however, while the vast majority of Muslims in Indonesia have pursued their political objectives through peaceful means, the extremists among them would go on to commit the largest acts of terrorism in Indonesia's history.

Similar to JI's origins, Aceh's secessionist movement was a direct response to the way in which Suharto attempted to realize the nation-building goals of Indonesian nationalism.[36] After more than a decade following the defeat of Darul Islam in the 1960s, the nucleus of what we now call GAM emerged in 1976 and demanded the creation of an independent state of 'Acheh-Sumatera'. GAM's political agenda differed from the 1950s revolt in three fundamental ways: (1) it was not led by religious figures, (2) it substantially sidelined the Islamic state issue, and (3) it sought independence from Indonesia rather than to take over the central government.[37] The newly found gas and oil fields in Aceh in the 1970s, and the related strong response by the security apparatus to ensure Jakarta's continued access and exploitation, provided the initial rationale and basis for the movement.

Jakarta quelled the movement with military operations, and by 1979 its leader, Hasan di Tiro, and several others were forced into exile in Sweden and Malaysia. However, popular support in Aceh for GAM did not dissipate as the province continued to face socio-economic problems. Although Aceh supplied close to 30 per cent of Indonesia's total oil and gas exports, the region remained impoverished as it received only a fraction of the natural resources' financial benefits.[38] Huge inequalities also existed between mostly Javanese migrants, who benefited from the development of gas exports, and the Acehnese.[39] GAM then resurfaced in the mid-1990s with more support from a fairly wide cross-section of the population. The Indonesian state's continued economic exploitation further drove many within the population to join or be a part of GAM's network and operations.[40]

Jakarta's favoured military approach to handle any unrest in the area did not improve conditions. Total estimates of the casualties of the Aceh conflict vary, but most accounts put the figures for 1976–2005 between 12,000 and 50,000 people.[41] During the particularly dire Military Operations Zone (DOM) period, it was reported that there were 3,000 widows or widowers and 16,375 orphans (1989–98).[42] Even after the DOM status was lifted in 1998, violence between GAM and Indonesian security forces returned in 2000. As the security forces resumed their operations and as human rights abuses mounted, support for GAM increased. Estimates vary, but GAM nearly tripled its fighting force between mid-1999 and mid-2001, and its supporters controlled roughly 70 to 80 per cent of all the villages in Aceh.[43] In short, it was both the exploitation of Aceh's natural resources by the state and the conduct of its armed forces that allowed the conflict to carry over into the post-Suharto period.

Taken as a whole, focusing on Aceh and JI provides a useful point of contrast. While both groups were initially descendants of Darul Islam, and while both arose partially as a consequence of the state's handling of internal threats, they have elicited different responses from the Indonesian state over time. JI, and the radical Islamic groups that preceded it, have at times been tolerated by the state, and at other times were resisted through law enforcement and other measures.[44] GAM, on the other hand, has been met with staunch military resistance almost from the beginning. This was true during the New Order and after, as we shall see in the next section. Exploring how the state has responded to these two groups allows us to place the development of Indonesian counterterrorism policies in their historical context.

Understanding contemporary Indonesian state responses to terror

We begin by fast-forwarding our discussion to today's terrorism threat. As of 2018, Indonesia has no major rebellion, no immediate border conflict, and no nationwide domestic repression. Indeed, its communal conflicts are largely resolved, even if grievances remain, and there is no public support for violence.[45] When it comes to terrorism, according to credible analysts, 'since a shootout with the police in Poso in 2007, JI had decided to end jihad operations in Indonesia. Several of its top leaders were in prison; those who were not were focused on religious outreach (*dakwah*) and education. ... All were counselling members against violence, not because jihad in Indonesia was illegitimate but because given the constellation of forces at the moment, it was too costly and did not help to further the goals of an Islamic state.'[46] Indeed, while JI may have been re-burnishing its reputation as a jihadi organization through its channels to Syrian Islamist rebels, violent extremism in Indonesia has continued to be low-tech and low-casualty.[47]

Meanwhile, the Aceh conflict ended with the 2005 Helsinki peace agreement, and the ensuing special governance laws and elections seem to have effectively contained any return to full-scale rebellion, particularly with GAM disbanded. Some violent splinter groups have, however, set up jihadi training camps in parts of the province (allegedly funded by Jemaah Anshorut Tauhid, or JAT, a new group that JI's Ba'asyir founded), though much of it was dismantled by the state in 2010.[48] While the threat of open rebellion has diminished, new patterns of local conflict have emerged recently, including: (1) conflicts among former GAM elites, (2) conflicts between former GAM elites and former GAM rank-and-file combatants, and (3) conflicts between the ethnic Acehnese majority and the diverse ethnic minority groups.[49] However, these conflicts are largely contained at the local level.

Overall, while one could argue that the post-Suharto state has largely been successful in responding to JI and GAM, we suggest that not only are the threats these groups initially posed intimately tied to the state itself (as previously shown), but the complex, incoherent and occasionally paradoxical manner in which the state managed to achieve the above conditions has ultimately left lingering concerns. In the following sections we will demonstrate that a more militaristic approach helped to perpetuate these conflicts, while a more constrained approach based in law enforcement has tended to reduce the antagonistic relationship between the state and those who support the objectives of JI or GAM.

Handling JI: From enemy-centric to population-centric?

Indonesian counterterrorism has undergone three periods of significant change: the 1998 democratic transition; the September 11, 2001, attacks and the 2002 Bali bombings. Suharto's removal in 1998 was accompanied by the separation of the national police from the military and the opening of the political party system, which effectively gave Islamic political parties access to the government. The separation of the police not only granted them autonomy, it also tasked the institution with internal security and law-enforcement duties, including counterterrorism. And, while Islamic groups had previously been the frequent targets of Suharto's repression, the post-Suharto revival of Islamic political parties meant that political elites would now find it difficult to establish any harsh policies against radical Islamic militants.[50] Together, the post-Suharto reforms sought a break from the military's dominant role and from repressive policies against specific elements of society; they also set the stage for a restrained response to Islamic extremism.

The second transformative moment was the 9/11 attacks. Whereas before 9/11 Indonesia's counterterrorism was mostly a domestic affair, the attacks introduced a transnational dimension in the form of foreign security aid, regional counterterrorist efforts, and pressure from the US, Australia and others to crack down on Islamic militants. While the Indonesian public's response to 9/11 was a mixture of disapproval and scepticism, the US invasions of Afghanistan and Iraq were viewed negatively across the board. This scepticism was reflected in Jakarta's tendency to overlook Islamic extremism prior to the Bali bombings.[51] Even immediately after 9/11, against pressure from the

US, Indonesia chose a more reserved strategy. The influence of Islamic political parties, the fact that the moniker 'Jemaah Islamiyah' can be translated as 'Islamic community' and a sceptical stance towards powerful governments all contributed to this reluctance. Indonesia's initial hesitancy to take a firm stance against terrorism can be seen in the initial failure of anti-terrorist legislation before the Bali bombings.[52] Overall, while 9/11 led to increased external attention to and aid for Indonesian counterterrorism, both official policy and political rhetoric were carefully designed to distance the state's fight against terrorism from the US 'global war on terror'.[53]

The third transformative event, the 2002 Bali bombings, in which 202 people were killed, significantly reshaped Indonesia's counterterrorism perspective. The immediate response was the onset of a criminal investigation and the issuance of two presidential decrees on 18 October 2002: the Government Regulation in Lieu of Law (GRL) no. 1 of 2002, concerning the eradication of criminal acts of terrorism, and GRL no. 2 of 2002, making GRL no. 1 retroactively applicable to the Bali bombings.[54] Notably, the new laws allowed security personnel to hold suspects for twenty days, and to possibly extend this for another six months.[55] President Megawati also established the Counter-Terrorism Coordinating Desk under the Office of the Coordinating Minister for Political, Legal and Security Affairs, designed to formulate and coordinate strategy across state agencies.[56] This desk would later be transformed into the National Counter-Terrorism Agency in 2010.

Overall, while the state spent a considerable amount of resources on counterterrorism (see figure 5.1), the police were the main benefactor by virtue of their counterterrorist role. Aside from a domestic budgetary boost, the police were also flooded with foreign aid. The most notable example was the creation of Detachment 88, a special police division dedicated to counterterrorism and funded through America's Anti-Terrorism Assistance Program.[57] Another example is the creation in 2004 of the Australian-funded Jakarta Centre for Law Enforcement Cooperation (JCLEC), located at the national police academy in Central Java, designed to provide a comprehensive curriculum in investigations, information analysis and specific litigation areas. Australian funding also strengthened the police's investigative capacity, especially pertaining to bombings.[58] Finally, the police were also the leading agency and benefactor in regional and international counterterrorism cooperation.[59]

This newfound funding for the police, however, heightened latent bureaucratic rivalries with the military carried over from their separation at the end of the New Order.[60] Exacerbating this relationship, Law no. 34 of 2004 on the Indonesian Armed Forces suggests that the military could involve itself in military operations other than war, including against separatist movements or terrorism.[61] Observers warned that involving the military in counterterrorism

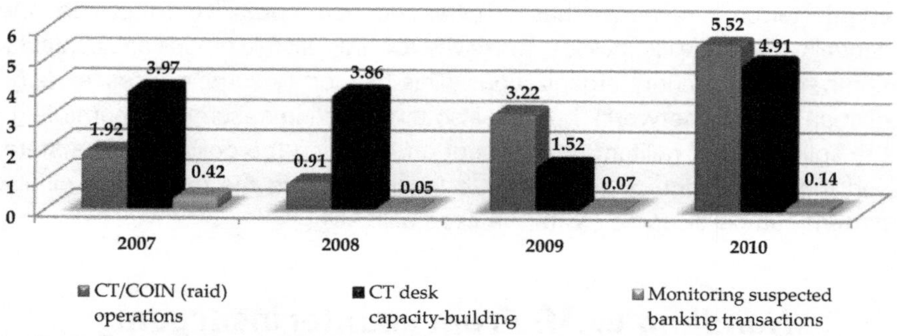

Figure 5.1 Indonesian national budget for counterterrorism (CT), 2007–10 (billions IDR). COIN, counterinsurgency.

could open the door for possible human rights abuses and a return to Suharto-style repression, and could diminish its overall readiness.[62] The debate over the role of the military has not been resolved, even as newly minted President Joko Widodo seems to have approved a larger role for the military than did the previous administrations.[63]

Overshadowing these rivalries, there is a growing realization among officials that the population is the 'centre of gravity' and that Indonesia needs to involve all sectors of the state and society to assist the police.[64] However, this is easier said than done. On the one hand, officials have held back counterterrorist efforts out of sensitivity to the Muslim community.[65] After all, even as moderate Muslim groups have condemned terrorist attacks, they reject overwrought state responses that risk overstepping their boundaries.[66] On the other hand, the police could not ignore the reality that the crux of the problem may lie within elements of the Muslim community. This dilemma is perhaps why the state has begun involving religious communities as part of a 'de-radicalization' campaign, and the police have turned to unconventional and non-coercive interrogation techniques. These include allowing detainees to meet their families, providing them with financial assistance or sending senior police commanders to have lunches with them.

Overall, domestic political changes have led to a contestation of the military's role and the ensuing centrality of the police in various counterterrorism efforts. While these developments appeared to strengthen the anti-terrorist hand of the state, bombings persisted in Indonesia throughout the 2000s.[67] Furthermore, as the police were part of the military under the New Order, the legacy of 'national resilience' remains central in the domestic orientation of the state's approach to terrorism and in the tensions among the now separate security organizations. In an attempt to move beyond its authoritarian past, Indonesia's counterterrorist response has emphasized non-repressive measures, the centrality of the police, political sensitivity towards Islamic groups and contestation between security organizations. This has led to some successes (e.g., dismantling JI's network), but has also left lingering security concerns (e.g., the splintering of militant groups bent on targeting the police and the state, and the reallocation of some counterterror duties to the military). A similar pattern can be discerned with the case of GAM.

Handling GAM: From counterinsurgency to peace talks

Aceh saw ebb and flow between a more repressive, militaristic approach to the ongoing insurgency and a more cooperative approach that prioritized a negotiated settlement. As we briefly mentioned above, the cycle of violence between Jakarta's security forces and GAM continued even after the end of Suharto's tenure; partially due to the 'democratic opening' and partially due to the success of the East Timor referendum.[68] As such, the domestic political constraints facing the new government under Suharto's protégé and vice president, B.J. Habibie, eventually forced Jakarta to end the DOM period and pass a new regional autonomy law. Initially, at least until late 1998, the military supported Habibie's policies, withdrew thousands of troops from Aceh, and granted amnesty to GAM prisoners.

However, as the presidential elections in June 1999 drew closer, violence in Aceh returned as the military's influence in Aceh policymaking rose under General Wiranto, which allowed key figures associated with repressive policies to dominate Jakarta's approach.[69] Habibie's East Timor debacle made it additionally unlikely that the president would extend an olive branch to GAM. By the end of 1998, *Operasi Satgas Wibawa*, the military's latest post-DOM operations, began in North and East Aceh.[70] By the end of Habibie's tenure, conflict with GAM had intensified, with over 70,000 Acehnese displaced.

This cycle of escalation and de-escalation continued under Habibie's two successors. Despite initially pursuing a confusing approach to Aceh, Habibie's first successor, Abdurrahman Wahid, brought in the Henry Dunant Center (HDC) as a third party mediator, which produced two peace initiatives.[71] The first was the 2000 Humanitarian Pause, which saw initial promise by the early autumn of that year.[72] By September, however, conflict resumed as GAM and Jakarta blamed each other for violations of the agreement. When popular support for Wahid's presidency crumbled, the TNI consolidated its hold over Aceh policy. Repressive security actions went into full swing in February 2001, and at the time of Wahid's impeachment in July, there were more security forces in Aceh than at any time since Suharto's downfall.[73] Peace talks effectively ceased at that point.

Megawati Sukarnoputri, Wahid's successor, initially adopted a 'dual track' approach in dealing with GAM – engaging in security operations while holding limited negotiations. This approach unravelled as GAM's military strength increased amid ongoing negotiations. The military, building on its strong personal rapport with Megawati, continued to increase its dominance over Aceh policy.[74] Nevertheless, the HDC still produced the Cessation of Hostilities Agreement (COHA) in 2002. The COHA was initially promising as violence abated and negotiations continued, but tensions had resurfaced by February 2003 as the planned GAM disarmament did not materialize and Jakarta's forces were not relocated to GAM's satisfaction. Violence returned as security disturbances were rising and widespread.

By that time, Megawati had already approved the promotions of hardline generals such as Endriartono Sutarto and Ryamizard Ryacudu in a 2002 reshuffle.[75] Also in 2002, the military decided that Aceh should be constituted as a separate regional military command. By the middle of that year, some 32,000 personnel were deployed to carry out security operations in Aceh, and Jakarta stepped up its security response.[76] In mid-2003, the government declared a military emergency (martial law) in Aceh. Subsequently, the TNI began its largest military operations in history. While official figures varied, the number of security force personnel (military and police) has been claimed to be around 55,000–60,000.[77] In total, there were 230 known security operations by the Indonesian Government during this period.[78] It should come as no surprise that all peace efforts ceased.

Susilo Bambang Yudhoyono entered office in October 2004 and inherited the Aceh quagmire. The military continued to dominate policymaking under martial law, as several influential generals were opposed to a reconciliatory approach.[79] But Yudhoyono, buttressed by a huge mandate as Indonesia's first-ever directly elected president and a strong domestic support for his cabinet, soon announced his intention to bring peace to Aceh.[80] As a first step, he removed hardline officers and filled key command positions with his close associates. But cognizant of the importance of Aceh to the officer corps' monetary bottom line, his vice president was tasked to address the military's 'financial needs' by providing a 'withdrawal fund' of as much as US$58.4 million.[81] Finally, while many attribute the end of the Aceh conflict to the 2004 Indian Ocean tsunami, secret contacts between GAM and Jakarta had already begun before the tsunami struck.[82] Under the auspices of the Crisis Management Initiative, a non-governmental organization led by former Finnish president Marti Ahtisaari, negotiators met in January 2005 for the first of what were eventually five rounds of negotiations over seven months.[83] Yudhoyono's ability to appease or remove potential 'spoilers' in the military got rid of any impediments to the Helsinki Agreement, which was signed in December 2005.

Overall, Jakarta's approach to GAM, similar to its approach to JI, did not waver from the fundamental baseline of maintaining state unity. Furthermore, the response also cycled between a militaristic approach and a cooperative one, similar to the debate over police versus military control of counterterrorism. In contrast to JI, however, GAM was seen as a direct threat to the state and therefore fell within the purview of the military, rather than the police. While the Helsinki deal seems to have muffled rebellious actions, the repressive manner in which the state responded prior to that agreement left lingering tensions and allowed local conflicts to develop. These measures, far from being an isolated response to the particular situation in Aceh, stem from historical state responses to internal threats, as regime change and security-sector reform have been unable to completely eradicate the New Order's legacy of 'national resilience' in the face of postcolonial vulnerability.

Conclusions and broader implications

While transnational terrorism has impacted Indonesia in the post-9/11 era, political violence, terrorism and the state's response have been rooted in Indonesia's domestic politics and historical narrative. As such, Indonesian counterterrorism has been different in both form and function to the reactions of the leading Anglo-American states in the war on terror. While the latter states committed their militaries abroad in an effort to exterminate foreign militants, Indonesia has crafted security responses representative of the tension between its authoritarian past and its efforts to move beyond it. This has led the state to be critical of the US global war on terror, to respond cautiously to its own domestic constituents, and to combine conventional counterterrorism policies with non-conventional and non-coercive ones.

However, contemporary counterterrorism and security policies in Indonesia still betray the legacy of the New Order's state-building projects and its inward-looking doctrine of 'national resilience'. Through these Suharto policies the actions of the Indonesian state also revived the Darul Islam movement and catalysed the precursors of contemporary Islamic terrorism. And, through its initial coercive response to GAM, the state arguably perpetuated the conflict in Aceh. It is perhaps the recognition of this cycle of responses to and catalysis of domestic political violence that has led the democratic Indonesia that came after the New Order to pursue security reform and non-coercive security and counterterrorist strategies. While the diminishing status of JI and the

Helsinki peace agreement signal the possible effectiveness of these efforts, the contested involvement of the military in counterterrorism and the state's mixed response to GAM suggest that the vulnerability and legacy of the New Order may not yet be passed. With between 300 and 700 Indonesians estimated to have joined the Islamic State in Iraq and Syria by 2016, and with an unknown number of those individuals having since returned to Indonesia as the Islamic State lost territory, Indonesia may again have to grapple with its history.[84]

Notes

1 While we often refer to the 'Indonesian state', we are not claiming that the state has been a consistently unified actor throughout its history.

2 Edward Aspinall, 'Ethnic and religious violence in Indonesia: A review essay,' *Australian Journal of International Affairs* 62:4 (2008): 558–72. Other scholars have provided different typologies of violence in Indonesia; see Mohammad Zulfan Tadjoeddin, *Explaining Collective Violence in Contemporary Indonesia: From Conflict to Cooperation* (London: Palgrave MacMillan, 2014).

3 At least a dozen groups launched attacks against the state during the first three decades of Indonesia's independence. See Dorodjatun Kuntjoro-Jakti and T.B. Simatupang, 'The Indonesian experience in facing non-armed and armed movements: Lessons from the past and glimpses of the future,' in K. Snitwongse and S. Paribatra (eds), *Durable Stability in Southeast Asia* (Singapore: Institute of Southeast Asian Studies, 1987), pp. 113–16.

4 See Andi Widjajanto and Artanti Wardhani, *Hubungan Intelijen dan Negara (1945–2004)* (Jakarta: Pacivis-UI, 2008), p. 39.

5 While exact figures are hard to verify, one estimate is that around 19,000 people lost their lives, with 1.3 million displaced, in civil wars, militia attacks, ethnic cleansings, terrorist bombings, political mobilizations and guerrilla insurgencies, or in the security force reprisals that these actions prompted, between 1997 and 2005. See Aspinall, 'Ethnic and religious violence in Indonesia,' p. 559.

6 These preliminary figures are from an unpublished database, 'The evolution of the Indonesian national security state', which is part of an ongoing project developed by the Centre for Strategic and International Studies, Jakarta, and managed by Evan A. Laksmana. The project measures contestations over the state by coding the cause being waged by the groups perpetrating violence in categories including separatism, disapproval over state ideology, and other issues related to the regime or state practices, rather than economic or ethnic grievances.

7 Figures taken from the unpublished database 'The evolution of the Indonesian national security state'. The data set initially stopped the coding at 2009 because that was the last year Indonesia saw a major suicide attack. Recent developments, including the early 2016 attack in Jakarta, have clearly changed the equation.

8 Vibanshu Shekhar, *The Politics of Islam, Nation-Building, Development: Ethnic Violence and Terrorism in Indonesia* (New Delhi: Anamika, 2011).

9 To minimize clutter in our narrative, we use 'TNI' to refer to the military, while acknowledging that the name was used after the separation of the police in 1999 and that the military has used different names since 1945. On how the Indonesian military dominated the Indonesian state, see Ulf Sundhaussen, *The Road to Power: Indonesian Military Politics, 1945–1967* (Kuala Lumpur: Oxford University Press, 1982).

10 Henk S. Nordholt, 'A genealogy of violence,' in F. Colombijn and J.T. Lindblad (eds), *Roots of Violence in Indonesia: Contemporary Violence in Historical Perspective* (Singapore: Institute of Southeast Asian Studies, 2002), pp. 33–62.

11 See for example, Alexander Wendt and Michael Barnett, 'Dependent state formation and third world militarization,' *Review of International Studies* 19:4 (1993): 321–47; Raju Thomas, 'What is third world security?' *Annual Review of Political Science* 6 (2003): 205–32.

12 See Leonard C. Sebastian, *Realpolitik Ideology: Indonesia's Use of Military Force* (Singapore: Institute of Southeast Asian Studies, 2006).

13 Jun Honna, 'Military ideology in response to democratic pressure during the late Suharto era: Political and institutional contexts,' in Benedict R.O'G. Anderson (ed.), *Violence and the State in Suharto's Indonesia* (Ithaca, NY: Cornell University Southeast Asia Program, 2001), p. 55. This particular 'developmentalist' ideology was also a deliberate choice to contrast Suharto's New Order with Sukarno's disastrous economics. For Sukarno's economic policies, see Howard Dick, 'Formation of the nation-state, 1930s–1966,' in Howard Dick, Vinvent Houben, Thomas Lindblad and Thee Kian Wie (eds), *The Emergence of a National Economy: An Economic History of Indonesia, 1800–2000* (Honolulu: University of Hawaii Press, 2002), pp. 111–52.

14 Honna, 'Military ideology.'

15 Officially, national resilience is 'a dynamic condition of will power, determination and firmness with the ability to develop national strength to face and overcome all manner of threats internal and external, direct or indirect, that may endanger the Indonesian national identity and the total way of life of the nation and its people, and to achieve the objectives of the national struggle': Daud Yusuf, quoted in Amitav Acharya, 'Culture, security, multilateralism: The "ASEAN way" and regional order,' *Contemporary Security Policy* 19:1 (1998): 70.

16 Nasution also believed that the military should not control the government, but play an equal role in running the country. See Adrian Vickers, *A History of Modern Indonesia* (Cambridge, UK: Cambridge University Press, 2013), p. 145.

17 See this evolution in David Jenkins, 'The evolution of Indonesian army doctrinal thinking: The concept of dwifungsi,' *Southeast Asian Journal of Social Science* 11:2 (1983): 15–30.

18 Vickers, *History of Modern Indonesia*, p. 282.

19 Robert E. Elson, 'In fear of the people: Suharto and the justification of state-sponsored violence under the New Order,' in Colombijn and Lindblad, *Roots of Violence in Indonesia*, pp. 173–95.

20 *Ibid.*, p. 173.

21 Yuhki Tajima, *The Institutional Origins of Communal Violence: Indonesia's Transition from Authoritarian Rule* (Cambridge, UK: Cambridge University Press, 2014), p. 43.

22 See the discussion in Robert Cribb, 'Not the next Yugoslavia: Prospects for the disintegration of Indonesia,' *Australian Journal of International Affairs* 52:2 (1999): 169–78; Edward Aspinall and Mark T. Berger, 'The break-up of Indonesia? Nationalisms after decolonization and the limits of the nation-state in post-Cold War Southeast Asia,' *Third World Quarterly* 22:6 (2001): 1003–24.

23 In 1976, GAM was established as the Aceh-Sumatra National Liberation Front (ASNLF) by Hasan di Tiro, grandson of Teungku Cik di Tiro, a hero of the anticolonial struggle against the Dutch. For its initial history, see Kirsten E. Schulze, *The Free Aceh Movement (GAM): Anatomy of a Separatist Organization* (Washington, DC: The East–West Center, 2004), pp. 4–5.

24 See the discussion of this history in Quinton Temby, 'Imagining an Islamic state in Indonesia: From Darul Islam to Jemaah Islamiyah,' *Indonesia* 89 (April 2010): 3.

25 Greg Fealy, 'Islamic radicalism in Indonesia: The faltering revival?' *Southeast Asian Affairs* (2004): 104–21.

26 These points on JI's origins were made by Sidney Jones, 'New Order repression and the birth of Jemaah Islamiyah,' in Ed Aspinall and Greg Fealy (eds), *Soeharto's New Order and its Legacy: Essays in Honour of Harold Crouch* (Canberra, Australia: Australian National University Press, 2010), pp. 39–40.

27 See Jones, 'New Order repression,' pp. 39–40; Temby, 'Imagining an Islamic state,' p. 10.

28 See Martin van Bruinessen, 'Genealogies of Islamic radicalism in post-Suharto Indonesia,' *South East Asia Research* 10:2 (2002): 128; Jones 'New Order repression,' pp. 39–40; Temby 'Imagining an Islamic state,' p. 26.

29 See the details of these policies towards weakening and repressing political Islam in Douglas Ramage, *Politics in Indonesia: Democracy, Islam, and the Ideology of Tolerance* (London: Routledge, 1995), p. 30; Donald J. Porter, *Managing Politics and Islam in Indonesia* (London: Routledge, 2002), p. 92.

30 Jones, 'New Order repression,' pp. 44–5.

31 Based on Presidential Decision no. 179/KOTI/1965, the agency had extrajudicial authority to exercise both military and non-military operations to restore and uphold the government's authority and integrity. See Pusat Sejarah dan Tradisi TNI (TNI centre for history and tradition), *Sejarah TNI Jilid IV (1966–1983)* (Jakarta: Indonesian Army Historical Research Center, n.d.), pp. 91, 97, 98.

32 Bilveer Singh, 'The challenge of militant Islam and terrorism in Indonesia,' *Australian Journal of International Affairs* 58:1 (2004): 53.

33 While it is agreed that they eventually found their way to Afghanistan in the 1980s and interacted with the Mujahidin, whether or not they established connections with al Qaeda is disputed. See Sidney Jones 'The changing nature of Jemaah Islamiyah,' *Australian Journal of International Affairs* 59:2 (2005): 172–4.

34 After Sungkar's death in 1999, it is believed that Ba'asyir took over control of the organization. See Singh, 'The challenge of militant Islam,' p. 54. In contrast, one scholar argues that JI is better described as 'a much hazier, messier picture of a loosely organized network of like-minded activists, acting together on an ad hoc basis': John T. Sidel, *Riots, Pogroms, Jihad: Religious Violence in Indonesia* (Cornell University Press, 2006), pp. 206–7.

35 Jones, *New Order repression*, p. 40.

36 We can observe similar patterns in Papua and East Timor. See Aspinall and Berger, 'The Break-up of Indonesia?'

37 John Braithwhite, Valerie Braithwaite, Michael Cookson and Leah Dunn, *Anomie and Violence: Non-Truth and Reconciliation in Indonesian Peacebuilding* (Canberra, Australia: Australian National University E-Press, 2010), p. 353.

38 Jacques Bertrand, *Nationalism and Ethnic Conflict in Indonesia* (Cambridge, UK: Cambridge University Press, 2004), p. 170.

39 *Ibid.*, p. 172.

40 See Geoffrey B. Robinson, '*Rawan* is as *Rawan* does: The origins of disorder in New Order Aceh,' *Indonesia* 66 (October 1998): 127–56; Ariffadhillah, 'The recent situation in Aceh after the joint understanding on a humanitarian pause for Aceh,' in Ingrid Wessel and Georgia Wimhofer (eds), *Violence in Indonesia* (Hamburg: Abera, 2001), p. 318.

41 The actual figure perhaps lies somewhere around 30,000. There have also been reports of 625 cases of rape and torture, 781 extrajudicial killings and 163 forced disappearances in 1999, along with an estimated 5,000–7,000 torture cases and 3,266 extrajudicial executions between 1999 and 2002. Figures from Braithwhite et.al, *Anomie and Violence*, p. 352.

42 Priyambudi Sulistiyanto, 'Whither Aceh?' *Third World Quarterly* 22:3 (2001): 443.

43 See Michael L. Ross, 'Resources and rebellion in Aceh, Indonesia,' in Paul Collier and Nicholas Sambanis (eds), *Understanding Civil War: Evidence and Analysis*, vol. II (Washington, DC: World Bank, 2005), p. 43.

44 There were other Islamic groups in the 1970s and 1980s that the Suharto regime also repressed violently under the pretext that they were threatening the state. See the details in Pusat Sejarah dan Tradisi TNI, *Sejarah TNI Jilid IV*.

45 Sidney Jones and Solahudin, 'Terrorism in Indonesia: A fading threat?' *Southeast Asian Affairs* (2014): 139–48.

46 *Ibid.*, 142.

47 *Ibid.*, 139.

48 See the full details in Sidney Jones, 'The ongoing extremist threat in Indonesia,' *Southeast Asian Affairs* (2011): 92–4.

49 See Mohammad Hasan Ansori, 'From insurgency to bureaucracy: Free Aceh Movement, Aceh Party and the new face of conflict,' *Stability* 1:1 (2012): 31–44.

50 As nearly 90% of the Indonesian population is Muslim and Islamic political parties have, combined, garnered 30%–40% of the electoral vote in Indonesia's elections since 1999, there is a strong check to prevent the government from alienating Islamic interests. See Greg Fealy, 'Indonesia's Islamic parties in decline,' *Inside Story*, 11 May 2009, available at: http://inside.org.au/indonesia%E2%80%99s-islamic-parties-in-decline (accessed 30 September 2014).

51 A series of bombings in Jakarta in 1999 are thought to have been the work of JI, but very little was done in response. Also, leaders of the FPI and Laskar Jihad – Islamic extremist groups – were arrested only after the Bali bombings. See Vickers, *History of Modern Indonesia,* p. 221.

52 Opposition to the law focused on its association with a US approach to counterterrorism and the possibility it could resurrect aspects of the authoritarian New Order state.

53 For more details see Senia Febrica, 'Securitizing terrorism in Southeast Asia: Accounting for the varying responses of Singapore and Indonesia,' *Asian Survey* 50:3 (2010): 569–90.

54 Both decrees were passed by a vote of 220 to 46, but the retroactive application of GRL no. 2 would later be struck down as unconstitutional. See Kent Roach, *The 9/11 Effect: Comparative Counter-terrorism* (New York: Cambridge University Press, 2011), pp. 152–3.

55 Singh, 'The challenge of militant Islam,' pp. 59–60.

56 See Leonard Sebastian, 'The Indonesia dilemma: How to participate in the war on terror without becoming a national security state,' in Kumar Ramakrishna and See Seng Tan (eds), *After Bali: The Threat of Terrorism in Southeast Asia* (Singapore: Institute of Defence and Strategic Studies, 2003), pp. 357–82.

57 The detachment has become the premier group detaining hundreds and killing dozens of militants, JI-linked or otherwise. See Ken Conboy, *Elite: The Special Forces of Indonesia 1950–2008* (Jakarta: Equinox, 2008), p. 141; Peter Chalk, Angel Rabasa, William Rosenau and Leanne Piggott, *The Evolving Terrorist Threat: A Net Assessment* (Arlington, VA: RAND, 2009), p. 154; Robert Tumanggor, 'Indonesia's Counter-Terrorism Policy,' *UNISCI Discussion Papers* 15 (2007): 97.

58 After the 2002 bombings, a national bomb task force – credited with many of the key JI arrests in 2002 and 2003 – was formed to assist in the investigation. See Chalk et. al, *The Evolving Terrorist Threat*, pp. 153–4; Greg Barton, *Jemaah Islamiyah: Radical Islamism in Indonesia* (Singapore: Singapore University Press, 2005).

59 This includes joint operations, intelligence exchanges and extradition agreements with Malaysia and Singapore; a memorandum of understanding on combating terrorism with Australia; a mutual legal assistance treaty with South Korea; an agreement on information exchange with Malaysia, the Philippines, Thailand, and Cambodia; and participation in the Associataion of Southeast Asian Nations (ASEAN) Plan of Action to Combat Transnational Crimes.

60 Zachary Abuza, *Political Islam and Violence in Indonesia* (New York: Routledge, 2006), p. 62.

61 The Law of the Republic of Indonesia No. 34 of the Year 2004 about the Indonesian National Armed Forces, ch. IV, 'Role, functions, and duties,' art. 7B. However, Law no. 2 of 2002 on the Indonesian National Police states that the police could 'request the assistance of the TNI in dealing with security issues that are regulated by a Presidential Decree': The Law of the Republic of Indonesia No. 2 of 2002 Concerning the Indonesian National Police, ch. VII, 'Assistance, relationship and cooperation,' art. 41(1), available at: http://policehumanrightsresources.org/wp-content/uploads/2016/08/Indonesia-Law-No-2-Concerning-the-State-Police-2002.pdf (accessed 2 May 2018). To put it differently, the TNI can only counter terrorism if the police request its assistance in doing so.

62 Under Law No. 15 of 2003 on Countering Criminal Acts of Terrorism, Indonesia adopts a criminal justice model of counterterrorism in which the National Police (POLRI) is the lead agency and the military can be seconded to assist on an ad-hoc basis as commanded by the president. As of early 2018, efforts are underway in the national legislature (DPR) to revise this law to give a wider role for the military in counterterrorism without being seconded to the police. If passed, the revision could effectively end Indonesia's criminal-justice approach to counterterrorism and perhaps even bring us back to the New Order era where the military handles domestic security. See the debate over this revision in Julie Chernov Hwang, 'The unintended consequences of amending Indonesia's anti-terrorism law,' Lawfare Blog website, 1 October 2017, available at: www.lawfareblog.com/unintended-consequences-amending-indonesias-anti-terrorism-law (accessed 2 May 2018).

63 In April 2015, the military staged a large-scale quick reaction force exercise in Poso, a hotbed of militant and terrorist activities in recent years. See 'Military restores security, order in restive Poso,' *Jakarta Post*, 17 April 2015, available at: www.thejakartapost.com/news/2015/04/17/military-restores-security-order-restive-poso.html (accessed 27 April 2018).

64 Private conversation with B.G. Tito Karnavian, then head of Detachment 88, Jakarta, 9 July 2010. This population-centric approach to counterterrorism suggests the assumption that counterterrorist aims can be achieved through the methods of counterinsurgency, when in fact those two strategies may not always work in concert; see Michael Boyle, 'Do counterterrorism and counterinsurgency go together?' *International Affairs* 86:2 (2010): 333–53. For a discussion of counterinsurgency and counterterrorism in Indonesia, see David J. Kilcullen, *Counterinsurgency* (Oxford: Oxford University Press, 2010).

65 President Megawati's absence at the Bali bombing memorial has been partially explained as distancing himself from international condemnation of Islamic extremism. See Anthony Smith, 'Terrorism and the political landscape in Indonesia: The fragile post-Bali consensus,' in Anthony Smith (ed.), *Terrorism and Violence in Southeast Asia: Transnational Challenges to States and Regional Stability* (Armonk, NY: M.E. Sharpe, 2005), p. 103.

66 This is particularly salient given that terrorism has been said to strengthen the intelligence agencies. For example, the State Intelligence Agency developed Directorate 43 to infiltrate jihadist organizations, counter militant messages, and monitor Islamist groups and their social networks. See Vickers, *History of Modern Indonesia*, p. 223; International Crisis Group, '"De-radicalization" and Indonesian prisons,' *Asia Report* 142 (19 November 2007): 159.

67 Targets of major bombings since 2002 include the J.W. Marriott Hotel in 2003, the Australian embassy in 2004, Tentena market in 2005, simultaneous attacks in Bali and Palu in 2005, the Marriott Hotel again in 2009, and a police mosque in 2011.

68 The immediate post-1998 democratic opening admittedly gave GAM political space to publicly make its demands for separation. Further, at that time, GAM used East Timor as a blueprint and inspiration in its public relations campaign. Kirsten E. Schulze, 'Insurgency and counter-insurgency: Strategy and the Aceh conflict, October 1976–May 2004,' in Anthony Reid (ed.), *Verandah of Violence: The Background to the Aceh Problem* (Singapore: National University of Singapore Press, 2006), p. 237.

69 Habibie appointed General Syarwan Hamid (who headed North Aceh military operations during DOM) as home affairs minister and Feisal Tanjung (TNI commander during DOM) as coordinating minister for political and security affairs. Several other officers who commanded or were previously stationed in Aceh were also assigned into key strategic and advisory positions. See Michelle Ann Miller, *Rebellion and Reform in Indonesia: Jakarta's Security and Autonomy Policies in Aceh* (London: Routledge, 2009), pp. 15–16.

70 *Operasi Sadar Rencong* (I and II) replaced *Operasi Satgas Wibawa* and included a 'Mass Riots Repression Force' and 'shoot on the spot' orders. See Rizal Sukma, *Security Operations in Aceh: Goals, Consequences, and Lessons* (Washington, DC: East–West Center, 2004).

71 Initially Wahid raised the possibility of a referendum in Aceh like the one in East Timor, and attempted to start dialogue, but undermined these efforts by trying to buy off GAM officers and permitting the military to step up security operations. See Tatik S. Hafidz, *Fading Away: The Political Role of the Army in Indonesia's Transition to Democracy 1998–2001* (Singapore: Institute of Defence and Strategic Studies, 2006), p. 160.

72 In the first three months only 69 civilians and 14 members of the security forces were killed (as opposed to the 300 dead during the previous four months). See Hashim Djalal and Dini Sari Djalal, *Seeking Lasting Peace in Aceh* (Jakarta: Centre for Strategic and International Studies, 2006), p. 52.

73 See Edward Aspinall, *The Helsinki Agreement: A More Promising Basis for Peace in Aceh?* Policy Studies 20 (Washington, DC: East–West Center, 2005), p. 52.

74 This rapport stemmed from her nationalist stance and her party's close relationship with the TNI, with as many as 150 retired generals as party members. See Sukardi Rinakit, *The Indonesian Military after the New Order* (Singapore: Institute of Southeast Asian Studies, 2005), p. 213.

75 Scholars pinpoint Ryacudu as the key spoiler of the Aceh peace process. See Edward Aspinall and Harold Crouch, *The Aceh Peace Process: Why It Failed* (Washington, DC: East–West Center, 2003), p. 24.

76 Damien Kingsbury, *Power Politics and the Indonesian Military* (London: Routledge, 2003), p. 227; Matthew N. Davies, *Indonesia's War over Aceh: Last Stand on Mecca's Porch* (London: Routledge, 2006).

77 Some put it around 58,000 just before the tsunami. See Damien Kingsbury, *Peace in Aceh: A Personal Account of the Helsinki Peace Process* (Jakarta: Equinox, 2006), p. xii.

78 Figures from Iis Gindarsah, 'Penyebab Defisit Keamanan di Aceh pada Masa Implementasi COHA dan Pemberlakuan Keadaan Darurat Militer 1' (Causes of security deficits in Aceh during the implementation of COHA and the First Military Emergency) (Master's thesis, University of Indonesia, 2009).

79 Marcus Mietzner, *Military Politics, Islam, and the State in Indonesia: From Turbulent Transition to Democratic Consolidation* (Singapore: Institute of Southeast Asian Studies, 2009), p. 294.

80 It should be noted that, upon assuming office, Yudhoyono did not immediately change the repressive Aceh approach that had been in place since May 2003. See Miller, *Rebellion and Reform*, p. 151.

81 Parliament also approved another US$25 million for non-combat activities. See Marcus Mietzner, *The Politics of Military Reform in Post-Suharto Indonesia: Elite Conflict, Nationalism, and Institutional Resistance* (Washington, DC: East West Center, 2006), p. 51.

82 Michael Morfit, 'The road to Helsinki: The Aceh agreement and Indonesia's democratic development,' *International Negotiation* 12:1 (2007): 117.

83 The most detailed accounts of the Helsinki rounds can be found in Kingsbury, *Peace in Aceh*, and Hamid Awaludin, *Peace in Aceh: Notes on the Peace Process between the Republic of Indonesia and the Aceh Freedom Movement in Helsinki* (Jakarta: Centre for Strategic and International Studies, 2009).

84 *BBC News*, 'The Islamic State group's influence in Indonesia,' *BBC News*, 20 July 2016, available at: www.bbc.com/news/world-asia-35312624 (accessed 2 May 2018).

PART III

South Asia

6

Counterterrorism in India: An ad hoc response to an enduring and variable threat

Rashmi Singh

Introduction

On 26 November 2008, the world watched in horror as ten armed men in a series of coordinated attacks wrought havoc on the Indian coastal city of Mumbai. Terrorism in India had made the headlines – again. While these were neither India's, nor indeed Mumbai's, first major terrorist attacks, their sheer scale and innovation, the high number of foreigners killed, and the inability of India's security apparatus to respond in a timely and effective manner quite rightly focused the world's attention upon India's counterterrorism (CT) infrastructure. Since its inception in 1947, India has been the victim of a remarkably diverse range of terrorist violence. Not only has the country produced an extraordinarily large number of home-grown terrorist groups but it has also been targeted by cross-border and transnational terrorist

---

This chapter is the product of an ongoing project by the author focusing on Indian terrorism and counterterrorism. It builds upon and further develops some of the ideas and concepts also discussed in Rashmmi Singh, 'India's experience with terrorism,' in Nicolas Blarel, Sunit Ganguly and Manjeet Pardesi (eds), *The Oxford Handbook of India's National Security* (Oxford: Oxford University Press, 2018).

organizations. According to the University of Maryland's Study of Terrorism and Responses to Terrorism (START) programme's *Country Reports on Terrorism 2015*,[1] although there was no significant increase in the overall number of attacks in 2015, India continued to experience an incredibly high incidence of terrorism, ranking fourth in the world after Iraq, Afghanistan and Pakistan. At the same time, despite such substantial, diverse and long-standing challenges to its sovereignty and legitimacy, India's CT infrastructure and consequently its CT responses and policies remain remarkably myopic and underdeveloped.

Arguably, understanding India's long-standing experience with terrorism as well as its uneven response to the terrorist threat requires one to understand both how political violence interacts and intersects with key markers of identity within the country and how these markers have traditionally been politicalized by key stakeholders. In other words, terrorism in India is often engendered and propelled by tensions revolving around such issues as ethnicity, caste, religion and socio-economic concerns. In turn, the government's response (or the deliberate lack thereof) to various terrorist campaigns and manifestations of political violence also tends to be influenced by not only its own affinities but also how it chooses to manipulate these tensions for its own political ends. When placed against the backdrop of India's multiple other challenges, be they endemic corruption, the paucity of resources, or the abject lack of effective and adequate anti-terrorism legislation, this repeated privileging of partisan electoral politics not only ensures the absence of a long-term strategic response but also engenders a CT infrastructure that is both weak and heavily compromised. It is this combination of factors which also explains why, when viewed in the *longue durée*, India has had a consistently uneven, ad hoc and often contradictory response to the terrorist threats posed to its national security.

This chapter aims to broadly outline India's unenviable track record with terrorism within its sovereign borders as well as provide a critical overview and evaluation of its response to the same. In what follows, I first discuss how the unprecedented overlap between terrorism and insurgency within the subcontinent represents a key challenge to formulating an understanding of terrorism and counterterrorism in this context. I then briefly discuss the emergence and evolution of key terrorist groups in the country before moving on to critically evaluating India's uneven responses to these threats. Having provided this critical context, I conclude by categorizing terrorism in India as either '*pure terrorism*' – that practised by what are best described as 'incorrigible terrorist groups'[2] – or as a '*hybrid threat*' – a complex amalgamation of insurgency and terrorism utilized by what are essentially 'corrigible' groups.[3]

The challenge of studying terrorism and responses to terrorism in the Indian context

A key issue with the study of terrorism is the manner in which it tends to be conflated with various other kinds of political violence. This conflation is particularly evident in the case of insurgency and arguably not only rooted in the difficulties associated with defining terrorism but further exacerbated by the fact that insurgents tend to use similar types of violent actions for the same sorts of purposes as do terrorists. Moreover, given that neither terrorism nor insurgency is an entirely bounded concept, considerable overlap exists between the two and it is not entirely surprising that such confusion persists. However, it is incredibly misleading to categorize terrorism as insurgency or vice versa, and therefore imperative to clearly delineate these two very distinct phenomena. Such an endeavour is particularly relevant in the case of India, where this distinction is not only conceptually imperative but also important for understanding the key terrorist threats facing the country as well as the government's obfuscated CT responses to the same.

An insurgency is a 'protracted violent conflict in which one or more groups seek to overthrow or fundamentally change the political or social order in a state or region through the use of sustained violence, subversion, social disruption, and political action'.[4] Insurgencies therefore tend to involve violent action against the government or civil authorities in power undertaken by a 'group of armed individuals who operate as a military unit, attack enemy military forces, and seize and hold territory while also exercising some form of sovereignty or control over a defined geographical area and its population'.[5] Having said that, insurgencies need not be large popular movements and, in actuality, many insurgencies involve only small numbers of armed rebels.[6] Insurgencies tend to address concerns around identity, nation-building and economic underdevelopment, and often manifest as internal ethnic wars.[7] Unlike terrorism, insurgencies depend heavily upon local populations and consequently tend to involve a 'hearts and minds' component, whereby information and psychological warfare are used to co-opt or mobilize popular support. In an Indian context, the Maoist insurgents are an excellent example of this strategy. A loose collection of communist groups that initially fought for land reforms, the Maoists operate in the heavily forested areas of southern, central and eastern India, which are also home to India's eighty-four-million strong tribal population. These indigenous tribes have typically lived in extreme poverty and lack even basic amenities like safe drinking water, healthcare and education. The Maoist insurgents have gained tremendous local support by stepping in and providing the governance, amenities and services that the Indian

Government has not. Thus, it is not unusual to see the Maoists provide irrigation systems, fresh water, schools and clinics to local tribal communities in the jungles,[8] which in turn provide the insurgents with not only material and ideological support but also an unending supply of new recruits.

Terrorist groups, on the other hand, are more clandestine and are hence logically more isolated from local populations. Consequently, terrorist organizations – unlike insurgent armed units – both tend to operate covertly and rarely attempt to control territory (al Qaeda and the Islamic State are notable exceptions). Moreover, terrorist organizations are typically opportunistic; thus – quite unlike insurgent groups – they not only tend to avoid direct confrontation with their targets' military forces but also usually lack the resources required to undertake mass political mobilization. As a result, most terrorist groups rarely exercise direct control over a populace,[9] although of course there are several exceptions. To summarize the core difference between terrorism and insurgency, while insurgent groups can, and often do, use terrorist tactics, 'terrorists need not be insurgents.'[10]

India's case involves a complex amalgamation of what can be categorized as 'pure terrorism' on the one hand – groups which use the tactic of terrorism as a 'weapon system' without resorting to any other form of violent political contestation – and a significant number of insurgencies which have terrorism as their 'defining feature' on the other.[11] In fact, much of the terrorist activity in India is associated with insurgent movements, and groups that resort to pure terrorism tend to be comparatively few. Having said that, the imprecise conceptual boundaries between terrorism and insurgency make analysing terrorism and CT in India immensely challenging, and the confusion between these two categories is plainly reflected in India's CT and counterinsurgency (COIN) responses, which are at times indistinguishable, much to the detriment of both. Thus, rather incomprehensibly, India's CT doctrine tends to be framed in the population-centric 'hearts and minds' rhetoric that traditionally underpins COIN rather than CT strategies. At the same time, despite this hearts and minds rhetoric, India's response to both pure terrorism and insurgencies that use terrorist violence tends towards a lethal, kinetic response which is more characteristic of CT rather than COIN operations. One may argue that to some extent the state's use of a COIN rhetoric is understandable, given how much terrorist violence in India is insurgency related. However, this overlap neither explains nor mitigates the consequences of India's overwhelming reliance on lethal force and short-term kinetic action to what are widely divergent and distinctly different types of threats. In fact, one may argue that the confusion between these two concepts underpins not only India's woefully underdeveloped COIN response but also the continued absence of a holistic CT strategy that would incorporate, in addition to a kinetic response, non-kinetic elements such as counter-radicalization, de-radicalization and rehabilitation efforts. The Indian state has been able to deal with the fallout and costs of such muddled, underdeveloped and short-sighted COIN and CT strategies primarily because the vast majority of the threats to date have been geographically localized and/or peripheral and far removed from the country's heartland. However, as new and more diffuse threats emerge and/or mutate it is abundantly clear that India's current strategies are failing to safeguard its national security and need urgent reconsideration.

The complex case of terrorism in India

India has a remarkably large number of home-grown groups that use terrorism against the state. In 2013 alone there were at least sixty-six active terrorist groups in India.[12] In November 2015 the Government of India released a list of thirty-nine banned groups.[13] However, this list only included prohibited groups and excluded all organizations that were still active but not proscribed, inactive or involved in peace talks/negotiations with the government authorities. It is worth noting that the majority of these proscribed groups were domestically based and oriented, although this by no means undercuts the very serious threat of both cross-border and transnational terrorism that India faces. Given India's experience with Pakistani-sponsored irregular warfare and terrorism as well as a whole host of other insurgency- and terrorism-related challenges, it would not be an exaggeration to state that variegated political violence is an enduring reality of India's internal security. In short, India faces a complex amalgam of indigenous, proxy and transnational threats, which mark its experience with terrorism as highly unusual in scale, scope and complexity.

Given the sheer number of groups that have operated within India's borders it is impossible to provide an in-depth analysis of all of them. However, it is important to identify at least the key threats to the Indian state, both in the past and currently. To this end, what follows is a brief description of the regions most affected by a past, ongoing and/or contained conflict in India. Where more than one region or state is impacted by a particular variety of terrorism, the description below categorizes the violence on the basis of the broad ideological leanings of the groups involved as opposed to geographical location.

Jammu and Kashmir

Perhaps one of the best known and enduring conflicts in India is the one involving the state of Jammu and Kashmir (henceforth J&K). Located at the northernmost point of India, this region has been a source conflict among India, Pakistan and China since 1947, when British colonialism ended. Conflicting claims over J&K, an area with immense geo-strategic significance for all three states, have also engendered a number of military confrontations between India and Pakistan. Indeed, it would be no exaggeration to say that the 'Kashmir issue' remains a critical flashpoint between these two countries.[14] In 1998 this region came to be racked by an ethno-religious insurgency as a pro-independence secessionist group called the Jammu Kashmir Liberation front (JKLF) launched an armed campaign against the Indian state.[15] The rise of Kashmiri secessionism was closely correlated with fundamental demographic, economic and political developments in the region.[16] Thus, a dramatic increase in literacy rates combined with media exposure and increased access to higher education engendered a young and politically aware population that was both willing and able to challenge the existing order.[17] However, in less than two years what had begun as an armed campaign to achieve independence came to be hijacked first by local pro-Pakistan Islamist groups such as Hizb-ul-Mujahidin, which was supported by Pakistani intelligence, and then, by the mid-1990s, a host of cross-border Islamist groups which were also sponsored and encouraged by the Pakistani state to wage a jihad in Kashmir.[18]

From the very beginning, Pakistan sought to control the rising militancy in the state and systematically undercut pro-independence elements in favour of groups that were more inclined towards a merger with the Pakistani state. To this end, Pakistan deliberately supported multiple Islamist groups, or *tanzeems*, in Kashmir, thereby successfully preventing any one group from becoming dominant and challenging its ability to manipulate local groups for its own purposes.[19] Both the pro-Pakistan groups and the cross-border Islamist organizations that had been created and nurtured in Pakistan were supported by the Pakistani Inter-Services Intelligence Agency (ISI), with the external jihadis being used strategically to 'augment indigenous rebels'.[20] That Pakistan was fairly successful in undermining pro-independence groups is more than evident from the fact that by 1994 the JKLF had split several times and the largest remaining group had declared a ceasefire.[21] However, this by no means spelt the end of the insurgency, which was now propelled forward by a combination of local pro-Pakistani and cross-border groups. Pakistani state support for both the insurgent and terrorist groups operating in J&K can be explained through the lens of the long-standing historic conflict between India and Pakistan over this region. Having lost two conventional wars against India over the issue since the 1947 Partition, the Pakistani President General Muhammad Zia-ul-Haq adopted a policy of nurturing a host of radical Sunni militant groups in the late 1980s. These groups were to be used both to counter the perceived threat posed by Pakistan's Shia minority following the

Iranian revolution and, more importantly, as terrorist proxies to wage a jihad against India to achieve Pakistan's long- and short-term foreign policy aims.[22]

Hence, what developed in J&K can be best categorized as a complex amalgam of local insurgencies (represented by local groups with diverging demands and ambitions) that mutated into predominantly cross-border Islamist terrorism supported by Pakistan as part of its proxy war against the Indian state. It is important to underscore that towards the end of the 1990s, Pakistan lost control over the local *tanzeems* it supported in Kashmir, as several of these groups began to look beyond the ISI for support, funding and training.[23] This both augmented and further complicated Islamist terrorism within India. Furthermore, as will be discussed below, even Pakistan's militant proxies, such as Lashkar-i-Taiba and Jaish-e-Mohammad, which in the post-9/11 period had moved more decisively into al Qaeda's ideological orbit with concomitantly expanding global connections and ambitions, altered their modus operandi in India and extended their areas of operations well beyond the state of J&K.[24] However, irrespective of broader conceptual categorizations, what is worth remembering is that both local militants and cross-border fighters in Kashmir overwhelmingly relied upon terrorism to challenge the Indian state.

North-East India

The so-called 'North-East' is a generic term that encompasses the eight states of Assam, Arunachal Pradesh, Mizoram, Nagaland, Meghalaya, Sikkim, Tripura and Manipur. To call one of the most ethnically, linguistically and culturally diverse regions of the world merely the 'North-East' is an over-simplification of its incredible regional complexity. At the same time, when it comes to understanding the occurrence of terrorism there are sufficient similarities, linkages and overspills between these states to justify such a categorization.[25] Like J&K, much of the North-East has been plagued by violence since the very inception of the Indian state. Of course, international attention tends to be fixed on J&K, which is perhaps unsurprising given that the area is a flashpoint between two nuclear states. However, the incredibly complex political and social environment of North-East India,[26] combined with what are essentially competing political demands and a virtual kaleidoscope of insurgent groups that rely on terrorist tactics, often with vastly different agendas, suggests that political unrest in this region may be an even more intractable challenge for the Indian state than the conflict in Kashmir.[27] Located at its easternmost tip, this region is connected to the rest of India through a narrow land corridor and is sandwiched between Bangladesh, Tibet, Burma and Bhutan. A total of 98 per cent of this region's borders are international borders; as such, not only is the geo-strategic importance of the region more than obvious, but easy access to neighbouring safe havens lends a trans-border hue to much of the political unrest here.

The roots of political unrest in this region lie in its past. It was formerly an outpost of the British Empire, albeit one of vital importance thanks to the discovery of tea, and became part of the newly independent Indian state in 1947. However, under the empire this region had been categorized as a 'frontier' or 'tribal area' and remained outside the jurisdiction of British provincial legislature. This meant that even during the British Raj, a deep division existed between the culturally and ethnically distinct North-East and the rest of the country, and the region's predominantly tribal communities remained fairly disengaged from the socio-political events that ultimately led to India's independence,[28] and their own subsequent annexation into this new state. Consequently, it should not come as a surprise that the earliest armed secessionist movement in this region arose shortly after the formation of independent India, as the Nagas began a violent campaign demanding autonomy,[29] arguing that as the area had been administered separately by the British it should have been granted sovereignty. Other local insurgencies in Mizoram, Tripura and Manipur soon followed, and demands of nationhood tended to revolve around assertions of ethnic, cultural and, on occasion, religious differences with independent India. Despite long periods of containment, conflict management and arguably some headway by the Indian state, resentment continued to simmer and from the 1980s onwards almost all the states in the North-East have been impacted by ethnic insurgencies that are increasingly characterized by the use of terrorism. Consequently, North-East India has the unfortunate distinction of being one of the most volatile regions of the world. Over time, political violence in this region has steadily degenerated into pure terrorism. There has been a steady increase in terrorist attacks on infrastructure, civilians, security forces and political authorities.[30] To some extent this spike in terrorist violence is not only the result of the appearance of several new organizations in the North-East but also because a number of factions have broken away from the main insurgent groups. This makes peace efforts more complicated as the core groups no longer exercise a monopoly over sub-state violence in this region. It is also worth noting that the very particular location of the North-East has always lent a trans-border element to local insurgent movements, many of which operate out of the relative safe havens provided by the bordering countries of Myanmar, Bangladesh and Bhutan. This further complicates India's COIN and CT efforts against these groups, which always have the option of crossing the international border in order to escape any campaigns. The already tricky security situation in this region has been made even more complex by two more recent developments. First, in recent years the Maoist insurgency plaguing eastern and central India has managed to penetrate into the North-East as well. While the nature of the Maoist threat in the North-East remains unclear, the Maoists' relationship with local ethnic insurgent groups suggests the need for vigilance and certainly does not bode well for the already beleaguered Indian state. Second, there is a distinct trend of emergent Islamist terrorism in this area. Not only is this problematic in and of itself, but it also has dire repercussions for the local security situation given its clear cross-border links with organizations such as the Jamaat-ul-Mujahidin Bangladesh (JMB).[31] One would think that given the sheer durability, scale and scope of the security challenges in the North-East, the Indian Government would prioritize formulating strategies that would facilitate a swift and peaceful resolution to these multiple conflicts. However, somewhat unfortunately, the area continues to remain on the periphery of India's social, political and cultural imagination, and as such the 'costs of letting low-intensity conflicts proliferate and fester [here] are seen as affordable'.[32]

Punjab

The insurgency that convulsed the state of Punjab between 1978 and 1993 is often cited as a successful example of India's CT and COIN strategies.[33] It was perpetrated by groups who sought the creation of a separate Sikh state called Khalistan. Although the brutal campaign for an independent Khalistan was fought in the name of defending the Sikh faith and to avenge the injustices perpetrated by the Hindu community, over 61 per cent of the 11,694 people killed between 1981 and 1993 were Sikh.[34] While one can arguably trace the roots of the insurgency to Sikh nationalism, which considerably predates an independent India, the primary cause of the conflict was much more firmly grounded in the contemporary. The social and economic conditions in Punjab in the post-independence era produced by, among other factors, first Partition and then the coming to a head of the Punjabi Suba agitation created ripe conditions for unrest.[35] Finally, a bitter power struggle both within and between the two key political parties in the state – the Congress and the Akali Dal – essentially triggered the rise of religious extremism, as both parties deliberately fuelled communal discord between the Hindus and the Sikh, which became the foundational reason for the rise of terrorism. One of the Congress Party's strategies included covertly assisting the rise of a village preacher by the name of Jarnail Singh Bhindranwale,[36] a vocal and deeply conservative orthodox Sikh, against the Akali Dal. Bhindranwale proved to be a serious political miscalculation for the Congress. First, the competition that he represented served to drive the Akali Dal's Sikh supporters into the 'militant fold',[37] and further poisoned the political climate in Punjab; second, he quickly resorted to the use of terrorist tactics to target ideological and political opponents as well as to amass public support from the Sikh community. As a result, Sikh religious extremists essentially came to occupy the political space that was forsaken by the two main parties in Punjab in their bid for political primacy.[38]

Violence was sparked off in Punjab when Bhindranwale's orthodox extremist followers clashed in April 1978 with the Nirankaris, an unorthodox reformist movement within Sikhism often viewed as heretical by the Sikh orthodoxy. Over the following years, violence in Punjab grew exponentially as Bhindranwale incited violence and targeted both Nirankaris and dissident Sikhs, as well as Hindus and any of his critics. The lack of a firm response by the Punjab or central governments bolstered Bhindranwale's sense of political immunity and further emboldened his campaign of terrorism. He slowly began using the Golden Temple – the holiest Sikh shrine – for sanctuary, thereby strengthening his appeal amongst the Sikh population as a genuinely important religious leader. This situation was further complicated by the support provided by the Pakistani state as well as the diaspora Sikh population for the Khalistan movement.[39] However, despite the increasing violence, until 1984 what was clearly an emergent insurgency in the Punjab was still categorized as a mere law-and-order problem by the central authorities.[40] A key turning point in the conflict came with the controversial 1984 Operation Blue Star, in which Indian troops stormed the Golden Temple where the militants were holed up, killing Bhindranwale but damaging the shrine in the process. At the time, Operation Blue Star was only the second military-led CT operation in India. However, what made it particularly unusual was the fact that it was undertaken to regain control of the Golden Temple, the most important religious site in Sikhism, by flushing out the militants who were sheltering inside the complex. This engendered incredible resentment in the Sikh community, which felt that its holiest shrine had been desecrated, and instigated the assassination of Prime Minister Indira Gandhi by her Sikh bodyguards and, in turn, the violent anti-Sikh reprisal riots across India. If, prior to 1984, the primary objective of most of the militants was to secure a position within the existing power structure, after Operation Blue Star the objective became securing a fully independent Sikh state.[41] Consequently, far from resolving the situation, violence in Punjab rapidly spiked in 1984, despite the fact that after Bhindranwale no other central figurehead emerged and factionalism in the movement became rife. The weak and polarized police response combined with the central government's indecisive approach further aggravated this situation.

The next turning point in the conflict occurred in 1986 when command of the Punjab police was handed over to J.F. Ribeiro and K.P.S. Gill. Simultaneously there was also a clear shift in political will with the result that police numbers were augmented, weaponry improved and its administration streamlined.[42] In April 1988, the National Security Guard (NSG), a security force that had been created after Operation Blue Star with army, police and paramilitary personnel, organized and conducted Operation Black Thunder against militants, once again holed up in the Golden Temple. The operation was a resounding success and resulted in the surrender of a number of extremists. This not only served to ensure that the Sikh extremists lost the 'aura of invincibility' they had thus far enjoyed but also exposed their crimes and desecration of the Golden Temple to the Sikh populace.[43] Thus, 1988 spelled the beginning of the end for the Khalistan insurgency in India. As morale in the Sikh insurgency collapsed, the provision of extra manpower to assist the Punjab police, renewed political will at the centre to eradicate terrorism and what was essentially an intelligence-led police offensive combined to enable the successful culling of extremist ranks.[44] As a result, terrorist incidents, with their concomitant civilian casualties, declined sharply.[45] According to one estimate, the number of people killed in terrorist incidents in Punjab in 1992 was approximately 2,000; this figure dropped to 90 in 1993.[46] Thus, insurgency in Punjab died out before it could be fully formed. While a small fringe of extremists continue to survive in the state today and there is certainly an undercurrent of militancy, the threat that the Khalistan movement could be reignited within India remains negligible.[47] The ideology of an independent Khalistan is mostly kept alive by an active group of non-resident Indians, based in the USA, Canada and the UK, and to some extent it also continues to exist on Pakistan's radar.[48]

Naxalites

If Punjab is India's success story then the Naxalite problem is its recurring nightmare. Naxalites are essentially left-wing extremists who draw doctrinal inspiration from Marxism and Leninism and utilize Maoist tactics in order to create a 'new democratic revolution'.[49] The term 'Naxalism' references a large and dynamic armed movement which 'despite periods of cooperation and coordination ... has not been unified in different parts of the country'.[50] A movement that has existed for over fifty years, its fortunes have ebbed and flowed thanks to India's CT/COIN response. However, what began as a small militant peasant uprising in 1967 has since evolved into what has been categorized as 'India's greatest internal security threat'.[51] This is primarily because, unlike the conflicts in Punjab or the North-East that are territorially limited, the threat of Naxalism has steadily expanded across India. Currently, at least twelve Indian states and nearly 185 of its 602 districts are impacted by Naxal violence.[52]

The conflict first began as a peasant rebellion by members of the Santhal tribe in the Naxalbari district of West Bengal (hence its name) in 1967, and was spearheaded by leaders like Charu Mazumdar and Kanu Sanyal from the

Communist Party of India (Marxist) (CIP(M)).[53] The revolt began in response to long-standing exploitation and oppression by the landlords in the village who held large tracts of land, whereas the peasants who cultivated the land remained no more than landless labour. However, the conflict did not remain restricted to the Naxalbari; instead, it rapidly manifested as an armed peasant uprising and guerrilla warfare that spread across the rural areas of several states, including Andhra Pradesh, Bihar, Punjab, Uttar Pradesh and Orissa. From its very inception the movement resorted to murdering what it categorized as its 'class enemies', inviting the rapid deployment of security forces to address the threat.[54] Although the rural rebellion was brutally crushed using paramilitary forces, an urban insurgency had erupted in Calcutta (present-day Kolkata) by 1969. This, in turn, was subdued by the counterinsurgency efforts of the West Bengal state police forces and by 1973 the first phase of Naxalism had drawn to a close. However, towards the late 1970s and 1980s a significant number of Naxalite groups began to remobilize as the core grievances –the absence of land reform, class- and caste-based discrimination and exploitation, as well as disagreements about land and forest rights – remained and continued to resonate in society. Moreover, having learned from their past mistakes, many of these groups now embarked upon a concentrated effort to mobilize popular support, which they saw as necessary for waging a protracted people's war.[55] In addition to mass mobilization at the village level, by the 1980s Naxalite leaders had formed organizations to confront landlords, the police and paramilitary forces, as well as started holding territory in the inaccessible reaches of hilly and forested areas.[56] Thus, despite having been decimated in the late 1970s, the Naxalites had made a decisive comeback by the 1990s.

After 1999/2000, the movement had gained enough strength to exponentially expand and intensify its armed activities across several additional districts. Arguably this was the result of what can be best described as an inconsistent and deeply politicized COIN response by various states. India's federal political structure means that each state is responsible for its own CT and intelligence and the centre's role tends to be limited to one of advice and assistance. However, many state governments in the late 1980s and 1990s refused to acknowledge the underlying grievances that were engendering Naxalite violence and terrorism. Instead, they tended to ignore the threat for electoral gains and then resort to kinetic measures and intense state repression when Naxalite violence inevitably increased.[57] This sporadic, inadequate and inconsistent COIN response did no more than facilitate the growth of the Naxalite movement, as over time the insurgents learned how to organize and conduct their political and military operations much more effectively.[58] Since the turn of the millennium, the movement has continued to expand territorially and its armed activity has also intensified as groups have become progressively much more militarized.

To some extent, this growth can also be attributed to the merger of two key splinter groups in 2004.[59] What has resulted is the emergence of a 'red corridor' – contiguous tracts of land that are under Naxalite control and where the local population provides the movement's many groups with members, intelligence and logistical support. It is worth noting that after the 1990s the Naxalite movement also invested considerable time and energy into developing this stronger rural base. Furthermore, an analysis of two key Naxalite documents, the 2004 'Strategy and tactics of Indian revolution' and the 2007 'Urban perspective: Our work in urban areas', reveals that the movement also clearly recognizes that its collapse in the 1970s might be located in Naxalism's failure to take root in urban areas.[60] Hence, these documents clearly underscore the strategic importance of concomitantly developing urban bases,[61] from where the movement can 'mobilize and organize the proletariat in performing its crucial leadership role',[62] and thereby complement the struggle in rural areas. However, given that state power is weak in the countryside but entrenched in urban centres, the movement recognizes that it is the rural areas which play the primary role in its armed struggle. As such, the strategic control of rural areas is seen as a prerequisite to eventually surrounding and capturing urban centres.

Unlike other insurgencies in India, Naxalism is distinctive in that its use of terrorist violence targeting critical infrastructure as well as civilians and security personnel characterized the movement from its very inception. Not only has terrorist violence been endemic to the movement but it has steadily escalated as the Naxalites have consolidated their hold on territory and learned how to conduct more effective political and military operations. In more recent years, there is also a clear criminal element to the movement, with leaders profiting from illegal mining and deforesting industries. However, the fundamental reason for the longevity and proliferation of the movement is the consistent failure of the Indian state to provide effective governance to the underprivileged and exploited sections of society. Research has shown a clear correlation between high rates of illiteracy and poverty in some states and rates of popular participation in Naxal violent activity. Thus, Bihar and Jharkhand, which are economically the most underdeveloped states in India, tend to provide the core cadres for the movement.[63] In circumstances of continued disenfranchisement, the movement offers emancipation and an alternative system of governance through the use of armed force to the deeply disaffected, disenchanted and impoverished sections of Indian society. It is worth noting that the Indian Government sees development as a critical part of its security response. However, endemic corruption and a Kafkaesque bureaucracy often mean that this emphasis on development – as opposed to a more holistic CT strategy which would also incorporate long-term soft measures alongside kinetic measures *in addition* to development projects – inadvertently promotes alienation and violence. Thus, most development projects are top-down affairs with minimal local participation.[64] Furthermore, many development policies and projects are either woefully inadequate or so slowly implemented (if implemented at all) due to political and bureaucratic pressures and interests that they do little more than further aggravate local grievances and legitimize the insurgent/terrorist rhetoric of an ineffective and deceitful government. In all cases, the root cause of poor governance and the resulting underdevelopment remain unaddressed and serve to further alienate local populations. Hence, unless and until the government demonstrates genuine political will and implements consistent policies that translate into concrete results to address these core grievances, the threat from Naxalite terrorism promises to continue to escalate and destabilize India from within.

Islamist terrorism

Having discussed India's regrettably vast experience with various insurgencies that use and have used terrorism, we now turn to perhaps the one form of so-called 'pure terrorism' that exists in India: Islamist terrorism. While we touched upon one element of jihad in India while discussing the insurgency in Kashmir, it would be wrong to assert that all Islamist terrorism is in some way linked to Pakistan, although undoubtedly Pakistan has fuelled and manipulated local grievances for its own political and religious agenda. We can broadly divide India's experience with Islamist violence into the categories of cross-border terrorism, home-grown jihad and, finally, transnational global jihad.

As discussed previously, in Kashmir the local insurgency was divided quite sharply between pro-independence groups like the JKLF and pro-Pakistan groups like Hizb-ul-Mujahidin, with both enjoying the support of the Pakistani ISI. While the JKLF's ideology was grounded in a fairly secular understanding of Kashmiri nationhood, it did not hesitate to use Islamist language, symbolism and themes, including the language of jihad and martyrdom, in order to mobilize the population against the Indian state as well as J&K's Hindu population. However, the key internal impetus for Islamization originated in groups like Hizb-ul-Mujahidin and their ideologues. These ideologues not only deliberately linked Kashmiri nationalism to jihad but also situated the conflict in Kashmir within an 'Islamist paradigm', thereby discrediting and displacing the JKLF's agenda and 'providing a religious rationale for advocating Kashmir's accession to Pakistan'.[65] However, this initial competition between two competing visions for Kashmir – one secessionist and the other pressing for accession to Pakistan – was soon overtaken by an organized, expertly trained and well-funded cross-border jihad. Hence, by 1996 Pakistan was pumping significant numbers of Pakistani and other foreign militants into Kashmir, with the result that the predominantly ethnic Kashmiri terrorist groups in the region were overtaken by groups like Lashkar-i-Taiba (LeT), Jaish-e-Mohammad (JeM) and Harkat-ul-Mujahidin.

As has been mentioned previously, the cross-border Islamist terrorist groups operating in Kashmir can be understood through the lens of the long-standing historic conflict between India and Pakistan. Most of these Pakistani outfits tended to adhere to the Deobandi school of Sunni Islam, a clear exception being LeT which is an adherent of Ahl-e-Hadith, a puritanical strain of Islam that closely resembles the Wahhabism of the Arabian Peninsula. Hence, Pakistan's deliberate policy of fostering terrorist groups to be used as proxies against the Indian state bore fruit as various Pakistani groups initiated their jihad to liberate Indian-administered Kashmir in the 1990s. For many of these groups, any state that has historically experienced Muslim rule is considered an Islamic territory that must be liberated. In short, these groups espoused a pan-Islamist rationale to justify military action in Kashmir. By the early 2000s, several Pakistani groups involved in the proxy war in Kashmir had expanded their ambitions and area of operations to other parts of India. The earliest indicator of this was the combined JeM and LeT attack on the Indian Parliament in 2001. Developments in Pakistan and Afghanistan after al Qaeda's attacks on the United States in September 2001 also changed the militant landscape in the South Asian region. Consequently, groups like LeT assisted al Qaeda cadres to exfiltrate from Afghanistan, provided them with safe havens in Pakistan and also took over the running of al Qaeda's training camps whilst it regrouped. This sort of increasing interaction between these groups precipitated the evolution of LeT's ideology, including with regard to its global pan-Islamist agenda, as clearly evidenced by shifts in its tactics. Thus, with the 2008 attacks in Mumbai the LeT once again not only struck well beyond Kashmir but also conducted the kind of multi-site, simultaneous attack that is a hallmark al Qaeda. More significantly, for the first time in its years of operating in India, LeT also deliberately focused on attacking Western and Jewish targets.[66]

In addition, although the scale of the indigenous jihadism remains unclear, as do its ties to Pakistan-based groups, India undoubtedly faces an increasingly virulent home-grown Islamist threat. To some extent this threat is deeply rooted in India's historic past and the tension between the majority Hindu community and the Muslim community that represents its largest minority. A sense of discrimination and relative deprivation on the part of the Muslim population has created fertile conditions for radicalization and the turn towards terrorist violence. These factors gave rise to several home-grown jihadist groups beginning in the mid-1980s. It is worth noting that while some fringe elements of the Muslim community were, and continue to be, more vulnerable to radicalization and recruitment by terrorist organizations, Muslims in India have, on the whole, 'overwhelmingly resisted these efforts at subversion and radicalization'.[67] Having said that, a number of these home-grown jihadist groups which emerged in the mid-1980s not only engaged in criminal activities but, more critically, were provided assistance by the Pakistani ISI, sometimes directly and at other times through its militant proxies.[68] Thus, the makings of a home-grown Indian jihad were already in place when simmering communal tensions erupted onto the surface with the Ram Janm Bhoomi/Babri Masjid debacle in 1992. This dispute revolved around the contested location of the Babri Masjid – an old mosque said to be built on a site of supreme Hindu significance – the birthplace of the divine Lord Ram and the ruins of a temple that originally marked the site. In December 1992, after months of tension, a mob of Hindu right-wingers destroyed the mosque, which resulted in communal rioting across India. In the wake of these riots, in which hundreds of Hindus and Muslims were killed, there was a series of deadly retributive bombings across Mumbai in March 1993, which were traced back to the Pakistani ISI and their hand in India, Dawood Ibrahim, the Muslim head of a South Asian crime syndicate known as the D-Company. Yet another series of coordinated blasts hit several Indian cities in December that year. These were traced back to the Tanzim Islahul Muslimeen (TIM), an armed Muslim defence militia whose leaders were recruited and trained by a LeT operative in the early 1990s.[69] In the crackdown that ensued many TIM members fled the country to neighbouring Pakistan or Bangladesh. Those that were left behind in India began a recruitment drive, sending several new recruits to LeT training camps in Pakistan, mostly via Bangladesh.[70] Other groups like the Students Islamic Movement of India (SIMI) also came to function as suppliers for the expanding Indian jihadist movement, and served as recruiting pools for groups like LeT.[71] The Indian Mujahidin (IM), consisting of more militant SIMI members, also conducted a number of terrorist attacks as part of its militant jihad against the Indian state.[72]

The final threat of Islamist terrorism emerges from transnational organizations like al Qaeda and the Islamic State. India has featured as a key enemy and part of what has been viewed as the 'Crusader–Zionist–Hindu conspiracy' against Muslims in al Qaeda's rhetoric from the very beginning. Thus, various al Qaeda documents mention the importance of waging a jihad against the persecution of Muslims in Kashmir and in India more broadly. The aim of this jihad would be to wrest back lands which had once been under Muslim rule and to bring the subcontinent under sharia law. Hence India has been, for a very long time, a key part of al Qaeda's global jihadist ambitions. To this end, al Qaeda's current leader Ayman al-Zawahiri announced the formation of the group's newest regional branch, al Qaeda in India (AQIS), via a fifty-five-minute video in September 2014.[73] According to the first edition of al Qaeda's *Resurgence* magazine,[74] AQIS was the product of a merger of several regional jihadist groups, although it is unclear which groups these may be.[75] While it has been argued that AQIS was created in order to seize back the initiative from al Qaeda's key challenger – the Islamic State – al Qaeda has denied this and asserted that the formation of AQIS had been in the pipelines for several years.[76] AQIS's narrative is centred around the concept of *Ghazwa al-Hind* or the Battle of India,[77] which would free the subcontinent from apostate rule and occupation and re-establish a caliphate reminiscent of the erstwhile Mughal Empire. The concept of 'India' in AQIS rhetoric extends well beyond the borders of the present-day state to include areas of Afghanistan, Pakistan, Myanmar and Bangladesh. This seems to bear out in the fact that despite its name, thus far at least, AQIS has mostly been involved in conducting attacks in Pakistan and Bangladesh; although given its local base it would be folly to underestimate the threat that it continues to pose to India's national security and stability. More recently, a series of arrests have illustrated that the Islamic State now also has a footprint in India. Thus far the Islamic State has been making strategic use of social media for its propaganda in order to draw support from both individuals formerly associated with local terrorist groups, such as SIMI and IM, and other unaffiliated individuals. Since June 2014 several young men have also reportedly travelled to Syria and Iraq to fight for the IS.[78] Thus, while the full scope and scale of the transnational threat is at present unclear, it is more than evident that the spectre of global jihad does indeed threaten India. More significantly, the ties that these transnational groups have to local and regional groups make it imperative that we both acknowledge and address this peril.

The Indian state's response

From the above it is more than evident that India faces an enduring and unusually diverse terrorist threat. Yet despite being targeted by terrorism since independence, to date India's response remains remarkably underdeveloped, short-sighted, and not only inconsistent but often contradictory. India's response tends to be characteristically threat reactive and ad hoc, and rarely includes long-term preventive measures which address core grievances or develop programmes concentrating upon counter-radicalization, de-radicalization, rehabilitation or reintegration.[79] This weak response can be understood by exploring some of the challenges faced by the Indian state and the limitations of its CT infrastructure, which hamper both the formulation of consistent CT policies and an effective CT response.

Structural weaknesses

The first critical shortcoming of India's CT infrastructure is that it is woefully under-resourced and deeply fragmented. The absence of resources can be explained by not only the general state of India's developing economy but also what has been termed its 'selective poverty',[80] whereby authorities deliberately direct their resources towards development and other issues rather than national security. Thus, when compared with the budgets of even smaller developing countries, India does not supply nearly enough funds to its security agencies on a per capita basis.[81] This selective poverty is further exacerbated by India's endemic corruption and partisan politics, with the result that CT funding is uneven and ad hoc and, even when available, compromised and diminished. To some extent, India's threat-reactive CT stance can be attributed to this perennial lack of funding. Added to this mix is India's federal political structure, which further constrains its CT response. Thus, it is the responsibility of each state's police force to both maintain law and order in its territory and operate and organize counterterrorism and intelligence. The centre's role is essentially restricted to providing advice, training and financial support when requested by individual states. Although cooperation between the centre and federal agencies is both encouraged and desirable, especially with regard to an effective CT response, the absence of adequate resources makes it nigh on impossible to coordinate local police efforts with those of other agencies and departments. Hence, in reality states tend to be functionally siloed from the central government in New Delhi, making coordination both between local agencies and between New Delhi and each state incredibly challenging. Moreover, state and federal agencies tend to be in direct competition for the same scarce resources, which further hampers cooperation. On top of this, both central and state police agencies are not only poorly trained, ill equipped and technologically backward, they are also increasingly understaffed. The 2013 Bureau of Police Research and Development revealed that India has 136.42 police personnel per 100,000 citizens, which, although an improvement from previous figures, remains much lower than that in most countries.[82] The recruitment of personnel into the police is also influenced by political patronage, and further engenders corruption and incompetence in the agency. Thus, India's federal structure in combination with its paucity of resources and endemic corruption becomes a critical barrier to formulating comprehensive and coordinated CT policies and responses.

This situation is further exacerbated by the fact that India has an absolutely dizzying array of intelligence and physical security agencies with often unclear and/or overlapping functions. In New Delhi alone there are a huge number of intelligence, investigative and law-enforcement agencies responsible for collecting intelligence and conducting CT and COIN operations (kinetic and/or non-kinetic). India's national intelligence community comprises the Intelligence Bureau (IB), which comes under the Ministry of Home Affairs (MHA) and is responsible for domestic intelligence, and the Research and Analysis Wing (RAW), which is responsible for external intelligence and, as part of the Cabinet Secretariat, answers directly to the prime minister. The Defence Intelligence Agency (DIA) under the Ministry of Defence (MoD) and the Intelligence Directorates-General of the Armed Forces, also under the MoD, are responsible for collecting tactical intelligence in areas where CT operations are underway, such as J&K or the North-East.[83] New Delhi also has a number of physical security agencies which it uses in its COIN and CT operations,[84] to varying degrees and with different, on occasion overlapping, mandates. The Central Reserve Police Force (CRPF), the Border Security Force (BSF), the National Security Guards (NSG), the Central Industrial Security Force (CISF), Indo-Tibetan Border Police (ITBP), the SSB or Sashastra Seema Bal (formerly the Special Service Bureau), Assam Rifles, and so on – all come under the MHA and are responsible for not only fulfilling their own individual functions but also assisting state forces when requested to do so. Of these the NSG, which was created in the wake of Operation Blue Star, is specifically geared to provide a kinetic response to terrorist situations.[85] Both the CRPF and BSF are also called upon quite often to assist local state police forces conduct CT operations. The Cabinet Secretariat, on the other hand, oversees the functions of the Air Reconnaissance Centre (ARC), the Special Frontier Force (SFF) and the Special Protection Group (SPG), the latter deployed solely for the security of the current and former Prime Ministers of India.[86] India tends to also rely on its army when its police and other security forces cannot cope with a particular terrorist threat, as was seen in the case of Operation Steeplechase against the Maoists in West Bengal, Bihar and Orrisa in 1971, and again with Operation Blue Star in Punjab in 1984; although in some areas, such as J&K, the army has traditionally adopted the leading role.[87] The Multi-Agency Centre (MAC) and a host of other joint committees and task forces have been created to synchronize the intelligence gathered by this vast array of agencies and 'to generate shared threat perceptions and associated responses',[88] but in reality these bodies are so incredibly slow and bureaucratic as to be fairly ineffective. Immediately in the wake of the Mumbai attacks, India also established the National Investigation Agency (NIA) and the National Counter-Terrorism Centre (NCTC) to streamline its CT response. The NCTC was tasked with better coordinating the states' and centre's CT responses by integrating and analysing all terrorism-related intelligence held by the Indian Government. The NIA was created to take immediate action on the basis of this intelligence and can bypass state bureaucracy and directly target, arrest and prosecute those suspected of any terrorist activity. However, both bodies have been mired in controversy since their creation as state ministers see them as no more than a ruse by the centre to encroach on and intervene in federal matters.[89]

In short, a weak police force, too many agencies with overlapping mandates, and an abject lack of coordination or a joint strategic vision together translate into a compromised CT infrastructure and a muddled CT response. However, the story does not end here. These critical shortcomings are made even more complex by what is an underdeveloped legal system which not only lacks the required legislation to effectively address the terrorist threat but also tends to rely on laws that are ultimately short-sighted, reactive and draconian. To fully understand how this contributes towards producing an ineffective CT response on the part of the Indian state we need to understand both the history and key components of the CT legislation in India, as well as its contemporary handicaps.

To some extent, India's underdeveloped CT legislation can be attributed to the fact that its laws remain mired in its colonial past. Thus, we can trace the rationale of India's security policies and legislation to the 1793 East India Company law dealing with separatists and seditionists that allowed for preventive detention, including without trial, in cases where the security of the state was deemed to be threatened. The legal system in modern India continues to rely upon a modified version of this original preventive detention system as well as leaning heavily upon 'constitutionally and statutorily granted emergency powers [as well as] robust non-emergency criminal laws that authorise broad police powers and significantly curtail defendants' rights in a manner strikingly similar to that of emergency powers'.[90] This is more than evident in modern India's anti-terrorism acts. Throughout the 1970s and 1980s, both emergency and non-emergency powers were used to battle terrorism, with non-emergency criminal provisions incorporating expansive police powers, the ability to preventively detain suspects for long periods of time, and the ability to freeze the assets of all individuals and organizations deemed to be 'unlawful'. A prime example is the Terrorist Affected Areas Act of 1984 (TAAA) that was directed at controlling the Punjab insurgency and spurred by the fear that terrorist violence would spread throughout India.[91] Although TAAA was restricted to the Punjab, it expanded police and intelligence-gathering powers and enabled the use of special courts to try terrorist suspects, all of which led to serious human rights concerns regarding the due process of law. The assassination of Prime Minister Indira Gandhi by her two Sikh bodyguards in 1984 facilitated the repurposing and broadening of TAAA, and the Terrorist and Disruptive Activities (Prevention) Act (TADA) was passed in 1985. Although modelled on TAAA, TADA's jurisdiction was broadened beyond Punjab to cover all of India. TADA not only revitalized robust and expansive police powers, it also brought back many of the measures outlined in the 1971 Maintenance of Internal Security Act (MISA) and those used during the Emergency in India that lasted twenty-one months (1975–77). Thus, alongside preventive detention, TADA not only enabled the police to search and enter premises without warrants and wiretap suspects, it also permitted the use in a court of law of confessions obtained under questionable circumstances.[92] While TADA officially expired in 1995, its definition of terrorism as well as many of its provisions were duplicated in the 2002 Prevention of Terrorism Act (POTA), which was passed, at least partially, in response to the global changes occurring after the September 11th attacks in the United States. Once again, thanks to a series of human rights concerns and complaints, POTA was repealed in 2004. However, once again its key provisions came to be incorporated as amendments into the 1967 Unlawful Activities Prevention Act (UAPA)[93] which is the primary anti-terrorism law in force in India today.

India has a long and disastrous history of communalism and political gamesmanship, and therefore the legislature needs to carefully consider the potential for abuse of each law it passes. However, even a cursory review of the laws described above reveals a sordid history of misuse and abuse. For instance, POTA, which was repealed in 2004, applied such a broad and generalized definition of terrorism, imposed such severe penalties, and granted such sweeping powers of arrest and detention that it is almost surprising that there were not more human rights violations under the act. In empowering the executive to the extent that it did, POTA essentially opened the floodgates for the arbitrary and punitive detention of innocent civilians. 'Warning signs of POTA's susceptibility to abuse surfaced in the summer of 2002 [when] only four months after its effective date law enforcement officials had arrested 250 people nationwide under the Act'.[94] Only eight months later, in the seven states that were applying POTA this number had increased to 940 arrests, of which an astonishing 560 individuals were in prison. More significantly, the law was being applied erratically with enormous variation from state to state. Thus, in Jharkhand POTA became synonymous with the widespread detention of women, children and the elderly, so much so that more people came to be imprisoned in Jharkhand than in terrorism-plagued J&K.[95] Yet other states abused POTA by using it to deliberately target minorities and political opponents. The most glaring example of misuse emerged from Gujarat, where POTA was used to arrest 123 Muslims who had allegedly been involved in a vicious attack at Godhara on a train full of Hindu passengers returning from Ayodhya in February 2002.[96] However, the Gujarat Government refused to apply POTA against Hindus who were allegedly involved in killing and injuring over 2,000 Muslims in the Gujarat riots that followed the Godhara train attack.[97] But, perhaps more significantly, Gujarat was not the *only* state to use POTA to arbitrarily target minorities. In short, the empowerment of the executive and the uneven, selective and discriminatory application of the law facilitated by POTA not only raised alarm bells with regard to the violation of basic human and constitutional rights in India but also served to undermine and detract from an effective and accurate legal response to the terrorist threat by the Indian state. Furthermore, the misuse of the anti-terror law by the state also engendered deep resentment among different parts of the population and further served to delegitimize not only that specific law but CT-related legislation more generally as well. However, far from learning its lesson, instead of attempting to carefully design a more long-sighted and proportionate law after revoking POTA, India once again merely incorporated POTA's key provisions as amendments into the UAPA. Not only that, India's characteristically knee-jerk reaction to the 2008 Mumbai attacks saw the speedy introduction of new draconian anti-terror bills that quickly invited criticism from organizations like Amnesty International, which accused India of violating international human rights standards.[98] Perhaps somewhat predictably, a human rights movement is gathering force in India against the misuse of UAPA at the time of writing.[99]

All the laws discussed above have been passed and applied by the central government in New Delhi. However, the CT waters are muddied even further thanks to India's federal structure, which essentially means that a series of other laws passed by state legislatures are also used in conjunction with central laws to address the threat of terrorism. These include the Maharashtra Control of Organised Crime Act (MCOCA) applicable in Maharashtra and Delhi, the Karnataka Control of Organised Crime Act (KCOCA), and the Chhattisgarh Vishesh Jan Suraksha Adhiniyam (CVJSA). Most terrorism-related cases involve individuals being charged under multiple central and state laws.[100] Another key issue that then emerges is the direct conflict between provisions of the state law and the centre's law, which further serves to undermine and delay India's CT response. Thus, it is more than evident that India's legal system remains underdeveloped and poorly equipped to effectively address the enduring terrorist threat that it faces. Instead of using its legacy of terrorism to formulate a nuanced and long-sighted legal response, Indian legislation tends towards event-responsive emergency powers or depends upon non-emergency powers that are expansive and repressive. In addition to the human rights violations inherent in such an approach, this has also served to delegitimize the Indian state and weaken its CT and COIN response, all of which essentially bolsters the cause and rhetoric of non-state actors who use terrorism and insurgency against it.

The incessant overlap between terrorism and insurgency

As discussed previously, a long-standing and deep-seated conceptual and practical confusion between terrorism and insurgency in the subcontinent is clearly reflected in India's CT and COIN responses. Of course, this complication is grounded in the fact that the majority of India's terrorism is produced by insurgent movements which choose to use this particular tactic to challenge the state. However, as Boyle rightly argues, while COIN and CT operations need not be mutually exclusive, neither are they fully compatible or mutually reinforcing.[101] In other words, these are two very different models of warfare with diverging assumptions about the role of force and the need to (re-) establish robust governance structures, as well as the significance of winning local support and securing political legitimacy. Even more importantly, because of these divergent assumptions they can 'incur mutually offsetting costs at the strategic and tactical level'.[102] To some extent, this is precisely what we see happening in India.

To a large extent, India's CT doctrine is framed in 'hearts and minds' COIN language. However, when we look more closely at India's CT campaigns – both when they address pure terrorism and when they address the terrorism–insurgency hybrid, despite this rhetoric the state response tends to be overwhelmingly kinetic and reliant on the use of lethal force. Similarly, India's COIN approach marks a sharp departure from Western doctrine that advocates a 'population-centric' strategy to win 'hearts and minds'.[103] Once again, despite India's hearts and minds rhetoric and the insistence of those who claim that the state has always seen COIN as a 'political rather than a military problem',[104] in practice this is not the case. Hence, a closer look at India's COIN approach reveals a 'strategy of attrition' that is founded upon the coercive use of 'raw state power' and 'enemy-centric campaigns' that aim to 'suffocate the insurgency' in question through a 'saturation of forces'.[105] So the question that emerges is why does the Indian state use hearts and minds COIN language when *both* its CT and COIN responses are so overwhelmingly reliant on the use of lethal force? Is the government confused or deliberately disingenuous?

The answer seems to lie in the fact that the government lacks a holistic, long-term approach to either CT or COIN. Why? As discussed previously, India's already scarce resources tend to be directed towards development as opposed to national security. This also means that India lacks the funds to develop long-term programmes directed towards addressing key grievances and/or dealing with issues such as counter-radicalization, de-radicalization, rehabilitation and reintegration.[106] Similarly, India lacks the legislative structures to effectively implement a criminal-justice model of CT. Given these considerable challenges it should not come as a surprise that the Indian state tends to resort to kinetic, force-dependent, quick-fix responses, even if its language is one of political negotiation and reconciliation. However, it must be emphasized that kinetic efforts against the terrorism–insurgency hybrid threat tend to be complemented by other tactics and strategies. In the case of the Punjab insurgency, for instance, alongside decapitation insurgents were also co-opted and transformed into local assets. The police also conducted mass contact programmes that sapped popular support from the insurgency, which was already in a precarious position because of its deliberate targeting of Sikhs in the state.[107] Thus, arguably, the government's hearts and minds rhetoric is not intrinsically dishonest, as New Delhi has historically attempted to negotiate with insurgencies that use terrorism (or corrigible terrorists, if you prefer) within India's boundaries. Having said that, often agreements with local stakeholders fail to be implemented for reasons rooted in political expediency or corruption, thereby inadvertently bolstering the terrorists' position and generating more security problems. Once again, the centre's variable response to the Punjab insurgency provides an excellent example. In Punjab, Prime Minister Indira Gandhi feared the erosion of the Indian union as well as the centre's authority, and thus not only preferred 'strong central responses [but also] … refused to negotiate with provincial non-state actors'.[108] Her son and successor Rajiv Gandhi, on the other hand, negotiated a landmark accord with moderate Sikh leaders in the Akali Dal (Longowal faction), although he balked when it came to implementing this accord for fear of losing the Hindu vote in Punjab. Rajiv's retrenchment served to delegitimize the moderate Akali Dal leadership and expanded 'the political space for militants who benefited from Sikh anger over the centre's reneging',[109] thus further worsening the security crisis in the Punjab and once again forcing the government to harden its response. In his turn, Rajiv's successor, Prime Minister V.P. Singh, discontinued the campaign against Khalistani terrorism and adopted a more conciliatory approach. Once again this resulted in the resurgence of terrorist violence and forced the government to take a more hardline CT stance.[110] Thus, we can see how the government's inconsistency repeatedly compromised CT efforts and served to consistently push it towards adopting a more kinetic response to regain lost ground.

It is also important to note that while the state's response may perforce be overwhelmingly kinetic, it still tends to be weak as India's lack of resources means that its CT teams are poorly equipped and trained. In fact, it has been argued that India's forces are not sufficiently trained to undertake COIN operations, and are too poorly equipped to effectively conduct and fulfil CT duties.[111] Add to this the condition of India's police services, and it should also come as no surprise that a reliance on kinetic responses essentially translates into a reliance upon the military and/or special forces, with concomitantly higher civilian costs and accompanying accusations of human rights abuse. Some analysts have argued that this is a fundamental flaw in Indian CT because effective and efficient policing helps the state identify and neutralize any deviations and anomalies, thus forming both the foundation of a well-governed nation and the backbone of its CT response strategy.[112] This is a problem not only because of the generally poor state of India's police services but also because in cases where the police were modernized, militarized and placed in charge of leading kinetic operations (e.g., in Punjab), we've seen that the police structure remained 'bloated, inefficient and incapable of investigative police work more than a decade later'.[113]

It is worth mentioning that hearts and minds language is only utilized by the Indian Government in hybrid cases – in the cases of domestic insurgencies that are characterized by the use of terrorism. When addressing cases of pure terrorism, there is a palpable absence of such language and the emphasis tends to be fully upon a kinetic CT response. However, once again this kinetic response is subject to the same sets of challenges described above: political partisanship, a federal state structure that hampers a coherent CT policy, poorly trained and equipped forces that compromise a kinetic response, the absence of required legislation to prosecute those suspected of terrorist activity, and so on. In the case of pure terrorism these challenges become even more acute. This is primarily because pure terrorism in India tends to be practised by incorrigible terrorists – those who have such absolutist and maximalist aims that they cannot and will not be bargained with. While some of these terrorists have roots in local communities (e.g., home-grown Islamist terrorists, such as the Indian Mujahidin and SIMI) others are parasitic (i.e., cross-border and transnational terrorists, such as LeT and al Qaeda) and do not necessarily have the same degree of local support. Despite this variation, the threat posed by Islamist terrorism is considerable, and India's ability to counter it remains questionable for several reasons. First, unlike hybrid threats, in the case of pure terrorism India's traditional strategy of coercion, co-option and containment may well fall short of ensuring even partial success against this threat. Why? To begin with, and as clearly demonstrated during the Mumbai attacks, India's intelligence and kinetic-response capabilities remain well below par and, as yet, unable to effectively meet the tactical challenge posed by what are proving to be highly innovative Islamist groups. Second, India's traditional strategy of co-option is difficult given the ideologically absolutist and maximalist goals of these groups, as well as the fact that the majority of their members seem to share their pan-Islamist aspirations and are thus less vulnerable to co-option. Finally, unlike domestic insurgencies that use terrorism – and this includes the local insurgency in Kashmir – the threat posed by Islamist terrorism is not localized in any one geographical region of India, and as such is much more problematic to contain. In fact, attacks by incorrigible Islamist organizations – local and cross-border (the Indian homeland has, thus far, not fallen victim to an attack by a transnational group) – have occurred in cities as geographically disparate as Srinagar, Varanasi, New Delhi, Jaipur, Pune, Mumbai and Bangalore, to name just a few. In short, pure/Islamist terrorism may well be the biggest CT challenge faced by the Indian state to date and, given both the current state of its CT infrastructure and the ad hoc nature of its CT responses, may potentially prove the most difficult to undermine.

Conclusion

India faces a complex combination of indigenous, proxy and transnational terrorism. In order to understand this complexity one must first acknowledge that the Indian state has been involved in many low-intensity conflicts throughout its territory since almost the moment of its inception. Indeed, much of the terrorist activity that we see in India is the direct consequence of such protracted disputes. The roots of conflicts vary widely and each case is distinctly impacted and shaped by not only the prevailing local socio-economic conditions but also the area's particular geopolitical context. Not only are there multiple sources of violence and grievances in India, but the federal structure of the Indian state also enables a very particular response to each challenge. Thus, while over the years India has tended to opt for the use of physical force, it has also used strategies of negotiation and conciliation with various groups, with varying degrees of success. Grievances and violence in India intersect with caste, ethnic, religious and other social identity markers. As such, an already complicated phenomenon is made even more complex within the Indian setting. However, it is worth underscoring that despite the unusually formidable challenge that is terrorism in India, the state has endured. Undoubtedly, it would benefit from not only strengthening its existing architecture of CT and COIN, as well as its ground-level capabilities and capacities, but also understanding how these two models of warfare co-exist and interact. More importantly, it would benefit from fully understanding how to best formulate both COIN and CT strategies in India without incurring what may be mutually offsetting costs. Taken together this would allow India to finally achieve more holistic, national-level strategies and policies for countering the evolving threat of terrorism within its borders much more effectively.

Notes

1 START, *Annex of Statistical Information: Country Reports on Terrorism 2015* (Baltimore, MD: START, 2016).
2 P. Wilkinson, *Terrorism versus Democracy: The Liberal State Response* (London: Routledge, 2011), p. 4.
3 *Ibid.*
4 R.S. Moore, 'The basics of counterinsurgency,' *Small Wars Journal* (2007): 3, available at: http://smallwarsjournal.com/blog/small-wars-pleasures (accessed 27 September 2017).
5 B. Hoffman, *Inside Terrorism* (New York: Columbia University Press, 2006), p. 35.
6 Wilkinson, *Terrorism versus Democracy*, p. 8.
7 B. O'Neill, *Insurgency and Terrorism: Inside Modern Revolutionary Warfare* (Dulles, VA: Brassey's, 1990); D. Kilcullen, *The Accidental Guerrilla: Fighting Small Wars in the Midst of a Big One* (London: C. Hurst, 2009); A. Upadhyay, *The Dynamics of Terrorism in North East India: India's Fragile Borderlands* (London: I.B. Tauris, 2009).
8 Kamal Kumar, 'Analysis: India's Maoist challenge,' *Al Jazeera*, 24 August 2013, available at: www.aljazeera.com/indepth/features/2013/08/2013812124328669128.html (accessed 18 January 2018); Imran Garda, 'India's silent war,' *Al Jazeera*, 21 October 2011, available at: www.aljazeera.com/programmes/aljazeeracorrespondent/2011/10/20111019124251679523.html (accessed 18 January 2018).
9 Hoffman, *Inside Terrorism*; Kilcullen, *Accidental Guerrilla*.
10 M.G. Findley and J.K. Young, 'Fighting fire with fire? How (not) to neutralize an insurgency,' *Civil Wars* 9:4 (2007): 380.
11 Upadhyay, *Dynamics of Terrorism*, p. 24.
12 B. Jain, '66 terror groups active in India: Govt,' *Times of India*, 27 August 2013, available at: http://timesofindia.indiatimes.com/india/66-terror-groups-active-in-India-Govt/articleshow/22097789.cms (accessed 18 January 2018).
13 Government of India Ministry of Home Affairs (MHA), 'Banned Organisations,' MHA website, available at: http://mha.nic.in/bo (accessed 1 May 2016).
14 A. Misra, 'The problem of Kashmir and the problem in Kashmir: Divergence demands convergence,' *Strategic Analysis* 29:1 (2005): 16–43.
15 See, for example, V. Schofield, *Kashmir in the Crossfire* (London: I.B. Tauris, 1996); R. Wirsing, *India, Pakistan and the Kashmir Dispute* (London: Macmillian, 1998); Praveen Swami, *The Kargil War* (New Delhi: LeftWord Books, 1999).
16 R. Ganguly, 'India, Pakistan and the Kashmir insurgency: Causes, dynamics and prospects for resolution,' *Asian Studies Review* 25:3 (2007): 309–34.
17 S. Ganguly, 'Explaining the Kashmir insurgency: Political mobilization and institutional decay,' *International Security* 21:6 (1996): 76–107.
18 A. Evans, 'The Kashmir insurgency: As bad as it gets,' *Small Wars and Insurgencies,* 11:1 (2000); G. Garner, 'Chechnya and Kashmir: The jihadist evolution of nationalism to jihad and beyond,' *Terrorism and Political Violence* 25:3 (2013): 69–81.

19 V.G. Patankar, 'Insurgency, proxy war and terrorism in Kashmir,' in Sumit Ganguly and David P. Fidler (eds), *India and Counterinsurgency: Lessons Learned* (New York: Routledge, 2009), pp. 65–78.
20 T. Marks, 'India: State responses to insurgency in Jammu and Kashmir,' *Low Intensity Conflict and Law Enforcement* 12:3 (2004): 124.
21 Evans, 'Kashmir insurgency.'
22 R. Singh, 'Lashkar-i-Taiba: An al Qaeda associate in Pakistan?' in Manuel Almeida (ed.), *Al Qaeda after Bin Laden* (Dubai: al-Mesbar, 2012), ch. 5.
23 Patankar, 'Insurgency, proxy war and terrorism.'
24 Singh, 'Lashkar-i-Taiba'; R. Singh, 'Counter-terrorism in the post-9/11 era: Successes, failures and lessons learned,' in Richard English (ed.), *Illusions of Terrorism and Counter-Terrorism* (Oxford: Oxford University Press, 2015), ch. 2.
25 Upadhyay, *Dynamics of Terrorism*.
26 See, for example, S. Baruah (ed.), *Beyond Counter-Insurgency: Breaking the Impasse in Northeast India* (Oxford: Oxford University Press, 2009).
27 L.E. Cline, 'The insurgency environment in Northeast India,' *Small Wars and Insurgencies* 17:2 (2006): 126–47.
28 Upadhyay, *Dynamics of Terrorism*, p. 31.
29 N. Nibedon, *Nagaland: Night of the Guerrillas* (New Delhi: Lancer, 2000); S. Nag, 'North East: A comparative analysis of Naga, Mizo and Meitei insurgencies,' *Faultlines* 14 (2003): 67–79.
30 D. Srivastava, *Terrorism and Armed Violence in India: An Analysis of Events in 2008* (New Delhi: Institute of Peace and Conflict Studies, 2009).
31 W. Hussain, *India's North East in 2015* (New Delhi: Institute of Peace and Conflict Studies, 2015).
32 Baruah, *Beyond Counter-Insurgency*, p. 3.
33 See, for example, K.P.S. Gill, *Punjab: Knights of Falsehood* (New Delhi: Har Anand, 1997); P. Wallace, 'Countering terrorist movements in India: Kashmir and Khalistan,' in R.J. Art and L. Richardson (eds), *Democracy and Counterterrorism: Lessons from the Past* (Washington, DC: United States Institute of Peace, 2007), pp. 425–82; P. Mahadevan, 'The Gill Doctrine: A model for 21st century counter-terrorism,' *Faultlines* 19 (2008): 1–32, and *The Politics of Counterterrorism in India: Strategic Intelligence and National Security in South Asia* (London: I.B. Tauris, 2012).
34 Gill, *Punjab*.
35 *Ibid.*
36 V. Marwah, 'India's counterinsurgency campaign in Punjab,' in Ganguly and Fidler, *India and Counterinsurgency*, pp. 89–106.
37 *Ibid.*, p. 91.
38 J.S. Chima, *The Sikh Separatist Insurgency: Political Leadership and Ethnonationalist Movements* (New Delhi: Sage, 2010).
39 Mahadevan, *Politics of Counterterrorism in India*.
40 C.C. Fair, 'Lessons from India's experience in the Punjab, 1978–1993,' in Ganguly and Fidler, *India and Counterinsurgency*, pp. 107–26.
41 Marwah, 'India's counterinsurgency campaign in Punjab,' p. 92.
42 K.P.S. Gill, 'Endgame in Punjab: 1988–1993,' *Faultlines* 1 (1999), available at: www.satp.org/satporgtp/publication/faultlines/volume1/Fault1-kpstext.htm (accessed 31 January 2016).
43 Marwah, 'India's counterinsurgency campaign in Punjab,' pp. 97, 101.

44 Mahadevan, 'Gill Doctrine.'
45 Gill, 'Endgame in Punjab.'
46 V. Karan, *War by Stealth: Terrorism in India* (New Delhi: Viking, 1997), p. 151.
47 Gill, 'Endgame in Punjab.'
48 *Ibid.*
49 A.K. Mehra, 'Naxalism in India: Revolution or terror?' *Terrorism and Political Violence* 12:2 (2000): 37–66; J.L. Oetken, 'Counterinsurgency against Naxalites in India,' in Ganguly and Fidler, *India and Counterinsurgency*, pp. 127–51.
50 Mehra, 'Naxalism in India,' p. 36.
51 A. Ray, 'Tribal development and Maoism in India: A gendered perspective,' *International Journal of Diversity in Organizations, Communities and Nations* 11:5 (2012): 45–56.
52 N. Goswami, *Indian National Security and Counter-Insurgency: The Use of Force vs Non-Violent Response* (London: Routledge, 2014), p. 115.
53 G.D. Bakshi, *Left Wing Extremism in India: Context, Implications and Response Options*, Manekshaw Paper no. 9 (New Delhi: Centre for Land Warfare Studies, 2009).
54 Oetken, 'Counterinsurgency against Naxalites in India.'
55 S. Banerjee, *India's Simmering Revolution: The Naxalite Uprising* (London: Zed Books, 1984); R.K. Gupta, *The Crimson Agenda: Maoist Protest and Terror* (Delhi: Wordsmiths, 2004).
56 Oetken, 'Counterinsurgency against Naxalites in India.'
57 A. Sahni, 'Naxalism: The retreat of civil governance,' *Faultlines* 5 (2000), available at: www.satp.org/satporgtp/publication/faultlines/volume5/Fault5–7asahni.htm (accessed 5 March 2016).
58 Oetken, 'Counterinsurgency against Naxalites in India.'
59 U. Mukherjee, 'Maoists' urban perspective: An analysis,' Centre for Land Warfare Studies website, 13 November 2011, available at: www.claws.in/715/maoists-urban-perspective-an-analysis-uddipan-mukherjee.html (accessed 25 June 2016).
60 Mehra, 'Naxalism in India.'
61 CPI(M), 'Urban perspective: Our work in urban areas,' South Asia Terrorism Portal website, 2007, available at: www.satp.org/satporgtp/countries/india/maoist/documents/papers/index.html (accessed 25 June 2016); V.K. Ahluwalia, 'Strategy and tactics of the Indian Maoists: An analysis,' *Strategic Analysis* 36:5 (2012): 723–34.
62 Mukherjee, 'Maoists' urban perspective.'
63 Goswami, *Indian National Security*.
64 Namrata Goswami, 'India's counter-insurgency experience: The "trust and nurture" strategy,' *Small Wars and Insurgencies* 20:1 (2009): 66–86.
65 Garner, 'Chechnya and Kashmir': 423.
66 Singh, 'Counter-terrorism in the post-9/11 era.'
67 Ajai Sahni, *The World Almanac of Islamism* (Washington, DC: American Foreign Policy Council, 2017), p. 13.
68 S. Gupta, *Indian Mujahideen: The Enemy Within* (Gurgaon, India: Hachette India, 2011); S. Tankel, 'The Indian jihadist movement: Evolution and dynamics,' *Strategic Perspectives* 17 (2014): 1–33.
69 Sarfaraz Nawaz, *Jihadist Violence: The Indian Threat* (Washington, DC: Woodrow Wilson International Center for Scholars, 2013).

70 Stephen Tankel, *Storming the World Stage: The Story of Lashkar-E-Taiba* (London: Hurst, 2011).
71 C.C. Fair, 'On the Students Islamic Movement of India,' *Asia Policy* 9 (2010): 101–19; Gupta, *Indian Mujahideen*.
72 A. Roul, 'India's home-grown jihadi threat: A profile of the Indian Mujahideen,' *Terrorism Monitor* 7:4 (2009): 9–11.
73 S. Das, 'The emergence of al-Qaeda in the Indian sub-continent,' *International Security Observer* (2015), http://securityobserver.org/the-emergence-of-al-qaeda-in-the-indian-sub-continent (no longer available; accessed 28 June 2016); A. Reed, *Al Qaeda in the Indian Subcontinent: A New Frontline in the Global Jihadist Movement?* International Centre for Counter-Terrorism (ICCT) Policy Brief (The Hague: ICCT, 2015).
74 *Resurgence* 1 (2014), available at: https://azelin.files.wordpress.com/2015/04/resurgence-1.pdf (accessed 28 June 2016).
75 B. Roggio, 'Al Qaeda in the Indian subcontinent incorporates regional jihadist groups,' *Long War Journal* (2014), available at: www.longwarjournal.org/archives/2014/09/analysis_al_qaeda_in.php (accessed 28 June 2016); A. Chandran, 'Al Qaeda in the Indian subcontinent: Almost forgotten,' Critical Threats Project website, 3 September 2015, available at: www.criticalthreats.org/al-qaeda/chandran-al-qaeda-in-indian-subcontinent-backgrounder-september-3-2015 (accessed 28 June 2016).
76 Reed, 'Al Qaeda in the Indian subcontinent.'
77 H. Haqqani, 'Prophecy and jihad in the Indian subcontinent,' Hudson Institute website, 27 March 2015, available at: www.hudson.org/research/11167-prophecy-the-jihad-in-the-indian-subcontinent# (accessed 28 June 2016).
78 A. Roul, 'How Islamic State gained ground in India using indigenous militant networks,' *Terrorism Monitor* 14:9 (2016): 7–9.
79 E.B. Hearne, 'Re-examining India's counter-terrorism approach: Adopting a long view,' *Strategic Analysis* 36:4 (2012): 527–41.
80 Mahadevan, *Politics of Counterterrorism in India*, p. 26.
81 P. Staniland, 'Improving India's counterterrorism policy after Mumbai,' *CTC Sentinel* 2:4 (2009): 11–14.
82 'Police–public ratio in India is 136.42 per one lakh population,' *Zee News*, 22 July 2014, available at: http://zeenews.india.com/news/nation/police-public-ratio-in-india-is-13642-per-one-lakh-population_949338.html (accessed 29 June 2016).
83 B. Raman, 'Counter-terrorism: The Indian experience,' South Asia Analysis Group website, 1 April 2003, available at: www.southasiaanalysis.org/paper649 (accessed 16 May 2016).
84 M.G. Singh, former SFF officer and retired director of the Research and Analysis Wing (RAW), interview by Rashmi Singh, 1 May 2016.
85 *Ibid.*
86 *Ibid.*
87 *Ibid.*; Raman, 'Counter-terrorism.'
88 Staniland, 'Improving India's counterterrorism policy.'
89 P.R. Chari, 'National counter-terrorism centre for India: Understanding the debate,' Issue Brief, IPCS website, 1 March 2012, available at: www.ipcs.org/issue_select.php?recNo=435 (accessed 16 May 2016); G. Kanwal, 'India's counter-terrorism policies are mired in systemic weaknesses,' *Institute for Defence Studies and Analyses (IDSA) Comment*, 14 May 2012, available

at: https://idsa.in/idsacomments/IndiasCounterTerrorismPoliciesareMiredinSystemicWeaknesses_gkanwal_140512 (accessed 16 May 2016).

90 S. Setty, 'What's in a name? How nations define terrorism ten years after 9/11,' *University of Pennsylvania Journal of International Law* 33:1 (2011): 45–6.

91 *Ibid.*

92 N. Manoharan, *Trojan Horses? Efficacy of Counter-terrorism Legislation in a Democracy: Lessons from India*, Manekshaw Paper no. 30 (New Delhi: Centre for Land Warfare Studies, 2011).

93 Setty, 'What's in a name?'; Manoharan, *Trojan Horses?*

94 Christopher Gagné, 'Pota: Lessons learned from India's anti-terror acts,' *Third World Law Journal* 25:1 (2005): 273.

95 *Ibid.*

96 *Ibid.*; Christophe Jaffrelot, *Communal Riots in Gujarat: The State at Risk?* (Heidelberg: South Asia Institute, University of Heidelberg, 2003).

97 Gagné, 'Pota'; Jaffrelot, *Communal Riots in Gujarat*.

98 Amnesty International, 'India: New anti-terror laws would violate international human rights standards,' press release, Amnesty International website, 18 December 2008, available at: https://archive.amnesty.ie/news/india-new-anti-terror-laws-would-violate-international-human-rights-standards (accessed 2 March 2017).

99 Staff reporter, 'Rights activists' meet against misuse of UAPA,' *Hindu*, 2 February 2017, available at: www.thehindu.com/news/cities/kozhikode/Rights-activists%E2%80%99-meet-against-misuse-of-UAPA/article17143836.ece (accessed 3 March 2017).

100 Srijoni Sen, Rukmini Das, Raadhika Gupta and Vrinda Bhandari, *Anti-Terror Law in India: A Study of Statutes and Judgments, 2001–2014* (New Delhi: Vidhi Centre for Legal Policy, 2015), p. 15.

101 M.J. Boyle, 'Do counterterrorism and counterinsurgency go together?' *International Affairs* 86:2 (2010): 336.

102 *Ibid.*

103 David Kilcullen, 'Two schools of classical counterinsurgency,' *Small Wars Journal* (27 January 2007), available at: http://smallwarsjournal.com/blog/two-schools-of-classical-counterinsurgency (accessed 11 June 2016).

104 Rajesh Rajagopalan, 'Force and compromise: India's counterinsurgency grand strategy,' *South Asia: Journal of South Asian Studies* 30:1 (2007): 75.

105 Sameer Lalwani, 'India's approach to counterinsurgency and the Naxalite problem,' *CTC Sentinel* 4:10 (2011): 5–9.

106 Hearne, 'Re-examining India's counter-terrorism.'

107 M.G. Singh, interview, 1 May 2016.

108 Fair, 'Lessons from India's experience,' p. 108.

109 *Ibid.*, p. 109.

110 Mahadevan, *Politics of Counterterrorism in India*, p. 184.

111 Goswami, *Indian National Security*.

112 A. Sahni, 'Counter-terrorism: The architecture of failure,' *War Within Borders* (2011), available at: www.satp.org/satporgtp/ajaisahni/11AS-19Mumbai2611.htm (accessed 20 May 2016).

113 Lalwani, 'India's approach to counterinsurgency': 5.

Pakistan

7

Countering terrorism in Pakistan: Challenges, conundrum and resolution

Muhammad Feyyaz

Introduction

Pakistan has achieved a number of important successes in its bid to curb domestic terrorism.[1] Some analysts have described the country's counterterrorism struggle as a success attributed to the predominant role of the military.[2] Indeed, the degree of security produced by the military-led counterterrorism (CT) campaign is noteworthy; it is equally true that this effort has concomitantly been subverted by other important actors in the social and political arena.[3] The prevailing environment can be conceptually termed as an ouroboros (a self-cannibalizing serpent), wherein state institutions such as the armed forces and law-enforcement agencies are engaged in combating terrorism, while others present within the state system – political elites as well as society – are directly or indirectly enabling or for that matter sustaining it. The consequences have been (1) a state of uncertainty if not general despondency over the long-term prospect of eradicating the threat,[4] and (2) a growing scepticism among Western critics and governments (the United States in particular) about Pakistan's commitment to eliminate terrorism, due to its alleged use of militancy as a tool of foreign policy.[5]

Several factors account for this conundrum. Primarily, it is a multitude of conflicting viewpoints, policy attitudes and reactions against terrorism that have hampered the development of an articulate and coherent institution-based CT vision to effectively fight militancy.[6] Secondly, Pakistan is perhaps one of the more misunderstood countries abroad due to a lack of comprehension about its peculiar national security conditions, particularly its role in a conflicted neighbourhood that often spawns misperceptions about it. The problem is that despite the existence of a sizeable literature about Pakistan, most of it is policy driven and produced for specific countries (like the US), and is hence essentially reductive in scope.[7] The mainstream terrorism and conflict literature has also not systematically sought to understand the reasons for Pakistan's individual dynamics and constraints in its fight against terrorism. A more crucial scholarly void is the persistent ignorance of the country's chequered political history, its varied and competing socio-religious actors, and complex set of geopolitical relationships.[8] Besides, the post-9/11 military-minded 'war on terror' (WOT) has consumed much in its progress and blinded many to some of the important historical features of South Asia. The extant study of terrorism has consequently become increasingly focused on wide-angled, oversimplified and metrics-based methodology, thereby depriving the terrorism scholarship of much-needed context-specific and analytically objective research about inherently heterodox countries like Pakistan.[9] This chapter helps to fill this gap by using a longitudinal design.

It begins with a brief history of conflict in Pakistan to illuminate and objectively analyse the variables that have been in play since Pakistan's founding, especially the varied dispositions toward the conceptualization, espousal and application of non-state violence. This history is set in a regional context so as to provide an organizing lens to place subsequent conditions in perspective, as covered in the next section, which deals with the constructions of terrorism and CT at home. This historical review presents the prevailing security landscape in and around Pakistan as the country joined the WOT in September 2001. The discussion in the third section, about Pakistan's WOT, highlights why a war which could have been waged in such a way as to allow a good prospect of success was not, and has not been able to yield outcomes commensurate with the enormity of sacrifices rendered by the security and law-enforcement forces, as well as the destruction and misery suffered by the common citizenry.[10] It particularly points out how disparately terrorism is conceptualized and responded to in Pakistan by different socio-political actors and constituencies, and, importantly, how international players further compound the struggle to deal with terrorism. The discussion concludes by collating the reasons preventing a coordinated fight against terrorism, and highlights some policy implications. It is expected that the analysis will furnish useful input for scholars, analysts and practitioners in grasping the complexities of the CT paradigm of an important geopolitical actor – Pakistan – and further assist research in this important area, particularly in elucidating how Pakistan differs in its conceptions and responses from other geographical regions and liberal democracies.

'Counterterrorism' is not yet a clearly defined area in its fullest sense, and spans a number of other policy areas.[11] In this chapter, counterterrorism is understood theoretically as follows: (1) it is subset of a broader counterinsurgency (COIN) doctrine comprising proactive and reactive measures that enable a government to eliminate non-state terrorism, and effectively reduce the structural capacity of terrorist organizations to carry out terrorist acts;[12] and (2) the response structure should ideally constitute a cohesive assemblage of processes, instruments and implementing mechanisms flowing from a politico-legal framework. In the absence of these instruments, routine CT reactions are mere misconceptions of an ideal CT response, and hence can only be termed ad hoc, at best. Finally, these measures are meaningless if the effectiveness of CT is not measured. Accordingly, this chapter draws upon a few important determinants from the existing literature to ascertain the effectiveness of CT: the quality of national leadership, socio-political consensus and cohesion, international and domestic support, reduction in civilian (and rebel) casualties, and soft CT measures.[13]

Conflict history and genesis of indirect strategy

Violent conflict in one way or another has been intrinsic part of the political history of Pakistan since its inception. In order to understand the processes that have produced a securitized mindset, an examination of the conditions surrounding the country at the time of its creation, and major developments since then, is important.

All experts on South Asia agree that Pakistan as a country emerged from its birth in August 1947 with a lingering sense of insecurity.[14] The trauma of creation had its roots in the hastily drawn and controversial partition map of the subcontinent made under the notorious Radcliffe Boundary Award. This was still haunting the new state,[15] when two months later, on 26 October 1947, Kashmir (henceforth Indian-held Kashmir (IHK)) was subjected to Indian aggression. The movement of the Indian military into IHK was premised on a tribal invasion from the Pakistani side a few days earlier. Notwithstanding that many Pakistanis may have been sympathetic to this tribal offensive, scholarly opinion is divided on whether it was officially sanctioned by the Pakistani state or occurred in response to the precarious situation inside IHK due to repressive measures by the local Hindu raja.[16] Termed the First Kashmir War, this initial conflict between the two countries, later involving Pakistani armed forces, lasted for several months until a UN-brokered ceasefire took effect in January 1949, which led to the establishment of a Cease-fire Line

(CFL) and virtual territorial division of the State of Jammu and Kashmir. Later, India amassed forces along the western frontier, which came on the heels of a seizure of territory in early 1948 by the Indian Army in the area of the Patharia Reserve Forest on the East Pakistan–Assam border.[17] During July and October 1951, the Indian Army repeatedly transgressed into West Pakistan territory (approximately forty-eight times), coupled with dozens of violations of Pakistan's air space. Most of these incursions took place in Azad (free) or the Pakistani side of Kashmir, although similar violations occurred in East Pakistan.[18]

There were two important outcomes of these episodes. First, because the continued buildup and sudden proximity of Indian military to the hinterland of Pakistan critically endangered the territorial integrity of the new state, Kashmir assumed vital importance for Pakistan's survival and became the basis for perennial contention with India.[19] Secondly, some scholars maintain that since Pakistan succeeded in seizing part of Kashmir, a belief in the strategy of using irregular fighters took root among military planners.[20] Arguably, despite the fact that a predisposition for proxy warfare can be inferred from some Pakistani military writings during the 1950s,[21] there is no evidence to suggest any institutional espousal among state or government functionaries of the use of an indirect strategy against India for wider or more general foreign policy purposes.[22]

Unlike the First Kashmir War, when decision making came from sources chaotically diffused across government, 'Operation Gibraltar' in 1965 in IHK is generally believed to have involved the country's higher direction of war under President Mohammad Ayub Khan.[23] Nevertheless, Pakistani writers differ over whether this operation was authorized by Ayub, citing confusion over which operation – the Gibraltar or another subsidiary military offensive called Grand Slam in South Kashmir – was to be launched. Interestingly, both were disapproved by the army's command and staff hierarchy.[24] Nor has Ayub mentioned Gibraltar in his memoirs.[25] He is reported to have remarked during a high-level meeting that 'All I asked ... was to keep the situation in Kashmir under review. They [the foreign office and ISI (Inter Services Intelligence)] can't force a campaign of military action on the Government.'[26] The circumstances surrounding this intervention were not straightforward. The subcontinent was marked by fluid political conditions over the preceding three years due to political upheaval in IHK, and intense involvement of major powers – the US and Great Britain – to contain China.[27] On its part, Pakistan did not exploit the Indian military weaknesses afforded during India's tension with China, especially during the Indo-China war of 1962 when a vacuum along the CFL provided a great potential advantage.[28] Indeed, a tactical victory against India in August 1965 in the Rann of Kutch, a mangrove land bordering Pakistan's southern province of Sindh and India's Gujarat, had emboldened many in the Pakistan Army with a (false) sense of superiority concerning its ability to fight a war against India.[29] However, the actual Gibraltar Operation in August 1965 – which aimed to generate a popular uprising inside IHK with the purpose of unfreezing the Kashmir issue, a mission which entailed infiltration by regular troops of the Pakistan Army disguised as *mujahids* (freedom fighters) across the CFL – proved a fiasco and led instead to the eruption of war with India in September 1965.[30] The precursor to and consequences of Gibraltar may have 'marked a further stage in ... Pakistan's state use of irregular ... forces',[31] as has been suggested by some historians.

Nonetheless, the aftermath of 1971 war with India resulted in the dismemberment of Pakistan, which was noteworthy in heightening the sense of existential threat among the politico-military elite to a far greater level than had prevailed at the time of Pakistan's creation. It also fuelled a desire to avenge the humiliating defeat of the Pakistani Army.[32] Two important events marked the early period of that decade – the rise of the Baloch insurgency and the overthrow of the monarchy in Afghanistan by Mohammad Daoud in 1973, which forced Afghan religious hardliners (e.g., Ahmed Shah Massoud and Gulbuddin Hikmatyar) to seek shelter in Pakistan.[33] Daoud, who was viewed as the 'main Afghan exponent of Pakhtoonistan [greater Afghanistan]', soon after assuming power began assisting the insurgency in Balochistan, and extended shelter to some 30,000 Marri Baluch tribesmen who had escaped a Pakistani military crackdown against them in Baluchistan.[34] In turn, Zulifkar Ali Bhutto, the then prime minister of Pakistan (1971–77), armed and used the Afghan resistance movement to counter Daoud.[35] This political posture by Pakistan has been defined as proxy war by some authors.[36] The assertion is inaccurate because while the sheltering of and political support to Afghan dissidents can be conceptually framed as the use of an indirect strategy in COIN warfare, it was not a typical instance of waging war by proxies. For the most part, the immediate context of Afghan provocation was responsible for the retaliation.[37] The support for Afghan jihad against the USSR was built using the same human base. It was essentially a global effort to contain communism; Pakistan provided the operational base, and participated in the struggle driven entirely by a desire to protect its own survival.[38] Apart from the arrival and stationing of foreign fighters, several non-state groups came into being in Pakistan during this time, comprising ideologues and youths belonging to Karachi-based Deobandi seminaries, Jamiat Ulema-e-Islam (JUI), JI (Jamaat-e-Islami) and Salafists (i.e., Lashkar-e-Taiba, or LeT).[39]

The Afghan-Russo conflict had entered its intense phase in the early 1980s when the Sikh insurgency erupted in Indian Punjab. Pakistan promptly seized the opportunity to extend sustained support to the Sikh cause as a legitimate response to India's overt support of Bengali separatists in 1971.[40] However, more assertive retribution by Pakistan transpired later, with the quick support of an armed uprising by Kashmiris in 1989 against Indian rule. The goal was to bring India under pressure, despite it being the stronger power in the status quo, through deniable privatized jihad, while accepting a corresponding response by India in Sindh province.[41] Nawaz Sharif (former prime minister and head of a leading political party, PML(N) (the Pakistan Muslim League – Nawaz)) had based his entire election campaign during the early 1990s around nationalism and support for Kashmiri Mujahidin.[42] This political discourse resulted in nationwide popularization of the potential possibility of liberation of Kashmir through jihad.[43] The application of unconventional means by Pakistan against India can factually be evinced from this period onward.[44] Yet Praveen Swami, one of India's most prominent journalists, suggests instead that 'The stark reality, which hardly anyone cares honestly to face, is that armed militancy had reared its head in Kashmir at least 20 years before Zia-ul-Haq launched his covert operation there.' He further states that 'Terrorist groups ... those now operating in Jammu and Kashmir, were or are [not] simply pawns of Pakistan's military and intelligence services. ... Such groups had a variety of ideological motivations, and complex political objectives ... [and] their actions were rooted in history and politics.'[45] Yet when the 1999 cross-LOC (Line of Control, previously CFL) intrusion in Kargil Sector was presented by Pakistan as undertaken by the Mujahidin (or proxies), which was a near replay of Gibraltar, the claim was dismissed by former Indian army Chief General V.P. Singh.[46] Overall, these overtures show a deeper preoccupation with Kashmir among Pakistanis, and more so among the Punjabis and Pashtuns, who dominate the military, bureaucracy and political class. It may be of interest to Western readers that the letter 'K' in the acronym 'Pakistan' stands for Kashmir.[47] Therefore, moral and diplomatic support to the Kashmiris' right to self-determination has been a consistent policy pillar of all governments in Pakistan.[48]

Besides, the justification for supporting armed resistance is also inspired by universal declarations, resolutions and covenants such as are made by the UN, OIC (Organization of Islamic Cooperation) and International Islamic Fiqh Academy, a subsidiary of OIC that has debunked 'armed struggle against occupation as a terrorist crime' and clearly delineates the difference between terrorism and legitimate resistance for the purposes of removing tyranny and reclaiming lost rights through jihad as struggle (which is not terrorism), so long as that struggle follows the rulings of Islamic law and related international treaties.[49] Consequently, Pakistani governments and socio-political elites, and a major part of the population, have historically not regarded the liberation struggle in Kashmir or the support rendered to it as terrorism; rather, the violence against unarmed Kashmiris by the Indian security forces is termed open 'terrorism'.[50]

Similarly, Pakistani analysts have concluded that assistance to Afghan Taliban during the 1990s by Benazir Bhutto to dislodge unfriendly warriors in Kabul was more of a marriage of convenience between Pakistan and the Taliban than the result of any ideological affinity between the two.[51] In some ways it was a continuation of Bhutto's policies, without deploying proxies of Pakistani origin. Importantly, the age-old Indian role in the security politics of Afghanistan – that is, instigating the issue of Pakhtoonistan – was central to Pakistani perception of security risks from its western borders.[52] Some Western writers go even farther back, asserting that the key foundational reason behind Pakistan's support for Islamic militant groups does not reside only in Afghanistan's demand for an independent 'Pashtunistan', but was a response to a series of aggressions by that country during the 1950s and 1960s that shaped Pakistan's strategic calculations.[53] Pakistan's unwillingness to abandon the Afghan Taliban – specifically the Afghan jihad ally the Haqqani Network – since 2004 needs to be understood through this prism.[54]

Construction of 'terrorism' and counterterrorism (1947–2000)

It is extremely difficult if not impossible to trace the roots of CT in Pakistan. This difficulty derives from the convoluted history of construction of the terms 'terrorism' and 'terrorists', and the legal provisions instituted to combat them. The single most important determinant that has, over time, shaped the official vocabulary and history of dealing with perceived or actual home-grown violence in Pakistan resides in the exclusionary national identity built around Urdu and Islam as the overarching official foundations of Pakistani nationalism.[55] This national-unity narrative evolved by subsuming regional (ethnic) diversity and by accentuating the separateness of religious and sectarian minorities.[56] By default, the centralizing tendency ingrained a source of enduring social conflict, which in time, with increasing homogenizing measures (such as the One Unit Scheme of 1955), worked to essentialize, sharpen and aggravate group differentiation.

The first Baloch revolt by Khan of Kalat soon after independence, later taken over by his brother Agha Abdul Karim upon Khan's deposition (1948–49), and a series of subsequent Baloch uprisings inspired and led by different leaders under different Pakistani regimes – 1958–59, 1962–63, 1973–77 – germinated in reaction to this strategic idea.[57] Most researchers, military writers, government officials and global databases labelled Baloch dissidents as insurgents, outlaws, guerrillas, secessionists, separatists or insurrectionists.[58] However the terror tactics (as they are now understood) were also evident in attacks on the settlers by the Baloch tribes, and equally in oppression by the government, especially under the civilian rule of Bhutto.[59]

The precursor to the violent separatism in Balochistan in the 1970s was the explosive turmoil in East Pakistan led by Bengali nationalists, who were categorized as traitors and charged with treason designed to destroy the state of Pakistan.[60] Pakistani military officials have variously categorized them as mischief-mongers, saboteurs, infiltrators, militants, rebels and insurgents, while the enforcement actions by the Pakistan Army were called internal security operations.[61] Bengali writers generally consider the resistance fighters to have been rebels, guerrillas and insurgents.[62] Apart from high-handed state-directed suppression and equally gruesome excesses by the Bengali rebels, the Pakistani military-led government employed irregular counterinsurgents – the Al-Badhr Mujahidin group (from the Dhaka branch of Jamaat-e-Islami) – to quell the revolt.[63] Stephen Cohen sees this strategy more as a compulsion than a choice because the Bengali civilian Intelligence Bureau (IB) officers in East Pakistan were considered untrustworthy, necessitating calling upon ISI and the eventual recruitment of Islamist groups, including students, to undertake countermeasures.[64] It should be noted that the provincial government (of the National Awami Party (NaAP)) in Balochistan was sacked on the pretext of anti-Pakistani activities,[65] a rhetorical repeat of the 'traitor' labelling in East Pakistan. Were the contemporary lexicon in use in South Asia in those days, most of these acts and responses would have been called terrorism and counterterrorism. Yet the *Global Terrorism Database* has labelled only one exceptional violent incident by NaAP in 1975 as a terrorist act.[66]

The Suppression of Terrorist Activities Act of 1975 passed by Bhutto's regime emerged within this backdrop to deal with violent opposition and nationalist movements in the NWFP (North West Frontier Province – now Khyber Pakhtunkhwa – KP) and Balochistan provinces.[67] One of its immediate legal sources was the British emergency and anti-terrorism laws in force in Northern Ireland (NIEPA 1973) after the British Government took direct control of the region in 1972.[68] It was possibly inspired by the continuing practice of adapting legal regimes from colonial legacy in addition to having been a close ally with the US and Britain during the Cold War period, when all three countries shared an identical threat perception.[69] The term 'terrorism' was thus essentially imported into Pakistan.

Prior to this act, earlier governments in Pakistan had used a variety of British-crafted criminal-code, constitutional and judicial procedures to control political activity and suppress anti-state activities.[70] However, it was the 1975 Act that for the first time deployed and made known publicly the term 'terrorism' in Pakistan. After the Soviet invasion of Afghanistan and Pakistan's joining the global jihad, violent acts by hostile intelligence agencies became routine in Pakistan. But the expression 'terrorism' used by contemporary writers to describe those events is essentially a construction, because it is difficult to find the word 'terrorism' in the public media archives.[71] The 1975 Act subsequently led to two more enactments in 1990–92 – the Terrorist Affected Areas (Special Courts) Act X and the Special Courts for Speedy Trials Act IX – which in the preamble include terminologies of 'acts of terrorism, subversion and other heinous offences in the terrorist affected areas.'

It is instructive to note that, separately from foreign-sponsored violence in Pakistan, the mid-1980s had witnessed the onset and growth of sectarianism in the country. The genesis of a sectarian wave is assigned to an ambitious Islamization project and (narrow) drive for Sunnification of the state of Pakistan by General Zia to advance both a radical ideology of exclusion, incited primarily by his pretension of piety, and Deobandi conservatism and Saudi Wahhabism.[72] But it was also to prevent Shia mobilization inspired by the Iranian revolution.[73] While the sharpening of the sectarian divide drew influence from the entrenching of Sunni Islamism in Pakistan by the state through multiple institutional and legal means that had been under way since 1977, the primary provocation and inception of open Shia–Sunni confrontation owed a great deal to Tehran's eagerness to export revolution and active attempts by zealous emissaries of the Iranian revolutionary regime to organize Pakistani's Shias, including formation of the first Shia militant group – the Imamia Students Organization.[74] The Pakistani incumbent regime construed these assertive politics as a threat posed by Shias to governmental authority, thereby radicalizing hardline Sunni clergy.[75]

Guided by the millennial agenda of anti-Shia Deobandi group Sipah-e-Sahaba Pakistan (SSP – founded in 1986),[76] the arrival of other militant Deobandi organizations following the withdrawal of Soviets from Afghanistan, and the resultant patronizing by Gulf countries and Iran, sectarianism gained unparalleled momentum throughout the country.[77] The Afghan jihad proved to be propitious for foreign rivals – Iraq, Saudi Arabia and Iran – to deepen their commitment with their proxies inside Pakistan. The late 1980s and early 1990s increasingly witnessed the emergence of a plethora of sectarian and jihadi groups (Deobandi Harkat groups, Salafi LeT) across Pakistan,[78] mostly under the sway of ulama (clergy) of JUI, who were to later develop overlapping membership with al Qaeda and the Afghan and Pakistani Taliban.[79]

In addition to the courting of the religious right, in the late 1970s the ISI, organizationally bolstered by Zia, began to play up ethnic differences among Mohajirs and Sindhis to create a bulwark against the military regime's political opponents; namely, the Sindhi-led PPP (Pakistan People's Party).[80] The Muttahida Qaumi Movement (MQM), which claims to represent the Mohajir community of urban Sindh, was partially founded by the ISI, which also facilitated the party's lateral entry into provincial and national politics.[81] While the country was reeling from the sectarian chasm, identity politics also surged with full force onto the national horizon. MQM engaged in premeditated violent acts against its political and ethnic opponents, the army, and law-enforcement agencies (guerrilla tactics) on a large scale during the mid-1990s.[82] Indeed, this violence was more frequent than the sectarian terrorist attacks of the 1990s, and was more narrowly focused and concentrated primarily in the southern region of the country.[83] Only a military operation was able to contain the ethnic terrorism.

It was in the midst of these developments that the Anti-Terrorist Act (ATA) in 1997 was promulgated by the Government of Nawaz Sharif, to reign in a spate of ethnic terrorism and sectarianism.[84] Until this stage, non-state violence had been dealt with almost arbitrarily. The anti-terrorist laws enacted to this point by different governments were purely politically charged, which blurred the distinction between political dissent and non-state violence, a trend which still pervades national politics.[85] Ironically, despite laying out ATA, a conscious understanding and categorization of violent acts as terrorism and the countervailing measures as CT did not emerge at that time among the state or society more generally.

Meanwhile, al Qaeda had assumed concrete shape in neighbouring Afghanistan. Pakistani sectarian groups, mainly the LeJ (Lashkar-e-Jhangvi), sought shelter under Taliban rule in order to escape repression by the Sharif Government, which strengthened their pre-existing nexus with Arab Afghans.[86] Shortly afterwards, the consolidation of global Salafi jihad was proclaimed by Osama bin Laden in February 1998, symbolized by the formation of the World Islamic Front and declaration of jihad against Jews and crusaders.[87] Over the next three years, a wave of terrorist activity directed from Afghanistan spanned the globe.

In 1999 General Pervez Musharraf overthrew the civilian government of Sharif and imposed a benign martial law. Prior to the fateful attacks of September 11th, 2001, he expanded ATA through several amendments, largely to implicate political opponents but also entailing banning two notorious sectarian organizations – LeJ and SeM (Sipah-e-Muhammad) – while placing others under observation.[88] Despite the continuing tide of sectarianism – and the official backing of the leadership of SSP, which was cited by Shias as a proof of Musharraf's Government going soft on its anti-sectarian agenda – he remained hamstrung in politics and did not formulate a cohesive response to address violent episodes.[89] Ultimately, it was the shared sectarian agenda that was to produce a formidable coalition of terrorist groups in Pakistan.[90]

Counterterrorism 2001–18

When the US approached Pakistan on 12 September 2001 with demands for cooperation, the military elite – realizing that the country was militarily weak to confront the superpower – recognized an opportunity to dissuade the formation of an Indian-US alliance, to preserve the Kashmir cause, and to mitigate the prospect of Indian aggression (at the behest of or in unison with Western powers) degrading Pakistan's defence capability.[91] Joining the global fight against terrorism was hence inevitable. However, the common perception that Musharraf abandoned the Taliban when he joined the WOT is counterfactual. Ashley Tellis asserts that throughout the initial phase of Operation Enduring Freedom, General Musharraf and his cohort implored the United States to desist from decisively destroying Mullah Mohammad Omar's regime, or at least avoid destruction of the Taliban's traditional base in southern Afghanistan.[92]

In any case, Pakistan entered into an alliance with the international community to support US-led military operations in Afghanistan from a setting fraught with trouble. The expression 'counterterrorism' became fashionable in the official and political lexicon of Pakistan after 9/11.

Response by Musharraf's regime: 2001–8

The existing literature more often treats Pakistan's response to the solicitation of help by the United States and its CT effort either as an extension of America's WOT or as a single determination. This interpretation is inaccurate. An objective analysis reveals that Pakistan's decision to join the US-led alliance, and the dynamics emanating from military intervention in Afghanistan and Pakistan's response thereof, created different effects. Overall, the WOT created a two-front war scenario – one in mainstream (non-tribal) Pakistan, and the other in tribal areas; these merged subsequently to constitute a more formidable threat.

The incidence of terrorism in the country picked up soon after Pakistan joined the WOT.[93] The immediate outcome was the fragmentation of JeM (Jaish-e-Mohammad) and HuM (Harkat ul-Mujahidin), both of which had close ties with al Qaeda and the Taliban. By October 2001, hawkish elements of JeM were set on a collision course with the military regime.[94] The first demonstration of disillusionment with Pakistan's new course was a suicide attack on the Kashmir legislative assembly in Srinagar on 1 October 2001, which killed thirty-one people. The second was a Fedayeen assault on the Indian parliament on 13 December by JeM rebels. Both not only took the Pakistani military establishment and the JeM leadership by surprise, but also seriously undermined Pakistan's Kashmir cause, especially to portray Kashmiri groups as freedom fighters.[95] Between October and December 2001, there were several terrorist acts, gun battles with rebels and violent protest rallies by the Afghan Jihad Council.[96]

Public and media cynicism regarding the decision was widespread.[97] Some of the mainstream political parties, including the liberal elements and particularly the politico-religious entities, vehemently opposed the turnaround and have remained sceptical throughout due to what they see as the suspect nature of Pakistan's participation in the WOT.[98] There was strong dissent within the army's senior command, too, on rapid acceptance of US demands, not to mention continued existence of pro-Taliban officers in ISI, despite a sizeable purging before the US air strikes began, including the sacking of its chief, General Mahmud Ahmad.[99] These polarized conditions, including the opposition of many conservative former generals, made the start of Pakistan's participation in the WOT increasingly more ominous.[100] The situation was aggravated when Musharraf announced additional amendments to the ATA in January 2002. This move, coupled with efforts to curtail militants' cross-border activities in IHK, caused a number of factions to initiate a series of bombings across Pakistan, targeting minorities and the security forces, and including attempts on Musharraf's life.[101] The LeJ marked its re-emergence with the May 2002 car bomb outside Karachi's Sheraton Hotel that killed fourteen, including eleven French engineers.[102] The more aggrieved faction of JeM, led by Maulana Abdul Jabbar, retaliated by launching a series of terrorist attacks across Pakistan targeting Western nationals, Christians and Shia Muslims. Backed by Osama bin Laden, jihad was pressed against the 'slave' government of Pakistan.[103] Jabbar later formed a separate terror group, Jamaat-al-Furqan, consisting of renegades. The erstwhile pro-state 313 brigade also became an antagonist. A few renegades from JeM later provided the groundwork for founding militancy in Swat.[104] Besides, breakaway factions from LeT, HuM, HUJI and LeJ spawned a new breed of anti-state Punjabi Taliban, who declared Pakistan as a *Darul Harb* (abode of war).[105]

The stimulus provided by the US-led invasion of Afghanistan, on the other hand, generated the second set of pernicious conditions. For instance, soon after the American attack, JUI declared jihad against the US forces, and anti-American sentiment and hatred against the military regime intensified.[106] Simultaneously, Federally Administered Tribal Areas (FATA) were flooded by al Qaeda, its affiliates, other foreign militants and the Haqqanis, whereas most remnants of the Afghan Taliban found refuge in northwestern Balochistan. The veteran settlers of Afghan jihad among tribal society played an important role in further exacerbating local conditions in FATA.[107]

The assistance demanded for WOT included intelligence sharing, logistics facilitation, and operational deployments to stop al Qaeda at the borders or apprehend its cadres seeking sanctuary inside Pakistan, as well as severing diplomatic ties with the Taliban, if necessary.[108] The initial military movements in FATA and policing measures undertaken between December 2001 and March 2004 to apprehend foreign elements in mainland Pakistan were part of this agreed arrangement. Indeed, the tribesmen were contacted prior to movement of forces into their agencies.[109] It was for this reason that when the army went to the Kurram and Khyber agencies of FATA during December 2001 (Operation Al Mezaan) to secure the border with Afghanistan, and to block and apprehend terrorists fleeing that country, there was no resistance from the tribes.[110] However, when an expedition was made into to North and South Waziristan during June 2002 upon information of the presence of hostile elements, and with the commitment to allow the tribes to handle the local situation, the Ahmad Wazir elders warned that any military operation in tribal areas would be regarded as a declaration of war on the Pashtun tribes.[111] Besides, one of the underlying precipitants of the tribal reaction in providing refuge to foreign and Afghan fugitives had been the systematic extermination and persecution of the Afghans by Northern Alliance and US forces, which deeply angered their frontier brethren in Pakistan.[112] As the incidence of violence inside Afghanistan increased, the US forced Pakistan into robust operations against the militants inside FATA, while pointedly disparaging the usefulness of idle border deployments.[113] A major regional development during 2002 – a large-scale Indian mobilization along Pakistan's eastern borders, provoked by an attack on the Indian parliament and a defensive deployment by Pakistan, but also because of a reduction of troop levels through the deployments to FATA – further worsened the security challenges faced by the military regime.[114]

Meanwhile, after the October 2002 Pakistani elections and riding on anti-American sentiment, a pro-Taliban mullah-led political coalition – the Muttahida Majlis-e-Amal (MMA) – took control of the two provinces bordering Afghanistan – KP and Balochistan – who, besides altering internal Pakistani politics in favour of hardline Deobandi factions, became the principal purveyor of ideological and material provisions in the spread and acceleration of Talibanization in the Pashtun belts.[115] The installation of the MMA is blamed on ingenious politics by Musharraf to maintain a democratic facade while keeping afloat the threat for the coalition partners of a takeover of Pakistan by bigots to ensure their sustained support.[116] With the MMA in power, not only did sectarian and jihadi organizations obtain a new lease of life, the key political position of the coalition in these provinces removed any worries the Afghan Taliban may have had in matters of logistics, and especially manpower.[117] The rise under Fazlullah of the Swati Taliban, which later turned into a monster, is imputed to inaction by the MMA Government in KP.

Battles between the military and militant groups became increasingly common in FATA in 2003, when the tribes refused to hand over al Qaeda and Taliban militants to the army.[118] Thereafter the insurgency began to regularly target the Pakistani army presence in FATA, later expanding into settled areas of Khyber Pakhtunkhwa.[119] Throughout this period, a precipitous flow of US instructions and Pakistani knee-jerk adjustments in FATA, and battles followed by shady peace deals with local militants entailing significant concessions, became standard practice.[120] The impulsive attempts to implement US orders mostly resulted in aborted operations, seriously eroding overall morale and also undermining public confidence in the government's ability to deal with the growth of violence.[121]

Even though civilians were targeted by the Taliban in tribal territory, and more so from 2003 onwards, the primary contest was fought between the tribal militias, Taliban and tribesmen sheltering foreigners and the Pakistan Army. From this perspective, operations in FATA cannot be wholly conceptualized as anti-terror, but fall broadly under the rubric of tribal guerrilla warfare, not counterinsurgency in the military sense. Nevertheless, FATA at this stage was the centre of the militants' incubation, and the operational terrain of terrorism in Pakistan was under the reign of sectarian and jihadi renegades.

All the while, the country was fighting the scourge of non-state violence without a coherent counterterrorism strategy. Essentially, there was no clear objective or vision inside the government.[122] The country's past experience of counterinsurgency at home placed it in a fairly strong position when the WOT was declared,[123] but the initial reaction by Musharraf did not produce enough clarity to prosecute it. Moreover, the historical predominance in national security issues of the military, and its dictatorial style of governance, did not allow it to elicit consultation with civilian counterparts while devising strategies during the early phase of the insurrection.[124]

Whereas the arbitrary nature of the decision making (acknowledged by Musharraf)[125] was beneficial to the coalition partners, it was entirely ad hoc,[126] failing to articulate (even tentatively) a guiding framework to configure the response. The lack of a viable counterterrorism doctrine, let alone a counter-insurgency one, the presence of inexperienced senior commanders with no grasp of tribal dynamics, and the organizational inadequacy to fight sustained tribal warfare prior to Operation Enduring Freedom added to the professional problems involved in fighting a cohesive campaign against the battle-hardened militants.[127] It is not known if the army followed even its traditional standard operating procedure of issuing operational instructions. The Peshawar-based corps headquarters was the linchpin in the whole affair, and was supposedly left alone to conduct operations as it willed.[128] Akbar Ahmed, a well-known anthropologist, attributes the venture into Waziristan to military arrogance combined with ignorance of the cultural and historical context of the region, and is of the opinion that it was doomed from the start.[129]

On top of all this, the conflicting fatwas by the religious right and organizations denouncing both army operations against 'Mujahidin' and the soldiers as apostates added to the confusion.[130] Because of this, there was conflict of cause in the early years among the officers and men of the armed and para-military forces serving in FATA, over fighting 'terrorists' who were 'others' but Muslims nevertheless. In some instances, parents simply refused to receive the remains of their slain soldier sons.[131] A 'three Ds' strategy of *dialogue*, *development* and *deterrence* was frequently alluded to by Pervez Musharraf in 2004. The concept was never more than marginally helpful to the executants; given the dismal state of affairs on the ground, it certainly didn't turn out to be useful as events unfolded. It was never translated into a workable model, and Musharraf's attempt to homogenize public discourse through a strategy of 'enlightened moderation' also proved a farce.[132]

Between 2006 and 2008, Pakistan was overwhelmed by wanton violence. The triggers that generated a paradigm shift towards this spate of violence were provided by a US-led drone strike on a religious seminary belonging to Tehrik Nifaz Shariat-e-Muhammadi (TNSM) in the village of Chenegai in Bajuar Agency on 30 October 2006, killing up to sixty-nine children, and the storming of Lal Masjid (the Red Mosque) with the combined might of regular and para-military troops (Operation Sunrise) in Islamabad during July 2007.[133] The ideo-logues and terror groups, of diverse persuasions (including TNSM), abandoned their strategy of selective violence, and coalesced around Tehrik-e-Taliban Pakistan (TTP) to launch indiscriminate attacks. These attacks, inspired by vengeance, were the most terrifying development during December of 2007.[134] The Pashtun-driven militancy, prior to Operation Sunrise, evolved to comprise fresh and deadlier Punjabi renegades from further fractionalization and internal dissension of JeM, LeT, HuM, SSP and the reorganized jihadi outfits like 313 brigade under Ilyas Kashmiri.[135] Over 4,000 terrorism-related acts were carried out over the next two years, striking a variety of targets without sparing any region of the country.[136] A characteristic feature of this wave of terrorism was the terrorists' enhanced reliance, skill and outreach in perpetrating suicide attacks that – apart from destruction of property and infrastructure – killed, maimed and wounded over 5,300 citizens (figure 7.1),[137] including former Pakistani Prime Minister Bhutto who was assassinated in December 2007.

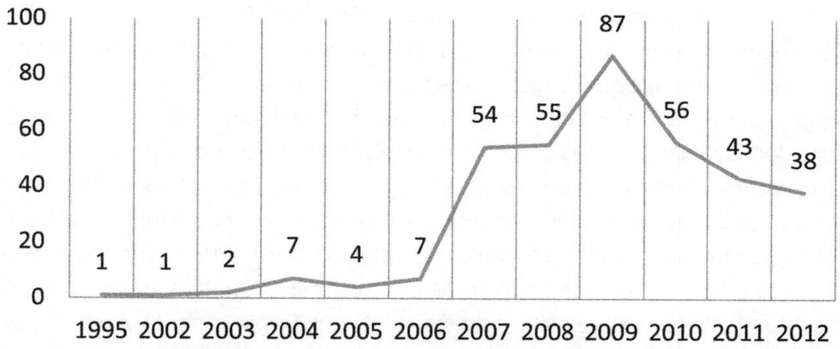

Figure 7.1 Annual aggregates of suicide attacks in Pakistan, 1995–2012.

District Swat of KP province was completely ravaged under an unrelenting regime of terror by Fazlullah. The halfhearted military drives failed to contain his brutalities. To be sure, in the meantime – and in addition to increased bickering among soldiers about the moral rationality of the WOT at home, which stifled their cause – more territory and internal sovereignty had been lost to the insurgents, who were now openly challenging the authority of the state across all major urban centres including the national capital.[138]

During the eight-year (2001–8) reign of terrorism, the military and intelligence network consistently maintained certain distinctions among non-state entities based on the utility offered and the threat posed to the state.[139] The Kashmiri groups (LeT, JeM, HzM (Hizbul Mujahidin)), who were regarded as freedom fighters due to the historical centrality of the Kashmir issue, and the 'good' (Pakistani) Taliban were treated in the former category, whereas al Qaeda, TTP and sectarian organizations were declared enemies of the state.[140] The justification rendered by analysts for the distinction between good and bad Taliban has been described as a 'realistic response of a smaller and weaker nation-state unable to either defy or influence the policies of the world's sole superpower, while trying to simultaneously protect its immediate and medium-to-long term national security interests.'[141] A more clear explanation of the regime's behaviour is that it was engaging in selective military action against hostile groups while constructively dealing with reconcilable others.[142] Within the sectarian groups, Musharraf's Government deliberately tolerated SSP due to its political utility; this organization remained relevant also because of its roots in society and sectarian support that includes the ranks of the police and bureaucracy.[143] The Afghan Taliban, who were fully resuscitated during 2004, transcended these criteria because they were a means for strategic influence in Afghanistan.[144] This has in turn been a crucial cause of tension in Pakistan–US relations.

The two relevant provincial governments during Musharraf's rule – KP and Balochistan under the MMA – had their priorities almost entirely opposed to those of the federal government. They remained aligned with sectarian organizations, and the Afghan as well as the Pakistani Taliban. The political right, led by Islamic conglomerates and PML(N), showed reluctance even to take responsibility for soldiers' deaths. Therefore, the absence of a unified national stand, political ownership or semblance of it during Musharraf's era on fighting extremism and terrorism should not be surprising.[145] The mishandling of the simmering Balochs which led to the assassination of an important tribal leader and well-known politician – Akbar Bugti – on 26 August 2006, which was hailed as the successful elimination of a terrorist by the military, sparked another full-blown Baloch anti-state war from 2006 onwards.[146] The insurgency contributed more woes to the already fragile war against terrorism. The only positive and widely acclaimed aspect of the military campaign was the apprehension and killing of several key cadres of al Qaeda. The pernicious role of India in discrediting Pakistan's efforts and the counterproductive part played by the US in accentuating governance difficulties, not least the lack of enthusiasm of NATO forces in Afghanistan to reciprocate Pakistan's efforts to seal the border, also told heavily on the war-waging efforts of Pakistan.[147]

Counterterrorism under the Zardari Government, 2008–13

The advent of democracy in March 2008 was hailed as the harbinger of change for the fragile state of security in Pakistan. The Pakistani Army under its new chief General Ashfaq Parvez Kiyani seemed willing to give the democratic experiment a chance, led by the fledgling civilian government of PPP, comprising a weak coalition of opportunistic parties. Apart from the lingering absence of politically inclusive strategy to deal with terrorism, conditions deteriorated due to growing socio-political fissures, a worsening economy and international pressure resulting from the 2008 Mumbai attacks. The sudden breakup of the ruling coalition soon after its formation was a major setback, but a more important one was Sharif's public opposition to Zardari's continuation of many policies once embraced by Musharraf, including his close relationship with the US in the WOT.[148] This tension between the two parties clearly established pro- and anti-Taliban camps.

The situation in FATA remained fluid, while in Swat it grew increasingly grave. The new provincial government of KP led by the Awami National Party (ANP) rashly concluded two peace deals during April–May 2008 with TNSM and the Taliban in Swat. The limited success gained by intermittent military operations, however, enabled the Taliban by early 2009 to install a parallel government in large parts of the Swat Valley.[149] Another peace accord in Swat was signed on 16 February 2009, followed by the promulgation of 'Nizam-e-Adl Regulation 2009' (sharia law) with the approval of the president of Pakistan.[150] All the peace agreements collapsed within few months, as previously in FATA, strengthening the belief that the deals comprised ratification of defeats on the ground.[151] This was evident from a remarkable spike in the scale of violence, and the audacity of the militants in striking strategic targets such as army headquarters.[152] The civilian government seemingly lacked competence to address this morass, and had practically ceded all strategic authority for organizing campaigns against insurgents to the army. The subsequent Swat operation (May–August 2009) was able to achieve its objectives due to strong political backup and popular support, although not from religious parties. South Waziristan was cleared later that year. Even though hugely important, these one-off interventions were not inspired by informed statecraft.[153] As a result, there were voices of concern in the international community over the spectre of Pakistan's nuclear assets falling into the hands of extremists.

One notable contribution by Kiyani was the establishment of army De-radicalization and Rehabilitation Centres in Swat and Tank, which were later rolled out across a few more locations. These facilities have successfully reintegrated hundreds of militants captured during active operations.[154] The effort, however, did not receive equal backing by the government. There are two particular achievements for which the PPP Government can nevertheless be credited. Firstly, it laid the organizational and legal foundation of the National Counterterrorism Authority (NACTA), which was formally established during March 2013, albeit without resolving problems of its administrative control and mandate due to vested political interests.[155] Second, it took total ownership of the WOT, although without an institutionalized response to the threat.[156] Official approaches to counterterrorism thus generally remained rhetorical, more often characterized by the 'three Ds' mantra instituted by Musharraf, but with little evidence on the ground of a practicable road map for achieving these goals.[157]

A recurring theme that previously made the fight against terrorism exceedingly difficult was the ubiquity of discourse on jihad that had been allowed to grow and flourish, spawning misperception and irrationality.[158] This was helped by a heightened pace of drone warfare from the Obama Administration in tribal areas, galvanizing more recruits for militants driven by vengeance over the increasingly reported killing of innocent civilians.[159] Furthermore, the public also saw itself as a victim of the American-led war, because of the routine violent backlash by the Taliban in Pakistani cities. The WOT in Pakistan thus seriously suffered. The country descended into further chaos due to other developments. For instance, as opposed to the anti-terrorism orientation of the centre, the provincial government in Punjab under the PML(N) went to the other extreme by brokering a deal with groups such as al Qaeda and TTP to save the province from attacks by terrorists.[160] What was more, the assassination of Governor Salmaan Taseer in January 2011 over alleged blasphemy and lionizing of his murderer produced a new ideological front consisting of activists of PML(N) along with Barelvis (the largest Sunni faction in Pakistan) and the TTP, which symbolized the inherent contradiction between what the government claimed to stand for – rejection of terrorism – and how a sizeable section of society negated this narrative.[161] The federal government and provincial government of KP also yielded to intense pressure by religious forces to shelve deliberations on amending the blasphemy laws and the curriculum modernization project, respectively.[162] Another monumental incident during 2011 was the killing of Bin Laden in Abbottabad. There were funeral prayers accompanied by anguish, grief and sorrow on his demise, which clearly revealed a sharp contrast in views on the identity of terrorists.[163] Because there was no structured, government-led strategic communication architect to control and contain the mounting wave of religious extremism, and because of the motivational campaign of terrorists and their supporters, discursive space was ceded to them unchallenged.[164]

The leadership of PML(N), the Pakistan Tehrik-e-Insaf (PTI; who had symbolically supported the Swat and South Waziristan operations) and the religious parties (JUI, JI) also gradually became more vociferous for ending support for the WOT and opening negotiations with insurgents. This stance invariably became integral to their upcoming election campaigns, evoking in return discrete favour from the Taliban.[165] The incessant terrorist campaign that was distinctly against the secular parties (PPP, ANP and MQM) while completely sparing the PML(N) and PTI clearly manifested the political preferences of the Taliban.[166]

During this time, the Baloch conflict that had raged since 2006 remained moderate compared with the violence perpetrated by religious terrorists. It could not, however, be resolved, despite conciliatory measures taken by the PPP Government during its tenure to address the causes of grievance of Baloch nationalists. CT continued with a heavy reliance on the military instrument but without much success.

Counterterrorism under the PML(N) regime, 2013–18

After the general election of 2013, a new government led by the PML(N) was installed in early June. Terrorist attacks were being carried out on a daily basis at the time. Paradoxically, while policies addressing other issues were emphasized by the ruling party, there was no attention to national security. Neither was the army in favour of talking to TTP. Despite the colossal loss of human life, the government did not react to any of the horrendous attacks launched from the start of its term, let alone contemplate a fresh military response to the onslaught.[167] Mediated peace negotiations with militants began in late 2013. The euphoria was, however, short-lived, due to unabated terrorist activity by TTP and its affiliates, including the targeted killing of a two-star general in Swat, although some politicians accused the government of a lack of sincerity in exploring prospects for a peaceful outcome.[168]

During March 2014, the Ministry of Interior (MOI) unveiled its National Internal Security Policy 2014–2018 (NISP), outlining a broad vision to deal with terrorism and extremism, to be implemented by the country's supreme CT coordination body, NACTA.[169] This was a major achievement by any government since the onset of the WOT. The policy document was highly ambitious in aiming to harness strategic intelligence organizations, given the history of complex civil–military relations, and to integrate functions of other ministries, all under the auspices of the MOI.[170] In a practical sense, the government did not show any keenness to attend to the issue of terrorism until foreign fighters attacked Karachi Airport in June 2014, triggering the army's long-awaited operation – Zarb-e-Azb in NWA (North Waziristan Agency). The real impetus for the military campaign was provided by the massacre of schoolchildren in Peshawar in December 2014, which led to the development of a twenty-point (extra-legal) National Action Plan (NAP) to combat violent extremism and terrorism, including setting up military courts to try civilians accused of committing terrorism through a constitutional amendment.[171] Backed by the unconditional support of all segments of society, the NAP created hope inside the country and also abroad that finally Pakistan had mustered the political will to eliminate the menace of terrorism once and for all, and was on course to become a 'normal' country.[172] Indeed, after the successful operation in Swat during 2009, Zarb-e-Azb was the first comprehensive military campaign by Pakistan, mainly on the initiative of the military, against domestic terrorism of all hues.

However, the incredibly slow and politicized response by the government in operationalizing NAP has led its detractors to term it the 'National Inaction Plan.'[173] Similarly, the state itself remained partially complicit in forsaking the prosecution of some of the most high-profile terrorists and allowing the revival of the jihad project by Islamic parties, which included the leadership of some proscribed organizations.[174] More significant, and where the Pakistani establishment and the religious polity seem largely firm, is the persistent support of the Afghan militants, although recent reports suggest serious cracks in the traditional equation between the two. It is a fact, however, that apart from a lack of 'matching and complementing governance initiatives' from the government to implement NAP, the 'whole-nation approach' so categorically stressed by the armed forces allowed for a subtle discretion in whom to label a terrorist, or otherwise.[175] There have therefore been mixed reactions from the US and Western scholars about support for Pakistan's WOT.

By the end of 2016, symptoms of terrorism were considerably reduced in Pakistan, prompting the politico-military leadership to claim the 'end' of terrorism.[176] A sense of complacency took root among the population, only for it to be rudely shocked, after a brief prelude, by the re-rearing of full-blown violence in early 2017. At the time of writing (October 2018), at least fifty-five terrorist incidents have occurred during the current year.[177] This tally indicates a marked reduction in violence in Pakistan; concurrently, however, violent extremism has spread more menacingly at the grass roots. The meteoric rise of, and the state's failure to curb vandalism by, Tehreek-i-Labbaik Ya Rasool Allah (TLYRA), a new violent sectarian movement, is one such example.[178]

The litany of failures by the PML(N) Government to effectively check the onslaught by terrorists, hate preachers and others who propagate divisive ideologies can be witnessed in a public indictment by the Justice Faez Isa Commission Report of December 2016.[179] Not only are the structures, motivations and ecosystem underlying terrorism far from addressed, which makes the sustainability of the claimed arrest in violence suspect, but also the ominous presence of transnational armed groups on Pakistani soil, specifically the increasing footprints of Daesh and the at-large splinters of TTP, threatens the prospect of stability in Pakistan any time soon.[180] The government's preoccupation with its alleged involvement – despite the ouster of Nawaz Sharif in illicit offshore assets, the so-called Panama leaks – also adversely affected its already tenuous predisposition toward opposing religious violence.[181] In the absence of a unified conceptualization of WOT, the provinces have evolved their own CT frameworks – for example, criminal justice in Punjab or the security approach (kill rather than capture) in Khyber Pakhtunkhwa – underpinned by diverse policy attitudes vis-à-vis the warfare orientation of the Pakistani armed forces to pursue the campaign against terrorism and violent extremism.[182] A notable trend since the evolution of NAP has also been an enhanced focus on military-led intelligence-based operations in the country.[183] While crediting them for certain degree of success, in principal all of these operational persuasions remain centred on the military, which reveals ambiguity about who is responsible for NAP.[184]

Further, it is not known to what degree other provinces or state institutions (barring the army) are engaging in strategic communication to neutralize terrorists' ideologies or reintegrate former militants. Punjab has established legal, discursive and organizational processes and mechanisms to address these issues,[185] but the impact of these initiatives remains undetermined.

Policy implications and conclusions

The main focus of this chapter has been to explore the reasons for Pakistan's inability to eradicate terrorism despite its cost to the country, as well as misperceptions about its sincerity in supporting the broader anti-terrorism cause. Three aspects have been systematically analysed: the conceptualization and role of violence in Pakistan's strategic thought within the regional environment, specifically the alleged practice of employing proxies; the evolution of the terrorism lexicon and instruments within this setting; and, finally, a comprehensive review of the WOT from 2001 to 2018.

Fundamentally, the discussion underscores two major findings. First, not only is the use of proxies by the Pakistani state a widely misunderstood issue but its association with the expression 'terrorism' is misplaced. Secondly, insofar as outcomes of the WOT are concerned, the analysis suggests that, regardless of some significant successes, overall the response behaviour by successive governments has been marred by a lack of political sense; civil–military tension over the issue of terrorism; and the uncertain, fluctuating levels of support from various provincial governments, political parties, vigilantes and society to take ownership of and prosecute the WOT.

In the case of the former, it comes out strongly that the use of or support for the application of proxies is not an institutionalized feature of Pakistani statecraft or of national politics. Both Gibraltar and Kargil were traditional military operations. The occasional use of proxies in Kashmir by the military regimes specifically of Zia, Nawaz Sharif and to a lesser degree by Musharraf cannot be denied, however. The fact remains that neither the armed struggle in Kashmir nor the Kashmiri jihadis are construed by the majority in Pakistan as terrorism or terrorists. Besides, the prevailing scholarly opinion seems to conflate logistical support – such as to Afghan religious groups during the era of Daoud, to the Taliban during the WOT and to Sikh dissidents – with the physical employment of agents by the state. This generalization is not borne out by empirical facts. This is because the backing of Afghan groups by the strategic elite has evolved from the troubled history of Pakistan–Afghanistan relations and the Indian role in managing Afghan policies towards Pakistan. What is further often ignored is that there exists a strong ethnic affinity between the Afghan and Pakistani Pashtun populations, as well as shared religious terrain between Deobandi politicians and their adherents in Pakistan with the Afghan groups. This support base is unlikely to diminish, despite the shifts in Pakistan's security calculus away from Afghan groupings. Secondly, transnational terror acts in India by Kashmiri groups are perceived in Pakistan separately from the armed freedom struggle in IHK, implying a different categorization of violent acts. The lack of understanding of these realities by scholars and policymakers abroad, without, however, discounting the adept diplomacy by India, has led to misperceptions about this country.

Admittedly, there is a conflict between Pakistan's national interests, underpinned by historical, security, psychosocial and cultural reasons and constraints, and the expectations of Western countries, notably the US. The latter country views the entire landscape of violence in South Asia through a linear lens, which overlooks intricate local and regional dynamics and tends to create friction in bilateral relations. A closer cooperation to counter terrorism can be fostered only if the geopolitical context is grasped, with an understanding that the route to stability in Afghanistan goes through Kashmir. The discussion reveals, though obliquely, that support for Afghan fighters by Pakistan may recede in the near future, and Pakistan may also reign in the Kashmiri jihadis, but without leaving the Kashmiris until there is strong ground for a resolution of the Kashmir problem.

In the WOT, possibly the most obvious deficiency has been the inadequate quality of leadership, from Musharraf through Zardari to Nawaz Sharif. Broadly, they have failed to conceptualize the raft of challenges, to create an enduring socio-political consensus against the WOT or to develop a coherent CT vision. Their approaches to contend with terrorism therefore have been devoid of objective substance. In essence, whereas countering terrorism and mitigating its fallout in an environment characterized by ideological, political and security complexity and polarization warranted its pursuit within a broader strategy of COIN, the military option was imposed right from the outset, which made the WOT a disjointed enterprise divorced from popular aspirations. This approach has been continued by successive governments without reflection, and without strengthening it with political measures.

Moreover, the realpolitik of the mainstream political parties and concomitant centre–province divergences in perception, preference and practice for or against WOT, under military as well as civil rule, have acted as a major obstacle to stemming terrorism and violent extremism. The analysis has highlighted not only that the military had to operate for a considerable time without political or public support,but also how key political actors with significant followings have encouraged ultra-right politics to the extent of the politicization of religion and embracing of known terror groups (i.e., the PML(N) and JUI). Musharraf, too, was drawn into eliciting political favours from the Taliban-friendly MMA and sectarian organizations to legitimize his rule. These deviant behaviours caused confusion and produced conflicting perceptions among the population about the country's strategic direction in countering violent acts, and thus led to the waxing and waning of public support. This situation was exacerbated by a contested understanding spawned by the varied framings of terrorism. It was only recently that some ownership of the WOT by the public became politically visible. Needless to say, foreign and regional powers – the US, India and partly the coalition partners – were also instrumental in subverting Pakistan's WOT, without due attention or regard for its domestic crises. The burden of blame therefore warrants judicious sharing by external actors.

An important finding that emerges from this enquiry is that non-military means to address the causes of the growth, proliferation and longevity of terrorism have been virtually ignored. In particular, strategic communication – including efforts to reintegrate militants – by and large has remained exceptional and without a national vision. Similarly, the successes gained in the WOT can be broadly attributed to post-Musharraf military leaders and popular resonance that they were able to create, especially in the wake of Operation Zarb-e-Azb. The political leadership has failed to meet the challenge. However, without exception, the military rulers have produced ethnic differentiations and nurtured sectarian ideologies and structures. Both have been detrimental to equitable social mobility and religious equilibrium in society. The reversal of these processes, however, is a mammoth undertaking.

The discussion in its entirety indicates that the management and resolution of terrorism in a country like Pakistan needs to be comprehended and addressed as a conflict, and not as a method. Besides, without a sound political vision clearly envisaging the end state of such challenges, popular support will remain divided. While the warfare approach has reduced the incidence of anti-state violence, it cannot alone eradicate the menace. Terrorism scholarship has amply proved that a decline in violence is not a reliable predictor of the waning of terrorism or terror organizations.[186] It would be prudent to harness and employ the best possible intellectual and expert resources to generate a long-term response. The NISP under civilian oversight could provide the starting point. The document lacks on several counts, which necessitates its reappraisal and recasting in the light of current threats and challenges to provide a guiding framework to develop a comprehensive COIN strategy. Nevertheless, CT policy and strategy should flow from it with due incorporation of relevant aspects of the NAP. The latter in any case should be shelved, since it does not have legal status. Moreover, the substantial presence of terrorism apologists in the country makes it all the more plausible to adopt a relatively pacifist approach, so as to obtain national consensus to deal with the menace and achieve enduring peace and stability. This also requires harmonizing the divergent CT efforts in play in the provinces.

A suitable CT model for Pakistan can be conceived based on broadening the existing understanding of CT by recasting focus away from the military to a civilian-led prevention approach based on law enforcement and soft power. It would require a major effort on the part of the state to transform the afflicted mindsets and to disengage those already committed and mobilized to commit violence. Conceivably, broad-based socio-economic and religion-driven reformation strategies, coupled with parallel endeavours to generate home-grown knowledge about political violence based on a rich reservoir of primary sources and field experience, will be helpful. A functional NACTA will be indispensable for this purpose. Finally, the international community, for on its part, needs to approach Pakistan within the characteristic regional environment of its functioning. It needs, therefore, to meaningfully engage India in a productive dialogue to reduce Pakistan's security concerns. In the end, the entire gamut of transnational non-state violence is linked at its root to achieving a resolution of the Kashmir issue, and the earlier the better. This will provide Pakistan with a sense of purpose and the opportunity to concentrate its resources to decisively act against all forms and manifestations of terrorism.

Notes

1 Institute for Economics and Peace, *Global Terrorism Index 2016: Measuring and Understanding the Impact of Terrorism* (Sydney: Institute for Economics and Peace, 2016), pp. 3, 12, 14; and see 'Foreword' in M.A. Rana (ed.), *Pakistan Security Report 2017* (Islamabad: Pakistan Institute for Peace Studies, 2017).

2 See, for example, P. Oborne and S. Agha, 'Pakistan is winning its war on terror,' *Spectator*, 30 December 2016; S. Lalwani, 'Actually, Pakistan is winning its war on terrorism,' *Foreign Policy*, 10 December 2015, available at: http://foreignpolicy.com/2015/12/10/actually-pakistan-is-winning-its-war-on-terror (accessed 2 May 2018); E. Haider, 'Counterinsurgency: The myth of Sisyphus?' in M. Yusuf (ed.), *Pakistan's Counter Challenge* (Washington, DC: Georgetown University Press, 2014), p. 78.

3 For a glimpse of this phenomenon, see Haider Imam, 'Pakistan two years after the APS massacre,' *Nation*, 17 December 2016.

4 A. Rashid, 'Viewpoint: Will Pakistan ever stamp out extremism,' *BBC News*, 1 February 2017, available at: www.bbc.co.uk/news/world-asia-38793330 (accessed 23 May 2018); A. Khattak, 'Back to private jihad?' *Nation*, 30 July 2016, and 'Reversal of NAP,' *Nation*, 11 June 2016; U.M. Younus, 'Are we really winning the war on terror?' *Express Tribune*, 20 November 2015.

5 M. Popovic, 'The perils of weak organization: Explaining loyalty and defection of militant organizations toward Pakistan,' *Studies in Conflict and Terrorism* 38:11 (2015): 919–37; T.V. Paul, *The Warrior State* (Karachi: Oxford University Press, 2014), p. 67; D.S. Markey, *No Exit from Pakistan: America's Tortured*

Relationship with Islamabad (Dehli: Cambridge University Press, 2014), p. 4; C. Gall, *The Wrong Enemy: America in Afghanistan, 2001–2014* (Boston, MA: Houghton Mifflin Harcourt, 2014); C.C. Fair, 'The militant challenge in Pakistan,' *Asia Policy* 11 (January 2011): 105–37.

6 M. Feyyaz, 'The discourse and study of terrorism in decolonised states: A case of Pakistan,' *Critical Studies on Terrorism* 9:3 (2016): 455–77.

7 C.C. Fair, *Fighting to the End: The Pakistan Army's Way of War* (Karachi: Oxford University Press, 2014); H. Abbas, *Militancy in Pakistan's Borderlands: Implications for the Nation and for Afghan Policy* (New York: Century Foundation, 2010); M.K. Mahsud, *The Battle for Pakistan: Militancy and Conflict in South Waziristan* (Washington, DC: New America Foundation, 2010); S. Nawaz, *FATA: A Most Dangerous Place* (Washington, DC: Center for Strategic and International Studies, 2009); D.S. Markey, *Securing Pakistan's Tribal Belt*, Council Special Report no. 36 (Washington, DC: Council on Foreign Relations, 2008).

8 Feyyaz, 'Discourse and study of terrorism.'

9 R. English, 'The future study of terrorism,' *European Journal of International Security* 1:2 (2016): 135–49; J.A. Sluka, 'The contribution of anthropology to critical terrorism studies,' in Richard Jackson, M.B. Smyth and J. Gunning (eds), *Critical Terrorism Studies: A New Research Agenda* (Abingdon, UK: Routledge, 2009), pp. 139, 152.

10 See 'Fatalities in terrorist violence in Pakistan 2003–2018,' South Asia Terrorism Portal website, [October 2018], available at: www.satp.org/satporgtp/countries/pakistan/database/casualties.htm (accessed 2 October 2018).

11 J. Argomaniz, O. Bures and C. Kaunert, 'A decade of EU counter-terrorism and intelligence: A critical assessment,' *Intelligence and National Security* 30:2–3 (2015), 191–206.

12 Yusuf, *Pakistan's Counter Challenge*, p. 5.

13 Leadership is included exclusively by this author; for details on the remaining parameters, see N. Morag, 'Measuring success in coping with terrorism: The Israeli case,' *Studies in Conflict and Terrorism* 28:4 (2005): 307–20.

14 Paul, *Warrior State*, pp. 45–8; P. Staniland, 'Explaining civil-military relations in complex political environments: India and Pakistan in comparative perspective,' *Security Studies* 17:2 (2008): 322–62; I. Talbot, *Provincial Politics and the Pakistan Movement: The Growth of the Muslim League in North-West and North-East India 1937–47* (Karachi: Oxford University Press, 1988); H.J. Morgenthau, 'Military illusions,' *New Republic* 134:12 (1956): 15–16.

15 Ishtiaq Ahmed, *Pakistan the Garrison State: Origins, Evolution, Consequences 1947–2011* (Karachi: Oxford University Press, 2013), pp. 73–8; Staniland, 'Explaining civil-military relations.' For a detailed account of the Radcliffe Commission, see A. Lamb, *Incomplete Partition: The Genesis of the Kashmir Dispute 1947–1948* (Rawalpindi, Pakistan: Services Book Club, 1991), pp. 81–3.

16 C. Jaffrelot, *The Pakistan Paradox: Instability and Resilience* (Haryana, India: Random House, 2015), p. 6; Ahmed, *Pakistan the Garrison State*, p. 65; A. Shah, *The Army and Democracy: Military Politics in Pakistan* (Cambridge, MA: Harvard University Press, 2014), pp. 40–2; A. Jalala, *The Struggle for Pakistan: A Muslim Homeland and Global Politics* (Cambridge, MA: Harvard University Press, 2014), pp. 68–9; M. Yusuf (ed.), *Insurgency and Counter-insurgency in South Asia: Through a Peacebuilding Lens* (Washington, DC:

United States Institute of Peace, 2014), pp. 25–6; S. Nawaz, *Crossed Swords: Paksitan, Its Army, and the Wars Within* (Oxford: Oxford University Press, 2008), p. 48; A.H. Dani, *History of Northern Areas of Pakistan* (Lahore: Sang-e-Meel, 2007); Victoria Schofield, *Kashmir in Conflict: India, Pakistan and the Unending War* (London: I.B. Tauris, 2000), p. 51; F.M. Khan, *The Story of the Pakistan Army* (Karachi: Oxford University Press, 1963), pp. 88–90; J. Korbel, *Danger in Kashmir* (Princeton, NJ: Princeton University Press, 1966), p. 95.

17 M. Razvi, *The Frontiers of Pakistan: A Study of Frontier Problems in Pakistan's Foreign Policy* (Karachi: Pakistan Institute of International Affairs, 1972).

18 Khan, *Story of the Pakistan Army*, p. 132.

19 K. Sarwar Hussain, *Kashmir Question* (Karachi: Pakistan Institute of International Affairs, 1966), p. 3; Khan, *Story of the Pakistan Army*, pp. 92, 96, 100; Korbel, *Danger in Kashmir*, pp. 93–6, 249–51, 256, 260–73.

20 Fair, *Fighting to the End*, p. 14.

21 *Ibid.*; S.P. Cohen, *The Idea of Pakistan* (Washington, DC: Brookings, 2004), p. 342.

22 See, for example, Cohen, *Idea of Pakistan*, p. 51; Lamb, *Incomplete Partition*, pp. 124, 136; P.I. Cheema, *Pakistan's Defence Policy 1947–58* (Lahore: Sang-e-Meel, 1998), pp. 86–7; A. Lamb, *Kashmir: A Dispute Legacy 1856–1990* (Karachi: Oxford University Press, 1992), p. 125.

23 Nawaz, *Crossed Swords*, pp. 205–6.

24 Ahmed, *Pakistan the Garrison State*, pp. 135–6, Nawaz, *Crossed Swords*, pp. 206–8.

25 M.A. Khan, *Friends not Masters* (Islamabad: Mr Books, 2006 [first published 1967]), pp. 169–72.

26 A. Gauhar, *Ayub Khan: Pakistan's First Military Ruler* (Lahore: Sang-e-Meel, 1998), pp. 320–1.

27 Cohen, *Idea of Pakistan*, p. 64; Khan, *Friends not Masters*, pp. 169–72; Lamb, *Kashmir*, pp. 252–60; W. Wilcox, 'Kashmir and the Indo-Pakistan War, 1965,' in Masuma Hasan (ed.), *Pakistan in a Changing World* (Karachi: Pakistan Institute of International Affairs, 1978), pp. 166–7, Josef, 337–40.

28 *Ibid.*

29 Ahmed, *Pakistan the Garrison State*, p. 135.

30 Nawaz, *Crossed Swords*, p. 206.

31 I. Talbot, *Pakistan: A New History* (Karachi: Oxford University Press, 2015), p. 88.

32 A. Rashid, *Descent into Chaos* (New York: Penguin Books, 2009), p. 111.

33 R.M. Khan, *Afghanistan and Pakistan: Conflict, Extremism, and Resistance to Modernity*, 2nd ed. (Karachi: Oxford University Press, 2012), p. 5.

34 'Baluch' or 'Baluchistan' was used prior to 1973 to denote this ethnicity residing in northwest/western Pakistan. The current constitutional usage is 'Baloch' or 'Balochistan'. Both are used, according to the historical period under discussion. See also Feisal Khan, 'Why borrow trouble for yourself and lend it to neighbors? Understanding the historical roots of Pakistan's Afghan policy,' *Asian Affairs: An American Review*, 37:4 (2010): 171–89.

35 A.H. Amin, 'Remembering our warriors: Babar 'the Great,' *Defence Journal* (April 2001), available at: www.defencejournal.com/2001/apr/babar.htm (accessed 11 May 2018).

36 Fair, 'Militant challenge in Pakistan.'

37 Khan, 'Why borrow trouble.'

38 Abbas, *Militancy in Pakistan's Borderlands.*

39 Jaffrelot, *Pakistan Paradox*, pp. 508–12.

40 Cohen, *Idea of Pakistan*, p. 228; I. Badhwar and T. Singh, 'Sikh terrorists: The Pakistan hand,' *India Today*, 15 May 1986.

41 K. Ahmed, 'South Asia's unresolved disputes,' *South Asian Journal* 7 (March 2005): 6–26; Khan, 'Why borrow trouble.'

42 H. Haqqani, *Magnificent Delusions* (New Delhi: Thompson India, 2013), pp. 272–4, 277–8, 281–2.

43 S. Tankel, 'Beyond FATA: Exploring the Punjabi militant threat to Pakistan,' *Terrorism and Political Violence* 28:1 (2016): 49–71; Ahmed, 'South Asia's unresolved disputes.'

44 Tankel, 'Beyond FATA.'

45 P. Swami, 'Failed threats and flawed fences: India's military responses to Pakistan's proxy war,' *India Review* 3:2 (2004): 147–70.

46 General V.P. Malik, *Kargil: From Surprise to Victory* (New Delhi: Harper Collins, 2006), pp. 263, 340–8.

47 K.B. Saeed, *Pakistan: The Formative Phase 1857–1947*, 2nd ed. (Karachi: Oxford University Press, 1969), pp. 105–6.

48 H. Abbas, *The Taliban Revival* (London: Yale University Press, 2014), p. 104.

49 For details see 'Resolution 154: Islam's position on extremism, radicalism, and terrorism,' *Amman Message* (Amman, Jordan, 2006) pp. 143–4; G. Ahmed, 'What is terrorism and what is not,' *Dawn*, 24 March 2005.

50 Newsdesk, 'Violence in Indian Kashmir is terrorism: Nisar,' *Express Tribune*, 4 August 2016; S. Yasmeen, 'Kashmir: The discourse in Pakistan,' *Economic and Political Weekly* 37:7 (2002): 611–13.

51 R.B. Rais, *Recovering the Frontier State: War, Ethnicity and State in Afghanistan* (London: Lexington Books, 2008), p. 15.

52 L. Dupree, *Afghanistan*, (Karachi: Oxford University Press, 2012 [first published 1973]), p. 491.

53 D. Ross and T. Vassefi, 'The forgotten history of Afghanistan–Pakistan relations,' *Yale Journal of International Affairs* (2012): 38–45; L. Montagno, 'The Pak-Afghan Détente,' *Asian Survey* 3:12 (1963): 616–24.

54 Paul, *Warrior State*, p. 67; Markey, *No Exit from Pakistan*, p. 4.

55 J. Levesque, 'Managing diversity in Pakistan: Nationalism, ethnic politics and cultural resistance,' book review, *South Asia Multidisciplinary Academic Journal* (online), available at: http://samaj.revues.org/3551 (accessed 2 May 2018).

56 K. Ahmed, *Sectarian War: Pakistan's Sunni–Shia Violence and its Links to the Middle East* (Oxford: Oxford University Press, 2011), p. xix.

57 M. Feyyaz, 'Constructing Baloch militancy in Pakistan,' *South Asian Journal* 40 (April–June 2013), pp. 114–35; M. Axmann, *Back to the Future: The Khanate of Kalat and the Genesis of Baloch Nationalism 1915–1955* (Karachi: Oxford University Press, 2008), pp. 226–8, 234, 286–7; A. Khan, *Politics of Identity: Ethnic Nationalism and the State in Pakistan* (New Delhi: Sage India, 2005), pp. 116–18.

58 *Ibid.*; B. Cloughley, *War, Coups and Terror* (Barnsley, UK: Pen and Sword Military, 2008), p. 19; Khan, *Story of the Pakistan Army*, p. 191.

59 Cloughley, *War, Coups and Terror*, pp. 18–19.

60 E. Murphy and A. Tamana, 'State terrorism and the military in Pakistan,' in E. Murphy, R. Jackson and S. Poynting (eds), *Contemporary State Terrorism: Theory and Practice* (London: Routledge, 2010), pp. 48–67; Ahmed, *Pakistan* *the Garrison State*, p. 192. See also F.Q. Quaderi, *Bangladesh Genocide and World Press* (Dhaka: Alaxandira, 1972), p. 19.

61 Major General H.A. Qureshi, *The 1971 Indo-Pakistan War: A Soldier's Narrative* (Karachi: Oxford University Press, 2012 [originally published 2002]), pp. 18, 32–3, 36–7.

62 Quaderi, *Bangladesh Genocide*, p. 175.

63 A.P. Schmid, *The Routledge Handbook of Terrorism Research* (London: Routledge, 2011), p. 600; S.V.R. Nasr, *The Vanguard of the Islamic Revolution: The Jama'at-i-Islamic of Pakistan* (Los Angles: University of California Press, 1994), p. 169.

64 Cohen, *Idea of Pakistan*, p. 100.

65 Khan, *Politics of Identity*, pp. 121, 126.

66 See Study of Terrorism and Responses to Terrorism (START), *Global Terrorism Database*, University of Maryland, available at: www.start.umd.edu/gtd/ (searching under 'Pakistan' for the years 1970–80).

67 S. Fayyaz, 'Responding to terrorism: Pakistan's anti-terrorism laws,' *Perspectives on Terrorism* 2:6 (2008): 10–19.

68 S.S. Raza, 'The anti-terrorism legal regime of Pakistan and the global paradigm of security: A genealogical and comparative analysis,' *Review of Human Rights* (October 2016): 1–38, available at: http://reviewhumanrights.com/anti-terrorism-legal-regime-of-pakistan/ (accessed 6 May 2018).

69 *Ibid.*

70 S. Fayyaz, *Responding to Terrorism: Pakistan's Anti-terrorism Laws* (Islamabad: Pakistan Institute of Peace Studies, 2008).

71 The author consulted veteran journalists and searched the accessible media archives in Lahore.

72 A. Rafiq, *Sunni Deobandi-Shi'i Sectarian Violence in Pakistan: Explaining the Resurgence since 2007* (Washington, DC: Middle East Institute, 2014); H. Abbas, *Pakistan's Drift into Extremism: Allah, the Army and America's War on Terror* (New York: M.E. Sharpe, 2005), p. 89; S. Alam, 'Iran–Pakistan relations: Political and strategic dimensions,' *Strategic Analysis* 28:4 (2004): 526–45.

73 Jaffrelot, *Pakistan Paradox,* pp. 488–90; International Crisis Group (ICG), *Reforming the Judiciary in Pakistan*, Asia Report no. 160 (Brussels: ICG, 2008).

74 Nasr, 'Islam, the state and the rise of sectarian militancy,' in Jaffrelot (ed.), *Pakistan: Nation, Nationalism and the State* (Lahore: Vanguard Books, 2005 [2002]), pp. 87–8.

75 *Ibid.*

76 M.A. Rana, *A to Z of Jehadi Organisations in Pakistan* (Lahore: Mashal Books, 2005).

77 M.A. Qadeer, *Pakistan: Social and Cultural Transformations in a Muslim Nation* (Abingdon, UK: Routledge, 2006), p. 174.

78 Talbot, *Pakistan*, pp. 162–3.

79 Jaffrelot, *Pakistan Paradox*, p. 489; Fair, *Fighting to the End*, p. 244.

80 A. Malik, *Political Survival in Pakistan: Beyond Ideology* (Abingdon, UK: Routledge, 2011), pp. 137–8.

81 'Zia had founded MQM, says Beg,' *Indian Express*, 28 May 2007, available at: http://archive.indianexpress.com/news/zia-had-founded-mqm-says-beg/32043 (accessed 1 May 2018); C. Sen, 'Pakistan's Beirut,' a review of

Karachi: A Terror Capital in the Making by Wilson Jhon, *Asia Times Online*, 17 January 2004, available at: www.atimes.com/atimes/South_Asia/FA17Df07.html (accessed 14 June 2018).

82 O. Bennett-Jones, 'Altaf Hussain, the notorious MQM leader who swapped Pakistan for London,' *Guardian*, 29 July 2013.

83 L. Saeed, S.H. Syed and R.P. Martin, 'Historical patterns of terrorism in Pakistan,' *Defense and Security Analysis* 30:3 (2014): 209–29.

84 Fayyaz, *Responding to Terrorism*.

85 *Ibid*.

86 Tankel, 'Beyond FATA.'

87 M. Sageman, *Understanding Terror Networks* (Philadelphia, PA: University of Pennsylvania Press, 2004), pp. 47–8.

88 'In Musharraf's words: "A day of reckoning,"' *New York Times*, 12 January 2002.

89 A.K. Behuria, 'Sunni–Shia relations in Pakistan: The widening divide, *Strategic Analysis* 28 (2004): 157–76.

90 M.A. Rana, 'Taliban insurgency in FATA: Evolution and prospects,' in Yusuf, *Insurgency and Counterinsurgency*, pp. 107–29.

91 S. Tankel, 'Beyond the double game: Lessons from Pakistan's approach to Islamist militancy,' *Journal of Strategic Studies*, available at: http://dx.doi.org/10.1080/01402390.2016.1174114 (accessed 6 May 2018); P. Musharraf, *In the Line of Fire* (London: Simon and Schuster, 2006), p. 201–5; O. Jones, *Pakistan: Eye of the Storm* (New Haven, CT: Yale University Press, 2002).

92 A.J. Tellis, *Pakistan and the War on Terror: Conflicted Goals, Compromised Performance* (Washington, DC: Carnegie Endowment for International Peace, 2008), p. 3; see also *BBC News*, 'Musharraf rallies Pakistan,' *BBC News*, 19 September 2001, available at: http://news.bbc.co.uk/2/hi/not_in_website/syndication/monitoring/media_reports/1553542.stm (accessed 7 May 2018).

93 'Major incidents of terrorism-related violence in Pakistan, 1988–2004,' South Asia Terrorism Portal website, available at: www.satp.org/satporgtp/countries/pakistan/database/majorinc2004.htm (accessed 3 May 2018).

94 Popovic, 'Perils of weak organization.'

95 *Ibid*.

96 'Pakistan timeline – 2001,' South Asia Terrorism Portal website, available at www.satp.org/Timelines.aspx?countries=pakistan (accessed 8 May 2018).

97 See Rashid, *Descent into Chaos*, pp. 117–19; C.H. Kennedy, 'Pakistan in 2004: Running very fast to stay in the same place,' *Asian Survey* 45:1 (January–February 2005): 5–111. See also S. Sengupta, 'Pakistan's leader faces increasing political challenges,' *New York Times*, 18 August 2006, p. 3; S. Fayyaz, 'Pakistan response towards terrorism: A case study of Musharraf regime' (PhD dissertation, University of Birmingham, 2010), p. 2; R. Srinivasan and J. Ray, 'Few Pakistanis perceive benefits from alliance with US,' *Gallup*, 3 October 2008, available at: www.gallup.com/poll/110926/Few-Pakistanis-Perceive-Benefits-From-Alliance-US.aspx (discussing a Gallup opinion poll conducted in June 2008).

98 Khan, *Afghanistan and Pakistan*, pp. 122–3; P. Hoodbhoy, 'Can the left become relevant to Islamic Pakistan?' *New Politics* XIII-1:49 (2010), available at: http://newpol.org/content/can-left-become-relevant-islamic-pakistan (accessed 24 May 2018).

99 Rashid, *Descent into Chaos*, p. 79; A.S. Zaeef, *My Life with Taliban* (Gurgaon, India: Hechette, 2010), pp. 147–8, 152.

100 The generals who were accused of being ideologically sympathetic to the Taliban and al Qaeda include Gen. Hamid Gul and Gen. Mirza Aslam Beg; for more detail, see D. Gartenstein-Ross, 'Musharraf gets tough,' *Weekly Standard*, 16 July 2007, available at: www.defenddemocracy.org/media-hit/musharraf-gets-tough/#sthash.JTOeaSi7.dpuf (accessed 4 May 2018).

101 Popovic, 'Perils of weak organization.'

102 ICG, *Reforming the Judiciary in Pakistan*; Tankel, 'Beyond FATA.'

103 Popovic, 'Perils of weak organization.'

104 Author's interview of Akhtar Ali Shah, additional inspector general of police, Khyber Pakhtunkhwa, 26 May 2016, Mardan, Pakistan; Feyyaz, 'Political economy of Tehrik-i-Taliban Swat,' *PIPS Journal of Peace and conflict Studies* 4:3 (2011): 37–60.

105 H. Abbas, 'Defining the Punjabi Taliban network,' *CTC Sentinel* 2:4 (2009): 1–4; Rashid, *Descent into Chaos*, pp. 230–2, 272.

106 Cloughley, *War, Coups and Terror*, pp. 164–6, 182–4.

107 N. Fiaz, 'Policy intervention in FATA: Why discourse matters,' *Journal of Strategic Security* 5:1 (2012): 49–62.

108 B. Woodward, *Bush at War* (London: Pocket Books, 2003), pp. 58–9; Abbas, *Pakistan's Drift into Extremism*, pp. 221–2.

109 Lieutenant General Mohmmad Jan Orakzi, commander of the Peshawar Corps, himself from tribal areas, briefed the tribes.

110 M.J. Orakzi, 'Situation in FATA: Causes, consequences and the way forward,' *Policy Perspectives* 6:1 (2009): 27–45.

111 A. Ahmed, *The Thistle and the Drone: How America's War on Terror Became a Global War on Tribal Islam* (Lahore: Vanguard Books, 2013), p. 69.

112 Rashid, *Descent into Chaos*, pp. 90–4, 240.

113 A. Basit, M.A. Rānā and S. Sial, *Dynamics of Taliban Insurgency in FATA* (Islamabad: PIPS, 2010), p. 60.

114 Abbas, *Taliban Revival*, p. 104.

115 M. Norell, 'The Taliban and the Muttahida Majlis-e-Amal (MMA),' *China and Eurasia Forum Quarterly* 5:3 (2007): 61–82.

116 Fayyaz, 'Pakistan response towards terrorism,' pp. 278–9; A.K. Behuria, 'Fighting the Taliban: Pakistan at war with itself,' *Australian Journal of International Affairs* 61:4 (2007): 529–43; W. Maley, 'The 'War against Terrorism' in South Asia,' *Contemporary South Asia* 12:2 (2003): 203–17.

117 Norell, 'Taliban.'

118 Basit et al., *Dynamics of Taliban Insurgency*, p. 60.

119 S. Qadir, 'The state's response to the Pakistani Taliban onslaught,' in Yusuf, *Insurgency and Counterinsurgency*, pp. 131–66.

120 S.H. Tajik, 'Analysis of peace agreements with militants and lessons for the future,' *Conflict and Peace Studies* 4:1 (2011): 1–18; K.A. Kronstadt and B. Vaughn, *Terrorism in South Asia*, CRS Report for Congress RL32259 (2004), available at: http://www.fas.org/irp/crs/RL32259.pdf (accessed 2 May 2018).

121 T. Masood, 'Pakistan's fight against terrorism,' *Defence Against Terrorism Review* 4:1 (2012): 13–30.

122 Qadir, 'State's response.'

123 For example, the Special Services Group has been involved in low-intensity operations throughout its history, i.e. from 1956. See S. Jones and C. Fair, *Counter Insurgency in Pakistan* (Santa Monica, CA: RAND, 2010), p. 38.
124 Qadir, 'State's response,' pp. 131–59.
125 Fayyaz, 'Pakistan response towards terrorism,' pp. 132–3.
126 Qadir, 'State's response,' pp. 136–7.
127 Jones and Fair, *Counter Insurgency in Pakistan*, pp. 34–6, 43–4; P.I. Cheema, 'Challenges facing a counter-militant campaign in Pakistan's FATA,' *NBR Analysis* 19:3 (2008): 83–90.
128 Author's interview with Brigadier Shahid Afzal (retired), former chief of staff of 11 Corps.
129 Ahmed, *Thistle and the Drone*, p. 69.
130 Haider, 'Counterinsurgency,' p. 72.
131 *Ibid.*
132 Fayyaz, 'Pakistan response towards terrorism,' pp. 279–81.
133 See C. Woods, 'The day 69 children died,' *Express Tribune*, 12 August 2011; 'Fidayeen (suicide squad) attacks in Pakistan,' 2006 (serial 6), South Asia Terrorism Portal website (n.d.), available at: www.satp.org/satporgtp/countries/pakistan/database/Fidayeenattack.htm (accessed 5 May 2018).
134 K. Iqbal, *The Making of Pakistani Human Bombs* (London: Lexington Books, 2015), pp. 7, 57, 71.
135 Ilyas Kashmiri was a Pakistani Kashmiri fighter. He created 313 brigade in 1991 for operations inside IHK. See A. Dolnik and K. Iqbal, *Negotiating the Siege of the Lal Masjid* (Karachi: Oxford University Press, 2016), pp. 229–30; Jaffrelot, *Pakistan Paradox*, p. 489; Fair, *Fighting to the End*, p. 512.
136 Feyyaz, 'Conceptualising terrorism trend patterns in Pakistan: An empirical perspective,' *Perspectives on Terrorism* 7:1 (2013): 73–102.
137 Iqbal, *Making of Pakistani Human Bombs*, pp. 6–7; H. Abbas, 'A profile of Tehrik-i-Taliban Pakistan,' *CTC Sentinel* 1:2 (2008): 1–4. For details on casualties, see 'Fidayeen (suicide squad) attacks in Pakistan: 2002–18,' South Asia Terrorism Portal website, n.d., available at www.satp.org/Datasheets.aspx?countries=pakistan (accessed 11 May 2018).
138 Dolnik and Iqbal, *Negotiating the Siege*, pp. 227–8; A. Mir, *Talibanization of Pakistan: 9/11 to 26/11* (New Dehli: Pentagon Security International, 2009), pp. xii–xiii, xviii.
139 Tankel, 'Beyond the double game.'
140 A. Siddiqa, 'Pakistan's counterterrorism strategy: Separating friends from enemies,' *Washington Quarterly* 34:1 (2011): 149–62; K. Ahmed, 'The fiction of "good" and "bad" Taliban,' *Friday Times*, 9–15 November 2012; H. Haqqani, *Pakistan between Mosque and Military* (Lahore: Vanguard Books, 2005), pp. 304–5.
141 Fayyaz, 'Pakistan response towards terrorism,' p. 302.
142 The participant observation of the author during two years' stay (2006–8) in North Waziristan as a brigade commander.
143 Tankel, 'Beyond FATA.'
144 Abbas, *Taliban Revival*, pp. 116–19; Haqqani, *Pakistan between Mosque*, pp. 304–5.
145 N. Ahmed, *Pakistan's Counter-Terrorism Strategy and Its Implications for Domestic, Regional and International Security*, FMSH-WP-2014-59

(Paris: Foundation Maison des Sciences de l'Homme, 2014), available at: https://halshs.archives-ouvertes.fr/halshs-00937552/document (accessed 11 May 2018).

146 Murphy and Tamana, 'State terrorism,' p. 61.

147 Feyyaz, 'Global war on terrorism in South Asia,' *Pakistan Horizon* 62:4 (2009): 39–53.

148 M.J. Nelson, 'Pakistan in 2008: Moving beyond Musharraf,' *Asian Survey* 49:1 (2009): 16–27.

149 Mir, *Talibanization*, pp. 397–8; Abbas, *Militancy in Pakistan's Borderlands*.

150 N.U. Haq and Y. Imtiaz, *Swat Peace Accord* (Islamabad: Islamabad Policy Research Institute, 2009); CNN World, 'Swat Valley: Ski resort to Taliban stronghold,' *CNN World*, 22 April 2009, available at: http://edition.cnn.com/2009/WORLD/asiapcf/04/22/pakistan.qa/index.html (accessed 30 April 2018).

151 Abbas, *Militancy in Pakistan's Borderlands*; B. Arnoldy and I. Ahmed, 'Pakistan's tenuous gains on Taliban,' *Christian Science Monitor*, 9 March 2009, available at: www.csmonitor.com/World/Asia-South-Central/2009/0309/p01s02-wosc.html (accessed 4 March 2018).

152 Saeed et al., 'Historical patterns of terrorism.'

153 Mir, *Talibanization*, p. 417.

154 Based on the author's interview with Dr Feriha Peracha, CEO of the Social Welfare Academics and Training organization (SWAaT), a Lahore-based charity working to prevent and counter violent extremism in Pakistan, on 23 October 2017. Also see F. Peracha, R.R. Khan, A. Ayub and K. Aijaz, 'Pakistan: Lessons from deradicalising young Taliban fighters,' in Tony Blair Faith Foundation, *How to Prevent: Extremism and Policy Options*, 48–55, available at: www.gcerf.org/wp-content/uploads/TBFF_How-to-Prevent_Global-Perspectives-Vol-2.pdf (accessed 12 May 2018).

155 T. Hussain, 'Cabinet approves NACTA bill for formation of anti-terrorism body,' *Pakistan Today*, 29 November 2012; see also Parliament act no. XIX of 2013, available at www.na.gov.pk/uploads/documents/1364795170_139.pdf (accessed 13 May 2018); M. Zaidi, 'What Nacta can do,' *Express Tribune*, 17 March 2013, available at: http://tribune.com.pk/story/521863/what-nacta-can-do (accessed 10 December 2017).

156 M.A. Rana, 'A review of national internal security policy (2013–18),' Pak Institute for Peace Studies (PIPS) website, 21 January 2013, available at: www.pakpips.com/article/2897 (accessed 14 June 2018).

157 S. Shams, 'The clash of narratives Swat military operation against the Taliban,' Working Paper Series #120 (Islamabad: Pakistan: Sustainable Development Policy Institute, 2011); Shuja Nawaz, 'The battle for Pakistan,' *Wall Street Journal*, 19 October 2009, available at: www.wsj.com/articles/SB10001424052748704500604574482973468887970 (accessed 14 June 2018).

158 Fiaz, 'Policy intervention in FATA.'

159 Z. Hussain, *The Scorpion's Tail: The Relentless Rise of Islamic Militants in Pakistan – and How It Threatens America* (New York: Free Press, 2010), pp. 148–50.

160 Shahbaz wanted to cut a deal with TTP as long they didn't conduct operations in Punjab. See 'CM Shahbaz wants Taliban to spare Punjab,' *Dawn*, 15 March 2010, available at: www.dawn.com/news/857697/cm-shahbaz-wants-taliban-to-spare-punjab (accessed 11 May 2018).

161 E. Friedland, 'The canonization of an Islamist killer,' Clarion Project website, 28 December 2016, available at: www.clarionproject.org/analysis/canonization-islamist-killer (accessed 6 January 2018).

162 Q. Butt, 'Shrinking space: K-P govt shelves plans for textbook reforms, JUI, JI protested against revised, secular syllabus,' *Express Tribune*, 6 April 2012.

163 *Daily Mail* Reporter, 'First the tears, now the anger: Pakistanis burn U.S. flags as backlash over Bin Laden's death grows,' *Daily Mail*, 4 May 2011, available at: www.dailymail.co.uk/news/article-1383011/Osama-Bin-Laden-dead-Pakistanis-burn-US-flags-backlash-grows.html (accessed 11 November 2017); R. Crilly, 'Osama bin Laden: Pakistan politicians mourn al-Qaeda leader,' *Telegraph*, 11 May 2011, available at: www.telegraph.co.uk/news/worldnews/al-qaeda/8506639/Osama-bin-Laden-Pakistan-politicians-mourn-al-Qaeda-leader.html (accessed 2 May 2018).

164 M. Feyyaz, 'Why Pakistan does not have a counter terrorism narrative,' *Journal of Strategic Security* 8:1 (2015): 63–78.

165 O. Guerin, 'Pakistan election: Sharif 'would end' war on terror role,' *BBC News*, 8 May 2013, available at: www.bbc.co.uk/news/world-asia-22460355 (accessed 14 June 2018); 'Imran Khan vows to end US-led war on terror in Pakistan,' *India Today*, 22 April 2013, available at: http://indiatoday.intoday.in/story/imran-khan-vows-to-end-us-led-war-on-terror-in-pakistan/1/266960.html (accessed 14 June 2018).

166 R. Jan, 'Taliban violence mars Pakistan's elections,' AEI Critical Threats Project website, 17 May 2013, available at: www.criticalthreats.org/pakistan/jan-taliban-violence-mars-pakistans-election-may-17–2013 (accessed 13 April 2017).

167 R. Jan, 'The future of Pakistan: What to expect from Nawaz Sharif's new government,' AEI Critical Threats Project website, 31 July 2013, available at: www.criticalthreats.org/analysis/the-future-of-pakistan-what-to-expect-from-nawaz-sharifs-new-government (accessed 11 May 2018).

168 Staff Reporter, 'Taliban had agreed to accept state writ, claims Fazl,' *Dawn*, 7 July 2014, available at: www.dawn.com/news/1117576 (accessed 7 February 2018); M. Golovnina and A. Ali, 'Peace talks between Pakistan and Taliban collapse after killings,' *Reuters*, 7 February 2014, available at: www.reuters.com/article/2014/02/17/us-pakistan-talibanidUSBREA1G0MP20140217 (accessed 7 October 2017).

169 Government of Pakistan, Ministry of Interior, *National Internal Security Policy: 2014–2018* (Author, n.d.), p. 85, available at: https://nacta.gov.pk/wp-content/uploads/2017/08/National-Internal-Security-Policy-2014.pdf (accessed 2 December 2017).

170 M. Yusaf, 'Flaws in INSP,' *Dawn*, 1 April 2014.

171 NACTA, 'National Action Plan, 2014,' NACTA website, 24 August 2017, last updated 12 October 2017, available at: https://nacta.gov.pk/nap-2014/. (accessed 14 June 2018).

172 Khattak, 'Reversal of NAP.'

173 I. Khan, 'National Inaction Plan,' *Dawn*, 28 August 2016.

174 'Punjabi Taliban chief unlikely to be tried in military courts,' *News*, 17 January 2015.

175 'Raheel Sharif recounts Pakistan's war against terrorism: "There is a method to this madness,"' *Dawn*, 17 January 2017; 'Gen Raheel stresses need for govt cooperation to counter terrorism,' *Dawn*, 10 November 2015.

176 See, e.g., 'Nation's resolve to eliminate terrorism cannot be deterred, says Nawaz,' *Express Tribune,* 23 February 2017; 'Pakistan has defeated terrorism, now in consolidation phase: Gen Qamar Bajwa,' *Dawn*, 29 December 2016; '2016 to see end of terrorism – Army Chief,' *Express Tribune*, 4 June 2016.

177 See 'Major incidents of terrorism related violence in Pakistan – 2018,' South Asia Terrorism Portal website, available at: www.satp.org/Datasheets.aspx?countries=pakistan (accessed 10 May 2018).

178 Q. Ali, 'Who is Khadim Hussain Rizvi?' *Dawn*, 3 December 2017.

179 A. Nasir, 'Thank you, Justice Isa,' *Dawn*, 17 December 2016; Younus, 'Are we really winning.'

180 *Ibid.*; see also Rana, *Pakistan Security Report*, p. 83.

181 F. Husain, 'Rise of the Shahbaz League,' *Express Tribune*, 22 October 2017; U. Jamal, 'After Panama papers scandal, Pakistani democracy's fate may be in the military's hands,' *Diplomat*, 28 May 2016.

182 This observation is based on insights gained during a prolonged discussion of the writer with various stakeholders in criminal justice dispensation of the Punjab Government, on 23 October 2017.

183 'Raheel Sharif recounts.'

184 See PIPS, 'Key points', in 'Pakistan security report 2017 full report,' PIPS website, 6 January 2018, available at: www.pakpips.com/article/book/pakistan-security-report-2017 (accessed 15 May 2018).

185 See R. Bole, 'Can Pakistani technology fight Pakistani terror?' *Diplomat*, 3 August 2017.

186 M. Becker, 'Why violence abates: Imposed and elective declines in terrorist attacks,' *Terrorism and Political Violence* 29:2 (2017): 215–35.

PART IV

Latin and South America

8

When the shoe doesn't fit: Brazilian approaches to terrorism and counterterrorism in the post-9/11 era

Jorge M. Lasmar

Introduction

More than ever, specialists are turning to regional specificities when trying to understand how particular terrorist groups think and act. Terrorist groups commonly adopt radicalized transnational ideologies and rhetoric. However, in most cases, we see that terrorist groups not only inscribe their local grievances onto the larger globalized rhetoric but also adapt their modus operandi to the regional realities of their particular theatre(s) of action.

The same can be said about governmental responses to terrorism. It is absolutely essential to understand that specific local grievances and distinct regional socio-economic realities influence the behaviour of terrorist groups. But it is also important to acknowledge that – in the terrorist mind – different countries play distinct roles in their overall struggle. Transnational terrorist groups choose specific countries to be the direct targets of their violent activity; still other countries are seen as targets for their political and ideological messages, while others are used to conduct supporting activities (financing, recruiting, etc.). In the same vein, national governments also face a vast array of specific local constraints that include, amongst other things, the cultural acceptance (or lack thereof) for specific anti-terrorism measures; domestic bureaucratic and political limitations; and, last but not least, the availability of relevant material and human resources. This is why it is vital for any anti- and counterterrorism approach to take into consideration the local realities and regional specificities in order to avoid 'one size fits all' responses.

With these parameters in mind, the reality of Brazilian counterterrorism (CT) makes for an interesting case study. At first glance and rather misleadingly, Brazil is not directly threatened by terrorism – transnational, international or domestic – and has consistently chosen to remain on the periphery of key debates on the issue.[1] In fact, most Brazilians themselves think of terrorism as a distant and even exotic reality. This (mis)perception is a direct result of the general view that international terrorists are not a local threat due to Brazil's pacifist nature and a foreign policy that overwhelmingly leans towards appeasement. Over the last thirty years, the country has not suffered a single high-profile terrorist attack. The *Global Terrorism Index* regularly categorizes Brazil among the countries with the lowest risk or impact from terrorist activities.[2] Even for those who question Brazil's pacifist nature, it is organized crime and drug trafficking – and not terrorism – that represent its chief security threats. This preoccupation with organized crime and drug trafficking is undoubtedly justifiable. In a recent report published by the United Nations, Brazil was responsible for 11.4 per cent of all assassinations in the world in 2012. In other words, there were 56,337 registered assassinations in Brazil that year – a figure four *times* higher than the overall world average.[3] However, although Brazil may have been free from terrorist attacks thus far, it is neither free from the presence of terrorist groups/individuals nor exempt from future attacks. Thus, Brazil faces both domestic and international challenges to its CT policies.

Herein lies an interesting contradiction. On the one hand, Brazilian policymakers are very proud of its skilful foreign policy, which, having successfully 'insulated' Brazil from international conflicts, ensures that the country is not involved in any violent conflicts outside its borders. As a result, having being supposedly insulated from international conflicts and security issues, Brazil's attention and resources have been traditionally directed towards issues within its own borders. However, at the same time, Brazil has been woefully ineffective in tackling its serious domestic violence and insecurity issues. One of the side effects of this paradox is a concrete lack of both a systematic strategy for countering international terrorism and a dearth of institutional and legal resources to address this issue. Nevertheless, as a result of mounting susceptibility to terrorist groups and individuals operating within its own territory and/or against its interests abroad, Brazil finds itself under increasing international pressure to become more active and aware in the fight against international terrorism, especially with regard to creating legal anti-terror instruments. The consequence is a sharply divided – and somewhat schizophrenic – governmental approach. The Brazilian Government is caught between those who strongly advocate the criminalization of acts of terrorism and those who strongly deny the existence of any terrorist threat within Brazilian territory and thus argue for the superfluity of any such legislation. As will be discussed below, this resistance can be partly explained by the presence of former leftist guerrilla fighters in the highest echelons of the current administration, many of whom were indeed categorized as terrorists and even tortured while fighting against the Brazilian military dictatorship (1964–89). Nonetheless, other local factors such as the daunting legal and bureaucratic structure, the chronic lack of material and human resources, the persistent lack of knowledge on the subject, and even the ever-present threat of violent organized crime are all also important elements that have a hand in shaping Brazil's approach to CT.

To understand the reality of Brazilian CT and the reasons underpinning the contradiction described above, this chapter will start by describing the reality of post-9/11 terrorism in Brazil. Next, it will go on to delineate the current scenario of Brazilian CT, by describing first the legal framework of Brazilian CT and then its institutional design. Having provided that critical background, this chapter will proceed to discuss the key historical and political factors which shape and/or limit Brazil's CT policies. Finally, it concludes by considering the anti-terror draft legislation that is currently under discussion in the Brazilian Congress.

The reality of post-9/11 international terrorism in Brazil

The widespread perception that Brazil is immune to terrorism could not be more misleading. A significant number of Brazilian policymakers have, time and again, demonstrated difficulty in understanding that the lack of terrorist attacks does not necessarily equate to the absence of terrorist activities, or indeed translate into immunity against future attacks. Partially, this misperception results directly from a broader lack of understanding of how terrorism works in reality. Many legislators in Brazil fail to understand that a terrorist attack is not an isolated event but rather the result of a long chain of interconnected planned actions. This (mis)understanding is further enhanced by two other local particularities. Firstly, many sectors of the Brazilian administration have adopted an attitude of 'denial' by publicly refuting the existence of any international terrorist activity in Brazil as well as strongly reacting against any claims to the contrary.[4] Secondly, at the time of writing, Brazil did not legally consider terrorism a self-standing crime, nor did it have consistent laws addressing the subject. Thus, over the past few years, several cases which were actually related to international terrorism had been perforce formally investigated under the guise of other crimes or administrative offences such as document forgery, racism or illegal immigration, making it difficult to identify them specifically as terrorism-related cases.

Nevertheless, despite these frequent denials there is growing evidence that a number of international-terrorism-related activities in fact have occurred, and continue to occur, within Brazilian territory. It is known, for example, that on several occasions the US federal police (FBI) has warned the Brazilian authorities of terrorist-related activities in Brazil.[5] Likewise, publicly available US Government documents provide de facto operational cooperation with the Brazilian Federal Police in the arrest and monitoring of individuals linked to international terrorist groups, in the sharing of evidence, and even in executing joint operations.[6] Similarly, a careful assessment of investigations undertaken by the Brazilian Federal Police as well as of public statements made by government authorities clearly point to the existence of terrorism-related activities in Brazil.

In fact, this is not a new phenomenon. Evidence shows that since the 1980s several Shia individuals, allegedly linked to the Iranian Government, have engaged in radicalization and recruitment activities within Brazil. It is known, for example, that in May 1984, an Iranian named Mohsen Rabbani (often considered to be the mastermind of several terrorist attacks) sent another Iranian, Mullah Mohamed Taghi Tabatabaei Einaki, to Brazil. During his stay, both the Iraqi and the Saudi Arabian ambassador to Brazil formally accused Einaki of recruiting individuals to join the Iranian terrorist network in cities such as São Paulo, Rio de Janeiro, and Curitiba.[7] The Federal Police investigated and eventually expelled Einaki from Brazil. It is worth noting that he was formally expelled under the charge of 'engaging in political activities different from those declared when entering the country',[8] even though the expulsion was, in reality, motivated by suspicions of his involvement with the Lebanese Hizbullah.[9] Einaki's presence in Brazil and his relationship with Rabbani have also been linked to the preparations for the terrorist attacks on the Israeli Embassy in Buenos Aires in 1992 and the suicide attack on the Israel Mutual Association–Argentina (AMIA) in 1994.[10] Shortly before his death, the Special Prosecutor Alberto Nisman released a report connecting the individuals involved in the attacks in Argentina with Brazil. According to Nisman, intelligence reports revealed that on 2 August 1994 Rabbani met with a Brazilian named Ghazi Iskhandar, who was allegedly connected to the Lebanese Hizbullah.[11] Similarly, the Brazilian press reported that another Brazilian, Rodrigo Jalloul, was the right-hand man of Rabbani and assisted him in his clandestine activities in Brazil.[12] These cases were not isolated incidents. The AMIA case investigation points to the continuity of extremist activities within Brazil. Nisman's reports also reveal that the Brazilian Federal Police have been consistently aware of the presence of group members from Hizbullah, Hamas, Islamic Jihad and Al-Islamiyah Gamat in the states of São Paulo, Paraná and even in the Distrito Federal (Federal District). These reports also mention that Interpol in Brasilia has been aware that Hizbullah members in São Paulo[13] have been engaged in procuring finances for the group.[14]

In much the same vein, it is known that both the Brazilian Intelligence Agency (ABIN) and the Federal Police investigated Khalid Sheikh Mohammed's visit to Brazil in 1995. Currently held in Guantanamo Bay, Sheikh Mohammed has not only been identified as the mastermind behind the 9/11 attacks but has also been linked to various other al Qaeda plots between 1993 and 2003. These include the plan to assassinate Pope John Paul II during his visit to Manila; the (in)famous Bojinka plot, which hoped to trigger the almost simultaneous explosion of twelve US-bound commercial flights; the attempt by Richard Reid to detonate a shoe bomb mid-flight to the United States and the horrific Bali bombings in 2002. According to the *9/11 Commission Report,* Sheikh Mohammed visited the city of Foz do Iguaçu (near the border with Argentina and Paraguay) in 1995 to meet with a contact given to him by Mohamed Atef (aka Abu Hafs), who was at the time the head of al Qaeda's Operational Branch.[15]

The Foz do Iguaçu incident helped construct the myth of the tri-border area (i.e., the border area between Argentina, Brazil and Paraguay) as a lawless safe haven for criminal organizations and terrorist groups alike. Even though there are various reports about organized crime in the region, in reality, the status of the tri-border as the national capital of terrorism remains highly questionable, albeit it is still a commonly held belief in many circles.[16] However, it is worth emphasizing that Brazilian intelligence and police officers who have served in the region have both publicly and privately denied, and consistently so, the presence of any terrorist activity in the region.[17] Regarding local crime, recent operations by the Brazilian police have increased security in the region. Local police operations have also resulted in the establishment of a special maritime police unit and the creation of an independent border and a drone operations unit. The outcome has been the movement of criminal activities to other, more porous, border areas along the Paraná River and Lake Itaipu.[18] However, as discussed below, most terrorism-related activities in Brazil have been located outside this region.

While most of the limited academic research on the topic of terrorism in Brazil focuses upon the triple border area, empirical evidence demonstrates that the problem of terrorism in Brazil extends well beyond this region. The Panorama Operation illustrates the geographical distribution of terrorism within Brazil rather well. This operation was directed towards identifying and detaining extremists with links to known foreign terrorist organizations,[19] and took place in the states of Paraná and Mato Grosso, in southern and western Brazil, on 7 June 2005. At the time, the Federal Police issued twenty-eight arrest warrants and detained nineteen extremists led by the Lebanese Jihad Chaim Baalbaki and the Jordanian Sael Basheer Yhaya Atari. Amongst those arrested, nine were caught in Foz do Iguaçu, four were picked up in Curitiba, four in Paranaguá, one in Matinhos and one in Cuiabá. However, due to the lack of specific legislation these individuals could not be charged with terrorism or terror-related offences under Brazilian law. Thus, all detainees had to be prosecuted for crimes and offences other than terrorism – for example, the use of forged visas and airline tickets, credit card fraud, mobile-phone cloning and the illegal use of mobile phones, smuggling, document forgery, illegal trade in firearms, and so on. In another operation in 2007, the Federal Police arrested a Sunni extremist who was suspected of supporting terrorism in the southern Brazilian state of Santa Catarina. He was detained and deported on the administrative charge of 'failure to declare funds when entering the country'.

The handful of examples cited above clearly demonstrate that individuals linked to extremist groups such as al Qaeda, Hizbullah and Al-Islamiyah Gamat are not only extant in Brazil but have also been consistently reported and investigated. The strongest evidence of such a presence is the public testimony of Daniel Lorenz, a former chief of the Intelligence Division of the Federal Police. At a public hearing in the Brazilian Congress, Lorenz confirmed that Khaled Hussein Ali, an individual criminally accused of racism in Sao Paulo,[20] had connections with al Qaeda and was one of the global leaders of the group's Jihad Media Battalion (JMB).[21] Ali allegedly used his internet cafe in São Paulo to coordinate JMB activities including disseminating propaganda for al Qaeda; offering a virtual space for recruitment, support, training and communication; and providing assistance for acts of terrorism committed outside Brazil. According to media reports, the FBI informed the Brazilian Federal Police about a red-flagged IP address that eventually led to Ali's arrest.[22] According to Coutinho, Ali was arrested as he was accessing his files in order to allow the police to read the encrypted material stored on his computer.[23] The material found on his computer included terrorist manuals and emails requesting the blocking of JMB access to individuals who had been arrested in Gaza by the Israeli Government.[24] Further analysis of his computer's content proved Ali was involved in disseminating propaganda, providing logistical support and engaging in recruitment activities for al Qaeda. Using what was found, the Federal Police charged Ali of the crimes of racism and anti-Semitism in Brazil. However, the fact that he was released twenty-one days after his arrest clearly demonstrated the practical problems inherent in Brazil's underdeveloped (or, more accurately put, nearly non-existent) terrorism legislation. Moreover, in a true reflection of the Brazilian attitude of denial, the prosecutor responsible for the case issued a number of public statements contesting media reports regarding Ali's involvement with terrorism.[25] Various other cases can be mentioned for São Paulo, including that of the Lebanese Kamed El Laouz, who was also identified as one of the coordinators of the JMB, and that of Hesham Ahmed Marhmoud Eltrabily, an Egyptian who was convicted for a terrorist act that left sixty-two tourists dead in Luxor, Egypt, in 1997. The Federal Police arrested El Laouz in March 2009,[26] but, in the case of the latter, the Brazilian Government denied the Egyptian request for extradition,[27] citing lack of evidence of Eltrabily's involvement in terrorism. Cases such as those of Ali and Eltrabily reveal the difficulties the Brazilian authorities face in dealing with terrorism-related charges in the absence of specific anti-terrorism legislation.

These cases also reveal the increasing presence of international terrorist activities within Brazil. In fact, according to Lorenz, the Federal Police have been identifying a growing terrorist threat in Brazil.[28] Initially, the Federal Police thought that international terrorists were merely using Brazilian territory to transit though or to hide. However, recent investigations have unearthed new evidence demonstrating that individuals linked to terrorist groups have, in fact, been actively seeking to establish permanent residence in Brazil through marriage or by adopting Brazilian children. The investigations have also identified a number of Brazilians who were attracted to extremist ideologies and the idea of martyrdom; some of these individuals travelled to Iran and the Middle East in what the Federal Police believes was a search for radical religious instruction. Finally, there is some evidence that a few of these individuals have been actively supporting terrorist groups outside Brazil with recruitment, financing, training, logistics and reconnaissance.[29]

More recently, a few cases have also raised red flags. In early April 2016, the Brazilian Federal Police and Interpol investigated the disappearance of a twenty-year-old student from the state of Pará. The police suspected that Karina Raiol had secretly travelled to Syria to join the Islamic State. According to the preliminary investigation reports, one day Karina told her family that she was going to university but instead secretly travelled to Istanbul via Morocco. The Federal Police discovered messages indicating sympathy for Islamic State on her computer, including a post where she stated that terrorism is the only way to fight injustice. They also discovered that her travel expenses had been covered from abroad by an unknown source. In another case, the Brazilian Federal Police monitored a student aged twenty-three in Santa Catarina, Ibrahim Chaiboun Darwiche, who spent three months with the Islamic State in Syria. According to the investigations, after his return to Brazil and in the run up to the Olympic Games in Rio de Janeiro, Darwiche began long-range target practice with a precision rifle late at night. After their investigation, the police suspected that he might have been planning an attack during the Olympic Games. As terrorism was not a category of crime in Brazil at the time, he could neither be arrested nor formally charged. Instead, the police managed to obtain an unprecedented court order temporarily banning Darwiche from airports, stadiums and schools, as well as obliging him to wear an ankle monitor.

Brazilian anti-terror legislation

Brazil lacks clear and comprehensive anti- and CT legislation. Whether or not one agrees with the purported dangers of creating anti-terror legislation, the fact remains that the absence of a specific legal framework has already posed serious problems for Brazilian CT. As mentioned above, terrorism-related activities are already taking place in Brazil. Hence, the specificities of the terrorist modus operandi as opposed to that of common criminals pose a serious challenge to the existing criminal law system – hampering investigations and criminal prosecution. While this author advocates that it is not necessary to replace or abandon criminal law to address cases of terrorism and terrorism-related activities, it is absolutely imperative that terrorism-specific legislation is enshrined within a human rights framework. As such, Brazil needs to rethink some of its existing criminal law institutes in the light of a specific anti-terrorism legislation so that it is able to address terrorism and terrorism-related activities much more efficiently.

Two examples of where such modifications are necessary are the laws on telephone tapping (9296/96 and 10217/01) and on police infiltration (12850/13). Both laws require the pre-existence of an ongoing criminal investigation and legal proceedings, consequently excluding the potential legal use of interception devices or infiltration for intelligence-gathering purposes. This seriously hinders preventive police action,[30] and once again forces a kinetic response on the part of the military and/or police. As regards existing terrorism legislation, the Brazilian Constitution considers the fight against terrorism as a central pillar of its foreign policy (Article 4, VIII). It also explicitly considers terrorism to be a heinous crime in which no bail, grace, amnesty or pardon is permissible (Article 5, inc. XLIII). Terrorism is also considered to be a crime against national security (7,170/83). However, all these provisions remain more theoretical than practical, particularly given that there is no legal definition of terrorism. Therefore, technically, *none* of these laws can be applied.

Another interesting example is Bill 10.744, by which the federal government assumes financial and civil liability in the stead of third parties in the event of a terrorist attack, act of war or related event against Brazilian civilian aircraft or against aircraft operated by Brazilian companies. But, perhaps most significantly, this bill actually offers a definition of terrorism. In paragraph 4 of Article 1, Bill 10.744 defines terrorism as 'any act from one or more persons, whether or not they are agents of a sovereign power, with political or terrorist ends, whether the resulting loss or damage is accidental or intentional'. However, as is amply clear, this is an exceedingly broad and confusingly vague definition and, as such, severely limited in its application. Interestingly, the bill also stipulates that the minister of defence must attest whether the act in question was committed with terroristic ends. Fortunately, so far Brazil has not witnessed such an attack and as such this bill remains theoretical. However, it is easy to understand that to confer such discretionary powers to the minister of defence can, once again, engender a whole host of problems.

At the time of writing, the last existing legal provision on terrorism and terrorism-related activities in Brazil was the recently passed Organized Crime Act (12850/2013). This law was created to guide investigations and prosecutions of criminal organizations and to establish what qualify as criminal offences.[31] Under its provisions, the law also applies 'to international terrorist organizations recognized as such through norms of international law in forums in which Brazil is a member and whose acts supporting terrorism, preparatory acts or terrorist acts, occur or may occur within the national territory'.[32] This article is groundbreaking as it not only admits the possibility of the presence of international terrorist organizations inside Brazil but also clearly includes 'preparatory acts of terrorism' and 'terrorism' as criminal offences. However, the law still leaves open what counts as a terrorist organization 'according to international law'. This ambiguity is important because this is exactly one of the points that is constantly criticized by Europe, the US, and international bodies such as the UN and the Financial Action Task Force (FATF), also known by its French name, Groupe d'Action Financière (GAFI), which complain that Brazil has frequently refused to publicly recognize groups such as the Fuerzas Armadas Revolucionarias de Colombia (FARC), Hamas or Hizbullah as terrorist organizations.[33] Finally, it is important to note that the law is directed towards tackling criminal (and/or terrorist) organizations, thereby excluding individual actors, such as lone wolves, from its scope.

In terms of international legal obligations, Brazil has ratified at least fifteen international conventions and protocols related to the fight against terrorism. However, Brazil – following a longstanding tradition that privileges its domestic laws over international ones – has done little to incorporate these treaties and relevant UN Security Council resolutions into its domestic legal system. To some extent this lack of integration can be explained by citing the very same reasons as for Brazil's opposition to creating anti-terror legislation that were discussed above – but two additional arguments deserve a mention.

First, it is argued that the blind application and incorporation of international norms into the domestic legal system would be a violation of Brazilian sovereignty; and, second, it is argued that incorporating international norms would signify a blind acceptance and application of foreign CT models to what is a very different social reality and set of interests. Without doubt, one cannot defend the unquestioning implementation of foreign CT models. However, it is also imperative to develop an institutional and strategic design that is aligned with both Brazil's international obligations and its particular social reality, resources and interests, because the blind absence of *any* legislation can be equally harmful.

In other words, the absence of domestic laws that incorporate and implement international norms can have potentially negative consequences. This is clearly observable in the case of laws related to countering terrorist financing. In 2005 Brazil ratified the UN Convention for the Suppression of the Financing of Terrorism. This treaty, together with resolutions 1373 (2001) and 1267 (1999) of the Security Council and combined with the requirement for mutual legal assistance in cases of terrorist financing that is stipulated in several other treaties to which Brazil is party, creates the obligation to criminalize various aspects of terrorist financing. However, Brazil has not consistently criminalized the financing of terrorism. On the contrary, Brazil has *decriminalized* it. The Brazilian Money Laundering Bill (12683/2012) abrogated the crime of financing terrorism which existed in older laws dealing with financial crimes. When asked to explain this puzzling action in international forums, the Brazilian authorities claimed that there was no need to criminalize terrorist financing since Brazil not only possesses good financial intelligence but also has a well-structured anti-money-laundering system. Moreover, they reasoned that the wording of the new bill was such that it also implicitly encompassed cases of terrorist financing. Finally, and perhaps most worryingly, the Brazilian authorities argued that the financing of international terrorism did not occur in Brazil. They based this claim on the fact that the Brazilian Financial Intelligence Unit, known as the Council for Financial Activities Control (COAF), had searched for persons and entities listed in the Security Council's resolutions 1267 and 1373 and that it did not find any listed goods, accounts or assets in Brazil.[34]

Nonetheless, internationally, the Brazilian Government has been heavily criticized for this position.[35] In fact, at least two recent cases involving the financing of terrorism have surfaced inside Brazil, and both the US Government and the FATF have renewed their objections to the Brazilian position in this matter. While recognizing Brazil's efforts regarding money laundering, the FATF often points out that Brazil has not yet criminalized the financing of terrorism in a manner consistent with its recommendations. For example, in its latest country report it repeatedly warned that Brazil's failure to criminalize the financing of terrorism 'seriously impacts [its] ability to investigate and prosecute terrorist financing. This also undermines their ability to adopt precautionary measures, confiscate property and provide international cooperation (extradition) in these cases'.[36]

According to the FATF, in order to establish an effective international network to fight the financing of terrorism, it is necessary that countries adopt, in addition to the criminalization terrorist financing itself, provisions of other related crimes, such as when goods, funds or assets in question: (1) will knowingly be used to fund a terrorist act, (2) are held by a terrorist organization for any purpose (i.e., not necessarily for a terrorist attack), (3) are held by a terrorist individual for any other purpose or, finally, (4) are held for the financing of a terrorist act that has not yet been committed or attempted. According to the FATF, Brazil's failure to implement this legislation severely limits its ability to freeze and/or seize assets, goods and funds linked to terrorist financing.

The FATF acknowledges that Brazil has incorporated the UN Security Council's resolutions 1267 and 1373 in its legislation, but simultaneously argues that it has not implemented the necessary means to make them effective. The FATF points out, for example, that Brazilian financial authorities lack the power to freeze assets linked to terrorism as there is no distinction made between the seizure of assets linked to terrorism versus any other criminal activity.[37] Therefore, any action taken in this regard perforce follows the procedures provided for cases of money laundering. In other words, the lack of specific legislation means Brazil has *no legal provisions* to authorize the freezing of assets on the grounds that these are merely related to a terrorist organization or individual with or without necessarily being connected to a terrorist act.[38] In short, Brazil lacks the legal provisions to comply with and implement FATF's provisions (2) (3) and (4) outlined above. The FATF has also been sceptical about Brazil's ability to freeze companies' and individuals' assets 'without delay' and 'within hours of their appointment by Al Qaeda Sanctions Committee and the Taliban Sanctions Committee', as required by resolution 1267 (1999) of the Security Council.[39] In addition, there is no specific provision in Brazilian law that allows for it continuing a freezing of assets that started abroad. Similarly, it lacks procedures for the listing and de-listing/thawing of assets and funds of individuals or organizations internationally listed as terrorist financers. The FATF also expresses doubts about whether the Brazilian authorities have the necessary instruments of control over non-governmental and non-profit organizations (NGOs). International authorities such as the UN's Counter-Terrorism Implementation Task Force, the European Commission and the International Monetary Fund have been increasingly concerned about the nexus between NGOs and terrorist financing. To this end, they have voiced fears that the Brazilian Government would have severely limited powers of investigation and action over NGOs operating within Brazil thanks to the lack of required legislation.[40]

Finally, given the international nature of the current financial system (both legal and illegal), the lack of legislation may also result in international cooperation issues. A clear example is that of extradition. It is true that Brazil can extradite individuals linked to terrorist financing and other related activities due to its broad interpretation of the principle of dual criminality.[41] However, there are limits to such a broad interpretation as well. An individual could be extradited for terrorism due to Brazil's flexible understanding of the institution of extradition, but it would only happen in cases where the terrorist act has already been committed or attempted. Thus, several gaps remain, for example, in situations in which the terrorist attack is in the planning stages and has not yet occurred, or in cases in which the terrorist group or individual holds assets or goods not intended to be directly used for terrorist activities. Furthermore, given that Brazil does not extradite its own nationals, situations in which the accused is a Brazilian citizen could also hinder international cooperation.[42]

The Brazilian institutional anti-terrorism design and its limitations

In Brazil, no single agency is in charge of preventing or coordinating the fight against terrorism. In reality, various governmental agencies have diffuse – and frequently overlapping – jurisdictions on terrorism-related cases.

ABIN and Interpol, for example, are responsible for monitoring and preventing terrorist threats. Their investigations are usually initiated after they receive relevant foreign intelligence from attachés, external intelligence agencies or other international bodies.[43] Once the Brazilian Federal Police receives intelligence from ABIN, Interpol or from its own intelligence-gathering network, it initiates the surveillance and investigation of suspects in order to 'prevent, obstruct, identify and neutralize terrorist conduct'.[44] The Federal Police also acts through its various internal divisions, such as the Judiciary Police Officers Division, the Anti-Terrorism Division, the General Coordination of Maritime Police Division, the Airport and Border Division, the General Coordination of Public and Social Order Division, the General Coordination of Combating Organized Crime Division, and the Special Investigations and General Coordination of the Tactical Operations Command Division.[45]

As with intelligence, surveillance and investigation, when it comes to the kinetic response to terrorist attacks, there exists a similarly complex and somewhat Kafkaesque division of jurisdictions. The Federal Police, the Military

Police and the Civil Police are all responsible for the police's kinetic response in terrorism-related cases. It is worth noting that in the case of both the Military Police and the Civil Police, each state in Brazil has its own distinct force, with widely varying levels of training, resources and preparedness. The Federal Police's Anti-Terrorism Division (DAT) and its Tactical Operations Command (COT) carry out the tactical response to terrorist attacks. The Military Police – which operates at the state level – responds to terrorist attacks through its special-ops units such as BOPE (Batalhão de Operações Especiais) and GATE (Grupo de Ações Táticas Especiais). The Civil Police – which also operates at a state level – also acts through its special-ops divisions such as the DOE (Divisão de Operações Especiais). Finally, the Ministry of Defence and the Army Command through its Special Operations Brigade (BOE) – and in the case of cyberterrorism through its Cyber Defence Centre (CDCiber) – are jointly responsible for the military response to terrorist attacks. In practice, it is highly unclear if there is any sort of hierarchy of response by different police and military forces and/or where the jurisdiction of one begins and the others ends.

Another institution that plays a key role in the fight against terrorism is the Brazilian Financial Intelligence Unit. Brazil, as a member of the FATF and its Money Laundering Division for South America (GAFISUD) and 'FATF Style Regional Bodies' (FSRB), established a working group within the Ministry of Justice to incorporate the recommendations of these bodies, which include multiple directives to combat the financing of terrorism. However, perhaps the most important organ involved in the fight against terrorist finance is the COAF. The COAF works to detect and fight the financing of terrorism through financial intelligence. It is also responsible for freezing funds and assets linked to terrorists or terrorist organizations listed in the freeze list issued by the UN Security Council in accordance with resolutions 1267 and 1373.

Yet, despite this institutional design these agencies do not have a clear division of roles and in addition lack inter-agency coordination – two elements that arguably represent the fundamental limitations of Brazil's CT institutional design. Additionally, these agencies are chronically short on material, technological, financial and human resources,[46] reflecting both a larger structural problem as well as the low political priority of this issue vis-à-vis the government's agenda. The problematic institutional architecture of departments involved in countering terrorism in Brazil is also a direct result of expanding the jurisdictions of pre-existing agencies without a corresponding increase in their already scarce human and material resources. Although this process of addition was seen as an easy solution, it also reflects another interesting cultural characteristic that may potentially be traced back to Brazil's military dictatorship. The trauma of dictatorship generated a deep mistrust of everything military. In spite of a relatively peaceful transition to democratic rule, the military (and much of the police as well) was highly discredited amongst civilians. Accordingly, since the 1990s the government has viewed security and defence as relatively low priority issues, reflecting perhaps an unspoken fear of the negative consequences of a strong military. Nevertheless, thanks to the extra funding secured for the 2014 World Cup and the 2016 Olympic Games, the army found –in the spheres of both CT and cyber-defence – a new source of material means and, more importantly, a way to reinvent itself and construct a more socially accepted presence. However, the unintended consequence has been that both legislative and security policies are unblinkingly focused upon what is an essentially kinetic response to terrorist attacks as opposed to their prevention. In this sense, Salvador Raza is right in pointing out that the pure and simple addition of new competences in the institutions acting for the prevention and combating of terrorism – such as the army – should not be seen as the answer to the historical problem of a disempowered military, but rather it should have resulted in an opportunity for a new design and restructuring of the military's doctrine and role.[47] The same can be said of all other government agencies.

One can further argue that, in addition to agency-level limitations, Brazil's institutional architecture is made even more complicated by its federal system. Therefore, a handful of states have enacted a series of state-level CT legislative and policy measures. For instance, the military police of the state of Minas Gerais is the first in Brazil to have developed and instituted a permanent CT course for its rapid-response team. However, while some states across Brazil may have implemented particular CT policy measures this has been done very unevenly and not without some conflict with the federal government. Perhaps the main points of clash between state and federal government relate to the confusion regarding jurisdiction: where one's jurisdiction ends and the other's begins and the allocation of already limited human and material resources, as well as the problems related to inter-agency cooperation as have already been discussed above.[48]

Hence, a key problem of Brazil's current CT institutional design is that it reflects the country's immensely complex federal system and echoes the lack of a national strategy to combat terrorism in a political environment in which the government does not see the need for one. The absence of a systematic institutional and legal apparatus, the lack of inter-agency cooperation and synergy, in addition to inter-agency disputes over new jurisdictions and resources, all reflect this short-sighted national strategy. This is not a trivial matter. Better inter-agency cooperation, a redistribution of jurisdictions, institutional redesign and a concentrated effort to integrate agencies engaged in the prevention and combat of terrorism should be key priorities. More importantly, a consolidated national strategy and specific legislation that facilitate it are important preconditions in the design of any anti- and counterterrorism policy, as it is this strategic and legal framework that will determine the policy's shape, reach and limits.

Counterterrorism meets politics: Understanding the limitations of Brazilian CT legislation

The picture painted above illustrates the reality of terrorism-related activities in Brazil, the awareness of the Brazilian authorities about the matter and the weaknesses of its CT. Thus, in light of so much evidence, how can we understand the government's adamant public denial of any terrorist activity in Brazil? What explains its inertia and refusal to formulate and/or adopt any concrete policies against the very real threat of terrorism? Upon closer study, one can identify several different views within the current administration. One of the main positions, especially voiced in congress and popular within the Brazilian-Muslim communities, argues that any explicit CT policy or legislation will only contribute to stigmatizing the Brazilian-Muslim population. Others argue that any official statement recognizing the existence of terrorist activities in Brazil is likely to negatively impact its tourism industry. Yet others go as far as to argue that the mere existence of anti-terrorism laws (no matter their content) would give the impression that Brazil both supports and is fully aligned with the United States in its 'Global War on Terror.'[49] They argue that international terrorist groups could perceive this supposed alignment as a provocation which would consequently *draw* terrorism to Brazil.[50] Congressman Raul Jungmann, for example, has expressed more than once his indignation towards an adviser to the then minister of justice, Tarso Genro, who argued that the approval of any anti-terrorism legislation would certainly bring terrorism into Brazil.[51] Astonishingly, this is not an isolated position. At a recent public hearing on the subject, one congressman emphasized that there is no need to create anti-terror laws in Brazil as terrorist attacks never happened in countries *without* such laws. The author D.N. Souza also points out that several high-level politicians see Brazil as a historically peaceful and tolerant country that, somehow, is immune to terrorism.[52] Indeed, questions such as 'Why would anyone want to carry out terrorist attacks in Brazil?' are, unfortunately, frequently asked in the government's many corridors.

It is, however, important to understand why there is such a firm stance – one could even say, a taboo – against openly dealing with anything related to terrorism in Brazil. For one, it is necessary to remember that Brazil suffered under a military dictatorship between 1964 and 1989. During this period, several left-wing leaders (who are now high-ranking politicians) engaged in violent activities while resisting the dictatorship. Various politicians were persecuted, and many were forced to go underground. Many were accused of being terrorists and either sought refuge abroad or, if they remained in the country, faced arrest and torture at the hands of the military regime. These politicians now occupy positions of leadership in key political parties as well as holding several seats in both houses of Parliament. Thus, it is understandable that CT is viewed with hostility by a significant proportion of the legislators (of *both* the upper and lower houses of Congress) and, consequently, draft bills related to CT tend not to be passed. This problem is further compounded by the very structure of the Brazilian presidential system. In Brazil, the president has significant power to influence both domestic and international policy. Both President Luiz Inácio Lula da Silva (Lula) and President Dilma Rousseff were jailed during the period of military rule due to their leftist activism. Lula's activism saw him participating in strikes and demonstrations, while Rousseff challenged the military dictatorship as a guerrilla fighter; indeed, it is a well-known fact that she was tortured by the regime while in prison. Arguably, it is this history of activism and struggle that made these two presidents particularly suspicious of and resistant to any strengthening of Brazil's CT policy.

Moreover, Lula and Dilma's labour party (Partido dos Trabalhadores, or PT) has had a historically close – albeit on occasion contentious – relationship with various local social movements which today constitute an important share of PT's political base. This is relevant for two reasons. Firstly, one of Brazil's largest social movements is the Landless Workers' Movement (Movimento dos Trabalhadores sem Terra, or MST), with an estimated 1.5 million members.[53] The movement's main goal is to achieve social justice via extensive agrarian reform. However, its radical ideology and its recourse to legally dubious actions have posed serious problems in the past. According to MST, it is justifiable to employ violence while mass-occupying rural lands it believes to be unproductive. This is because, in its opinion, the Brazilian judiciary is highly biased towards landowners. Thus, MST squatters (and the landowners in response) frequently resort to violence in order to force the government to expropriate the lands in their favour.[54] Therefore, in regard to terrorism-related legislation, if the government indeed criminalizes 'terrorism' as a self-standing crime then MST's actions could easily be framed as terrorism due to their potent combination of violence and political motivation. As one can imagine, the political implications of doing so would be immense for Brazilian domestic politics.

Secondly, starting in mid-2013, a series of spontaneous mass protests erupted across Brazil. These protests mobilized millions of people across the country. However, unlike traditional social movements, there was no single coherent identity or agenda or, indeed, even a recognizable leadership. They emerged instead as spontaneous expressions of widespread dissatisfaction and resentment with the general direction of Brazilian politics, addressing a vast array of issues ranging from corruption and high taxation to other, wider socio-economic and political policies. Although the frequency of these protests has considerably decreased over 2016–17, they have come to be recognized as a new form of expression in Brazilian politics. However, even though they have largely been viewed as an important expression of a healthy, functioning democracy, a segment of the protesters have either been linked to anarchist groups or used the cover of mass protests to practise hooliganism. Thus, on many occasions, mass demonstrations that began peacefully displayed episodes of riot-like violence which were accompanied by the large-scale destruction of private property and violent clashes with the police. So once again, with reference to terrorism, many Brazilians still remember the military dictatorship and fear that any anti-terrorism legislation created could be used to curb legitimate social movements and restrict freedom of expression and the right to congregate. The occurrence of violent activities in otherwise peaceful protests would, in their view, serve as an excuse for the government to crack down on what are essentially legitimate social movements. Many social movement leaders and political parties have actively voiced this fear. In fact, the Lower House report on the draft bill on anti-terrorism underscores the legitimacy of the 2013 social movements and protests, and dedicates almost two pages to justifying the consensus on the need to exclude social movements and protests from the law. Quoting a note by the Government Attorneys Association, the report even states that 'the acts of social movements, even when violent, do not have as a special objective the provocation of terror or panic' and thus should be excluded from the application of this bill.[55]

The Brazilian reluctance to adopt laws and policies on the subject is thus understandable. In the minds of the legislators, the social harm that could potentially be caused by anti-terror laws far surpasses any damage that may be caused by a – potentially 'unlikely' – terrorist attack on Brazilian soil. These domestic particularities thus not only deeply affect how the threat of terrorism is conveyed publicly to domestic audiences, but also impact and shape both the conceptualization as well as the practice of CT in Brazil.

Draft legislation

Finally, it is important to mention that at the time of writing several draft laws on the issue of CT were under discussion in the Brazilian Congress. Amongst them one can mention the draft legislation to deny visas to individuals linked to terrorism (introduced in 2011); the draft legislation on the definition of terrorism in the constitution (introduced in 2013); the penal code reform bill, which includes a section relating to international crimes and acts of terrorism (introduced in 2012); and the draft for defining and combating terrorism during the World Cup (introduced in 2011). However, as is more than evident by the dates on which these draft bills were first introduced for discussion, there seems to be a distinct lack of will on the part of congress to discuss, much less approve, these laws. The United States, for example, is explicit in its criticism when it argues that the main failure of Brazilian CT is that these anti-terrorism and anti-money-laundering draft bills have been ready for several years but have yet to be put to the vote, mainly due to the lack of political will. According to the US, this deliberate inertia is the result of historical and ideological apprehensions that this kind of legislation could be used against legitimate opposition and social movements.[56] In addition to the resistance against adopting any sort of CT legislation, an analysis of the contents of these draft bills – and the discussions around them – clearly demonstrates that the majority of those who support the creation of CT legislation tend to focus excessively upon the criminalization of terrorist attacks while excluding other key aspects, such as prevention, the provision of assistance to victims and post-facto investigations.

However, there is a caveat. On account of recent events, this scenario will most likely shift in the not-too-distant future. Unexpectedly, a combination of both international and domestic pressures has created what can be best called an 'issue synergy linkage' that is very likely to generate the conditions necessary to finally facilitate the approval of anti-terrorism legislation in Brazil. On the one hand, there has been mounting pressure from the FATF-GAFI, which is threatening to adopt sanctions against Brazil. This pressure has resulted in a concentrated effort on the part of the Brazilian financial authorities to try to mobilize Congress to approve at least some CT legislation.

This move has recently resulted in Congress tagging two specific CT bills as urgent matters, which means that they have to be put to the vote before all other non-urgent issues and bills. Here an interesting political twist comes into play. Brazil is currently in the middle of a political crisis where the ruling party has lost its majority in Congress and several high-level members of the government are facing grave corruption charges. The current leader of the Lower House of Congress is a member of the opposition party, and has recently also been implicated in the corruption scandal. In response, he has mobilized the Lower House of Congress, which is dominated by the opposition and is threatening to push for the approval of various laws that would further undercut and weaken the current government. However, because two CT bills have already been tagged as urgent he cannot push forward with this plan until and unless these bills are put to the vote. In short, this unprecedented, two-levelled pressure may well create the necessary political conditions for Brazil to finally shift its stance regarding the approval of at least some CT laws.

Unfortunately, it must also be stressed that due to the high heterogeneity of domestic interests in this subject, the above-mentioned confluence of factors probably still will not be sufficient to design a set of coherent, integrated standards. Nor will it be sufficient to create a normative architecture that is aligned with both a broader strategy to prevent and combat terrorism as well as Brazil's particular socio-economic reality. In all probability, we will see patchwork legislation being approved which will essentially reflect strongly divergent political interests and encompass provisions that will exclude labour syndicates and social movements from its reach.

Conclusion

This chapter describes how international terrorism has impacted Brazil and discusses the structural and institutional design of anti-terrorism in the country, while also outlining its key limitations. The uniqueness of Brazil's domestic cultural and political settings is key to understanding the both the Brazilian Government's historical inertia as well as its occasionally puzzling position vis-à-vis this subject. Thus, specific domestic material limitations and what is an extremely complex institutional and political scene both heavily impact Brazilian CT processes.

Although most Brazilians see terrorism as a distant reality, the fact remains that Brazil is not immune to this threat nor to its consequences. However, somewhat paradoxically, Brazil still continues to lack anti-terrorism and CT policies and legislation. Amongst the many causes identified that could explain this absence, one can emphasize the dearth of expertise on the subject, the lack of a consolidated strategy to guide institutional actions and the inexistence of a systemic legal framework to structure CT policies.

Simultaneously, two divergent forces hamper Brazilian CT. First, domestically, there is strong pressure to not create any legislation on the subject. The issue – perceived as peripheral – has not yet been able to overcome historical and ideological domestic political barriers and move up the government's political agenda. The political bargaining currently underway at the Brazilian Congress significantly constrains any political debate around the theme of terrorism. This is not only due to widespread ignorance about the subject, but also (and most importantly) due to the great heterogeneity of domestic political interests, which do not overlap sufficiently to form an acceptable 'win set' for the majority of policymakers. Thus, the issue has become heavily politicized and linked to matters that are very loosely related (or indeed completely unrelated) to terrorism, thereby greatly reducing any possibility of reaching an agreement in Congress. Consequently, the current political deadlock around other pressing domestic issues and interests disaggregates the linkage of terrorism with topics important enough to receive the attention of Congress. Thus, the current domestic political game ends up precluding any convergence of interests and preferences around the subject.

Second, international society has been progressively pressuring Brazil to create CT legislation. Increasingly, the lack of legislation has been interpreted as a deliberate unwillingness on Brazil's part to cooperate in the fight against terrorism. This is important because terrorism can, and does, have an important transnational component. Thus, the fight against terrorism arguably requires greater cooperation between the intelligence, police and criminal justice offices of multiple countries.[57] This is not only because can terrorists prepare future attacks from different countries, but also because, despite being recognized as a threat to international peace and security, terrorism is not yet legally recognized as an international crime. Thus, terrorism becomes a *national* crime of *international* concern, as the responsibility for bringing terrorists to justice falls firmly under domestic jurisdictions.[58] However – whether or not one agrees with the need to create CT legislation in Brazil – it must not be seen as voluntary defector from the international fight against terror. Rather, Brazil may best be viewed as a reluctant collaborator which, due to the complex political-domestic scenario described above, becomes what Putnam calls an 'involuntary defector'.[59]

Author's note

At the time of editing, several important changes occurred in Brazil which are relevant for this chapter. As mentioned above, the two anti-terrorism bills that had been tagged as urgent were finally approved amid a domestic political storm. In March 2016, the anti-terrorism bill (13.260), which criminalizes acts of terrorism, entered into force and later that year so did the bill regulating the procedures for freezing assets identified by the UN Security Council (13.170). On the political front, President Dilma (a member of the Labour Party) was impeached in April 2016 under accusations of criminal responsibility for administrative misconduct and disregarding the federal budget. The impeachment, combined with a series of corruption scandals involving high-level Labour Party members, pushed PT out of power at the national level. This change in the political scene is relevant because the new administration, under President Michel Temer (Dilma's former vice president) has a more conservative stance and therefore may well pose less resistance on terrorism-related issues. This is especially important given that the Brazilian political system grants the president significant powers to influence policy. However, as the political maelstrom and corruption scandals evolve and spill over to involve and implicate politicians of various other parties, including several of Temer's new ministers, any changes become highly unlikely. Political survival, inter-party struggles, the economic crisis and domestic violence will, in all probability, take precedence for this administration, and thus leave very little space for the government to press forward with any legislation that may be controversial and/or come with a high political and social cost, as is the case with anti-terror laws. Furthermore, there is a widespread perception that in the aftermath of the Olympics the terrorist threat is once again very low, if not negligible, in Brazil. Thus, the issue of terrorism has lost considerable synergy and capacity to forge links with other issues that could help mobilize the multiple interests in the National Congress, thus providing the conditions under which further CT-related legislation could be approved.

It is also important to note that – as mentioned above – the approval of the two most recent bills by no means creates a coherent, integrated standard of anti- and counterterrorism in Brazil. Undoubtedly, this anti-terrorism bill represents a major advance as it criminalizes acts of terrorism, support for terrorism offences, the preparation of terrorist acts, recruiting, training abroad and also the financing of terrorism. Nevertheless, the bill has major flaws. According to its Article 2, terrorism:

> consists in the practice by one or more individuals of the acts foreseen in this article, for reasons of xenophobia, discrimination or prejudice of race, colour, ethnicity and religion, when committed with the purpose of provoking social or generalized terror, exposing to danger persons, property or the public peace and safety.[60]

This definition of terrorism is very controversial as only an act motivated by reasons of xenophobia, discrimination or prejudice of race, colour, ethnicity or religion could be considered an 'act of terrorism'. Thus, a purely politically motivated or even environmentally motivated terrorist act would not be considered 'a crime of terrorism'. The bill also focuses upon the criminalization of such acts and does not deal with other important aspects of anti- and counterterrorism such as the operational and investigative needs of the police, the intelligence and legal systems, or procedural law issues such as witness and victim protection, extradition, and so on. It also does not address the wider issue of an anti-terrorism institutional design or strategy. Another point worth mentioning is that its Article 2, section 2, expressly excludes the liability of labour syndicates as well as social and religious movements from the application of this bill. While undoubtedly legitimate social movements and syndicates should not be persecuted under the guise of terrorism, this exclusion clearly hints at how the anti-terrorism issue is deeply sensitive and heavily impacted by the ever-changing domestic political game.

Finally, it is important to mention Operation Hashtag. In the months prior to the Olympic Games, Brazilian intelligence and police services were on high alert due to a new Islamic State channel in Portuguese that used the Telegram application, and also direct threats made to Brazil on Twitter by a French member of the Islamic State, Maxime Hauchard. The Brazilian Federal Police and intelligence agency began monitoring social media after receiving information from foreign intelligence agencies that Brazilian citizens were in contact with the Islamic State. In this joint investigation, the Brazilian intelligence agency, the Federal Police and the military monitored and arrested in July 2016 eight (later rising to fifteen) persons who formed a group called Ansar al-Khalifah Brazil. Using the application Telegram to avoid being monitored, the members of this group were spread over ten different Brazilian states and planned, among other things, to travel to Syria to receive combat training, to acquire weapons in Bolivia, to chemically contaminate a water reservoir in Rio de Janeiro during the Olympic Games and to attack the gay pride parade in São Paulo. The prosecution charged the suspects of being motivated by 'reasons of religious discrimination', and under the new law formally accused them of the crimes of 'preparatory acts of terrorism' and 'being a member of a terrorist organization' (Islamic State). So far, the case is ongoing and being conducted in secret, but we know that five alleged suspects continue to be detained. This is the first case – and so far, the only one – being conducted under the auspices of Brazil's new anti-terrorism law.

Notes

1 There exists a very sparse historical literature about Brazil's own leftist guerrilla movements of the 1960s and 1970s, and an even scanter literature about the tri-border area (i.e., the common frontier between Brazil, Paraguay and Argentina) and the threat that this poses to Brazilian security in the contemporary era.

2 Institute for Economics and Peace, *Global Terrorism Index: Capturing the Impact of Terrorism in 2002–2011* (New York: Institute for Economics and Peace, 2012), p. 5; *Global Terrorism Index 2014: Measuring and Understanding the Impact of Terrorism* (New York: Institute for Economics and Peace, 2014).

3 Julio J. Waiselfisz, *Mapa da Violência* (Rio de Janeiro: FLACSO, 2014).

4 American Embassy in Brasília (AEB), *08brasilia43* (Brasilia: AEB, 2008), p. 1.

5 AEB, 'Counterterrorism in Brazil: Looking beyond the tri-border area,' Cable 08BRASILIA43 (Brasília: Wikileaks, 2008), available at: https://wikileaks.org/plusd/cables/08BRASILIA43_a.html (accessed 6 June 2016); 'Brazil: 2009 country report on terrorism,' Cable 09BRASILIA1540 (Brasília: Wikileaks, 2009), available at: https://wikileaks.org/plusd/cables/09BRASILIA1540_a.html (accessed 6 June 2016); 'Brazil: Police publicly admit al Qaeda's presence,' Cable 09BRASILIA1206 (Brasília: Wikileaks, 2009) available at: https://wikileaks.org/plusd/cables/09BRASILIA1206_a.html (accessed 6 June 2016); US Department of State (USDoS), *Country Reports on Terrorism 2013* (Washington: USDoS, 2014).

6 *Ibid.*, 208.

7 Alberto Nisman and Marcelo M. Burgos, *Amia Case* (Buenos Aires: Investigations Unit of the Office of the Attorney General, 2013), p. 409.

8 Alberto Nisman and Marcelo M. Burgos, *Summary: Amia Case* (Buenos Aires: Investigations Unit Office of the Attorney General, 2013), p. 9.

9 Nisman and Burgos, 'Amia Case,' p. 409.

10 *Ibid.*, p. 409.

11 *Ibid.*, p. 489.

12 Douglas Farah, *Back to the Future: Argentina Unravels* (Alexandria, VA: Transparency and Financial Investigations International Assessment and Strategy Center, 2012), p. 20.

13 Nisman and Burgos, 'Summary: Amia Case,' p. 27.

14 Nisman and Burgos, 'Amia Case,' p. 558.

15 9/11 Commission, *Final Report on 9/11 Commission Recommendations* (Washington: National Commission on Terrorist Acts Upon the United States (9/11 Commission), 2005), p. 148.

16 For example, the 2005 *Country Report on Terrorism* states that the tri-border area is 'an area where terrorism financing occurs'. USDoS, *Country Reports on Terrorism 2005* (Washington: USDoS, 2006), p. 270; *Country Reports on Terrorism 2015* (Washington: USDoS, 2016), p. 291. For a similar argument, see also Adriano M. Barbosa, 'Combating terrorism in the Brazilian tri-border area: A necessary law enforcement strategic approach' (PhD thesis, Naval Postgradute School, Monterey, CA, 2007).

17 Paulo de T. R. Paniago, 'Uma cartilha para melhor entender o terrorismo internacional: Conceitos e definições,' *Revista Brasileira de Inteligência* 3:4 (2007): 17; Álisson C. Raposo, 'Terrorismo e contraterrorismo: Desafios do século XXI,' *Revista Brasileira de Inteligência* 3:4 (2007): 50. This stance is also borne out by my conversations with various military, intelligence and police personnel who have been stationed in the tri-border region (non-attributable, off-the-record interviews and conversations held between January 2013 and December 2015).

18 USDoS, *Country Reports on Terrorism 2009* (Washington: USDoS, 2010), p. 152.

19 Author's conversation with an anonymous government source, 2015.

20 Unlike in the US where racist speech is not criminalized unless and until a hate crime occurs as a corollary, in Brazil both general acts of racism and racist slurs count as crimes in and of themselves (see bill 7.716/1989 and article 140 of the Brazilian Criminal Code).

21 Comissão de Segurança Pública e Combate ao Crime Organizado: Câmara dos Deputados, *Debate Sobre a Atuação de Membros de Grupos Terroristas no Território Brasileiro* (Brasília: Câmara dos Deputados, 2009).
22 Leonardo Coutinho, 'A Rede do Terror no Brasil,' *Veja* 44:14 (2011): 88–96.
23 *Ibid.*
24 *Ibid.*, 91.
25 AEB, *09brasilia1206* (Brasilia: AEB, 2009), p. 2.
26 Coutinho, 'A Rede do Terror no Brasil.'
27 *Ibid.*
28 Câmara dos Deputados, *Debate Sobre a Atuação.*
29 *Ibid.*
30 Priscila Brandão and Vladmir Brito, 'Terrorismo, Inteligência e Mecanismos Legais: Desafios para o Brasil,' in Carlos S. Arturi (ed.), *Politicas de Defesa, Inteligência e Seguranca* (Porto Alegre, Brazil: UFRGS Editora, 2014), p. 181.
31 Government of Brazil, Organized Crime Act, law no. 12850/2013, Article 1.
32 *Ibid.*, paragraph 2, II.
33 AEB, *08brasilia43*, p. 2.
34 *Ibid.*
35 FATF and Grupo de Ação Financeira da América do Sul (GAFISUD), *Mutual Evaluation Report: Anti-Money Laundering and Combating the Financing of Terrorism – Federative Republic of Brazil* (Paris: Financial Action Task Force/ Financial Action Task Force on Money Laundering in South America, 2010), p. 43; AEB, *08brasilia43*, p. 2.
36 *Ibid.*, p. 26.
37 *Ibid.*, p. 54.
38 *Ibid.*, p. 55.
39 *Ibid.*, p. 58, Special Recommendation III.
40 *Ibid.*, p. 219.
41 *Ibid.*, p. 244.
42 *Ibid.*
43 AEB, *08brasilia43*, p. 1.
44 Wantuir F.B. Jacini, 'Terrorismo: Atuação da Polícia Federal,' *CEJ* 18 (2002): 76.
45 *Ibid.*, 75.
46 Delanne N. Souza, 'Brazil's role in the fight against terrorism,' *Revista Brasileira de Inteligência* 5 (2009): 33.
47 Salvador Raza, 'Terrorism in the southern cone: "Prosfictional" view and power politics,' *SCSRC Discussion Paper* 5:55 (2005): 6.
48 However, while this undoubtedly reflects the complexity inherent in Brazil's federal political system, by no means can one argue that the national government's CT policy is inadequate *because* it relies on local state governments to undertake the job. Nor can one credibly argue that individual states across the board reflect the centre's stance vis-à-vis downplaying the threat of terrorism.
49 AEB, *08brasilia43*, p. 2.
50 AEB, *09brasilia1206*.
51 Câmara dos Deputados, *Debate Sobre a Atuação*, p. 16.
52 Souza, 'Brazil's role,' 32.
53 Arthur Zimerman, 'Land and violence in Brazil: A fatal combination,' *LASA paper* (2011): 9.

54 *Ibid.*
55 Câmara dos Deputados, *Parecer da Comissão de Relações Exteriores e Defesa Nacional da Câmara dos Deputados Sobre o Projeto de Lei 2.016* (Brasilia: Câmara dos Deputados, 2016), p. 2.
56 AEB, *09brasilia1206*, p. 1.
57 United Nations Office on Drugs and Crime (UNODC), *Handbook on Criminal Justice Responses to Terrorism* (Vienna: UNODC, 2009), p. 5.
58 *Ibid.*, p. 9.
59 Robert D. Putnam, 'Diplomacy and domestic politics: The logic of two-level games,' *International Organization* 42:3 (1988): 427–60.
60 Government of Brazil, Bill 13.260/16, Article 2.

Colombia

9

The changing meaning of 'terrorism' in Colombia: A matter of discourse

Oscar Palma

Introduction

Discourses on terrorism are not foreign to Colombian society. The word is used every day by politicians, state officials, academics, journalists, analysts and people in the streets. Every Colombian has grown up understanding that terrorism is part of everyday life. The people have been victims of a wide range of actors, including drug kingpins, paramilitary squads, guerrillas and even state forces. Car bombings, armed assaults in towns, assassinations, kidnappings and massacres are common themes in the daily news.

However, determining the dimensions of terrorism in Colombia has never been easy, given the absence of a concrete understanding of what terrorism actually is. The Centro Nacional de Memoria Histórica has recorded about 95 terrorist attacks with 1,566 victims from 1988 to 2012. This is a conservative estimate, since other forms of violent attack, like armed combat, are not included. Over roughly the same period there have been about 716 combats, 16,340 targeted killings, 27,023 kidnappings, 5,138 cases of attack to civilian property, 1,982 massacres with 11,751 victims, 10,189 victims of landmines and 25,007 victims of forced disappearance.[1] If we consider all of these acts as terrorism, as some actually do, then its incidence grows exponentially.[2]

It is precisely this high exposure of Colombians to terrorism which ironically clouds the issue of constructing a concrete understanding of the phenomenon.

The term has been used to describe so many actors and so many types of actions that it has lost its explanatory power over a specific phenomenon. Were drug lords terrorists? Are guerrillas who have existed since the 1960s terrorist organizations? How can we understand terrorism in Colombia?

The word has different meanings for different observers. Far-left movements, radicalized groups and anarchists, not to mention guerrillas, see the military and the police as agents of systemic state terror. Rightist politicians and the bulk of society categorize insurgents, mainly the Revolutionary Armed Forces of Colombia (FARC) and the National Liberation Army (ELN), as terrorist organizations. Others see, rather, the actions of Pablo Escobar and major drug cartels to be proper terrorist acts. Many will speak about former paramilitary groups, often the Autodefensas Unidas de Colombia (AUC) and its heirs – the so-called criminal bands, or BACRIMs – as the real terrorists.

This is due to the subjective nature of terrorism. More than being an objective reality, what society understands as terrorism is constructed through discourse. In the line of the critical discourse analysis approach to the subject, terrorism is here understood not as an objective, freestanding, self-evident phenomenon, but as a discursive construction that, although loaded with assumptions, cultural biases and moral charges, is used uncritically and unreflectively with considerable consequences.[3]

This chapter explains how the discourse has driven the understanding of terrorism in Colombia, and the ways in which the state has responded. The use of the concepts of terrorism and narcoterrorism has varied through time, describing a disparate group of actors such as cocaine traffickers, guerrillas, paramilitary organizations and even state institutions. Constructing the perception of an agent as a terrorist is not simply a matter of semantics, it brings relevant policymaking effects, usually in the legitimation of the state response. The discourse of a global 'War on Terror' that emerged after 9/11 was appropriated by the leaders in Colombia to legitimize the waging of a more forceful war against insurgent groups.

For this purpose, the chapter first discusses conceptions on terrorism from a critical discourse perspective and how they can be observed in Colombia. With a brief review of the history of violence in the country, it then explores the discourse on narcoterrorism, which was the first example of the concept of terrorism being used systematically in public discourse. It then explores the transition towards the characterization of insurgents, particularly FARC, as terrorist groups, with the demise of major drug cartels and the increased operational capabilities of guerrillas. Finally, it analyses how the discourse of a global war on terrorism was appropriated in Colombia to increase the military offensive against insurgents, with stronger support from the population.

A complex concept

It is worth pointing out that to approach terrorism as a discursive construction, which is applied to certain acts (and not others) in a specific socio-political context as well as geographical and temporal settings, is not the same thing as arguing that acts of terrorism are not real, that real people do not harm or kill other people. Rather, it is to say that the representation of real acts of violence as terrorism is conditioned by a complex series of political, social and discursive practices located in a specific context. In other words, 'The actions and pronouncements of politicians, academics, lawyers and others transform a particular act of violence – such as a bombing or murder – into an act of "terrorism."'[4] This is precisely what we see in Colombia, through the categorization of specific actors as terrorists according to the circumstances.

The problem begins with the definition of terrorism itself. There is no agreed definition and no common list of terrorist groups worldwide. The impossibility to distinguish between terrorism and the use of terror, the subjective and politically motivated categorization of actors as terrorists, a belief in having the moral high ground, the historical evolution of the concept, and the proliferation of definitions have made it almost impossible to advance.[5]

What counts as terrorism and who is a terrorist are typical subjects of debate and have generated mixed responses in the Colombian case. The changing meaning of the word over time, as has been explained by several authors,[6] has also been an obstacle for the construction of a concrete understanding of the concept. This is why a critical discourse analysis approach provides the ideal framework to address the importance of the discursive dimension of terrorism by providing an analysis of discourses and discerning the often opaque connections between language and other elements in social life.[7] This is the most appropriate pathway to understand why certain actors and acts have been categorized as terrorists and terrorism throughout Colombia's history: principally because of the politically motivated interest of delegitimizing an agent. This is especially evident with the strengthening of a global discourse against terrorism after the attacks of 11 September 2001.

To follow Andreas Feldmann and Victor Hinojosa's argument, terrorist acts have existed in Colombia for more than a century. Kidnappings, massacres and systematic persecution have been common practices through Colombian history since the republican wars of the nineteenth century. The One Thousand Days War (1899–1902) was a violent confrontation between centralists and federalists, after the colonial era, to decide the form of the nascent republic. These two blocs gave origin to Colombia's main parties, Liberal and Conservative, which have continued a hostile dynamic. During the 1930s, differences increased considerably between factions, materializing in a violent sectarianism not only between elites but among citizens because of their affiliation. These tensions exploded with the assassination of Liberal presidential candidate Jorge Eliécer Gaitán in 1948, triggering systemic clashes between the conservative government and liberal self-defence forces that would later evolve into proper guerrilla movements. This period became known as *La Violencia*; one of the most intensely violent episodes in Colombia's history, lasting until the late 1950s.

Throughout these years, the country experienced the forms of violence that Feldmann and Hinojosa categorize as terrorism. Their argument is that these acts constitute terrorism, and so Colombia has experienced terrorism since its independence. From their point of view, Colombia registered the highest incidence of terrorism in the world from 1970 to 2004.[8] Could this account of terrorism be considered objective? Is it undebatable that Colombia has experienced terrorism since its formation? As argued above, terrorism is a discursive construction, applied only to certain acts and in specific socio-political, geographical and temporal contexts. Back when these acts occurred they were not categorized as terrorism, they were simply observed as excesses of war. There is no terrorism without it being referred to as such.

This perspective creates a new narrative, seen from the present, about something that happened in the past, reinterpreting facts to argue that terrorism has existed for decades, when a discourse presenting such events as acts of terror did not previously exist. As seen from critical discourse analysis, framing an event as 'terrorism' is not a natural act, nor is it neutral, and alternative framings are always possible, but sometimes these are slow to emerge.[9] The acts observed through Colombia's history could well be understood as war crimes, crimes against humanity or violations of international humanitarian law. At the time they occurred they weren't interpreted as acts of terrorism, so why should one argue that terrorism has existed ever since? Rather than being linked to the actor or the act, the existence of terrorism depends on the discourse.

Before the 1970s the concept was barely part of public discourse. With the appearance of drug cartels through the 1980s and 1990s the word was popularly used to describe the actions of Pablo Escobar and the Medellin and Cali Cartels. It was during this period that the concept of narcoterrorism became prevalent in the discourse.[10] Armando Borrero, former presidential security advisor and now professor at the Colombian Joint War College, refers to this form of violence as 'criminal terrorism'.[11]

With the demise of the major drug cartels and the assassination of Pablo Escobar by the mid-1990s, leftist guerrillas began to be referred to as terrorists. The concept of 'terrorism to support guerrilla actions' appeared.[12] This notion referred to guerrillas using terrorism in order to achieve their strategic objectives.

But there is a very thin line between this categorization and labelling guerrillas entirely as terrorists. In the first case, we would assume that guerrillas use several warfare methods, including (but not limited to) terrorism. In the latter, the organizations would employ exclusively terrorist tactics. This distinction is clearer when the problem is observed from an academic perspective, but in political and popular discourse the line is more blurry. Political leaders, especially those fighting rebels, and people on the street, do not care about this difference. If a group makes a terrorist attack, whatever its strategic circumstances it will immediately be perceived as a terrorist organization, even if it employs other operational means. An objective approach to understanding the organization is lost through the discourse portraying the agent as a terrorist.

Besides discourses portraying guerrillas and criminals as terrorists, state responses to these phenomena, which will be explored below, have also been categorized as terrorism in many cases. This has also clouded the issue of creating a concrete understanding of terrorism.

Terrorism and the drug cartels

It is difficult to date the specific moment when use of the concept of terrorism appeared in Colombia. Before the 1980s it was rarely used, but was not inexistent. Guerrillas were still referred to as bandits, rebels, subversives or even as groups using terrorism, but not as terrorists. Garry Leech, an author and journalist who spent several years in Colombia, evidences this perception of insurgents as bandits during the 1960s, when discussing so-called 'independent republics', which were self-governed peasant communities who controlled territory and were profoundly influenced by communism:

> By declaring these republics as shortcuts for communist bandits, the government came up with the excuse to launch military attacks against them, to condemn them politically, and to block them economically.[13]

It was with the major attacks by drug cartels, and more specifically by the Medellin Cartel, that the use of the concept spread. The state responded to this violence by elevating the discourse portraying cartel's actions as terrorism, and presenting it as a threat to national security. President Virgilio Barco (1986–90) argued:

> Drug cartels have declared a total war on us. This war declaration goes against all nations. Against those who see the future of their youth destroyed

> by drugs as well as those, like Colombia, who see their democracy and institutions threatened by violence and terrorism. There are no borders for the death created by this dirty business, no country could be considered safe from drug-dealing terrorism.[14]

Evidently, the categorization of drug-related violence as terrorism was not one that happened without discussion. In theory, and as has been delineated by Bruce Hoffman, one of the most recognized scholars of terrorism, the concept refers to politically motivated violence.[15] Criminals are not interested in changing the social order or the political system, they are only concerned with the continuation of their business in order to make more profit. So the question is: to what extent could the cartels' actions be considered political?

Violence did increase as a result of Escobar's actions – he plagued Colombia with bombings and targeted killings. Car bombings, for example, hadn't been common before, but Escobar made this practice routine in Colombia. In November 1989, for the first time, a commercial airliner was blown up mid-flight, killing 110 people. Bogotá experienced its worst period of terror with a sequence of bombings against civilian and state targets: of *El Espectador*, one of the leading newspapers in Colombia; of the offices of the Department of Security (DAS) in 1989, killing 52 and injuring about 1,000 people; of the Centro 93 shopping centre in 1993, killing 8, injuring 250 and causing about US$ 700,000 in damage; of the commercial district of Chapinero and even of the city centre.[16]

The targeted killing campaign was aimed at journalists, politicians, judges, presidential candidates and police officers. The director of *El Espectador* Guillermo Cano, presidential candidate Luis Carlos Galan and justice minister Rodrigo Lara were all murdered because they supported extradition. The number of policeman killed is astronomical. President César Gaviria said that just in Medellin, in January 1990, about 400 police officers were killed. The statistics are contested, however, and more conservative estimates have been made.[17] But the lack of clear figures demonstrates that the phenomenon went beyond all normal parameters, proving the intensity of the violence.

Whereas the main objective of the cartel is inherently economic, the purpose of these attacks could be understood as political because several of its acts had political veneer. In theory, criminals want to continue making profit. Confronting the state could be counterproductive, because the criminals are likely to lose in the long term. However, criminal enterprises may grow to a size where a struggle against the state is simply inevitable. Escobar's activities began to compete with the state itself in many locations. In Medellin and the province of Antioquia, *El Patron* became the provider of services, from energy to recreation. In order for his enterprise to grow it was necessary to buy state and police officials, causing his political influence to rise astronomically through corruption. A war with the state began when the idea of extradition of drug dealers to the United States took form. The possibility of being jailed in the US enraged several drug dealers, who came together under an organization known as Los Extraditables. Their opposition to extradition motivated many of their terrorist attacks and the assassination of prominent politicians. These actions were political in essence. An expression of opposition to a state act is political by definition. When criminals control territory, regulate population activities, provide services and clash with the state, they are acting politically.

When this political dimension is taken into account, the concept of terrorism seems to be more applicable to the case. Armando Borrero agrees that by the end of the 1980s, this form of 'criminal terrorism' acquired a more political nature, in its struggle against extradition, the media, the police and the judicial system.[18]

In fact, this was the origin of the concept of narcoterrorism. Introduced by US ambassador to Colombia Lewis Tambs, it has been further developed by scholars. Rachel Ehrenfeld defines narcoterrorism as 'the use of drug trafficking to advance the objectives of certain governments and terrorist organizations'.[19] The concept quickly became part of the Colombian political discourse, although referring first to drug cartels and not to guerrillas. Tambs did refer to FARC as a narcoterrorist organization back in 1985, but given the primary focus on the cartels, this conception of guerrillas didn't take root. President César Gaviria stated:

> Drug dealing is a threat to peace, not as tangible as tanks or fighter jets, but equally real and no less devastating, and it has become one of the worst enemies of social integrity and democratic stability. Sooner or later we will destroy narco-terrorism, but if the rest of the international community does not make any sacrifices comparable to those done by Colombia, humanity will never be free from drug-dealing and its disastrous consequences.[20]

This kind of violence waged by cartels could have been categorized in a different manner, but through the discourse it became almost universally recognized as narcoterrorism. This became the dominant narrative to explain systemic violence in Colombia. A simple word count on 'narcoterrorism' in Colombia's leading newspaper, *El Tiempo*, since 1990 demonstrates the centrality of the concept in the public debate. This is shown in figure 9.1 in comparison to a similar count in the *New York Times*, in order to illustrate how widespread it became in the Colombian debate.

In Colombia, the use of the concept peaked through the early and mid-1990s, due to intense cartel violence. The curve in figure 9.1 demonstrates that

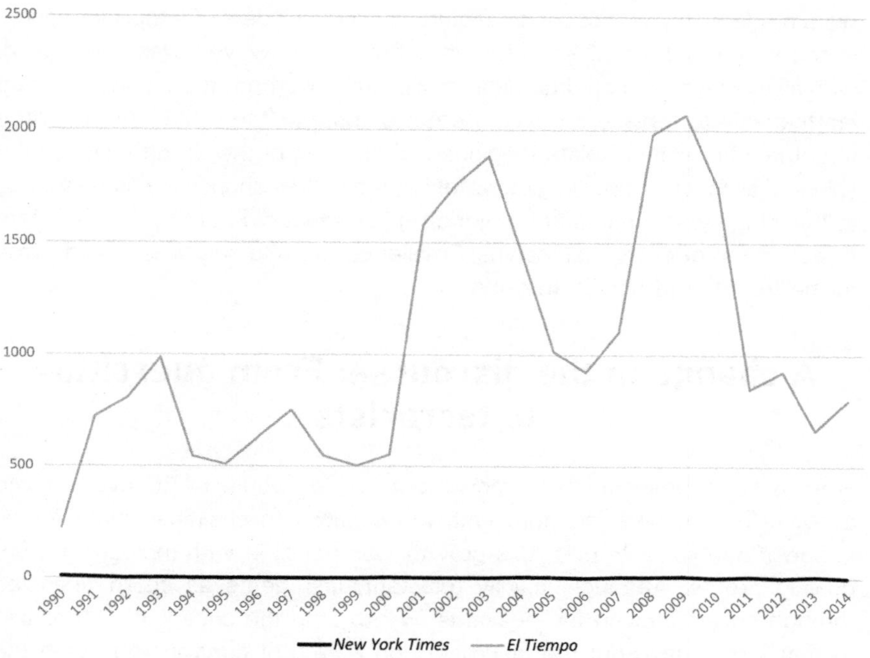

Figure 9.1 Word count for 'narcoterrorism' in the *New York Times* and *El Tiempo*, 1990–2014.

through the late 1990s the use of the concept faded away as major cartels were disbanded, only to reappear strongly in the early 2000s with the emergence of a discourse on the global war on terror, but in Colombia's case, referring to guerrillas. The highest peak in the curve, though, appears more recently, in the late 2000s, as the official discourse during Alvaro Uribe's Government emphasized guerrilla actions as terrorism and narcoterrorism, a transformation that is analysed more thoroughly below. In the United States, however, the use of the concept was not as widespread as it was in Colombia. Variations in the *New York Times* curve are not even noticeable, with fewer than ten entries per year.

Now, looking into the practicalities of state responses, the struggles against drug dealing, cartels and guerrillas were initially understood as separate enterprises. Since terrorism was associated with drug cartels through the discourse, they received more public attention as a more imminent threat. A 'beheading' strategy was thus implemented, targeting mafia bosses. The national police created elite units with the support of the United States to track Escobar, combining intelligence and operations assets. Enormous efforts were made by the authorities to capture or kill the leaders of important figures in the cartels. The problem of coca cultivation, however, was overlooked, with all eyes focused on drug dealers. Several government programmes tried ineffectively to replace coca with other crops, but the lack of proper infrastructure connecting isolated regions with the rest of the country caused the failure of all these efforts. In general terms, then, the response to narcoterrorism at this stage was a pursuit of major drug lords that did not have a significant effect on the markets themselves. Smaller cartels and guerrillas would come to the forefront of narcotrafficking.

A change in the discourse: From guerrillas to terrorists

From a small peasant-based movement in the 1950s, FARC evolved into a powerful army-like structure with the capacity to challenge state forces in specific regions. In part, this growth was possible with increasing drug-dealing profits. Although initially reluctant, insurgents accepted financing through cocaine, given the peasants' will to crop the coca leaf. Opposition to that would have put the insurgents on a path of confrontation with the population. In the Seventh Guerrilla Conference in 1982, FARC approved the cultivation of coca in its areas of influence, only with the creation of a tax known as *gramaje*, charged to dealers. It was initially 10 to 15 per cent of the profits.[21]

The tax was ideal for FARC's growth and expansion plans, and it provided the necessary resources for its period of greatest strength, during the 1980s and 1990s. The insurgents' participation became evident with the discovery of production complexes such as Tranquilandia in the jungles of the province of Caquetá, where the bulk of the Medellin Cartel's drugs were produced with protection from the insurgents.[22]

Since the mid-1980s, FARC has progressively increased its involvement in the cocaine-producing trade chain. Links with drug lords were disrupted and confrontation with the cartels began around that time. FARC started to take over link after link of the production process: from taxing to becoming the prime buyers at the lowest stages of the chain, and even becoming traders themselves.[23] Taxation was expanded to cultivators and croppers, and it was kept for smaller drug dealers and landing-strip users.[24]

From 1996 to 1998 FARC gained total control of the drug trade in Putumayo and Caquetá. It eliminated local drug dealers and introduced fixed prices for the coca paste. It forced farmers to sell only to the local Front, and began storing and trading large amounts of cocaine with multiple new micro-cartels.[25]

Since then, FARC's involvement in the drug trade has not been homogeneous throughout the territory; it varies from region to region.[26]

This increased participation in the drug trade, together with the decline of major cartels, progressively led to FARC's classification as a narcoterrorist organization. Through the discourse, the insurgents began to be presented as the main terrorist threat against the nation. The ELN would also be portrayed as a terrorist group, but its participation was more marginal, and its military capabilities were not comparable to FARC's.

Between 1996 and 1998, FARC reached its historical zenith in terms of manpower and strategic capability. Over two years, several operations against military and police units proved that FARC had reached a superior military capability. For most of their history, the insurgents had only managed to use guerrilla tactics to harass military forces in isolated regions, but they progressively acquired the strength to fight in more conventional terms, challenging state control in specific areas of the territory. In the southeast, FARC was able to conduct successful attacks against elite military units. General Carlos Alberto Ospina, former joint commander of the military forces, explains this progress through a curve based on the number of soldiers or policeman killed in each operation over time (figure 9.2). The first part of the curve shows an increasing number of casualties for the military forces and a qualitative escalation according to the type of target. The second part shows a decrease of insurgent capabilities as the state regains the strategic initiative.[27]

Were these attacks terrorist actions? Is this the typical behaviour of a terrorist organization? If these questions are answered from a strategic studies perspective, we could be speaking about the evolution of the operational

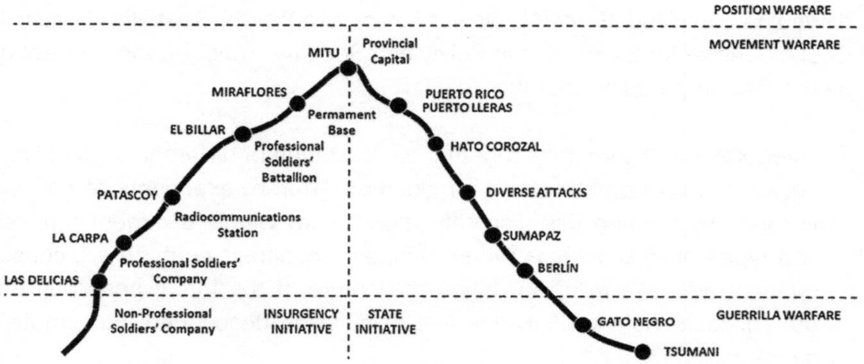

Figure 9.2 Progression of FARC attacks. The vertical axis represents the number of soldiers or policemen killed in each operation; the horizontal axis represents time.

capability of the organization, advancing from irregular to regular warfare tactics. These actions could be understood as proper acts of war: an army-like structure fighting the positions of an enemy by military means. Considering that the targets were not civilian, and that the objective was not to create fear through an audience beyond the immediate target, it could be argued that such actions were not terrorist acts.

However, these were not the only type of operations undertaken by FARC. In many cases, the insurgents took over towns by force and terror, destroying houses, threatening the population, harassing civilians and killing thousands of innocent individuals, including women and children. For example, in the town of Bojayá, FARC killed 79 civilians, burning and destroying houses and a cathedral in a turf war against the paramilitary in 2002.[28] In Bogotá, FARC placed a car bomb at the elite social club El Nogal, killing 36 and injuring more than 200;[29] beyond these attacks, thousands of landmines were planted, and hundreds of attacks were made on the energy and oil infrastructure. From the point of view of many, such attacks could correctly be understood as terrorist actions and not as war operations.

The definition of insurgents as narcoterrorists is debatable. The political objective behind such categorization is obvious. Presenting guerrillas as narcoterrorists implies that the group is opposed to the people. Since insurgency scenarios are dialectical competitions between the state and the rebels to win the support of the population, portraying FARC in these terms is useful for the state as it delegitimizes the guerrillas.

If we analyse the rigour of this categorization, portraying FARC and the ELN as narcoterrorist organizations does not have much logic. The origin, interests and natures of drug cartels and insurgents are so different that placing them within the same group is actually misleading, and could end in flawed policymaking. Grant Wardlaw, a senior fellow at the Australian Research Council Centre for Excellence in Policy and Security, criticized the concept of narcoterrorism, arguing that it:

> categorizes and combines together a wide range of different sorts of links between drug traffickers and a myriad of different exponents of political violence by treating this disparate group, with widely divergent motives and types of relationships with drugs, as a coherent entity. [As a consequence] we have failed to define the nature of the threat posed by the drug/political violence linkages and have often descended into emotive name-calling.[30]

Whichever position is assumed in this debate, and as analysed from the critical discourse perspective, the representation of violent acts as terrorism is conditioned by practices in a specific context. It is because of the context of the end of the 1990s that FARC began to be presented as a terrorist group. But that representation would only become more prevalent with the appearance of a discourse on the global war on terrorism.

Effects of the global discourse against terrorism

Andrés Pastrana's administration (1998–2002) tried new negotiations with FARC but, as in previous cases, the attempt failed. Presidents Betancur (1982–86), Barco (1986–90) and Gaviria (1990–94) tried to respond to the decades-long threat of insurgencies through dialogue. At a moment when FARC wasn't necessarily weak, and after a lack of advancement in counter-insurgency during Samper's Government, widely perceived as illegitimate given its presidential campaign connections with the Cali Cartel, Pastrana appeared with an interesting proposition. A negotiated solution seemed to be a logical path to follow at a moment in which the 'military option' didn't seem plausible. But FARC went to the negotiations in a position of relative strength and without a clear intention of achieving peace. Reasons for the failure of the process include FARC's use of the demilitarized zone created for these negotiations (an area the size of Switzerland) to hide hostages, produce cocaine, strengthen its operations, meet foreign representatives, recruit and rest, and the state's incapacity to deal with paramilitary organizations.

The insurgents pointed to the state's supposed preparations for war as another reason for the failure. Pastrana intended to respond to the problem of the drug trade through a comprehensive plan, Plan Colombia, which included a military component. Formulated in 1998, its main objectives were to reduce areas cultivated with drug crops by half in four years, to increase the manual eradication of crops, to strengthen criminal intelligence in order to capture drug dealers and intercept cargo more efficiently, and to strengthen economic and social structures to disrupt the criminal economy, allowing the integration of communities to licit economic processes.[31] The Plan was a resource pool to which Colombia, the United States and the international community contributed with funds. By 2000, adaptations to the Plan had made it more compatible with American interests, focusing more on strengthening state capabilities and the military.[32] FARC interpreted the Plan as a military build-up parallel to negotiations, which eroded trust between the actors.

Plan Colombia required US$ 7.5 billion. Of this, Colombia contributed US$ 4 billion and the international community US$ 3.5 billion. The United

States alone provided US$ 1.3 billion: US$ 700 million for military aid, and US$ 600 million for crop substitution, public services and strengthening democracy. Military aid was increased later to US$ 1 billion.[33]

It is interesting to note that as a response of the state to these phenomena, the struggles against narcotics and insurgency were still conceived of as separate enterprises, but the anti-narcotics strategy was heavily militarized. Aid channelled through Plan Colombia couldn't initially be used in the fight against insurgents. The United States didn't want to become immersed in a counterinsurgency struggle against Colombian guerrillas. But this would change with the September 11th attacks. The emergence of a global war on terror was not only the creation of a coalition to destroy al Qaeda and to deploy troops to Afghanistan and Iraq. It was also the construction of a discourse presenting the struggle against terrorists worldwide as a priority in international politics. As was explained by Bartolucci and Gallo, the representation of the September 11th events as 'acts of terrorism' has allowed the reframing of a discourse in a way that has been uncritically accepted and widely reproduced, up to the point of it becoming one of the principal security discourses at the global level.[34]

This discourse has been replicated worldwide, creating a global systemic response against organizations that would then be more firmly qualified as terrorist groups. Leaders in several countries appropriated the discourse within their own internal struggles, to justify a more radical fight against enemies, increasing the legitimacy of their responses. They argued that they were waging their own wars on terror. As Bartolucci explains, this has been the case in Spain against the Basques; China against the Uyghurs; Sri Lanka against the Tamils; Russia against the Chechens; Mauritania against Islamists; and in Algeria, Mali and Niger against the Tuareg and the Tubu.[35]

Colombia wasn't an exception. The response of the administration of Alvaro Uribe (2002–10) to FARC and ELN was precisely to intensify their portrayal as terrorist (and narcoterrorist) groups. Uribe appropriated the global War-on-Terror discourse to describe the Colombian struggle against FARC and ELN, and to develop a heavily militarized response to defeat them. As explained by Diana Rojas, researcher at the Universidad Nacional de Colombia, 'This campaign to discredit insurgencies [by labelling them as terrorism] contributed to reaffirm the idea that the Colombian conflict is part of the global war on terror with the consequential legitimation of Uribe's Democratic Security Policy.'[36]

FARC had been listed as a terrorist organization by the United States in 1997,[37] and by the European Union in 2002.[38] The AUC and the ELN followed soon after. Uribe capitalized on this inclusion. '[His] policy focus [was] to cast the armed conflict as an "antiterrorist fight" by re-labelling the guerrillas as terrorists and promoting international and regional initiatives to support this policy':[39]

> Today, FARC is transformed into the world's biggest cartel, a terrorist group that commits crimes against humanity. Their political purpose is a disguise more than a reality.[40]

Uribe was successful in portraying the decades-old problem of violence in Colombia merely as a terrorist threat. Structural causes like land tenancy, income distribution, political marginality, abandonment of remote regions and illicit economy cycles, among other things, became irrelevant in the discourse. Colombia would refer only to the narcoterrorism of FARC as the cause of insecurity.

The official discourse quickly spread through the population. Almost everyone in Colombia sees FARC as a terrorist group, and not as an insurgent, guerrilla or bandit group, as it was considered in the 1960s. Other perspectives on the insurgency were silenced, and those challenging the notion of FARC as a terrorist group were even defamed as supporters. The popularity of this perspective is proven by a strong appropriation of the concept through the public discourse. Figure 9.1 has already demonstrated that since the 2000s the use of the word 'narcoterrorism' has increased significantly, and this has been especially in relation to FARC. A word count on 'terrorism' leads to similar conclusions (figure 9.3). Comparing the *New York Times* and *El Tiempo* curves, it is possible to observe that in 2001 there was a dramatic rise in the use of the concept in both newspapers. This is logical considering the importance of the 'terrorist issue' after 9/11. However, from the mid-2000s, whereas the use of the term decreases in the *New York Times*, it reaches a higher peak in the Colombian newspaper. This demonstrates the deep penetration of the concept in the public debate. The peak in 2008 can be explained by the most successful special operations against FARC, and the multitude of popular mobilizations against the insurgents. News related to the insurgency proliferated in that year.

The most significant achievement of the appropriation of this discourse is related to the transformation in state responses to terrorism. The United States was finally convinced that the struggles against narcotics and guerrillas were the same; that the war against narcotics would never be successful if insurgencies were not challenged. Hence, military aid was finally channelled to fight insurgencies too. 'In August 2002, George Bush signed a Bill that allowed past and present aid to support a unified campaign against both drugs and Colombian groups on the list of terrorist organizations.'[41] As a consequence, military aid increased in the years following 9/11. In spite of a peak in 2000,

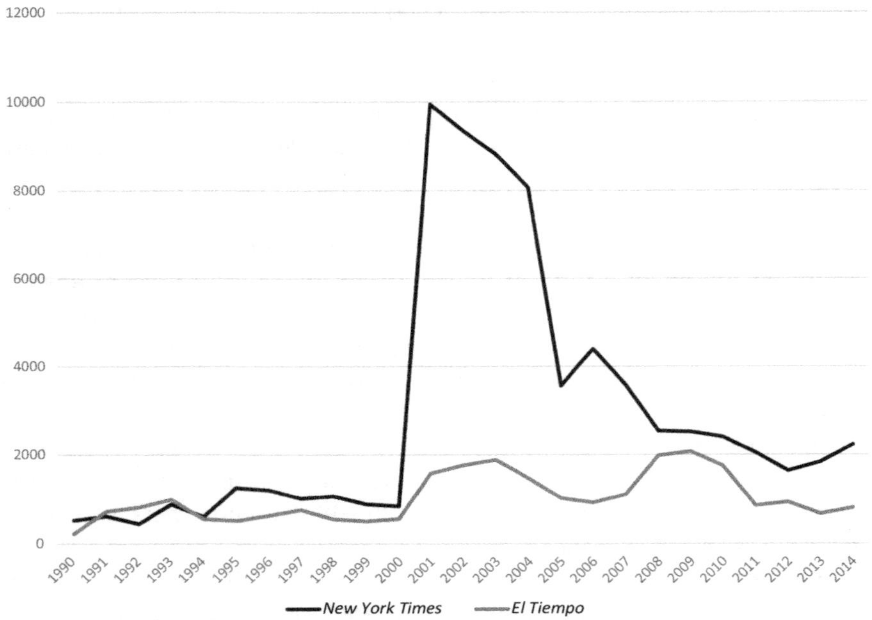

Figure 9.3 Word count for 'terrorism' in the *New York Times* and *El Tiempo*, 1990–2014.

amounts demonstrate higher contributions from the United States in the post-9/11 era than before (table 9.1).

In order to channel these funds into the defeat of insurgencies, Uribe formulated the Democratic Security Policy (DSP). It was a comprehensive strategy for state institutions, not just the military, to gain control of the entire territory and to build state institutions. It was a different conception of the state response, understanding the emergence of insurgency and criminal phenomena as a consequence of weak state institutions in isolated regions. As such, it required military might, but also the participation of all state institutions. It is a similar conception to the British 'comprehensive approach' of counterinsurgency, which included a development dimension as a hoped-for definite solution to the problem.

Plan Patriota was the military component of the DSP designed to attack FARC in its strongest areas. Plan Colombia had left the military with greatly increased strength. The number of professional soldiers increased from 22,000 to 55,000, regular soldiers from 46,000 to 73,000. Smaller and more flexible, rapidly deployable units began to be implemented, and were stationed in the areas of strong insurgent presence. The Rapid Deployment Force (FUDRA),

Table 9.1 Increase in US military aid to Colombia following 9/11

Year	Amount of Aid (US$ million)
1996	64
1997	87
1998	115
1999	310
2000	772
2001	224
2002	389
2003	606
2004	611
2005	596
2006	589
2007	619

Source: Adam Isacson and Gimena Sanchez, 'President Trump and Colombia's Santos to meet this week,' Washington Office on Latin America (WOLA) website, 15 May 2008, available at: www.wola.org/analysis/president-trump-colombias-santos-meet-week/ (accessed 12 May 2018).

with 5,000 soldiers, was created as an elite army counterinsurgency unit composed of three Mobile Brigades and a Brigade of Special Forces; it was prepared to act in any geographical setting. A River Brigade was created as part of the marine infantry, with five River Battalions deployed across the national territory and a river warfare school. Five new Mobile Brigades were later created, with 2,500 soldiers each. Combat helicopters increased from 18 to 30, and transportation helicopters from 126 to 223, while 5 silent aeroplanes with night vision were acquired. Rifles increased from 120,000 to 180,000.[42]

Army aviation was repowered with 50 Black Hawks, 30 Huey IIs, and 11 UH-1Ns for a total of 114 helicopters. A total of 83 Black Hawks were given to the air force and the police.[43] The air force also received 25 Super Tucanos, 12 Attack Huey IIs, 4 Casa C-295s for transportation, 4 Beechcraft 350 Super King Air (2 transportation, 2 intelligence platforms), 5 Cessna caravans as intelligence platforms and 25 for basic training, 13 last generation K-firs and the modernization of 11 more.[44] Heavily equipped military units were created specifically to regain control of cocaine-producing areas. A new anti-narcotics brigade (BRACNA) with three battalions was created. The air force base of Tres Esquinas, a hub for offensive actions in the south, was modernized.

All of these adaptations enabled the military to change the balance of power against FARC. Before Plan Colombia, the capacity to fight from the air was almost nil. Given FARC's lack of anti-aircraft defence capabilities, the military obtained a strong advantage against the insurgents. Air bombardments were the key to both weaken FARC's control of specific territories and erode the command structure by attacking top leaders' campsites. Similarly, a qualitative and quantitative increase of army capacities, including professional soldiers, specialized jungle and mountain units, informer networks, and local soldiers with a deep knowledge of their communities provided capacities that the army had previously lacked, reducing FARC's spaces of action, cutting mobile corridors and pushing it out of its historical regions of domination.

Statistics demonstrate that the strategy was successful. In the period between 2001 and 2010 insurgent groups were reduced to their weakest point in history. FARC had gone from 20,000 combatants at the end of the 1990s to 8,000–10,000 by 2010.[45] Likewise, from 2002 to 2009 there were 12,294 demobilizations, of which 1,128 were middle-rank commanders with more than ten years of experience: an increase from one in twenty-seven in 2002 to one in three in 2008.[46] Other indicators are shown in table 9.2.

However, not everything about this particular state response under Uribe's administration was positive. The need to defeat the terrorists through military means systematically pressured the military to produce results. In many cases, commanders resorted to the killing of civilians to present them as FARC casualties. This phenomenon, which had existed before Uribe's administration, is known as *falsos positivos*, and it increased 150 per cent from 2002 to 2010, according to a study published by two prestigious universities in Bogotá.[47] These kinds of practices, and not forgetting other aspects like the historical synergy that has existed between the state and paramilitary squads in certain regions, have been the basis for the notion of 'state terrorism'. This is also a popular discourse in Colombia, although more concentrated at the left of the political spectrum: non-governmental organizations, trade unions, student groups

Table 9.2 Indicators of the weakening of FARC following the introduction of the Democratic Security Policy (DSP)

Indicator	Change after DSP
Homicides	45% reduction 2002–9
Terrorist attacks	71% reduction 2002–10
Kidnappings	93% reduction 2002–9
Mass kidnappings	100% reduction 2002–9
Coca crops	33% reduction 2002–9
Cocaine production	40% reduction 2002–9
Drug seizure	113% increase 2002–9

Source: David Spencer, *Colombia: Camino a la Recuperacion: Seguridad y Gobernabilidad 1982–2010*. (Washington: Centre for Hemispheric Defense Studies, 2011). p. 81.

and communist movements. Nonetheless, the vision of paramilitary groups as terrorist organizations is more common than the idea of state terrorism.

The categorization of insurgents as terrorists became so deeply rooted in policymaking that an obvious rift emerged with neighbouring countries which refused to recognize them as such. A left-leaning bloc emerged during the early 2000s in Latin America, with the most radical among them in Ecuador, Bolivia, Nicaragua and Venezuela. These so-called Bolivarian governments rejected American influence, neoliberal economic models and global trade institutions. Their alliance clashed with Colombia's position as the main US ally in the region. The Bolivarians shared political, economic and social views with FARC, making the Colombian Government deeply suspicious about linkages between the rebels and these governments. The permissiveness of Correa in Ecuador and Chávez in Venezuela towards the guerrillas, and Uribe's undiplomatic way of resolving their differences, triggered the worst crisis in the bilateral relations between Colombia and Venezuela and Ecuador, when Uribe decided to bomb FARC's campsite on Ecuadorian territory without the consent of Correa's Government.

For the governments of Hugo Chávez in Venezuela and Rafael Correa in Ecuador, FARC and ELN were not terrorist organizations. They were rebels in arms with legitimate causes to fight for. Addressing the National Assembly, Chávez argued that 'FARC and ELN are no terrorist corps, they are real armies. [...] They are insurgent forces with a political project, a Bolivarian project that is respected here.'[48] Similarly, María Isabel Salvador, Ecuadorian minister of foreign affairs, argued that 'Ecuador will not consider Colombian guerrillas, FARC and ELN, as belligerent, neither will it qualify them as terrorists. It will keep its qualification as irregular groups.'[49]

But how accurate is it to categorize insurgents as terrorists? After 9/11, the discourse on terrorism proved to be so strong that all sorts of organizations – including guerrillas, paramilitary groups and drug gangs – were quickly qualified as such. However, as with 'narcoterrorism', observing diverse types of agents through the same lens can be misleading. Alfredo Rangel, a security researcher who became a senator for the right-wing Centro Democratico party agrees with this idea. He argues:

> The conflict in our country which has so many faces, so many forms, and one main dynamic, the guerrilla warfare waged against the Colombian state, cannot be reduced to one of its faces, which is evidently, terrorism.[50]

It is not the objective of this chapter to determine whether insurgents are terrorist organizations. That is a political opinion that will place the observer on one of the sides of the political debate. If we define terrorists as those organizations which resort to terrorist methods, even if they also employ other types of tactics, then FARC can easily be classified as such. But if we focus on the actor itself, and not on its methods, the perspective may be different. FARC is an insurgent group that has carried out terrorist attacks in many cases, but also acts via guerrilla and even conventional warfare. What is interesting in this case is that whatever the strategic circumstances of the organization, in the discourse, FARC became profoundly identified as a terrorist organization, and this understanding brought certain policymaking consequences.

The people's appropriation of a discourse

One of the most interesting effects of the diffusion of the discourse portraying insurgents as terrorists was the deep penetration it had through the nation, among civilians and Colombians without any formal political affiliation. This is evidenced by the appearance of spontaneous online social network movements strongly rejecting FARC. 'Colombia soy yo' appeared in 2008 as the initiative of a group of students and young professionals, with a Facebook group. With mottos like 'no more terrorism', 'no more lies', 'no more kidnapping', 'no more murders' and 'no more FARC', their popularity spread rapidly. Once they gained a critical mass, the media and politicians joined the chorus to promote an iconic massive mobilization on 4 March 2008, entitled 'One million voices against FARC'. It was one of the biggest demonstrations in Colombian history, with attendance in every major city in Colombia and overseas.

As a spontaneous movement, Colombia soy yo didn't truly evolve into an influential organization. Its leadership unfolded into smaller movements without much strength, but the manifestations had a great echo in European countries, where FARC had managed to portray itself as freedom fighters. Social networks were a key instrument for the diffusion of the discourse. There were many Facebook groups vociferously opposing FARC as a terrorist group, including Las FARC: terroristas y mentirosos (FARC: terrorists and liars), No más FARC (No more FARC), and One million voices against FARC. The description of the latter says:

> Note for the audience of this page. To FARC adulators, promoters of terrorism, intolerant defenders of Havana, friends of FARC impunity and sponsors of the country's submission to the world's biggest cartel, we warn you, you are not welcome in this group, you are in the wrong place, and your posts will be deleted and your accounts blocked, as a tribute to the thousands of FARC's victims that are waiting for justice today, no impunity.[51]

Other Facebook groups demonstrate an ardent support for Uribe as a kind of saviour of Colombia. In line with Latin American messianic politics, Uribe's discourse was so powerful that sectors of the population were convinced that the destruction of FARC was the key to the solution of violence in Colombia, whatever the structural causes of conflict, and that Uribe was the one indicated for this job. It is not a coincidence that his approval ratings were the highest in Colombian history, ranging from 63 per cent to 85 per cent, compared to 53 per cent for Gaviria, 30 per cent for Samper and 21 per cent for Pastrana (1998–2002) by the end of their terms.[52] Even after his presidency, people claim he should still be in charge. Examples of these groups are Yo le creo a Uribe: Salvemos a Colombia (I believe in Uribe: Let's save Colombia), Doctor Alvaro Uribe Velez mil gracias!!!!! (Doctor Alvaro Uribe Velez many thanks!!!!!) and Alvaro Uribe idolo del pueblo (Alvaro Uribe people's idol).

This sector of society radically opposes the peace process that Juan Manuel Santos (2010–) established with the insurgents. Given their perspective of FARC as a terrorist organization, they do not conceive a negotiated solution as a proper way out of the conflict. They see Santos as a traitor, and negotiations as showing the weakness of the state. A comment from a citizen in a Facebook group called Gracias Presidente Uribe – Primero Colombia exemplifies the deep penetration of the discourse:

> The ego and arrogance of FARC Manuel Santos[53] has made him stupid. ... Like never in the history of Colombia, a president is competing for the first place of the worst president in South America, with his colleagues of Brazil and Venezuela. [...] Even if it hurts the communists in this country, Uribe had a popularity of 82 percent of approval of the Colombian people, he left the country with a good economy, security and a more calmed atmosphere, meanwhile with FARCSANTOS this territory is full of coca, delinquency, unemployment, and pessimism, we reach the top of stupidity when now on TV the FARC rats appear saying that we have to pay an extortion or *vacuna*[54] because it is stipulated in the laws of FARC's constitution (sic). [...] in the hands of Uribe this would be different, instead of giving them 10 seats in Congress he would give them 10 graves.[55]

By 2016, negotiations with FARC had advanced to an unprecedented historical point. The agenda had practically been discussed in full, and the atmosphere signalled that the agreement was about to be signed. Uribe's party, Centro Democratico, and its supporters have become the main obstacle to an agreement in Havana. The categorization of FARC as a terrorist agent has made it difficult for this sector to conceive any kind of political concessions and any alternative besides FARC's strict submission to law. Juan Manuel Santos, however, has built on a different perspective, explaining conflict in Colombia beyond a mere 'terrorist threat', and insurgencies beyond the narcoterrorism framework.

Conclusion

Contrary to what we might think, terrorism isn't necessarily an objective phenomenon that can be observed and understood in a concrete manner. Our understanding of who is a terrorist and what constitutes terrorism itself is a subjective construction based on the discourse, and generally following political interests. This is why if we want to understand terrorism in Colombia, and the responses that have been created around it, an analysis from a critical discourse approach is more appropriate.

As has been explained, the conception of terrorism in Colombia has changed over the years, according to which actors have challenged the state more significantly at each specific point in time and have generated more violence. The discourse was initially more focused on major drug cartels – specifically, the Medellin Cartel and Pablo Escobar. The conception of narcoterrorism appeared as a state response to place the enemy at the centre of the public debate, and to concentrate the efforts of institutions against it. With the demise of the major cartels and the preponderance of guerrillas both in drug dealing and in violence, these guerrillas began to be recognized as terrorist organizations. Although at the beginning they were seen as bandits and guerrillas, by the end of the 1990s, with the increase of their operational capability, they began to be referred to as terrorists.

The most significant evolution came with the construction of a global discourse of a war against terrorism after the 9/11 attacks in the United States. This construction was appropriated in Colombia by the Government of Alvaro Uribe to explain the struggle against insurgents, and particularly FARC, as part of this global War on Terror. The policy effects were astounding. Foreign aid given for anti-narcotics was finally channelled to fight insurgents, and the legitimacy of this response increased considerably within Colombia. Uribe has been regarded as the most successful president in recent years, and the strength of his discourse can still be appreciated at the time of writing, eight years after the end of his term, in the form of a robust opposition to the peace process in Havana. Notwithstanding, some of the historical responses of the state to the phenomenon of insurgencies – through excesses, transgressions of the law and alliances with paramilitary squads – have been categorized by some as state terrorism. These variations in the conception of terrorism have rendered a single, concrete understanding of the phenomenon in Colombia impossible.

Notes

1 Centro Nacional de Memoria Histórica, '¡Basta Ya! Colombia: Memorias de Guerra y dignidad,' Centro Nacional de Memoria Histórica website, 2012, available at: www.centrodememoriahistorica.gov.co/micrositios/informeGeneral/estadisticas.html (accessed 23 April 2016).

2 This position is expoundeded by Andreas Feldmann and Victor Hinojosa, 'Logic and sources of a multidimensional ubiquitous phenomenon,' *Terrorism and Political Violence* 21:1 (2009): 46–61.

3 Valentina Bartolucci and Georgio Gallo, 'Terrorism, systems thinking and critical discourse analysis,' *Systems Reseach and Behavioural Science* 32 (2015): 15–27; Valentina Bartolucci, 'Terrorism rhetoric under the Bush administration,' *Journal of Language and Politics* 11:4 (2012): 562–82; Richard Jackson, Marie Breene Smyth, Jeroen Gunning and Lee Jarvis, *Terrorism: A Critical Introduction* (London: Palgrave Macmillan, 2011); Richard Jackson, 'The core commitments of critical terrorism studies,' *European Political Science* 6:3 (2007): 244–51.

4 Jackson et al., *Terrorism*, p. 3.

5 Pamela L. Griset and Sue Mahan, *Terrorism in Perspective* (London: Sage, 2003); Walter Laqueur, *The New Terrorism* (Oxford: Oxford University Press, 1999); Gus Martin, *Understanding Terrorism* (London: Sage, 2006), pp. 45–61.

6 Bruce Hoffman, *Inside Terrorism* (New York: Columbia University Press, 2006), pp. 3–17; Annette Hubschle, 'The T word: Conceptualizing terrorism,' *African Security Review* 15:3 (2006): 2–18.

7 Norman Fairclough, *Analysing Discourse: Textual Analysis for Social Research* (London: Routledge, 2003).

8 Feldmann and Hinojosa, 'Logic and sources.'

9 Bartolucci and Gallo, 'Terrorism.'

10 Diego Tarapués, 'An overview of the terrorism in Colombia: Context, national legislation and anti-terrorism measures,' *[Con]textos* 1:4 (2012): 29–37.

11 Armando Borrero, 'Terrorismo, Narcotráfico y Delincuencia.' *Revista Criminalidad* 49 (2006): 134–8.

12 Borrero, 'Terrorismo, Narcotráfico y Delincuencia'; Tarapués, 'Overview of the terrorism.'

13 Garry Leech, 'Colombia: Cincuenta años de violencia,' *Rebelión*, 29 June 2002, available at: www.rebelion.org/hemeroteca/plancolombia/leech290602.htm (accessed 5 February 2015).

14 Virgilio Barco, 'Discurso del Presdiente Virgilio Barco a la 44 Asamblea de las Naciones Unidas,' *Revista* 8 (October–December 1989): 32–7.

15 Hoffman, *Inside Terrorism*.

16 *El Tiempo*, 'Historia de otras bombas,' *El Tiempo*, 12 November 1999, available at: www.eltiempo.com/archivo/documento/MAM-949482 (accessed 5 February 2015).

17 German Jimenez, 'Pablo Escobar mató a 400 policias en enero del 90: Gaviria,' *El Universal*, 2 December 2013, available at: www.eluniversal.com.co/

colombia/pablo-escobar-mato-400-policias-en-enero-del-90-gaviria-144017 (accessed 9 January 2016).
18 Borrero, 'Terrorismo, Narcotráfico y Delincuencia,' 134–8.
19 Rachel Ehrenfeld, *Narcoterrorism* (New York: Basic Books, 1990), p. xiii.
20 César Gaviria, 'Discurso del Presidente Cesar Gaviria ante la ONU,' *Revista* 11 (July–September 1990): 29–33.
21 International Crisis Group, *War and Drugs in Colombia: Latinamerica Report, 11* (Bogota; International Crisis Group, 2005).
22 Nadia Lizarazo, 'Papel de las Fuerzas Armadas en la Politica Antidrogas 1985–1990,' in Alejo Vargas, *El Papel de las Fuerzas Armadas en la Politica Antidrogas Colombiana* (Bogota: Universidad Nacional de Colombia, 2008).
23 Eduardo Pizarro, *Una Democracia Asediada* (Bogota: Norma, 2004).
24 International Crisis Group, *War and Drugs in Colombia.*
25 *Ibid.*
26 *Ibid.*
27 Carlos Ospina, 'Insights from Colombia's long war: Counterinsurgency lessons learned,' *Journal of Counterterrorism and Homeland Security International* 12:3 (2006): 26–33.
28 Diana Duran, 'En Bojayá fueron 79 no 119: Gonzalo Sanchez,' *El Espectador*, 2 December 2011, available at: www.elespectador.com/noticias/judicial/bojaya-fueron-79-no-119-gonzalo-sanchez-articulo-314712 (accessed 5 February 2015).
29 *El País*, 'Mañana se cumplen 10 años del atentado al Club El Nogal,' *El País*, 3 February 2013, available at: www.elpais.com.co/elpais/colombia/noticias/manana-cumplen-10-anos-atentado-club-nogal (accessed 5 February 2015).
30 Grant Wardlaw, 'Linkages between the illegal drug traffic and terrorism,' *Conflict Quarterly* 8:3 (1988): 5–26.
31 León Valencia, *Adios a la Politica, Bienvenida la Guerra* (Bogota: Intermedio, 2002), p. 204.
32 Ingrid Vaicius, 'Una perspectiva hacia el entendimiento del Plan Colombia,' in Jorge Estrada (ed.), *Plan Colombia y la Instensificación de la Guerra* (Bogota: Universidad Nacional de Colombia, 2002), pp. 21–2.
33 Rafael Pardo, *Historia de las Guerras* (Bogota: Ediciones B, 2004), pp. 564–5.
34 Bartolucci and Gallo, 'Terrorism.'
35 Bartolucci, 'Terrorism rhetoric.'
36 Diana Rojas, 'Balance de la politica internacional del gobierno Uribe,' *Análisis Político* 19:57 (May–August 2006): 92.
37 US Department of State, 'Foreign Terrorist Organizations,' US Department of State website, available at: www.state.gov/j/ct/rls/other/des/123085.htm (accessed 5 February 2015).
38 Paul Ames, 'Unión Europea agrega a las FARC a su lista terrorista,' *La Nación*, 18 June 2002, available at: wvw.nacion.com/ln_ee/2002/junio/18/ultima8.html (accessed 15 February 2015).
39 Mirko Sossai, 'The internal conflict in Colombia and the fight against terrorism,' *Journal of International Criminal Justice* 3 (2005): 253–67.
40 Caracol Radio, 'Lea aquí el discurso completo del presidente Uribe,' *Caracol Radio*, 28 October 2012, para. 7, available at: http://caracol.com.co/radio/2012/10/28/nacional/1351437960_786666.html (accessed 21 April 2016).
41 Adam Isacson, 'Optimism, pessimism and terrorism: Colombia and the United States,' *Brown Journal of World Affairs* 10:2 (2004): 245–55.

42 Valencia, *Adios a la Politica.*
43 Juan Manuel Santos, *Jaque al Terror: Los Anos Horribles de las FARC* (Bogota: Planeta, 2009), p. 180.
44 *Ibid.*, p. 192.
45 *Semana*, '¿Que les queda a las FARC?' *Semana*, 6 June 2008, available at: www.semana.com/conflicto/multimedia/que-queda-farc/141008–3 (accessed 22 March 2009).
46 Fundación Ideas Para la Paz, 'Las Farc: Un año después del jaque,' *Siguiendo el Conflicto: Hechos y Análisis* 55 (July 2009): 1–29.
47 Reported in *Semana*, 'Falsos positivos aumentaron mas del 150% con Uribe,' *Semana*, 7 February 2014, available at: www.semana.com/nacion/articulo/falsos-positivos-aumentaron-154-en-gobierno-de-uribe/376423–3 (accessed 21 January 2016).
48 Quoted in *La Nación*, 'Chavez: Las FARC "no son terroristas,"' *La Nación*, 10 January 2008, available at: www.lanacion.com.ar/978386-chavez-las-farc-no-son-terroristas (accessed 5 February 2015).
49 Quoted in *Semana*, 'Se destapó Chavez,' *Semana*, 1 December 2008, available at: www.semana.com/nacion/articulo/se-destapo-chavez/90424–3 (accessed 5 February 2015).
50 Alfredo Rangel, 'Conflicto Armado y Terrorismo en Colombia,' *Revista de Derecho Público* 16 (June 2013): 59–68.
51 'One million voices against FARC,' *Facebook* page, available at: www.facebook.com/onemillionvoices/?fref=ts (accessed 11 May 2016).
52 Jorge Londoño, 'La de Uribe una histórica popularidad,' *El Colombiano*, 5 August 2010, available at: www.elcolombiano.com/la_de_uribe_una_historica_popularidad-HVEC_99428 (accessed 15 February 2015).
53 This is a common word play used by opposers of Santos, replacing 'Juan' with 'FARC' in his name. The nickname FARCSANTOS is also popular.
54 The Spanish word for 'vaccine', a colloquial word used in Colombia to mean 'extortion'.
55 Comment on 'Gracias Presidente Uribe – Primero Colombia,' *Facebook* group, 5 May 2016 (8.43 a.m.), available at: www.facebook.com/groups/722582224537914 (accessed 5 May 2016).

PART V

Middle East and North Africa

10

Algeria's response to violent extremism

George Joffé

Introduction

The independent Algerian state was born through extreme violence and, during its more than five decades of independent existence, has experienced repeated episodes of violent political convulsion. Indeed, since 1980, violence has been the leitmotif of Algeria's political evolution and, since the mid-1980s, this has often taken the form of non-state terrorist extremism,[1] particularly during the 1990s when the country was plunged into civil war. Since the civil war ended at the start of the twenty-first century, the country has continued to experience low-level 'residual terrorism',[2] and, in the context of the post-2011 North African world, has seen this violent residuum meld with the generalized extremist chaos that has erupted throughout the Sahara and the Sahel. Violent extremism in Algeria, however, cannot be considered in isolation from the political system there, for both are linked in a dialectic of mutual engagement in that the instruments by which the state seeks to combat extremism have moulded it and have been influenced by it in turn. This chapter, therefore, after having provided a brief history of extremism in Algeria since 1980, also addresses the parallel issue of the country's political history, and will seek to demonstrate how these two strands of the history of the state are intertwined and what the effect of this interrelationship has been on the structure of the contemporary state and on its struggle against extremism.

The background to violence in Algeria

Violence has always been an intrinsic factor in the organization of Algerian society. In precolonial times, in the absence of an effective state in the Weberian sense, war was recognized as a legitimate mechanism through which local potentates could amass resources and impose power.[3] In realist terms, therefore, precolonial Algerian society depended on the close interrelationship between power and violence to determine its political culture and the political environment in which it could develop, outside the usual confines of the normative monopoly of legitimate violence that would have prevailed, had there been an effective state. In large part, this was an outgrowth of the spontaneous social structures that had developed, ironically enough, to diffuse social violence in the absence of the power of an effective state. However, the segmentary lineage structures, inherent to Algeria's tribes, that were mobilized to achieve this outcome also lent themselves to local notables amassing power within their immediate hinterlands through repressive violence, thus setting a generalized culture of wealth accumulation through violence.[4]

Colonialism was a further statement about the efficacy of violence as an expression of power, albeit that, in this case, the agency articulating violence and imposing itself on Algerian society was now an alien state and society. Nonetheless, the 132 years of colonial domination was, in essence, a statement about the subjugation of Algerian society to a set of externally imposed criteria about authority and power, designed to impress on Algerians themselves their own moral, intellectual and cultural inferiority – the infamous *complexe d'infériorité* between the indigenous and settler *colon* populations – and their ultimate dependence on the vagaries of the dominant and alien (in religious and cultural terms) attitudes of the settler *pied-noirs*. Inevitably, therefore, the eventual war for independence was couched in similar terms, for it was, in essence, a conscious attempt to reverse this equation in order to restore Algerian self-respect and its sense of agency in a postcolonial world. Violence, in essence, was to be the means by which this could be achieved – as Frantz Fanon, a psychiatrist from Martinique who became a major theoretician of the Algerian revolution until his death in 1961, was well aware.[5] There can be little surprise, therefore, if violence has acquired the informal status of being the ultimate mechanism of legitimization for the acquisition of material assets and cultural capital, sanctified as it has been by a long tradition of success.

In effect, the significance of the means by which Algeria acceded to independence was, inevitably, primarily conditioned by its experience of French colonialism, alongside its precolonial heritage. Yet Algeria's French colonial experience was unique in two important respects. Algeria was to become a colony of settlement after its occupation in 1830, in which the colons were determined to seize control of resources, so the territory that France had acquired was administratively integrated into France as three separate *départements* in 1848. This was a consequence of the defeat of the 'Abd al-Qadir rebellion in western Algeria,[6] and a result of the new constitution drawn up in 1848 after the revolution had replaced the Louis-Philippe monarchy with a new republic.[7] Native Algerians and the European colons thus became part of the metropolitan territory of France, returning senators and deputies to the metropole's governing institutions in Paris. The picture, however, was complicated by subsequent provisions for internal administration inside Algeria itself, for these came under the terms of the two *sénatus-consultes* issued by Napoleon III in 1863 and 1865 respectively, after he had seized power in 1852 and had created France's Second Empire. Both decrees were intended to remove ambiguities over the status of indigenous Algerians as a result of the integration of their territories into France and the tensions they experienced with the ever-enlarging colon settler population.

The first, in 1863, essentially confirmed that Algeria's tribes were the rightful owners of the lands they occupied. It also introduced new administrative and legal mechanisms designed to bolster indigenous rights and to revive the Algerian educational system, which had been decimated by the occupation. The second, two years later, offered Algerians French citizenship, provided they accepted French personal-status laws over matters such as inheritance and marriage. The two decrees, taken together, were an attempt to establish Algerians as full citizens in their own land and thus avoid the fate of subject status under colon domination. They represented the replacement, in effect, of the settler policy of the *assimilation* of Algerians into a single society that the settlers would dominate with one of *association* between two different but equal societies within a single state.[8]

Unfortunately, both decrees contained flaws that meant that their purpose would eventually be subverted. Despite the confirmation of indigenous rights to land ownership under the 1863 *sénatus-consulte*, it did not reverse the provisions of the 1848 law over land ownership in which all forest was taken into the state domain and private (*milk*) and collective (*'arsh*) land ownership were recognized as separate categories. In general, however, traditionally land had simply been held in indivision – collective ownership by village and tribal groups whereby only the usufruct was individually controlled and subject to regular redistribution – and, since the authorities demanded all fallow *'arsh* land be handed over to state domain, Algeria's tribes had been deprived of the majority of their traditional land, whether for cultivation or as forest grazing land. Thus, although compensation was proposed under the decree for tribes unjustly dispossessed of their lands, the mechanisms by which the settler colons had acquired vast tracts of land remained in being, to be subsequently exploited by the colon community to further marginalize the tribes on the land. After the collapse of the Second Empire in 1871, that is what it progressively did, culminating in 1873 in the *Loi Warnier* – which, by ordaining that individual land rights should replace collective ownership, effectively destroyed the economic sinews of tribal society. By 1898, settler colons had acquired control through the law of almost 1.5 million hectares, three times as much as had been alienated between 1830 and 1870, despite the aspirations of the 1863 *sénatus-consulte*.[9]

This physical dispossession of Algeria's indigenous population was paralleled by its socio-political marginalization as a result of the unanticipated outcomes of the 1865 *sénatus-consulte*. The fact that the decree, despite offering full citizenship to indigenous Algerians, placed on them the obligation of abandoning their Islamic personal status meant that few were able to take advantage of the process of naturalization it offered. Indeed, by 1875, only 371 Algerian Muslims had done so,[10] and by 1936 the number had only risen to 2,500.[11] With the collapse of the empire and the restoration of the colon policy of assimilation after 1871, the opportunity to do so effectively vanished, creating a situation that was to be perpetuated almost up to the end of the French presence in Algeria. The consequent religious and cultural alienation was paralleled by a separate and repressive legal code, the Code de l'Indigenat, and both patterns of alienation fed into a widespread indigenous sense of inferiority to the settler society that dominated them. That, in turn, provoked a collective psychological inversion of absolute rejection of the French civilizational paradigm that Fanon was subsequently to so accurately identify, and to claim that violence would be the only meaningful route to recovery.[12]

The upshot during the colonial era, however, was that Algerians effectively became strangers in their own land, suffering economic alienation, social isolation and political marginalization. As Jules Cambon, then governor general in Algiers, reported to the French senate in 1894, Algerians had become 'a sort of human dust' as a result of France's policies of eliminating the natural patterns of leadership inside Algerian society.[13] This process of profound alienation was to be completed during Algeria's war of independence between 1954 and 1962, when France, having relinquished control of Morocco and Tunisia in 1956, attempted to retain its presence in Algeria for strategic and atavistic reasons related both to the administrative and sovereign integration of the country into France itself and to colons' insistence on their economic and political rights to the country, to the deprivation of Algerians themselves. Indeed, in many respects, the peculiar violence that attended the birth of independent Algeria in that war was a reflection of that deprivation, as much as France's reluctance to accept such an outcome reflected its unique political and historical investment in its project there, in contrast to its engagements in Morocco and Tunisia.

The collective anger that that deprivation caused can be sensed in Algeria even today. Kamel Daoud captures its essence in his Algerian counterpart novel to Albert Camus's encapsulation of the *pieds-noirs* settlers' attitudes towards Algerians in *L'Etranger*, when he remarks, 'We [Algerians] were the ghosts in this country when the settlers were exploiting it and bestowing on it their church bells and cypresses and swans.'[14] The consequence of such a sentiment, Lewis Gordon points out in his study of Fanon, would be that, 'Colonialism's victory would be continued violence; the colonized's victory would be, to the colonial forces, violence incarnate.'[15] And Frantz Fanon himself, in the first sentence of his last work, written in 1961, *Les damnés de la terre,* argued that, 'National liberation, national renaissance, returning the nation to the people: whatever the rubric or new formulations introduced, decolonisation is always a violent phenomenon.'[16]

He went on to point out that violence was the means through which 'the colonized man' found freedom,[17] and that violence 'unifies the people', while being a 'cleansing force' for the individual.[18] Such experiences, however, then become internalized as a dominant mechanism of achieving political action which will persist through time. This has indeed been the Algerian experience and is, in essence, the substance of this chapter. A prime example of this process of internalization was the appalling and terrifying punishment of the *harkis*, those Algerians who had worked with the French army during the war for independence, after the Evian Accords, which brought the war to an end, were signed.[19]

Such patterns of behaviour have thus become a political culture, defined by Baker as: 'the set of discourses or symbolic practices by which ... [competing] claims [about politics] are made',[20] where culture itself is best captured by Clifford Geertz's definition of it as 'an historically transmitted pattern of meanings embodied in symbols, a system of inherited conceptions expressed in symbolic forms by means of which men communicate, perpetuate, and develop their knowledge about and their attitudes toward life'.[21] The consequence is, as Andrew Hussey suggests in discussing the implications of the Algerian war for independence in the 1950s and 1960s and the violence of the Algerian migrant community in France today, that 'Torture, collective killings and ethnic cleansing were all deployed by the French in North Africa as weapons of war. On the Muslim side, insurgency, terrorism and assassination were legitimized as tools against the European oppressor.'[22] He could equally well have been talking about the 132 years of French colonial oppression that preceded the war, and that thereby set a paradigm for the contemporary world.

The history of violence in Algeria

The nature of the Algerian war for independence and, particularly, events immediately at its conclusion, predetermined the propensity of the independent Algerian state and its opponents to settle their disputes through violence. For instance, the Front de Libération Nationale (FLN), the body created to lead the struggle for Algerian independence, determined early on that it would not tolerate competing movements directed towards the same ends. It therefore forced them to amalgamate with itself and, if they refused, eliminated them. This did not, however, eliminate disputes and disagreements over strategy and tactics; it merely internalized them within the corpus of the FLN, which led to a series of bloody settlings of accounts within the movement.[23] Even the decisions of the Soummam Conference in 1956, setting up political control of the struggle on the basis of collegiality, did not eliminate these power struggles, which were to plague the movement right up to the end of the war in 1962.[24] This pattern of resolving disputes has effectively persisted up to the present day and, alongside the FLN's open espousal of terrorism against the European settler population and those Algerians who resisted it, explains much of the dialectic of violence that characterizes the contemporary state.[25]

In parallel to these ongoing tensions – and partly because of them – the revolutionary movement also created a military-controlled security system, the Securité Militaire, which since 1990 has been known as the Direction de Renseignements de Securité (DRS) and is the most occult and unaccountable part of the Algerian government system today. Until very recently, although its head was formally accountable to the defence and interior ministries, in reality he was a dominant element in Algeria's 'deep state', as part of what Algerians call *Le Pouvoir* or *Les Décideurs*, the *nomenklatura* where the key decisions affecting national policy are really taken outside the formal structure of government. The security service he headed, therefore, also served the 'deep state' in the first instance and was closely allied to the corrupt economic elites that Algerians know as the *mafia*. Its lack of accountability has enabled it to use whatever techniques it wished to enforce the security of the state (which it is often accused of confusing with its own interests) and it thus represents a direct pattern of descent of the violence of the struggle for independence into the contemporary political order of the country. As part of the 'deep state', it also forms part of what Rachid Tlemcani has called the 'military-bureaucratic oligarchy' of Algeria, even today.[26] The organization itself had been founded during the struggle for independence as a component of what came to be known as the Ministère de l'Armement, des Liaisons Générales et des Communications, the MALG.

This had its origins in a major struggle over the military direction of the FLN in 1956 between Abane Ramdane and Belkacem Krim (which Krim won when Ramdane was assassinated in late December 1957), and a subsequent struggle over the same issue in 1958 when Krim was forced to share military oversight with two former military commanders inside Algeria, Lakhdar Ben Tobbal and Abdelhafid Boussouf, the latter having been the commander previously of Houari Boumediènne (later to become army commander and then president) in *Wilaya 5*,[27] along Algeria's western border with Morocco. Boussouf eventually controlled communications and intelligence – which were to become the core activities of the MALG – as minister for communications in the first Gouvernement Provisoire de la République Algérienne (GPRA) in 1958.[28]

A second consequence of the tensions innate in the war of independence was the way in which independence was eventually achieved. With the end of the actual war and the Evian Accords in March 1962, the unity that the struggle had imposed on the FLN and the GPRA began to collapse. Indeed, in some respects, this appearance of unity, in theory imposed by the decisions of the Soummam Conference in 1956, had always been fictitious. Now, however, the tensions between the *wilaya* commanders and the political leadership of the FLN became overt, as did tensions within the leadership itself. In October 1956, five of the nine *chefs historiques* of the FLN – the nine men who had planned the original uprising against France on 1 November 1954 – had been hijacked to Algiers whilst flying from Rabat to Tunis, thereby decapitating the core FLN leadership and marginalizing its most important figures.[29] Yet with the signing of the Evian Accords which brought an end to the conflict five and a half years later, they resumed their leadership roles upon their release from French custody, thus exacerbating the tensions that already existed between them and the political leadership that had maintained the struggle in their absence.

The struggle emerged in the Conseil National de la Révolution Algérienne (CNRA), the ruling body of the FLN, just after the movement had established what its programme for independence would be in the Tripoli Charter, and pitted its leadership in the CNRA's Bureau Politique under Ahmed Ben Bella with most of the other *chefs historiques* against the GPRA leadership under Benyoucef Ben Khedda. The actual dispute focused around the issue of the future role of the Algerian army, which was in exile, in effect, in Morocco and Tunisia as a result of France's construction of two electrified fences along the Moroccan and Tunisian borders with Algeria – the Lignes Morice and

Challe – in 1957 and 1958 respectively. The GPRA leadership, feeling that its control of the army had lapsed, sought to replace its commander, Houari Boumediènne, and two of his subordinates who were close to the Ben Bella group, which, in consequence, rejected its initiative. The army in Morocco, which was under Boumediènne's direct control, marched in response on Algiers, the capital of the new state, effectively marginalizing the GPRA leadership under Ben Khedda and its military allies among the autonomous *wilaya* units which had actually borne the brunt of the fighting against French forces and resented the army's pretentions.[30]

The eventual outcome was to be Ben Bella's installation as head of the new state, an event that was to lead to a further split inside the FLN leadership as first Mohamed Boudiaf and then Hocine Aït Ahmed moved into clandestine opposition, since Ben Bella had usurped power from the FLN's collective leadership because of his military backing. This, in turn, left Ben Bella dependent solely on the support of the army. Yet, one of the key decisions of the Soummam Conference had been that the political leadership should supervene over the military leadership. Now that principle was permanently reversed, placing real power exclusively in the hands of the army leadership, backed up by the security services. Three years later, in a further dispute over its leadership, Boumediènne mounted an army-backed coup against Ben Bella as president, replacing him as Algeria's titular leader. For our purposes, the net consequence of these complex manoeuvres within the governance processes of the new state was to establish the army and its propensity for violent action as the ultimate arbiter within Algeria. Constitutional government, as originally envisaged for the new state, was, in short, replaced by the arbitrary power of the army, the 'shame-faced sovereign' in Hugh Roberts's memorable phrase, which nonetheless has stood behind virtually every political evolution and rupture in Algeria ever since, except, perhaps, for the brief experience of democratic politics between October 1988 and December 1991.[31]

Violence in Algeria, however, is an antiphonal and dialectical process, for the arbitrary violence of the state is mirrored by the violent actions of non-state actors, too. These began to become significant contributors to political action in 1980, with the advent of the 'Berber Spring' in April of that year.[32] This began as a mass movement of protest against cultural repression in the predominantly Imaghzen region of Kabylia in northern Algeria, which quickly transmuted into a protest over political repression. The Chadli Bendjedid presidential regime responded by introducing timid economic liberalization, but tried to contain political protest by encouraging Algeria's nascent Islamist movement to react against attempts to redefine Algeria's cultural identity from one of an Arabo-Islamic nation state into one recognizing the nationally specific complexities of Algeria's cultural and political heritage. The struggle also had a political dimension in that countering cultural protest implied countering demands for political liberalization as well, but there were also two unexpected and unwanted consequences. The first was that an indigenous semi-clandestine Islamist movement began to contest the official narrative of the state, and the second was the emergence of a violent challenge to the state itself.

The Islamist movement itself began in 1930, with the creation of the Association des Oulemas Musulmans Algériens (AUA), a body created by Abdulhamid Bin Badis as part of the Algerian Islah movement which emerged in the 1920s in response to the growth of anti-colonial *salafiyya*[33] sentiment throughout the Middle East and North Africa.[34] The AUA had been absorbed into the FLN during the war and, even though the Algerian struggle was not overtly 'Islamic' in terms of its self-image, the presence of the AUA within it served as a guarantor that one of the ultimate purposes of the struggle for independence would be the revival of independent Algeria as a culturally authentic Muslim society. Thus, although the FLN was to be reduced to a vehicle through which Algeria's military regime communicated with the wider population once victory had been achieved, care was taken by Algeria's rulers to ensure that the formal role of Islam inside the new Arabo-Islamic state was preserved, although autonomous Islamist activity was rigidly excluded. Although an Islamic association, the al-Qiyam (values), was permitted in the early 1960s under the patronage of a charismatic journalist and political thinker, Malek Bennabi,[35] and a former *chef historique* of the revolution, Mohammed Khider, the Boumediènne regime had suppressed it by the end of the decade as a potential threat to its own hegemonic power.

The Boumediènne regime, however, had also introduced a widespread Arabization programme to counter the cultural and linguistic persistence of French as the dominant medium of communication throughout the country. Given the lack of indigenous instructors capable of facilitating the programme, large numbers of Egyptians were recruited to do this and, with them, came the Muslim Brotherhood, another variant of the salafiyya movement. The movement, known in Algeria as the Ahl ad-Daw'a, quietly spread throughout the urban petty bourgeoisie and skilled labour force, despite official disapproval, so that by the mid-1980s it represented a powerful, if informal, political voice within the country, with its own recognized spokesmen. It was this body which was covertly mobilized by the Bendjedid regime to confront the francophone cultural and political dissidents in the aftermath of the Berber Spring.[36] The confrontations, which were violent, led to repressive state action and a growing alienation between the Islamist movement and the state, to which the latter responded by trying to placate the movement through the 'Islamization' of public space and, in 1984, introducing legal measures to bring personal-status law into line with sharia.[37]

However, in the mid-1980s, Algeria's external economic environment worsened as countries in the Organization of Petroleum-Exporting Countries (OPEC), led by Saudi Arabia, increased oil output at the cost of global price declines in an attempt to marginalize non-OPEC producers. The effect on Algeria, however, was to reduce its external revenues and push it towards a significant trade deficit. To avoid this, the government severely restrained imports, which, in turn, exacerbated public discontent, leading to riots in Constantine in 1986, ostensibly over issues of student housing but, in reality, highlighting widespread economic hardship.[38] Islamists took a leading part in the demonstrations, given Constantine's reputation as a centre of Islamic studies, but the incident, although justified in economic terms, also marked the beginning of public resentment of the role of the FLN in abetting regime policy but failing to honour its original pledge of recreating the promised culturally authentic Islamic society in Algeria.

As significant was the fact that these events took place against the backdrop of the Iranian revolution in 1979, which had revived popular interest in an alternative Islamic political narrative, even though there Shia Islam had been involved, and in the Soviet invasion of Afghanistan in the same year, together with the American- and Saudi-promoted Mujahidin response to it. By 1986–87, young Algerians who had been recruited into the Mujahidin in Afghanistan, to resist the Soviet occupation of the country, had begun to return to Algeria where they formed a quite specific group within the wider, *salafiyya*-dominated Islamist movement who became known as the 'Afghanistes'. There they subsequently coalesced with disgruntled members of the FLN, frustrated by the movement's broken promises over the Algerian future. The group that had been formed by the former FLN members, the Mouvement Algérien Islamique Armé (MAIA), had been created in 1982 by Mustapha Bouyali and had decided to use violence to force the state to alter its policies after it failed to gain support from other *salafiyya* Islamist groups the previous year. Between late 1982 and 1987, the MAIA waged an intermittent campaign of violence in the Blida plain, south of Algiers. Eventually Bouyali was killed in an ambush in 1987 and the authorities were able to bring an end to his organization, making some 200 arrests, although the group was estimated to have had 600 sympathizers.[39]

What was striking about the MAIA experience was that it would prove to have been a paradigm for the much more extensive campaign of violence that was to emerge a few years later and which would morph into the Algerian civil war of the 1990s. It reflected the way in which the arbitrary violence and repressiveness of the state provoked a corresponding display of violence among its opponents, and underlined the degree to which other forms of protest and challenge to it were ultimately doomed to irrelevance. It also demonstrated that the Islamist political narrative in Algeria carried increasing legitimacy against the failures of the FLN. Not surprisingly, therefore, when the real crisis arose a year later, in 1988, it would be the Islamist movement that would come to embody resistance to the repressive hegemony of the state.

The Algerian civil war

In October 1988, the political and economic tensions that had been mounting in Algeria came to a head in countrywide riots that forced the regime to transform its approach to the governance of the country. Almost overnight, the presidency persuaded a sceptical and reluctant army command to replace single-party rule with a pluralist democracy. Its calculation was, apparently, that in such a fragmented political environment, it would become the essential mediator and arbiter of the political process and thus retain its hegemonic position. In the event, it was soon to discover that this position was challenged by the country's dominant Islamist movement, the Front Islamique du Salut (Jabha Islamiyya li'l-Inqath – FIS), once it had been registered as a political party. It proved to be an extremely popular movement, largely because it could claim a legitimacy that the FLN had lost; namely, in its objective of restoring the Islamic socio-cultural environment, originally promised by the FLN but a promise that successive governments and the party had betrayed.[40] It was a legitimacy that was summed up in the slogan, popular in Algiers at the time: '*Le FIS est le fils de l'FLN*' – a play on words which meant 'The FIS is the son of the FLN.'

Of course, the FIS had much more explicit political objectives too, not least (for some of its members at least) of creating an Islamic state in Algeria once it had won control of the legislative assembly, as it appeared poised to do after the first round of legislative elections in December 1991.[41] Indeed, its electoral success in municipal elections in June 1990, combined with the declared objectives of its more radical members, had already alarmed Algeria's secular elites, the army command and the security services, and its promises of constitutional change appear to have been the last straw.[42] At the start of 1992, a coterie of leading army officers, some of them also involved in government,[43] forced President Chadli Bendjedid to resign, instituted a collective presidency around the figure of a former *chef historique*, Mohamed Boudiaf, who had been in exile in Morocco since 1963, suspended the electoral process – a second, run-off round had been due – and banned the FIS, rounding up thousands of its supporters and interning them in camps in the Sahara.

The violent reaction of the state to the FIS's electoral successes – its leadership had been imprisoned the previous June – and the brutality with which it treated the movement's rank and file in the internment camps were to provide the spark for the civil war.[44] Yet, despite the regime's subsequent claims, it was not FIS militants as such who actually unleashed the violence, for the movement had overtly rejected violence as a principle of political practice.[45] Instead it was former activists from the MAIA, released from prison by Chadli Bendjedid in 1989, who were responsible. For them, the Algerian state was tyrannical (*taghrut*) and arrogant (*hoghra*), as well as having betrayed its Islamic duty. Violence, through jihad to eliminate it as a *takfiri* (apostate) state, was therefore legitimate. Although scattered violence from isolated armed groups began in November 1991 in Guemar, and reached the capital, Algiers, in February 1992 when six policemen were killed in the casbah, the organized movement only emerged in January 1992 when a former Bouyali activist, Mansour Miliani, took over a group of 'Afghanistes' – Algerians who had fought with the Mujahidin in Afghanistan in the 1980s and who had returned to Algeria. This marked the beginning of what was to become known as the Groupes Islamiques Armés (GIA – Jama'at Islamiyya Musalha), a coalition of groups that eventually accepted the common agenda of replacing the Algerian state.[46]

Alongside this coalition, another group emerged which was also derived from the MAIA, the Mouvement Islamique Armé (MIA) which later transmuted into the Armée Islamique du Salut (AIS – Jaysh Islami li'l-Inqa<u>th</u>) in 1994. This was founded by Ahmed Chebouti, formerly a colleague of Mansour Miliani in the MAIA, who, like him, had been released from prison in 1989. The MIA rejected the extremist solutions of the GIA – the violent replacement of the Algerian state and the physical elimination of all those it perceived as hostile to its objectives, often in the most brutal ways. Instead, it looked towards coercing the military-backed regime that now controlled Algeria into restoring the electoral process that had been ruptured by the coup and to ensuring that the eventual outcome would be respected by it. This was also an agenda endorsed by the remnants of the FIS, most of whose leading cadres were either under arrest or had fled the country but, whereas the FIS leadership sought to do this through persuasion and negotiation, as in the 1995 initiative led by the Christian NGO network in Rome, the Sant' Egidio Community,[47] the MIA was prepared to use violence. Eventually, on 1 October 1997, the AIS, now led by Madani Mezrag, declared a truce with the Algerian army, the result of an accord negotiated between its leadership and the army command the previous July, and dissolved itself on 4 January 2000. Its membership, estimated at between 800 and 3,000 men, took advantage of a presidential pardon to return to normal life.[48]

The AIS had been formed when attempts to form a united front between the GIA and the MIA broke down, particularly after Mohammed Sa'id and Abderrazak Rejam – two leading members of the FIS, but acting on their own initiative, who had joined the GIA with the objective of defining common goals and moderating the increasingly violent behaviour of the GIA itself – were killed at the end of 1994. Thereafter the two movements were at daggers drawn with each other, a factor that contributed to the AIS's eventual decision to accept the Algerian army's initiative for a truce in June 1997. In fact, as time passed, the GIA became increasingly violent and indiscriminate in the campaign it waged against the regime in power and the wider Algerian population. The paramount leadership of the group also rapidly changed under the pressure of army onslaughts upon it and because, it was increasingly suspected, the DRS had managed to infiltrate the leadership and influence its strategy and tactics as a counterterrorism strategy designed to discredit it. Massacres of civilians became its increasingly favoured option, a tactic which fed the suspicions of DRS infiltration because of growing popular antagonism towards it as a result.[49] Subsequently a series of accounts from victims and even practitioners have hardened these suspicions.[50]

In September 1997, the GIA finally split under the pressure of the extreme violence that it had adopted. The new splinter group, the Groupe Salafiste de Prédication et du Combat (GSPC – Jama'a Salafiyya li'd-Daw'a wa'l-Jihad), formed by Hassan Hattab after the GIA itself had been censured for its extreme violence by al Qaida's deputy leader, Ayman al-Zawahiri, expressly disavowed the indiscriminate massacres of the GIA and, in Kabylia, focused on attacking the army and institutions of the state alongside a campaign of robberies and kidnappings to ensure its financial base. By the end of the 1990s, the old GIA had faded away, leaving only the GSPC as the vehicle of 'residual terrorism', which proved impossible to completely eradicate, with an estimated 800 supporters that were constantly replenished by volunteers, despite the inroads the army made into its strength. Whether or not the GIA had, in reality, been penetrated and effectively taken over by the DRS, its failure highlighted the fact that its leadership had convinced the rank-and-file membership of extremist views that were simply out of touch with the reality on the ground, and that it had, as a result, lost wider support, thus making it an easy target for the army as the population at large was more than happy to see it destroyed.[51]

By the time that the civil war was considered to have effectively ended at the close of the twentieth century, at least 100,000 persons were believed to have died in the conflict – many observers consider that the true figure is between 150,000 and 200,000. The army, in an international conference in October 2002, claimed that up to 27,000 persons had joined the terrorist movements and that 15,000 of them had been killed during the decade-long struggle between 1992 and 2002, together with 30,200 civilians. This gives a figure for total losses of 45,200 – just under half the total stated by the president, Abdelaziz Bouteflika, who had formally admitted that there had been 100,000 deaths in a television broadcast some months before when he announced a limited amnesty for those who had been involved.[52] The violence involved, however, was not merely confined to the struggle between the security forces and the extremist groups opposing them, for the period of the conflict was also marked by infighting within the regime and by mysterious killings of regime opponents who were not implicated in extremist violence.

Thus, in late June 1992, the then president, Mohamed Boudiaf, was assassinated in Annaba by a member of his bodyguard, Lembarak Boumaarafi. His assailant was subsequently arrested and alleged to have been an Islamist extremist who had infiltrated the presidential guard, although he was never put on trial. Popular suspicion fell, however, on the interior minister, for the president had begun an anti-corruption investigation which had already led to the arrest of one army general, and he was also supposed to be fostering contacts with the moderate FIS leadership. In late January 1997, Abdelhak Benhamouda, the secretary general of the Union Générale des Travailleurs Algériens (UGTA) and a vocal opponent of the regime, was killed while trying to form a new political party, the Rassemblement Nationale Démocratique (RND), which the army-backed regime had wanted to use for its own purposes and which it subsequently transformed into a loyal vehicle of regime support, a position that it still occupies today. Just six months later, Abdelkader Hachani, the last leader of the FIS before it was banned, was shot in Algiers. Although his alleged assassin, Fouad Boulemia, was declared a member of the GIA and was tried for the offence and sentenced to death, he was then inexplicably released, raising a wave of suspicion as to what his real function and connections had been, especially as Mr Hachani was an extremely popular figure, despite having served a five year prison term for his role in the FIS. These are just three examples of far wider violence practised against the Algerian population, apparently by the institutions of the state. In addition, the Algerian Government has admitted that over 6,000 people were 'disappeared' by the security authorities and has paid their families compensation – a sure indication of the degree of official complicity in the violence that marked the civil war.[53]

The aftermath

Although the civil war effectively ended at the turn of the millennium, the problems of arbitrary governance and inherent state violence still persist.

Admittedly, with the collapse of the GIA, the army was able to alter its tactics from countering what was, in many parts of Algeria, a rural insurgency towards the more typical policing function of counterterrorism more appropriate for dealing with marginalized and isolated terrorist networks in urban and rural areas, except for Kabylia. 'Residual terrorism' in the official phrase is, however, endemic in Kabylia and can spill over on occasion into surrounding provinces. It occasionally flares up into a major terrorist incident, as occurred at the Tiguentourine gas facility close to In Amenas in eastern Algeria in January 2013, although on that occasion the source of the violence was located outside the country, albeit having originated from the sequelae of the civil war. Ten years before, the GSPC had extended its area of activities into the Sahara, where it carried out a spectacular kidnapping of some thirty European tourists who were eventually ransomed for a rumoured €5 million.

This southward extension of the movement has subsequently proliferated into northern Mali, around the ancient salt mines of Taoudenni, where it has been protected by the local notability, and has become enmeshed in the smuggling networks of the Sahara. Its three splinter groups there – the Algerian-dominated al Qaida in the Islamic Maghrib (AQIM), its Sahelian correlate, Mujao,[54] and a parallel Tuareg Islamist movement, Ansar ad-Din, together with a dissident branch of AQIM led by Mokhtar Belmokhtar, who was responsible for the In Amenas attack, al-Murabitun – act as a pole of attraction for the disaffected and alienated throughout the Sahel as well as in Algeria itself, and they have fed off the chaos in Libya after the civil war there in 2011 which culminated in the overthrow of the Gaddafi regime. In 2006, these Saharan offshoots of the GSPC declared their allegiance to al Qaida and, in 2015, some allegedly switched to support Daesh (the Islamic State). Their opportunity to exploit the new possibilities offered by the political chaos in Mali emerged in 2012 when a Tuareg movement, the MNLA,[55] which had supported the Gaddafi regime during Libya's civil war, returned to Mali to lay claim to its own autonomous homeland, Azawad, whilst the Malian capital, Bamako, was in the throes of the aftermath of an army-backed coup against the government.

Piggybacking on the Tuareg initiative –which was purely nationalist in inspiration and had nothing to do with extremist political Islam – the three groups took over the major towns in northern Mali – Gao, Kigal and Timbuktu – and instituted a harsh Islamic regime there. In the January of the following year, they attempted a lightening attack on the Malian capital, Bamako, only to be frustrated by Mokhtar Belmokhtar's separate attack on In Amenas as a consequence of his disagreements with the AQIM leadership, with the result that France intervened to protect the Malian Government, sending troops to force the three extremist groups out of their northern Malian fastnesses. French forces, now buttressed by an African Union peacekeeping force, remain there and, although Islamist extremists have regrouped, they have been unable to recover control of the urban areas they once held. Mokhtar Belmokhtar, ever the maverick, has continued to make his presence felt, with attacks on French interests in the uranium mines at Arlit in Niger in 2013, on a hotel in Bamako in 2015 and in Burkina Faso in the same year.[56]

Of course, these groups are remote from the Algerian heartland but they act as a constant warning that the civil war in Algeria could break out anew. The Algerian Government has concentrated on ensuring that they do not penetrate Algeria itself, offering instead to mediate between them and the Malian Government. Yet the generalized threat that they offer to northwest Africa has forced Algeria into making a more muscular response as well. It has, as a result, attempted to organize a regional military response to militant extremism in the region, as well as excluding such violence from its own frontiers through sophisticated monitoring of its immensely long borders. It has also, albeit reluctantly, had to recognize that it can no longer operate in the region to the exclusion of other interested powers, not least the United States and France. During the civil war, it managed to keep foreign engagement covert; France, on occasion – as with the 24 December 1994 hijack of an Air France airliner at Algiers, or when embassy personnel in Algiers were kidnapped by the GIA – did intervene with Algerian agreement, and America's AFRICOM military command in Stuttgart quietly collaborated with the DRS. However, in general, Algeria's struggle against terrorist violence has remained a domestic affair and its government has criticized European governments, in particular, over their toleration of Algerian extremists in exile, who were, it claimed, acting against its interests.

However, with the growth of extremism in the Sahel, this picture has begun to change. The attack on the In Amenas facility in January 2013 resulted in thirty-seven deaths of foreigners held by the extremists, and serious complaints from foreign governments about the behaviour of the Algerian army and the DRS. External pressure resulted in changes in the reporting structures of the DRS and of its senior personnel, together with reluctant Algerian cooperation, first with France about over-flight rights to Mali during the AQIM-inspired sweep on Bamako at the same time as the In Amenas incident and, second, with AFRICOM about subsequent extremist attacks in West Africa. The picture has also been complicated by Algeria's difficult relations with its western neighbour, Morocco, with the result that Algiers is being gradually melded into a regional response to extremism, as it cooperates with Tunis over border security and extremism in the Djabal Chambi/Kasserine region of Tunisia and uneasily eyes the growing chaos in Libya and covert foreign intervention there. Despite its reluctance, in short, Algeria now seems condemned to regional and wider collaboration with neighbouring states, Europe and the United States as it attempts to control the violence that surrounds it.

Indeed, violence remains implicit within the Algerian state as well. The complexities of the 'deep state' still reflect the reality of government, even if Algerians no longer fear immediate arrest for voicing opinions of which the authorities disapprove, provided they cross no 'red lines'. Issues of legitimate and transparent governance have not been solved – the presidency has arbitrarily breached its constitutional limits and a succession crisis looms. As in the past, it is the army and the security forces that determine the broad lines of official policy, despite presidential attempts to wrest power from them. Administration is so inefficient that the riot has become the major means of forcing local government to respond to local need. In 2010 alone there were 9,200 such incidents, and during 2015 there were serious incidents in Ghardaia and in Insalah in which the army had to intervene, despite a constitutional ban on its operations within Algerian territory outside issues such as those of the civil war. Indeed, it is only the memory of the civil war that seems to have prevented similar violence from breaking out again. Now, as oil prices fall, Algeria faces another financial crisis for which it is ill prepared, which suggests that either the deep state cedes power through democratic transition in an attempt to rid the country of the arbitrary system of violence that has governed it since independence, if not long before, or a replay of the violence of the civil war will re-emerge.

Notes

1 By 'extremism' here is meant the active adoption of an ideology and associated praxis to challenge the state and its ruling elites through violence in order to replace them – in effect, through asymmetric warfare, which in turn enables the state to characterize such behaviour as aberrant and criminal. This is in contrast to radicalism, which is an attempt to engage in political contention with the hegemonic discourse of the state in order to modify it, usually through a social movement. See G. Joffé, 'Introduction: Antiphonal responses, social movements and networks,' in G. Joffé (ed.), *Islamist Radicalisation in North Africa: Politics and Process* (London: Routledge, 2012), pp. 1–8.

2 This is the term preferred by Algerian politicians in describing the ongoing low-level violence that is the daily reality in parts of Kabylia, eastern Algeria and the Sahara. What is meant by 'terrorism' here is the use of 'coercive intimidation' to achieve political ends by the inculcation of fear through the threat of physical violence; see P. Wilkinson, *Terrorism and the Liberal State*, 2nd ed. (London: Macmillan, 1986), p. 51. The Algerian Government's characterization of this as 'residual terrorism' merely reflects the difficulty it has had in eliminating the clandestine groups involved and in preventing them from engaging in recruitment – a feature that illustrates its failure to attract political loyalty amongst marginal segments of the population.

3 L. Martinez, *The Algerian Civil War 1990–1998* (London: Hurst, 2000), pp. 9–14.

4 Viz R. Montagne, *The Berbers: Their Social and Political Organisation*, trans D. Seddon (London: Frank Cass, 1973).

5 F. Fanon, *The Wretched of the Earth*, trans C. Farringdon (Harmondsworth, UK: Penguin, 1967), p. 28.

6 Emir 'Abd al-Qadir, a *sharif* or descendent of the Prophet Muhammad born in 1808, was an adherent of the Qadiriyya Sufi order in Algeria who in 1832 organized tribal resistance to the French occupation of Algeria as *Emīr al-Muminīn* (commander of the faithful). After a brief truce in 1834, hostilities resumed until, by the time that peace was restored in 1837, the emir controlled western Algeria and much of central Algeria as well. Hostilities broke out once again two years later and French forces under General Bugeaud launched a scorched-earth campaign to break Algerian resistance. In 1842, the emir retired to Morocco, where French forces crushed his Moroccan support at the Battle of Isly in August 1844. By 1847 he was forced to surrender and was imprisoned in France. In 1852, he was pardoned by Napoleon III and retired, first to Bursa in Turkey and then, in 1855, to Damascus where he died in December 1883. He is today considered the symbol of Algerian resistance to foreign domination. See J.W. Kisa, *Commander of the Faithful: The Life and Times of Emir Abd el-Kader, a Story of True Jihad* (Rhinebeck, NY: Monkfish Book, 2008).

7 Ch.-R. Ageron, *Modern Algeria: A History from 1830 to the Present*, trans M. Brett (London: Hurst, 1991) p. 28.

8 Ageron, *Modern Algeria*, pp. 38–40. The term was later used by Algerians seeking equality within French society as citizens of a single country.

9 *Ibid.*, pp. 58–9.

10 *Ibid.*, p. 39, n. 6.

11 A. Horne, *A Savage War of Peace: Algeria 1954–1962* (Harmondsworth, UK: Penguin, 1977), p. 35.

12 Fanon, *Wretched of the Earth*, p. 28.

13 Quoted in Horne, *Savage War of Peace*, p. 38.

14 K. Daoud, *The Mersault Investigation*, trans J. Cullen (London: Oneworld, 2015), p. 11.

15 L.R. Gordon, *What Fanon Said: A Philosophical Introduction to His Life and Thought* (London: Hurst, 2015), p. 118.

16 Fanon, *Wretched of the Earth*, p. 28.

17 *Ibid.*, p. 68.

18 *Ibid.*, p. 74.

19 Horne, *Savage War of Peace*, pp. 537–8. Of the 250,000 Algerians who had supported the French army's operations in Algeria during the war, only 15,000 escaped to France at its end. The majority, who were abandoned by the French army on General de Gaulle's orders, were either worked to death as forced labour clearing minefields or killed as traitors to the cause of Algerian independence by the victors.

20 K.M. Baker, *Inventing the French Revolution: Essays on French Political Culture in the Eighteenth Century* (Cambridge: Cambridge University Press, 1990), p. 19.

21 C. Geertz, 'Religion as a cultural system,' in *The Interpretation of Cultures* (New York: Basic Books, 1973), p. 89.

22 A. Hussey, *The French Intifada: The Long War between France and Its Arabs* (New York: Farrar, Straus and Giroux, 2014), p. 14.

23 R. Tlemcani, *State and Revolution in Algeria* (London: Zed/Boulder, CO: Westview, 1986), pp. 59–65; see also M. Harbi, *Le FLN, mirage et réalité: des origins à la prise du pouvoir (1945–1962)* (Paris: Editions Jeune Afrique, 1980), pp. 143–68.

24 For the report of the conference, see M. Harbi, *Les archives de la Révolution Algérienne* (Paris: Editions Jeune Afrique, 1981), document 33, pp. 160–8; for a discussion, see Harbi, *FLN*, pp. 173–83.

25 This use of terrorist violence to achieve political ends was justified by the movement as a mechanism for balancing out the overwhelming military force available to France. This imbalance is the narrative that underlies the dramatic tension in Gillo Pontecorvo's 1966 film, *The Battle of Algiers* (Casbah Film/Igor Film), a strikingly effective recreation of the harrowing of the 'casbah' in Algiers by the French army in 1957 when French forces under General Massu made widespread use of torture, as confirmed in 2001 by Paul Aussaresses, a former general; P. Aussaresses, *Services spéciaux, Algérie 1955–1957* (Paris: Editions Perrin, 2001). See also C.A. Jones, 'The Battle of Algiers,' *Millennium* 35:2 (2007): 445–52.

26 Tlemcani, *State and Revolution*, p. 62.

27 The *wilaya*s (the word actually means 'province') were the revolutionary military districts during the war, each of which, because of the exigencies of the struggle, operated virtually autonomously from the central revolutionary authorities or the army command, which were located outside Algeria, in Morocco and Tunisia, as a result of French military action.

28 See E. O'Ballance, *The Algerian Insurrection 1954–1962* (London: Faber and Faber, 1967), p. 142; J. Ruedy, *Modern Algeria: The Origins and Development of a Nation* (Bloomington and Indianapolis, IN: Indiana University Press, 1992), p. 174; and K. Adamson, *Algeria: A Study in Competing Ideologies* (London: Cassell, 1998), pp. 78–9.

29 Horne, *Savage War of Peace*, p. 159.

30 Tlemcani, *State and Revolution*, p. 76.

31 H. Roberts, 'The struggle for constitutional rule in Algeria,' *Journal of Algerian Studies* 3 (1998): 19–30.

32 S. Mezhoud, 'Glasnost the Algerian way: The role of Berber nationalists in political reform,' in G. Joffé (ed.), *North Africa: Nation, State and Region* (London: Routledge, 1993), pp. 142–69.

33 The *salafiyya* movement, inspired by Jamal al-Afghani in the 1860s and propagated throughout the region by personalities such as Mohamed 'Abduh, sought to find in the region's Islamic heritage the inspiration to create a viable intellectual alternative vision to counter the Western cultural project embodied in colonialism.

34 G. Joffé, 'Trajectories of radicalisation: Algeria 1989–1999,' in Joffé, *Islamist Radicalisation*, pp. 114–37.

35 See S.J. Walsh, 'Killing post-Almohade man: Malek Bennabi, Algerian Islamism and the search for a liberal governance,' *Journal of North African Studies* 12:2 (2007): 203–22.

36 In fact, the Imaghzen population of Kabylia was not so much 'francophone' as opposed to the Arabization of Algerian public life. French was therefore a convenient lingua franca to render the public use of modern literary Arabic (*fusḥa*) in administration and education unnecessary. The other languages spoken in Algeria – *darija* and Berber languages – were not written for no standard transliteration system was available, and they were not, at that time, recognized by the state as national languages. They are now.

37 M. Willis, *The Islamist Challenge in Algeria: A Political History* (Reading, UK: Ithaca, 1996), pp. 90–4.

38 *Ibid.*, pp. 99–100.

39 *Ibid.*, pp. 72–84.

40 The promise was made at the beginning of the war of liberation when, on 31 October 1954, the FLN had published a proclamation which, overlooking the fact that no formal Algerian state had ever existed before, promised to 'restore' Algeria as a sovereign, democratic and social state within the framework of Islamic principles. M. Harbi (ed.), *Les archives de la revolution Algérienne* (Paris: Editions Jeune-Afrique, 1981), pp. 101–3.

41 Joffé, 'Trajectories of radicalisation,' pp. 124–6.

42 In the municipal elections, the FIS won control of 853 of Algeria's 1,539 municipal councils and 31 of the country's 48 provincial councils, virtually double the FLN's score; *ibid.*, p. 134, n. 27. In the first round of the legislative elections it won 188 of 231 seats, more than ten times the number won by the FLN; D. Nohlen, M. Krennerich and B. Thibaut, *Elections in Africa: A Data Handbook* (Oxford: Oxford University Press, 1999), p. 54.

43 The group comprised General Khaled Nezzar, minister of defence; Larbi Belkhair, interior minister and former general; General Mohamed Lamari, army chief of staff; General Mohamed 'Toufik' Mediène, head of the DRS; and General Mohamed Touati.

44 Joffé, *Islamist Radicalisation*, pp. 131–2, n. 58.

45 J.N.C. Hill, *Identity in Algerian Politics: The Legacy of Colonial Rule* (Boulder, CO: Lynne Renner, 2010), p. 141.

46 G. Joffé, 'Informal networks in North Africa,' in D.M. Jones, A. Lane and P. Schulte (eds), *Terrorism, Security and the Power of Informal Networks* (Cheltenham, UK: Edward Elgar, 2010), pp. 72–3.

47 Algeria-Watch, 'La Plat-forme de Rome,' Algeria-Watch website, 13 January 1995, available at: www.algeria-watch.org/farticle/docu/platform.htm (accessed 1 November 2015).

48 Algeria-Watch, 'Dissolution de l'Armée Islamique du Salut,' Algeria-Watch website, 5 January 2000, available at: www.algeria-watch.org/farticle/ais/aisdissolut2.htm (accessed 1 November 2015).

49 See B. Izel, J.S. Wafa and W. Isaac, 'What is the GIA?' in Y. Bedjaoui, A. Aroua and M. Ait-Larbi (eds), *An Inquiry into the Algerian Massacres* (Geneva: Hoggar Books, 1999), pp. 373–457, for a discussion of this aspect of the violence.

50 See, for example, H. Souadia, *La sale guerre* (Paris: Editions La Découverte, 2001); M. Samraoui, *Chronique des années de sang* (Paris: Editions Denoël, 2003); N. Yous, *Qui a tué à Bentalha?* (Paris: Editions La Découverte, 2000); H. Aboud, *La mafia des généraux* (Paris: Editions J-C. Lattès, 2002).

51 As Hafez suggests, it had constructed an anti-system collective ideological framing argument for its activities which was exclusivist and out of touch with reality – a fatal step for a network that purported to be a social movement; M.A. Hafez, 'From marginalisation to massacres: A political process explanation of GIA violence in Algeria,' in Q. Wiktorowicz (ed.), *Islamic Activism: A Social Movement Theory Approach* (Bloomington IN: Indiana University Press, 2004), p. 38. See also M.M. Hafez, 'Armed Islamist movements and political violence in Algeria,' *Middle East Journal* 54:4 (2000): 572–91.

52 In fact, some years later, on 21 February 2005, the president admitted that 150,000 people had died and the civil war had caused US $40 billion of damage. See *Al Jazeera*, 'Algeria puts strife toll at 150,000,' *Al Jazeera*, 23 February 2005, available at: www.aljazeera.com/archive/2005/02/200849155453867369.html (accessed 1 November 2015).

53 G. Joffé, 'National reconciliation and general amnesty in Algeria,' *Mediterranean Politics* 13:2 (2008): 217.

54 *Jamā'at at-tawḥīd wa'l-jihād fī'l-'ifrīqīyyā al-gharbiyya*; Mouvement pour l'unicité et le jihad en Afrique de l'Ouest (Movement for uniqueness and jihad in West Africa).

55 Mouvement national pour la libération d'Azawad.

56 R. Marchal (ed.), *Le Sahel dans la crise malienne* (Paris: Sciences-Po/CERI, 2013).

11

Extremism in moderation: Understanding state responses to terrorism in Egypt

Dina Al Raffie

Introduction

If it can be agreed that one of the greatest threats facing the world today is that of Salafi jihadism[1] (henceforth 'jihadism' or 'jihadist'), then few countries serve as good an example of the movement's evolution than the Arab Republic of Egypt. The recent episode of jihadist hostilities in the Sinai is but one in a series of episodes that stretches back almost ninety years in the country's contemporary history. Though the current study on Egyptian counterterrorism (CT) responses is primarily preoccupied with post-independence Egypt, the trajectory of modern-day jihadism traces its intellectual, ideological roots to late nineteenth-century Islamic reformers and, more concretely, to the founding of the Jama'at al-Ikhwan al - Muslimun (the Muslim Brotherhood, henceforth Ikhwan). However, it would be misleading to present jihadism in general as the primary threat to Egyptian national security interests. Although Islamic extremism has arguably constituted the primary *terrorist* threat to the nation state since its independence, the Egyptian conceptualization of terrorism and the way in which its vocabulary has today developed cannot be understood without taking into consideration how key historical events in the country's contemporary history have shaped it.

More importantly, the Egyptian case study challenges a number of assumptions on the relationship between state and society under authoritarian regimes.

Existing literature often overemphasizes the role of repressive measures in Egyptian CT strategies, and inaccurately portrays the terror dynamic as a simplistic cause-and-effect cycle, whereby both the cause of terrorism and its reoccurrence are primarily responses to said repressive measures. However, in doing so, the literature not only overlooks important soft measures that have been consistently employed throughout regime CT strategies over the past seventy years, but also downplays the significance of the state's interaction with mainstream society and external actors for the development of the state's discourse on terrorism. Simply put, despite its generally authoritarian nature, the Egyptian state's approaches to CT are much more nuanced and cannot be understood without taking into consideration the state's relations vis-à-vis a wide range of actors.

This case study thus reviews how Egyptian CT responses have developed since the country's independence from British colonial rule in 1952 to the present day. The first section summarizes the history of terrorism in Egypt, understanding it as one of several national security threats that will be referred to throughout where they intersect with terrorism. The second section will address the CT measures adopted by the state to respond to the threat. These measures will be discussed in an order such that they roughly correspond to the successive regimes that ruled Egypt, starting with that of Gamal Abdel Nasser through to Hosni Mubarak's. This is because, despite glaring similarities and consistencies in the general approach, specific policies and state responses have varied over time depending on an evolution in the capabilities of the state's security apparatus, but also – and perhaps more importantly – the interaction of four variables: state (regime), society, opposition and the prevailing geopolitical context of the time period in question. The chapter focuses primarily on the above-mentioned regimes due to the fact that the duration of their tenure provides a more solid basis for the analysis of CT strategy trends. The aborted presidency of President-elect Mohamed Morsi and the relatively short tenure of President Abdel Fattah el-Sisi prevent the making of determinate statements on their respective approaches to CT, although references will be made to both where relevant.

Domestic terrorism in Egypt

Shaped by European notions of statehood and self-determination, a number of political movements and parties emerged in the decades preceding Egyptian independence that championed alternative conceptions of statehood for a future Egypt. A large number were nationalist oriented, yet an equally growing force was the Islamic revivalist movement. Both developed in tandem with prevailing domestic and geopolitical concerns of the time, of which the demise of the Ottoman Empire and the continuing presence of the British were arguably two of the most important.[2]

In Egypt, the most prominent Islamist current organized under Hassan al-Banna's Ikhwan, founded in 1928. Similar to several revivalist initiatives being established elsewhere across the Muslim world, the Ikhwan's *raison d'être* was the safeguarding of Muslims' religious identity and the Islamic nature of Egypt against the perceived 'economic and cultural imperialism' of Western secularism.[3] The Ikhwan built on the critique of its intellectual predecessors whose main concern was the failure of religious institutions to provide spiritual guidance corresponding to the requirements of modernity. This generation of revivalists felt that reform within a secular constitutional framework was feasible, and took to task religious authorities for implementing reform to better accommodate the modern state of world affairs. However, the Ikhwan adopted a contrary position. Although it similarly sought (and actively fought for) independence from British colonial rule – and therefore anticipated an independent Egyptian state within the Westphalian sense – their envisioned state was to be a purely Islamic one, with a stated hope for the resurrection of the caliphate.[4] In a sense, the Ikhwan preached an exclusivist Islamic worldview that argued for a return to Islamic fundamentals as a basis and *necessity* for progress in the Islamic world.

It is this form of Islamic revivalist thinking that has come to broadly define the contemporary Islamist movement. The academic discourse on contemporary Islamism is large and beyond the scope of this chapter,[5] as is a discussion on Egyptian Salafism, whose movements do share a degree of ideological affinity to Islamists like the Ikhwan. Suffice it to say that there are several Salafi movements in Egypt that have existed in tandem with the Ikhwan and the other groups mentioned below, that have never developed full-fledged political and/or violent arms.[6] That being said, an overview of the ideological basis of Islamism in the Egyptian context is necessary as it was Islamism that helped lay the ideological groundwork for the generations of violent Islamist/jihadist movements to follow.

The Ikhwan's main goal at its founding was to initiate an Islamic re-education of the masses through the provision of social services and aggressive religious preaching (*da'wa*) to spread the organization's message and philosophy. Its preoccupation was based on the belief that, besides the corrupting effects of Western cultural influence on Islam, the reason for the regression of Islam in the public sphere was due to the religious slacking of the masses. Thus, in concert with the more organized, political elements of the group (that would later attempt to realize their Islamic ambitions for the Egyptian state through conspiring with Gamal Abdel Nasser to overthrow the Egyptian monarchy), the Ikhwan stressed the need for renewed religious zeal among the masses that would both reinforce and elicit public demand for an Islamic state project. This did not prevent it from setting up an armed wing, more commonly known as the 'Special Apparatus', whose establishment was avowedly for the Palestinian and Egyptian cause, yet is documented as having eventually turned inwards against internal opposition, thus provoking a backlash from the Ikhwan's erstwhile co-conspirators in the overthrow of the monarchy.[7]

This led to lengthy clashes with Nasser's Revolutionary Command Council (RCC), and the outlawing of the movement, with many of its supporters arrested and sentenced. Despite several sentences being shortened or repealed, a division in opinion occurred within the Ikhwan – both inside and outside prison – as to how the group should proceed. Despite there being a number of leadership figures whose opinions were of importance to the discourse, the division can best be summarized by the writings of two key Ikhwan figures: the Ikhwan's second general guide (*murshid 'am*) Hassan al-Hudaybi's *Preachers, Not Judges* (*Du'at la Qudat*),[8] and Sayyid Qutb's *Milestones* (*Ma'alim fi al-Tariq*).[9]

Preachers is widely held to be the Ikhwan's response to a rising radical tendency amongst Ikhwan elements that propagated violence as the only solution to realizing the organization's political vision.[10] This tendency was based on Qutb's interpretation, most starkly laid out in *Milestones*, of apostasy (*takfir*), which held that since the state was not implementing God's law (*hukm Allah*), its rulers – and, by extension, society for not demanding it of the state – had become unbelievers (*kuffar*) living a reality akin to the pre-Islamic period of *jahiliyya*. The litmus test for belief thus shifted from individual measures of faith to collective belief/disbelief depending on the nature of rule within a society. In contrast, *Preachers* laid out an argument responding to a number of Qutb's claims, particularly those on *takfir*, by raising the bar by which Muslims could be made apostates. It maintained the need for the eventual establishment of a true Islamic state, based on sharia, yet stressed that *da'wa* and the reformation of society to bring it slowly 'into accordance with *hukm Allah*'[11] were the essence of the Ikhwan's mission and the appropriate means to fulfil its goals.

Thus, a conclusion shared by all within the Islamist current under the Nasser regime – a conclusion that would repeat itself with subsequent governments – was that the Islamic project was undesirable and that the government was willing and capable of responding with force greater than that with which the Islamists could successfully resist in conventional confrontation. However, the issue on which Islamist opinion diverged, and that influenced the evolution of disparate groups within the Islamist camp, was on how to proceed and on what means were appropriate in further pursuing the Islamic project. The outcome was a split in the organization that produced three broad Islamist clusters that remain to be active today.

The first – and arguably largest – remains the Ikhwan, whose leadership largely followed the advice and method forwarded in *Preachers*, and reorganized along the lines of influencing the 'political system through negotiation, policymaking, and political maneuvering'.[12] As such, the core of the Ikhwan has remained non-violent and instead pursued the desired change largely through legitimate social and political avenues. Despite only being officially designated a terrorist organization in December 2013, the Ikhwan has always been a 'banned organization' (*gama'a mahzura*) for a number of reasons, of which its ideological ties with its more violent offshoots is one. Due to this, and the fact that it has always constituted the largest organized opposition to the regime, we will frequently return to the Ikhwan as a non-terrorist organization that nevertheless played a significant role through its interactions with the government in the development of CT policies and discourse over the years.

The second cluster can be described as the radical offspring of the Qutbian *takfiri* ideological strand that favours asymmetric violence against the state and its interests.[13] This strand's adherents initially belonged to disparate cells that largely operated underground, and would later merge into the Egyptian Islamic Jihad (Tanzim al-Jihad). A number of the Tanzim's leadership – though not all – were previously Ikhwan members, and include the current al Qaeda (AQ) leader Ayman al-Zawahiri and the author of one of the most popular jihadist tracts, 'The neglected duty' (*Al-Farida Al Gha'iba*), Muhammed Abdel Salam Faraj.[14] This is one of the reasons why successive Egyptian regimes, including the current one, have often insisted that there are no moderate Islamists, only non-violent ones. An assertion that is not entirely unfounded, even in literature on the topic. For example, in his interviews with jailed militants in the 1970s, Egyptian-American sociologist and human rights activist Saad Eddin Ibrahim found that, 'In terms of religious dimensions of ideology, their reading of history and their overall vision for the future, the militants expressed no differences with the Muslim Brotherhood.'[15]

It is important to note that one of the defining features of this cluster was that a number of prominent figures within its leadership were members of the Egyptian Armed Forces (EAF) who had either defected or were working as double agents for the jihadist movement. A case in point is the assassination of the second Egyptian President Anwar el-Sadat in 1981, which was organized and carried out by First Lieutenant Khalid al-Islambouli. The attempts of Egyptian jihadists to infiltrate the army are well documented, and were driven by the recognition that the state's centre of gravity was the armed forces, ergo the institution that had a monopoly on arms.

However, the outcome of the jihadists' confrontations with the state forced many of the group's members to flee or go further underground, assuming they had not already been arrested and/or sentenced. Many Tanzim members that fled Egypt either sought asylum in Western states or else found refuge in countries sympathetic to the Islamist cause, like the Sudan. Many more members, including Zawahiri and Sayyid Imam al-Sharif (aka 'Dr Fadl') – a Tanzim leadership figure and prominent spiritual ideologue of the global jihadist movement – ended up in Afghanistan, where they became deeply involved with the anti-Soviet Mujahidin. Although the Egyptian Government benefited from the redirection of jihad efforts to Afghanistan, the latter also served jihadists well in that it provided them with a theatre of conflict in which they were not only allowed, but also actively encouraged, and supported to hone their warfare skills. This included both conventional and asymmetric warfare techniques that Tanzim members – among Egyptian jihadists from other *takfiri* groups – wasted no time putting into use back home in the 1990s.

A third and final cluster includes groups and movements that occupied a midway position between the violent revolutionary underground and the more moderate Ikhwan. The most prominent is al-Gama'a al-Islamiyya (the 'Islamic group'), which was mostly active in Upper Egypt, and combined *da'wa* and the provision of social services with a more hardline imposition of Islamic (sharia) laws through *hisba* at the community level.[16] Though it was vocal about its rejection of the state's politics for being un-Islamic, the group did not initially challenge the authority of the state head-on. Instead, it substituted for the state in the poorer Upper Egyptian districts by exerting itself as a de facto Islamic government whose mission it was to realize an Islamic Egypt – and thus God's will – in piecemeal fashion, one province at a time.

However, the Gama'a did not last long. Its demise was as much a result of its own behaviour vis-à-vis its constituencies as it was a matter of overstepping the tolerance threshold of the state. The larger and more powerful the group became, the more brazen its actions and rhetoric. Besides the clear threat it presented to the Egyptian authorities, the group's behaviour towards its own constituencies became increasingly violent and oppressive, leading to a loss of popular support that played into the hands of authorities.[17] Skirmishes between the police and members of the group eventually escalated into what can be considered a years-long counterinsurgency against the group, which culminated in the loss of its support base, the incarceration of a significant number of its leadership cadre and supporters, and the exile of its leader Omar Abdel Rahman (aka 'the Blind Sheikh'), who eventually landed in jail in the United States for his role in the 1993 World Trade Center bombings.

The most violent episodes in the twentieth century for Egypt played out from the mid-1970s to the late 1990s. Under Nasser, the ideological foundation of the more violent, revolutionary clusters were laid. Under Sadat, the Tanzim organized and the Gama'a gained ground in Upper Egypt, with sporadic violence occurring in the last few years of Sadat's reign and spilling over into Hosni Mubarak's. A short respite followed in the years covering the anti-Soviet Afghan war, which was then followed by renewed insurgent and terrorist activity in the 1980s and 1990s that eventually culminated in the calling for a ceasefire by the incarcerated spiritual leaders of the two largest terrorist organizations – the Tanzim and the Gama'a. These events roughly coincided with the emergence of AQ on the global scene, and the strategic shift championed by the latter, which called for refocusing jihadist efforts against the 'far enemy'. Thus, the groups were split into two broad camps: those inside Egypt who abided by the principles of the ceasefire, and those who remained in exile and chose to fight on behalf of the newly established AQ vanguard. With the onset of the 'Global War on Terror', Egyptian jihadists in exile became further removed from the domestic front as a number of them proceeded to take up various leadership positions in AQ-affiliated organizations abroad.

For Egypt, the twenty-first century broke with a lull in jihadist activities, albeit intermittently interrupted by sporadic jihadist attacks in the Sinai. The situation has now changed due to widespread instability in the region. The current terrorist threat is multipronged and multidirectional, emerging simultaneously from within Egypt and spilling over from across the borders. Along both its Libyan border in the Western Sahara and on the Sinai, Egypt faces a terrorist threat from the Islamic State (IS)-affiliated terrorist group Wilayat Sina' (the 'Sinai Province') and an assortment of jihadist militias that have links to a host of global jihadist organizations, including AQ.[18] IS-affiliated militias have also claimed attacks on the mainland, along with a host of independent, non-affiliated cells.[19] Commonly referred to as the 'Allied Popular Resistance Movement',[20] these independent calls have been held responsible for hundreds of attacks against security and government personnel and infrastructure, as well as civilian objects such as 'transportation, power infrastructure, and private property'.[21] Sources point to the movement partly comprising disenfranchised, 'rogue' Ikhwan adherents that have split with the old guard.[22] Curiously, elements within the movement have denied belonging to the jihadist fringe and some have issued their own theological treatise laying out an argument for violence against the state. Using another term derived from Islamic theology, seditionists (*ahl baghy*), the movement has managed to create yet another category for classifying the state – and justifying attacks against it – that lies between sin and apostasy; in other words, it has potentially created a fourth ideological cluster within the Egyptian Islamist current.

Besides clashes with terrorist elements, the collapse of the Gadaffi regime and the souring of relations with the Palestinian Hamas have led to a spike in arms smuggling, with un-intercepted contraband finding its way into militants' hands from Greater Egypt to the Sinai and beyond. From the country's south, the Sudan has been an Islamist-sympathetic government since the 1990s as well as a key smuggling transit state for arms dealers to militant groups in the Sinai, Palestinian militias including Hamas, and – most importantly – Iran.[23] With the help of Sinai Bedouin tribes and the occasional bribery of Egyptian border-control police officers, arms have continued to flow through the Sudan into Egypt and onwards.

Consistencies in CT measures over the decades

'Securitocracy' is the term that comes closest to describing power relations in Egypt, and refers to a 'system of security elites (intelligence and security services, military, and police forces), that, at the executive level, use either direct or indirect political power and influence in matters related to a state's foreign and security policy, internal security, and even in the economic sectors.'[24] Security elites play an important role in maintaining the political status quo through the appointment of local factions sympathetic – or at least acquiescent – to their political programme, combined with repressive measures to keep the opposition in check. The political programme in question is not always so much based on an 'elaborate and guiding ideology'[25] as it is on the elites' interest-driven desire for power consolidation – that is, the regime type can generally be considered authoritarian. Perceived challenges to the status quo are not tolerated, and opposition is only allowed insofar as it does not seriously upset the power balance nor infringe upon the ruling regime.

There are many differences in the CT strategies of the governments that have ruled Egypt since Nasser, yet the continuation of authoritarian rule in Egypt has delivered consistency in many areas. Most notably in the repressive measures employed, but also certain legal measures adopted in cases and situations deemed to present a national security threat. These measures, and the institutions that employ them, are extensions of those that existed under British colonial rule. For example, the General Intelligence Services (GID) created during Gamal Abdel Nasser's rule was little more than a window-dressed version of that which existed under British-occupied Egypt. The Egyptian intelligence culture and work ethic, as well as various interrogation techniques that persist until this day, are arguably an outcome of the close cooperation and training of Egyptian intelligence units with and by Soviet and former German Democratic Republic (DDR) intelligence outfits.[26]

The State Security Investigation Service (SSIS), the Egyptian General Intelligence Services (EGIS) and the Military Intelligence Department (MID) (which come under the umbrella term *mukhabarat*) have always been among the most potent tools for state repression and national security. This is primarily due to the latter's broad powers, that include powers of (extrajudicial) arrest and detainment of suspects, who can be held for indefinite periods before officially being registered at a prison or given access to legal representation. Arrests are often not limited to specific subjects who are under investigation, but can also include the subject's immediate social network and family. This has almost always been the case with members of the organized Islamist opposition – regardless of their relationship to violence – where group members are literally swept up in mass raids along with the accused, despite there being insufficient evidence to either hold or prosecute them. There are several well-documented examples of how this tactic was used against Islamist militant groups like the Gama'a.[27] Prior to it being driven out of its enclaves, the group enjoyed a measure of popular support that afforded its members a degree of anonymity. From the government's perspective, targeting the surrounding population was just as important as targeting the accused for the purpose of flushing out co-conspirators and aides within the populace.

This tactic serves a number of purposes. Absent concrete evidence, the use of torture and other so-called 'enhanced interrogation' techniques can serve to secure a confession or obtain further information that the state needs for a prosecution. The same measure is also meant to have a deterrent effect: to remind outside members and those supporting terrorist organizations of the extent of the state's power, as well as demonstrate the potential risks of collaborating in state-sanctioned forms of dissent. In this vein, a particularly culture-specific measure occasionally adopted against the opposition – including the jihadist opposition – is the detention of female relatives of suspects. Because of the patriarchal honour code that governs gender relations in Egyptian society, this can be an effective technique in either obtaining information from suspected terrorists held in custody, or else pressuring fugitives to surrender in exchange for the women and girls.

Enabling the extrajudicial use of force are various emergency laws and parallel judicial authorities in the form of military or non-military courts that fall outside the purview of regular judicial institutions like the Supreme Constitutional Court. The former build on the Emergency Law of 1958, which held that the president could declare a state of emergency 'whenever public security or order were threatened'.[28] Although the initial law states that emergency powers can only be enforced for a limited period, the approval of an extension by a People's Assembly largely consisting of pro-regime figures has ensured compliance with the almost uninterrupted extension of the Emergency Law in all its adaptations. The most relevant element of the law to national security and, by extension, CT is that it exempts the president from following the provisions set by the constitution's Criminal Procedure Code (CPC), which are 'provisions that, inter alia, require warrants for searches and limit post-arrest detention'.[29]

The Mubarak regime retained similar powers in the 2007 constitutional revisions by effectively constitutionalizing the exemption from the CPC for CT-related operations. During Mubarak's rule especially, the Emergency Law was invoked on the grounds that the country faced a terrorist threat – a not entirely unfounded claim – and that the latter posed an existential threat to the state. The reality of terrorism thus greatly benefited the Mubarak regime, especially as it was increasingly used to justify the implementation of extraordinary measures in the face of external diplomatic pressure from human rights organizations and foreign states. Further, and another tradition inherited from the Nasser regime, is the use of military and emergency courts for the trial of civilians whose crimes are, broadly speaking, political. The referral of cases to such courts was also integrated into the revised 2007 constitutional amendments, and gives the president the right to decide which court should handle a case categorized as political or 'acts of sovereignty'.[30] Many of these legal exemptions have been further institutionalized under the current regime of Abdel Fattah el-Sisi through select amendments, and the introduction of new laws that build on the latter under the pretext of protecting the nation from security threats.[31]

Another takeaway from the Nasser era for the evolution of the Egyptian intelligence community is its encounters with the then nascent state of Israel. The GID's discovery of several successful efforts of intelligence infiltration by Israel prompted the strengthening of human intelligence (HUMINT) sources, which have since developed into an elaborate network of informants that remains one of the most powerful tools in the government's intelligence arsenal today. As Wolfgang Lotz explains of the 1960s, informants 'sat on every corner, outside every door, outside every ship, idly watching. ... It was as if the whole city was a slumberous, watching animal.'[32] The same can be said of informants today, who can be anyone from contracted doormen (*bawabs*) to taxi drivers.

HUMINT was also useful for Nasser's multiple forays into neighbouring countries, where sources were planted for the purpose of collecting intelligence, but also in supporting rogue elements or movements for subversive purposes. The latter included launching radio stations – most famously, Voice of the Arabs – that broadcast government propaganda both inside and outside Egypt for the purpose of manipulating public opinion.[33] The creation and dissemination of propaganda by the government through state-controlled media organs is yet another consistent tactic of successive governments that we will return to when discussing the various regimes' soft power strategies.

Ironically, the effect of the very policies that Nasser often employed against other states – including subversion – along with the reality of defections and suspected mutiny within both the army ranks and intelligence services generated an atmosphere of institutional insecurity. In his seminal work on the history of the Egyptian *mukhabarat*, Owen Sirrs explains that the history of the services is replete with instances of distrust among the various intelligence outfits that hinders intelligence sharing and leads to the frequent reshuffling of individuals as well as the compartmentalization of information.[34] Similarly, the modern history of the EAF is characterized by instances of attempted infiltration and mutiny of anti-regime figures, of which many are jihadists. As a result, a general ban on individuals with ties to Islamist movements from taking up jobs in any of the state's security institutions has been applied and is exercised to this day. This ban is not a formally documented policy but rather a tradition that has grown within Egyptian security administrations as a result of experience. Earlier examples of it include pre-coup attempts to purge the Free Officers movement of Ikhwan sympathizers. This unwritten policy seeks to protect the state not only from anti-regime coups instigated from the inside, but also from the potential radicalizing effect of Islamists on the 'inside' if they are allowed into the various corps.

At this point it is worth noting that one of the fundamental differences between Western responses to Islamist extremism and Egyptian ones is that Egypt does not distinguish between the violent and non-violent strands of Islamism and sees them as two sides of the same coin. This has not meant that both strands have been dealt with in the same manner. Islamist organizations have been given limited room to manoeuvre within the political realm, and their role in aiding CT efforts while also bolstering the state's legitimacy and cementing their own power will be discussed in the following passages. In Nasser's era, terrorism did not fully materialize and the most prominent of the Islamist current spent the majority of Nasser's rule incarcerated, reflecting, or regrouping into future terrorist cells.

Finally, Egypt's earlier experiences with Israel, the various attempted coups, and the general mistrust and suspicion that pervade the military and intelligence culture have helped define the way in which the state continues to respond to terrorism today. Egypt maintains one of the largest conventional militaries in the region, and continues to perceive external threats posed by nation states – most notably Israel – as some of its primary national security threats. As a result, there has been little progress in developing smaller, more agile units that are more adequately fit to respond to counterinsurgencies. The outcome, as is clearly observed in the Sinai insurgency, is the disproportionate and largely indiscriminate use of conventional military means that lead to unnecessary loss of civilian life, but also of officers' lives.

The general incapability and unwillingness to develop smaller units more capable of effectively carrying out counterinsurgency (COIN) operations relates to the trust factor. As Byman explains, 'Decentralization and small-unit initiative are important for success, but authoritarian regimes are less likely to trust their forces in such circumstances.'[35] Because small-unit initiatives require a degree of delegation and independence from larger bureaucratic military structures, they also prevent 'coup-proofing',[36] which is standard practice in many authoritarian militaries and intelligence services. Egypt is no exception. Yet the resistance from the state to downsizing and professionalizing its army in a manner more relevant to the current threats posed by jihadists partly also comes from the perception that such a move would weaken its conventional forces and leave it vulnerable to attacks by other conventional militaries.[37]

That being said, the use of repression and indiscriminate violence always has its limits. And in almost every state campaign, such measures have always been accompanied by softer measures to try to bring the violence down to an acceptable level. For example, the Mubarak regime's efforts to suppress the terrorist campaign of the 1990s involved the imprisoned leadership of both the Gama'a and Tanzim and culminated with the release of ideological revisions that led to the disengagement of many of the groups' followers outside prison.[38] If that particular case study proved anything, it is that certain soft measures for CT or COIN campaigns are just as important for authoritarian regimes as they are for Western secular democracies. What's more, literature on the Egyptian state portrays its government as being totally uninterested in its citizens' public opinion due to its intermittent crackdowns on human rights, including freedom of speech and political participation. However, this is a flawed assessment, as it equates the abuse of globally accepted human rights with an automatically ineffective 'hearts and minds' campaign back home. Yet, depending on how clever governments are in manipulating how their citizens feel and think and, more importantly, what constitutes 'good' feeling and thinking, a successful 'hearts and minds' campaign is possible. And even when this strategy is unsuccessful, public campaigns *can* help deliver public acquiescence through casting the regime as the best of the available options, thus winning passive support.

The following sections aim to show just how central public opinion has been to the development of CT policies and the conceptualization of terrorism. It highlights the contextual differences in the CT environment under the regimes of Gamal Abdel Nasser, Anwar el-Sadat and Hosni Mubarak, while also pointing out where relevant the trends that continue under the current regime of Abdel Fattah el-Sisi.

Gamal Abdel Nasser: conspiracy

The political atmosphere of the Nasser period contributed to the construction of various master narratives and a popular mentality that would later constitute the primary discursive playing field in which terrorism would be conceptualized. The most significant narrative relates to the collective failure of Egypt and its Arab neighbours to prevent the creation of the state of Israel, and the state's repeated military failures to redeem the dignity of the Arabs. This had a rather emasculating effect on the Arab armies, and is widely held in the collective memory of the Arab world especially as the catastrophe, or *nakba*. Within this atmosphere, a discourse of conspiracy emerged in which Israel and the Jews were the primary protagonists. Arguably, the most important function of these conspiracies was to concoct alternative explanations that would offset the Egyptian – and collective Arab – sense of failure, as well as furnish a common adversary against which to create a rally-around-the-flag effect, thus further deflecting criticism from the state. As Jeffrey T. Kenney notes, 'anti-Jewish rhetoric – ranging from simple portrayals of the Jews as historic enemies of Islam to more anti-Semitic demonizing of the Jews – was a weapon in the war against Israel, and opposition to Israel was an essential part of the nationalist cause'.[39] The Zionist design was the ultimate bogeyman whose primary goal was the partitioning of the region and Egypt through subversive activities for territorial gains and eventual world domination.

To understand how this conspiracy narrative became relevant to CT in Egypt, it is important to summarize how the state has communicated it to the people over time. In a nutshell, there is an omnipresent Zionist conspiracy that could manifest in any number of shapes and forms. The state's primary job is to prevent the conspirators, whose identities conveniently evolve to represent contenders to state power. As the institutions most capable of performing defence functions are those tasked with protecting national security, the argument that the state has persistently made is that certain extraordinary measures are required to respond adequately to the threat. Civil liberties are guaranteed by the constitution insofar as they do not infringe on capabilities the state deems necessary to contain the threat. The most important message sent to the people is one of 'United we stand, divided we fall.' Unity and the collective national good can only come at the expense of individual civil liberties, whose unrestrained practice will only have the effect of creating fissures in society that the enemy can easily infiltrate and capitalize on.

Despite the losses sustained, and the fact that none of Egypt's wars against Israel can be termed victories, they have nevertheless been propagated as such by a state whose propaganda created heroes and martyrs out of the soldiers that courageously fought, and collective victims out of a nation whose losses were the cause of conspiracy and not incompetence. Similarly, despite the general failure of Egypt to make good on its promise to recover the lands lost to Israel and realize a Palestinian state, the fact that the army engaged the Israelis in battle earned it respect among the population that opposing groups have found difficult to challenge. Taken together, consecutive Egyptian governments have used a combination of conspiracy theories as well as the reputation of the army to boost the legitimacy of their rule and delegitimize the Islamist opposition. On the one hand, Egyptian jihadists and Islamists have employed the same anti-Semitic and anti-Zionist rhetoric, yet have never physically confronted the state of Israel, giving the state the opportunity to cast them as insincere, hypocritical liars who would not be able to provide security or stability to the nation in the face of the Zionist threat were they to come to power. On the other hand, the unrest caused by jihadist terror and the insecurity that results from having to relocate state resources in battling it have often been framed as an externally supported attempt to weaken and destabilize the country, thus implicitly or explicitly implying that the jihadists are acting as agents of a foreign plot.

Conspiracies aside, the state has always attempted to challenge the jihadist and Islamist opposition on its own religious terms. The co-optation of religious authorities like Al-Azhar started prior to Egyptian independence but was invigorated under Nasser, who also established complementary state-controlled religious institutions for the dissemination of official state-sponsored Islam.[40] By seizing on the reputation of Al-Azhar as one of the most prestigious and authoritative religious institutions in the Muslim world, Nasser sought to boost his own religious credentials and thus delegitimize the *takfiri* narratives making the rounds in the more radical Islamist circles. The state's control of the religious endowments (*awqaf*) budget also assured the acquiescence of the community of religious scholars and laymen to the regime's political activities and rule, at times directing the said institutions to publish rejoinders to *takfiri* narratives and condemn violence against the state. However, the condemnation of Al-Azhar and other state-sponsored institutions was not merely a matter of state coercion. In establishing itself as an Islamic movement, the Islamist current posed a threat to the authority of the religious clergy or *ulama* in having the final say on all matters religious. It was within affiliated journals

– like the Supreme Council of Islamic Affairs' *Minbar al-Islam*, among others – that some of the strongest attacks against the Islamist current were levelled.

For example, in its response to Qutb's *Milestones*, by way of a review in the above mentioned journal, the head of the *fatwa* commission at the time, Sheikh Abd al-Latif Sibki, accused Qutb and – by extension – the Ikhwan of *Kharijism*.[41] Although the etymology of the term is complex, it holds irreligious, negative connotations in the collective Muslim conscience. By revolting against the Muslim Caliph Ali, the *khawarij* were effectively cast as outsiders to Islam; the root letters of the sect's name literally mean 'to leave' or 'to go out'. In its contemporary sense, the term implies a form of Muslim excommunication as the radical takfirism of the *khawarij* has historically legitimated the shedding of their blood to prevent the civil strife and discord (*fitna*) they sow in Muslim societies. Kenney traces its first official usage in Nasser's Egypt to Sibki,[42] who castigated Qutbian thought for bearing similarity to that of the *khawarij*. Likening the Islamist current to the *khawarij* not only served the function of undermining the credibility of its religious narrative, but also simultaneously emphasized obedience to the ruler (i.e., the regime) as a religious duty by invoking a specific event from Islamic history and applying it to the modern day. Most importantly, it served to validate the security measures adopted by the state against the Islamists.

Arguably, then, Egypt was already engaging in countering-violent-extremism (CVE) approaches long before it became a trend and a necessity in the West. Similar to what the West is experiencing today, however, this strategy has had mixed results in the state's fight against extremism. For one thing, jihadists have been able to challenge the credibility of the religious authorities by writing them off as corrupt government mouthpieces that fail to confront the authorities about their irreligious practices. On a more basic level, the silence of laymen on the excessive violence of the state against all forms of opposition has provided yet another avenue for challenging the credibility of those religious authorities. Another shortcoming of this specific approach that has endured over the decades is the lack of oversight of the activities of the religious institutions. Although the state has traditionally obsessively guarded its security institutions from infiltration, the same vigilance has rarely been extended to the religious sphere. And so, despite a historically strong Sufi orientation, the curricula and teachings of Al-Azhar have developed over the years a more hardline Sunni orientation, with external Saudi funding playing a considerable part in influencing the development of its religious doctrine;[43] the authorities tasked with providing counter-narratives have thus become partially complicit in propagating extremism. Examples of this will be discussed below.

Anwar el-Sadat: the 'believing president'

The religious nature of the state's response to terror took an even more dramatic turn when Sadat came to power. Whereas Nasser tried to balance the Islamists' claim to religious superiority through capitalizing on the reputation and prestige of religious authorities, Sadat attempted to equal it by presenting himself as the 'believing president', reconciling with the imprisoned Brotherhood, and allowing Islamism to re-establish itself as a political and social force. Two main reasons arguably drove this approach. The first was Sadat's desire to discredit and challenge the popularity of secular political movements. As a figure unknown to the public, and one whose appointment surprised many in the intelligence community, joining forces with the Islamists provided him an immediate constituency. But, more importantly, a sentiment championed by the Islamists and their more radical counterparts was that the continuous successes of Israel on the battlefield against the Muslims were the result of the strong religious character that underpinned its political character; the opposite of which was true for Egypt. This argument gained significant ground in the aftermath of Egypt's 1967 defeat against Israel and, instead of attempting to challenge it, Sadat rode the sentiment.

An important economic element likely also drove both Sadat and his successor's decision to allow for Islamist activity, albeit to differing degrees. Sadat's adoption of an economic 'open-door' policy effectively pulled the public safety net out from under large segments of the population that had previously relied on the state for the provision of various goods, subsidies and land. While the government and business elites benefited from Sadat's open-door policy, the majority of the population did not. Those unable to secure jobs in the Gulf or abroad were left in dire circumstances that the government halfheartedly responded to with food and public utility subsidies. However, an important source of social services for the poor were the Islamists. Until recently having many of its assets frozen and businesses dismantled, the Ikhwan was among the largest provider of public services and commodities at discounted prices. But even more radical groups like the Gama'a were left to operate in Upper Egypt, despite the state's knowledge of their *takfiri* tendencies. As the trend was and always has been, as long as the activism was restricted to the areas in which they operated and did not cross the threshold of violence against the state and its interests, the extra provision of services was welcomed. More importantly, it helped relieve the burden to a government that had repeatedly needed to put down food riots and protests. As Darwisheh contends, the state encouraged 'Islamic services to the extent that it consider[ed] their services to be a contribution toward placating the masses'.[44]

Sadat's era perhaps serves as a good example of the dangers of nurturing non-violent Islamism. If his method of governance has taught us anything, it is that the leeway provided to the largely non-violent Islamists at the time did not have the moderating effect perhaps hoped for by Sadat and the modern-day West. In Gehad Auda's contribution to the Fundamentalism Project, the author traces the success of the Islamists in rebuilding their constituencies on university campuses and professional syndicates, and in the growing Islamization of society.[45] Neither did the religious rhetoric of the president nor the compromises made at the societal level by making Egypt more Islamic in nature appease the more radical among the Islamists, who would later conspire to assassinate him. In failing to understand the depth of the population's hostility towards Israel – one that had been intentionally fuelled by Sadat and his predecessors – Sadat effectively placed himself in a 'traitor' category – one that he and his predecessor had spent years perfecting as a strategic tool against all forms of opposition – as a result of his signing of the Camp David Accords peace treaty with Israel.

More importantly, Sadat's policy of ceding ground to the Islamists was naive in that he believed that his compromise in allowing religion to more aggressively pervade the public sphere would be met with compromises from the Islamists on his methods of governance. This belief was based on a logic similar to that of the academic inclusion–moderation hypothesis: that the inclusion of Islamist parties in the political process could lead to their moderation and a larger willingness for compromise.[46] In Egypt's case, it is difficult to argue that this has worked in the case of either the Gama'a or the more moderate Ikhwan, during either the latter's time in politics prior to the Arab Spring, or its one-year rule under President-elect Mohamed Morsi. In the latter case, a plethora of articles highlight how the Ikhwan continued a number of oppressive practices characteristic of authoritarian rule, yet with an eye to establishing a theocracy.[47]

Sadat did eventually initiate a renewed crackdown on Islamists, as well as creating an Anti-Islamic-Terror Department in the Interior Ministry to counter the threat,[48] but his apparent religiosity and faith in Allah interceding on his behalf to protect him blinded him to the dangerous realities he faced. He was assassinated on 6 October 1981, and his Vice President Muhammad Hosni Mubarak assumed office eight days later.

Hosni Mubarak: extremism in moderation

One would have thought that, given the experiences and fate of his predecessor, Mubarak would continue the suppression of the Islamist movement and deny it the space to manoeuvre. To some extent, this was the case. The leadership of the Tanzim and Gama'a that were sentenced and imprisoned would remain in prison, some until the Arab Spring in 2011. The coincidence of the Afghan-Soviet War with the start of Mubarak's presidency was advantageous in that it redirected the efforts of many jihadists to Afghanistan and other theatres of conflict. Those that remained, however, were allowed to continue their activities – be it the Gama'a in its Upper Egypt enclaves, or the Ikhwan, which was afforded the usual limited room to manoeuvre the political scene while continuing its *da'wa* efforts and social services.

Mubarak only allowed the gloves to come off in the security forces' clashes with the Gama'a when the latter increased its harassment of police officers and security officials. In this respect, the use of excessive force had two effects on the insurgency. On the one hand, the lack of interest of the state in employing methods to discriminate between civilians and insurgents led to a decrease in support for the insurgents. Because 'regardless of previous sympathies, it is the climate of fear ... and the saturation of security forces that compel cooperation, even if passive, with the state.'[49] Further, as the insurgents suffered losses, they became increasingly vengeful against their erstwhile supporters, whom they often accused of collaborating with the authorities.

The primary question at this point is why the Egyptian state continued, and continues, to tolerate groups it alleges are extremist or dangerous. To some extent, the answer lies in the state's desire to avoid further hostilities with an Islamist current that has displayed both a willingness and a capability to resort to violence, absent any viable means of political or social expression. In Egypt, this extends to the Ikhwan due to the fact that a number of its former members constitute some of the most important ideological figureheads of the jihadist movement. For example, Sayyid Qutb's various treatises on Islam are still popular among jihadists today, despite the fact that they do not explicitly call for violence. More importantly, there is recognition that, regardless of the olive branches extended to the Islamist opposition, both the violent and non-violent ends of the spectrum persist in their view that the nature of governance is un-Islamic. The difference is a matter of belief, laid out in ideological nuance, on the permissibility of using violence to correct the situation. Thus, in making limited compromises, supplemented by the occasional use of hard power, the government attempts to control a large-scale spillover into violence.

For example, the government's tactic of collectively punishing both violent and non-violent Islamists for the latter's actions has incentivized the Ikhwan to condemn terrorist acts for fear of being targeted by the state. By doing so, it not only distances itself from its ideological brothers in arms – and pits the various factions against one another – but also lends indirect support to the state. Being the largest and best-organized Islamist movement in the country, the anticipated outcome is a redirection of would-be violent Islamist dissenters to the largely non-violent Ikhwan ideological strand. The idea is to provide enough leeway for non-violent Islamists to perceive that their goals are best met through peaceful, legitimate means, while simultaneously instituting political roadblocks – like barriers to entering parliament and creating political parties – that prevent them from gaining power. Of course, the results of Egypt's first free elections prove the limits of this strategy, due to its fixation on power at the expense of curbing the *ideological* influence of the Islamist opposition on the masses. However, by way of limiting excessive violence, it has at times been successful.

Like Sadat, Mubarak likely also understood the resilience and resonance of the Islamist message with the Muslim-majority population. Realizing the resurfacing of Islam as a defining marker of both national and individual social identities, Egyptian governments have found it prudent to continue engaging from an Islamic platform in order to counter the holier-than-thou effect of the Islamists.[50] Successive governments' political platforms have consisted of strengthening Islamist opposition at the expense of all other ideologies, then attempting to outdo the Islamists through co-opting elements of their political agenda. Yet this plan has always been bound to failure as the realities of modern-day governance and state relations necessitate a measure of secularism in state operations that contradicts the standards and requirements promoted by Islamists. Even the Kingdom of Saudi Arabia, with its strict imposition of sharia-ordained *hudud* punishments, has come under attack or been apostatized by both Salafis and jihadists for its political dealings, of which many are perceived by the latter as *shirk* for not following certain sharia standards for governance.[51]

Paradoxically, the results of these policies contradict the oft-stated position of the Egyptian Government that it is unsound to differentiate between violent and non-violent Islamists for it is the essence of the ideology, not its tactics, that count. Which brings us to another area where the responses of the Egyptian state presumably differ from those of modern Western democracies. Whereas the latter formulate their CT policies with the long-term safety and prosperity of their populations in mind, the Egyptian state has played a balancing act where the disadvantages of allowing the controlled flourishing of extremism are weighed against the interests of the ruling party. For, while it may appear paradoxical, the policy of tolerating – and even encouraging – a certain level of extremism does have its benefits, whether or not this constitutes an official governmental strategy.

Both the government and the Islamists share a fear of an empowered democratic populace, albeit for different reasons. The Islamist current plays a significant role in demonizing democratic secular ideologies through portraying them as godless, un-Islamic and morally corrupt, thus helping the state defend against the infiltration of Western democratic ideals and norms that would challenge the state's authoritarian rule. This demonization of the West has been particularly useful for the manipulation of public opinion and geopolitics since 9/11. Coalescing with and building on a public conspiratorial mindset (that the state has championed for decades) both the Mubarak (and, more recently, Abdel Fattah el-Sisi's) regime and Islamists have, through their respective media organs, framed the West's push for democratization as an imperial design for regional domination, but also used the same narrative to implicate one another.

Drawing on a plethora of geopolitical issues, like the Palestinian question or the wars in Iraq and Afghanistan, both the state and Islamists have forwarded explanations for the latter that centre on a shared understanding that US and Western policies are to blame, and are part of an intentional US-led plot underway to further cement US hegemony and realize 'Zionist' and US expansionist goals in the Muslim world. However, whereas Islamists have generally held the ruling regimes complicit in the latter's ability to inflict suffering on Muslims, the Egyptian state has altered the same argumentation to frame terrorism in ways that deflect attention from its domestic root causes.

In the first vein, terrorism is explained as the logical consequence of Western encroachment on Muslim lands, and the continuing support of the US and West to Israel. For example, Behr and Berger show how in the widely circulated *Al-Ahram* newspaper (majority owned by the Egyptian Government), 'out of 46 relevant opinion pieces [to the study of discourse on terrorism] ... 26 presented Israel as a direct cause or beneficiary of the attacks, while 27 blamed the U.S./Western policies and racism'.[52] The purpose of which is to 'externalize the "root causes" of Islamist terrorism',[53] and thus counter the West's notion that the latter is the result of a 'lack of venues for peaceful participation, the increasing dominance of narrow interpretations of anti-modern religious thinking as well as the anti-Western hegemonic debate itself'.[54]

The Mubarak regime's tactic of externalizing the causes of Islamic extremism was also a standard response to international pressures to democratize. Besides explaining extremism away as a by-product of Western aggression, the Mubarak regime simultaneously capitalized on the growing threat of jihadism to US and Western interests to extract dispensation from the fulfilment of certain democratization indicators in return for guaranteeing cooperation and assistance in the US War on Terror. More importantly, the fact that the best-organized opposition in Egypt has always been of an (at best) illiberal and (at worst) violent, Islamist nature, enables the military-backed regimes to present themselves as the better alternative, both to their secular allies and the population. Using examples of states where the dismantling of an authoritarian regime led to jihadist insurgencies and instability – that in many cases had also increased the threat level to Western interests – the Mubarak regime could make an argument for why Egypt's fate would be similar. An unchecked democracy would lead to an inevitable win for the Islamists, whose illiberal and blatantly anti-Western agenda would cost Western allies an important partner in the region and, more importantly, for the US, one of the few allies who has a working relationship with Israel. And so a domestic policy of allowing a degree of extremism, as defined by the Egyptian Government itself, has its benefits as it bolsters an undesirable political alternative as *the only* alternative, providing an overall legitimate argument for why democratization and human-rights reforms are not only infeasible, but also not in the interest of international allies.

Domestically, externalizing the root causes of Islamism in general and jihadism in particular plays an important role in delegitimizing the ideology. Jihadists are framed as serving the interests of Israel through their actions, in that their violence, while 'understandable',[55] only serves to weaken the homeland through fragmenting it. Under the Mubarak regime, this accusation was more balanced in that it did not directly accuse jihadists of collaborating with Israel. In recent years, this accusation has been replaced with a more active one that places most notably the Ikhwan – now a designated terrorist organization – and the jihadists in the centre of newer versions of the age-old conspiracy theory. The punchline, and an ultimate jab at the credibility of the wider jihadist movement, is that jihadism is not only the outcome of US intervention, but also the creation of it and its various co-conspirators in a bid to justify its interventions and occupation of the Muslim world. As such, jihadist terrorism becomes a tool used by Israel and the Zionist-supporting West to justify infringing upon the sovereignty and territorial integrity of the Islamic world in general and Egypt in particular.

This narrative resonates deeply with an Egyptian public that is increasingly aware of the instability and wars that abound in neighbouring countries, with Syria and Iraq becoming the latest perfect examples of states on the verge of breaking up. It is immaterial to the Egyptian public that Muslim-majority countries in and immediately beyond the Middle East and North Africa (MENA) region have played an equal, if not larger, role in influencing the outcome on the ground today. The public's anti-Western sentiment and the bias against the Western outsider as an agent of change trump the facts on the ground and are powerful rhetorical tools for simultaneously delegitimizing jihadism and the democratization agenda. For many ordinary Egyptians, the result of military interventions in the region and the greater Muslim world by allegedly democratic states has been neither freedom nor democracy. These failures, and the resulting increase in jihadist activity since 9/11, have only served to vindicate the belief that jihadism is a foreign creation. Given both the deep-seated hostility among Egyptians for Israel, and the latter's close relationship to the US, it becomes easier to sell to the public the narrative of a Western-backed conspiracy targeting the region's and state's stability in favour of Israel. Ironically, the state through its media organs sells the AQ 'Crusader–Zionist' conspiracy line, albeit in an informal fashion.

The notion of terrorism being a foreign design was also strongly pushed in movies that were produced during the 1980s and 1990s, around the same time that the jihadist campaign was taking off in Egypt. In many, the terrorists were involved with foreign elements or else received their funding from abroad. In the movie *Explosion* (*Infijar*),[56] for example, the terrorist mastermind is paid to execute a number of assassinations for a Western group whose origins are left to the audience's imagination. In another, *National Security* (*Amn Dawla*),[57] a female prisoner is tasked by state security to infiltrate an Islamist terrorist organization that is operating from abroad. In one of the scenes, the agent asset happens upon terrorists dealing in illicit materials, after which a 'shalom' is exchanged and they part ways; again suggesting Jewish/Israeli complicity in the Islamist terrorist phenomenon. Another feature of this and many later films is the lack of engagement with the ideological element of terrorism. This slightly changed in the 1990s when a connection was suggested between religious extremism and poverty, the lack of opportunities or else brainwashing by other extremists. Overall, however, few serious attempts have been made in Egyptian cinema to critically examine the religious discourse underlying terrorist ideology or the influence of the state's security measures on radicalization and recruitment into terrorist organizations. Nor has Egyptian cinema necessarily been the most suitable medium to address these issues.

More recent attempts by the likes of television presenters Islam al-Beheiry (before he was jailed), Bassem Youssef (before his show was stopped) and Ibrahim Issa to do the same have faced significant challenges from the state's various censorship mechanisms, but also, at times, from Egypt's religious authorities. Beheiry is a good case in point. In a string of episodes in his television show *With Islam* (*Ma'a Islam*),[58] the presenter and Islamic scholar argued for a reformed reading and interpretation of Islam that acknowledges the fallibility of the scholars who compiled what are now accepted as the four most authoritative doctrines (*madahib*) of Sunni Islamic jurisprudence (*fiqh*). As the argument goes, in accepting that these *madahib* are by no means the direct word of God, Muslims can move past the perceived obligation of abiding by the interpretations they offer and thus shed the traditions held within them that could (and do) provide theological justifications for Islamic extremism and terrorism. The argument forwarded by Beheiry is controversial, yet is by no means isolated. In his television show, Ibrahim Issa similarly criticizes the apologists among the Islamic clergy, pointing out that many of IS's actions can and do find justification in the conventional *fiqh* preached and taught in mainstream religious institutions.[59]

Despite such critique effectively responding to Egyptian President Abdel Fattah el-Sisi's call for a 'religious revolution',[60] there appears to be little appetite – particularly among the religious orthodoxy – for real reform or religious introspection. It was Al-Azhar that filed a lawsuit against Beheiry's show, accusing him of 'insulting religion, slandering Al-Azhar, propagating extremist ideology, insulting Islamic scholars, and attempting to undermine national security'.[61] What becomes clear in particularly the last accusation – undermining 'national security' – is that the university and religious seminary does not hesitate to employ elements of the state's narrative to protect its own interests against potential usurpers of its religious authority and power when it suits. More worrying perhaps are the recent refusals of Al-Azhar to apostatize ISIS for its action in Syria and Iraq, yet, as pointed out in the following quotation by Issa, Al-Azhar 'never ceases to shoot out statements accusing novelists, writers, thinkers – anyone who says anything that contradicts their views – of lapsing into a state of infidelity'.[62] Whether this is simply a tactic of using its religious authority to respond to criticism, or else a testament to a degree of radicalism within the institution, is debatable.

Externalizing the root causes of extremism works to absolve the remainder of the non-violent Muslim populace of the responsibility to reflect upon and self-critique the potential religious sources of extremism. This means that a discursive vacuum exists in not only the political realm in Egyptian society, but also the religious. The dangers of this are clear in that, by downplaying the very real religious roots of the problem, the population is left uneducated on the narratives of the extremists and the many ways in which they manipulate and dominate a religious discourse that feeds into terrorism. The rhetoric provided by both the state and the religious authorities is gravely lacking as it provides no long-term solution to an otherwise enduring ideology, which largely explains the episodic cycles of violence that need to occur to put down the inevitable resurgence of terrorism.

The current regime of Abdel Fattah el-Sisi bears many similarities in its CT approaches to those that have preceded it. The counterinsurgency in Sinai follows the same battlefield logic as that of previous regimes in its reliance on conventional military methods, with a new CT law that criminalizes the distribution of unauthorized information on security operations, or else information that is deemed threatening to national security. A recent example of a related prosecution is that of investigative journalist Hossam Bahgat, who was arrested late last year and charged with 'publishing false news that harms national interests and disseminating information that disturbs public peace'.[63] Bahgat had reported on an apparently secret military trial of twenty-six army officers who were allegedly conspiring to instigate a coup. For a military-backed regime whose legitimacy depends on its ability to provide stability and security, releasing such information clearly presents a threat to its legitimacy by undermining the cohesiveness of the military and, by extension, the government. The silencing of dissent and the state's need to censor, as well as control, the flow of information to the public continues unabated.

Finally, despite its designation of the Ikhwan as a terrorist organization, and Article 74 in the 2014 constitution on the banning of religious parties, the Sisi regime has left significant wiggle room for parties like the Salafist Al-Nour party, which pragmatically distanced itself from the Ikhwan-backed Morsi regime after the latter was toppled. It remains to be seen what the role of Islamist and Salafist parties will be in the future of Egypt, but recent efforts at reinvigorating the relationship between Egypt and Hamas in Gaza (at one point even mediated by the Palestinian Islamic Jihad (PIJ)),[64] as well as the continued courting of Salafists by the government, suggests that little will change by way of finally surrendering the state's toxic relations with political Islam.

Conclusion

The CT response of the Egyptian state today continues to heavily depend on military might and a robust set of repressive measures more than any comprehensive approach to decrease the likelihood of terrorism recurring in society. The latter necessitates the involvement of an empowered civil society, which is prevented from flourishing due to the challenge it would pose to the government's claim to power. An empowered civil society with a diversified political environment would also undermine political Islam, whose perpetuation has been vital to successive regimes' political narratives.

The policy of allowing extremism in moderation – be it intentional or not – may have delivered political benefits to the state, yet the failure to develop a counter-narrative to it in the form of a durable social contract and vision of nationhood at times renders even repressive measures ineffective. Popular Egyptian television presenter Ibrahim Issa explains this best in an episode in which he discusses political Islam. He explains, 'There is a political void in the country … and the government thinks it will be able to fill it with silence. But instead, both political Islam and the likes of IS invest in this political void and fill it, and are the ones that stand to gain the most from it.'[65] The reason, according to Issa, is that political Islam as an idea in all its manifestations has four elements that Egyptian authoritarian regimes do not: a doctrine (*'aqida*), a plan, the will to sacrifice for the doctrine and persistence in pursuing it.[66] Lacking these elements, the state relies on abstract principles of nationhood based on rhetorical political manoeuvring and polemics. Building on the collective memory of the nation, conspiracy theories and the politics of fear only go so far in securing loyalty to a regime or figures within it. Coupled with the economic malaise and the repressive measures used to counter riots and protests propelled by it, political Islam and its jihadist offspring will continue to have fertile ground.

What remains, then, is something akin to Israel's policy of 'mowing the grass',[67] where the state is unwilling or incapable of providing a counter to jihadist ideology, through addressing its root causes, but is periodically forced to respond with enough force to impel a ceasefire until the next round of hostilities is initiated. However, as is the case with Israel, this 'cumulative deterrence' is only effective in ensuring periods of calm, yet 'as long as fundamental political realities persist, deterrence might fail at one point or another'.[68] In Egypt today, at the time of writing, the regime of Abdel Fattah el-Sisi is engaged in the latest round of Islamist-inspired violence, proof that absent a comprehensive approach that entails not only reforming the religious narrative, but also the overall political environment of the state, it is unlikely that the future of Egypt will be anything more than the continuation of cyclical episodes of violence.

Notes

1 Salafi jihadism is the violent manifestation of Salafism, which is an Islamic doctrine whose adherents seek to emulate the examples and teaching of first three generations of Islam – i.e., the *salaf*. Salafis reject the blind imitation of any one of the mainstream canonical schools of Islamic jurisprudence, and urge to the roots of Islam as the truest and purest example of Islamic conduct.

2 For an in-depth account of the development of Egyptian nationalist thought and the concept of 'territorial nationalism', see Israel Gershoni and James P. Jankowski, *Egypt, Islam, and the Arabs: The Search for Egyptian Nationhood, 1900–1930* (Oxford: Oxford University Press, 1986).

3 Tara Povey, *Forces of Change: Social Movements in Egypt and Iran since the 1990s* (London: Palgrave Macmillan, 2015), p. 107.

4 For example, in the writings of the fifth Ikhwan General Guide Mustafa Mashhur, preaching (*da'wa*) has six phases, of which the sixth involves the collective effort of reformed Muslims to 'establish the state and return the caliphate'; Carrie Rosefsky Wickham, *Mobilizing Islam: Religion, Activism, and Political Change in Egypt* (New York: Columbia University Press, 2002), p. 145.

5 For an excellent overview see Christoph Schuck, 'A conceptual framework of Sunni Islamism,' *Politics, Religion, and Ideology* 14:4 (2013): 485–506.

6 See, for example, Richard Gauvain, 'Salafism in Modern Egypt: Panacea or pest?' *Political Theology* 11:6 (2015): 802–25.

7 Omar Ashour, *The De-Radicalization of Jihadists: Transforming Armed Islamist Movements* (New York: Routledge, 2009): 37–9.

8 The work, published in Arabic, does not seem to be available in English translation, but is overviewed in Barbara Zollner, 'Prison Talk: The Muslim Brotherhood's Internal Struggle during Gamal Abdel Nasser's Persecution, 1954 to 1971,' *International Journal of Middle East Studies* 39:3 (2007): 411–33.

9 Sayyid Qutb, *Milestones*, International Islamic Federation of Student Organizations (Chicago: KAZI, 2003).

10 Zollner, 'Prison Talk,' 423.

11 *Ibid.*, 423.

12 *Ibid.*, 421.

13 For an overview, see Jeffrey A. Nedoroscik, 'Extremist groups in Egypt,' *Terrorism and Political Violence* 14:2 (2010): 57–70.

14 For an overview of Faraj's views, see Walter Laqueur, *Voices of Terror: Manifestos, Writings, and Manuals of al Qaeda, Hamas, and other Terrorists, from around the World and throughout the Ages* (New York: Reed, 2004), pp. 401–2.

15 Saad Eddin Ibrahim, 'Egypt's Islamic militants,' in Nicholas Hopkins and Saad Eddin Ibrahim (eds), *Arab Society* (Cairo: American University in Cairo Press, 1998), p. 500.

16 *Hisba* is an Islamic term that means enjoining the good and forbidding the evil in the observance of Islamic conduct. It is a form of moral policing that has existed through the history of Islam, and is typically the responsibility of the state. In contemporary Muslim-majority states that have limited or dismantled the practice, groups like the Gama'a have sometimes taken it upon themselves to re-establish it in their areas of control.

17 Stefan Malthaner, *Mobilizing the Faithful: Militant Islamist Groups and their Constituencies* (Frankfurt/New York: Campus, 2010).

18 Emily Dyer and Oren Kessler, *Terror in the Sinai* (London: Henry Jackson Society, 2014).

19 For an overview, see Mokhtar Awad, 'The Islamic State's pyramid scheme: Egyptian expansion and the Giza Governorate cell,' *CTC Sentinel*, 22 April 2016.

20 This movement is composed of a number of cells operating on the mainland and active in different governorates. These include 'Revolutionary Punishment, Popular Resistance Movement(s), Execution Battalion, Beni Suef Revolutionaries Movement, and Helwan Brigades'; Tahrir Institute for Middle East Policy (TIMEP), *Egypt Security Watch Quarterly Report: January–March 2016* (Washington, DC: TIMEP, 2016), p. 16, available at: https://timep.org/commentary/quarterly-report-2016-q1-2/ (accessed 16 June 2016).

21 *Ibid.*, p. 9.

22 Mokhtar Awad, 'Egypt's new radicalism: The Muslim Brotherhood and jihad,' *Foreign Affairs*, 4 February 2016, available at: www.foreignaffairs.com/articles/egypt/2016-02-04/egypts-new-radicalism (accessed 5 April 2016).

23 Eran Zohar, 'The arming of non-state actors in the Gaza Strip and Sinai Peninsula,' *Australian Journal of International Affairs* 69:4 (2015): 438–61.

24 Juha P. Mäkelä, 'The Arab Spring's impact on Egypt's securitocracy,' *International Journal of Intelligence and Counterintelligence* 27:2 (2014): 218.

25 Juan J. Linz, 'An authoritarian regime: The case of Spain,' in Yrjo Littunen and Eric Allardt (eds), *Cleavages, Ideologies and Party Systems* (Helsinki: Academic Bookstore, 1964), p. 297.

26 Owen L. Sirrs, *The Egyptian Intelligence Service: A History of the Mukhabarat, 1910–2009* (London: Routledge, 2010), p. 38.

27 See, for example, Mary Anne Weaver, *A Portrait of Egypt: A Journey through the World of Militant Islam* (New York: Farrar, Straus and Giroux, 2000), and Malthaner, *Mobilizing the Faithful*.

28 Sadiq Reza, 'Endless emergency: The case of Egypt,' *New Criminal Law Review* 10:4 (2007): 537.

29 *Ibid.*, 538.

30 *Ibid.*, 548.

31 Amr Hamzawy, 'Legislating authoritarianism: Egypt's new era of repression,' Carnegie Endowment for International Peace website, 16 March 2017, available at: https://carnegieendowment.org/2017/03/16/legislating-authoritarianism-egypt-s-new-era-of-repression-pub-68285 (accessed 27 August 2017).

32 Wolfgang Lotz, *The Champagne Spy* (New York: St. Martin's, 1972), pp. 24–5, cited in Owen L. Sirrs, 'Reforming Egyptian intelligence: Precedents and prospects.' *Intelligence and National Security* 28:2 (2013): 236.

33 Sirrs, *Egyptian Intelligence Service*, p. 46.

34 *Ibid.*, p. 80.

35 Daniel Byman, '"Death solves all problems": The authoritarian model of counterinsurgency,' *Journal of Strategic Studies* 39:1 (2015): 83.

36 *Ibid.*

37 This author has come across this in televised interviews in the Egyptian media with members of the EAF or other national security institutions – e.g., Tony Khalifa, 'Akeed Amro Ammar yakshef qa'imat al-'omala' wa al-taboor al-khames fi misr fi ajra' al-kalam "ala al-qahira wa al-nas"' (Colonel Amro Ammar uncovers the agents and fifth pillar in Egypt on [talk show] *Bold Talk* (Cairo and the People)), *YouTube*, 9 March 2014, available at: www.youtube.com/watch?v=AkvnUdS7ydg&app=desktop (accessed 26 August 2017).

38 Dina Al Raffie, 'Straight from the horse's mouth: De-radicalization claims of former Egyptian militant leaders,' *Perspectives on Terrorism* 9:1 (2015): 27–48.

39 Jeffrey T. Kenney, 'Enemies near and far: The image of the Jews in Islamist discourse in Egypt,' *Religion* 24:3 (1994): 254.

40 Dietrich Jung, Mary Juul Petersen and Sara Lei Sparre, *Politics of Modern Muslim Subjectivities: Islam, Youth, and Social Activism in the Middle East* (New York: Palgrave Macmillan, 2014), p. 113.

41 Jeffrey T. Kenney, *Muslim Rebels: Kharijites and the Politics of Extremism in Egypt* (New York: Oxford University Press, 2006).

42 *Ibid.*

43 Housam Darwisheh, 'Survival, triumph and fall: The political transformation of the Muslim Brotherhood in Egypt,' in Khoo Boo Teik, Vedi Hadiz and

Yoshihio Nakanishi (eds), *Between Dissent and Power: The Transformation of Islamic Politics in the Middle East and Asia* (London: Palgrave Macmillan, 2014), p. 112.

44 Sohair A. Morsy, quoted: *ibid.*, p. 117.

45 Gehad Auda, 'The "normalization" of the Islamic movement in Egypt from the 1970s to the early 1990s,' in Martin E. Marty and R. Scott Appleby (eds), *Accounting for Fundamentalisms: The Dynamic Character of Movements* (Chicago: University of Chicago Press, 1994), pp. 374–412.

46 For an overview of literature, see Ashour, *De-Radicalization of Jihadists,* pp. 26–8.

47 Yasser El-Shimy, 'The Muslim Brotherhood,' in Emile Hokayem and Hebatalla Taha (eds), *Egypt after the Spring: Revolt and Reaction* (London: International Institute for Strategic Studies, 2016), pp. 75–104; Ashraf El-Sherif, *The Egyptian Muslim Brotherhood's Failures* (Washington, DC: Carnegie Endowment for International Peace, 2014), available at: http://carnegieendowment.org/files/muslim_brotherhood_failures.pdf (accessed 6 June 2016).

48 Ephraim Kahana and Sagit Stivi-Kerbis, 'The assassination of Anwar al-Sadat: An intelligence failure,' *International Journal of Intelligence and CounterIntelligence* 27:1 (2014): 183.

49 David H. Ucko, '"The people are revolting": An anatomy of authoritarian counterinsurgency,' *Journal of Strategic Studies* 39:1 (2016): 47.

50 For a good example of how this worked under Sadat, see Hassan Hanafi, 'The relevance of the Islamic alternative,' *Arab Studies Quarterly* 4:1/2 (1982): 54–74.

51 *Shirk* is an Islamic term that denotes the deification or worship of anything or anyone besides God. Although it relates to spiritual worship, Islamists extend it to governance through arguing that ruling with laws other than those ordained by God amounts to *shirk*, as it replaces God's laws with man-made ones, and is thus tantamount to varying degrees of sin or else is a form of apostasy.

52 Hartmut Behr and Lars Berger, 'The challenge of talking about terrorism: The EU and the Arab debate on the causes of Islamist terrorism,' *Terrorism and Political Violence* 21:4 (2009): 541.

53 *Ibid.*, 542.

54 *Ibid.*

55 *Ibid.*

56 Saeed Mohamed Marzouk, *Infijar* (Explosion) (Cairo: Hassan Yacoub, 1990).

57 Nader Galal, *Amn Dawla* (National security) (Cairo, 1999).

58 Broadcast on Al-Kahera Wel Nas (Cairo and the people) network, 2013–15.

59 Ibrahim Issa, 'Egyptian TV host Ibrahim Issa: Nobody dares to admit that ISIS crimes are based on Islamic sources,' Middle East Media Research Institute TV Monitor Project, clip #4773, 3 February 2015, available at: www.memri.org/tv/egyptian-tv-host-ibrahim-issa-nobody-dares-admit-isis-crimes-are-based-islamic-sources (accessed 10 July 2016).

60 Mada Masr, 'Preacher Islam al-Beheiry sentenced to one year for insulting Islam,' Mada Masr website, 29 December 2015, available at: www.madamasr.com/en/2015/12/29/news/u/preacher-islam-al-beheiry-sentenced-to-one-year-for-insulting-islam/ (accessed 26 August, 2017).

61 *Ibid.*

62 Raymond Ibrahim, 'Dr. Ahmed Al-Tayeb: Meet the world's "most influential Muslim,"' *Frontpage Mag*, 24 August 2016, available at: www.frontpagemag.com/fpm/263946/dr-ahmed-al-tayeb-meet-worlds-most-influential-raymond-ibrahim (accessed 26 August 2017).

63 *Al Jazeera*, 'Egypt military arrests journalist in "blow for freedom,"' *Al Jazeera*, 9 November 2015, available at: www.aljazeera.com/news/2015/11/egypt-military-arrests-journalist-blow-freedom-151108194121623.html (accessed 26 August 2017).

64 Al-Masry Al-Youm, 'Palestinian Islamic jihad movement visits Cairo,' *Egypt Independent*, 17 July 2017, available at: www.egyptindependent.com/palestinian-islamic-jihad-movement-visits-cairo/ (accessed 5 June 2018).

65 Ibrahim Issa, '#ma'a Ibrahim Issa: saytarat al-irhab 'ala tanzimat al-Islam al-siyasi wa qanun al-i'lam al-mowahad 24 mayo' (#with Ibrahim Issa: terrorism's control over political Islam and the law of unified media 24 May), *YouTube*, 25 May 2016, available at: www.youtube.com/watch?v=k7WH_qIB-i0 (accessed 26 August 2017).

66 *Ibid.*

67 Efraim Inbar and Eitan Shamir, '"Mowing the Grass": Israel's strategy for protracted intractable conflict,' *Journal of Strategic Studies* 37:1 (2014): 65–90.

68 *Ibid.*, 76.

12

Contending notions of terrorism in Lebanon: Politico-legal manoeuvres and political Islam

Bashir Saade

لائحة الإرهابتبعكم، بلّوهاواشربوا مَيتّها

(This 'terrorism list' of yours, soak it and drink its water; Hassan Nasrallah, widely broadcast speech, 25 May, 2013)

Introduction

Lebanon, like many other places in the world, has known deadly attacks against civilian areas that carried specific political messages. But unlike most other places, especially in the West, Lebanon's political tradition has been mired with car-bomb attacks, targeted assassinations and deadly plots of various kinds. Sporadic security incidents have rocked the capital and several key towns in the country since the close of the civil war in the early 1990s. Civil peace was intermittently disturbed by bombings and various types of assassinations throughout the 1990s, mostly targeting political figures, but also involving small-scale wars pitting Hizbullah and Israel in the south of Lebanon. The existence of a low level of armed organization and action in Lebanon has shaped what are dubbed 'terrorist' actions in different ways.

The purpose of this chapter is to map the field of terrorist actions in relation to the security environment in Lebanon. The chapter argues that, depending on the institutional and organizational setting available to each local political actor or coalition, contending understandings of terrorism have been deployed and have produced leverage by framing each respective political 'Other'. In the absence of a strong executive power or a unified national vision built into the security rationale of state institutions, different Lebanese political groups have interacted in this climate by offsetting each other, or at times coming to compromises, or even at other times reaching all-out armed confrontations. The politics of naming or branding in this context comes as a useful tool to create real effect on the ground. In his study of the Italian Communist Party facing the challenge of switching its name to 'Social Democrat', David Kertzer persuasively argues that naming is not just epiphenomenal to other more real events, but shaped the rationale for political actions and the relationship with Communist supporters.[1] Likewise, the branding of acts as terrorist triggers the formulation of public policy and has social repercussions for the relationship of the different parties in Lebanon and their constituencies. For example, an armed political party such as Hizbullah is bound by its popularity and has organic links with a population that votes for its presence in parliament and municipalities and, more importantly, that may decide to join the organization's military wing.

Two instances of terrorism labelling will be explored in this chapter. One is the anti-Hizbullah political coalition leading the charge to label the killings of prominent Lebanese politicians carried out from 2005 onwards as terrorist acts, and possibly pointing the finger towards Syria and Hizbullah as the chief instigators of these acts, while mobilizing an armada of international institutions resulting in the setting up of a UN-sponsored special tribunal. The other is the attempt by Hizbullah to frame an enemy present on Lebanese and Syrian soil and more generally in the Middle East as a threat to its 'Resistance project', and ultimately as a threat to Islamic values and 'the Prophet's legacy'.

The terrorist attacks that Lebanon has known have in many ways not shared the typical characteristics of such attacks in other countries in the region and around the world. That may be due to an overly politically charged climate, where a heightened security situation involves competing groups delineated by sect, different nationalist visions, and different representations of enemies and the political Other. In a sense, Lebanon's political regime could be thought of as a pure oligarchy or a quasi-anarchy where no solid executive power exists as the different political groups and coalitions offset each other through the vaguely defined and overlapping prerogatives of a prime minister and a president. What has been called somewhat optimistically the 'consociational democracy model' – mostly consecrated during the Taif Agreement of 1989 where the various warlords of the country war-torn since 1975 hashed out a working solution to different conflicting national visions under the aegis of a regionally fragile consensus between Saudi Arabia, Syria and the US – among other things and for the purposes of this essay, permitted several security rationales to exist. This has manifested both at the political level through disagreements among parliament, the president and the prime minister on basic national priorities, and also in different state institutions, occupied by different political groups, pushing for divergent policies (for example the Lebanese army and the Lebanese internal security forces, especially after 2005). This is important because the rationale for terrorist activities or operations of violence that involve the targeting of civilians leads to ongoing conflicts between the different local protagonists. Regional actors can exploit these conflicts, but it is also often the case that Lebanese groups draw these regional and international powers into propping up their local positions, and this includes another – 'hybrid' – actor that emerges from both local and global contexts and that has been dubbed 'Sunni jihadi' radical organizations and individuals.

Background

In order to explain this further, one needs to understand the current Lebanese political system. Since the end of the 'civil war' in 1990 and the signing of the Taif Agreement that put an end to the hostilities, Syria imposed itself as the main power broker in Lebanon. The various militia formations emerging from the war faced the choice of accepting the agreement, disarming and accommodating to the new political formula, or becoming pariahs of the emerging system. For example, the main leaders of the Christian militias were excluded. One, Michel Aoun, an army general, was exiled in Paris after Syria executed a whole contingent of the Lebanese army division he was commanding near the presidential palace in Baabda,[2] and the other, Samir Geagea, the leader of the Lebanese forces, was put in prison in 1994 after an explosion in a church close to the capital killing fifteen civilians was attributed to him. A few years later, a third Christian leader, Elie Hobeika, who led a pro-Syrian branch of the Lebanese forces and was considered partly responsible for the Sabra and Chatila massacre of 1982 and the failed CIA assassination attempt of Muhammad Husayn Fadlallah, was killed in a booby-trapped car in 2002. Some reports argue that the possibility of a trial of Ariel Sharon in Belgium could have been related to his killing.[3]

But not all armed groups were disbanded. The 1990s sealed a new security formula that permitted Hizbullah to continue its Islamic Resistance against Israel, which was occupying large areas of the south of Lebanon. After a few years of occupation and after intense negotiations with Iran, the 'pax Syriana'[4] had to make room for an armed actor whose sole rationale for bearing weapons was to fight to free land from Israeli occupation. It is crucial to remember in this regard that relations between Hizbullah and Syria had been quite tense since the formation of the party and until 1992. Noteworthy was the massacre of Fathallah in 1987, where the Syrian army attacked a Hizbullah position in the southern suburbs of Beirut in retaliation for the latter's support of Palestinians in the War of the Camps. Nevertheless, the pax Syriana and Resistance contained in the south of Lebanon proved to be very durable and highly beneficial to the development of Hizbullah's military project. The Syrian regime mostly managed to exert influence and control through its different allies in the country – particularly its Lebanese political and security allies – and was highly dependent on the latter's personal interests. The exact dynamics of Syrian control of Lebanon tend to be oversimplified in the literature. While the Syrians had the upper hand on security questions – yet were strengthened by a committed Lebanese intelligentsia – they had to govern through an intricate system of negotiations between the various Lebanese parties. Reinoud Leenders examines in his *Spoils of Truce* the complex corruption practices that linked various Lebanese and Syrian groups and factions.[5]

Ultimately, the pax Syriana could only work as a result of a specific regional consensus. The renewed internationalization of Middle East politics of the post-9/11 period drastically changed settled regional arrangements. In Lebanon, through the Taif Agreement, Saudi Arabia promoted the ambitious and rich entrepreneur Rafic Hariri as prime minister of the country, and Iran backed Hizbullah's Resistance project. While Syria dominated through an intricate alliance of Lebanese oligarchs and military officers, the US had to accept that the pax Syriana was the least troublesome alternative for the time being. This consensus became more and more fragile when the various parties involved could not accommodate their more and more pressing differences. A strong rivalry developed between Prime Minister Rafic Hariri and the president and former general of the Lebanese army Emile Lahoud, which resulted in regular vetoing of each other's initiatives and policy proposals. As mentioned earlier, the main issue with the consensual model concocted in Taif was that the prime minister and the president were given almost identical powers, or at least the text was vague enough to assume it was so. The original purpose of establishing a kind of sectarian parity and distribution of powers among the various sects of the country ended up backfiring and compromising the possibility of taking comprehensive executive and national decisions. This situation meant that all parties in Lebanon had to rely, even more so than in the past, on foreign parties in order to bargain their positions on the inside, but most of the time to no avail. On the eve of Hariri's assassination in 2005 it was considered that he had joined the 'anti-Syria' camp in Lebanon, while

Lahoud and the security structure, along with Hizbullah, represented those who were aligned with the Syrian regime.

The assassination of Rafic Hariri and its consequences

On the 14 February 2005, former Lebanese Prime Minister Rafic Hariri's convoy exploded, one tonne of TNT killing him and twenty-one others, triggering a series of drastic political changes including the withdrawal of the Syrian army on 30 April 2005, and a long tug of war between the various Lebanese political factions. Based on a presidential statement following the attack, a UN-sponsored fact-finding mission (FFM) was formed, headed by Peter Fitzgerald, a deputy commissioner of the Irish police. The FFM interviewed different political and security actors, investigated the scene of the crime and published its report, which, although admitting that it could not identify the likely culprits, put the blame squarely on the Syrian regime and its allies in the Lebanese security apparatus, which the FFM advised to be totally reformed. The report was published towards the end of March 2005, preceded by a few weeks by the total withdrawal of the Syrian army from Lebanon and the imprisonment of four Lebanese generals suspected to be complicit in the assassination.

The pressure on Syria to withdraw from Lebanon, and Bashar al-Assad's regime's likely involvement in the assassination of Hariri, split Lebanon into a pro-Syrian camp dubbed 'March 8' and an anti-Syrian one known as 'March 14', the names referring to demonstrations that took place during 2005. The March 8 and March 14 camp appellations referred to cross-sectarian political coalitions that were split on their nationalist visions, mainly over foreign policy questions and the fate of the weapons of Hizbullah. Once Syria withdrew militarily from Lebanon, and its key security service allies were imprisoned, the issue of Hizbullah's weapons became the foremost point of contention. A short-lived coalition between the various actors for legislative elections produced a majority vote for Hariri's son Saad, who became the first prime minister after the Syrian withdrawal. General Michel Aoun, who had just returned from exile in May 2005, hailed the anti-Syrian demonstrations that had been taking place in downtown Beirut since 14 March 'the Cedar revolution', and joined the nascent anti-Syrian coalition, signing a Memorandum of Understanding with Hizbullah in early 2006.

By December 2005 and after a wave of targeted assassinations and explosions rocking Beirut, the Lebanese Government, then headed by an anti-Syrian coalition, asked the UN to set up an international tribunal to follow up on the

FFM. The UN and the Lebanese Government signed an agreement for the Special Tribunal for Lebanon (STL) on 23 January 2007. The agreement was handed to the Lebanese parliament to ratify. The speaker of parliament, Nabih Berri – allied with Hizbullah and its various allies, which formed a bloc against the anti-Syrian coalition – refused to convene parliament to hold a vote on its ratification. Nevertheless, a majority of members of parliament from the anti-Syrian camp signed a petition, which the then Prime Minister Fouad Siniora handed to the UN secretary general, requesting that the Security Council form the tribunal, which it did through Resolution 1757, a step considered by some to be unconstitutional.[6] Although the STL was initially planned as a treaty-based institution, meaning as an agreement between the government and the UN, it was argued that 'a Security Council resolution adopted under Chapter VII of the UN Charter is an instrument of subordination'.[7] It was another two years before the STL opened its doors, in 2009. One of its first rules of order was the release of the four Lebanese generals, as there was no persuasive evidence to keep them in custody. In June 2011, and after a complex analysis of the mobile-phone network activity just before the assassination, four Hizbullah members were named as suspects and were summoned to face interrogation in the Hague.

The legal basis of the STL remained a subject of controversy, and the literature on the subject has been extensive.[8] One point of contention was the juridical validity and sovereignty of a tribunal that extracted its legitimacy simultaneously from domestic and international law, first in the absence of a formal parliamentary ratification and second in light of a legal problem in merging the two legal systems. Crimes like the assassination of Hariri, which appeared to be a political assassination, had never been tried under international law, which normally deals with much wider acts that affect whole populations. Articulating a working legal notion of 'terrorism' became the most important requirement for an international institution to prosecute such crimes. And while international law does not have such legal precedents, Lebanese domestic law (like that of several other countries in the world) had legally conceptualized terrorist acts as early as 1958, in the aftermath of popular revolts that led to confrontations with the state and finally a US military intervention to restore civil peace. In effect, Lebanon would be the first country to provide a working definition of terrorism that could be used by an international institution to try such crimes, falling in this murky zone between political assassination and civil threat.[9]

But there were political undertones to a legal initiative attempting to understand terrorism. As Robert Bosco puts it, 'The argument that the Hariri tribunal has a moral function, i.e. to redress wrongs, to rehabilitate Lebanon's system of justice, and to further strengthen the international norm against political assassination, depends in large part on blurring the distinction between political assassination and terrorism.'[10] Terrorism as a specific type of crime, especially as defined by Lebanese domestic law, involves significant speculation over the intentions of the perpetrator, who, to meet the definition, would need to have aimed 'to terrorize a group of people, even if the crime did not cause the death or harm of anybody'.[11] Yet in the case of the assassination of Hariri and the few other attacks that took place up to the end of 2005, there was a clear indication that political figures were the targets. The killing of civilians and the instilling of fear are controversial points, since it is hard to know whether the latter is a by-product of an act or part of an initial objective. As Talal Asad points out, the US 'War on Terror' was predicated on a clear distinction between acts of war and terrorism, which main difference seems to be one of (hierarchical) moral intentions.[12]

In effect, institutional and political parties' efforts to develop notions and labels of terrorism are part of an ongoing political process of asserting different types of gains and influence, or reacting to various threats and opportunities. Political entities resort to different symbolic articulations to frame their enemies or the political Other, depending on the institutional and ideological settings in which they operate. The ruling coalition that emerged after the assassination of Rafic Hariri definitely fought first Syrian political influence and second the latter's resilient ally Hizbullah, as well as its various aligned groups, through the use of such international mechanisms. Given that Hizbullah was part of the Lebanese parliament, and while its military project, Hizbullah's 'Islamic Resistance', was considered legislatively legitimate, the use of an international institution to frame activities as terrorist was a convenient way to confront it in the only arena where it was possible to do so. Constructing a working definition of terrorism was highly instrumental to this politics.

The STL was also thought to be politicized because it unilaterally favoured a single thesis that informed the investigation. Yet, there were other theses that also proposed an understanding of terrorism, and thus could have been politicized or framed the political Other in different ways. Hizbullah's Secretary General Hassan Nasrallah vehemently criticized the STL's mandate and the way it was being conducted, primarily reproaching investigators for never taking into consideration the possibility that it could have been Israel that had conducted the operation. In August 2010 and in an eloquent, almost scholarly, ordered presentation, Nasrallah argued for considering such a track by revealing how Hizbullah's system of surveillance had infiltrated Israeli systems, and how the latter had meticulous coverage of Lebanese airspaces, especially that area where Hariri was assassinated.[13] While this may have just been an attempt by Hizbullah to shift the blame to Israel and provide the party with political cover, Nasrallah's impressive presentation did make a persuasive case that international investigators should be looking in several directions before indicting. The STL investigation continued moving in the opposite direction, however, clinging to the Hizbullah inculpation thesis. The final chapter in this saga was the death of Mustafa Badreddine, a top Hizbullah commander who was among the four suspects apprehended by the STL. Yet the trial continued 'pending further information' on Badreddine's death, a move considered by and large as another compromising blow to the STL's reputation.[14]

Another important path to follow is that of the Sunni jihadi militancy, as, although still a controversial point, it was initially believed that the blast was caused by a suicide bomber named Ahmed Abu Adass. Moreover, the attack was claimed by a 'little-known group calling itself Victory and Jihad in Greater Syria'.[15] The STL prosecution argued that Adass was lured by the Hizbullah suspects, but still did not resolve the question of the suicide bombing. For one thing, the Sunni jihadi track facilitated the construction of an enemy that was wholly outside of the system, as opposed to other political formations that are all part of the Lebanese arena and who do fight through violent means. The jihadi track, as will be seen below, involves rogue Muslim elements who may come from different places in the Middle East and who may be linked to the Afghani or Iraqi legacy of jihadism, with ties to looser organizations such as al Qaeda or important figures such as the Jordanian jihadist Zarqawi. Yet, a similar strategy is followed when trying to inculpate Hizbullah and labelling the latter as a 'terrorist' agent. This strategy is closely associated with the idea that the organization has a foreign agenda or is being moved by a foreign entity, in this case Iran.

Sunni jihadism and the making of a terrorist

Whereas the attacks mentioned above that targeted political figures could roughly be described as political assassinations even if they did involve collateral civilian damage, those that have targeted the highly civilian areas of the southern suburbs of Beirut since 2016 resemble more what is conventionally labelled a terrorist attack, and they have most often involved suicide operations. Yet, ironically, these attacks have not received the same attention from international legal institutions. Moreover, although the period covered by the tribunal was up to the end of 2005, it was potentially able to extend its jurisdiction beyond 2005 only if the Security Council and the Lebanese state agreed on such a move. In effect, a significant number of attacks have taken place up to the time of writing this chapter. Some attacks targeted specific political or military figures (such as the assassinations Gebran Tueni, Pierre Gemayel, Walid Eido, Antoine Ghanem, Francois Elias Hajj, Wissam Eid, Wissam al-Hassan and Mohammad Shatah, all considered to be part of the March 14 camp, but also other assassinations such as of Mahmoud al Majzoub of the Palestinian Islamic Jihad, or the pro-Syrian Druze politician Saleh Aridi), and others targeted civilian areas, mostly the north of Lebanon, such as the bombings in Tripoli in 2008 and 2013, and in the southern suburbs of Beirut, one of Hizbullah's strongholds, in 2013 and 2014.

In addition to all these attacks, it is important to mention that a full-scale war broke out in May 2007 between the Lebanese army and a radical jihadi organization that called itself Fath al Islam, when the latter attempted to take over the Palestinian camp of Nahr al Bared on the coastal north of Lebanon after the former slaughtered twenty-seven Lebanese army soldiers in their sleep. Earlier the same day, the police had raided a house used by Fath al Islam militants in the town of Tripoli. What followed from these confrontations was a massive military onslaught of the camp that lasted until September 2007, and that resulted in its total destruction and the fleeing of the key Fath al Islam leaders. On the eve of the Nahr al Bared confrontations, two explosions took place in Beirut, both targeting commercial areas (the ABC Mall and the area of Verdun), on 20 and 21 May. And, before these explosions, another series of bus bombing had taken place in the largely Christian area of Bikfaya. The four Syrians arrested at the time confessed to being part of the Fath al Islam organization.

What Lebanon witnessed in the full-blown war against Fath al Islam had a long historical precedent. As the country discovered an instance of a militant Sunni jihadi organization, commentators were split between understanding it either as a proxy of Syrian intelligence (as the March 14 camp would see it), or as Saudi or US funded (as per the March 8 camp). But even though Fath al Islam had benefited from the goodwill and strategic connivance of various actors, including those just mentioned, it had its own agenda and did not depend on any patron to operate, as Bernard Rougier persuasively claims.[16] Most radical organizations that emerged before and after Fath al Islam were at different points in time co-opted, surveilled or constrained by security institutions, but the latter never had a full control over them. One interesting implication here is that the Lebanese army onslaught of the Nahr al Bared camp was more akin to a full-blown military, rather than a 'counterterrorist', operation.

Rougier explains that since the 1990s these Sunni radical groups and individuals have been deterritorialized, loosely or not connected, and highly mobile, moving across different countries such as Iraq, Syria and Lebanon, settling mostly in Palestinian camps such as in the Lebanon, where the power vacuum and the prevailing non-state-security situation made a fertile ground for their organizing and mobilizing.[17] Other areas of loose security in Lebanon were conducive to the training or settling of militants, such as Dinniyeh in the north of Lebanon or, more recently, the northern border town of Arsal, which has witnessed fierce confrontations between Jabhat al-Nusrah and Islamic State (IS) militants as well as the Lebanese army. But, as Rougier argues, 'Jihadi' militants are ideologically fluid, shifting political priorities and alliances according to context. If 'anti-imperialism' or 'anti-Western' is a general rallying slogan, it may involve drastically opposite implications. Those who thought that Israel and the US presence were the main problems, grew closer to Hizbullah, Iran and the 'Axis of Resistance', especially in the 1980s. One of the main irredentist Sunni Islamist parties, the group al-Tawhid, was trained mostly by the Iranian Pasdaran during this period. Yet al-Tawhid was fiercely fought by Syria, who, when not bloodily suppressing it, arrested most of its members or forced others to flee to Western countries such as Denmark, Sweden and Australia; the Gulf; or Pakistan – where, in all cases, they would be heavily influenced by Salafi movements.[18]

Indeed, it is the nature of the relation between the prevailing states or dominant powers – in this case mainly Syria, who mostly controlled security questions – and those organizations that would partly explain their ultimate ideological directions. Whereas Hizbullah, after a period of bitter confrontations with the Syrian regime, found a compromise brokered by Iran, the other much looser, more unruly and more unpredictable Sunni militant organizations did not find a similar happy deal. A tumultuous relationship with Syria would slowly shift many of these militants and political actors from being allied with Iran to more nebulous Salafi-inspired, Gulf-financed, 'Sunni'-centred movements. These individuals who responded to more 'Sunni' grievances would argue that targeting 'Shia' interests or even populations is key to gain influence and challenge dominant powers. This last narrative found its most extreme and murderous expression with Abu Musab al-Zarqawi and his al Qaeda in Iraq, which subsequently became IS. But even though these sets of grievances could be shared by various groups and individuals, they translate into very different political practices, of which IS and al Qaeda are extreme forms.

Although, traditionally, Sunni militant politics is partly shaped by the experience of Palestinian camps, which would make it more sympathetic to the Palestinian cause and thus to the 'Axis of Resistance' modus operandi, the deterritorialized and pariah status of the camps, exacerbated by waves of migration to other regions of the world, reinforces an alienation from the state or dominant powers in place. On the other hand, its conflictual interaction with the Assad Syrian regime makes the relation more one of either subservience or dissent. But, all in all, Sunni politics across the spectrum from moderate to more radical was bound to become the arch enemy of the Syrian regime, first for sectarian reasons as the latter consistently followed a politics of protection of minorities in Lebanon while controlling, dividing or suppressing what was considered to be a majority. One of the first bombing operations that qualifies as a terrorist act, given that it was targeting a completely civilian area, took place in 2003. Although the blowing up of a McDonald's restaurant shortly before the assassination of Hariri was made possible by the same transnational networks of 'Salafized' Lebanese diaspora that had fled the north in the mid-1980s, it received no interest from the STL investigation.[19] And yet again the aftermath of the Iraqi war saw a gradual upsurge in foreign fighters, who had been already present in Pakistan and Afghanistan, but were now attracted to other areas where weak state sovereignties struggled to control territory, such as in Lebanon, Syria and Iraq. These foreign fighters were slightly different from those emerging from Palestinian camp experiences, although some of them may have spent time in these camps.[20] They were younger and more radical, their political objectives much less linked to a specific territory.

It is noteworthy that not all Salafi movements are sympathetic to militant and violent actions. Most shield themselves from political processes and prefer to work at a social level to spread a set of religious values and practices, yet it is precisely their reluctance to engage in politics and their hostility towards 'national' boundaries that constitute a tipping point towards armed alternatives. But in the prevailing political context, the connection between Salafism and jihadism, especially in the case of north of Lebanon, is an important one. The city of Tripoli is a case in point, with a long history of sectarian feuds between Alawites and Sunnis, exacerbated by the Syrian presence since 1976.[21]

After the fall of Saddam Hussein in 2003, some Salafi currents across the world pushed militants to go and fight the occupation in Iraq, while Syrian intelligence turned a blind eye to the border crossings. Salafi religious credibility and popularity were formed in this way, as Salafis were still a minority group in Tripoli, in Lebanon.[22] And, as mentioned before, it was in Iraq that the first sectarian strategies started emerging, as Iran and Hizbullah were present also as early as 2003 and were pushing for a specific balance of power that did not benefit more nebulous organizations. The Syrian uprisings and their almost immediate militarization should be read in light of a gradual 'sectarianization' of politics stretching from 2003 to 2011, for which Iraq would be the main arena, and where Lebanon, as seen above, would experience a more tamed yet still important confrontation that would dramatically intensify after the beginning of Hizbullah's military involvement in Syria.

Moreover, the case of Sheikh Ahmed al-Assir – who started as a Salafi preacher, involved in what is called 'tablīghi' (preaching) and social and religious work in the city of Saida in the south of Lebanon – is a relevant one. Al-Assir became politically active over a short space of time. In 2012, he had organized a sit-in in Saida to protest against the fact that Hizbullah was a military organization. In April 2013, however, al-Assir was urging his followers to go and fight in Syria, in Qusayr and in Homs,[23] and footage has emerged of him in combat gear allegedly in Qusayr,[24] after Hizbullah's military intervention there; later that year, in June, his group clashed with the Lebanese army in Saida in heavy street fighting. It is unclear what triggered the change, but it definitely involved the changing political context as described above, as well as probable regional backing from states such as Saudi Arabia. Al-Assir managed to escape these confrontations but was later arrested as he was attempting to flee from Beirut airport in 2015.

In effect, Hizbullah decided to formally render public its intervention in Syria on 25 May 2013 during 'Liberation Day', which annually remembers the withdrawal of the Israeli army from the south of Lebanon. Hizbullah's Secretary General Hassan Nasrallah appeared on television to make the case for fighting in Syria against what he argued was a new form of threat in the region. In this speech, Nasrallah also explained the rationale behind his organization's backing of the Assad regime, which mostly involved backing the 'Axis of Resistance' and confronting this new enemy, 'the Takfiri' threat. Takfirism, in the words of Nasrallah and as disseminated by the dominant press and social media, is a label given to those Sunni jihadi groups who consider any other Muslim sects or currents, even within Sunni Islam, as unbelievers, or *kuffar*. Takfirism can be traced back to the rise of Zarqawism rather than al Qaeda as such, although Salafi currents of Wahhabi inspiration have held anti-Shia attitudes. This can be traced to the founder of this highly puritan religious movement that spread across the Arab peninsula in the latter part of the nineteenth century, helped by the house of Saud, a powerful family of the region who founded the state of Saudi Arabia in 1932. While the relationship between the more radical brands of Salafism and the Saudi state is complex,[25] the two do share certain characteristics, such as an anti-Shia attitude and an obsession with a literalist understanding of the faith, along with a tendency to support civil violence in order to protect their dogmas.[26]

Hizbullah had just started its military operations before this official declaration; if anything, in his speech Nasrallah deplored what he thought was a belated move. According to him, the militarization of the Syrian uprisings had started much earlier, and an important base for supplying and funding an armed Syrian opposition was Lebanon. Rougier confirms this, and describes well the way the Sunni-led Mustaqbal party and the Lebanese internal security forces (at the time led by the enigmatic Wissam al-Hassan, who died in yet another massive car explosion in Beirut in 2012)[27] planned and helped arm and train a 'moderate' opposition that they helped cross the northern border of Lebanon into Syria.[28] As this operation got out of hand and opposition groups multiplied and became unruly, the dominant narrative of Nasrallah is that the appellation of 'moderate and radical' did not apply to these armed groups, which according to him all engaged in ethnic cleansing and sectarian tactics.

In Qusayr, Syria, Hizbullah fought the Farouq Battalion, a heteroclite group of 'Islamist' fighters with complex ideological backgrounds and shifting allegiances, mostly originating from the larger Homs area. As Hizbullah and the Syrian army prevailed in these border regions to the east of Lebanon, fighters of these mostly Sunni groups escaped and found safe haven in the bordering town of Arsal in the north of Lebanon. These various fighters have gradually been integrated into larger, more successful or effective organizations, such as Jabhat al-Nusrah or IS. For Hizbullah, all these groups and individuals have a similar political rationale, which uses sectarian politics as a strategy for influence. As also happened in Iraq from 2003 onwards, for Hizbullah, Syria becomes an arena where similar tactics are being deployed in order to challenge the existing powers. In Iraq the gradually forming Shia-dominated state and in Syria the Alawi regime of Bashar al-Assad are both similar targets, and both are backed by Iran.

The Dahieh bombings and the case of Arsal

After Hizbullah began its military intervention in Syria, bombing attacks increased gradually, targeting dense civilian areas, commercial areas and sometimes mosques. The latter half of 2013 was bloody. A series of bombings rocked not only the southern suburbs of Beirut, but also Tripoli. On 9 July 2013, a car bomb exploded in the Bir el-Abed district of Dahieh without causing loss of life, but leaving fifty people wounded. Just a month later a more deadly explosion, this time in Roueiss, another district of Dahieh, again targeted what is considered to be a Hizbullah stronghold. A few days later in Tripoli, on 23 August, bombs exploded simultaneously in two different mosques, killing at least forty-two people. Then, on 19 November, a large explosion hit the Iranian cultural centre in Bir al Hassan on the outskirts of Dahieh, killing at least twenty-two people. It was also during this year that a senior Hizbullah commander, Hassan Lakkis, was killed by two gunmen in Beirut, and Mohamad Chatah, a former minister close to the Mustaqbal party known as Hizbullah's political rival, was killed by a car bomb.

The year 2014 saw an increase in the wave of suicide attacks and other bombings, not just targeting civilian areas in different districts of Dahieh but also military barracks (especially in the Bekaa and the eastern frontier with

Syria), and the town of Arsal. In the previous year, this town, situated in the northeast of Lebanon close to the border with Syria, had been the centre of an intensive war between the combatants fleeing Qusayr and the Qalamoun region and the Lebanese army subsequently morphing into Jabhat al-Nusrah or IS. At times, al-Nusrah and IS were fighting each other in a destructive war over territory and leadership in the town. Roadside bombs, ambushes and kidnappings were the main tactics used. Interestingly, as Hizbullah ended its military campaign in Syria and the Lebanese army isolated the Sunni jihadi problem in 2015, virtually no attacks occurred during that year or the year following, a proof of the military rationale for such operations (see table 12.1). During 2015 and 2016, most military skirmishes took place in and around Arsal, except the occasional assassination of political or intelligence figures.

That the Lebanese army was fighting Sunni jihadi groups was not a new thing, as was mentioned with Fath al Islam. The alignment of interests between the Lebanese army and Hizbullah, who was also fighting the same groups in Syria, spreads over a decade of tacit cooperation. The army has traditionally been close to Hizbullah, especially since Lahoud's term in the mid-1990s. In May 2008, this relationship was tested when Hizbullah decided to 'invade' Beirut (as it would be described by its opponents), and capture the weapons held at the al-Mustaqbal party offices. This was in response to a gradual build-up of pressure on Hizbullah, in the aftermath of July 2006, to demilitarize, the last measure being the arrest of the security chief of Beirut's international airport, Brigadier-General Wafik Shoukeir, over accusations he had allowed Hizbullah to set up spy cameras inside the airport. The broader strategy of the Lebanese cabinet was to dismantle Hizbullah's landline telephone network, which was strategic to its military operations.

During the few days when this was happening, and as it threatened to deflagrate into a sectarian conflict, the Lebanese army's official position was to remain 'neutral'. But in so doing, the army was mainly just letting Hizbullah achieve its military goal. Hizbullah handed the weapons over to the army as soon as they seized al-Mustaqbal's offices and the various Lebanese political forces signed an agreement in Doha that toned down the escalation of animosity. Clearly, the army was not happy with the removal of Shoukeir, and did not share the cabinet's opinion that Hizbullah's telecommunications network was a threat to national security. But, then again, it was its general, Michel Sleiman, who would become president, though only after toning down his pro-Resistance rhetoric and growing closer to Saudi Arabia and March 14, after the Doha Agreement towards the end of May 2008.[29]

This may partly explain why Sunni radical organizations targeted the Lebanese army from the Sheikh al-Assir incident to the more recent and significantly more intense operations in Arsal and in the Bekaa. Many Sunni army officers

Table 12.1 Attacks in Lebanon since Rafic Hariri's assassination

	Date	Place	Target	Method	Casualties
2005	1-Feb	Beirut	Rafic Hariri convoy	Truck bomb	21
	19-Mar	New Jdeideh	Civilian and commercial area	Car bomb	
	23-Mar	Kaslik	Shopping centre	Car bomb	3
	26-Mar	Sad el-Bouchrieh	Factories	Car bomb	
	1-Apr	Broumana	Resort	Bomb	
	7-May	Jounieh	Radio station	Car bomb	
	2-Jun	Beirut	Samir Kassir	Car bomb	
	21-Jun	Beirut	George Hawi	Car bomb	
	12-Jul	Antelias	Elias Murr (attempt)	Car bomb	2
	22-Jul	Beirut	Restaurant	Car bomb	
	22-Aug	Zalka	Shopping centre	Bomb	
	17-Sep	Beirut	Jeitawi area, civilian	2 car bombs	1
	25-Sep	Beirut	May Chidiac (attempt)	Car bomb	
	12-Dec	Beirut	Gebran Tueni	Car bomb	3
2006	25-May	Saida	Mahmoud al Majzoub	Bomb	
	Jul–Aug	**Israel and Hizbullah war**			
	21-Nov	Beirut	Pierre Gemayel	Gunman	
2007	13-Feb	Bikfaya	Civilian bus	Bomb	3
	20-May	Beirut	ABC commercial centre	Explosives	1
	23-May	Aley	Civilian area	Explosives	
	13-Jun	Beirut	Walid Eido	Car bomb	9
	19-Sep	Beirut	Antoine Ghanem	Car bomb	5
	12-Dec	Beirut	Francois Hajj	Remote-control car bomb	4
2008	15-Jan	Beirut	Wissam Eid	Suicide car bomb	10
	7-May	**Hizbullah military operation in Beirut to seize weapons in Mustaqbal party offices**			
		Doha Agreement			
	25 Jul–29 Sept	**Armed clashes between Sunni and Alawite militants in Tripoli**			**23**
	13-Aug	Tripoli	Civilian bus	Car bomb	16
	10-Sep	Beirut	Saleh Aridi	Car bomb	
	29-Sep	Tripoli	Military bus	Car bomb	5

Table 12.1 Attacks in Lebanon since Rafic Hariri's assassination (Continued)

	Date	Place	Target	Method	Casualties
2012	19-Oct	Beirut	Wissam al Hassan	Car bomb	9
2013	9-Jul	Bir el Abed	Civilian	Car bomb	
	15-Aug	Roueiss	Civilian	Car bomb	27
	23-Aug	Tripoli	Taqwa and Sahwa mosque	Car bomb	42
	19-Nov	Bir Hassan	Iranian cultural centre	Car and motorcycle bomb	22
	3-Dec	Beirut	Hassan Lakkis	Gunmen	
	27-Dec	Beirut	Mohammad Chatah	Car bomb	5
2014	2-Jan	Haret Hreik	Hizbullah political offices	Car bomb	4
	16-Jan	Hermel	Civilian	Suicide car bomb	42
	21-Jan	Haret Hreik	Civilian	Suicide car bomb	4
	1-Feb	Hermel	Civilian	Suicide car bomb	4
	3-Feb	Dahyeh	Civilian van	Suicide attack	
	19-Feb	Bir Hassan	Iranian cultural centre	Suicide car bomb	8
	22-Feb	Hermel	Army post	Suicide car bomb	3
	29-Mar	Arsal	Army post	Suicide car bomb	3
	20-Jun	Dahr el Baydar	Checkpoint	Suicide car bomb	1
	24-Jun	Beirut café	Checkpoint	Suicide car bomb	
	27-Jun	Beirut hotel	Civilian	Suicide car bomb	
	6-Aug	Tripoli	Checkpoint	Home-made bomb	1
	19-Sep	Arsal	Military	Suicide car bomb	2
	20-Sep	Bekaa	Hizbullah checkpoint	Suicide car bomb	?
	14-Nov	Arsal	Military	Roadside bomb	

Table 12.1 Attacks in Lebanon since Rafic Hariri's assassination (Continued)

	Date	Place	Target	Method	Casualties
2015	10-Jan	Tripoli	Jabal Mohsen café	Double suicide attack	9
	26-Jan	Zgharta	Ghassan Ajaj	Gunman	
	2-Mar	Damascus	Ali Eid	Gunman	
	5-Oct	Border	Hizbullah bus	Roadside bomb	
	5-Nov	Arsal	Muslim committee	Motorcycle suicide bomb	6
	6-Nov	Arsal	Military	Roadside bomb	
	12-Nov	Borj al-Barajneh	Civilian	Double suicide attack	43
	5-Dec	Deir al-Amar	Civilian/military	Suicide attack	3
2016	24-Mar	Arsal	Military	Roadside bomb	1
	12-Apr	Ain el Helweh	Fathi Zaydan	Explosion	
	12-Jun	Verdun	BLOM Bank	Explosion	
	27-Jun	Qaa	Civilian	4 suicide bombers	5
	15-Aug	Arsal	Military	Roadside bomb	

have voiced discontent as to what they perceive as a Hizbullah infiltration of the Lebanese army.[30] It is not clear to what extent this threatens the unity of the army, as these tensions have not destabilized it so far, and its 'war on terrorism' is still focused and ongoing.

Does Hizbullah have a notion of terrorism?

Whether it is the Lebanese army, or Hizbullah or any other party in Lebanon, it is now clear that no one single party can frame a fully exhaustive national notion of terrorism. The contested political terrain under which Hizbullah and other political groups operate in Lebanon has led to an intensified symbolic battle over definitions, naming and labelling of militant or violent acts. Although most political groups and coalitions agree that the enemy the army is fighting has engaged in so-called terrorist activities, some, especially among the Sunni community, are close to Jabhat al-Nusrah and IS, such as the Committee of Muslim Scholars, composed of prominent Lebanese Salafi sheikhs of Tripoli. Moreover, some political groups, especially those opposing Hizbullah, would argue that Sunni jihadi radical formations are in reaction to either the Syrian regime's repressive policies or Hizbullah's actions in Syria.

In this context, Hizbullah's attempt at explaining terrorism goes through an Islamic appraisal. The argument is that such groups do not understand the spirit and ethics of the Prophet's legacy, and this is an accusation especially launched towards the Wahhabi order predominant in Saudi Arabia, and now more widely thanks to Saudi resources. *Al-irhāb al takfīri* (takfīri terrorism) is the term most commonly used by Hizbullah officials,[31] and the media is sympathetic with the party. The symbolic battle fought here is not just a by-product of the more material conflict of interest but is at the heart of how enemies are framed and perceive themselves. For example, Hizbullah's statement against the Brussels attacks of March 2016 did link Takfiri groups with terrorist acts. Hizbullah 'considers that these bombings are an aggravation of the danger posed by terrorist Takfiri groups who carry out these acts based on hatred of humanity and on their bloody ideals'. However, as is typically the case, here Hizbullah denounced 'the regional and global powers that stand behind [Takfiri groups] and provide them with ideological, moral and financial support'.[32]

Although Hizbullah condemns these attacks it also accuses specific states of being behind them. For example, in a speech given on 1 March 2016, Nasrallah declared that the car bombs that exploded on the roadside of the Bekaa region (especially in Hermel, see table 12.1) were 'under Saudi administration'.[33] Nasrallah sees a continuing Saudi policy of 'annihilating' Hizbullah since the July 2006 war with Israel. Meanwhile, Saudi Arabia has lobbied hard at the Arab League for the other Arab countries to pass a resolution naming Hizbullah a 'terrorist organization', as it argues that Hizbullah trained the Huthi Ansarullah group in Yemen against which Saudi Arabia has been engaged in a war since 2015. Although Saudi Arabia was not able to gain the votes of most Arab countries, it did push through the smaller Gulf Cooperation Council a declaration that Hizbullah is a terrorist organization, a declaration which would involve sanctions, although the nature of those is still not clear. Saudi Arabia has also stopped its funding of the acquisition of French military supplies by the Lebanese army.[34]

Ultimately, Hizbullah links Saudi actions to a wider US political strategy in the region, which involves its alliance with Israel. In a recent interview, Nasrallah justified Hizbullah's intervention as a direct continuation of the July 2006 war. Nasrallah stated that the US 'from the admission of its own officials says it created IS', Nusra and all these groups to fight 'the Resistance'.[35] 'We are still fighting July 2006, and these are our feelings and understandings of the situation, and that of our combatants and families.'[36] For Hizbullah, then, there is a clear delineation of the various political phenomena it is facing. On the one hand, there is a regional situation legislated by realist politics and in which states and non-state actors interact. On the other, there is a cultural or ideological battle being fought against an enemy that puts into question the ideological foundation not just of an Islamic political group such as Hizbullah but the Shia sect at large. Facing the enemy involves a fierce media-related battle to reclaim the legacy of the Prophet and the Islamic tradition at large.

Conclusion

Depending on the varying institutional and social context, political groups develop different strategies of action to produce leverage and gain. Framing notions of terrorism and labelling them in such a way is just a continuation of struggles fought at the diplomatic and military levels. For the March 14 camp, 'internationalizing' the tribunal was a way to escape the ongoing impossibility of facing Hizbullah and the Syrian regime on the ground. For Hizbullah, understanding the 'Takfiri' threat as another facet of terrorism helps relate to specific populations affected by these actions, whether it is Hizbullah's constituency that needs justification for their continuing support to the party, or people across the Arab and Muslim world who are likely to find IS's cause resonant with their sets of grievances.

Notes

1 D.I. Kertzer, *Politics and Symbols: The Italian Communist Party and the Fall of Communism* (New Haven and London: Yale University Press, 1996).

2 Marius Deeb, 'Lebanon since 1979: Syria, Hizballah, and the war against peace in the Middle East,' in Robert Owen Freedman (ed.), *The Middle East Enters the Twenty-First Century* (Gainesville, FL: University Press of Florida, 2002), p. 214.

3 Trevor Mostyn, 'Elie Hobeika,' *Guardian*, 25 January 2002, available at: www.theguardian.com/world/2002/jan/25/israelandthepalestinians.lebanon (accessed 9 January 2018).

4 For a good overview of the complex politics of this period, see Rola El-Husseini, *Pax Syriana: Elite Politics in Postwar Lebanon*, 1st ed. (Syracuse, NY: Syracuse University Press, 2012).

5 Reinoud Leenders, *Spoils of Truce* (Ithaca, NY: Cornell University Press, 2012).

6 'Siniora sent a letter to Ban for the adoption of a binding decision by the Security Council,' *Al-Akhbar*, 15 May 2007 (issue 226), www.al-akhbar.com/node/145963 (no longer available; accessed 9 January 2018).

7 Bardo Fassbender, 'Reflections on the international legality of the Special Tribunal for Lebanon,' *Journal of International Criminal Justice* 5 (2007): 1091–105.

8 For example, see John Cerone, 'Politics of international justice: US policy and the legitimacy of the Special Tribunal for Lebanon,' *Denver Journal of International Law and Policy* 40:1–3 (2011–12): 44–63.

9 This is drawn from an insight shared with the author by Omar Nashabe, a criminal justice analyst and a close observer of the development of the STL and its proceedings.

10 Robert M. Bosco, 'The assassination of Rafik Hariri: Foreign policy perspectives,' *International Political Science Review* 30:4 (2009): 349.

11 Nidal Nabil Jurdi, 'The subject-matter jurisdiction of the Special Tribunal for Lebanon,' *Journal of International Criminal Justice* 5:5 (2007): 1125–38, quote 1133.

12 Talal Asad, *On Suicide Bombing* (New York: Columbia University Press, 2007).

13 Maha Barada, 'Nasrallah reveals Hariri murder "evidence,"' *BBC News*, 10 August 2010, available at: www.bbc.co.uk/news/world-middle-east-10922045 (accessed 9 January 2018). The full press conference can be found in Halomaster 7, "Sayyed Nasrallah – Hariri assassination evidence expose: Full press conference," *YouTube*, 11 August 2010, available at: www.youtube.com/watch?v=5odeTwU2zjw (accessed 9 January 2018).

14 STL, 'STL judges: Trial continues pending further information on the death of Mustafa Badreddine,' STL website, 1 June 2016, available at: www.stl-tsl.org/en/media/press-releases/5022-stl-judges-trial-continues-pending-further-information-on-the-death-of-mustafa-badreddine (accessed 9 January 2018).

15 *BBC News*, 'Beirut blast "was suicide attack,"' *BBC News*, 15 February 2005, available at: http://news.bbc.co.uk/1/hi/world/middle_east/4266587.stm (accessed 9 January 2018).

16 Bernard Rougier, *L'Oumma en fragments: Contrôler le sunnisme au Liban* (Paris: Presses universitaires de France, 2011).

17 Bernard Rougier, *Everyday Jihad: The Rise of Militant Islam among Palestinians in Lebanon* (Cambridge, MA, and London: Harvard University Press, 2007).

18 Bernard Rougier, *The Sunni Tragedy in the Middle East: Northern Lebanon from al-Qaeda to ISIS* (Princeton, NJ: Princeton University Press, 2015), p. 15.

19 *Ibid.*, pp. 26–7.

20 For an exhaustive account of Muslim foreign fighters since the 1980s, see Thomas Hegghammer, 'The rise of Muslim fighters: Islam and the globalization of jihad,' *International Security* 35:3 (2010): 53–94.

21 For a great historical overview, see Tine Gade, 'Sunni Islamists in Tripoli and the Asad regime 1966–2014,' *Syria Studies* 7:2 (2015): 20–65.

22 Rougier, *Sunni Tragedy*, p. 64.

23 *Al Arabiya*, 'Lebanese Sunni cleric calls for jihad to aid Syrian rebels against Hezbollah,' *Al Arabiya*, 23 April 2013, available at: http://english.alarabiya.net/en/News/middle-east/2013/04/23/Lebanese-Sunni-cleric-calls-for-Jihad-to-aid-Syrian-rebels-against-Hezbollah.html (accessed 9 January 2018).

24 'Lebanese Sheikh al-Assir filmed fighting in Syria,' LiveLeak website, 1 May 2013, available at: www.liveleak.com/view?i=91b_1367406014 (accessed 9 January 2018).

25 For a history of the tumultuous relationship between Wahhabi clerics, Salafis in general and the Saudi ruling clan, see Stephane Lacroix, *Awakening Islam: The Politics of Religious Dissent in Contemporary Saudi Arabia* (Cambridge, MA: Harvard University Press, 2011).

26 Alastair Crooke, 'You can't understand ISIS if you don't know the history of Wahhabism in Saudi Arabia,' *Huffington Post*, 27 August 2014, available at: www.huffingtonpost.com/alastair-crooke/isis-wahhabism-saudi-arabia_b_5717157.html (accessed 9 January 2018).

27 Elias Muhanna, 'The many faces of Wissam Al-Hassan,' *New York Times* (Latitude blog), 22 October 2012, 8.23 a.m., available at: http://latitude.blogs.nytimes.com/2012/10/22/the-many-faces-of-wissam-al-hassan (accessed 9 January 2018).

28 Rougier, *Sunni Tragedy.*

29 The author gained a sense of this through a series of short interviews conducted with General Sleiman as the date of his election approached.

30 Tine Gade and Nayla Moussa, 'The Lebanese army after the Syrian crisis: Alienating the Sunni community?' in Are John Knudsen and Tine Gade (eds), *Civil-Military Relations in Lebanon: Conflict, Cohesion and Confessionalism in a Divided Society* (London: Palgrave Macmillan, 2017).

31 Hizbullah's parliamentary member Hassan Fadlallah declared this on television after the Borj el Barajneh suicide bombing attack on 12 November 2015.

32 'Hezbollah condemns Brussels attacks: Terrorism knows no borders,' Almanar TV website, 22 March 2016, available at: http://english.almanar.com.lb/adetails.php?eid=261985&frid=23&seccatid=14&cid=23&fromval=1 (accessed 9 January 2018).

33 Hassan Nasrallah, speech, 1 March 2016, widely broadcast on television and the Internet.

34 *Al Jazeera*, 'GCC declares Lebanon's Hezbollah a "terrorist" group,' *Al Jazeera*, 2 March 2016, available at: www.aljazeera.com/news/2016/03/gcc-declares-lebanon-hezbollah-terrorist-group-160302090712744.html (accessed 9 January 2018).

35 While there may be no definite proof of such a conspiracy theory, it is noteworthy that Nasrallah deploys it in a manner to frame the enemy fought in Syria within a larger 'international politics' scheme.

36 *Alahednews*, 'Sayyed Nasrallah: If there is a new war on Lebanon, resistance will win. Turkey must accept the end of the war project in Syria,' *Alahednews*, 19 August 2016, available at: http://bit.ly/2bESmXY (accessed 9 January 2018).

Saudi Arabia

13

Islam and Saudi Arabia's counterterrorism strategy

Roel Meijer

Introduction

This chapter will analyse the Saudi counterterrorism discourse in the period between 2003 and 2010. Much was written on these programmes at the time, but the religious side of the programme has seldom been investigated in depth.[1] This period is an interesting one, because for the first time Saudi Arabia was itself confronted with terrorism. It developed a two-pronged strategy: a 'soft' ideological one and a 'hard', repressive one. It is especially the soft measures and the counterterrorist religious discourse of the state that has been considered successful and has attracted much positive attention, and on which this chapter will concentrate.[2] The soft counterterrorism measures can be divided into two. The broader measures are directed to the general public and intended to discredit the terrorists and undermine their legitimacy. The government has done this by orchestrating a clever campaign for the hearts and minds of the population by portraying the terrorists as 'misguided'.[3] It appeared benevolent and offered amnesties in 2004 and mid-2006, and

---

Elements of this chapter have been republished from Roel Meijer, 'Saudi Arabia's war on terrorism: Combating passions, ignorance and deviation,' in Jeevan Deol and Zaheer Kazmi (eds), *Contextualizing Jihadi Thought* (London/New York: Hurst/ Columbia University Press, 2012), pp. 165–90.

organized mediation to allow terrorists to hand themselves in. Included in this approach is the Intellectual Security Program that warns the population against the dangers of violence and how to detect its early symptoms.

The more narrow soft approach is represented by the rehabilitation program, which is divided into prevention, rehabilitation and post-release care (PRAC). The last two in particular are believed to have 'generated very positive and intriguing results'.[4] One of the reasons for this positive response is that the counselling programmes were not based on revenge but on 'benevolence' that has its roots in the assumption that (most) suspects are 'naive' and have been 'lied to and misled by extremists'.[5] The general impression is that the Saudi state is capable of winning the 'war of ideas' and that former terrorists and potential terrorists have proclaimed 'loyalty, recognition of authority, and obedience to leadership [the king]'.[6] Many international experts have been duly impressed by the successes of this approach.[7] Also, in official US sources, Saudi Arabia has been praised for its counterterrorism discourse.[8] Few commentators at the time, however, realized that the Saudi soft approach was based on Wahhabism, the Saudi version of Salafism, itself an important source of religious radicalism, exclusion and intolerance.[9]

As the Saudis try to base their counterterrorism discourse on a religious discourse, they have taken their definition of terrorism (*irhab*) from the Qur'an, which condemns wanton destruction of people and sources of income as 'corruption on earth' (*ifsad fi-l-ard*).[10] Corruption on earth is directed against the five essential human conditions for life, which are protected in Islamic law: religion (*din*), soul (*nafs*), intelligence (*'aql*), honour (*'ird*) and possessions/wealth (*mal*).[11] In line with this religious creed, the minister of defence at the time, Prince Sultan, defined terrorism as 'every action which has the aim to instil fear in innocents, to bring corruption on earth, or is organized to achieve these ends'.[12] The term 'corruption on earth' has a longer official history, and was used in 1989 by the Council of Senior Ulama,[13] after the attacks in Riyadh on 13 November 1995,[14] and after the first attacks in Riyadh by al Qaeda on the Arabian Peninsula (AQAP) in August 2003. Anyone found guilty of these crimes could be sentenced to death.[15]

There is also another reason why the Western concept of terrorism is not well liked in official Saudi discourse. This is because the Western definition regards violence against innocent citizens as the end of a line of development contained in such concepts as intolerance and rejection of the humanity of others, and holds equality (regardless of race, religion or gender), pluralism, democracy and the practice of negotiation as the only means of eliminating its causes – all of which are anathema to Wahhabism. In the Saudi discourse, the causes of violence are sought in another logical sequence of steps beginning with religious ignorance (*jahil*), irrationality/passions (*ahwa'*), deviation (*inhiraf*) and extremism (*ghuluw*), leading to political involvement (*hizbiyya*) and violence (*'unf*). In this discourse the believer is the central figure, and the concept of the 'victorious sect' (*al-ta'ifa al-mansura*), to which all Salafis/Wahhabis belong, is by definition unequal. It also assumes a priori that Islam (Wahhabism) and terrorism are mutually exclusive.[16] Thus, 'terrorism', according to minister of interior Prince Nayef, 'is the work of the devil; it is not anchored in religion, is not supported by knowledge of people and human values and harms others for narrow personal reasons and closed ignorant concepts'.[17] During the International Conference on Terrorism held in Riyadh in 2005, Prince Nayef stated that terrorism is perpetrated by a 'miscreant minority'.[18]

Not only does the Western definition of terrorism and its adjacent counter-concepts pose a threat to official Wahhabism and its support of such potentially ambiguous or threatening concepts as *al-wala' wa-l-bara'* (loyalty to Muslims and disavowal of non-Muslims) jihad and *takfir* (excommunication) – even in their moderate decontested forms – and the total rejection of politics as a separate autonomous field to solve basic conflicts of interest, Western definitions also condemn all those national liberation struggles Saudi Arabia supports in Palestine, Chechnya and Afghanistan.[19]

Finally, the difference with Western definitions of terrorism is that the Saudi counterterrorist discourse buttresses the Saudi patrimonial system of rule. The linchpin in this narrative is the theory of obedience to the ruler (*wali al-amr*). Article 6 of the Basic Law states that citizens should obey the ruler.[20] But the Qur'anic concept goes much further than obedience to the ruler alone and underpins a hierarchy of authority (the son to his father, the wife to her husband, the employee to his or her employer, etc.) and non-critical attitudes demanded of the Saudi population.[21] Its religious dimension dovetails with traditional notions of loyalty and allegiance to the social and political order. As the Saudi state has its roots in tribal society, the concept is overlaid with tribal customs associated with patriarchy and patronage, expressed in royal claims to wisdom, benevolence, generosity, munificence and forgiveness, and direct accessibility through the royal council (*majlis*) to the king. The royal family legitimizes its position in conveying a feeling of responsibility for the well-being not only of the individual Saudi citizen but also of his family, his clan and the tribe to which he belongs. This entails a concept of the Saudis not as citizens (*muwatinun*) with inviolable rights, but as subjects (*raaya*), who are dependent on the ruler's personal generosity and benevolence (*makrama*) and can gain from his patronage if they prove themselves loyal, pliant and 'obedient'. It is therefore not surprising that the success of the individual rehabilitation programme is measured not only by the inclusion of former terrorists into the religious fold but that religious repentance (*tawba*) is accompanied by a renewed oath of allegiance (*bay'a*) to the ruler.

The rest of the chapter investigates the background and the terminology of the Saudi counterterrorism discourse. Because Wahhabism is itself the source of terrorism, this is as much a battle with itself – to contain its inner demons – as a battle with the 'terrorists'.

The danger of extremism, deviation and passions

Counterterrorism narratives

Although the Saudi authorities pride themselves on the success of their 'battle of ideas', they are extremely reticent in allowing outsiders to see the literature or manuals their personnel or volunteers use in the de-radicalization courses. I have relied on two official Saudi compilations on terrorism, containing interviews with ministers and articles,[22] together with a host of interviews with and statements by governmental officials and religious clerics in public speeches, in addition to newspaper articles which confirm the ideological content of the two books. There also exists a considerable literature against extremism and terrorism written by Saudi clerics and translated into English, which since 9/11 has been part of the international counterterrorism strategy of the Saudi state.[23]

Deviation

First of all, in Saudi Arabia the terrorist is not regarded just as someone who did not abide by the law and used violence, but is defined as someone subject to 'deviation' (*inhiraf*).[24] Rather than being regarded as rational beings who have inalienable rights and can be held legally accountable for the political goals they pursue and the havoc they wreak, terrorists are treated as wayward sons who should be reprimanded or 'given advice' (*nasiha*) – that is, counselled – but in the end are forgiven if they accept the patronage and munificence of the ruler and return to the 'straight path'. In this view the relationship between terrorist/deviator and ruler/patron/patriarch is a direct one, often literally so, as between 2003 and 2009 terrorists were offered amnesty in personal interviews with the minister or deputy minister of interior after making personal demonstrations and utterances of 'repentance'.[25] This direct relationship also accounts for the ruthless retribution if the 'terrorist' does not comply with the demands of subservience this relationship makes and thereby shows disloyalty. Rejection of patronage is seen not just as a crime but also as a personal insult to the benevolence of the monarch. In punishment, the wayward son is excommunicated and is placed outside the law, a status which in

Islamic law is conceptualized as 'corrupters on earth' (*munfasidun fi-l-ard*). Once placed in this category, they not only can be gunned down in the street or blown up in their houses, but their memory and their families and tribes are humiliated by the exposure of their mutilated bodies to the public in gory pictures on television and in newspapers, demonstrating the wrath of the ruler as expressed in the machinery of the state. As 'corrupters on earth' they have no rights and can be imprisoned indefinitely and are not included in the rehabilitation programmes.

Extremism

The most important way to define the terrorist is to associate terrorism with 'religious extremism' (*ghuluw/tatarruf*).[26] This is not just a discourse of the Saudi state but goes back to the first time of dissension (*fitna*) in AD 661 after the assassination of 'Ali. The Saudi state has taken over this concept by taking the core concept of extremism and closely interlocking it with such terms as exaggeration (*mujawaza*), excess (*mubalagha/ifrat/irtifa'*) and zealotry (*tashaddud*).[27] This focus on religion as the source of extremism excludes political, social, economic or cultural origins of violence, and therefore side-tracks any rational political debate on the background of violence in Saudi Arabia and puts it in the hands of the *ulama*.

Part of this terrorist counter-narrative has the purpose of giving back to the *ulama* their authority over society based on their religious knowledge (*'ilm*). People who have the audacity to think for themselves are accused of suffering from ignorance (*jahl*): 'Ignorance [of true religion] is one of the most important reasons to deviate from truth, reject it and distance oneself from it, [leading to ideological] difference [*ikhtilaf*] and [political] divisions [*tafarruq*].'[28] Ignorance thus lies at the origins of misguidance (*dalala*) and innovation (*bid'a*),[29] which can lead to excommunication (*takfir*) as the main religious legitimization of the use of violence against the deviant.[30] Rejecting the proof (*dalil*) that the *ulama* provide and following one's own unguided reason (*'aql*) can also constitute sources of misguidance (*dalala*).[31] Finally, engaging in politics and joining 'groups' or 'parties' questions the authority of the religious establishment and the obedience to the king (*wali al-amr*).[32]

Passions

But not just religious misguidance and ignorance can lead to extremism (*ghuluw*). Uncontrolled emotions and behaviour can also lead to deviancy.[33] An important element in the discourse on extremism is the theory of inclinations and passions (*hawa/ahwa'*). These emotions, in turn, are related to other sources of deviation, such as desires (*shahwa/shahawat*) and corrupted reasoning and sophistry (*shubha/shubahat*). Imposing correct behaviour and strict morals is therefore imperative as a means to combat terrorism.[34]

With the theory of passions Wahhabism comes closest to propounding a religious psychology of terrorism. There are several steps that have to be made in this process. Thus, according to then minister of interior Prince Nayif (who died in 2012), 'terrorism does not issue from a people or a creed, it originates in an individual person'.[35] He suggested that the most potent means of countering it was to 'create a psychological barrier around Muslims and their creed [*'aqida*]'.[36] Likewise, Shaykh Salih bin Fawzan al-Fawzan, one of the leading *ulama* in Saudi Arabia at that time, argues that terrorists are 'those individuals who ride their passions/inclinations and have chosen the road to error out of stubbornness and haughtiness'. He concludes with the remark that 'they seek a means to fulfil their ambitions hastily',[37] suggesting that religious guidance and the virtue of patience can only be acquired from the *ulama*.

A number of negative passions are named that mislead the believer. They manifest themselves particularly in such emotions as envy (*hasad*) and hatred (*hiqd*). In a typical characterization of extremism, which brings the negative connotations of uncontrolled emotions, bad faith and one of the main mortal sins of Wahhabism, religious innovation (*bid'a*), together, Sulayman Aba al-Khayl, dean of the Islamic University of Muhammad ibn Saud and teacher of Islamic jurisprudence (*fiqh*) in the Higher Institute for Judges, states that extremist groups 'try to prove their passions with the *shari'a* and deform the texts and proofs to agree with their innovations'. In this manner, he argues, 'their opinions and their minds have become the primary sources [of finding the truth] and the *shari'a* has become subordinated to it'.[38]

This unholy alliance of unguided reason and wanton passions is represented by the general Wahhabi definition of deviationists as the 'people of passions and innovations (*ahl-al-ahwa' wa-l-bid'a*)'.[39] From this term it is clear that passions, innovation and deviation are closely linked, and each follows from the others, and this provides the core concept of extremism (*ghuluw*) with its specific connotation as opposed to the Truth. The only remedy, according to Sulayman Aba al-Khayl, is a de-politicized moral dictum: 'to rein in one's emotions, control them, distance oneself from them, and look at the Truth [*haqq*] and keep a balance'.[40]

The problem with this disciplining discourse of passions is that it is very imprecise and can be used against all kinds of people who do not fit the Wahhabi mould. The complex process of radicalization is brought down to basic feelings and is left unanalysed. For instance, Shaykh Rabi' al-Madkhali, one of the most conservative Saudi *ulama*, believed the violence of the Algerian civil war of the 1990s had its origins in 'enmity, hatred, and power of the resentment and passions, desirous of degradation [of the other] and spilling of blood'.[41]

But not only Muslims can be misled by passions. The West is also accused of being led by passions and inclinations when it regards Islam as the source of terrorism.[42] However, from the frequent references to the subject, doubtless the main culprit of self-indulgence, disobedience and revolt against the order of things is unguided youth. Youths, as the *'classes dangereuses'*, are liable to go astray because they are ignorant, gullible and stubborn. From the many references to youths, they are the main political, religious and cultural threat to stability and correct morals because 'new generations reject completely the existing *turath*' (tradition).[43]

Not surprisingly, the fourth group that is regarded as a threat is the intellectuals (*muthaqqafun*) – Westernized independent thinkers, as opposed to *ulama*. They resemble terrorists because they 'spread banalities and superficialities and are holders of passions (*ashab al-shahawat*)', and in the heat of public debates they can be proclaimed apostates.[44] The broadness of the terms basically means that all opponents of the conservative *ulama* can be accused of 'deviation' and 'passions', and therefore be just one step removed from being 'terrorists'.

The median way

Another method to contain Wahhabism's radical strains has been to introduce new definitions of Islam as moderateness (*i'tidal*) and the middle-of-the-road, or median, way (*wasatiyya*),[45] or use such terms as balance (*ittizan*). In this way, common Islamic terms such as justice (*'adl*), ease (*yusr*) or facilitation of belief (*taysir*) can be used to counter extremism. This discourse is not part of Wahhabi ideological make-up but derives from Yusuf al-Qaradawi (although the Saudi state will not acknowledge it), but since 9/11 has been brought within the parameters of its ideological range and has been transported to its core to buttress the decontested peaceful nature of its four contestable concepts and enhance the credibility of its struggle against extremism.[46] Like the concept of passions (*ahwa'*), the concept *wasatiyya* gives specific flavour and colour to the Saudi counterterrorist discourse by means of the richness of its adjacent terms, which supposedly resonate with the values of a conservative society that finds its legitimation in Wahhabism.

The core of this discourse of normality is constituted by the discourse of correct manners/attitudes and ethics (*akhlaq*), based on the Sunna of the Prophet. This is a general Muslim discourse but is given a Wahhabi twist by relating it to the 'right creed'. If the right creed (*'aqida*) represents the truth in doctrine, and terms like 'balance' and 'facilitation' are meant to convey moderateness, having the correct moral behaviour (*hasan al-khulq*) is their reflection in practice (*manhaj*) in daily life, and refers to more precisely defined values and attitudes that oppose extremism and restrain passions. Thus religion and behaviour are entwined, for 'religion is ethics [*khulq*]', and it is believed that 'whatever increases your morals will increase your religiosity'.[47]

Walking the straight path or the median way (*wasatiyya*) means that the believer must not deviate to either side of the straight path, and the two alternative pitfalls are also described. For instance, justice in this context does not mean equality before the law or getting your rightful share, but is expressed in avoiding two extremes: wastefulness/exaggeration (*ifrat*) on the one side, and negligence (*tafrit*) on the other. It is furthermore related to such virtues as open-handedness, generosity and munificence.[48] Other virtues mentioned are wisdom (*hikma*), friendliness (*rifq*) and flexibility (*lin*).

Saudi counterterrorism strategy

The advisory committees

Saudi counterterrorist discourse in the first decade of the twenty-first century was not just a discourse but was also translated into a policy, as is apparent from the language applied and the practices implemented in the more specific rehabilitation programs and the broader Intellectual Security campaign. One of the most conspicuous elements is the close cooperation of the religious and political authorities in these campaigns. The Advisory Committees (al-Lijan al-Munasiha wa-l-Ra'aya) were founded after the first attacks occurred in Saudi Arabia in May 2003. They were established – like all the other counterterrorist initiatives – by Muhammad ibn Nayef, deputy minister of interior and son of Nayef ibn 'Abd al-'Aziz, the minister of interior.[49] The programmes were implemented in five specialized prisons around Riyadh dealing with terrorism, and cost a total of 1.7 billion riyals.[50]

From the beginning, the religious establishment was heavily represented in this counterterrorism programme. We are told that the programme consisted of four sections: religious knowledge (*'ilm*), security (*aman*), social work and media, but the balance was in favour of the religious side. It consisted of 160 *ulama* but only 40 psychologists and social workers.[51] The first section was manned by *ulama* and religious experts and was directed at 'correcting thought'. Its goal was to combat spurious arguments (*shubahat*), 'wrong convictions' and the 'wrong understanding' of religious texts by prisoners.[52] In essence, refutation (*tafnid*) of deviation was its main task and it is exactly this aspect of the programme that has been regarded as highly successful. We are furthermore informed that whereas at first the prisoners were reluctant to talk to the 'ulama rooted in knowledge', once their trust was won they competed to join the course because they understood that 'the only goal of the correct explanation of the *shari'a* was to reach the truth'.[53] Wholly in line with the official discourse, the head of the project, Ali bin Shai'a al-Nafisa, stated that the prisoners realized that their deviation derived from 'wrong explanations' and 'provocative *fatwas*' (*al-fatawa al-tahridiyya*) of *ulama* of 'aggressive organizations' who led them to adopt wrong ethics/habits based on 'excitement', 'delusions', 'utopian thought' and 'restrictive thinking'; in short – as explained above – passions (*ahwa'*).[54] The psychological dimension is reflected in the sentence 'who becomes mixed up in his heart by spurious reasoning (*shubahat*) and whims/greed (*shahawat*) can use them for evil ends.' In order to counter 'enthusiastic' videos on the Internet and provocative lectures, these sources must be 'closely controlled by the rules of the *shari'a* [otherwise they] can develop into a violent storm.'[55]

As part of the de-radicalization programme prisoners were offered special religious sessions (*dawrat*) on exactly these crucial and contested, ambivalent and potentially extremist topics, such as *takfir* (excommunication), *al-wala' wa-l-bara'* (the principle of loyalty to one's community, i.e. Muslims/Salafis, and disavowal of non-Muslims/non-Salafis), *jihad*, the spilling of innocent blood, the ruler and the community (*al-imama wa-l-jama'a*), and allegiance (*bay'a*) and obedience (*ta'a*) to the (wrong) leaders instead of to the correct ruler (*wali al-amr*). The whole course covered twenty sessions and lasted seven weeks.[56] Total ideological de-programming, called revision (*muraja'a*) of radical ideas, is regarded as a necessary precondition for taking part in the subsequent social reintegration stages of the programme,[57] which included courses on law, culture, psychology, sports, medicine, and other subjects.[58]

The ultimate goal of the programme, according to Shaykh 'Ali al-Nafisa, is reconversion and 'repentance and a return to God'. Once the prisoners had understood that they had been led astray, he explained that 'some youth wept tears of remorse, [...] describing themselves as if they were half drunk or fools who had missed the manifest truth that the counselling shaykhs had given to them'. The expression 'breaking down in sobs' seems to suggest that ulama and psychologists work together to bring about a catharsis of the prisoner in a combination of religious indoctrination and psychological techniques.[59]

Aside from the intellectual dimension, the rehabilitation programmes also have a financial dimension. The Ministry of Interior has paid 115 million riyals (£14.7 million) to detainees and their families to help them, for example, in repaying debts and obtaining healthcare.[60]

Intellectual security

The Intellectual Security (*al-aman al-fikri*) programme, as the words suggest, derives from the same discourse as the Advisory Committees. It also adopts the terminology of religious psychology, of waging war against 'malicious' and 'envious people'. In contrast to the Advisory Committees, however, it is a preventive programme for the general public. It aims to 'raise consciousness' (*taw'iya*) and present 'correct arguments' to counter extremism.[61] It is also more blunt in that it combines Islam and security explicitly. A prominent cleric, Shaykh Salih bin Fawzan al-Fawzan, demonstrating the close connection between the state and the religious establishment, stated that Islam not only ensures stability (*istiqrar*) but is also 'the religion of belief and security [*aman*]'.[62]

The Intellectual Security programme probably started in 2007. It is part of a religious campaign to protect culture and society from threats to Islam.[63] Some even speak of 'creating a blockade' against deviant thought.[64] The programme is especially focused on those sections of society where the main threat – youth – can radicalize (in families, schools, universities) and is intended to educate parents, teachers, university professors, imams of mosques, policemen and the military to detect he first symptoms of radicalization. The purpose is to gain a return of obedience to the ruler along the principles of *wali al-amr*. For those sections of society are regarded the first in line for '*immunization* [*tahsin*] of people against deviant thoughts'.[65]

As an example, on 15 May 2007, the Ministry of Education organized a week-long session of lectures on the subject of 'security and the nation' for 166 secondary schools around Riyadh and schools belonging to the teachers' training institute, and meetings with 100 directors of the schools. Also, the dean of the Teachers' College, Dr 'Ali al-'Afnan, organized a fifth session on *al-aman al-fikri* with teachers.[66] In August of that year a seminar was organized by the Committee Commanding Good and Preventing Wrong (religious police) in the province of al-'Asir on the role of the *ulama* and *du'a* (call) in rooting intellectual security, and the role of helpers in countering ideas 'which weaken the role of the family, undermine the authority of the parents, and spread forbidden deeds [*mankurat*] and ideas of *takfir* and revolt against the ruler'.[67] But one of the purposes is to limit the chaos in fatwas. In May 2010 a conference was held for 700 mosque preachers, who were asked to limit their fatwas and refer those who seek guidance to the 'people of knowledge'. The Friday preachers had an important task in implanting the notion of *wasatiyya* and pointing out the dangers of *takfir*.[68] 'Abd al-Rahman al-Hadlaq stated that intellectual security was important for teachers and supervisors in the massive Qur'an-remembering sessions to detect early signs of extremism.[69] That it is also directed against radical imams is clear from the warning of the undersecretary of Islamic affairs, who stated that imams who did not moderate their campaigns against journalists could be fired.[70]

Another difference is that the Intellectual Security campaign also has a stronger 'scientific' component. Although the *ulama* still play a crucial role in the campaign and Prince Nayef constantly refers to them as 'the vanguard in the anti-terrorist struggle',[71] a third party is involved in this phase of the war against deviation; namely, the universities, who try to reinvigorate the campaign and give it international respectability. The close involvement of the state is apparent from the endowment of the Prince Nayef Chair of Intellectual Security Studies in May 2008 at the University Imam Muhammad bin Saud with the aim of supervising this project.[72] Since its foundations this institute has organized a host of seminars on intellectual security,[73] and as a highpoint it organized a three-day national conference on intellectual security in May 2009. In an interview with the chair, Dr Khalid bin Mansur al-Daris, he reiterated the common themes of the doctrine of *ghuluw* (extremism). The scientific content, however, does not consist in analysing violence in an objective, detached manner, but in applying a security plan to all sections of life, especially schooling, in order that the student eventually walks 'the straight path'.[74] In an interview with the newspaper *al-Hayat*, the combination of science and religious language is clearly present when al-Daris tried to show the links between members of families who became involved in terrorism for emotional reasons and religious terminology by calling this way of thinking 'misguided thought' (*al-fikra al-dalla*) and promoting 'hatred' (*hiqd*).[75] In an earlier interview he had pointed out the new role of women in the organization.[76] The campaign has also extended to television broadcasts.

A glance at the programme of the three-day conference in May 2009 shows that papers with religious topics dominated most sessions, which were chaired by the highest religious dignitaries of the kingdom. The panels had such titles as 'Tactics in persuasion', 'The Qur'an and intellectual security', 'Finding signs of extremism among sons' and 'The role of the family in supporting security thinking of sons'.

This campaign has also gained attention outside Saudi Arabia. The US 2009 annual report on terrorism for Saudi Arabia notes that the minister of interior has warned citizens to be 'vigilant' even within families, and to report 'deviant' behaviour.[77]

Conclusion

How successful are these programmes? In order to evaluate them one must keep in mind that the Saudi state is waging a 'battle of ideas' and has set its sights on the highest goal, de-radicalization.[78] Also, one must realize that Saudis define terrorism as religious deviation and regard re-conversion and recognition of the *wali al-amr* as the ultimate success and condition for release.[79] Disengagement (from radical organizations, without ideological de-radicalization) is not the official goal, but is accepted if the former prisoner is no longer willing to use violence.[80]

From the above, it appears that the intellectual content of the Saudi programme is extremely weak even in its own terms, and can only appeal the most non-ideologically motivated 'terrorists'. The *ulama* who support this type of discourse suffer from a lack of credibility. Since the death in 1999 of Bin Baz, the previous mufti of Saudi Arabia, who enjoyed great prestige, no *alim* has been able to replace him. The present mufti has little authority, but, more importantly, in Salafism *ulama* who are not independent lack authority. This also explains the desperate search to find radicals who have revised their ideas (*muraja'a*),[81] like Sheikh Humayda, who is given ample television time to present his version of *ghuluw*.[82] Both for the lack of content and the shortage of authority it is unlikely that the state will be successful in combating terrorism or radicalism with this discourse on extremism (*ghuluw*). Also, the fatwa by the Council of Senior Ulama in April 2010, although applauded by the West,[83] is ambiguous and is regarded by specialists as ineffective.[84]

This is all the more problematic as there are powerful counter-ideologies that are readily available on the Internet. Ideologues like Yusuf al-'Uyairi, the first leader of al Qaida on the Arabian peninsula, would not be impressed by this approach. To him the rulers are corrupt and unable to defend Islam, like the *ulama*, who have betrayed the pure forms of *tawhid* (the Oneness of God) in toning down jihad and *al-wala' wa-l-bara'* (loyalty to one's community) and propagating an effeminate *akhlaq* (ethics) of defeatism. He believes that the urgency of the moment calls for self-sacrifice and total war. In place of their *'aqida* (creed) and *manhaj* (practice) of moderation and the median way, he proposes following a praxis in which the harsh reality of a transnational jihad determines whether one is a Muslim or not. Eventually this leads to a completely different definition of the 'victorious sect', as anyone who has studied jihadism knows.[85] Others, like the jihadi Salafi ideologue Abu Muhammad al-Maqdisi, have thought more deeply, teasing out the radical strains in the Wahhabi tradition. In a classical example of contesting the official version and then de-contesting in a more radical form such a crucial concept as *al-wala' wa-l-bara'*, he gives Salafism a completely different morphology than the subservient one the Saudi state promotes.[86] Although the radical 'shuyaibi school' might no longer exist, and there are no religious leaders inside Saudi Arabia to take its place, its ideas are still accessible on Internet.[87] Other research has pointed out the creative ways in which religion is turned against the state.[88] The weakness of the counterterrorism discourse could explain the 10 per cent of prisoners who do not take part in the counselling programme,[89] although the diehards are only a very few.[90]

This scepticism does not of course rule out that counsellors, through a combination of psychological methods and religious admonishing or simply out of the respect for elders in a conservative society, are capable of convincing prisoners who are not ideologically motivated to 'repent' and no longer take part in violent action. For this reason, less ideologically driven detainees might accept the second pillar on which this policy is based, that of *wali al-amr*, including the *bay'a*, *imama* (allegiance to the ruler). This could account for the 1,400 prisoners who have been released, according to official information. But the Amnesty International human rights report on political prisoners and the abuses of counterterrorism measures should make us wary of giving much weight to these numbers. Terrorism is defined so unclearly (deviancy, passions, etc.) that one does not really know if the detainees were in any way involved in actual 'terrorism'. In the end, the hard approach seems to have been the reason why the Saudi counterterrorism strategy between 2003 and 2009 was successful. Only one terrorist, Muhammad al-Awfi, returned to Saudi Arabia in 2009 and repented. Most of the other eighty-five members of AQAP on the list the Saudi Government published in February 2009 were arrested or killed.

Notes

1 See especially Thomas Hegghammer, 'There is nothing soft about Saudi counterterrorism,' *Foreign Policy*, 11 March 2010, available at: http://foreignpolicy.com/2010/03/11/there-is-nothing-soft-about-saudi-counterterrorism/ (accessed 10 June 2011). The most laudatory reports were published in the media; see, for instance, Jeffrey Fleishman, 'Saudi Arabia tries to rehab radical minds,' *Los Angeles Times*, 21 December 2007, available at: http://articles.latimes.com/2007/dec/21/world/fg-rehab21. For a more sceptical article, see David Ottaway, 'Saudi effort draws on radical clerics to combat lure of al-Qaeda,' *Washington Post*, 7 May 2006. For a compliant analysis of the programmes, see also Abdullah F. Ansary, 'Combating extremism: A brief overview of Saudi Arabia's approach,' *Middle East Policy*, 15 (summer 2008): 111–42. For a thorough analysis of the programmes, which limits itself to only those programmes, see Christopher Boucek, 'Extremist re-education and rehabilitation in Saudi Arabia,' in Tore Bjørgo and John Horgan (eds), *Leaving Terrorism Behind: Individual and Collective Disengagement* (London/New York: Routledge, 2009), pp. 212–23. For another laudatory article, which does not refer at all to the ideological content of the rehab-programmes, see Jessica Stern, 'Mind over matter,' *Foreign Affairs* (January/February 2010), pp. 95–108. See also Marisa L. Porges, 'The Saudi deradicalization experiment,'

Council on Foreign Relations website, 22 January 2010, available at: https://www.cfr.org/expert-brief/saudi-deradicalization-experiment (accessed 11 May 2018).

2 See, for instance, Tom Quiggin, 'Understanding al-Qaeda's ideology for counter-narrative work,' *Perspectives on Terrorism* 3:2 (2009): 18–24; William D. Casebeer and James A. Russell, 'Storytelling and terrorism: Towards a comprehensive "counter narrative strategy,"' *Strategic Insights* 4:3 (2005), available at: http://www.au.af.mil/au/awc/awcgate/nps/casebeer_mar05.pdf (accessed 11 May 2018).

3 Thomas Hegghammer, *The Failure of Jihad in Saudi Arabia*, Combating Terrorism Center at West Point, Occasional Paper Series, 25 February 2010, available at: https://ctc.usma.edu/the-failure-of-jihad-in-saudi-arabia/ (accessed 11 May 2018), pp. 18–21.

4 Christopher Boucek, *Saudi Arabia's 'Soft' Counterterrorism Strategy: Prevention, Rehabilitation and Aftercare*, Carnegie Papers, Middle East Program no. 97 (Washington, DC: Carnegie Endowment for International Peace, 2008), p. 1. For a thorough analysis of the programmes see Boucek, 'Extremist re-education,' pp. 212–23.

5 Boucek, *Saudi Arabia's 'Soft' Counterterrorism Strategy*, p. 11.

6 *Ibid.*, p. 15.

7 Stern, 'Mind over matter.' Also, the report by the United States Government Accountability Office (GAO) expresses satisfaction with Saudi efforts at countering ideology, as the target of 'public condemnation of terrorism' has been met; see GAO, *Combating Terrorism: US Agencies Report Progress Countering Terrorism and Its Financing in Saudi Arabia, but Continued Focus on Counter Terrorism Financing Efforts Needed*, GAO-09-993 (Washington, DC: GAO, 2009), pp. 20, 26–32, available at: www.gao.gov/new.items/d09883.pdf (accessed 9 January 2018). See also Rob Wagner, 'Rehabilitation and deradicalization: Saudi Arabia's counterterrorism successes and failures,' *Peace and Conflict Monitor*, 1 August 2010, available at www.monitor.upeace.org/innerpg.cfm?id_article=735 (accessed 13 January 2018); Aidan Kirby Winn, 'Can Gitmo's terrorists be rehabilitated?' *Commentary*, 29 June 2009, available at: www.rand.org/commentary/2009/06/29/CSM.html (accessed 13 January 2018).

8 United States Department of State (USDS), *Country Reports on Terrorism 2008* (Washington, DC: USDS Office of the Coordinator for Counterterrorism (OCC), 2009), available at: www.state.gov/documents/organization/122599.pdf (accessed 18 May 2018); Chap. 5.3, 'Collaboration with Saudi Arabia,' in *Country Reports on Terrorism [2007]* (Washington, DC: USDS OCC, 2008), available at: www.state.gov/j/ct/rls/crt/2007/104112.htm (accessed 18 May 2018).

9 There is some confusion about the relationship between Salafism and Wahhabism. This is compounded by the rejection of the Saudis of the term Wahhabism because it would mean they were named after the founder of the movement, Muhammad ibn 'Abd al-Wahhab (1703–92), which is regarded as an insult and a rejection of their claim to follow the only correct form of Islam. The followers of 'Abd al-Wahhab call themselves the *muwahhidun*, the believers in the Oneness of God (*tawhid*), the central tenet of Wahhabism/Salafism. Like Salafism, Wahhabism wants to return to the golden age of Islam, the first four generations of Muslims, the so-called 'pious forefathers' (*al-salaf al-salih*) who lived according to the original, uncontaminated rules of Islam. Regaining this pristine purity in doctrine and practice is the goal of Salafism/Wahhabism. The difference between Salafism and Wahhabism is that Wahhabis still follow the Hanbali law school, whereas Salafis do not follow any law school but directly study the Qur'an and especially the Hadith (the sayings of the prophet Muhammad). Salafism is a convergence of different revivalist movements originating throughout the Islamic world. It is often regarded as intolerant because it condemns all forms of Islam other than its own, advising its followers to stay away from contact with other, non-Salafi Muslims, let alone non-Muslims. The doctrines that are most controversial are: the 'victorious sect' *al-ta'ifa al-mansura* (saved sect), the idea that only Salafis will be saved and go to heaven; *al-wala' wa-l-bara'* (exclusive loyalty to one's own sect and disavowal and withdrawal from contact with non-members of all other sects); *takfir* (excommunication of Muslims who do not belong to the Salafi sect); and *jihad*, holy war, which was fought to establish the Saudi state. These elements reappear in different forms in the three currents that Salafism has developed over time: *quietist Salafism*, which focuses exclusively on purification of doctrine and practice and whose members are obedient to the powers that be; the *politicos*, who have been influenced by the Muslim Brotherhood and strive for an Islamic state; and *jihadism*, which states that only through jihad can the purification of Islam be achieved. Naturally, the Saudi state supports the first and combats the other two, but especially the second. During the Afghan war 1979–90, it supported jihadism as long as jihad was waged outside Saudi Arabia. Many Saudis also support the jihad of the Islamic State in Iraq and Syria. The danger is always that jihad can be turned against the Saudi state, which explains the deeply ambivalent attitude of the Saudi government towards jihadism in its counterterrorism program.

10 See, for instance, Qur'an, *suras* 2:204–5, 5:64, 10:81 and 5:33.

11 Sulayman bin Abdallah bin Hamud Aba al-Khayl, *Mawqif al-Mamlaka al-'Arabiyya al-Sa'udiyya min al-irhab:Dirasa shar'iyya 'ilmiyya watha'iqiyya* (The position of the Kingdom of Saudi Arabia towards terrorism: a legal scientific documentary study) (Riyadh: no publisher, 2003), p. 139. Also mentioned by Shaykh Abdallah bin Muhammad bin Ibrahim Al al-Shaykh (no date), *ibid.*, p. 521.

12 Cited in Aba al-Khayl, *Mawqif al-Mamlaka*, pp. 298 and 428.

13 'Aqil bin 'Abd al-Rahman bin Muhammad al-'Aqil, *al-Irhab afat al-'asr: Madha qala 'anhu al-'ulama wa-l-mashayikh wa-l-mufakkirun wa-l-tarbiyyun wa-bi-madha wa wasafuhu* (Terrorism plague of the times: what do the ulama, shaykhs, thinkers and educators say about it and how do they describe it) (Riyadh: no publisher, 1425 [2004]), p. 17; Aba al-Khayl, *Mawqif al-Mamlaka*, pp. 426–7. The *suras* in the Qur'an quoted on the principle of corruption on earth (*ifsad fi-l-ard*) are 5:32–3, 2:204–5, 6:151, 13:25, 27:48–9 and 28:77.

14 al-'Aqil, *al-Irhab afat al-'asr*, p. 19.

15 Amnesty International, *Saudi Arabia: Assaulting Human Rights in the Name of Counter-Terrorism* (London: Amnesty International Publications, 2009), pp. 18, 20–4, available at: www.amnesty.org/download/Documents/48000/mde230092009en.pdf (accessed 11 May 2018). The report quotes fatwa no. 148 of the Council of Senior Scholars from August 1988.

16 This has been the official Saudi counter to the accusation after 9/11 that Wahhabism is at the root of terrorism. See, for instance, the response to this criticism from Congress, *Khatab ila al-Gharb: Ruy'a min al-Sa'udiyya* (Response to the West: a Saudi point of view) (Riyadh: Dar al-Ghayna' li-l-Nashr, 2003).

17 Cited in Aba al-Khayl, *Mawqif al-Mamlaka*, pp. 311–12. Prince Nayef consistently uses a religious counterterrorism discourse. He, for instance, makes clear 'that the nation as a whole is based on this creed (*'aqida*) and that it cannot exist without it', in Muhammad 'Ali al-Harafi, 'al-Amir Nayif wa qadaya al-mujtama'' (Prince Nayef and the issues of society), *al-Watan*, 21 April 2008.

18 Prince Nayef, 'Opening address,' in the *Final Report of the Counter-Terrorism International Conference*, Riyadh, Saudi Arabia, 5–8 February 2005, pp. 6–7.

19 Lecture of Salih bin Fawzan al-Fawzan, reported in Aba al-Khayl, *Mawqif al-Mamlaka*, pp. 492–4.

20 Amnesty International, *Saudi Arabia*, p. 13.

21 The Qur'anic concept is mostly based on *sura* al-Nisa', 4:59 and 83. Textbooks on politics and Islam written for Saudi students are a good illustration of the strongly hierarchical interpretation of this concept that requires subservience. See, for instance, Sa'ud bin Salman Al Sa'ud, Khalid Mansur al-Daris, Taysir bin Sa'ud Abu Hamid, Sulayman bin Qasim al-'Aid, 'Abd al-'Aziz bin Sa'ud al-Dayji, et al., *al-Nizam al-Siyasi fi-l-Islam*, 4th ed. (Riyadh: Madar al-Watan li-l-Nashr, 2009), pp. 87–93. In this textbook the main emphasis is on obedience (*ta'a*), and obedience to the ruler is like obedience of man towards his creator (p. 92). Madawi Al Rasheed's assertion that Wahhabi scholars 'failed to produce a single treatise on the nature of the Islamic state and political authority' is certainly wrong. See Madawi Al Rasheed, *Contesting the Saudi State: Islamic Voices from a New Generation* (Cambridge, UK: Cambridge University Press, 2007), p. 46.

22 The two important Saudi compilations of texts on extremism I have used are: al-'Aqil, *al-Irhab afat al-'asr*, and Aba al-Khayl, *Mawqif al-Mamlaka*.

23 A visit to a Salafi bookshop in Great Britain will provide numerous books against extremism and terrorism. See, for instance, *'The Brothers of the Devils': Islamic Condemnation of Terrorists, Hijakers and Suicide Bombers*, trans. SalafiPublications.com, 2nd ed. (Birmingham: Salafi Publications, 2003), original in Arabic: *al-Irhabiyyub ikhwan al-shayatain: Atharuhum 'ala al-afrad wa-l-umam* (n.p., n.d.); Shaykh AbdulMuhsin ibn Hamad al-Abbad, *According to Which Intellect and Religion Is Bombing and Wreaking Havoc Considered Jihaad?* (n.p.: Daarul-'Itisaam, 1425 AH[2004]). Some organizations are specialized in de-radicalization programmes – such as SalafiManhaj, based in Brixton in the UK, which makes many translations. See for instance, Shaykh Saalih bin 'Abdul 'Azeez Aali Shaykh, *A Warning Against Extremism*, trans. AbdulHaq al-Ashanti (Amman: Jamiah Media, originally published as lecture in 1424 AH [2003]); Shaykh Dr Baasim bin Faysal al-Jawaabirah, *Extremism: The Causes, Effects and the Cure*, trans. SalafiManhaj (Brixton, UK: SalafiManhaj, 2008), originally published in 1428 AH [2006] as *Takfir fi daw' al-Sunnah al-Nabawiyya*.

24 Human-rights activists regard the term as onerous, because it can be used for anything and can stand above the law. For instance, when a judge hears that the *wali al-amr* does not agree with a verdict he has made, he will have to overturn his verdict; personal communication from Muhammad al-Qahtani, founder of the Saudi Civil and Political Rights Association (ACPRA),16 October 2010. He was sentenced to ten years' imprisonment in 2013 for his human rights activism in Saudi Arabia.

25 For a positive analysis of this phenomenon as a means of defeating al Qaeda, see, Bernard Haykal, 'Al-Qaida stumbles in Saudi,' *Guardian*, 27 September 2009, available at: www.guardian.co.uk/commentisfree/2009/sep/27/saudi-al-qaida-prince-muhammad (accessed 13 January 2018).

26 *Ghuluw* is a term that occurs repeatedly in the Qur'an. One of the most quoted *ayas* is: 'Ghuluw in religion, an increase [exaggeration] in religion is perhaps worse than too little'; *suras* 4:171 and 5:77; also *sura* 20:81. The source for ignorance is based on *sura* 7:138 and 7:33.

27 The *ghuluw* literature is vast and is a genre in itself. I have used Khalid bin Hamad al-Kharif, *al-Ghuluw fi-l-din wa atharuhu fi-l-umma* (Extremism in religion and its influence on the umma) (Riyadh: Maktaba al-Rushd, 2005), and sections in Aba al-Khayl, *Mawqif al-Mamlaka*, and al-'Aqil, *al-Irhab afat al-'asr*.

28 Al-Kharif, *al-Ghuluw fi-l-din*, p. 22.

29 *Ibid.*, p. 22.

30 *Ibid.*, p. 12.

31 *Ibid.*, pp. 27–30.

32 *Ibid.*, p. 32.

33 This is confirmed by 'Abd al-Rahman al-Hadlaq, head of the counselling programme, with his statement 'your behavior is a reflection of your ideology'. Taken from a long discussion that the author had with Abd al-Rahman al-Hadlaq and Turki al-Mansur at Riyadh on 17 October 2010.

34 Others have pointed out the extreme social moralism and surveillance in Saudi Arabia as a deflection from real political claims. See especially Al Rasheed, *Contesting the Saudi State*, pp. 24–5, and the remark by Gwenn Okruhlik that 'The problem is not with conservative morality but that the very idea of morality has been trivialized. It is conflated with the codification of social absurdities, demonstrated by religious rulings that regulate the plucking of an eyebrow, the use of nail polish, and the length of gowns, rather than grapple with explicitly political issues that revolve around distributive fairness, governmental accountability, and social justice.' Quoted in 'State power, religious privilege and myths about political reform,' in Mohammed Ayoob and Hasan Kosebalaban (eds.), *Religion and Politics in Saudi Arabia: Wahhabism and the State* (Boulder, CO: Lynne Rienner, 2009), p. 95.

35 Prince Nayif, interview published in *Majalla al-Da'wa*, 4 October 2001, cited in Aba al-Khayl, *Mawqif al-Mamlaka*, p. 321.

36 Prince Nayef, interview probably after 9/11, cited in Aba al-Khayl, *Mawqif al-Mamlaka*, p. 316.

37 Shaykh Salih bin Fawzan al-Fawzan, lecture published in *Majalla al-Da'wa*, 24 October 2002, cited in Aba al-Khayl, *Mawqif al-Mamlaka*, p. 498.

38 Aba al-Khayl, *Mawqif al-Mamlaka*, 'Introduction,' p. 123.

39 Al-Kharif, *al-Ghuluw fi-l-din*, p. 23.

40 Interview with Sulayman Aba al-Khayl on passions and their influence and dangers, printed in al-'Aqil, *al-Irhab afat al-'asr*, pp. 212–13.

41 Rabi' al-Madkhali, *Nasiha ila al-umma al-Jaza'iriyya sha'ban wa-hukuma* (Advice to the Algerian people and government) (n.p.: 14/1/1422 HA [2001]), p. 1.

42 For instance, the attempt of the West to connect Islam to terrorism is rejected by the mufti as a form of being led by passions and inclinations in Aba al-Khayl, *Mawqif al-Mamlaka*, p. 522.

43 On Saudi youth, see Mai Yamani, *Changed Identities: The Challenge of the New Generation in Saudi Arabia* (London: Royal Institute of International Affairs, 2000).

44 Aba al-Khayl, 'Introduction,' in *Mawqif al-Mamlaka*, pp. 58–9. See also my article on gender segregation: Roel Meijer, 'Reform in Saudi Arabia: The gender segregation debate,' *Middle East Policy* 17: 4 (2010): 80–100.

45 Prince Sultan, in Aba al-Khayl, *Mawqif al-Mamlaka*, pp. 291–2.

46 Bettina Gräf, 'The concept of *wasatiyya* in the work of Yusuf al-Qaradawi,' in Jakob Skovgaard-Petersen (ed.), *Global Mufti: The Phenomenon of Yusuf al-Qaradawi* (London: Hurst, 2009), pp. 213–38.

47 For a comprehensive explanation of this widespread discourse, see Aba al-Khayl, *Mawqif al-Mamlaka*, pp. 173–81. See also Rabi' Hadi al-Madkhali, *Mudhakkira al-hadith al-nabawi fi-l-'aqida wa-l-ittiba'i* (Cairo: Dar al-Manhaj, 1424 [2004]; originally published 1406 [1985]), p. 37. The discourse is based also on *suras* 28:50 and 45:23.

48 Aba al-Khayl, *Mawqif al-Mamlaka*, 'Introduction,' p. 176.

49 Khalid al-Ghanami, 'Najaha rijal al-aman wa fashalat lijan al-munasiha' (Success of the security police and failure of the Advisory Committee), *al-Watan*, 30 April 2007, available at: www.alwatan.com.sa/news/writerdetail.asp?issueno=2404&id=238&Rname=53 (accessed 20 August 2009).

50 Turki al-Sahayl, 'Saudi Arabia: Grand mufti describes terrorism as "alien,"' *Asharq al Awsat*, 13 May 2010, available at: www.aawsat.com/english/news.asp?section=1&id=20929 (accessed 19 July 2009).

51 Turki al-Suhayl, 'Dahaya da'awi al-jihad fi-l-Iraq' (Victims of propaganda of jihad in Iraq), pt 4, *al-Sharq al-Awsat*, 21 July 2007, available at: www.aawsat.com/details.asp?issueno=10462&article=428975 (accessed 13 January 2018).

52 Turki al-Suhayl, 'al-Sa'udiyya: Jawla hasima ma'a al-takfiriyyin min khilal al-munasiha wa-l-ifraj 'an al-mawqufin amaniyyan' (Final round of the takfiris through the Advice Council and the release of those imprisoned), *al-Sharq al-Awsat*, 5 November 2005, available at: www.aawsat.com/details.asp?section=43&article=331928&issueno=9839 (accessed 9 September 2009). See also Walid Mahmud, '"al-Munasiha" al-Sa'udiyya bi-sujun al-Iraqiyya' (Saudi advice for Iraqi prisons), Islamonline website, 16 February 2008, available at: www.islamonline.net/servlet/Satellite?c=ArticleA_C&cid=1201957953553&pagename=Zone-Arabic-News%2FNWALayout (accessed 20 February 2009).

53 Al-Ghanami, 'Najaha rijal al-aman.'

54 Shaykh Ali bin Shai'a al-Nafisa combines a religious education with one in security and law. He graduated from the Faculty of Sharia in 1974, was appointed a member of the rehabilitation programme of the Ministry of Interior and obtained an MA in security and law ten years later. See interview with him in al-'Aqil, *al-Irhab afat al-'asr*, pp. 301–2.

55 There is a revealing interview with Ali bin Shai'a al-Nafisa in *al-Riyadh*, 9 December 2005, available at: www.alriyadh.com/2005/12/09/article113922.html (accessed 30 August 2009).

56 *Ibid.*

57 Asma' al-Muhammad, 'Fi-khidam al-intiqadat 'ilamiyya li-l-Lijan al-Munasiha: al-takfiriyyun fi sujun al-Sa'udiyya yabda'una fi-tadwin muraja'atihim' (In the sea of media critique of the committees of advice: Takfiris in prison are starting to write down their revisions), al-Arabiyya website, 20 June 2007, available at: www.alarabiya.net/articles/2007/06/20/35699.html (accessed 12 September 2009); al-Suhayl, 'Dahaya da'awi al-jihad fi-l-'Iraq.'

58 *Ibid.*

59 *Ibid.*

60 Nick Fielding and Sarah Baxter, 'Saudi Arabia is hub of world terror,' *Times*, 4 November 2007, available at: www.timesonline.co.uk/tol/news/world/middle_east/article2801017.ece (accessed 19 July 2009).

61 Abdallah al-Ghanami, 'Amir al-Nayif yad'u al-a'ima wa-l-khutaba' ila al-tawiya bi-l-aman al-fikri' (Prince Nayef calls the imams and preachers to raise awareness [of the dangers of terrorism] by means of intellectual security), *al-Watan*, 10 May 2010, available at: www.alwatan.com.sa/Local/News_Detail.aspx?ArticleID=1586&CategoryID=5 (accessed 13 January 2018).

62 Quoted in al-'Aqil, *al-Irhab afat al-'asr*, p. 76. The mufti made the same remark, stating that Islam cannot support terrorism because it 'protects security [*aman*] of society, defends the rights of individuals and has all kinds of laws regarding security, justice [*'adl*] and stability [*istiqrar*]'; quoted in Aba al-Khayl, *Mawqif al-Mamlaka*, p. 525. At the same time, *suras* are quoted of the evil intentions of Christians and Jews; e.g. *suras* 2:120 and 127, 4:89 and 3:119. Interestingly, most of these *suras* are also quoted by jihadis like Abu Muhammad al-Maqdisi and Abu Baseer al-Tartusi.

63 'Ali al-Khashiban, 'al-Thaqafa al-hakima..wa-marhala al-'inaya al-fikriyya' (The ruling culture and the stage of interest in thought), *al-Watan*, 13 April 2007, available at: www.alwatan.com.sa/news/writerdetail.asp?issueno=2387&id=79&Rname=34.

64 Qaynayn Abdallah al-Ghamidi, 'al-Aman al-fikri wa-tullab wa-talabat' (Intellectual security and male and female students), *al-Watan*, 20 May 2009, available at: www.alwatan.com.sa/news/writerdetail.asp?issueno=3155&id=11494&Rname=319 (accessed 9 September 2009).

65 *al-Jazira*, 13471, al-Jazirah website, 16 August 2009, www.al-jazirah.com/156795/ln4d.htm (no longer available; accessed 1 September 2009).

66 Article in *al-Watan*, 15 May 2007.

67 Hamza Qablan al-Mazini, 'Abhath 'an "al-Shamagh,"' *al-Watan*, 9 August 2007, www.alwatan.com.sa/new/writerdetail.asp?issueno=2505&id=1674 (no longer available; accessed 9 July 2009).

68 'Nadwa al-aman al-dini wa-l-fikri tutalibu al-khutaba' bi-l-turayyith fi 'ifta' al-musalin' (Seminar of religious and intellectual security asks preachers to act prudently in giving fatwas), *al-Hayat*, 14 May 2010, www.daralhayat.com/ksaarticle/140846 (no longer available).

69 See *al-Hayat*, 26 April 2010, www.daralhayat.com/ksaarticle/134553 (no longer available).

70 See the warning of the undersecretary of the Ministry of Religious Affairs, *al-Hayat*, 11 April 2010, www.daralhayat.com/ksaarticle/129322 (no longer available).

71 The 'person whose *'aqida* has been shocked, like in a earthquake, and his thought deviated can be exposed to currents with false thoughts that will lead him to destruction and loss, and expose his life and that of his society to danger'; see www.sahab.net/forums/showthread.php?t=363276.

72 The discourse of Nayef also remains largely religious. In a speech of 30 March 2009 he called upon 'ulama, shaykhs and *ahl al-fikr wa-l-ray'* [people of thought and opinions] to participate in the opposition against [extremism]'.

73 That the chair is not based on a secular research on terrorism is clear from a speech given by Dr Salih Hamid, a member of the Majlis al-Shura, entitled *al-Aman al-fikri fi dhu' maqasid al-shari'a* (Intellectual security in the light of the goals of the sharia), and also from the participation of the mufti Shaykh 'Abd al-'Aziz ibn 'Abdallah Al al-Shaykh in the seminars.

74 From a long interview with Khalid bin Mansur al-Daris, no date, www.ksu.edu.sa/sites/KSUArabic/UMessage/Archive/960/dialogue/Pages/Main_T3.aspx (no longer available).

75 Nasir al-Haqbani, 'al-Sa'udiyya: usar al-matlubina amaniyyan bi'a murashshiha li-l-tatarruf al-fikri' (The families of the wanted persons are the nearest candidates for extremist thought), *al-Hayat*, 10 June 2010, available at: www.daralhayat.com/internationalarticle/154007 (accessed 10 July 2010).

76 Nasir al-Haqbani, 'al-Mutawarrutun bi-l-irhab yalja'una ila masahira li-kasb da'm ma'nawi li-isti'ada nishatihim' (Those involved in terrorism use marriage relations to gain support for the activities), *al-Hayat*, 27 February 2010, www.daralhayat.com/ksaarticle/113556 (no longer available).

77 USDS, *Country Reports on Terrorism: Saudi Arabia* (Washington, DC: USDS OCC, xxxx), available at: www.saudi-us-relations.org/articles/2009/ioi/090502-country-report.html.

78 This was confirmed by 'Abd al-Rahman al-Hadlaq during our long discussion on 17 October 2010.

79 From the interview with 'Abd al-Rahman al-Hadlaq and Turki al-Mansur, 17 October 2010.

80 For more on these concepts see Bjorgo and Horgan, *Leaving Terrorism Behind*.

81 For more on revisionism, see Roel Meijer, 'The Jama'at in Egypt,' in Roel Meijer (ed.), *Global Salafism: Islam's New Religious Movement* (London: Hurst, 2009), and Omar Ashour, *De-radicalizing Jihadists: Transforming Armed Islamist Movements* (New York: Routledge, 2009).

82 Interview with 'Abd al-Rahman al-Hadlaq, 17 October 2010.

83 See, for instance, the positive response by David Ignatius, 'Saudis act aggressively to denounce terrorism,' *Washington Post*, 13 June 2010, available at: www.washingtonpost.com/wp-dyn/content/article/2010/06/11/AR2010061104395.html (accessed 13 January 2018).

84 Tom Peter, 'Saudi Arabia religious leaders call terrorism financing un-Islamic,' *Christian Science Monitor*, 19 May 2010, available at: www.csmonitor.com/World/Middle-East/2010/0519/Saudi-Arabia-religious-leaders-call-terrorism-financing-un-Islamic (accessed 13 January 2018).

85 See, for instance, Roel Meijer, 'Yusuf al-Uyairi and the making of a revolutionary Salafi praxis,' *Die Welt des Islams* 47:3–4 (2007): 422–59.

86 See the many articles by Joas Wagemakers; for example, 'The transformation of a radical concept: *al-Wala' wa-l-bara'* in the ideology of Abu Muhammad al-Maqdisi,' in Meijer, *Global Salafism*, pp. 81–106.

87 See Thomas Hegghammer, *Jihad in Saudi Arabia: Violence and Pan-Islamism since 1979* (Cambridge, UK: Cambridge University Press, 2010), pp. 83–98.

88 Al Rasheed, *Contesting the Saudi State*.

89 Interview with 'Abd al-Rahman al-Hadlaq and Turki al-Mansur, 17 October 2010.

90 According to Sean Keely, interviewed by the author in Riyadh on 24 October 2010, the number who refuse all cooperation is very small.

14

The state and terrorism in Iran

Ali M. Ansari

Introduction

For a state that regards itself as the intellectual heir to the French Revolution it is unsurprising that the ideas of 'terror' and 'terrorism' remain central to the controversies surrounding the nature of the Islamic Republic of Iran.[1] From an American perspective, the seizure of the US embassy on 4 November 1979 transformed Iran from an intimate ally into the leading 'state sponsor' of terrorism; an appellation that even the thaw in relations under the Obama administration has done little to change.[2] The revolutionary state's exercise of terror to subjugate the population and, in its eyes, restore order, has likewise confirmed the belief among extensive sections of the Iranian population – especially those who are politically active – that the application of terror remains a key, and regrettably common, means of state control. Yet, for all this, Iranian political activists and their government share a discomfort at the tidy distinctions and definitions imposed by the West on the rest of the world with regard to the use of terror. For many in Iran the distinctions are not as clear as the hypocrisy of Western countries who take a position that condemns acts that affect the West, but find themselves less moved when they or their allies are implicated directly or indirectly in acts of terror.[3] This applies not only to regional actors but to the pre-revolutionary monarchy in Iran itself, where the application of torture and terror, if not officially condoned, was not condemned.

A critical opportunity emerged in the aftermath of 9/11, when then President Mohammad Khatami expressed his willingness to cooperate with the Western coalition being built to combat the Taliban in particular and terrorism in general, if the United Nations could agree to a common definition of terrorism.[4] Regrettably, this approach was dismissed by the United States, arguably fearful that a definition would either be restrictive or find itself and its allies culpable. This absence of clarity causes enormous problems, not only for Western strategy but also for political strategy within Iran, where activists seeking to entrench rights and diminish, if not eradicate, the use of terror against citizens find themselves repeatedly undermined by a Western logic that is increasingly incoherent and contradictory.

Terror and the state

The use of terror to subjugate and frighten its subjects has a long pedigree in Iran, where vast territories, poor communications, basic administration and an absence of the rule of law ensured that autocrats resorted to highly visual and physically symbolic punishments to maintain order. The point was not simply to punish the criminal, the seditionist or the rebel, but to ensure that the memory of that punishment remained for some time to come, such that it would give subsequent troublemakers pause for thought. Perhaps the most prolific practitioner of state terror in recent memory was the founder of the Qajar dynasty, Agha Mohammad Khan (r. 1789–97), and it says something to the extent of the violence he exercised that some two centuries later his name still strikes fear in certain quarters. His brutality, more calculated than popular memory appreciates, effected the stability he sought to achieve in a state wracked by nearly a century of war, and insofar as some argued that the ends (stability) justified the means (terror),[5] application of terror by the state was tolerated and accepted as a legitimate means of statecraft, if never enthusiastically endorsed. Indeed, if for much of the nineteenth century Iran could be said to occupy a pre-modern mentality, in the Foucauldian sense of the word, when it came to application of discipline and punishment, as the century wore on and Enlightenment ideas took hold, an aversion grew, most obviously among intellectuals, against the arbitrary brutality of the state. This became all the more acute when it was apparent that European observers, who might once have justified and then tolerated such actions, increasingly found the practices being pursued to be well below the standards they might expect of a civilized and enlightened society. The pogroms against the fledgling Babi movement were particularly brutal, and in one celebrated passage (which appears to have had an impact on the imaginations of subsequent British diplomats),[6] Lord Curzon recounted:

> Nothing is more shocking to the European reader, in pursuing his way through the crime stained and bloody pages of Persian history during the last and, happily to a lesser degree, during the present century, than the record of savage punishments and abominable tortures, testifying alternately to the callousness of the brute and the ingenuity of the fiend. The Persian character has ever been fertile in device and indifferent to suffering; and in the field of judicial executions it has found ample scope for the exercise of both attainments. Up until quite a recent period, well within the borders of the present reign, condemned criminals have been crucified, blown from guns, buried alive, impaled, shod like horses, torn asunder by being bound to the heads of two trees bent together and then allowed to spring back to their natural position, converted into human torches, flayed while living. The latest case which I have heard of robbers being walled up alive in pillars of brick and mortar was in 1884.[7]

Greater engagement with Europe mitigated some of the worst excesses, but it was clear that a state that had little practical means of enforcing its authority regarded such visual expressions of violence as one of the few means available to it to maintain order and retain stability. Moreover, fear of authority was generally accepted to be the only realistic way to secure this. It was only with the absorption of radical new Enlightenment ideas by Iranian intellectuals at the end of the nineteenth century that attitudes about the nature of government, and its relationship with society, began to change. Though it must be stressed that the determining factor for many was the strengthening of the state via the reinvigoration of the 'nation', and that the new, more humane relationship was very much incidental to this primary goal. Consequently, while these new ideas were promoted vigorously by leading intellectuals, they never succeeded in institutionalizing them in the wider political culture.

However, for a brief moment narratives of the Enlightenment triumphed and in the aftermath of the Constitutional Revolution in 1906, these new ideas dictated that Iranians, as citizens of the new national state, enjoyed rights and should be treated with dignity, and above all should not be coerced into submission to the state but should willingly consent to the authority of a state whose purpose was to serve the people.[8] Although such high-minded ideals were rarely put into practice, at least not in an unqualified manner, one of the striking developments to occur in the reign of the first Pahlavi monarch, Reza Shah (r. 1925–41), was penal reform, which saw all forms of torture and physical abuse abolished, for political prisoners in particular and most others except common criminals, suspected spies and those charged with attempted regicide.[9] As Ervand Abrahamian points out, the regime may have been 'brutal and even deadly, but [was] not one that tortured'.[10] One political prisoner, reflecting on the cordial nature of his relations with his prison guards, noted that they were 'European-trained products of the Constitutional Revolution'.[11] He added that 'his interrogator had pointed out to the Shah in 1930 that advocating socialism was not a crime in itself. After his 1941 release, Ovanessian remained on cordial terms with his interrogators. One even phoned in 1944 to congratulate him on his election to parliament.'[12] Nevertheless, even this was to prove but an interlude between the violence of the nineteenth century and the brutality of the Cold War, where ideological conflict transformed political threats into existential ones.

Indeed public protestations aside, the reign of Mohammad Reza Shah (1941–79; the son of Reza Shah Pahlavi, mentioned above) witnessed the return of torture and violence as a means of political control. British embassy staff found themselves in receipt of unwelcome information when they were invited to attend a lunch with the then head of the military government in Tehran, General Bakhtiar. The military government (the precursor to the state security services (SAVAK)) had been established in the aftermath of the coup of August 1953, when the American CIA and British MI6 had orchestrated the overthrow of the nationalist prime minister Dr Mohammad Mosaddeq. Mosaddeq was a quintessential 'European-trained product of the constitutional revolution', and had continued the enlightened penal policy noted above. Following his fall, and in the politically fractious atmosphere that ensued, the monarchical establishment, taking full advantage of the febrile environment born of the Cold War, resorted to old and trusted methods to re-establish authority and, in their view, stability. Rumours abounded of the *hammam* (public baths) that was used by the military authorities to extract confessions, but the stories of more exotic methods used to terrorize the citizenry into submission were generally regarded as exaggerations, as General Bakhtiar tried to explain:

> For example, the bear had only been used once. (I understand this to be full-grown specimen which is kept in a cage in the grounds of the Second (Armoured) Division of which general Bakhtiar is the commanding officer). Even then the bear had not been allowed to molest the person concerned. This had been a man who, at the time of the Murdad troubles of 1953, had sent a telegram to Mosaddeq strongly supporting his policy, attacking the Shah and suggesting that the grounds of the Royal Palaces should be turned into zoological gardens. They thought the bear would be an appropriate

> punishment for such sentiments and the man had been put in the cage, much to his terror, but taken out after he had expressed rapid repentance and before the bear had actually got its claws on him.[13]

What is striking about this passage – quite apart from its complacency – is that the violence was threatened not for the purposes of extracting a confession (he had already confessed) but to terrify the recipient into submission. What was quite modern about this particular use of state terror was that violence was implied rather than enacted and the focus was psychological and on the humiliation of the individual. It may be, of course, that since physical violence was not used those in authority did not consider this to be torture, and did not consider humiliation to be an act of terror, but in a culture that values pride and dignity, ridicule of this nature could be a potent tool. Thus, for example, recalcitrant and incarcerated clerics were often required to shave their beards, and were then photographed so that they could reminded of their humiliation should their subsequent behaviour require it.[14]

The scale of the political violence used against opponents is a matter of some debate, and some of the more dramatic claims made, for example, by Amnesty International against the shah's rule, published in 1976, have been heavily criticized for too uncritically repeating the claims of the shah's opponents. Yet arguments about the scale miss the central point that such tactics were used at all, and that their use marked a retrograde step even by modest Iranian standards. Moreover, the growth in power of the late Pahlavi state – facilitated by dramatic economic growth and developments in technology – ensured that while the harsh government of the past might have been tolerated, the systematic oppression of the present was proving suffocating. While Mohammad Reza Shah dramatically expanded the investment in education begun by his father, he failed to complete the legal reforms initiated, with the consequence that while the power of the state grew exponentially, the rights of the citizen were woefully neglected. As result, in the 1970s, more radicalized elements in society reacted.

Political assassinations

Political assassinations had been part and parcel of Iranian political life for centuries, and a number of rulers had found themselves at the sharp end of an assassin's dagger or, latterly, gun. Naser al Din Shah had been assassinated in 1896, while a series of leading lights from either side of the Constitutional Movement, including clerics, had been murdered in the political turbulence following 1906. A young Mohammad Reza Shah found himself the target of a Tudeh Party (the communist 'toilers' party) attempt on his life in 1949. But it was perhaps the radical religious group, the Fedayin-e Islam (sacrificers of Islam) who most obviously exercised political violence as a means of terrifying opponents into silence. In 1946 they assassinated the outspoken Iranian nationalist Ahmad Kasravi, whose disdain for organized religion was well documented, while in 1951 they took a more overtly political step by assassinating Prime Minister Ali Razmara as he entered a mosque for prayers, for daring to consider a compromise on the question of the nationalization of the Anglo-Iranian Oil Company. The scandal of Razmara's murder was compounded by the fact that few found it prudent to publicly condemn it, while some clerics refused to preside over his funeral.[15] Whether this was out of fear of retribution or because clerics found Razmara insufficiently Muslim to warrant proper treatment, a paradigm had been established by which 'apostates' were legitimate targets for religiously sanctioned violence.

In a similar vein in 1965, the shah's Prime Minister Hassan Ali Mansur was gunned down by religious extremists (the shah himself survived no less than three assassination attempts, an achievement that only served to reinforce his religious self-belief). But, in 1971, the Fedayin-e Islam were joined by a new left-wing derivative, the Fedayin-e Khalq (the sacrificers of the people), who launched a bold, if politically inconsequential, attack on a police station in Siahkal in the Caspian province of Gilan, killing three police officers in the process. The attack was dismissed by the government as an act of left-wing terrorism, but its symbolic value far outweighed the immediate political consequences, as indicative of the rise of left-wing-inspired guerrilla activity (terrorism) against a government that perceived itself as legitimate, and who the people believed to be unassailable.[16] The scene was set for the emergence of what the shah described as 'Black Reaction' and 'Red Revolution', united in their opposition to the monarchy, but ultimately to turn on each other in Iran's very own revolutionary terror.

Revolutionary terror and the impact of the Iran–Iraq War

Given the intellectual affinity of many in the Islamic Revolution for the French Revolution, it should come as little surprise that 'terror' was regarded by many young radicals in the vanguard of the revolution as the means by which 'corruption' (a concept that was reinforced through Shia theology) could be purged and revolutionary purity maintained. It should also be unsurprising, therefore, that the vast majority of casualties during the Islamic Revolution in Iran occurred after the departure of the Shah on 16 January 1979 and reflected the struggle between the two increasingly divergent wings of the revolutionary movement. In the absence of the rule of law, order had been maintained through the authority of the shah, backed by a powerful security apparatus. But with the shah gone, and Ayatollah Ruhollah Khomeini's charismatic authority yet to make itself felt, the 'revolutionary spring of freedom' of early 1979 was at risk of crossing over into anarchy. As unity gave way to factional infighting – once the unifying figure of the shah had departed the scene – so too the dangers of social and political breakdown increased: a prospect made all too palpable by the existence of rival *komitehs* (committees) modelled on the French experience, who sought to establish order in their particular areas while frequently descending into internecine fighting and extortion rackets.[17] Thus, with no little irony, a revolution that had identified itself as the antithesis of the arbitrary power and perceived brutality of the shah, was itself quick to resort, on a far grander scale, to the very methods that it had initially intended to relegate to history.[18]

The fledgling Islamic Republic had sought to cement unity by diverting attention towards an external enemy, the first an invented one in the form of the US embassy, seized on 4 November 1979, the second, far more serious and real, the invasion of Saddam Hussein's Iraq in 1980. The existence of an external threat made the necessity of establishing internal order all the more urgent, particularly in the border areas where ethnic groups seeking greater autonomy – most obviously the Kurds – found themselves subjected to a brutal crackdown. But the use of terror in the traditional sense came to the fore when domestic rivalries spilled over into violence following the bombing of the Islamic Republican Party Headquarters on 28 June 1981 (at Haft-e Tir); the religious authorities took the opportunity to indulge in a reign of terror against the political forces of the Left in the country, targeting the most organized – and by extension most dangerous – of these groups, the Mojahedeen-e Khalq (MEK/MKO), deemed by many to have been responsible for the outrage. Order was eventually re-established – not before another president and prime minister (Mohammad-Ali Rajai and Mohammad-Javad Bahonar) were assassinated – but at a terrible cost, and while precise figures of the numbers executed vary, they are generally agreed to have been in the thousands.

Perhaps more troubling, however, was the means by which the 'terror' was imposed, the ad-hoc nature of the arrests and executions, whose chief function was to restore order through fear. While many Iranians tired of disorder and worried about the onset of war were willing to tolerate a degree of violence, the retribution exacted by the state essentially institutionalized a blood feud between the MEK and the authorities of the Islamic Republic which lasts to this day, with each side obsessing about the existential threat posed by the other (blaming the other for any attack, however improbable) and taking measures accordingly. For the revolutionary authorities the MEK became the epitome of terrorism and the template for all future designations of existential threat. Its members were labelled *monafeqin* (hypocrites), considered worse than unbelievers in that they pretended to be Muslims. One official paper at the time went so far as to suggest that Imam Ali (the first and most venerated of the Shia imams) had 'warned the faithful to be on guard against hypocrites who deceive, deviate, dilute religion, consort with the Devil, and resort to *teroryism*.'[19]

The MEK relocated to Iraq during the Iran–Iraq War and were effectively tarnished as traitors by most Iranians, while, at the end of the war in 1988, the Islamic Republic committed one of its more egregious sins by engaging in a purging of the prisons, which saw anything up to 5,000 political prisoners, mainly members of the MEK, being summarily executed.[20] While the executions later became notable for Ayatollah Hussein-Ali Montazeri's (Khomeini's then heir apparent) public protestations, it says something of the bloodletting that occurred during this war that this particularly brutal event barely raised any interest in a wider society that was fatigued by the prolonged conflict. It has since, however, come back to haunt officials,[21] especially as the war has receded into memory and political demands have changed. Indeed, what might have been tolerated in a war situation was clearly no longer acceptable for a state and society that sought a transition to a stable and durable peace. But for many in the Islamic Republic the 'war' was to continue.

The legacy of Rushdie and the idea of terror in the Islamic Republic

Among the more persistent charges levelled against the Islamic Republic has been its support for terrorism, especially through proxies such as the Lebanese Hizbullah.[22] The authorities in Iran counter that Hizbullah is a legitimate resistance movement against the real sponsor of state terror, Israel, and point to the fact that Hizbullah would not have been founded had Israel not invaded Lebanon in 1982. While opposition to the existence of the state of Israel can be sourced to the peculiarly hybrid Islamic–Marxist ideology of the Islamic Revolution (marrying sectarian and secular ideas), which regarded Israel as a quintessentially anti-Islamic colonial state and equated Zionism with racism, the Iran–Iraq War further invigorated these ideas by suggesting that the opposition to Israel was actually part of a wider geopolitical struggle for the survival of the revolution. To ideology was therefore added a peculiar realist dimension to the opposition, and support for various groups (Hamas, Islamic Jihad) was regarded in some quarters as a legitimate exercise in defence and deterrence. It mattered little that this argument was circular and tended to contradict itself.

The function of ideologies is to reconcile such contradictions into a coherent whole. Given the growing alliance – tacit or otherwise – that appeared to be emerging against Iran during the war in support of Iraq, Iran considered these countries as legitimate targets for retaliation. This explains its regional activities, seen by governments as seditious, and its retaliation against governments and individuals seen as supportive of Iraq. Perhaps the most notorious incident ascribed to Hizbullah and by extension Iran was the 1983 bombing of the US marines' barracks in Beirut. Hizbullah has repeatedly denied any involvement in this particular attack and, while Iran's guilt is an article of faith among many in the United States, there has been some scepticism voiced even in the US.[23] Be that as it may, for many Iranians these constituted legitimate targeting of military personnel during wartime. Similar arguments were made for the many dissidents – the chief targets of Iranian state terrorism – that were targeted in these years, on the basis that they were undermining the war effort, though needless to say the war allowed the authorities to conflate national, revolutionary and, at times, personal interests.

The problem was that when the war ended, these operations continued, perhaps the most notorious being the murder of former Iranian Prime Minister Shahpour Bakhtiar in Paris in 1991. The crime was especially vicious because his assailants, who had cultivated his friendship, stabbed him several times in an act of calculated brutality intended to send a clear message. It gained further notoriety from the apparent incompetence of the French authorities in nearly allowing the assailants to get away. In the event, one of the assailants was caught as he somewhat clumsily sought to cross the French border into Switzerland, resulting in considerable embarrassment all round.[24] Iran naturally denied any involvement, as it was by then regularly doing when the assassination of other dissidents, principally members of the MEK and the Kurdish Democratic Party of Iran (KDPI), came to light. Privately, officials would complain that they were not doing anything that intelligence and security services the world over (and not least those of Israel) did not do when the security of the state was under threat.

Such arguments gained less traction as the war receded into history, but Iranian denials laboured under a much more difficult problem of perception following the decision in 1989 of the then Supreme Leader Ayatollah Khomeini to issue a fatwa (religious judgement) sentencing the Indian-born British novelist Salman Rushdie to death for blasphemy. This single act, further sullied by the fact that a bounty of some $3 million was offered as a reward to anyone who succeeded in killing the author, probably did more than any other in tarnishing Iran with the label of state sponsor of terror. The fatwa against Rushdie could not be explained in terms of either revolutionary politics or the necessities of war. This was a religious judgment, in which the citizen of another country was sentenced to death and consequently forced into hiding. In inciting people to murder, it was not only an infringement of the principles of freedom of speech, but flatly contradicted the laws of most Western countries, and for all the initial ambivalence towards the fatwa by British politicians, it soon became a cause célèbre among activists and politicians in the West. This was not least because the fatwa was soon discovered to be much more than simple rhetoric for the purposes of domestic political consumption, but an edict that many Muslims around the world (though, significantly, few Iranians) were eager to operationalize.

In Iran the initial enthusiasm for the fatwa among the revolutionary establishment began to wane once it became apparent that it was proving a major obstacle to the full normalization of relations with Europe, not least because the question of Rushdie increasingly topped any discussion between the two sides. But, perhaps more pertinently, officials increasingly regarded the fatwa as morally problematic, and it is indeed worth bearing in mind that then President Ali Khamenei had initially commented that, if Rushdie apologized, the matter could be put to rest (although not frequently voiced, another issue over the fatwa was that Rushdie had previously been feted by the literati of the Islamic Republic as a 'third-world' anti-imperial writer). He was swiftly corrected by Ayatollah Khomeini, who stressed for good measure that even if Rushdie repented and 'became the most pious man of all time', it was the duty of all Muslims to kill him.[25] Khomeini's death some six months after the fatwa effectively closed down any opportunity to have the fatwa revised or removed.

The problems were accentuated by the fact that the fatwa appeared to legitimize the continued use of violence against dissidents, including those resident in the country, whose crimes were not political per se but cultural, and the targets were not political activists or agitators but intellectuals who were, through the 1990s, challenging the boundaries of what was acceptable in the Islamic Republic. For some in the hardline revolutionary establishment, these cultural challenges were just as, if not more, damaging to the purity and long-term stability of the revolution as any overt political challenge. A long obsession with the threat posed by the 'cultural onslaught' principally from Western civilization was over time re-articulated as a 'soft war' which had to be confronted, and for which cosmopolitan intellectuals served as a fifth column. These ideas would reach full and destructive expression during the presidency of Mahmoud Ahmadinejad, but initially they were faced with robust political and intellectual opposition from within.

The presidency of Hashemi Rafsanjani (1989–97) continued to see the targeting of dissidents abroad, especially in Europe, including most notoriously the gunning down of Kurdish dissidents in the Mykonos restaurant in Berlin in 1992. Vigorous denials of involvement by the Iranian Government, along with increasing popular incredulity that the MEK was actually behind the attack, led to suppositions that 'rogue' elements in the intelligence ministry had been involved in an effort to tarnish the image of a presidency seeking better relations with the outside world. Matters came to head when revelations appeared of intelligence officials targeting intellectuals within Iran, and exposed the murder of four distinguished political activists from the defunct National Front, in brutal conditions similar to those of the murder of Shahpour Bakhtiar in Paris in 1991.[26] These revelations over several months in 1998 coincided with, and were no doubt encouraged by, the election in 1997 of the reformist Mohammad Khatami, who won a dramatic landslide election victory on a platform of political reform, including civil rights and the rule of law. (One of the first things the Khatami administration did was to come to a resolution of the Rushdie crisis, committing the Iranian Government to abandoning pursuit of the implementation of the fatwa: a decision that effectively conceded the separation of state and religion in Iran.) While Rafsanjani might have been prepared to conduct an internal enquiry into what had transpired, Khatami was dangerously keen on transparency and accountability. The scandal of what became known as the 'chain murders' uncovered a series of attacks on intellectuals along with reported lists of further targets,[27] and resulted in the most thorough purging of 'rogue' elements from the Ministry of Intelligence to have occurred in Iran before or since.

Yet the promise of greater accountability was to prove short-lived, in large part because the more unsavoury elements simply relocated to other agencies, in particular the intelligence office of the judiciary and, most notoriously, the counterintelligence of the Islamic Revolutionary Guard Corps (IRGC), where their preoccupation with cultural fifth columnists and soft war could be nurtured and developed. Khatami's reformist administration, keen on greater transparency and the democratization of the political economy of the country, found itself the target of systematic attack by hardline conservatives, principally through the judiciary and parliament. But, in 2000 after the reformist landslide in parliament, opponents took to more direct means, and in late 2000 the chief strategist of reform, Saeed Hajarian (himself a former deputy minister in the Ministry of Intelligence), was badly injured and left quadriplegic following a failed assassination attempt.[28] This act of 'terror' (to borrow the language from Persian) had the desired effect of severely shaking the reformist administration, not least Khatami himself who later admitted that the attack had caused him to pause to think about the merits of pursuing the course he had taken. Indeed, from 2000 on, the reformist government, which had been on the offensive as far as political and economic reform were concerned, now found it had effectively lost the initiative.[29]

The inculcation and instillation of fear among reformists in particular and society in general was a major part of the strategy of recovery for conservative hardliners. Hardliners wanted to make the reformist government appear impotent in the face of a wider societal breakdown, while also suggesting themselves as the solution to the problem (that they had helped create). In the aftermath of the revelation of the 'chain murders', reformist intellectuals, many of them clerics, had sought to challenge the intellectual bases and justifications for the use of political and extrajudicial murder. Mohsen Kadivar, an astute critic of the structural weaknesses of the Islamic Republic, argued that while such activities might be permissible in a state that was not 'Islamic' *and* had effectively declared war on the religious authorities (an important distinction), after the victory of the Islamic Revolution, all such edicts would have to be processed through the proper legal channels. A fatwa might be issued but it could neither be secretive nor be applied outside the legitimate channels of the state, and, as with all fatwas, the target would be allowed a defence.[30] Ministers of intelligence had always been drawn from the *ulama* on the basis that in extreme circumstances they could issue fatwas and authorize the elimination of any individual considered a threat to the state. The problem was not so much that this facility was being too broadly interpreted but that other hardline clerics were issuing fatwas on their own initiative and without any reference to the institutions of the state. It reflected the dual nature of the Islamic Republic, with the orthodox government battling for authority with the revolutionary deep state that was unwilling to relinquish control, and the attempt on Hajarian's life was just one example of the conflict at hand.

Equally serious, and of more consequence, was the attempt to destabilize society at large by creating a climate of fear. Originally this had been led by state-tolerated (and to some extent sponsored) Islamic vigilantes, known as the Helpers of the Party of God (Ansar-e Hizbullah), whose modus operandi was to disrupt meetings (often violently) between individuals and groups regarded as cultural fifth columnists, though this effectively included everyone who did not subscribe to their reading of revolutionary Islam. But during Khatami's administration this extended to the murder of those individuals considered impure, with a number of serial murders taking place in Tehran, Mashhad and most notoriously in Kerman. The Tehran case was the most straightforward, insofar as the culprit was caught and condemned to death. Similarly in Mashhad, although by this stage the mood had shifted, with a number of conservative commentators showing some sympathy for the murderer, whose motives they argued were pure. Neither of these, however, compared to the legal quagmire that emerged out of the Kerman serial murders committed in 2002, when a group of young Islamic militia (*basij*), apparently at the behest of an ayatollah,[31] had decided to distribute summary justice to a number of individuals who they deemed to have transgressed religious law – taking the notion that in Islam the righteous must promote good and eliminate wickedness to an unfortunate extreme. The travesty of the situation, though it carried with it profound implications for the governance of the state, was that while the zealous youths had been convicted by the local court, the verdict was overturned on appeal to the higher court in Tehran, on the basis that it was up to the victims to prove their innocence. As the lawyer representing the (dead) victims protested, such a judgement not only made a travesty of the law, but essentially meant that it was open season for vigilantes.[32]

Ultimately, through repeated appeals to higher courts this problematic judgement was overturned, although when that occurred the perpetrators of the crimes managed to avoid incarceration through the reported payment of 'blood money' by way of compensation. But a principle had been effectively established which was to bear terrible fruit during the protests against the re-election of Mahmoud Ahmadinejad in 2009, which many Iranians considered had been fraudulent. In the increasingly tense environment it became clear that the government and the regime felt genuinely threatened by the popular upheaval, the courage of which appeared to suggest that any emotional attachment the people may have had for the Islamic Republic was on the wane. Recognizing that affection may be difficult to engender in the populace at this stage, the decision appears to have been taken that the regime's salvation lay in the reconstitution of fear. To achieve this the regime turned to the very hardline ayatollah who had been the ideological architect of the conservative resurgence during Khatami's presidency and the reported author of the fatwa that had led to the Kerman serial murders: Ayatollah Misbah-Yazdi.

Not only did Misbah-Yazdi articulate a reading of Islam that was narrow and tied to a 'belief' in the Guardianship of the Jurist, an additional 'pillar of the faith' calculated to alienate most orthodox Shias, he also added – extraordinarily – that obedience to Khamanei, and by extension Ahmadinejad (as the approved president), was the equivalent to obedience to God.[33] This remarkable claim caught many in the Iranian press (even sympathetic conservative organs), by surprise, but its purpose was essentially to distinguish *authentic* Muslims (by their new standards) from superficial or false Muslims (akin to the 'hypocrites' or *monafeqin*, the label normally applied to the MEK), who were by consequence 'beyond the pale' and not subject to legal protections. By designating those who did not subscribe to this new definition of Islam as unbelievers, or *kuffar*, Misbah-Yazdi was providing religious sanction to those hardline institutions to take whatever action they required without fear of retribution.[34] Many members of the *basij* did just that, with the most famous, though by no means the only, casualty of this new reign of terror being Neda Agha-Soltan, who was shot while attending a demonstration, either by a member of the *basiji* militia, or, for those in the government, as a victim of an elaborate CIA plot. For six months after the election the regime battled with protestors until fear took hold once again in society, inaugurating a period of repression not experienced since the onset of the revolution itself. The period has become known, in the official narrative, as the 'sedition' (*fitna*), and the level of paranoia within the regime reached such heights that at one of the many show trials of 'seditionists' that took place, the (long dead) German sociologist Max Weber found himself indicted.[35] Laying the new 'security state' to rest was one of the pillars of Hassan Rouhani's presidential campaign in 2013, and it says something of the limits of terror that Iranians rediscovered their voices, and found themselves in part protected by the reality that the regime was acutely anxious to avoid a rerun of the disturbances of 2009.

The (il)logic of the West

The use of political violence in the Islamic Republic had largely been justified by and predicated on a determination to combat Western encroachments and protect the revolution. The perceived widespread existence of torture in the shah's prisons had been one of the ideological linchpins justifying not only the revolution itself but also the increasingly extreme measures it took to protect the revolution. For some, the lesson was that the fall of Mosaddeq in 1953 was in part caused by his inability to take decisive action. As one Hojjat-ol Eslam[36] Ali Khamenei pronounced, 'We are not liberals like Mosaddeq and Allende whom the CIA can easily snuff out. We are willing to take drastic action to preserve our new-born Islamic Republic.'[37] Combating the enemy without – in this case the monarchists, and by extension their backer, the United States – provided one platform in the fight against 'terror'. Combating the other, the enemy within – in this case largely, though not exclusively, the MEK – was a much more vicious struggle, in large part because the enemy was not only more difficult to identify, but also, unlike the Americans who were simply trying to pursue their own interests (however misguided), constituted individuals who were clear and present traitors to the revolution and the faith.

For the better part of the first two decades following the revolution, these two facets of the struggle were occasionally identified with each other but never intimately so. The US was vigorously criticized for its support of Israel and Saddam Hussein, its previous support of the shah – whose sins were gradually transferred onto the US – and of course its actions in the Iran–Iraq War, most obviously the tragic shooting down of the Iran Air airbus by the *USS Vincennes* in 1988. The fact that Captain Will Rogers subsequently received a medal for his service in the Persian Gulf only confirmed the worst suspicions of many Iranians about US double standards with respect to terrorism, human rights and the use of political violence.[38] Still, this did not preclude the exploration of economic and occasionally political relations by both sides, most obviously exposed during the Iran–Contra affair and subsequently during the presidency of Hashemi Rafsanjani, when Iran took the bold step of offering an oil contract to the US oil company Conoco.

Indeed, the fact remains that, for all the rhetoric, the cold war between the United States and Iran was regarded by many Iranians as something that could eventually be overcome, an understanding made real by the election of Mohammad Khatami in 1997 and his subsequent attempt to 'break down the wall of mistrust' between the two countries. The real obsession remained the enemy within, and this was largely, though not exclusively, focused on the MEK. Indeed, two of the regular criticisms of US double standards with regard to terrorism were the platform it continued to give the MEK, and the failure of the US authorities to designate the MEK a terrorist organization – despite the fact, as Iranian officials reiterated, that the MEK was the one organization to have actually assassinated US officials, albeit in the 1970s. Much of this was to change during the presidency of Mohammad Khatami, and most obviously in the aftermath of 9/11, when the two narratives became increasingly and dangerously aligned.

For many hardliners in the regime, sympathetic to vast and complex conspiracy theories, there was never any doubt that the challenges faced by the Islamic Revolution and Republic were intimately related. But it was difficult for such views to gain traction in society at large, and indeed one of the reasons for Khatami's election in 1997 had been increasing public concern at the growing strength of hardliners within the political system and their propensity to use violence against perceived political opponents (see the 'chain murders', above). Khatami's landslide victory signalled that this tendency was in retreat, though it had by no means been defeated. As it reorganized to undermine the reformist platform, the decision of the Bush administration to launch the 'Global War on Terror' in the aftermath of 9/11 provided this hardline tendency with hitherto unforeseen opportunities, facilitated by the spectacular hubris of the Bush–Cheney White House.

If the wars in Afghanistan and Iraq initially put hardliners on the back foot, the ensuing military and political quagmires encouraged and empowered them. With the United States and the 'West' no longer the 'superpower' they aspired to be, elaborate narratives of deceit and decline could be articulated with ever more forcefulness (one being the cause of the other). Not only could hardliners who had decried the perfidy of the West point to the recklessness of the Iraq war and the travesty of Abu Ghraib, they could now use these developments to convince their more sympathetic compatriots that their sympathies had been misplaced. But the decision of the Bush White House to identify Iran as part of an 'axis of evil', despite the assistance afforded by the Khatami administration to the war in Afghanistan (especially with regard to intelligence on the Taliban), ensured that those officials who had staked much on better relations with the West (not least Khatami himself) were now dangerously vulnerable to the charge of naiveté, stupidity or, at worst, complicity;[39] especially as neo-cons in the United States could barely disguise their enthusiasm for regime change in Tehran to follow swiftly on the heels of that in Baghdad. All this ensured that any sympathy for the West could now be identified with treason.[40] Added to this was the emerging revelation that the United States was applying methods in its war on terror that included torture, extraordinary rendition and 'targeted killings', which allowed the charge of hypocrisy to be levelled with even greater efficacy.[41] It was one thing for the West to support brutal regimes on the basis of realpolitik, but to participate in these methods themselves while preaching against them to others severely undermined a moral logic by the which the 'West' – for all its flaws – had traditionally been regarded as a reference point and ideal. That it might fall short could be tolerated, but on this occasion the fall appeared profound.

There is little doubt that hardliners exploited this incoherence to great effect, taking advantage of the destabilization of the region to argue effectively for a greater securitization of the state, pointing out the costs of 'anarchy', while using methods that seemed to be shared widely and for which there could now be little coherent criticism. The West, and the United States in particular, long held culpable for turning a blind eye to terrorism in the form of the MEK and 'state-sponsored' terrorism by Israel, could now be held directly responsible for supporting and fostering terrorism, either by its own forces or by its proxies in the region.[42] Not only was the United States regarded as complicit in the assassination of Iranian nuclear scientists – widely assumed to have been murdered by Israeli agents – but in imposing the most severe sanctions against the country for its nuclear programme, it was accused of seeking to 'terrorize' the Iranian population into submission. Perhaps most damningly, it was accused of selectively backing uprisings during the Arab Spring and turning a blind eye to Bahraini repression of its democracy activists, while seeking the removal of Assad in Syria through the cultivation of radical groups, including ISIS (Islamic State). It mattered little if this were true, the

United States was guilty either by association or by incompetence, and as such the narrative could gain traction.

The consequences of the use of terror in Iran have been manifold. It has not only empowered but effectively legitimized activities that had hitherto been considered exceptional and/or problematic. The narratives of the 'enemy without' and the 'enemy within' have not only converged, they have become increasingly entrenched, such that in the aftermath of a nuclear accord that was meant to reset US–Iran relations and place them on a new trajectory – however slow and incremental – the security state that Rouhani argued had to be dismantled is in fact being reinforced. The West, and the United States in particular, has been identified as a supporter of terrorism, not only through its proxies but directly through its mishandling of Iraq after 2003 and its incoherent handling of the Syrian opposition after 2011. With the United States credibly seen as both complicit and incompetent, those elements within Iranian politics and society that were regarded as sympathetic to the United States have become guilty by association – either through naiveté or wilfully – the former description often being more pernicious since it requires 're-education'.[43] The template was the same as, and had echoes of, the reaction against Khatami, but the circumstances were now dangerously different. The practical consequences are that the Iranian state justifies its fight against terror with terror. An irony that draws it far closer to its American nemesis in means, methods and paranoia than it could ever have imagined.

Notes

1 While definitions of terror and terrorism remain contested, and are regularly politicized, this chapter will adopt the broad definition provided by Richard English: 'Terrorism involves heterogeneous violence used or threatened with a political aim; it can involve a variety of acts, of targets, and of actors; it possesses an important psychological dimension, producing terror or fear among a directly threatened group and also a wider implied audience in the hope of maximizing political communication and achievement; it embodies the exerting and implementing of power, and the attempted redressing of power relations; it represents a subspecies of warfare, and as such it can form part of a wider campaign of violent and non-violent attempts at political leverage.' Richard English, *Terrorism: How to Respond* (Oxford: Oxford University Press, 2009), p. 24.

2 US Department of State (USDS), *Country Reports on Terrorism 2013* (Washington, DC: USDS Office of the Coordinator for Counterterrorism, 2014), available at: www.state.gov/j/ct/rls/crt/2013/ (accessed 1 October 2015). In US political culture, the belief in Iran as *the* leading state sponsor of terrorism remains entrenched.

3 See, for example, Ali Khamenei's comments in 'Khotbeh-ye namoz-e eid Fetr' (The sermon on the occasion of the prayers for Eid Fetr), Khamenei.

ir website, 27 Tir 1394 [18 July 2015], available at: www.farsi.khamenei.ir/speech-content?id=30331 (accessed 1 September 2015). Also, his comments in a meeting with the members of the Assembly of Experts, 'Bayanat dar didar rais va ozaye Majlis khobregan rahbari' (Pronouncements on the occasion of meeting the chair and members of the Assembly of Experts), Khamanei.ir website, 12 Shahrivar 1394 [3 September 2015], available at: www.farsi.khamanei.ir/speech-content?id=30653 (accessed 30 August 2015); here he draws attention to the murder of Iranian nuclear scientists, which he says the Israelis have all but admitted.

4 It does not help that in Persian the word for assassination is 'terror'.

5 John Malcolm, *History of Persia*, vol. II (London: Longman, 1815), pp. 182–3.

6 The National Archives of the UK (TNA), FO 248/1569 Foreign Office, 'Torture in Iran,' 10117/1/56 (11 March 1956).

7 G.N. Curzon, *Persia and the Persian Question*, vol. I (London: Frank Cass, 1966; first published 1892), pp. 456–7.

8 See, in this regard, Mohammad Ali Foroughi, 'Hoquq-e Asasi: ya adab-e mashruteat-e dol' (Fundamental laws or the rules of constitutionalism of states), reprinted in I. Afshar and H. Homayunpur (eds), *Siyasatnameh-ye zoka-ol-molk, maqale-ha, nameh-ha, va sokhanrani-ha-ye siyasi-ye Mohammad Ali Foroughi* (The *Book of Politics* of Zoka ol Molk, the political articles, letters and speeches of Mohammad Ali Foroughi) (Tehran: Ketab-e Roshan, 1389 [2010], originally published Tehran: 1325–26 (lunar) [1907–8]), pp. 5–62.

9 Ervand Abrahamian, *Tortured Confessions: Prisons and Public Recantations in Iran* (Los Angeles: University of California Press, 1999), p. 41.

10 *Ibid.* p. 72.

11 *Ibid.*, p. 39.

12 *Ibid.*, p. 38.

13 TNA, FO 248/1569. In seeking to contextualize these developments the British diplomats were quick to refer to their copy of Curzon, *Persia*.

14 One such victim was reportedly Ali Khamenei. See E. Sciolino, *Persian Mirrors: The Elusive Face of Iran* (New York: Touchstone, 2000), p. 85.

15 TNA, FO 248/1514, 'Internal situation 1951,' 10101/78/51 (11 March 1951); see also 10101/65/51 (12 March 1951), where the British diplomat Francis Shepherd noted, 'It is however surprising that that he [the assassin] could so easily have succeeded in his design. Mr Alam did not see him break through the police cordon but he must have done so.'

16 On the emergence of guerrilla activities, see E. Abrahamian, *Iran between Two Revolutions* (Princeton, NJ: Princeton University Press, 1981), p. 480.

17 Abrahamian, *Tortured Confessions*, argues that these were in fact modelled on the Soviet experience (p. 124). Both revolutions, it would seem, informed the Iranian experience.

18 *Ibid.*, pp. 13 and 167.

19 *Ibid.*, p. 147.

20 For a detailed discussion see Abrahamian, *Tortured Confessions*, pp. 209–22. See also Iran Human Rights Documentation Center, 'Deadly fatwa: Iran's 1988 prison massacre,' Iran Human Rights Documentation Center website, n.d., available at: www.iranhrdc.org/english/publications/reports/3158-deadly-fatwa-iran-s-1988-prison-massacre.html (accessed 13 January 2018).

21 See, for example, G. Robertson, 'Iranians involved in 1988 massacres remain in public life,' *Sydney Morning Herald*, 14 June 2010. A key individual reportedly involved was the minister for justice in Rouhani's first administration, Mostafa Pourmohammadi, who was also rumoured to have been involved with the murder of dissidents abroad. In a press conference which Iranian news agencies subsequently edited, Pourmohammadi drew attention to the executions and argued that they could not be understood outside the context of the Iran–Iraq War: 'Defah-e vazier-e dadgostari az edam-ha-ye 68' (The minister of justice's defence of the executions of 68), IranWire website, 2 September 2015, available at: https://iranwire.com/fa/features/2684 (accessed 2 September 2015).

22 Many of the terrorist actions against the United States and its allies, including Saudi Arabia and Israel, have been ascribed to the Lebanese Hizbullah, and various offshoots (although it is not at all clear whether the links between these groups are anything but tenuous). These include attacks in Lebanon, Argentina and the Khobar Towers in Saudi Arabia, all of which Hizbullah, and by extension Iran, has strenuously denied.

23 On this see, PBS, 'Terrorist attacks on Americans, 1979–1988', PBS *Frontline*, n.d., available at: www.pbs.org/wgbh/pages/frontline/shows/target/etc/cron.html (accessed 13 January 2018).

24 See 'Ali Vakili Rad: The perfect murder and the imperfect getaway,' France 24 website, 19 May 2010, available at: www.france24.com/en/20100518-ali-vakili-rad-perfect-murder-imperfect-getaway-shapour-bakhtiar (accessed 3 September 2015).

25 See Andrew Antony, 'How one book ignited a culture war,' *Observer*, 11 January 2009.

26 H. Kaviani, *Dar jostejoye mohafal jenayatkaran* (Investigating the murderous associations) (Tehran: Negah-ye Emruz, 1378 [1999]), p. 30. The revelations were rumoured to have been leaked by disgruntled intelligence officers; see, for example, M.A. Zekryai, *Hijdahom Tir Mah 78 beh raviat jenahaye siyasi* (The 18th Tir 78, from the perspective of political factions) (Tehran: Kavir, 1378 [1999]), p. 58.

27 Kaviani, *Dar jostejoye mohafal jenayatkaran*, p. 38.

28 See *Akhbar-e Eqtesad* (Economic News), 23 Esfand 1378 [13 March 2000], p. 1. Hardliners were swift to blame the attempt on the United States; see M.A. Zakrayi, *Terror-e Hajarian beh ravayet-e jenaha-ye siyasi* (The assassination of Hajarian in the perspective of the political factions) (Tehran: Kavir, 1379 [2000]), pp. 267–9.

29 For further details of the rise and fall of the reform movement see A.M. Ansari, *Iran, Islam and Democracy: The Politics of Managing Change* (London: Royal Institute of International Affairs, 2006), p. 327.

30 This latter point clearly jarred with the fatwa against Rushdie in which the latter was clearly not allowed any response. See M. Kadivar, *Baha'ye Azadi: defa'at Mohsen Kadivar* (The price of freedom: the defence of Mohsen Kadivar) (Tehran: Ghazal, 1378 [1999]), pp. 183, 188, 201–2.

31 Generally considered to be Ayatollah Misbah-Yazdi.

32 See, in particular, Nehmat Ahmadi, 'Negahi beh parvandeh-ye ghatl-haye mahfeli-e kerman az aghaz ta konoon' (A look at the file of Kerman serial murders from the beginning to the present), *Etemad*, 29 Farvardin 1386 [18 April 2007]. For the background to these developments see A.M. Ansari, 'Iran under Ahmadinejad: Populism and its malcontents,' *International Affairs* 84:4 (2008): 683–700.

33 'Misbah-Yazdi: "eta'at az rais jomhur, eta'at az khodast!"' (Misbah Yazdi: 'obedience to the president is obedience to God!'), *Tabnak*, 22 Mordad 1388 [13 August 2009].

34 The moderate Ayatollah Sanei famously spoke out against these developments and was marginalized as a consequence. See, for example, 'Sokhanraniye ayatollah sanei dar mored "haroomzadeh gishe dorugh mige"' (The speech of Ayatollah Sanei on the subject of the 'bastard who tells lies'), YouTube website, 18 August 2009, available at: www.youtube.com/watch?v=IwzG4vwi0ms (accessed 3 January 2010); for an abridged version with English subtitles, see MEMRI TV, 'Prominent Iranian Ayatollah Yousef Sanei slams Iranian leadership over handling of protests,' YouTube website, 12 August 2009, available at: www.youtube.com/watch?v=ceHREFzgp10 (accessed 15 May 2018).

35 See, in this regard, Charles Kurzman, 'Reading Weber in Tehran,' *Chronicle Review*, 1 November 2009.

36 Hojiat-ol-Eslam (proof of Islam) is one level below ayatollah (sign of God).

37 Quoted in Abrahamian, *Tortured Confessions*, p. 137.

38 For a detailed account of this tragedy, see the BBC documentary *The Other Lockerbie* (BBC TV, 2000).

39 Many conservatives and hardliners used Bush's State of the Union address in 2002 to call for the implementation of martial law; for details, see Ansari, *Iran, Islam and Democracy*, p. 235.

40 In echoes of more recent developments, for example, the judiciary suddenly decreed that discussions about dialogue with the US would henceforth be considered illegal, a decree that caused widespread outrage and was soon overturned, see *Nowruz*, 5 Khordad 1381 [26 May 2002], p. 1.

41 On the rejection of an anti-torture bill on 'Islamic grounds' at the very time when the West appeared to be endorsing the limited use of torture, see *Nowruz*, 19 Khordad 1381 [9 June 2002], p. 1.

42 'Iran sees US as main backer of terrorism, drug trafficking,' *Tasnim* (English), 6 November 2015, available at: www.tasnimnews.com/en/news/2015/11/06/908745/iran-sees-us-as-main-backer-of-terrorism-drug-trafficking (accessed 6 November 2015); Reuters Staff, 'Iran says no co-operation with US in "fight against terrorists,"' *Reuters*, 4 November 2015, available at: https://www.reuters.com/article/us-mideast-crisis-syria-iran-idUSKCN0ST1XB20151104 (accessed 1 September 2015).

43 Up to and including, in this case, the president. See S. Lucas, 'Supreme leader slaps down Rouhani's "naïve" foreign policy and talks with the US,' *Enduring America*, 7 October 2015. See also H.R. Gholamzadeh, 'Soft war vs soft power,' *Mehr News*, 14 October 2015.

PART VI

Africa

15

Counterterrorism in Kenya: Security aid, impunity and Muslim alienation

Jeremy Prestholdt

Introduction

In late September 2013, four militants associated with the Somali insurgent group al Shabaab walked into an upmarket shopping centre in Nairobi. Armed with automatic weapons and grenades, the gunmen made their way through Westgate Mall firing on those trapped inside. They claimed that their actions were retribution for Kenya's military operations in Somalia and the recent assassinations of Kenyan Muslim clerics. The attackers would kill more than sixty people at the mall, including the nephew of Kenya's President Uhuru Kenyatta. Most of the victims died before security forces entered the building.[1]

More than three hours after the massacre began, an elite paramilitary unit of the Kenyan police, the General Service Unit (GSU) Reconnaissance Company (RC), attempted to wrest control of the building from the gunmen. Soon thereafter Kenya Defense Force (KDF) soldiers entered the building as well. But a firefight broke out between the two contingents and both withdrew.[2] After the exchange, one soldier and three members of the GSU-RC lay dead. The militants retreated as well, and over the following days the KDF laid siege to the mall. They also engaged in extensive looting.[3] On the third day the Kenyan military fired anti-tank rockets towards the last known position of the gunmen. The volley set fire to the mall and ultimately collapsed a large section of the building. After nearly seventy-eight hours, Kenyan security forces regained control of Westgate. Witnesses and the Kenyan media speculated that the attackers had escaped, but subsequent evidence suggested that all four assailants had died inside the mall.[4]

The calculated brutality of al Shabaab's attack shocked Kenyans and others around the world. Yet the assault on Westgate Mall was the culmination of years of intensifying political violence in Kenya and a harbinger of an increasingly deadly internal conflict. More precisely, it evidenced the interrelation of circumstances in Kenya and the civil war in Somalia. Al Shabaab staged simultaneous bombings in Uganda in 2010, and in the year preceding the mall attack it carried out bombings and other targeted killings inside Somalia with increasing frequency. In the wake of the Kenyan military's 2011 incursion into southern Somalia, al Shabaab and its affiliates launched a retaliatory campaign in Kenya that included over ninety attacks before the 2013 Westgate assault.[5] Militants used small arms, grenades and improvised explosive devices (IEDs) to target security installations, particularly military garrisons and police posts in proximity to the border with Somalia. They also carried out attacks on bars, transportation hubs, markets and churches. Though the attack on Westgate Mall was more deadly than those that immediately preceded it, it repeated an established pattern of al Shabaab actions.

Events at Westgate encapsulated the recurring dynamics of terrorism and counterterrorism in Kenya. First, the attackers chose a 'soft' target. As in the past, this resulted in maximum media attention and a high number of civilian deaths, non-Muslims in particular. Second, despite warnings that such an attack was imminent, the assault evidenced a slow and uncoordinated response by security forces.[6] Finally, the attackers imagined their actions to be retaliation for those of Kenyan security forces domestically and in neighbouring Somalia. Kenya's invasion of Somalia – the nation's first aggressive foreign action – and a decade and a half of extreme counterterrorism measures had deepened the historical grievances of many Kenyan Muslims. In Westgate and subsequent attacks, al Shabaab militants conflated these grievances with events in Somalia.[7] Specifically, al Shabaab and its Kenyan sympathizers referenced abuses by security forces, including communal punishment in Kenya and the KDF's actions in Somalia, as a means to appeal to young Kenyan Muslims and win recruits in Kenya. By taking such a tack, al Shabaab believed it could destabilize Kenya and force a withdrawal of the Kenyan military from Somalia.

Since the 1998 US embassy bombing in Nairobi, the Government of Kenya's response to terrorism has been multifaceted. Yet it has privileged the use of force over subtler measures. Government efforts have relied on both civil authorities and the military. The Kenyan police have employed measures such as profiling, detention and prosecution. The Kenyan military has conducted operations in Kenya and Somalia. These strategies have contributed to the apprehension of terrorist suspects and weakened al Shabaab in Somalia.

However, counterterrorism efforts in Kenya have been hampered by minimal coordination among agencies, the use of heavy-handed tactics, disregard for human rights, insufficient engagement with civil society organizations and a culture of corruption within the security forces. Moreover, two defining features of Kenyan counterterrorism efforts have emerged. First, counterterrorism in Kenya has clear socio-cultural dimensions. In the late 1990s, security forces responded to the threat of terrorism by focusing intently on Kenya's alienated Muslim communities, both in the Somali-majority north and at the Swahili-speaking coast. As a result, the response to terrorism in Kenya reflects communal divisions and animosity within Kenyan society that precede contemporary counterterrorism. Second, Kenya's invasion of neighbouring Somalia created two overlapping fronts: one within Kenya and the other across the border in Somalia. The actions of Kenyan policymakers and al Shabaab thus contributed to a more complete integration of the conflict in Somalia and internal tensions in Kenya.

The extrajudicial practices and other abuses of security forces in Kenya are not unique to the field of recent counterterrorism operations. Indeed, the colonial government and British military engaged in Kenya's most extreme form of systemic violence: the suppression of the Mau Mau insurgency (1952–60). Colonial security forces developed a programme of mass detention and forced relocation, or 'villagization'. Violence against civilians also included torture, rape and extrajudicial killings. These actions had unambiguous ethnic dimensions as security forces targeted Kikuyu specifically.[8] Moreover, counterinsurgency in Kenya offered political and economic benefits to those who remained loyal to the colonial administration. Independence followed shortly after the defeat of the Mau Mau insurgents, and Kenya's postcolonial elite adopted many policies of the colonial state, particularly when addressing perceived internal threats.[9]

In the postcolonial era, human rights organizations have regularly criticized the Kenyan police and military for their disregard for domestic law and basic human rights.[10] In the context of counterterrorism, the security forces have carried forward a number of tactics used against earlier insurgents, dissidents and communities. For instance, since 1998 authorities have subjected terrorist suspects to extrajudicial practices such as extraordinary rendition, intimidation, torture, bribery and disappearance. Recent investigations by journalists and human rights organizations additionally claim that in the years since the Westgate attack Kenyan authorities have engaged in the extrajudicial killing of terrorism suspects. These dimensions of counterterrorism praxis have limited the efficacy of legitimate investigative procedures, alienated Kenyan Muslims, deepened popular distrust of the authorities, and intensified a spiral of violence and recrimination.

This chapter will trace the development of counterterrorism policy in Kenya and its consequences since the end of the 1990s. Specifically, it will outline how domestic priorities and international pressure to pursue a robust counterterrorism agenda have exacerbated communal tensions and increased the sense of alienation within Kenya's Muslim minority communities, particularly among people of Somali, Swahili and Arab backgrounds. To appreciate the complexity of contemporary circumstances, two overlapping periods are identified in the history of counterterrorism in Kenya: 1998–2010 and 2011–present. These periods are typified by differing terrorist threats and have therefore occasioned contrasting state responses. The first period, which began with the US embassy bombing in Nairobi, was largely defined by the response to al Qaeda attacks against prominent foreign targets in Kenya. Initially during this period, the Kenyan Government did not perceive counterterrorism to be a national priority. However, significant external pressure, notably from the United States, encouraged greater commitment to a counterterrorism agenda. The second period, beginning in 2011, has been defined by a dramatic increase in terrorist activity, a greater interdependence among events in Somalia and Kenya, and the recruitment of Kenyans by al Shabaab and its affiliates to carry out attacks on Kenyan soil. The post-2010 campaign of terror in Kenya has prompted domestic demands for increased security. This, along with other political calculi, resulted in a new counterterrorism impetus that entailed overlapping internal and external dimensions. Al Shabaab's Kenyan campaign and the radicalization of young Kenyan Muslims now pose a multidimensional challenge to Kenyan security, one that has domestic, regional, and global as well as potentially long-term reverberations.

Al Qaeda in Kenya and the state response

In the early 1990s al Qaeda strategists identified potential US targets in East Africa. US embassies in the region employed minimal security, and thus a small group of mostly foreign al Qaeda operatives developed plans for attacking both the embassies in Dar es Salaam, Tanzania, and Nairobi, Kenya. In August 1998 the group succeeded in simultaneously detonating truck bombs outside the US embassies in Tanzania and Kenya. The blast in Nairobi killed over 200 people and injured thousands more, the vast majority of which were Kenyans.[11] Yet, since the intended targets were Americans, many policymakers in Nairobi saw the event as an external affair. Ensuing investigations turned up one of the bombers, British-born Mohamed Rashed Daoud Al-Owhali, who the Kenyan police delivered to the American authorities. President Daniel arap Moi also allowed FBI agents to work directly with Kenyan security forces. In the days following the embassy bombing, multinational investigative teams focused on Kenyan Muslim communities. Specifically, Kenyan security forces carried out investigations in Mombasa's majority-Swahili neighbourhoods, notably Old Town and Majengo. Many Swahili and Arab Muslims reported being detained and interrogated, sometimes by American investigators, but no Kenyans were consequently charged in relation to the attack.[12] Though it would later become evident that foreign operatives were largely responsible for the attack, counterterrorism efforts focused on specific ethnic communities. Moreover, the harassment of coastal Muslims in 1998 exacerbated historical grievances extending back to the late colonial era.

At the end of the colonial era, many Muslims at the coast and in the majority-Somali northeast region feared discrimination in a majority-Christian Kenya. These fears, and the coast's status as a protectorate under Zanzibari sovereignty, seeded a separatist movement led by prominent Arab, Swahili and Digo Muslims. Though the separatists were unsuccessful, the movement divided coastal communities and soured relations with Nairobi. At the same time, the full integration of the coast with Kenya engendered bitterness at the coast.[13] Moreover, after Kenyan independence in 1963 a Somali irredentist movement in the northeast sparked what came to be known as the Shifta War (1963–68). The civil war in North Eastern Kenya precipitated a great number of abuses by Kenya's security forces against the region's Somali majority. Adapting many of the counterinsurgency practices of the Mau Mau era, Kenyan forces developed a programme of mass internment, or forced 'villagization'.[14] The practice of collective punishment of Somali communities continued well after the formal cessation of hostilities. In 1984, for instance, Kenyan security forces massacred perhaps as many as 5,000 Somali men at the Wagalla airstrip near Wajir.[15] Additionally, in the 1980s Muslim leaders across Kenya voiced alarm over increasing economic marginality, political underrepresentation and chronic discrimination. In the 1990s mounting Muslim grievances contributed to the rise of the Islamic Party of Kenya (IPK). The party became a popular political platform for the voices of young Muslim urbanites, particularly in Mombasa. In response, state and non-state actors employed a variety of means to suppress the party, including police and vigilante raids on neighbourhoods perceived to support the IPK. With aid from local political elites, the Moi administration succeeded in neutralizing the party 1997.[16] Thus, police actions in Mombasa after the 1998 embassy bombing appeared to many an extension of a longer history of repression. Ultimately there was little evidence to link IPK activism with support for al Qaeda, and the efforts of the security forces in the late 1990s yielded only modest results.

Al Qaeda continued to operate in Kenya into the 2000s. Though the Moi administration did not rank counterterrorism as a high priority, some in State

House recognized its political utility. Specifically, the embassy bombing offered the opportunity to rebuild Kenya's formerly close relationship with the US, which had been strained in the early 1990s by American criticism of the Moi Government's rampant corruption and heavy-handed dealings with opposition activists. In an effort to partner with the US once again, Kenya's National Security Intelligence Service (NSIS) accommodated American security requests following the attacks of 11 September 2001. After receiving a list of suspects whom the FBI believed to be linked to al Qaeda, the police arrested more than fifty people. Most were interrogated and held for weeks without charge.[17] Well-known businessmen and opposition-party activists were among those arrested, suggesting a degree of political intimidation alongside counterterrorism. The Moi administration also complied with US requests to scrutinize the passport applications of Kenya's Asian and Arab citizens. The authorities began to enforce guidelines requiring citizens of Asian and Arab descent – including Swahili of mixed African, Arab and Asian ancestry who can trace their ancestry on the coast back indefinitely – to present their grandfather's birth certificate before they could receive or renew their passports.[18] Many Muslim leaders saw Kenya's enforcement of the passport regulation as an act of open discrimination against Muslims of Arab and Asian descent.[19]

External pressure to pursue a more robust counterterrorism agenda continued to mount after the 2002 al Qaeda bombing of an Israeli-owned hotel and attempted downing of an Israeli airliner near Mombasa. The attacks and subsequent travel advisories issued by Western embassies crippled Kenya's tourist sector. Yet, additional security aid was forthcoming, particularly from the US. As a result, newly elected President Mwai Kibaki found himself performing a delicate political balancing act. He protested Western warnings about Kenya's insecurity while embracing the new aid streams and bowing to US pressure to aggressively pursue terrorists. To salvage Kenya's image, identify the violence as manageable and appease US critics, the Kibaki administration narrowly defined the issue of terrorism as emanating from the coastal Muslim community. The new verve with which Kenyan authorities approached counterterrorism resulted in notable successes, including the capture of a suspected terrorist and cache of weapons in 2003, but it also led authorities to contravene and attempt to alter domestic law. For instance, the 2003 Suppression of Terror Bill defined terrorism so vaguely that it could include most acts of political dissent. The bill also proposed to curtail many freedoms, ease restrictions on extradition and do away with requirements for proof of intent. Effectively, the bill aimed to create an alternative criminal justice system for terrorism suspects. The Suppression of Terror Bill foundered in Kenyan parliament, but the Kibaki administration received increased counterterrorism support from the United States, Britain and Israel.[20]

In the years following the embassy bombing Kenya possessed neither the material resources nor the investigative capabilities to tackle the threat of international terrorism. In 2003 this changed. Security aid flowed into Kenya and the resources available to the counterterrorism forces grew exponentially. Foreign aid came in many forms, including police training and equipment as well as assistance for the expansion of judicial capabilities. In the year 2003 alone, the newly formed, semi-autonomous Anti-Terrorism Police Unit (ATPU) received nearly $10 million in aid from the US.[21] The NSIS, the GSU of the Kenyan police and other Kenyan civil authorities likewise received funding, equipment and training. In 2004 the US established the multistate East African Counterterrorism Initiative, and the bulk of its funding went to Kenya, some $88 million. In 2006 the US State Department's Antiterrorism Assistance programme provided the Kenyan Maritime Police Unit with equipment and constructed an anti-terrorism assistance camp at Manda Bay on the northern coast.[22] The United States similarly assisted in the training of the Kenyan military and invited hundreds of Kenyan security agents to America for specialized courses. The US even helped to create a new Kenyan army unit: the Ranger Strike Force. However, the most ambitious American project was the Partnership for Regional East Africa Counterterrorism, a multilateral body designed to build the capacity of East African partner nations and harmonize efforts among military, law enforcement and development actors, particularly in Kenya.[23]

Aid and diplomatic pressure expanded Kenya's security infrastructure. Yet, the effect of this infrastructure on the authorities' ability to identify terrorists, foil terrorist plots and bring criminals to justice was unclear. In the 2000s counterterrorism efforts continued to hinge on a combination of limited intelligence gathering and racial or ethnic profiling. The security forces also continued to flout domestic law with impunity. For instance, bribery and detention without charge remained common practices. According to human rights investigators, forced confessions and threats after release continued as well.[24] The paucity of evidence against Kenyan terror suspects meant that counterterrorism efforts yielded few indictments or convictions. When Kenyan courts did indict terrorism suspects, subsequent trials often suggested that the indictments might have been perfunctory responses to American criticism. The trial of several men suspected of involvement in the 2002 bombings offers a case in point. After continued US charges of inaction, the Kenyan authorities indicted several men from the small island town where an al Qaeda operative involved in the 1998 bombing of the US embassy in Nairobi, Fazul Abdullah Muhammad, lived in hiding. The defendants languished for two years in Kenya's most notorious maximum-security prison, a facility that once held Mau Mau detainees and later political prisoners. The trial came to an abrupt end when the Criminal

Investigations Department officer who led the investigation admitted that there was no conclusive evidence linking the defendants to the bombing.[25] After the trial one defendant, Sheikh Aboud Rogo, became an outspoken critic of the Kenyan Government. He would also voice sympathies for Somali jihadists and be among the first high-profile clerics to be murdered.

By the mid-2000s it seemed that ordinary Kenyans with no perceptible link to terrorism were bearing the greatest cost of counterterrorism. This was the case at least in part because the political and economic risks in targeting middle- and lower-class Kenyan Muslims were negligible, while external pressure to capture and convict terrorists was great. Therefore, as foreign security aid helped the Kenyan authorities to build a more robust security infrastructure, it also effectively rewarded them for abridging the rights of Kenya's Muslim citizens. Moreover, the Kenyan authorities and their international allies rarely acknowledged abuses by the security forces. When they did publicly recognize Muslim complaints of ill treatment, representatives of multiple governments suggested that Muslim grievances contributed to a 'home-grown' terrorist problem. As the decade wore on, Kenyan investigators continued to seek international recognition for domestic counterterrorism operations. One strategy was to time high-profile counterterrorism operations with events of diplomatic significance. For instance, during the Kenyan security minister's visit to Washington in 2007, the authorities responded to American criticism of Kenyan inaction by targeting the imam of one of Mombasa's largest mosques, Kwa Shibu. Police surrounded the residence of Sheikh Ibrahim Mohammed Obeidilla, and after tear-gassing the neighbourhood they ransacked three houses and arrested several people, including Obeidilla. The authorities justified their actions by claiming that since Sheikh Obeidilla was from the Comoro Islands, the birthplace of terrorist Fazul Abdullah Muhammad, he was either harbouring Fazul or had information on his whereabouts. Obeidilla denied any association with the wanted terrorist, but the police instructed him to sign documents confirming their association. Though investigators could not establish a link between Obeidilla and Fazul, they arranged for the sheikh's deportation. As the police prepared to deport Obeidilla, Kenya's High Court ruled the expulsion to be illegal. Despite this ruling, the police bundled off Sheikh Obeidilla to the Comoros.[26]

By 2007, events in neighbouring Somalia would begin to directly affect circumstances in Kenya. The previous year a militant coalition called the Islamic Courts Union (ICU) came to power in Mogadishu. The ICU was a loose confederation of clan leaders, Islamists and authorities in Somalia's Islamic court system, which had been the only administrative body to maintain a semblance of order during the war. The coalition was able to challenge Somalia's unpopular Transitional Federal Government (TFG) and take the capital,

Mogadishu.[27] Given the ICU's reported links to al Qaeda operatives, Ethiopian and American policymakers were deeply suspicious of the coalition. Intelligence sources were particularly concerned about an element of the ICU that was gaining influence: *al Shabaab*, or 'the youth'. Al Shabaab was instrumental in the ICU's expansion of control over Mogadishu and much of the rest of the country.[28] In early January 2007 the Ethiopian army unilaterally invaded Somalia and routed the ICU, including al Shabaab. Stripped of its moderate ICU leadership, al Shabaab was reborn in the Ethiopian occupation, during which it gained supporters and embraced a more extremist stance. Soon, the al Shabaab fringe became precisely what Ethiopian and US policymakers feared most: a radical pan-Islamist insurgent group that sought strong links with al Qaeda. The Ethiopian invasion therefore had the opposite of its intended effect.

Immediately after the Ethiopian invasion of Somalia, the Kenyan Government engaged in a programme of extraordinary rendition that further raised the ire of Kenya's Muslim community. During the Ethiopian invasion, hundreds of refugees crossed from Somalia to Kenya. Though most of these refugees entered Kenya without incident, the Kenyan authorities detained roughly 150 people from more than eighteen nations.[29] The Kenya Police then transferred the detainees to Nairobi, where Kenyan and American investigators vetted them. Most were held without charge for weeks. Before the detentions could draw a concerted response, the Kenyan authorities, with US assistance, transferred at least ninety of the detainees, including thirty-four women and children and several Kenyan citizens, to Mogadishu where most were handed over to the Ethiopian military. The Ethiopians in turn delivered the detainees to facilities in Addis Ababa that came to be known as the 'African Guantanamo'.[30]

While in Ethiopian custody the detainees underwent weeks, and in some cases more than a year, of confinement and interrogation. Most were denied access to a lawyer. Some detainees were subjected to solitary confinement, stress positions and psychological as well as physical torture.[31] The Kenyan Government refused to acknowledge that any of its nationals were held in Ethiopia. Only after significant pressure from Kenyan civil society, the release of damning reports on Ethiopia's detention facilities and the publication of the passenger lists from the rendition flights did the Kenyan Government retrieve its citizens from Ethiopian detention. Despite international outrage, the practice of extraordinary rendition persisted. For instance, in 2011 reporter Jeremy Scahill interviewed Ahmed Abdullahi Hassan, a Kenyan citizen of Somali descent rendered to Somalia by the Kenyan Government in 2009. According to Scahill, the US authorities had relayed concerns about Hassan to the Kenyan ATPU. The Kenya Police then collected Hassan and delivered him to Mogadishu, where he was held without charge.[32]

In late-2000s Somalia, al Shabaab was able to wage a relatively successful campaign against the Ethiopian forces and a coalition dubbed the African Union Mission in Somalia (AMISOM). The insurgents captured substantial territory in southern and central Somalia, including much of Mogadishu. Yet, al Shabaab relied on extreme brutality and a strict application of Islamic law. This made them unpopular in many areas under their control.[33] Al Shabaab also extended the war beyond Somalia. After the Ethiopian withdrawal in January 2009, Ugandans constituted a substantial proportion of the AMISOM force. In response to the presence of Ugandan troops in Somalia, al Shabaab launched simultaneous attacks in Kampala. In July 2010 al Shabaab suicide bombers targeted a Kampala restaurant and nightclub during the World Cup Finals. The World Cup bombings were the deadliest terrorist attacks in East Africa since 1998, and several suspects were Kenyan. The bombings foreshadowed al Shabaab's campaign of terror in Kenya.

By 2010, foreign security aid to Kenya had produced meagre results in the fight against terrorism. Moreover, human rights investigators continued to expose civil and human rights abuses by Kenya's security forces, including torture and disappearances. These excesses stoked a general sense of humiliation and alienation on the part of Muslims. Before the late 2000s, few Kenyan Muslims had advocated resistance to the authorities, but continued police impunity and a handful of outspoken Kenyan critics contributed to a gradual change in attitude in some quarters. Moreover, al Shabaab began to promote an ideology that interpreted the war against the Somali Government and AMISOM as a theatre in a larger confrontation between Muslims and the West.[34] As al Shabaab gained Kenyan sympathizers, members of the emerging coalition argued that Kenyan Muslims were duty-bound to join al Shabaab.

One proponent of this idea was Aboud Rogo, the Kenyan preacher acquitted of terrorism charges in 2005. In his widely circulated sermons, Rogo argued that the war in Somalia was not an attack on al Shabaab or Somalis per se. Somali insurgents, he suggested, were targeted because they were the only group in the region that followed Islam faithfully. Rogo's sermons similarly criticized Kenya's harsh counterterrorism tactics and the actions of US security forces elsewhere in eastern Africa. He concluded that Kenyans should take up the cause of al Shabaab.[35] Because of these incendiary messages the United Nations and United States included Aboud Rogo on their respective sanctions lists. Aided by the messages of radicals such as Rogo, in the late 2000s al Shabaab actively recruited young Kenyans. The Nairobi-based Muslim Youth Center (MYC) proved a key partner in this endeavour. Under the leadership of Ahmad Iman Ali, members of the MYC adopted a radical stance in favour of al Shabaab that drew supporters from Nairobi, Mombasa and elsewhere in Kenya.[36] Some of these adherents would later join al Shabaab's Kenyan affiliate, al Hijra, an offshoot of the MYC led by Ahmad Iman Ali after his departure for Somalia in 2009.[37] In the early 2010s, estimates of the number of Kenyans that had joined al Shabaab ranged as high as 700.[38]

War in Somalia, counterterrorism in Kenya

Border security dogged Kenya in 2010 and early 2011. A series of cross-border kidnappings and the bombing of a Kampala-bound Nairobi bus encouraged Kenya to take more forceful counterterrorism measures. The most significant of such measures came in late 2011, when Kenya unilaterally invaded the part of Somalia controlled by al Shabaab. The official objectives of the invasion, Operation Linda Nchi (protect the nation), were to aid African Union troops in the war against al Shabaab and create a buffer zone in southern Somalia. Encountering minimal resistance from al Shabaab, the KDF, assisted by local militias, quickly seized the strategically important port of Ras Kamboni.[39] The invasion soon proved lucrative for the Kenyan military as it pushed through to the larger port city of Kismayo. There the KDF taxed the export trade in charcoal, which created a revenue stream for the Kenyan forces.[40] Moreover, in June 2012 the KDF was integrated into AMISOM and paid standard European Union wages that were significantly higher than official Kenyan military pay. Security aid from Washington continued to flow as well. According to the US ambassador to Kenya, Robert F. Godec, by the middle of 2014 Kenya was one of the greatest recipients in the world of US civilian counterterrorism assistance.[41]

However, the real price of Kenya's actions in Somalia was evident soon after Kenyan troops crossed the border. Within days of the invasion, al Shabaab and its Kenyan allies began a bombing campaign in Kenyan cities targeting buses, shops, restaurants, bars, casinos, churches and many other public spaces. For example, militants linked to al Shabaab staged a coordinated attack on two churches in Garissa, North Eastern Province, which killed seventeen people and injured a great many others. The frequency of attacks in cities such as Nairobi, Mombasa, Mandera and Garissa increased in 2012, suggesting that the dynamics of terrorism in Kenya were changing significantly.[42] Indeed, al Shabaab did everything in its power to destabilize Kenya from within, including enticing Kenyans to join the insurgent group with promises of great material gain.[43]

Terrorism was now a significant concern for both Kenyan policymakers and the Kenyan public. Officials moved to double the national counterterrorism budget.[44] Yet the tactics of the security forces remained largely the same. The most notable exception was that counterterrorism efforts began to focus more intently on radical Muslim leaders and specific mosques. Before and immediately after the 2013 Westgate attack, a number of outspoken Kenyan clerics and other radicals were accused or indicted of terrorism-related crimes. Some were murdered. Many alleged that the assassinations were the work of the Kenyan security forces. Though the government denied any involvement, a 2014 Al Jazeera investigative report featured interviews with Kenyan 'death squad' members who claimed to be affiliated with multiple branches of the security forces.[45] Regardless of the identities of those behind the killings, the murder of Sheikh Aboud Rogo had the greatest reverberations. In August 2012, Rogo was killed in a hail of bullets as he drove along a major artery in suburban Mombasa. His death led to several days of rioting in Mombasa and drew condemnation from human rights groups and political leaders alike. In the ensuing riots, five churches were destroyed and three police officers were killed. Soon thereafter, several other preachers were gunned down in what appeared to be a purge of al Shabaab sympathizers.[46] In the following months many suspects were killed and their family members intimidated.[47]

Efforts to clamp down on radical voices led to further clashes. As the violence escalated, radicals in Mombasa and Nairobi attempted to gain control of symbolically important mosques.[48] This expanded political rifts within the Muslim community. Young radicals began attacking moderate Muslim leaders who they imagined to side with the Kenyan Government, including outspoken critics of the government's counterterrorism programme. Several moderate imams at the coast and in northeast Kenya were assassinated. Though the killers' identities remained obscure, a number of informants and police officers were similarly gunned down. In February 2014 police in Mombasa responded by raiding the mosque where Aboud Rogo once preached, Masjid Musa, as well as two other nearby mosques. They arrested hundreds of young Muslim men during the raids, several of whom subsequently disappeared. In the days that followed the Masjid Musa raid, the police banned all public gatherings in Mombasa.[49] As in the past, the use of excessive force by the authorities and the disappearance of a prominent cleric fortified radical voices.

In March 2014 police in Mombasa foiled the bombing of a local shopping mall, but at the end of the month gunmen attacked a Mombasa church, killing four. In the days that followed, Kenyan security forces embarked on the largest concerted domestic counterterrorism operation in several decades, a campaign dubbed Operation Usalama Watch (safety watch). Police rounded up more than a thousand ethnic Somalis in Nairobi and held them at Kasarani Stadium. Others were forced to pay bribes in order to avoid detention. Moreover, all Somali nationals in Nairobi and Mombasa – some 50,000 people – were ordered to refugee camps.[50] The government was returning to a familiar policy of collective punishment, reminiscent of that employed during and after the

Shifta War (see above).[51] In Mombasa, the county commissioner issued shoot-to-kill orders for terrorist suspects. The commissioner stated that 'if we find any of them, we will finish them on the spot. They are not people to take to court.'[52] In the months that followed, several other outspoken figures were murdered, including Abubaker Shariff Ahmed, known as 'Makaburi', an associate of Aboud Rogo. In a particularly brazen assault, Makaburi and an associate were gunned down as they exited a courthouse in suburban Mombasa.[53]

Indignation, fear and paranoia exacerbated the divide within Kenya's Muslim community. Most radicals belong to a generation that has seen joblessness and repression, both of which they understand as forms of religious persecution. Goaded towards radicalism by international currents of militancy and outspoken figures linked to al Shabaab's Kenyan confederate al Hijra, some young Muslims now see few prospects for change in conventional politics and put little stock in pacifism. Kenyan radicals have embraced a union of religion and politics that conceptually links historic grievances with counterterrorism in Kenya and the global war on terrorism. Specifically, al Shabaab and its supporters aim to capitalize on the outrage stirred by the killing of clerics, mosque raids and other counterterrorism measures. For instance, in the wake of Operation Usalama Watch, one senior al Shabaab commander made a direct appeal to Kenyans. He declared, 'We are urging all the Muslims in Kenya ... to fight the government of Kenya inside that country, because Kenyans killed your people including children.'[54] Al Shabaab and its allies wager that by reciting Muslim grievances, exploiting historically rooted socio-economic divisions and encouraging excessive reprisals they can pit Kenyan Muslims against the Kenyan Government and the nation's Christian majority. They calculate that this could significantly weaken the resolve and ability of counterterrorism forces in Kenya and Somalia.

Al Shabaab and its Kenyan allies broadcast their message through various channels. Videos produced by al Shabaab's media platform, al Kataib, have featured lectures in Swahili from Kenyans such as Ahmad Iman Ali (see above).[55] Their most sophisticated product is the magazine *Gaidi Mtaani* (the terrorist in the neighbourhood). The magazine is designed specifically for East Africa, using both Swahili and English to reach a wide audience. *Gaidi Mtaani* seeks to rationalize al Shabaab's attacks in Kenya by playing on Kenyan Muslims' feelings of alienation and addressing the logic of jihad. Additionally, *Gaidi Mtaani* frequently praises Kenyan radicals and emphasizes the virtues of violence. A 2012 cover story focused on Aboud Rogo, referring to him as an 'agent for change'.[56] Al Shabaab recruitment videos such as *Mujahideen Moments* have taken a similar tack. They feature Swahili-speaking Kenyan insurgents who emphasize themes such as the humiliation suffered by Muslims in Kenya, Christian 'occupation' of coastal land, revenge for the killing of prominent Kenyan preachers and the liberating potential of violence. These and other media feature Kenyan voices and portray violence as the only means to address the indignities suffered by Muslims.

In a related strategy to paint itself as allied with Kenyan Muslims, in many of its Kenyan operations al Shabaab has explicitly targeted Christians. Though the Westgate attackers spared some Muslims, no single event evidenced this strategy better than al Shabaab's chilling assault on several towns in northern Kenya. In June and July 2014, a modest al Shabaab militia that included Kenyan and Somali nationals terrorized counties in the northern coastal region. The militia killed more than eighty people, almost all of whom were Christian. In Mpeketoni, a small, isolated town populated largely by Christians – some of whom migrated to the coast as part of government land-settlement schemes – militants torched buildings and engaged the police in a pitched battle. Once the attackers gained control over the town they began to identify and murder Christian men, specifically. The police were slow to mount a counteroffensive, and in the hours that followed scores of men of multiple ethnic backgrounds were killed. As in the Westgate attack, many Muslims were spared. The assailants also left a message that portrayed their actions as an attempt to address Kenyan Muslims' grievances. A hastily composed statement, written in Swahili and English, appealed to local Muslims by declaring, 'This is your land.' The author argued that Kenyan Muslims could no longer look to the opposition party or the separatist organization the Mombasa Republican Council to champion their cause. Rather, the author concluded, Muslims should 'wake up and fight' to 'kick Christians out [of the] coast'.[57]

The attack at Mpeketoni, similar assaults in other coastal towns, the massacre of passengers on a regional bus in July 2014 and subsequent attacks in Lamu County demonstrated that Kenyan efforts to increase border security and decrease al Shabaab activity were having limited effect. They also showed that al Shabaab and the Kenyans in its ranks believed their actions to be a response to a host of Kenyan domestic concerns.[58] Indeed, this strategy of linking the plight of Kenyan Muslims with the war in Somalia was now explicit. Al Shabaab named one of its units the Nabhan Brigade in honour of Saleh Ali Saleh Nabhan, a Kenyan al Qaeda operative who was killed by US Navy SEALs in 2009. After the same brigade routed Kenyan forces at El Adde, Somalia, in 2016 – Kenya's greatest military defeat to date – al Shabaab used images of the 2014 Masjid Musa raid and the murdered cleric Aboud Rogo's words in a celebratory video of the assault.[59]

In 2015 al Shabaab targeted another isolated Christian population in northern Kenya. The attack would prove to be deadliest in East Africa since the 1998 embassy bombing. In the early hours of 2 April, a small group of militants stormed Garissa University College, about 200 kilometres from the Somali border. Much as with earlier attacks, gunmen targeted Christians, killing 147 people in all, most of whom were students. A spokesman for al Shabaab claimed that the university was chosen as a target since it was located 'on Muslim land colonized by non-Muslims', a reference to Garissa University College's majority non-Muslim student body.[60] Later reports suggested that the planner was Kenyan and a former University of Nairobi law student.[61] Though the authorities' response to the massacre was slow, it was better coordinated than those during Westgate and the 2014 coastal attacks. The outcome was also less ambiguous: the police killed most of the attackers and apprehended several others. Yet, as in the past, the Kenyan Government used the attack to silence its critics. Soon after the massacre, the government froze the assets of two of the most influential human rights organizations in Mombasa, Muslims for Human Rights and Haki Africa. Though the White House had recently invited the executive director of Haki Africa to participate in a summit on countering violent extremism, Kenyan Government officials stated that they intended to categorize the two organizations, along with many other groups and outspoken critics, as 'terrorist entities'. Nevertheless, a few weeks before President Barack Obama's 2015 visit to Kenya, the High Court in Mombasa ruled that the two human rights organizations could not be declared terrorist groups as there was no evidence linking them to terrorism.[62]

External pressure on Nairobi to address the excesses of Kenya's security forces had begun to build as well. In this regard, President Barack Obama's visit Kenya in July 2015 – the first by a sitting US president – may mark a new chapter in US–Kenya relations. Amid remarks on counterterrorism assistance during a televised speech, President Obama called on the Kenyan Government to make a 'commitment to uphold the rule of law, and respect for human rights, and to treat everybody who's peaceful and law-abiding fairly and equally'.[63] At the same time, the Obama administration continued to see Kenya as a key ally against al Shabaab. Specifically, the US affirmed its support for Kenya's counterterrorism programme, both during President Obama's visit to Kenya and through the multi-agency Security Governance Initiative (SGI) inaugurated in late 2014. Under the rubric of SGI, Kenya, along with five other African nations, was slated to receive multifaceted security assistance.[64] Echoing the president's comments, SGI also aimed to 'enhance police human resources management' and assist Kenya's justice system to increase 'public confidence in security institutions' and 'prevent the marginalization of segments of Kenya's population'.[65] In the latter years of the Obama administration, US policymakers seemed more attuned to the critiques of Kenyan counterterrorism initiatives made by human rights groups and other civil society organizations. The extent to which this pressure to address impunity will continue and the degree to which it will affect Kenya's counterterrorism praxis is not yet clear.

Conclusion

Counterterrorism repeats and elaborates a deeper history of misconduct by Kenya's security forces. Since the 1998 embassy bombing, security forces have engaged in politically motivated persecution and collective punishment, notably of Kenyan Somalis. Thus, the counterterrorism project in Kenya, much like counterinsurgency efforts in the late colonial and early postcolonial eras, has had socio-cultural dimensions. But there is also a notable difference between earlier abuses and the actions of the security forces in the counterterrorism field: the contemporary incentives and politics of counterterrorism are *both* domestic and international. More precisely, the organs of counterterrorism that have developed since 1998 are to some degree the consequence of foreign pressure and assistance. Social and political frictions within Kenya have also been exacerbated by events in Somalia. Thus, while Kenya faces an internal crisis, it is not entirely of Kenyans' own making. Rather, it is the result of a confluence of America's war on terrorism, a harrowing conflict in Somalia, al Shabaab's calculated brutality beyond Somalia's borders, the misconduct of the Kenyan security forces and the historic alienation of many Kenyan Muslim communities. The recent emergence of other militant groups in East Africa, such as al Mujahiroun and Jahba East Africa (an Islamic State affiliate) may complicate circumstances in Kenya further.[66]

Efforts to address violent extremism in Kenya after the 1998 embassy bombing were hamstrung by the limited capacities of the civil authorities. While external aid and increased domestic spending in the 2000s ensured that these agencies no longer lacked kinetic capacity, fundamental deficiencies in counterterrorism policy remained. Weaknesses in investigative procedure such as limited inter-agency coordination, poor evidence collection and a lack of sustained partnership with Muslim communities have compromised the efforts of the security forces. Corruption, including regular bribery by the security forces, and discrimination have contributed to a deep distrust of the security forces among Muslims. Moreover, external aid has incentivized counterterrorism, including heavy-handed and ineffective tactics, but it has not promoted accountability. Nevertheless, recent signs indicate that American policymakers harbour concerns about abuses by the Kenyan security forces. The Obama administration and other aid providers recognized that Kenya's counterterrorism praxis has alienated and angered Kenyan Muslims. Many Muslims feel more marginalized than ever before, and young people now question the prospects for change through conventional politics. As a result, some have turned to violence. By scapegoating Kenyan Muslim communities and engaging in acts of collective punishment, the security forces have helped to fortify radical thinking. The murder of high-profile clerics further amplified these sentiments. Indeed, the targeting of figures of leadership and authority encouraged and even invigorated younger, radical voices. The ensuing cycle of recrimination has left increasingly little room for moderates.

Kenya's current crisis has international, domestic, communal and intercommunal dimensions. The 2011 invasion of Somalia and al Shabaab's response opened a Pandora's box of violence within Kenya's borders, creating a level of instability contingent on domestic as well as international dynamics.[67] Unlike in the 1990s and early 2000s, recent violence has been driven by internal disillusionment and frustration. Kenya therefore faces the difficult task of developing a security programme that both protects its citizens and diminishes the appeal of extremism. To date, the Kenyan authorities have concentrated on the use of force, including collective punishment and a range of extrajudicial actions. This approach has largely neglected strategies of prevention that emphasize accountability, the rule of law, social justice and civil society engagement. Ultimately, the way in which the Kenyan state, its international allies and civil society respond to the current dynamics of insecurity – Muslim alienation and youth radicalization, in particular – will determine whether extremist messages fall on deaf ears or give rise to even more deadly internal conflict.

Notes

1 New York City Police Department (NYPD), *Analysis of al-Shabaab's Attack at the Westgate Mall in Nairobi, Kenya* (New York: NYPD, 2013); Peter Walker and Guy Alexander, 'Nairobi shopping mall attack: Kenyan president's nephew among the dead,' *Guardian*, 22 September 2013, available at: www.theguardian.com/world/2013/sep/22/nairobi-attack-kenya-president-nephew (accessed 28 April 2016); *BBC News*, 'Nairobi Westgate attack: The victims,' *BBC News*, 26 September 2013, available at: www.bbc.com/news/world-africa-24195845 (accessed 8 May 2016).

2 Tristan McConnell, '"Close your eyes and pretend to be dead": What really happened two years ago in the bloody attack on Westgate Mall,' *Foreign Policy*, 20 September 2015, available at: http://foreignpolicy.com/2015/09/20/nairobi-kenya-westgate-mall-attack-al-shabab/ (accessed 28 April 2016).

3 CCTV footage showing soldiers looting Westgate Mall caused public outrage. The KDF responded by accusing the police and a firefighter of also looting. Sam Kiplagat, 'Firefighter first to loot at Westgate Mall, says KDF,' *Star*,

13 January 2014, available at: www.the-star.co.ke/news/article-150425/firefighter-first-loot-westgate-mall-says-kdf#sthash.Wd05Tivm.dpuf (accessed 18 January 2014).

4 Republic of Kenya, Kenya National Assembly, *Report of the Joint Committee on Administration and National Security; and Defence and Foreign Relations on the Inquiry into the Westgate Terrorist Attack and Other Terror Attacks in Mandera in North-Eastern and Kilifi in the Coastal Region* (Nairobi: Clerk's Chambers, 2013); *Aftenposten*, 'PST har ventet på FBI. Nå er konklusjonen i Westgate-saken klar,' *Aftenposten*, 3 September 2015, available at: www.aftenposten.no/nyheter/iriks/PST-har-ventet-pa-FBI-Na-er-konklusjonen-i-Westgate-saken-klar-8149381.html (accessed 10 September 2015).

5 National Consortium for the Study of Terrorism and Responses to Terrorism (START), *Background Report: Al Shabaab Attack on Westgate Mall in Kenya* (Baltimore, MD: START, 2013), available at: www.start.umd.edu/sites/default/files/publications/local_attachments/STARTBackgroundReport_alShabaabKenya_Sept2013.pdf (accessed 28 April 2016); Republic of Kenya, Kenya National Assembly, *Report of the Joint Committee on Administration and National Security; and Defence and Foreign Relations on the Inquiry into the Westgate Terrorist Attack and Other Terror Attacks in Mandera in North-Eastern and Kilifi in the Coastal Region* (Nairobi: Clerk's Chambers, 2013), pp. 12–15.

6 *Reuters*, 'Kenyan security agencies ignored warnings before Westgate attack: Report,' *Reuters*, 26 January 2014, available at: www.reuters.com/article/us-kenya-westgate/kenyan-security-agencies-ignored-warnings-before-westgate-attack-report-idUSBREA0P09620140126 (accessed 27 January 2014).

7 On the continuities of police impunity, politically motivated persecution and corruption over time, see Truth, Justice and Reconciliation Commission (TJRC), *Report of the Truth, Justice, and Reconciliation Commission*, vol. IIA, 17 May 2013 version (Nairobi: TJRC, 2013), available at: http://digitalcommons.law.seattleu.edu/tjrc/6 (accessed 21 April 2015).

8 David Anderson, *Histories of the Hanged: The Dirty War in Kenya and the End of Empire* (New York: W.W. Norton, 2005); Caroline Elkins, *Imperial Reckoning: The Untold Story of Britain's Gulag in Kenya* (New York: Henry Holt, 2005); Daniel Branch, *Defeating Mau Mau, Creating Kenya: Counterinsurgency, Civil War, and Decolonization* (New York: Cambridge, 2009).

9 Daniel Branch, 'Loyalists, Mau Mau, and elections in Kenya: The first triumph of the system, 1957–1958,' *Africa Today* 53:2 (2006): 27–50; 'The politics of control in Kenya: Understanding the bureaucratic-executive state, 1952–78,' *Review of African Political Economy* 107 (2006): 11–31.

10 On extrajudicial executions and disappearances as well as impunity enjoyed by the security forces, see Kenya National Commission on Human Rights, *'The Cry of Blood': Report on Extra-Judicial Killings and Disappearances*, September 2008, available at: file.wikileaks.org/file/kenya-the-cry-of-blood/crimes-against-humanity-extra-judicial-killings-by-kenya-police-exposed.pdf (accessed 20 December 2014); United Nations Human Rights Council, 'Report of the Special Rapporteur on extrajudicial, summary or arbitrary executions, Philip Alston: Addendum: Mission to Kenya,' 26 May 2009, available at: reliefweb.int/sites/reliefweb.int/files/resources/15D4D9C184ADDBAA492575C90024524F-Full_Report.pdf (accessed 26 May 2018).

11 Harmony Project, *Al-Qaida's (Mis)Adventures in the Horn of Africa* (West Point, NY: Combating Terrorism Center at the US Military Academy, 2007).

12 *Independent Online*, 'FBI interrogations incur Muslim wrath', *Independent Online* (South Africa), 30 May 2000, available at: www.iol.co.za/news/africa/fbi-interrogations-incur-muslim-wrath-39059 (accessed 26 May 2018); Katy Salmon, 'Muslims say FBI targets them,' *Inter Press Service*, 6 March 2003, available at: https://advance.lexis.com/document/?pdmfid=1516831&crid=130a91f8-61c7-42c4-83ee-3dbf31c12ab7&pddocfullpath=%2Fshared%2Fdocument%2Fnews%2Furn%3AcontentItem%3A4835-1MF0-001G-V1K6-00000-00&pddocid=urn%3AcontentItem%3A4835-1MF0-001G-V1K6-00000-00&pdcontentcomponentid=8001&pdteaserkey=sr0&pditab=allpods&ecomp=Ly3k&earg=sr0&prid=36c564de-98d1-46fd-a2b2-c4682c23b44b (accessed 26 May 2018).

13 Jeremy Prestholdt, 'Politics of the soil: Separatism, autochthony, and decolonization at the Kenyan coast,' *Journal of African History* 55:2 (2014): 249–70; James R. Brennan, 'Lowering the sultan's flag: Sovereignty and decolonization in coastal Kenya,' *Comparatives Studies in Society and History* 50:4 (2008): 831–61.

14 Keren Weitzberg, *We Do Not Have Borders: Greater Somalia and the Predicaments of Belonging in Kenya* (Athens, OH: Ohio University Press, 2017); Hannah Whittaker, 'Legacies of empire: State violence and collective punishment in Kenya's North Eastern Province, c. 1963–present,' *Journal of Imperial and Commonwealth History* 43:4 (2015): 641–57; *Insurgency and Counterinsurgency in Kenya: A Social History of the Shifta Conflict, c. 1963–1968* (Leiden: Brill, 2014); 'Forced villagization during the shifta conflict in Kenya, c. 1963–8,' *International Journal of African Historical Studies* 45:3 (2012): 343–64.

15 David M. Anderson, 'Remembering Wagalla: State violence in northern Kenya, 1962–1991,' *Journal of Eastern African Studies* 8:4 (2014): 658–76.

16 Hassan Juma Ndzovu, 'The politicization of Muslim organizations and the future of Islamic-oriented politics in Kenya,' *Islamic Africa* 3:1 (2012): 25–53.

17 Francis Thoya, 'Suspects go to court to halt FBI extradition bid,' *Daily Nation*, 13 November 2001.

18 Timothy Kalyegira, 'Kenya's Muslims protest new passport laws,' *United Press International*, 26 November 2001, available at: https://advance.lexis.com/document/?pdmfid=1516831&crid=d7e5944d-8ace-41fb-b2ad-0e55f5268dd2&pddocfullpath=%2Fshared%2Fdocument%2Fnews%2Furn%3AcontentItem%3A442W-JFD0-00RC-81SM-00000-00&pddocid=urn%3AcontentItem%3A442W-JFD0-00RC-81SM-00000-00&pdcontentcomponentid=8076&pdteaserkey=sr0&pditab=allpods&ecomp=Ly3k&earg=sr0&prid=d9492301-6a1f-46fe-a948-2e1b59250e62 (accessed 26 May 2018).

19 For a wider perspective on the experiences of East African Muslims after September 11th, see Faraj Abdullah Tamim and Malinda Smith, 'Muslims in post-9/11 East Africa,' in Malinda Smith (ed.), *Securing Africa: Post-9/11 Discourses on Terrorism* (Burlington, VT: Ashgate, 2010), pp. 99–125.

20 Ahmed Issak Hassan, 'Pitfalls of the anti-terrorism bill,' *Daily Nation*, 27 June 2003. A modified bill, the Prevention of Terrorism Act No. 30, passed nearly a decade later. Thomas Harding and Mike Pflanz, 'Kenyan troops accused of torture "were trained by SAS,"' *Telegraph* (UK), 28 July 2008, available at:

www.telegraph.co.uk/news/worldnews/africaandindianocean/kenya/2466432/Kenyan-troops-accused-of-torture-were-trained-by-SAS.html (accessed 10 April 2015); 'Kibaki signs historic anti-terrorism bill,' *Standard*, 14 October 2012.

21 United States Department of State (USDS), *The Anti-Terrorism Assistance Program: Report to Congress for Fiscal Year 2003* (Washington, DC: USDS, 2004) available at: www.state.gov/documents/organization/35833.pdf (accessed 6 September 2012), pp. 2–3; Greg Mills, 'Africa's new strategic significance,' in John Davis (ed.), *Africa and the War on Terrorism* (Burlington, VT: Ashgate, 2007), pp. 17–30.

22 USDS, *Country Reports on Terrorism 2008* (Washington, DC: USDS Office of the Coordinator for Counterterrorism, 2009); Cyrus Ombati, 'US envoy hands over anti-terror unit to Kenya,' Standard Digital website, 31 March 2014, available at: www.standardmedia.co.ke/article/2000108323/us-envoy-hands-over-anti-terror-unit-to-kenya (accessed 2 April 2014).

23 S.L. Aronson, 'United States aid to Kenya: Regional security and counterterrorism assistance before and after 9/11,' *Student Pulse*, 2 March 2011, available at: www.studentpulse.com/a?id=393 (accessed 23 August 2011); Alice Hills, 'Trojan horses? USAID, counter-terrorism and Africa's police,' *Third World Quarterly* 27:4 (2006): 629–43. On the continuities of military aid between the Cold War and the War on Terrorism, see Elizabeth Schmidt, *Foreign Intervention in Africa: From the Cold War to the War on Terror* (Cambridge, UK: Cambridge University Press, 2013).

24 Muslims for Human Rights (MUHURI), *Impact of Insecurity on Human Rights at the Coast* (Mombasa: MUHURI, 2007).

25 Jeremy Prestholdt, 'Kenya, the United States, and counterterorrism,' *Africa Today* 57:4 (2011): 12–14.

26 *Nation* Correspondent, 'Police defend raid on three Muslim houses,' *Daily Nation*, 28 April 2007; *Standard* Reporter, 'State deports Muslim cleric,' *East African Standard*, 7 May 2007. In June 2011 Fazul Abdullah Muhammad was killed at a government checkpoint in Mogadishu as he was crossing from al Shabaab territory into a suburb controlled by the Transitional Federal Government; H. Omar, 'Somali soldier who killed al-Qaeda leader is shot in retaliation,' *Bloomberg*, 17 August 2011, available at: www.bloomberg.com/news/2011-08-17/somali-soldier-who-killed-al-qaeda-leader-is-shot-in-retaliation.html (accessed 2 September 2011).

27 C. Barnes and H. Hassan, 'The rise and fall of Mogadishu's Islamic courts,' *Journal of Eastern African Studies* 1:2 (2007): 151–60.

28 Stig Jarle Hansen, *Al-Shabaab in Somalia: The History and Ideology of a Militant Islamist Group* (New York: Oxford University Press, 2013).

29 Human Rights Watch, *Why Am I Still Here? The 2007 Horn of Africa Renditions and the Fate of Those Still Missing* (New York: Human Rights Watch, 2008).

30 A. Kimathi and A. Butt (eds), *Horn of Terror: Report of US-Led Mass Extraordinary Renditions from Kenya to Somalia, Ethiopia and Guantanamo Bay, January–June* (Nairobi: Muslim Human Rights Forum, 2007); Xan Rice, 'Africa's secret: The men, women and children "vanished" in the war on terror,' *Guardian*, 23 April 2007.

31 Human Rights Watch, *Why Am I Still Here?*

32 'Jeremy Scahill reveals CIA facility, prison in Somalia as US expands covert ops in stricken nation,' *Democracy Now*, 13 July 2011, available at:

www.democracynow.org/2011/7/13/jeremy_scahill_reveals_cia_facility_prison (accessed 16 July 2011).

33 Hansen, *Al-Shabaab in Somalia.*

34 Roland Marchal, 'A tentative assessment of the Somali Harakat Al-Shabaab,' *Journal of Eastern African Studies* 3:3 (2009): 381–404; Stig Jarle Hansen, 'Revenge or reward? The case of Somalia's suicide bombers,' *Journal of Terrorism Research* 1:1 (2010): 15–40.

35 Aboud Rogo, 'Mawaidha,' *YouTube*, n.d., available at: www.youtube.com/watch?v=i1UPnkYRn7E (accessed 3 March 2015).

36 Nyambega Gisesa, 'The making of a Kenyan terrorist commander,' *Daily Nation*, 22 January 2012.

37 David M. Anderson, 'Why Mpeketoni matters: Al Shabaab and violence in Kenya,' Norwegian Peacebuilding Resource Centre, September 2014, http://peacebuilding.no/eng/Regions/Africa/Publications/Why-Mpeketoni-matters-al-Shabaab-and-violence-in-Kenya (no longer available; accessed 1 May 2016); Fredrick Nzes, 'Al-Hijra: Al-Shabab's affiliate in Kenya,' *CTC Sentinel* 7:5 (2014): 24–6.

38 David M. Anderson and Jacob McKnight, 'Understanding al-Shabaab: Clan, Islam and insurgency in Kenya,' *Journal of Eastern African Studies* 9:3 (2015): 544; Stephanie Findlay, 'Kenya faces homegrown threat from al-Shabaab,' *Time*, 1 July 2014, available at: http://time.com/2941402/kenya-faces-homegrown-threat-from-al-shabab (accessed 2 May 2016).

39 David M. Anderson and Jacob McKnight, 'Kenya at war: Al Shabaab and its enemies in eastern Africa,' *African Affairs* 114:454 (2015): 1–27.

40 Anderson and McKnight, 'Kenya at war.'

41 'Press statement by US Ambassador to Kenya Robert F. Godec on security in Kenya,' US Embassy in Kenya website, 21 June 2014, available at: https://ke.usembassy.gov/press-statement-by-us-ambassador-to-kenya-robert-f-godec-on-security-in-kenya (accessed 26 May 2018).

42 *Times Live*, 'Islamists blamed for Nairobi church killing,' *Times Live*, 30 April 2012, available at: http://somaliamediamonitoring.org/april-30-2012-daily-monitoring-report/ (accessed 26 May 2018); Human Rights Watch reported the beating, torture and rape of hundreds of Somali refugees after these attacks; Human Rights Watch, 'World report 2014: Kenya,' Human Rights Watch website, n.d., available at: www.hrw.org/world-report/2014/country-chapters/kenya (accessed 13 January 2018).

43 Anderson and McKnight, 'Understanding al-Shabaab,' 536–57; Mark Lowen, 'Kenya al-Shabab terror recruits "in it for the money,"' *BBC News*, 29 January 2014, available at: www.bbc.com/news/world-africa-25934109 (accessed 5 April 2014).

44 Jonathan Horowitz, *Counterterrorism and Human Rights Abuses in Kenya and Uganda: The World Cup Bombing and Beyond* (n.p.: Open Society Justice Initiative, 2012), p. 22, available at: http://reliefweb.int/sites/reliefweb.int/files/resources/counterterrorism-human-rights-abuses-kenya-uganda-20121127.pdf (accessed 10 April 2015).

45 *Al Jazeera*, 'Inside Kenya's death squads,' *Al Jazeera*, 8 December 2014, available at: http://interactive.aljazeera.com/aje/KenyaDeathSquads/#film (accessed 18 April 2016); Joseph Akwiri, 'Kenya to investigate Al Jazeera allegations of "death squads,"' *Reuters*, 10 December 2014, available at: www.reuters.com/article/us-kenya-security-media-idUSKBN0JO1OV20141210 (accessed 13 January 2018).

46 For instance, soon after the Aboud Rogo murder, an associate who also preached at Masjid Musa, Sheikh Ibrahim Omar Rogo, and three others travelling with him were killed in a similar manner; Jonathan Horowitz, 'Assassinations, disappearances, and riots: What's happening in Mombasa?' Open Society Justice Initiative website, 29 August 2012, available at: www.soros.org/voices/assassinations-disappearances-and-riots-what-s-happening-mombasa (accessed 11 September 2012).

47 *Jicho Pevu*, Kenya Television Network, 23 March 2013. For additional cases of alleged police abuse, including extrajudicial executions, in the years that followed, see Haki Africa, *What Do We Tell the Families?: Killings and Disappearances in the Coastal Region of Kenya, 2012–2016*, Haki Africa website, December 2016, available at: hakiafrica.or.ke/wp-content/uploads/2017/02/HakiAfricaWDWTTF_V14.pdf (accessed 9 December 2016), and the Open Society Justice Initiative and Muslims for Human Rights, *'We're Tired of Taking You to the Court': Human Rights Abuses by Kenya's Anti-Terrorism Police Unit* (New York: Open Society Foundations, 2013).

48 Philip Mwakio, 'Muslim youth extremism out of hand, warn leaders,' *Standard*, 24 December 2013, available at: www.standardmedia.co.ke/thecounties/article/2000100745/muslim-youth-extremism-out-of-hand-warn-leaders (accessed 4 January 2014).

49 William Oketch, Ngumbao Kithi and Philip Mwakio, 'Foreigners among Mombasa mosque chaos suspects,' *Standard*, 6 February 2014, available at: www.standardmedia.co.ke/?articleID=2000104030&story_title=foreigners-among-mombasa-mosque-chaos-suspects&pageNo=2 (accessed 30 March 2015).

50 Amnesty International, 'Somalis are scapegoats in Kenya's counter-terror crackdown,' Amnesty International website, 27 May 2014, available at: www.amnesty.org/en/documents/AFR52/003/2014/en (accessed 11 April 2015).

51 Bosire Boniface, 'Kenya's collective punishment plan draws praise and alarm,' AllAfrica website, 21 January 2015, available at: http://allafrica.com/stories/201501220325.html (accessed 7 April 2015).

52 Simon Ndonga, 'Kenya: Shoot to kill order against Likoni attackers,' *Capital FM*, 26 March 2014.

53 'Gunned down in Mombasa: The clerics that have died,' UN Integrated Regional Information Networks website, 28 July 2014, available at: www.irinnews.org/report/100412/gunned-down-in-mombasa-the-clerics-that-have-died (accessed 20 December 2014).

54 AFP, 'Somalia's Al-Shabaab chief says war "shifting to Kenya,"' *East African*, 22 May 2014.

55 'A message by brother Ahmad Iman Ali regarding the Bay'ah of the Mujahideen,' Al Kataib Media, 25 April 2012, available at: https://archive.org/details/messahmad0412_kataib (accessed 29 April 2016).

56 *Gaidi Mtaani*, issue 3, 2012, available at: jihadology.net/2013/03/03/new-issue-of-the-magazine-gaidi-mtaani-issue-3 (accessed 30 March 2015).

57 Hussein Khalid, *Mpeketoni Killings: Human Rights Fact Finding Report*, July 2014, available at: http://hakiafrica.or.ke/wp-content/uploads/2017/02/Haki%20Africa%20-%20Mpeketoni%20Booklet%20FINAL.pdf (accessed 25 May 2018); Mary Harper, 'Kenyan coastal region of Lamu hit by deadly attacks,' *BBC*

News, 6 July 2014, available at: www.bbc.com/news/world-africa-28181246 (accessed 8 July 2014).

58 Hassan Mwakimako and Justin Willis, *Islam, Politics, and Violence on the Kenyan Coast*, Observatoire des Enjeux Politiques et Sécuritaires dans la Corne de l'Afrique, note 4, July 2014, available at: www.lam.sciencespobordeaux.fr/sites/lam/files/note4_observatoire.pdf (accessed 4 December 2014).

59 'Propaganda is effective weapon as al-Shabaab makes resurgence,' *PBS News Hour*, 22 April 2016, 7.43 p.m. EDT, transcript available at: www.pbs.org/newshour/bb/propaganda-is-effective-weapon-as-al-shabab-makes-resurgence (accessed 27 April 2016); Tomi Oladipo, 'What happened when al Shabaab attacked a Kenyan base in Somalia?' *BBC News*, 22 January 2016, available at: www.bbc.com/news/world-africa-35364593 (accessed 27 April 2016).

60 Elsa Buchanan, 'Kenya Garissa University: Death toll "as high as 150" and 315 unaccounted for as al-Shabaab siege ends,' *International Business Times*, 2 April 2015 (updated 14 July 2016), available at: www.ibtimes.co.uk/garissa-university-attack-four-dead-40-wounded-gunmen-storm-kenyan-college-1494693 (accessed 20 May 2018).

61 *Daily Nation*, 'Monster who led Shabaab mass killers is unmasked,' *Daily Nation*, 5 April 2015.

62 Hussein Khalid, 'Kenya's wrongheaded approach to terrorism,' *Washington Post*, 1 May 2015; *BBC News*, 'Kenya court rules Haki Africa and MHR not terrorists,' *BBC News*, 11 June 2015, available at: www.bbc.com/news/world-africa-33092786 (accessed 27 August 2015).

63 Barack Obama, 'Remarks by President Obama to the Kenyan people,' 26 July 2015, available at: www.whitehouse.gov/the-press-office/2015/07/26/remarks-president-obama-kenyan-people (accessed 25 April 2016).

64 White House, Office of the Press Secretary, 'Fact Sheet: Security Governance Initiative,' White House, President Barack Obama website, 6 August 2014, available at: www.whitehouse.gov/the-press-office/2014/08/06/fact-sheet-security-governance-initiative (accessed 28 April 2016).

65 Bureau of African Affairs, *Security Governance Initiative, 2015 Review*, US Department of State website, 2 March 2016, available at: www.state.gov/documents/organization/254115.pdf (accessed 28 April 2016).

66 Lizzie Dearden, 'Isis: New terrorist group Jahba East Africa pledges allegiance to "Islamic State" in Somalia,' *Independent*, 8 April 2016.

67 *Star*, 'Kenya: Insecurity hammers tourism as arrivals plunge by 31 percent,' *Star*, 21 April 2015, available at: http://allafrica.com/stories/201504210127.html (accessed 28 April 2015).

16

A vicious cycle: The growth of terrorism and counterterrorism in Nigeria, 1999–2016

Jennifer Giroux and Michael Nwankpa

Introduction

Most discussions about terrorism in Nigeria – and, indeed, Africa more broadly – tend to be about the Nigerian-based group referred to as Boko Haram – and for good reason. Formed in the early 2000s out of a small religious sect in the northeast of Nigeria, over the years Boko Haram has become an increasingly violent force that evolved into a full-blown insurgency in 2009 – a year that is also notable as it marked the decline of a completely different insurgency in Nigeria's Niger Delta region in the south. Since then, sustained violence has resulted in over 20,000 deaths,[1] and caused more than two million people to flee their homes and many more to live in a constant state of fear.[2] In fact, due to the volume and brutality of its tactics – which include mass abductions, suicide bombings and indiscriminate killings – Nigeria soon found itself at the top of global terrorism statistics. According to the Institute for Economies and Peace (IEP) *Global Terrorism Index*, Nigeria experienced 7,512 fatalities in 2014 – 6,644 of which were attributed to Boko Haram. Notably, this was an increase of over 300 per cent from 2013. As the IEP reported, Nigeria experienced the largest increase in deaths from terrorism in 2014 and became home to the deadliest terrorist group in the world.[3] In another report, the Institute for National Security Studies (INSS) also found that the 'number of suicide attacks in Africa soared 157 per cent in 2015', largely due to Boko

Haram who carried out 122 suicide attacks – 96 of which took place in Nigeria (up from 32 in 2014) and 'the rest in Cameroon (13), Chad (8), and Niger (5)'.[4] Interestingly, women (mostly teenage girls) carried out nearly half of these suicide attacks – a trend that has concerned and perplexed many.[5]

Apart from volume and brutality, another factor that has kept Boko Haram top-of-mind in conversations about terrorism in Nigeria is the way in which the group has evolved. Boko Haram grew in international prominence after its leader Abubakar Shekau pledged allegiance to ISIL (Islamic State in Iraq and the Levant, but also known as IS and ISIS) and it subsequently became known as Wilayat West Africa (more or less a combination of affiliated groups). Indeed, this development highlights one of the key aspects that distinguishes Boko Haram from other domestic groups: its links to a broader narrative of conservative beliefs and Western oppression espoused by other Islamic fundamentalist groups, many of which are carrying out deadly attacks in Syria and Iraq, among other countries. In addition, Fulani militants – a group of individuals from the Fula ethnic group who operate in the middle belt and northeast regions in Nigeria as well as parts of the Central African Republic – ramped up their own violent activities.

Against this backdrop it thus makes sense why the literature on terrorism in Nigeria has focused so intensely on Boko Haram. Studies have dissected various dimensions of the group, such as its history,[6] tactics,[7] and theories of expansion;[8] others have argued for counter-strategies,[9] or critiqued the government's responses,[10] as well as the way in which security policies have evolved.[11] But while such analyses are clearly important for any conversation on terrorism in Nigeria, they provide a limited view and understanding of terrorism in Nigeria. Indeed, since the early 1990s, terrorism has been part of various violent conflicts that cut across the country, typically accompanied by harsh and aggressive government responses that increasingly sit under the banner of counterterrorism. Before Boko Haram turned to violence, for example, the oil- and gas-producing Niger Delta region (in the south) was home to numerous violent non-state groups that used various tactics, including terrorism, as part of their politically violent campaigns for resource control and regional development. In fact, that continues to this day. In early 2016 the 'Niger Delta Avengers' (NDA) launched and became a group that, like many before it, targeted oil and gas infrastructure as a way to terrorize the energy industry, air its grievances and hit the government where it hurts: in its pockets.[12] The Nigerian Government responded – as it has done in the north – by deploying the military, leading some to see this as an emerging extension of its fight against terrorism.[13] However, despite such national dynamics and trends, terrorism in Nigeria continues to be seen as isolated phenomena that have regional dimensions rather than as connected dots in a broader pattern of violence. This leaves a critical gap in the understanding of terrorism in Nigeria.

Beyond Boko Haram: Making sense of the growth of terrorism in Nigeria

Between 1999 and 2018 there have been four consecutive democratically elected presidents – all of whom have struggled with various and often overlapping violent phenomena – criminal, intra- and inter-communal, ethno-sectarian, political, and separatist – that stretch across the country, at times impacting the stability of specific regions and at other times the very stability of the state.[14] Within this there have been a few notable developments. On the one hand, terrorism has increasingly become a tactic that various non-state groups, not just those in the northeast, use in their violent campaigns.[15] On the other hand, over time, the government has become more prone to referring to various expressions of violence – even violent robberies – as acts of terrorism.[16] This has encouraged the formation of a counterterrorism framework within its national security agenda. In addition, rather than addressing the grievances that fuel violence, government responses to violence have increasingly involved the military. Indeed, the fact that Nigerian military personnel are now deployed in twenty-eight out of the thirty-six states is illustrative of this trend.[17] As former National Security Advisor Colonel Sambo Dasuki shared in 2013: 'From mere intervention to assisting the police quell domestic violence; the military is now fighting the scourge of insurgency and terrorism. Thus, the military presence in our society is becoming routine.'[18]

Considering these domestic security trends, the period 1999–2016 is important for another reason. In 2001, the September 11th terrorist attacks on Washington, DC, and New York ushered in an era of aggressive policy responses aimed at countering terrorism, with a focus on radical Islamist groups like al Qaeda. With the US leading the charge via its global 'War on Terror' (GWOT), states and intergovernmental organizations created a number of counterterrorism initiatives and programmes that have since grown and expanded. The US took an early interest in improving security in Africa, with a particular focus on Nigeria, which it considers a key strategic partner.[19] Not only is the US the largest bilateral donor in Nigeria – providing more than $600 million annually in recent years – but since 2001 it has consistently provided the country, and the region more broadly, with support and resources that are targeted towards improving security and countering terrorism.[20] While it's certainly interesting to question how the US conceptualization of terrorism – and, within that, its counterterrorism activities – has influenced Nigeria's own understanding of terrorism, it also raises another key question: why has this increased support not led to an improved security situation in Nigeria?

This chapter aims to make sense of the growth of terrorism in Nigeria, and in doing so trace how the conceptualization of terrorism has changed over time. By examining security challenges in Nigeria over the period 1999–2016, this chapter will show how the increase of domestic terrorism is connected to a broader story of violence that cuts across the country – one in which weak policing and legal authority, combined with the heavy-handed military responses that are increasingly used to quell violence, are actually major drivers of violence.[21] In addition, it will show how international, particularly US, counterterrorism initiatives and programmes have played a role in Nigeria, but rendered little return in the form of an improved security environment.

As follows, the analysis is conceptualized into four key phases or, rather, waves of violence. The first and second phases (1999–2001 and 2002–5) examine the societal impact of Nigeria's transformation from military to democratic rule, the violence that characterized this period and how the GWOT that emerged following 2001 began to impact the country. Following this the chapter delves into the third phase (2005–9), where it places a spotlight on the escalation of violence in the Niger Delta and reveals the role that terrorism played both in the insurgency and in policy debates. Finally, in the fourth phase (2009–16) it shows how terrorism has not only become a defining tactic of violence used in the northeast and Middle Belt regions, but also reached the level of daily discourse – one in which terrorism has become a blanket term for various expressions of violence. It bears mentioning that the understanding of terrorism used here aligns with the academic literature, which broadly defines terrorism as a tactic of political violence that includes the use, or threat of use, of violence/force against civilians, with political motivation and the intent to induce fear in a population to force some form of (re)action.[22] Importantly, this definition will be used in the analysis to compare and contrast this understanding to the way that terrorism is framed both in public discourse (e.g., in the media) and in policy.

From military to civilian rule (1999–2001)

As Swampson and Onuoha note, 'Nigeria has a history of violent acts that could have been labelled as terrorism';[23] however, it wasn't till the 1990s that (counter)terrorism began to have a place, though nebulous, in national security. Following the annulment of the 1993 general elections and during General Sani Abacha's abusive and corrupt regime (1993–98), there were a few noteworthy politically motivated – indeed, terrorist – attacks. The first was the October 1993 hijacking of a Nigerian airliner (travelling from Lagos to Abuja) that was claimed by the Movement for the Advancement of Democracy (MAD), whose mission, according to its leader, was to 'terrorise the few people who have terrorised us politically and economically (in order) to recover the money stolen from us.'[24] Following this, in 1995–97, there was a series of bombings in a number of major cities such as Ilorin, Lagos, Kaduna and Onitsha.[25] Such attacks, as well as the growing public frustration with the government, prompted Abacha to create a 'Task Force on Terrorism' (also referred to as the 'Task Force on Bomb Blasts and Terrorism').[26] Though arrests were made through this task force, it's unclear how it, or the government for that matter, conceptualized terrorism or distinguished it from any other violent act. The fact that terrorism was not even found in the country's penal code, although the police were arresting individuals for alleged terrorist acts, reveals perhaps another motive – one in which the authorities conceptualized terrorism as a way to label and indeed demonize perceived enemies of the state, rather than as a term that distinguished one violent act from another. In fact, one of the key criticisms of the task force was its targeting of journalists and human rights activists – actors who were leading the criticism of Abacha's regime and advocating for change.[27]

When Nigeria returned to civilian rule in 1999 with the election of Olusegun Obasanjo, it was the beginning of a new era on many fronts. First, it marked the end of the US ban on aid to the Nigerian military[28] – a ban that began during the Abacha regime due to its human rights abuses – and the beginning of a new era of bilateral relations between the two countries in which counterterrorism would play a major role. Second, it was the start of a more serious continental counterterrorism dialogue – one that was driven by the impact of the 1998 US embassy bombings in Kenya and Tanzania. In light of these attacks, the US ramped up its counterterrorism efforts in East Africa while the Organization of African Unity (OAU, but now AU) adopted the Convention on the Prevention and Combating on Terrorism, which both defined terrorism and marked the first continental legislative instrument on countering it.[29] Nigeria not only joined in this convention but it also ratified the International Convention for the Suppression of the Financing of Terrorism – both measures taken as it celebrated its own democratic achievements, yet still lacked its own internal understanding of terrorism. Third, and finally, it marked the beginning of domestic security challenges that would eventually fuel the growth of terrorism in the country.

A kaleidoscope of security challenges takes shape

Shortly after the 1999 elections, violence began to increase in various parts of the country as ethnic groups began to compete – both with each other (e.g. the Ijaw versus Itsekiri, Tiv versus Jukun, Ife versus Modakeke) and also with the Nigerian state – for power and influence. This was largely due to the fact that when Obasanjo took office the country was in a very fragile state, with poor socio-economic and divisive political structures. Despite the tremendous potential of its economy and large natural-resource (oil and gas) wealth, years of corruption and poor governance had not only robbed the state but also paralysed any form of meaningful development. Roads were abysmal, jobs were few and electricity was largely absent. Added to this, the country was also reeling from nearly twenty years of brutal and corrupt military rule, during which the government mishandled and fuelled over sixty conflicts that occurred throughout the country, resulting in nearly 9,000 fatalities between 1985 and 1999 alone.[30] Indeed, such brutality left an indelible mark on the populace – one which Imobighe and Eguavoen characterize as a public 'psyche that embraces force, routine violence, and instinctively shies away from debate and dialogue, the two all-important props without which a truly democratic edifice cannot stand'.[31] It was therefore not long after the transition to civilian rule that aggrieved people took advantage of the greater freedom and less repression that democracy offered by expressing their discontent against the Nigerian state and other community/ethnic groups, largely through violent means.[32]

Amid rising tensions, weak institutions that lacked the capacity to uphold the law and a growing sense of insecurity, various ethnic and geopolitical groups formed and became active in vigilantism, or what locals referred to as 'people', 'jungle', 'rough' or 'instant' justice. For example, in the southwest, the O'odua People's Congress (OPC), which sought to protect the interest of the Yorubas, gave birth to a more radical faction headed by Gani Adams, who led the group as it burned down police stations, killed law-enforcement officers and stole arms. Meanwhile, in the southeast states of Abia, Imo and Anambra, the Bakassi Boys (carved out of the Onitsha Trade Association vigilante group) carried out a string of extrajudicial killings as part of their mission to combat violent crime in the region. In the South South, or Niger Delta, region, the 1995 government execution of Ken Saro-Wiwa and eight other Ogoni activists – who protested economic exploitation, marginalization and abusive oil extraction practices – led the Ijaw, the largest ethnic group in the region, to organize and protest similar grievances.[33] By 1999, groups such as the Ijaw Youth Council and Egbesu Boys were formed to fight and advocate for greater resource control and environmental sustainability. And, finally, in the north, the Arewa People's Congress, allegedly formed by disgruntled northern political and military elites, was established to protect the interests of the Muslims in the region,[34] while several other state-led vigilante groups (known as Hisbah groups) were formed to enforce adherence to sharia (Islamic) law, which had been established by twelve northern states between 2000 and 2001[35] – a decision that fuelled ethnic conflicts in the North Central, or Middle Belt, region.[36]

Vigilantism – or the act of undertaking law enforcement without legal authority – emerges out of a context of insecurity and lawlessness. As Smith aptly notes, 'Vigilantism is a common response to ambiguities and ambivalence regarding authority of the state,'[37] and, for Nigeria in particular, years of military rule not only 'normalized violence' but also 'created an expectation that violence is an acceptable means for dealing with threats to social order'.[38] The formation of multiple vigilante groups around or shortly after 1999 was the public's way of dealing with a corrupt and abusive political system – one in which the police, and to a lesser extent the military, are not trusted and are often complicit in the very crimes that plague daily life. Such vigilante groups are typically made up of people from a community that share ethnic and/or religious ties. For a group like the Bakassi Boys, even though they did not have a clear ethnic and political agenda, they tapped into Igbo interests, pride and, ultimately, trust.[39]

Acts of violence carried out by such groups intensified over time and included public executions of criminals and destruction of property. In one extreme example, in May 2001 the Bakassi Boys publicly killed more than thirty alleged criminals – an act that prompted praise by local leaders but concern within the federal government.[40] The rise of such groups is an important component of this analysis, as they not only brought together many individuals who would later inspire or form violent movements that would use terrorism but also triggered harsh state responses from the federal government which wanted to bring an end to vigilante violence and quell the growing public disorder. Shutting down such movements was not simple, however, given their local popularity as well as a weak police force that lacked local trust, often perpetrated crimes and simply did not have the capacity to deal with the situation. This left the military – a stronger institution but one with its own set of problems; namely, that it was part and parcel of the history of oppression and human rights abuses that the Nigerian people had endured for over twenty years. It is thus unsurprising that as Obasanjo began to deploy the military to deal with community protests and violence it escalated matters. For instance, on 20 November 1999, six months into the first tenure of Obasanjo's presidency, the Odi massacre occurred in the Niger Delta region. Amid the rising protests in the region – much of it led at the time by the Ijaw Youth Council (IYC) and the Egbesu Boys – multiple small groups began to take shape. After an unknown armed gang killed a group of Nigerian policemen in Odi (Bayelsa state) President Obasanjo sent troops into Odi (and surrounding communities) where they destroyed buildings and homes, killed tens of unarmed civilians (with some estimates claiming over 2,000) and carried out acts of sexual violence.[41] In a similar situation just north of the Niger Delta region, the army killed over 100 civilians in Zaki Biam, Benue state, in 2001. This was yet another act of retaliatory justice – this time in response to the murder of nineteen soldiers by the Tiv ethnic militia group. In response, Human Rights Watch released the following statement: 'The security forces have a duty to protect, not to attack, the population. The murder of the 19 soldiers should certainly be condemned, but their deaths do not justify the slaughter of civilians by the Nigerian army.'[42]

By the end of 2001, while the world began to shift its attention to international terrorism in the wake of the September 11th attacks, the Nigerian Government was increasingly sending the army to deal with a range of violent phenomena that should have been managed by local officials. Consequently, law enforcement incapability and the army's heavy-handed approach meant that the issues and grievances fuelling the violence went unaddressed, and in most cases drove groups to adopt more aggressive tactics at a time when the fight against terrorism was becoming an international phenomenon.

Terrorism defined (2002–5): More 'security' but less secure

In late 2001, as Nigeria dealt with its own domestic security challenges, terrorism was elevated to the top of global security challenges. On the heels of the launch of the GWOT, as well as UN Security Council Resolution (UNSCR) 1368, 1373, and 1377 (which established the international community's commitment to combating terrorism), an international counterterrorism regime took shape and created new security partnerships and initiatives. This had a major impact for African countries, as the continent was put on the list of places to concentrate counterterrorism efforts – citing its ungoverned spaces and porous borders as potential havens for terrorist activity.[43]

Nigeria responded to the 9/11 attacks in two notable ways. On the one hand, its State Security Services (SSS), which suspected that there were al Qaeda affiliates or supporters in the north, began arresting suspected terrorists – one arrest in 2001 of seven Pakistanis in Ogun state and another arrest in

2002 of an Algerian.[44] Such arrests, however, were few and far between and none led to prosecution in court. On the other hand, not only did Nigeria ratify the OAU Convention on the Prevention and Combating of Terrorism, which went into force in 2002, but it also criminalized terrorism via the Economic and Financial Crimes Commission Act of 2002. In Article 40, it defines terrorism as:

> (a) any act which is a violation of the Criminal Code or the Penal Code and which may endanger the life, physical integrity or freedom of, or cause serious injury or death to, any person, any number or group of persons or causes or may cause damage to public property, natural resources, environmental or cultural heritage and is calculated or intended to (i) intimidate, put in fear, force, coerce or induce any government, body, institution, the general public or segment thereof, to do or abstain from doing any act or to adopt or abandon a particular standpoint, or to act according to certain principles, or (ii) disrupt any public service, the delivery of any essential service to the public or to create a public emergency, or (iii) create general insurrection in a state; (b) any promotion, sponsorship of, contribution to, command, aid, incitement, encouragement, attempt, threat, conspiracy, organization or procurement of any person, with the intent to commit any act referred to in paragraph (a) i, ii, and iii.[45]

In other sections, particularly Article 14 (1–2), terrorism financing and participation in or facilitation of a terrorist attack are also criminalized.

This conceptualization is not only incredibly broad but also influenced by the international and sub-regional context – one in which Nigeria jumped on board the emerging international counterterrorism movement and was soon pushed to comply with the OAU convention and UNSCR 1373 by creating the legislative framework to criminalize terrorism. But rather than developing its own conceptualization of terrorism, Nigeria adopted the same definition, nearly word for word, of the OAU convention.[46] In other words, there was no internal debate on defining terrorism, nor even a perceived domestic need to codify terrorism within Nigeria's penal code, despite growing security challenges in the country as well as the alleged arrests by the SSS. While this may suggest that Nigeria was adopting a sub-regional perspective on terrorism, it also points to institutional weakness and a lack of internal understanding. At this time, violence was – and in many ways continues to be – viewed through the lens of politics, poverty, ethnicity, and so on. Terrorism was not seen as a tactic of political violence but rather as a form of profiling or demonizing one group or one cause, or distinguishing it from another. By adopting the same definition as the OAU convention, Nigeria was able to do its 'global duty' by criminalizing terrorism, while also avoiding an internal debate on what terrorism actually means.

Radical Islamism finds a home in the north while violence escalates in the Niger Delta

The rising global counterterrorism movement came at a time when frustrations and violence in Nigeria were beginning to escalate. In the north, Muhammed Yusuf, a Qur'anic scholar and preacher in Maiduguri, Borno state, launched a radical Islamist group in 2002 known as Jamā'at Ahl as-Sunnah lid-da'wa wal-Jihād (JAS; Arabic for 'the congregation of the people of tradition for proselytism and jihad'). JAS, which would later become known as Boko Haram, was made up of ethnic Kanuri in Nigeria's poverty-ridden north, where it sought to establish an extremist Islamic state with a strict adherence to its own version of sharia law, which included forbidding Western education, particularly to females. Such views, while extreme, were not uncommon in a region where religious and political extremism dates back to the 1970s. At that time the Maitatsine movement, which also opposed modernization and Western civilization, was formed and used shared grievances, such as economic and political marginalization, to mobilize local, mainly impoverished, communities and sow divisions. In a region where more than 70 per cent of the population lives in poverty, young, unemployed and unengaged men were – and continue to be – particularly susceptible to indoctrination.

While JAS initially emerged as a non-violent political organization that advocated for an Islamic government and criticized police brutality and political corruption, JAS members became increasingly frustrated by police harassment and unfulfilled promises from politicians to address grievances. Consequently the group splinted into more radical factions, such as the one led by Abubakar Shekau (who would later lead Boko Haram), and began to engage in more violent confrontations with local authorities. As one International Crisis Group (ICG) report described: 'In December 2003, the group, then called the Nigerian Taliban, attacked Kanamma, looted the police arsenal and burned down the station and some government buildings. A smaller faction then proceeded to Dapchi, where it attacked the police station and carted away additional arms; Babbangida town, where it burned down the local government secretariat and a government lodge; and Damaturu, where it stormed a police station, took guns and killed an officer.'[47] In response, the government sent in the army, which often led to more deaths than arrests. By 2005 this had only emboldened Yusuf, who hardened his message against the government and thus became more celebrated among the local population.

On a domestic level, JAS emerged out of a regional context of extremism in which many states in the north were instituting sharia law. As discussed, this fuelled religious tensions and gave political actors seeking regional autonomy a way to drive conflict. On an international level, however, JAS emerged as part of the 'global radicalization surge' inspired by al Qaeda, during which Osama bin Laden called on Muslims in countries like Nigeria to rise up in rebellion.[48] Naturally, northern elites were sensitive to any potential affiliation, perceived or otherwise, between al Qaeda and JAS and, more broadly, of Islam with terrorism. In fact, a draft counterterrorism bill that was presented to the Nigerian Senate in 2005 was withdrawn 'due to opposition from northern Senators who argued that the motivation for such a bill was anti-Muslim sentiment'.[49]

While tensions were heating up in the north, at the other end of the country – in the Niger Delta – protests and conflict that had emerged in the 1990s continued and began to shape-shift into other expressions of violence. The Niger Delta, which is made up of nine states in the south, is home to 140 different ethnic groups – most of whom live among the country's large oil and gas reserves. Like the north, the region was (and continues to be) poverty-ridden and underdeveloped due to years of government abuse and mismanagement. As Asuni notes, 'The federal government virtually ignored the Niger Delta during the 1990s, leaving development in the hands of the oil companies in an era when corporate social responsibility meant little.'[50] Though President Obasanjo attempted to address regional grievances in 2000 by increasing resource control (in the form of revenue) from 3 per cent to the current 13 per cent by replacing the Oil Minerals Producing Areas Development Commission (OMPADEC) with the Niger Delta Development Commission (NDDC), such measures failed to address the larger issues of oil exploitation, underdevelopment and environmental degradation.[51]

By 2002, as JAS emerged in the north, years of political manipulation, poor community engagement practices within the oil industry, and communal and ethnic conflicts had encouraged the formation of armed groups and arms proliferation in the Niger Delta. On the one hand, this led to an increase in threats to energy infrastructure by groups who demanded additional benefits from oil companies; on the other hand, it fuelled fights between ethnic groups over land, economic benefits or political power – sending communities into a tailspin. For example, between 1997 and 2003, the oil-producing city of Warri (Delta state) was the site of serious fighting, known as the 'Warri Crisis', between the Urhobo, Itsekiri and Ijaw ethnic groups.[52] In 2001, the government set up a 'Special Security Committee on Oil Producing Areas' and began deploying military personnel to the region, largely to protect oil installations. By 2003, however, the conflict was so bad that Shell and Chevron shut down much of its land-oil production. In response, the government ramped up the militarization of the region by sending in more security forces and establishing the Joint Task Force (JTF), which is made up of the army, police, navy, air force and the Department for State Security (DSS).

Though the influx of forces contributed to the restoration of order, it did not result in a more peaceful region overall. As a 2003 Human Rights Watch report on the Warri Crisis described, 'The government has not only failed to ensure that its security forces effectively protect civilians, but also that the police arrest, investigate and prosecute those guilty of murder and other crimes in relation to the violence.'[53] Such security tactics exacerbated underlying grievances and only pushed violence to other areas, where individuals found their way into the violent and criminal systems – some motivated by political grievances, others motivated by economic gains. In 2003, anti-corruption chief Nuhu Ribadu stated that 70 per cent of Nigeria's oil wealth was negatively affected by criminal activity, while the Nigerian National Petroleum Company (NNPC) reported that there were 400–500 yearly attacks on the oil industry, resulting in nearly US $1 billion in annual losses.[54] But such losses for the state meant economic gains for very powerful criminal groups, who vied for control. In 2004, the Niger Delta People's Volunteer Force (NDPVF) was launched in Rivers state, with the aim of securing local control of natural resources and political power. As other armed groups soon fell under its umbrella, the NDPVF escalated its oil-theft activities, which stimulated fights with other groups who were competing for power and money in the region. At the end of 2004, the NDPVF threatened to carry out a major attack aimed at all oil companies operating in the Niger Delta, if the government did not address the fundamental grievances in the region. While this threat led some in the media to label this an act of terrorism,[55] government actors looked at the violence in socio-economic terms and resisted giving it that label (similar to trends emerging in the north). Instead, fearful that the NDPVF would follow through on its threat, President Obasanjo quickly brokered a peace deal that included the allocation of jobs and other benefits. Unfortunately, corruption soon took hold of this process and unravelled the peace deal, thus reshuffling the deck and paving the way for new groups to form. As more JTF troops flooded the region, violence continued to escalate until it reached a full-blown insurgency in 2005.

Greater investments in security render small returns

During this period, as violence escalated in these two different regions, political actors were hesitant to use the word 'terrorism' for fear that counterterrorism efforts may be perceived as regional profiling and discrimination. Instead, the government responded to violent phenomena by either ignoring grievances – meaning it did not address the underlying socio-economic drivers of violence – or sending in the army, particularly when violence became potentially destabilizing or threatened state economic interests. The deployment of the army to handle various expressions of violence and civil disorder, however, was not just a problem because of the harsh tactics that military personnel would use but also because of the corruptive practices that came with them, such as extortion at checkpoints.[56] Meanwhile, the interest and will to professionalize the local police forces was lacking.

Granted, institutions do not change overnight; however, while Nigeria was grappling with significant domestic security challenges it was also participating in global counterterrorism efforts that brought increased funding for its security programs and initiatives, such as capacity building and training of public security personnel. In 2002 alone, the US established the Combined Joint Task Force (CJTF) Horn of Africa (HOA) to combat terrorism in the region; replaced the Africa Crisis Response Initiative, created in 1997, with the Africa Contingency Operations Training and Assistance (ACOTA) to enhance support of humanitarian and peace-building operations;[57] and launched the Pan Sahel Initiative (PSI), which sought to improve regional partnership and coordination of counterterrorism activities, as well as the security capabilities in Chad, Niger, Mauritania and Mali. In 2005, the US ramped up counterterrorism investments yet again, and expanded PSI into the Trans-Saharan Counterterrorism Initiative (TSCTI) in order to provide security training and support to a broader range of countries that stretched across the Sahel. As a leader in peacekeeping missions for the Economic Community of West African States (ECOWAS) and host of a peacekeeping centre in Jaji Military Cantonment (Kaduna), Nigeria became a key partner for the US and other nations supporting counterterrorism and security initiatives in Africa. In addition, its security officials participated in onshore and offshore security training and engagement activities with other member states.

With such capacity-building initiatives, one would assume that the Nigerian security agencies would become more effective over time in responding to and managing internal security challenges. The opposite seems to be true. If anything, by the end of 2005 security in Nigeria seemed to be worsening. But while we attempt to show how government responses to organized violence in Nigeria are the common denominator in conflict escalation, it is not hard to see how GWOT efforts reinforced this behaviour. Many of the programmes that were born out of the GWOT were largely driven by military efforts that employed harsh tactics, and came under review in 2004 via the UN High Commissioner for Human Rights.[58] In the following discussion, we return to the northeast and Niger Delta regions, where terrorism began to play more prominently in conflict theatre and security discourse, which in turn drove the government to further develop its own conceptual understanding of terrorism.

Terrorism in the age of insurgencies

With the government militarizing the Niger Delta and ignoring its development and environmental degradation, armed groups intensified the frequency and ferocity of attacks in the region. By the end of 2005, several militia groups had formed the Movement for the Emancipation of the Niger Delta (MEND) – an umbrella organization that was created with the intention to use military force to attack the oil and gas industry. The operative term here is 'military force'. Given the presence of the JTF, the armed groups resorted to stepping up attacks in order to force the government to address its regional grievances. After a small inaugural attack in December 2005, MEND kidnapped four foreign oil workers in January 2006 and demanded local resource control, a ransom payment of $1.5 billion (to be paid by Shell to Bayelsa state) and the release of prisoners. Soon after this attack, many more followed, sending the region into a full-blown insurgency.

By the end of the first quarter of 2006, the Nigerian Government had lost around US $1 billion in oil revenue due to MEND's attacks.[59] Beyond the sheer economic losses from these attacks, what was also notable about MEND was its use of terrorism in its violent campaign. For example, it bombed oil facilities and carried out kidnappings with the specific intent to target civilians in the energy industry, for a clear political cause, and with the intention to induce fear in the industry and government such that its demands would be met. After one attack in 2006, the group released the following statement: 'It must be clear that the Nigerian government cannot protect your workers or assets. Leave our land while you can or die in it. [...] Our aim is to totally destroy the capacity of the Nigerian government to export oil.'[60] Despite this, within Nigeria, a debate emerged around MEND's tactics and whether they constituted terrorism. For example, as MEND ramped up its attacks, Senator Emmanuel Paulker stated that 'the Senate would be mistaken to relate the genuine agitation of the Niger Delta people for justice to terrorism,'[61] while others examined its tactics and determined that the group was in fact committing acts of terrorism.[62] Essentially, many people, like Senator Paulker, sought to avoid labelling MEND's activities as terrorism for fear that it would delegitimize the real socio-economic grievances in the region.

In light of the tactics used by MEND as well as violence in other regions, the government returned to the terrorism debate and proposed another counterterrorism bill in 2007–8.[63] Interestingly, while one of the key contentions of previous debates was that the definition of terrorism was too broad and problematic, views began to shift during this period. During this debate, Senator Anyim Ude stated, 'With the high rate of militant activities in [the] Niger Delta, attack[s] on oil installation[s], kidnapping and other violent activities in the region, one wonders if we have not acquired a terrorist status. We need this bill to end it all.'[64] Alongside this debate, the government made other strides. For one, in 2007 it formed an inter-agency task force to improve coordination and communication on terrorism-related matters between the legislative and executive branches, and upgraded its airport security with US-funded body scanners. By the end of 2008, the heads of Nigeria's intelligence and security services were examining the terrorist threat in the region, while the police force launched an anti-terrorism squad (ATS) that was deployed to parts of the Niger Delta, as well as Lagos and Kano.

Although the government was making progress in conceptualizing terrorism, this shift had little impact on how it actually dealt with violence. Sending in the military was still the main strategy and aggressive tactics were the norm. This meant that the Niger Delta was soon flooded with more military personnel, many of whom were carrying out indiscriminate attacks on communities alleged to be hosting MEND or its affiliates. Meanwhile, offshore, the Nigerian navy increased its activities in the region, with the notable presence of thirteen warships, four helicopters and four boats patrolling the coast and waterways. Such efforts not only came with public complaints of abuses but they also failed to contain MEND's growth and reach – attacks persisted and oil revenue was cut by 50 per cent due to related losses.[65]

In spring 2009 the government ramped up its military efforts yet again – this time sending helicopters, ground troops and warships to attack MEND. Consequently, thousands of civilians fled their homes as communities were decimated by the bombings. Fortunately, after this the federal government proposed and reached an amnesty deal with MEND. In exchange for handing over arms, ammunition and equipment to the government and renouncing violence, the government promised reforms and other immediate benefits to the members of the armed groups that were costing more than $400 million every year. In this light, the amnesty programme is a payment scheme and tool of control rather than a solution to the Niger Delta crisis.[66]

As one insurgency ends another starts, and terrorism continues to grow

After 9/11, a global counterterrorism regime took shape and Nigeria, because of its size and influence in Africa, was a clear beneficiary of the increase in funds and support – through, for example, security training and capacity building – that came with it. The US increased its military assistance to Nigeria to US $11.1 million per year. In addition, Nigeria became the foremost beneficiary of ACOTA, which supported the training of 9,463 peacekeepers and 586 (peacekeeper) trainers, as well as providing a channel for bilateral assistance from international organizations like the UN Office for Drugs and Crime Terrorism Prevention Branch (TPB).[67] Despite this, its domestic security challenges were growing and becoming more complex by the day. In 2009, clashes emerged in the northeast, triggering an armed insurrection that brought a harsh military crackdown, which led to over 800 being killed. Yusuf was subsequently arrested and executed at police headquarters – paving the way for a more radical and violent leader, Abubakar Shekau, to assume control, and thus Boko Haram was born. It bears mentioning that at this time the government had the chance to crush the group and negotiate a deal to address key grievances;[68] however, in typical fashion it deployed more troops to the region – again, the parallels with the Niger Delta are striking.

Shortly after the 2009 clashes and the military clampdown, Shekau and other members of Boko Haram retreated to the Sahel and North Africa, where they reorganized and trained, in some cases with those affiliated with al Qaeda in Islamic Maghreb, al Shabaab and the Tuareg rebels in Mali. It wasn't until the death of President Umaru Musa Yar'Adua in 2010 that a new wave of violence emerged, and this soon moved to other areas. For instance, in 2011 Boko Haram carried out at least four major attacks in Abuja alone – including a Christmas Eve bombing of St Theresa's Catholic Church, and an attack aimed at the United Nations building where twenty-one persons died and about seventy-three were injured. In response, then US Secretary of State Hillary Clinton noted, 'We will stand with Nigeria as it faces serious security issues. The bombing of the UN headquarters in Abuja last month was a horrific and cowardly act, and we want to work with Nigeria and West Africa to improve security and to make sure that we also address the legitimate needs of people before extremists have a chance to exploit them.'[69] However, despite this pledge, the situation only worsened.

As Boko Haram carried out daily attacks,[70] the government ramped up its own use of force, as in the Niger Delta, which in turn drove Boko Haram to adopt more violent tactics aimed at public places, which included car and suicide bombings. In terms of tactical behaviour, this indicated a shift from focusing on security personnel and government targets to more direct and gruesome attacks on civilians. Terrorist attacks became its primary modus operandi. Consequently, the government returned to its terrorism debate and, in 2011, the Senate passed the Terrorism Prevention Act (TPA), the country's first anti-terrorism act, which shifted all terrorism cases to the federal level. In addition, government actors began to use the terrorism label more liberally when speaking about violence. For example, violent robberies carried out by criminal groups such as Sara Suka in Kaduna have increasingly been (mis) labelled terrorism.[71]

In 2012, the JTF was able to push Boko Haram to the outskirts of Maiduguri, but this came at a cost. The success of the government forces failed to conceal the human rights violations committed by the JTF – marked by collective punishment, including house burning, dragnet arrests, unlawful and prolonged detention without trial, torture, and extrajudicial killing of Boko Haram suspects and sympathizers.[72] Such gross violations blossomed with the greater powers that the JTF acquired in a new state of emergency declared in Borno, Yobe and Adamawa states on 14 May 2013. During this time the government captured large numbers of alleged Boko Haram members and detained them, without trial, at the Giwa barracks in Maiduguri.[73] According to Amnesty International, the barracks was not built as a detention facility yet it held upwards of 2,000 detainees – 1,900 beyond capacity – who were underfed and mistreated. As the mistreatment of those detained and the impunity of the government forces persisted, Boko Haram attacked Giwa in 2014 and set free hundreds of detainees, which prompted another harsh government response that led to an alleged 600 detainees being killed.

The accusations of gross human rights violations and corruption levelled against the Nigerian military put a strain on the counterterrorism partnership between Nigeria and its foremost partner, the US. Although the US designated Boko Haram a foreign terrorist organization in 2013, it repeatedly blocked weapon deals with Nigeria due to the military's tactics and its incapacity to protect its arsenal of weapons against Boko Haram raids.[74] In response, Nigeria suspended military training with the US. Following the Chibok kidnapping, which captured international attention, the US continued to challenge Nigeria's efforts to secure arms, even though it sent more than eighty marines to assist the Nigerian security agencies,[75] and supported the formation of a coalition of countries (known as the Multinational Joint Task Force, or MJTF) bordering northern Nigeria – including Chad, the Niger Republic, Cameroon and Mali – to combat Boko Haram.

With the situation spiralling out of control, northern elites pressured the government in 2011 and again in 2013 to host a committee on dialogue and security challenges in the north in order to consider an amnesty deal, inspired by the Niger Delta effort. Both attempts were unsuccessful, as the stronghold of Boko Haram refused to negotiate with the federal government (some negotiations with a government team had taken place, but Boko Haram denied that these were with its own authorized representatives). But, more critically, the motivations and logic behind the committee were flawed. What was good for the goose in the case of the Niger Delta was not good for the gander in the case of Boko Haram.[76] Nevertheless, this approach followed a recognizable pattern – one where the Nigerian Government has a tendency to create ad hoc advisory bodies to address security challenges and concerns, but these are often unsuccessful due to diversionary and corrupt practices. For instance, the main security forces responsible for the extrajudicial killings of Yusuf and Alhaji Baba Fugu are yet to be prosecuted, despite the recommendations of the presidential advisory committee investigating these incidents. To this day, compensation is yet to be paid, despite an injunction from a Borno High Court in April 2010.

By 2015 not only did civilians in the northeast fear attacks from Boko Haram and other criminal groups, but they also lived in a context where the Nigerian military had extrajudicially executed more than 1,000 people, arrested at least 20,000 people and tortured countless others.[77] Added to this, the security forces showed a shocking incapacity to defend civilians. As a result, similar to the vigilante movements that emerged and became so powerful in 1999 and 2000, people in the northeast resorted to self-help mechanisms and formed vigilante groups – the most prominent being the Civilian Joint Task Force (CJTF) – to push back against Boko Haram, and in some cases against corrupt and abusive security forces. But, as discussed earlier, while vigilante movements in Nigeria may initially take shape as a way to deal with lawlessness, they are also part of the equation that feeds the cycle of violence.

Conclusion

As of 2017, the future of the northeast is unclear. At the time of writing, the Nigerian Government continues to counter violence with brutal aggression, and violent phenomena continue to percolate and shape-shift from one group to the next, and from one region to another. What is clear, however, is the extraordinary shift in terrorism discourse and practices that has occurred in Nigeria since the turn of the millennium. Employing a historical tracing approach allowed this chapter to critically examine how the conceptualization of terrorism evolved with each wave of violence, while also factoring in the role that post-9/11 global initiatives have played in Nigeria's counterterrorism efforts. While the chapter has illustrated the influence that international actors have had on terrorism discourse within the country, it has also revealed how conceptualizing terrorism has been a near fifteen-year process – one that has been marked by repeated efforts to pass counterterrorism legislation as well as develop other counter measures. That said, such efforts have had little impact on how violence is actually treated in the country. The only discernable counter-violence strategy seems to be one that involves deploying the military, which has only driven armed groups to adopt more sophisticated violent tactics.

Looking ahead, although the government has made some progress in its effort to end the northern insurgency, it is likely that the violence will only shift to another region. Currently, there is no indication that the government's reliance on the military to manage domestic security challenges – regardless of size – will change. But without creating a more productive relationship between the public and security officials – one that involves engaging and leveraging community involvement without resorting to vigilantism – armed groups will continue to flourish, and terrorism will thus probably continue to grow in the country.

Notes

1 *BBC News*, 'Nigeria Boko Haram: Scores of refugees starved to death – MSF,' *BBC News*, 23 June 2016, available at: www.bbc.co.uk/news/world-africa-36603419 (accessed 12 July 2016).
2 Patricia Taft and Nate Haken, *Violence in Nigeria: Patterns and Trends* (New York: Springer, 2015).
3 Institute for Economics and Peace (IEP), *2015 Global Terrorism Index Report* (New York: IEP, 2015).
4 Daria Schitrit, Elinav Yogev and Yoram Schweitzer, 'Suicide attacks in 2015,' *INSS Insight* 789 (26 January 2016): 1–4.
5 Dionne Searcey, 'Nigeria vexed by Boko Haram's use of women as suicide bombers,' *New York Times*, 11 February 2016.
6 J.O. Abimbola and S.A. Adesote, 'Domestic terrorism and Boko Haram insurgency in Nigeria – issues and trends: A historical discourse,' *Journal of Arts and Contemporary Society* 4 (2012): 11–28; Freedom C. Onuoha, 'The Islamist challenge: Nigeria's Boko Haram crisis explained,' *African Security Review* 19:2 (2010): 54–67; Abimbola O. Adesoji, 'Between Maitatsine and Boko Haram: Islamic fundamentalism and the response of the Nigerian state,' *Africa Today* 57:4 (2011): 98–119; Nathaniel Daniel Danjibo, 'Islamic fundamentalism and sectarian violence: The "Maitatsine" and "Boko Haram" crises in Northern Nigeria,' *Peace and Conflict Studies Paper Series* (2009): 1–21.
7 Hakeem Onapajo and Ufo Okeke Uzodike, 'Boko Haram terrorism in Nigeria,' *African Security Review* 21:3 (2012): 24–39; J. Peter Pham, 'Boko Haram's evolving threat,' *Africa Security Brief* 20:6 (2012): 1.
8 Daniel Egiegba Agbiboa, 'Why Boko Haram exists: The relative deprivation perspective,' *African Conflict and Peacebuilding Review* 3:1 (2013): 144–57.
9 James J. Forest, *Confronting the Terrorism of Boko Haram in Nigeria*, JSOU report 12-5 (MacDill Air Force Base, FL: Joint Special Operations Univerisity, 2012); Niyi Awofeso, Jan Ritchie and Pieter Degeling, 'The Almajiri heritage and the threat of non-state terrorism in northern Nigeria: Lessons from Central Asia and Pakistan,' *Studies in Conflict and Terrorism* 26:4 (2003): 311–25; Hussein Solomon, 'Counter-terrorism in Nigeria,' *RUSI Journal*

157:4 (2012): 6–11; Iro Aghedo and Oarhe Osumah, 'The Boko Haram uprising: How should Nigeria respond?' *Third World Quarterly* 33:5 (2012): 853–69.

10 Amnesty International, *Stars on Their Shoulders. Blood on Their Hands: War Crimes Committed by the Nigerian Military* (London: Amnesty International, 2015); Human Rights Watch, 'Spiraling violence: Boko Haram attacks and security force abuses in Nigeria,' Human Rights Watch website, 11 October 2012, available at: www.hrw.org/report/2012/10/11/spiraling-violence/boko-haram-attacks-and-security-force-abuses-nigeria (accessed 30 October 2015).

11 Isaac Terwase Sampson and Freedom C. Onuoha, '"Forcing the horse to drink or making it realise its thirst"? Understanding the enactment of anti-terrorism legislation (ATL) in Nigeria,' *Perspectives on Terrorism* 5:3–4 (2011): 33–49.

12 In 2016, attacks by the NDA resulted in a decline in production by as much as 60 per cent; John Campbell, 'Nigerian security developments: Niger Delta Avengers, Boko Haram, and new police inspector general,' *CFR Blog, Africa in Transition*, 22 June 2016, available at: www.cfr.org/blog/nigerian-security-developments-niger-delta-avengers-boko-haram-and-new-police-inspector (accessed 1 July 2016).

13 Andrew McGregor, 'Nigeria expands its "war on terrorism" to the Niger Delta,' *Jamestown Foundation Terrorism Monitor* 14:18 (2016): 7–11.

14 Taft and Haken, *Violence in Nigeria.*

15 For example, during the insurgency in the Niger Delta (2006–9) studies on terrorism in Nigeria focused on the tactics of political violence in this region.

16 Joseph Midat, 'Sara-Suka, black spot: Kaduna outlaw groups of terror,' *Leadership*, 16 January 2016.

17 Omeiza Ajayi, 'Insecurity: Military now involved in 28 states,' *National Mirror*, 5 July 2013.

18 Quoted, *ibid.*

19 Lauren Ploch, *Nigeria: Current Issues and US Policy*, Report for Congress (Washington, DC: Congressional Research Service, 2013).

20 *Ibid.*, 20.

21 To note, the government regularly uses the military to deal with matters such criminal gangs, which should be reserved for the police; Judith Asuni, *Understanding the Armed Groups of the Niger Delta*, working paper (New York: Council on Foreign Relations, 2009).

22 Alex P. Schmid and Albert J. Jongman, *Political Terrorism: A New Guide to Actors, Authors, Concepts, Data Bases, Theories, and Literature* (New Brunswick and London: Transaction, 1988); Jackson Nyamuya Maogoto, 'War on the enemy: Self-defence and state-sponsored terrorism,' *Melbourne Journal of International Law* 4 (2003): 406.

23 Isaac Terwase Sampson and Freedom C. Onuoha, '"Forcing the horse to drink or making it realise its thirst"? Understanding the enactment of anti-terrorism legislation (ATL) in Nigeria,' *Perspectives on Terrorism* 5:3–4 (2011): 33.

24 US Bureau of Citizenship and Immigration Services, *Nigeria: MAD, Arrests of Political Opponents following the Death of Ibrahim Abacha*, NGA98001.ZLA (Washington, DC: US Bureau of Citizenship and Immigration Services, 14 April 1998), available at: www.refworld.org/docid/3df0a9a34.html (accessed 10 June 2016).

25 See Immigration and Refugee Board of Canada, *Nigeria: Bombing Incidents at Lagos Airport between June 1996 and November 1997*, NGA31152.E (Ottawa: Immigration and Refugee Board of Canada, 1 February 1999), available at: www.refworld.org/docid/3ae6ab4d1c.html (accessed 10 June 2016).

26 Human Rights Watch, *World Report 1999: Events of December 1997–November 1998* (New York: Human Rights Watch, 1999), p. 57.

27 Rotimi Sankore, 'Top level military arrests stun Nigeria,' *Guardian*, 9 December 1999.

28 Femi Omotoso, 'Governance crisis and democracy in Nigeria, 1999–2012,' *Mediterranean Journal of Social Sciences* 4:14 (2013): 126.

29 It's important to note that prior to this there was no such continental definition; Martin Ewi and Kwesi Aning, 'Assessing the role of the African Union in preventing and combating terrorism in Africa,' *African Security Review* 15:3 (2006): 32–46.

30 Annalisa Zinn, 'Theory versus reality: Civil war onset and avoidance in Nigeria since 1960,' in P. Collier and N. Sambanis (eds), *Understanding Civil War: Africa*, vol. 1 (Washington, DC: World Bank, 2005), pp. 89–121.

31 Thomas A. Imobighe and Agatha Eguavoen (eds), *Terrorism and Counterterrorism: An African Perspective* (Ibadan, Nigeria: Heinemann Education Books (Nigeria), 2006), p. 282.

32 Shedrack Gaya Best and Dimieari Von Kemedi, 'Armed groups and conflict in rivers and plateau states, Nigeria,' in Nicolas Florquin and Eric G. Berman (eds), *Armed and Aimless: Armed Groups, Guns, and Human Security in the ECOWAS Region* (Geneva: Small Arms Survey, 2005), p. 14.

33 Augustine Ikelegbe, 'The economy of conflict in the oil rich Niger Delta Region of Nigeria,' *Nordic Journal of African Studies* 14:2 (2005): 215.

34 Florquin and Berman, *Armed and Aimless*.

35 Adeyemi Bukola Oyeniyi, 'Terrorism in Nigeria: Groups, activities, and politics,' *International Journal of Politics and Good Governance* 1:1 (2010): 1–16.

36 For example, between February and May 2000, at least 2,000 people died in Kaduna, while in 2001 a reported 1,000 died in Jos, and hundreds more were killed in the clashes between Christians and Muslims in Kano.

37 Daniel Jordan Smith, 'Violent vigilantism and the state in Nigeria: The case of the Bakassi Boys,' in Edna G. Bay and Donald L. Donham (eds), *States of Violence: Politics, Youth, and Memory in Contemporary Africa* (Charlottesville, VA: University of Virgina Press, n.d.), p. 128.

38 *Ibid.*, p. 130.

39 *Ibid.*, p. 140.

40 *Ibid.*, pp. 136–8.

41 Human Rights Watch, *The Destruction of Odi and Rape in Choba* (New York: Human Rights Watch, 1999).

42 Human Rights Watch, *Nigeria: Soldiers Massacre Civilians in Revenge Attack in Benue State* (New York: Human Rights Watch, 2001).

43 James J. Forest and Jennifer Giroux, 'Terrorism and political violence in Africa: Contemporary trends in a shifting terrain,' *Perspectives on Terrorism* 5:3–4 (2011): 5–17.

44 John Campbell, *Nigeria: Dancing on the Brink* (London: Rowman and Littlefield, 2013), p. 60.

45 United Nations Office for Drugs and Crime (UNODC) Terrorism Prevention Branch, *A Review of the Legal Regime Against Terrorism in West and Central Africa*, working document (Vienna: UNODC, October 2008), pp. 138–9.

46 For the OAU definition see: OAU, *OAU Convention on the Prevention and Combating of Terrorism*, 14 June 1999, p. 207.

47 International Crisis Group (ICG), *Curbing Violence in Nigeria (II): The Boko Haram Insurgency*, report no. 216/Africa (Brussels: ICG, 2014), p. 10.

48 Michael Olufemi Sodipo, 'Mitigating radicalism in northern Nigeria,' *Africa Security Brief* 26 (August 2013): 1–8.

49 US Department of State (USDS), 'Africa overview,' in *Country Reports on Terrorism 2007* (Washington, DC: USDS Office of the Coordinator for Counterterrorism, 2008), p. 23.

50 Asuni, *Understanding the Armed Groups*, p. 6.

51 Oluwatoyin O. Oluwaniyi, 'Post-amnesty programme in the Niger Delta: Challenges and prospects,' *Conflict Trends* 4 (2011): 46–54; Michael Nwankpa, 'The politics of amnesty in Nigeria: A comparative analysis of the Boko Haram and Niger Delta insurgencies,' *Journal of Terrorism Research* 5:1 (2014): 67–77.

52 Asuni, *Understanding the Armed Groups*, p, 11.

53 Human Rights Watch, *The Warri Crisis: Fueling Violence* (New York: Human Rights Watch, 2003), III, 'Violence in 2003.'

54 Michael Watts, 'Petro-insurgency or criminal syndicate? Conflict and violence in the Niger Delta,' *Review of African Political Economy* 34:114 (2007): 637–60; Taft and Haken, *Violence in Nigeria.*

55 Rueben Abati, 'Warlords of the Niger Delta,' *Guardian (Lagos)*, 4 October 2004.

56 William Rosenau, Peter Chalk, Renny McPherson, Michelle Parker and Austin Long, *Corporations and Counterinsurgency*, occasional paper OP-259 (Santa Monica, CA: Rand Corporation, 2009), p. 10.

57 US Africa Command Public Affairs, Stuttgart, Germany, 'Africa Contingency Operations Training and Assistance (ACOTA),' *DISAM Journal* (December 2008): 5.

58 Sampson and Onuoha, 'Forcing the horse to drink.'

59 Augustine Ikelegbe, Omobolaji Olarinmoye and Steve Okhomina, *Youth Militias, Self Determination and Resource Control Struggles in the Niger-Delta Region of Nigeria* (Dakar, Senegal: Codesira, 2011); Watts, 'Petro-insurgency or criminal syndicate?'

60 *BBC News*, 'Shell evacuates Nigeria workers,' *BBC News*, 16 January 2006, available at: http://news.bbc.co.uk/1/hi/4615890.stm (accessed 10 June 2016).

61 Emmanuel Aziken and Shuaibu Inalegwu, 'Nigeria: Niger Delta senators bicker over Anti-Terrorism Bill,' *Vanguard*, 17 September 2008, available at: http://allafrica.com/stories/200809170491.html (accessed 10 June 2016).

62 Ibaba Samuel Ibaba, 'Terrorism in liberation struggles: Interrogating the engagement tactics of the movement for the emancipation of the Niger Delta,' *Perspectives on Terrorism* 5:3–4 (2011): 18–32.

63 Kelechi A. Kalu and George Klay Kieh (eds), *United States–Africa Security Relations: Terrorism, Regional Security and National Interests* (New York: Routledge, 2014).

64 Quoted in Aziken and Inalegwu, 'Nigeria.'

65 Erich Marquardt, 'The Niger Delta insurgency and its threat to energy security,' *Terrorism Monitor* 4:16 (2006): 3–6.

66 Mark Davidheiser and Kialee Nyiayaana, 'Demobilization or remobilization? The amnesty program and the search for peace in the Niger Delta,' *African Security* 4:1 (2011): 44–64; Nwankpa, 'Politics of amnesty.'

67 UNODC, *Review of the Legal Regime*, p. 143.

68 David Cook, *Boko Haram: A Prognosis* (Houston, TX: James A. Baker III Institute for Public Policy, Rice University, 2011), available at: http://hdl.handle.net/1911/70549 (accessed 2 January 2015).

69 Hillary Rodham Clinton, 'Remarks with Nigerian Foreign Minister Olugbenga Ashiru after their meeting,' US Department of State website, 29 September 2011, available at: https://2009-2017.state.gov/secretary/20092013clinton/rm/2011/09/174818.htm (accessed 2 January 2015).

70 For a list of notable attacks, see US Department of State, Office of the Spokesperson, 'Boko Haram and US counterterrorism assistance to Nigeria,' factsheet, US Department of State website, 14 May 2014, available at: https://2009-2017.state.gov/r/pa/prs/ps/2014/05/226072.htm (accessed 30 March 2017).

71 *Citizen*, 'Police uncover new terror group, Sara Suka, in Kaduna,' *Citizen*, 22 May 2015.

72 Amnesty International, 'Annual report: Nigeria 2013,' Amnesty International USA website, 23 May 2013, available at: https://www.amnestyusa.org/reports/annual-report-nigeria-2013/ (accessed 2 January 2015).

73 Nathaniel Allen, 'Western partners can't provide military assistance to fight Boko Haram, but here's what they can do,' *African Arguments*, 25 September 2015, available at: http://africanarguments.org/2015/09/25/western-partners-cant-provide-military-assistance-to-fight-boko-haram-but-heres-what-they-can-do-2/ (accessed 28 October 2015).

74 Michael Nwankpa, 'The political economy of securitization: The case of Boko Haram, Nigeria,' *Economics of Peace and Security Journal* 10:1 (2015): 32–9.

75 Lori Hinnant and Sylvie Corbet, 'Summit combats Boko Haram funds, arms, training,' *Kokomo Tribune*, 18 May 2014; Corina Simonelli, Michael Jensen, Alejandro Castro-Reina, Amy Pate, Scott Menner, et al., *START Background Report: Boko Haram Recent Attacks* (College Park, MD: National Consortium for the Study of Terrorism and Responses to Terrorism, 2014), available at: www.start.umd.edu/pubs/STARTBackgroundReport_BokoHaramRecentAttacks_May2014_0.pdf (accessed 2 January 2015).

76 Nwankpa, 'Politics of amnesty.'

77 Amnesty International, *Stars on Their Shoulders*.

17

Counterterrorism in Museveni's Uganda

Emma Leonard Boyle

Introduction

Uganda's counterterrorism policy can only be understood in the context of President Yoweri Museveni's national and regional ambitions. Throughout his long tenure as president of Uganda, Museveni has courted the support and aid of the West in order to strengthen his position as president and to increase his stature within East Africa. While economic development dominated the 1990s in Uganda, the focus of the 2000s has been security and, more specifically, terrorism. In the immediate aftermath of the 9/11 attacks, Museveni was the first African leader to speak with US President George Bush. In this telephone call, he sympathized with Bush over their joint fight against terrorism (in Uganda's case, from the Lord's Resistance Army) and offered the US unequivocal support. Because Uganda was already a 'darling of the West' due to the high economic growth rates of the 1990s,[1] there was little hesitation from the US in making Uganda a key ally in the 'War on Terror'.

Being a key ally in the War on Terror has allowed Museveni to consolidate his position within Uganda and to fashion himself as a regional leader. Museveni's regional ambitions can be seen clearly in two episodes. First, in his initial support for an East African federation with Kenya, Tanzania, Rwanda and Burundi. This would have produced a political union between these countries with sovereignty split between the federation and the national governments. Museveni's attempts to drum up support for such an enterprise caused alarm in the other East African countries, and his tone was likened to that of a candidate on the campaign trail, with the implication that Museveni fully intended to become the first president of the East African federation.[2] Second and more recently, his regional ambition can also be seen in his decision to send troops to Somalia with the African Union mission (AMISOM). Driven by a desire for Uganda to play a role within the international community and continue as a favoured ally of the US, Museveni doubled down on Uganda's commitment to the AMISOM peacekeeping mission in Somalia, even after al Shabaab killed seventy-six people in Kampala in 2010.[3]

Being a key ally and sending troops into Somalia has made Uganda an attractive target for extremist Islamist groups, who see attacks on Uganda as also hitting the US. The fear post-9/11 is that Islamist groups will attack vulnerable US targets in weaker countries, such as Uganda, if they do not have the strength to attack the US directly. This had already happened in the 1998 al Qaeda embassy bombings in Nairobi and Dar es Salaam. An attack against a US target in Uganda would serve the dual purpose of attacking the US and potentially persuading the Ugandan Government that the price of such a close relationship with the US is too high to pay. Al Shabaab used the same rationale in their 2010 attacks. Museveni, however, has not backed down in the wake of these attacks, solidifying Uganda as a steadfast ally of the US but also as an attractive target for further attacks.

This chapter begins by charting how Uganda came to be such a strong ally of the US and a key regional player in the War on Terror. It details the results of this policy, both within Uganda and across the wider region, before discussing how this has impacted the conceptualization of terrorism within Uganda. It concludes by arguing that the term 'terrorism' has become very confused within Uganda. Because of Museveni's strategic use of the term for political gain, no clear consensus has been established as to its exact meaning within the Ugandan context.

Background

Understanding how Museveni came to power and why he was able to rebuild the country's political system in the manner he did are key to understanding how he has been able to persuade both the citizens of Uganda and the international community that his continued stay in power is in the interest of the country. This would not have been possible without the violent chaos that Uganda experienced prior to Museveni becoming president. He came to power at the head of a rebel group, the National Resistance Army/Movement (NRA/M), and brought an end to the civil war that had been raging throughout

Uganda during the early 1980s. However, the civil war was the result of a much longer process of attrition against the Ugandan state infrastructure that began not long after independence.

When Uganda became independent from the British Empire in 1962, it had a parliamentary system of democracy and Milton Obote was elected as the first prime minister of the country, with the *kabaka*[4] of Buganda as the ceremonial head of state. However, it did not take long for a power struggle to develop between the two men and Obote increasingly became reliant on the army, and on violence, to secure his position. In 1966, he forced changes to the Ugandan Constitution through parliament and became president of Uganda. After this point, violence became the tool by which Obote ruled, mainly perpetrated by the army, which was led by Idi Amin. Obote remained Uganda's president until 1971, when Amin staged a coup and took power for himself.[5]

The Amin era (1971–79) accelerated the destruction of the state in Uganda, to the point where there was no policy process and ministers would listen to Amin's public addresses on the radio in an attempt to find out what policies they should be implementing.[6] After he was removed from power by the combined efforts of the Tanzanian army and exiled Ugandan rebels (of which Museveni was a part), there was a power vacuum in Uganda which various men attempted to fill. Between 1979 and 1986, Uganda was ruled by six presidents (Yusuf Lule, Godfrey Binaisa, Paulo Muwanga, Milton Obote, Bazilio Olara-Okello, and Tito Okello) and a Presidential Commission. From 1981 to January 1986, Uganda also experienced a bitterly fought civil war between the Uganda National Liberation Army and Museveni's NRA/M. Despite the signing of a peace agreement in Nairobi in 1985 between the two sides, the NRA/M quickly resumed the fighting and overthrew the government in January 1986, when Yoweri Katuga Museveni became president of Uganda.

Close to five years of instability and civil war in Uganda devastated a country that was once referred to as the 'pearl of Africa'. There was no longer a functioning government structure and almost no formal economy left. The wildlife stocks were devastated, and there were small rebel groups in most regions of the country. Museveni and the NRA/M had a huge task ahead if they were to rebuild the country.

Improving the security situation in Uganda was the first task the NRA/M approached, using a mixture of incentives and coercion to persuade rebel groups to lay down their arms and disband. Relatively quickly most areas of Uganda were pacified, with exceptions being the north (where the precursor groups to the Lord's Resistance Army continued to operate) and the northeast, where the Karimojong continued to resist state interference until 2011.[7] Government institutions were rebuilt as semi-democratic. Rather than move straight into multiparty elections, Museveni argued that Uganda was not ready for such a potentially divisive system, and instead implemented a 'no-party system', where individuals stood for election without a party affiliation.[8] This system remained until the 2005 referendum, which restored multiparty politics within Uganda, although the recent abolition of term limits and the intimidation of the opposition that has taken place in recent elections have left questions over how democratic Uganda now is.[9]

From the mid-1990s onwards, Uganda experienced both domestic terrorism and transnational Islamist terrorism. Domestic non-state terrorism arrived in 1996 in the form of the Allied Democratic Forces (ADF), who began by attacking border posts along the Uganda–Democratic Republic of Congo (DRC) border and swiftly graduated to planting bombs in Kampala.[10] More controversially, a number of people, including Museveni, have also argued that the violence of the Lord's Resistance Army (LRA) should be seen as domestic terrorism.[11] The 1998 attacks against the US embassies in Nairobi and Dar es Salaam were the first experience that East Africa had with significant transnational Islamist terrorism, and there is evidence that an attack on the US embassy in Kampala was pre-empted just one month later.[12] This section details each of these terrorism threats in turn.

The ADF was created in 1995 from the remnants of the National Army for the Liberation of Uganda (NALU), disaffected Muslim youth who had travelled from Kampala to the Ugandan-DRC border, and individuals who had fought with the Rwandan army or the Interahamwe.[13] This rebel group was initially situated in the Rwenzori Mountains of western Uganda, but was later driven into the more volatile eastern regions of the DRC, from where it launched attacks across the border into Uganda. Initially attacks were concentrated in the Kasese District of Uganda, which borders the DRC, but within only a couple of years the ADF had graduated to planting bombs in Kampala.

Some of the most remarkable ADF attacks took place in 1999. These included a series of attacks within Kampala, and a spectacular prison break. Between April and June 1999, the ADF launched seven separate attacks in Kampala, using bombs and hand grenades. Eleven people were killed and a further forty-two were injured.[14] Then in December 1999 around 200 ADF rebels attacked the Katojo Prison in western Uganda, from where they abducted 365 prisoners. As well as the psychological victory of successfully attacking a government prison, this also provided practical benefits to the ADF. The abducted prisoners replenished the depleted ranks of the ADF, and the Ugandan military was distracted from its attacks against ADF positions in the Rwenzori Mountains and was diverted to help the prison regain control of the remaining prisoners. It has also been suggested that the actual purpose of the attack was to target Ugandan Chief of Staff Brigadier James Kazini, who was visiting the prison at the time.[15] This period of activity by the ADF came to an end with the withdrawal agreement between the ADF and the Ugandan Government in January 2001. This came about after a series of military successes against the ADF in 2000, combined with a change in the regional climate. In July 1999, the governments fighting in the Second Congo War signed the Lusaka Ceasefire Agreement, which encouraged Uganda to withdraw its military units from the DRC, thus making negotiations with the ADF more palatable to the Ugandan Government.

Since 2001, there have been two other periods of ADF activity, although the group has not subsequently targeted civilians with bombs and grenades as it did during the first period of its existence, even though the Ugandan Government persuaded the US to include the ADF on the Terrorist Exclusion List in December 2001.[16] In 2007–8 there was heightened activity as the ADF increased incursions into western Uganda, and the Ugandan military counter-attacked. Once again there were ceasefire negotiations between the two sides, and in December 2007 around 200 ADF fighters surrendered to the Ugandan authorities. Violence once again flared in 2013 and has continued to the present. This time the ADF targeted civilians much more directly, burning villages and abducting civilians in both Uganda and the DRC. By the end of 2014 the violence was mostly directed within the DRC, and it was the DRC military conducting most of the operations against the ADF.

The Lord's Resistance Army (LRA) is currently conducting one of the longest running insurgencies within sub-Saharan Africa, which began in 1987. The LRA was created by Joseph Kony, who took advantage of the distrust of the people of Acholiland in Northern Uganda of the new Museveni Government. Having pacified most of the rest of the country, Museveni and the NRA turned their attention to the north, where there were still a number of rebel groups. Some of these groups claimed to represent the people of the region, and some were supporters of previous presidents (many of whom came from the north) who wished to see their patrons restored to power. All, however, remembered when Idi Amin had ordered northern soldiers to the barracks, only to have them massacred, and when Museveni ordered that these groups congregate at the barracks to be disarmed few believed Museveni's promise that this would not also be a massacre. Instead, many decided to fight the new government. The most successful and spectacular was the Holy Spirit Movement led by Alice Lakwena. This movement attracted widespread international attention, both for the fact that it was led by a female rebel and due to the mystical aspects of the group. Coming within fifty miles of the capital before being defeated, this group was seen as the precursor to the LRA. Joseph Kony claimed kinship with Lakwena (although the exact relationship has never been established) and explicitly stated that he was continuing her fight.

Although the LRA did not put out a detailed rationale for the insurgency, Kony argued that Uganda should be run as a Christian theocracy, with a government that was based on the Ten Commandments. However, when the people of Acholiland failed to support the LRA, the LRA turned on them ferociously, and the conflict quickly became dominated by LRA attacks on civilians rather than confrontations with the government. After promising peace talks failed in 1994, there was a considerable escalation of the conflict,[17] and in 1996 the Ugandan Government, under international pressure to do more to protect civilians in the north, implemented a policy of 'protected villages' within the conflict-affected area. Civilians were moved, sometimes forcibly, into these villages away from their farms and livelihoods, with the promise that the military would offer protection from LRA attacks. Unfortunately this did not happen, and many 'protected villages' suffered from repeated LRA attacks. It was this focus on attacking civilians that led many commentators to label the LRA a 'terrorist' group rather than a 'rebel' group.[18]

Around this time it was starting to become apparent that the US had been supporting the Ugandan Government in its fight against the LRA. While the relationship between the two countries was complicated by the fact that the US Government wanted to see more substantive movement towards democracy,[19] it was also becoming clear that geopolitical concerns were beginning to overtake a preference for democracy in Uganda. In 1997, the *Monitor* (a Ugandan newspaper) reported that 'President Yoweri Museveni, after years of denials, has finally acknowledged United States assistance in its protracted northern war with Sudan-backed rebels [the LRA].'[20] Support from the Clinton administration quickly followed, as Madeleine Albright, the US secretary of state, visited Uganda and publicly praised Museveni's Government for the progress it had made over the last decade.[21] Susan Rice, US assistant secretary of state for Africa, added her support for the Ugandan Government's military approach to defeating the LRA when she told Congress in July 1998, 'It is frankly difficult to imagine a negotiated settlement with a group like the LRA.'[22]

Throughout the 2000s the LRA became a regional problem rather than simply a Ugandan problem. As the LRA found it increasingly difficult to operate in Northern Uganda, the group spread its operations to neighbouring countries, such as Sudan, the DRC and, more recently, the Central African Republic. Its modus operandi, however, has remained the same. The LRA has studiously avoided confrontation with any of the national armies of the countries in which it operates, and instead attacks civilians, abducting children and levelling villages.

In addition to experiencing terrorism at the hands of these two domestic groups, Uganda has also experienced transnational terrorism. Al Qaeda announced its presence in East Africa in August 1998 with the twin embassy bombings in Nairobi and Dar es Salaam. There have been suggestions that the US embassy in Kampala was also due to be targeted that day, but that this attack and another plot the following month were foiled.[23] The Ugandan foreign minister, Amama Mbabazi, claimed that the Ugandan intelligence services were able to disrupt these plots as they had experience in dealing with the violence of multiple rebel groups throughout the 1990s, and the Clinton administration termed these claims 'credible'.

The Ugandan intelligence services were not as successful in 2010, when the Somali Islamist group al Shabaab planted two bombs in Kampala. The twin bombings during the World Cup Finals in 2010 were designed to kill and injure many, as civilians gathered to watch the football, and succeeded in killing seventy-four and injuring seventy. Al Shabaab, which had pledged allegiance to al Qaeda in 2009, targeted Uganda because of the presence of Ugandan troops in the African Union Mission in Somalia (AMISOM), as an al Shabaab spokesman later confirmed: 'We are sending a message to Uganda and Burundi, if they do not take out their Amisom troops from Somalia, blasts will continue and it will happen.'[24]

Uganda's counterterrorism policy

Prior to 2001, the response from the Ugandan Government to each of these situations was ad hoc. After the foiling of the bombing of the US embassy in Kampala in 1998, the Ugandan Government did not have an obvious further response to the threat of transnational terrorism on its soil until the 9/11 attacks changed the international situation. For domestic groups, the military provided the first line of response. The Ugandan People's Defense Forces (UPDF) were sent to the west to deal with the ADF and, by about 2002, was seen as successful in destroying the bases and infrastructure of the group. After the ADF again regrouped in 2007, it was the UPDF that was sent to once again pacify it, although the military has only been able to reduce the threat from the ADF and not eliminate it entirely.

For the LRA, the strategy again rested mainly on the military, but was combined at various points with attempts at peace negotiations. The first major military move against the LRA was Operation North, launched in March 1991. Part of this operation was to create local self-defence groups, known as 'Arrow Groups', of civilians who were then armed with bows and arrows. This campaign ultimately failed, amid increasing violence against civilians by both sides.[25] After this operation the minister for Northern Uganda, Betty Bigombe, attempted to negotiate a peace agreement with the LRA and was able to initiate contact with Joseph Kony in June 1993. Although it seemed for a while as though the negotiations might be successful, these talks ultimately failed as well. Bigombe had come very close to bringing two sides with deep mutual distrust to an agreement, but this mistrust proved too difficult to overcome, and in February 1994 Museveni gave the LRA an ultimatum to surrender before the government once again began military action.[26]

After the failure of these talks, the conflict took a regional turn and attracted the attention of the US. Westbrook argues that 'The actions and words of the US government must be seen in the context of the motivations of the US in the region as well as its overwhelming influence on the Ugandan government.'[27] By the mid-1990s the US was already concerned about the rise of Islamist extremism and the threats that this posed, and Sudan in particular was identified as a 'central hub of terrorist activity'.[28] Omar al-Bashir came to power in a bloodless military coup in 1989 and has been president of Sudan ever since. Although some elections have taken place since, most recently in April 2015, these have been viewed as nothing more than rigged elections to rubber-stamp his leadership. Al-Bashir has often been considered a religious extremist, and has implemented parts of sharia law within Sudan,[29] so it is perhaps not surprising that Osama bin Laden was based in the East African country from 1991 to 1996, developing the network that became al Qaeda. After Bin Laden declared war on the US in 1996, Sudan came under increasing pressure to expel him in exchange for no longer being referred to as a 'state sponsor of terrorism'. Bin Laden went from Sudan to Afghanistan, and continued to develop al Qaeda, which subsequently announced its presence on the world stage with the 1998 embassy bombings in Nairobi and Dar es Salaam.

So just how does the Ugandan Government's fight against a relatively small and weak rebel group fit into this nascent War on Terror? The key to explaining this is that the LRA enjoyed substantial material support from the Sudanese Government. From the mid-1990s and into the 2000s, Uganda and Sudan waged proxy war against each other as each provided support to rebel groups fighting the other government. After the Ugandan Government began to fund the Sudan People's Liberation Army (SPLA) fighting against the Sudanese Government, the latter retaliated and provided funding to the LRA. Sudanese funding to the LRA actually served two purposes. The first was to continue the proxy war against the Ugandan Government, the second to build up the LRA to the point where the group could also fight against the SPLA, distracting that group from its fight against the Sudanese Government. Because the Ugandan Government was an ally of the US and the Sudanese Government was of concern to the US, the US authorities took the decision to provide funding to the Ugandan Government in the fight against the LRA.

Until 1996, concerns over the progress Uganda had made in democratizing were paramount to the US, and the conflict in the north was secondary.[30] This began to change in the late 1990s, and Museveni acknowledged in 1997 that Uganda was receiving US support in the fight against the LRA.[31] In December 1997 US Secretary of State Madeleine Albright made her visit to Uganda, where she praised Uganda on its progress and made clear, in a meeting with SPLA leader Johan Garang, that the US wanted to see regime change in Khartoum.[32] This was followed by a visit from President Bill Clinton in March 1998.

US interest in this conflict increased post-9/11, as President Museveni positioned himself as a key ally in the War on Terror, and a stable presence in eastern Africa on which the US could rely. Professor Paul Omach, at Makarere University in Uganda, argued that the United States chose to partner with Uganda in the war on terror because of President Museveni: 'Museveni is one who is ready. He looks at himself as a revolutionary. He has actually said these things – "We are revolutionary, we are going to change the region." He takes the risk. But you see, he also doesn't have these democratic encumbrances when the body bags start coming.'[33] This view is supported by a 2006 statement in which the US Department of State commented that 'Uganda has a strong regional voice in opposing international terrorism and supported US counter-terrorism initiatives.'[34] Given the relative peace and security there compared with many of the surrounding countries, Uganda subsequently became the regional focus of the counterterrorism measures implemented by the US.

That Museveni would have positioned Uganda thus, and as quickly as he did, is not surprising when his history of working with the international donor community and his clear regional ambitions are reviewed. After initially stating that Uganda would follow a path of mixed socialism and capitalism, Museveni quickly changed this and Uganda accepted a structural adjustment programme in 1987.[35] Repositioning Uganda as an ally of the West in the final years of the Cold War allowed Uganda access to significant amounts of donor aid and, as the country became increasingly peaceful, Uganda entered something of an economic boom. From 1986 to 1996, Uganda experienced an average annual real gross domestic product rate of 7.7 per cent, and from 1996 to 2006 it grew at an average rate of 6.55 per cent annually, with a couple of years of over 8 per cent growth and one year of over 10 per cent growth.[36] In addition to GDP growth, the percentage of the population living below the absolute poverty line fell from 56.4 per cent in 1992/93 to 2.5 per cent in 2009/10.[37] This makes Uganda one of the few sub-Saharan African countries to achieve the first Millennium Development Goal of halving extreme poverty by 2015. The World Bank in 2007 identified the reason for this success as the 'careful sequencing and determined implementation of the most far-reaching stabilization and structural reform programme in Africa, and one of the most comprehensive reform efforts in the world'.[38]

The economic success experienced by Uganda and the relationships Museveni cultivated with many donor countries led to the president being considered a 'safe pair of hands' within East Africa, especially in the 1990s when many other countries in the region were experiencing conflict.[39] This perception was reinforced by the claims that the Ugandan intelligence services had foiled two attacks on the US embassy in Kampala in 1998. Reno argues that this combination of factors led donors to tolerate certain behaviours within the Ugandan political elite that would not have been tolerated in other donor-dependent countries.[40] Just as donor countries ignored Ugandan incursions into the DRC so that they could continue to point to an African structural adjustment programme success, Museveni has used Uganda's role as a key ally of the US in the War on Terror to enhance his regional position.

The aftermath of the 9/11 attacks and the beginning of the subsequent War on Terror impacted Uganda's conflict with the LRA in a number of ways. First, the LRA was designated a terrorist organization and the way that donor governments responded to the group changed. The US Department of State included the LRA in its list of foreign terrorist organizations and, according to Dolan, there 'was talk of using the Terrorism Act of January 2002 against the LRA members in the UK'.[41] For the first time, humanitarian aid was not the only type of foreign aid directed towards the conflict. The US donated $1.7 million to the Ugandan army for vehicles, spare parts and radios, and began to sponsor the training of 6,000 Ugandan troops who would be dedicated to fighting the LRA.

Second, in recognition of the geopolitical reality in East Africa it became imperative to bring Sudan into the process of defeating the LRA. In bilateral talks facilitated by UK Secretary of State for International Development Clare Short, President Museveni and President al-Bashir 'agreed on UPDF incursions into southern Sudan, with the stated aims of rescuing abducted children and capturing or killing Kony and his key commanders'.[42] The Ugandan Government then launched Operation Iron Fist in March 2002, in another attempt to defeat the LRA by military means. Ultimately, this operation also failed and the LRA intensified its attacks across Northern Uganda, widening the theatre of war to include areas of Langi and Teso that had previously been unaffected by the conflict.

During this period, Museveni expanded his methods of dealing with the LRA and attempted to bring an end to the conflict through legal means. He referred the LRA to the International Criminal Court (ICC) on 16 December 2003 for crimes against humanity and war crimes. After investigation, the ICC indicted Joseph Kony and his four top commanders, issuing sealed arrest warrants in July 2005 and unsealing these in October 2005. None of these commanders were arrested until Dominic Ongwen surrendered in January 2015, and he is currently awaiting trial. These arrest warrants did, however, complicate the resolution of the conflict. In 2006 the Juba peace negotiations began, and offered what seemed like the best prospect for peace in the twenty years since the conflict began.[43] However, ultimately these talks were also unsuccessful and one of the main reasons they broke down was that the Ugandan Government refused to guarantee that the indicted LRA leaders would not be prosecuted by the ICC. The government did not actually have the authority to guarantee this, as it had surrendered authority on this issue to the ICC after it referred the case.[44]

Even though the talks had failed, by the mid-2000s the LRA was no longer really a problem for Uganda, having moved its base of operations to the DRC and the Central African Republic. At this point, in terms of terrorism, Uganda turned its attention more fully to the War on Terror. In 2002 the Ugandan Government enacted the Anti-Terrorism Act, and for the first time the country could prosecute people for acts of terrorism, rather than attempt to pursue terrorists through other charges. This imposed a mandatory death penalty for terrorists, and a potential death penalty for sponsors and supporters of terrorism. The act created a list of proscribed terrorist organizations, which included al Qaeda, the LRA and the ADF.

The government had also created the Joint Anti-Terrorism Task Force in 1999, which was designed to coordinate responses to terrorism with the military and police across the country. However, both of these initiatives have been criticized. Human Rights Watch said the following of the 2002 legislation:

> [Dissidents are labelled] 'opponents of the state,' thus making those in the media and public life who have divergent views suspect. The terrorism law contains rather sweeping provisions. For example, possession of unlicensed firearms is tantamount to terrorism. ... Clause 14 empowers ministers to declare an organization 'terrorist,' without challenge in court.[45]

The potential for abuse became real in the aftermath of the 2001 elections. Supporters of the opposition leader and main challenger for the presidency, Kizza Besigye, went into exile after the election. Although Museveni later said that they were free to return, he had also accused Besigye of being a terrorist, and threatened to capture and kill all terrorists.[46] The Joint Anti-Terrorism Task Force was accused of 'prolonged incommunicado detention of terrorism and treason suspects at the JATT headquarters in Kololo, and the routine use of torture during interrogations'.[47]

These criticisms did not, however, stop the US from partnering with Uganda on a number of counterterrorism initiatives in East Africa. The first of these, the Eastern Africa Counterterrorism Initiative (EACTI), was announced in June 2003 and was designed to 'expand and accelerate [counterterrorism] efforts with Kenya, Ethiopia, Djibouti, Uganda, Tanzania, and other countries'.[48] In practical terms, this meant the US provided resources to improve policing and judicial capabilities, and provided counterterrorism training to senior-level decision-makers. Uganda's central role in the EACTI was clear in April 2004, when all of the participating nations, as well as G8 representatives and observers from neighbouring states, were invited to attend a conference in Kampala to review the initiative. The aim of this conference, according to the US Department of State, was to 'strength regional ties, particularly in the area of information sharing, and [help] to increase international donor interest and coordination in fighting the long-term battle against terrorism'.[49] In 2009, the United States established another regional body for counterterrorism efforts in East Africa, known as the Partnership for Regional East Africa Counterterrorism (PREACT). This is designed to 'build the capacity and cooperation of military, law enforcement, and civilian actors across East Africa to counter terrorism in a comprehensive fashion'.[50]

The US has also partnered with Uganda on a series of other regional and country-specific initiatives to increase Uganda's counterterrorism capabilities. In 2004 the US worked with Kenya, Uganda and Tanzania through the Safe Skies programme to create a regional civil aviation safety structure. In June 2009 the US Anti-terrorism Assistance Program (ATA) conducted an assessment of the Ugandan Government's counterterrorism capabilities. This concluded that counterterrorism efforts were hampered by limited resources and corruption.[51] The US Department of State also recommended that Uganda enact comprehensive anti-money-laundering legislation and improve coordination and information sharing between the security services,[52] despite the presence of the Joint Anti-Terrorism Task Force, which was supposed to do exactly that. In 2009, the US also provided funding to Uganda through the Terrorist Interdiction Program/Personal Identification Secure Comparison and Evaluation System Program (TIP/PISCES), which was designed to help countries at risk of terrorist activity enhance their border security capabilities. It did this through providing a computerized watch-list system and training operators in Uganda to identify suspect travellers.[53]

Conclusion

Uganda has a complicated history that impacts how terrorism is viewed within the country. Some of the incidents that the country has experienced, such as the 2010 World Cup bombings and the ADF bombings in Kampala, fit a very traditional understanding of what terrorism is. Others, such as the LRA attacks against civilians are more ambiguous, and have often been considered acts of conflict rather than terrorism. Further confusion has been caused in the public discourse of what terrorism is in Uganda by the tendency of the Museveni regime to label its opponents 'terrorists' and to threaten them with consequences under the Anti-Terrorism Act.

There is some concern that Uganda will continue to be a target for terrorist attacks, with the government expressing fears that refugees from areas like Somalia may pose a security threat.[54] Museveni recently suggested that Ugandan troops may be pulled out of Somalia, although this appeared to be a response more to the recent decision by the EU to cut funding to AMISOM than to any threats from al Shabaab. Museveni has previously been able to change donor behaviour by laying out undesirable responses to donor proposals, although it remains to be seen if funding will be restored to AMISOM. It is, however, unlikely that Museveni will withdraw troops from the Somalia conflict due to threats from al Shabaab, as the role of regional leader who is tough on terrorism is not one that Museveni will want to relinquish.

Notes

1 *BBC News*, 'Yoweri Museveni: Uganda's president profiled,' *BBC News*, 17 February 2016, available at: www.bbc.com/news/world-africa-12421747 (accessed 9 March 2017).

2 Kasaija Phillip Apuuli, 'Regional integration: A political federation of the East African countries?' *African Journal of International Affairs* 7:1–2 (2004): 21–34.

3 Nick Young, 'Uganda: A pawn in the US's proxy African war on terror,' *Guardian*, 25 September 2010, available at: www.theguardian.com/commentisfree/cifamerica/2010/sep/25/ugandas-proxy-war-on-terror (accessed 2 November 2015).

4 Often translated as king.

5 A.B.K. Kasozi, *The Social Origins of Violence in Uganda: 1964–1985* (Montreal: McGill-Queen's University Press, 1994).

6 Henry Kyemba, *State of Blood: The Inside Story of Idi Amin's Reign of Fear* (London: Corgi, 1977).

7 Pulitzer Center, 'Karamoja: Broken warriors,' Pulitzer Center website, 6 April 2011, available at: http://pulitzercenter.org/projects/karamoja-uganda-poverty-violence-disarmament-drought (accessed 23 January 2016).

8 To be distinguished from a one-party system in two ways. First, the individuals standing for election could run on their own policy platforms and did not have to toe any party line, or gain a party nomination to run. Second, all citizens of Uganda were members of this system by virtue of their citizenship. Expulsion from the system could not be used as a punishment.

9 See, for example, Human Rights Watch, 'Uganda: Not a level playing field: Government violations in the lead-up to the election,' Human Rights Watch website, 2001, available at: www.hrw.org/reports/2001/uganda (accessed 23 January 2016); and 'Uganda: Ensure free and fair elections: Unimpeded media, police accountability critical to campaigns,' Human Rights Watch website, 8 November 2015, available at: www.hrw.org/news/2015/11/08/uganda-ensure-free-and-fair-elections (accessed 23 January 2016).

10 Kristof Titeca and Koen Vlassenroot, 'Rebels without borders in the Rwenzori borderland? A biography of the Allied Democratic Forces,' *Journal of Eastern African Studies* 6:1 (2012): 154–76.

11 See Emma Leonard, 'The Lord's Resistance Army: An African terrorist group?' *Perspectives on Terrorism* 4:6 (2010), available at: www.terrorismanalysts.com/pt/index.php/pot/article/view/129/html (accessed 15 January 2018).

12 Kenneth J. Menkhaus, 'Constraints and opportunities in ungoverned spaces: The Horn of Africa,' in Michael A. Innes (ed.), *Denial of Sanctuary: Understanding Terrorist Safe Havens* (Westport, CT: Praeger Security International, 2007), pp. 67–82.

13 Lindsay Scorgie, 'Peripheral pariah or regional rebel? The Allied Democratic Forces and the Uganda/Congo borderland,' *Round Table* 100:412 (2011): 79–93.

14 International Crisis Group (ICG), *Eastern Congo: The ADF-NALU's Lost Rebellion*, Africa briefing no. 93 (Nairobi: ICG, 2012).

15 *IRIN*, 'ADF abducts 356 inmates in attacks on prison,' *IRIN*, 10 December 1999, available at: www.irinnews.org/news/1999/12/10/adf-abducts-365-inmates-attack-prison (accessed 18 April 2016).

16 Suranjan Weeraratne and Sterling Recker, 'The isolated Islamists: The case of the Allied Democratic Forces in Ugandan-Congolese borderland,' *Terrorism and Political Violence* 30:1, epub ahead of print (9 February 2016), available at: www.tandfonline.com/doi/full/10.1080/09546553.2016.1139577 (accessed 15 January 2018).

17 Chris Dolan and Lucy Hovil, *Humanitarian protection in Uganda: A Trojan Horse?* Humanitarian Policy Group background paper (London: Overseas Development Institute, 2006).

18 Jeffrey Kaplan, 'The Fifth Wave: The new tribalism?' *Terrorism and Political Violence* 19:4 (2007): 545–70.

19 *Economist, Uganda Country Report*, 1995 no. 4 (London: *Economist*, 1995).

20 Quoted in Chris Dolan, *Social Torture: The Case of Northern Uganda, 1986–2006* (Oxford: Berghahn Books, 2009), p. 47.

21 *Economist, Uganda Country Report*, 1998 no. 1 (London: *Economist*, 1998).

22 Quoted in David Westbrook, 'The torment of Northern Uganda: A legacy of missed opportunities,' *Online Journal of Peace and Conflict Resolution* 3:2 (2000), available at: www.trinstitute.org/ojpcr/3_2westbrook.htm (accessed 15 January 2018).

23 *Washington Post*, 'Embassy in Uganda may have been a target,' *Washington Post*, 6 October 1998, available at: www.washingtonpost.com/archive/politics/1998/10/06/embassy-in-uganda-may-have-been-a-target/11a05e0a-

81ef-4006-b524-29d4f0614a83/?utm_term=.1dc39596f802 (accessed 30 July 2016).

24 *Al Jazeera*, 'Al-Shabab claims Uganda bombings,' *Al Jazeera*, 13 July 2010, available at: www.aljazeera.com/news/africa/2010/07/201071121252082 6984.html (accessed 30 July 2010).

25 Human Rights Watch, 'Trail of death: LRA atrocities in northeastern Congo,' Human Rights Watch website, 28 March 2010, available at: www.hrw.org/report/2010/03/28/trail-death/lra-atrocities-northeastern-congo (accessed 15 January 2018).

26 Billie O'Kadameri, 'LRA/government negotiations 1993–94,' in Okello Lucima (ed.), *Protracted Conflict, Elusive Peace: Initiatives to End Violence in Northern Uganda,* (London: Conciliation Resources, 2002), available at: www.c-r.org/resources/protracted-conflict-elusive-peace-initiatives-end-violence-northern-uganda-original-accord (accessed 30 July 2016).

27 Westbrook, 'Torment of Northern Uganda.'

28 John Davis, 'The Clinton model: Sudan and the failure to capture bin Laden,' in John Davis (ed.), *Africa and the War on Terrorism* (Aldershot, UK: Ashgate, 2007), p. 129.

29 Peter Walker, 'Profile: Omar al-Bashir,' *Guardian*, 14 July 2008, available at: www.theguardian.com/world/2008/jul/14/sudan.warcrimes3 (accessed 1 November 2015).

30 *Economist, Uganda Country Report* (1995).

31 Chris Dolan, 'Understanding war and its continuation: The case of Northern Uganda' (PhD thesis, London School of Economics and Political Science, 2005).

32 *Economist, Uganda Country Report* (1998).

33 Quoted in *Voice of America*, 'US military involvement in Uganda yields mixed results,' *Voice of America*, 2 August 2012, available at: www.voanews.com/content/us-military-involvement-in-uganda-yields-mixed-results/1453697.html (accessed 2 November 2015).

34 US Department of State (USDS), *Country Reports on Terrorism 2005* (Washington, DC: USDS Office of the Coordinator for Counterterrorism, 2006), available at: www.state.gov/documents/organization/65462.pdf (accessed 15 January 2018).

35 Ellen Hauser, 'Ugandan relations with Western donors in the 1990s: What impact on democratization?' *Journal of Modern African Studies* 37:4 (1999): 621–41.

36 Sarah Ssewanyana, John Mary Matovu and Evarist Twimukye, 'Building on growth in Uganda,' in Punam Chuhan-Pole and Manka Angwafo (eds), *Yes Africa Can: Success Stories from a Dynamic Continent* (Washington, DC: International Bank for Reconstruction and Development/World Bank, 2011).

37 *Ibid.*

38 World Bank, *UGANDA, Moving beyond Recovery: Investment and Behavior Change, for Growth* (Washington, DC: World Bank Poverty Reduction and Economic Management Unit, 2007).

39 Hauser, 'Ugandan relations.'

40 William Reno, 'Uganda's politics of war and debt relief,' *Review of International Political Economy* 9:3 (2002): 415–35, available at: www.tandfonline.com/doi/pdf/10.1080/09692290210150671 (accessed 15 January 2018).

41 Dolan, 'Understanding war and its continuation,' p. 53.

42 *Ibid.*

43 *BBC News*, 'Uganda rebels drop truce demand,' *BBC News*, 14 August 2006, available at: http://news.bbc.co.uk/1/hi/world/africa/4790049.stm (accessed 15 January 2018).

44 As a compromise the Ugandan Government created the International Crimes Division of the High Court of Uganda in July 2008, with the intention that the five commanders under indictment from the ICC would be tried in Uganda. This was based on the principle of 'complementarity' within the Rome Statute: the ICC would prosecute crimes that the individual country signatories were unable or unwilling to prosecute, but if the country demonstrated willingness and the capacity to prosecute at home then jurisdiction would be returned from the ICC to the country.

45 Human Rights Watch, 'State of pain: Torture in Uganda,' *Human Rights Watch Reports* 16:4(A) (2004): 16, available at: www.hrw.org/sites/default/files/reports/uganda0304.pdf (accessed 15 January 2018).

46 Aili Mari Tripp, 'The changing face of authoritarianism in Africa: The case of Uganda,' *Africa Today* 50:3 (2004): 3–26.

47 Human Rights Watch, 'Open secret: Illegal detention and torture by the Joint Anti-Terrorism Task Force in Uganda,' Human Rights Watch website, 8 April 2009, available at: www.hrw.org/report/2009/04/08/open-secret/illegal-detention-and-torture-joint-anti-terrorism-task-force-uganda (accessed 15 January 2018).

48 USDS, *Patterns of Global Terrorism 2003* (Washington, DC: USDS, 2004), p. iv, available at: www.state.gov/documents/organization/31912.pdf (accessed 22 January 2016).

49 USDS, *Country Reports on Terrorism 2004* (Washington, DC: USDS Office of the Coordinator for Counterterrorism (OCC), 2005), p. 29, available at: www.state.gov/documents/organization/45313.pdf (accessed 15 January 2018).

50 USDS, 'Programs and initiatives,' USDS website, n.d., available at: www.state.gov/j/ct/programs/index.htm#PREACT (accessed 15 January 2018).

51 USDS, *Country Reports on Terrorism 2009* (Washington, DC: USDS OCC, 2010), available at: www.state.gov/documents/organization/141114.pdf (accessed 15 January 2018).

52 *Ibid.*, pp. 34–5.

53 *Ibid.*, p. 228.

54 Pascal Kwesiga, 'Refugees from terror-ridden nations worry Uganda,' *New Vision*, 16 June 2016, available at: www.newvision.co.ug/new_vision/news/1427157/refugees-terror-ridden-nations-worry-uganda (accessed 17 September 2016).

18

Understanding South Africa's confused and ineffective response to terrorism

Hussein Solomon

Introduction

That South Africa increasingly plays a key role in global terror networks, from the provision of safe houses or the acquisition of fraudulent identity documents to the raising of funds, is beyond doubt.[1] Al Qaeda, the Palestinian Hamas, Lebanon's Hizbullah and Somalia's al Shabaab all have a presence in the country.[2] The danger this poses to South Africa was evident in the September 2009 lockdown of the US embassy, its consulates and the offices of the United States Agency for International Development (USAID) when a credible threat against US interests in the country was received, emanating from al Shabaab's cell based in Cape Town.[3] For instance, a 2010 National Intelligence Agency (NIA) document leaked in 2015 noted that there were jihadi training camps at Zakariyya Park in Lenasia in Gauteng Province, at a farm in Port Elizabeth in the Eastern Cape and in KwaZulu-Natal.[4] In the 1990s, the Western Cape experienced a wave of urban terror conducted by local terror groups.[5] The malevolent nature of the threat was underlined by the repeated discovery of new paramilitary training camps in South Africa,[6] as new recruits were trained in the deadly arts accompanying the rise of militant Islam across the African continent. For all these reasons, an effective counterterrorism policy is essential.

If one examines the country's legislative framework, on the face of it South Africa does have a clear and comprehensive counterterrorism strategy. The

US State Department's June 2015 *Country Reports on Terrorism* argues that the South African Police Service (SAPS) Crime Intelligence Division, the Directorate for Priority Crime Investigation, the South African State Security Agency (SSA), the SAPS Special Task Force and the National Prosecuting Authority 'possess the knowledge, resources, intelligence capabilities and techniques to effectively implement South Africa's counter-terrorism legislation'.[7] At the level of implementation, however, and from statements emanating from South African officials, the policy is far more ambiguous. This gap between promise and performance has resulted in South Africa's counterterrorism strategy being rightly viewed by international partners as lacking credibility.[8] This chapter briefly explores the country's current counterterrorism policies, examines their implementation and provides reasons for the clear discrepancy between adoption and implementation.

South Africa's rhetoric on terrorism

In the aftermath of 9/11, Pretoria immediately denounced the terror attacks on American soil, and offered Washington both humanitarian assistance and the full cooperation of its security agencies.[9] The 9/11 attack, meanwhile, was one of the catalysts for South Africa to re-examine its own domestic terror laws. 'While the world unites to condemn those dastardly acts in the United States, we have to skirt around the issue. We go around making promises to co-operate with everyone but as our law stands, we cannot deal with terrorism. We are the only country that refuses to look terrorism in the face as a unique crime,' said South Africa's minister of safety and security in 2004, in support of specific anti-terrorism legislation.[10]

According to its Protection of Constitutional Democracy against Terrorist and Related Activities Act, 2004, the South African Government shall:

- condemn all acts of terror
- take all lawful measures to prevent acts of terror and bring to justice those involved in acts of terror
- undertake to protect foreign citizens from acts of terror in South Africa
- in the event of an act of terror in a foreign country and involving a South African citizen, cooperate with the host government to resolve the matter
- not make concessions that would encourage extortion by terrorists
- not allow its territory to be used as a haven to plan, direct or support acts of terror

- support and cooperate with the international community in their efforts to prevent and combat acts of terror
- use all appropriate measures to combat terrorism
- support its citizens who are victims of terrorism.[11]

The need for such legislation came not only from such seminal events as 9/11, but also the urban terror campaign that ravaged the Western Cape in the late 1990s, which witnessed amongst other things the bombing of Planet Hollywood in August 1998 and the targeting of moderate Muslim academics speaking out against the extremists. Interestingly, the bombing of Planet Hollywood was not motivated by any local grievance. It was the result of Muslim rage following US President Bill Clinton's 1998 decision to bomb Sudan. However, after security forces targeted People against Gangsterism and Drugs (PAGAD), the local Islamist group responsible, it in turn targeted the police and the state prosecutor responsible for the case.[12] The 2004 Protection of Constitutional Democracy against Terrorist and Related Activities Act of the Republic of South Africa also sought to integrate the country's numerous pieces of anti-terrorism legislation into one coherent and comprehensive law, and to align this with international instruments to counter terrorism.[13] The most important of these international instruments includes United Nations Security Council Resolution 1373, which affirms that any act of international terrorism constitutes a threat to global peace and security, and calls on member states to:

- deny all forms of financial support for terrorist groups
- suppress the provision of safe havens, sustenance or support for terrorists
- share information with other governments in the investigation, detection, arrest and prosecution of those involved in terrorist activities
- criminalize active and passive assistance for terrorism in domestic laws and bring violators of these laws to justice
- become party, as soon as possible, to the relevant international conventions and protocols relating to terrorism.[14]

Given the propinquity between organized crime syndicates and international terror networks, South Africa also enacted the Financial Intelligence Control Act in 2001 to stem money laundering, and joined the Financial Action Task Force and the Eastern and Southern African Anti-Money Laundering Group.[15] In addition to these multilateral commitments and its domestic anti-terror legislation, South Africa also brought the issue of terrorism to the fore through its bilateral relations. In October 2006, during a meeting with the Indian prime minister, Manmohan Singh, at the Union Buildings, former South African President Thabo Mbeki declared that the two countries would share intelligence to help prevent terrorist attacks.[16] This underscored the notion that terrorism constitutes a global threat and that only by acting in partnership can the international community eradicate this scourge. Following the al Shabaab twin bombings of the Ugandan capital, Kampala, in July 2010, the head of the South African delegation visiting Uganda condemned terrorism as evil and urged the international community to work together for its elimination. The South African official went on to state: 'As South Africa, we remain committed to continuing to discharge our responsibility – individually as a country and as part of the international community – to combat terrorism in all its manifestations.'[17]

Whatever the rhetoric emanating from Pretoria, the threat perception varied considerably among the security agencies. Two statements bear this out. Tshepo Mazibuko, the spokesperson for South Africa's embassy in Washington noted, 'Our security agents who frequently do security analysis have not yet come up with anything that says that there is al Qaeda activity in South Africa.'[18] Yet the security agents he refers to seem to have a different take. Gideon Jones, the former head of the Crime Investigation Unit of the SAPS responded to a question posed on terrorism in the country by noting that, '[South Africa] is a perfect place to cool off, regroup, and plan your finances and operations. The communications and infrastructure are excellent, there is a radical Muslim community, and our law enforcement is overstretched.'[19]

Clearly, despite the formal legislative framework, confusion continues to reign among government officials. This gap between promise and performance, and rhetoric and reality, has resulted in South Africa evincing a credibility gap in the area of terrorism. Perhaps it is easier to enact legislation than implement it, or to sign international agreements than actually destroy terrorist infrastructure. This glaring contradiction is also evident in the operational sphere.

From promise to performance

The promise that South Africa's counterterrorism legislation and attendant structures hold was not to be realized operationally; the ambiguity among policymakers in Pretoria was to have negative consequences. Two cases demonstrate the confusion and ineffectiveness of the South African counterterrorism strategy. The first of these is Mustafa Jonker and the Muizenberg cell. Just before dawn on 25 January 2008, Police Superintendent Noel Zeeman led his officers on a raid of two homes in Muizenberg, outside Cape Town. Three of the men targeted were Mustafa Mohamed Jonker, his brother-in-law Omar Hartley and Sedick Achmat. They stood accused of being part of a group planning to overthrow the government by means of blowing up specific targets. The men had been downloading material on how to make explosives. Other members of the group were Mahomed Davids, Abdul Rasheed Davids and Rafiek Osman. Despite the nature of the items seized in the raid, and the gravity of the charges – high treason; terrorism; conspiracy to commit murder; and unlawful possession of firearms, ammunition and explosives – none of the men were arrested. Indeed, the Davids brothers subsequently left South African shores.

It would seem that the men's Internet activity – visits to various jihadi websites – and a tip-off prompted the raids. Zeeman was to claim in court papers that the raid discovered chemicals, computers and videos containing brutal beheadings.[20] According to police explosives expert Captain Bester, the chemicals in the men's possession – hydrochloric acid, acetone and peroxide, which were hidden the under bed of one of the accused – were according to the formula downloaded from the Internet to make improvised explosive devices.[21] The accused men in turn referred to the chemicals as 'pool cleaner, paint remover and bleach'.[22] As for the Internet downloads from jihadi websites, Jonker stated that the information that he downloaded was freely available and legal to download.[23]

Jonker and Hartley went to court to challenge the search and seizure warrants issued by the magistrate, with their lawyer demanding the full disclosure of the contents of the affidavit that led to the warrant being issued.[24] Zeeman, meanwhile, asked the judge to place a 'gag' on certain parts of the affidavit used to grant the search warrants as it contained 'sensitive information'.[25] However, in March 2008 when the case went to court, the presiding judge, Justice Bennie Griesel, told the men's lawyers that he had not seen the state's opposing papers. It subsequently emerged that a deal was struck between the accused men and the state that resulted in the case being dropped and the material seized in the raid being returned.[26]

For researchers attempting to analyse the risk posed to South Africa by terrorists, situations like these raise more questions than they provide answers. The state seemed confident of its case, yet refused to file opposing papers and then struck a deal with the accused before the case went to court. So, did Zeeman want to protect the 'very reliable source'[27] that had tipped him off about the Muizenberg cell? And was he afraid that the affidavit being made public would compromise his source? Or, on the other hand, could the accused be innocent? According to their lawyer, the raids were part of a conspiracy by a 'Third Force to spread fear of Muslim culture and justify the establishment of US military and Israeli secret services bases in South Africa'.[28] It should be stated that no evidence was provided to prove such an assertion. Despite the promise of South Africa's counterterrorism legislative framework and the institutions it established, this certainly was not realized in the case of this Muizenberg cell.

However problematic we may believe the Muizenberg case was, worse was to come in the second case: the strange case of the two South Africans caught in an al Qaeda safe house in Pakistan. On 10 July 2004, Dr Feroz Abubaker Ganchi and Zubair Ismail travelled together to Pakistan, the latter ostensibly to pursue his Islamic education and the former to do welfare work.[29] They entered Pakistan on passports that were exact copies of ones seized in British anti-terror raids in London.[30] In Pakistan, local contacts assisted them to a house in Mohallah Islam Nagar that sheltered Islamists from Kenya and Sudan, as well as senior al Qaeda operative Ahmed Khalfan Ghailani.[31] Ghailani was alleged to have purchased the truck used in the 1998 vehicle bombing of the US embassy in Dar es Salaam, Tanzania, in which more than 200 people were killed. On 16 December 1998, a New York court indicted Ghailani for his role in this terrorist act, which resulted in him being on the FBI's list of twenty-two most-wanted terrorists.[32]

Following a tip-off,[33] Pakistani security forces surrounded the house and a fierce twelve-hour gun battle ensued. Fighting only ceased after Pakistani commandos broke down the wall and roof of one of the rooms and fired tear-gas canisters into the house after the men inside had run out of ammunition. The Pakistani security services discovered ten Kalashnikov rifles, pistols, hand grenades, laptop computers, chemicals, and atlases and maps in the house.[34] Given the length of the gun battle and its ferocity, as well as the subsequent confessions from the South Africans, the Pakistani authorities believe that they were 'trained terrorists'. Indeed, the Pakistani newspaper *Dawn* also stated that the South Africans had received training in Afghanistan and Iran.[35] Pakistan's law minister, Raja Basharat, stated that all of the twelve men arrested were operatives in Osama bin Laden's al Qaeda network.[36] Media reports indicated that both South Africans had confessed to the Pakistani authorities that their mission was to carry out terror attacks in South Africa. Among the alleged targets were the Carlton Centre, the Johannesburg Stock Exchange, Parliament, the Union Buildings, the Victoria and Alfred Waterfront, the Sheraton Hotel, and the US embassy in Pretoria.[37]

The confusion in this saga stems from the South African Government's reaction – once more highlighting the ambiguity amongst South African policymakers and security officials. When the news first broke, the Department of Foreign Affairs (DFA) spokesperson Ronnie Mamoepa questioned whether Ismail and

Ganchi were indeed South African; he pointed out that there were several cases of forged South African passports being used by international criminals and terrorists.[38] When it emerged that they were indeed South African citizens and the circumstances of their arrest came to light, then Deputy Foreign Affairs Minister Aziz Pahad stated, 'With the involvement of Ghailani, the case has taken on a more serious security aspect. What was earlier a foreign affairs issue is now an international security one.'[39] In August 2004, South Africa's NIA sent a team to Pakistan to question the two South Africans personally. The subsequent statements from then NIA Director-General Vusi Mavimbela were most interesting: 'We wanted to know whether it was true that there were plans to attack South Africa. This was all we wanted to know and we found that there was no evidence of such plans. ... We are not interested in why they are in Pakistan. South Africa is our only interest.'[40]

As in the case of the Muizenberg raid, there are more questions here than there are answers. Did South African intelligence agencies factor in why these men travelled on passports that were exact replicas of the ones seized in a British anti-terror raid in London, or how these men came to be in an al Qaeda safe house in Pakistan with a senior al Qaeda terrorist? The NIA seemed not to be interested in finding out the reasons for this. Moreover, the NIA did not seem to want to ask what the motivation would be on the part of Pakistani government officials to lie when they stated that the men were planning to attack targets in South Africa. On the other hand, what assurances did Mr Mavimbela have that these men were not going to strike at targets in South Africa?

These questions certainly demanded answers. The men eventually returned to South Africa, only to have the media probing any connection between the two men and the alleged al Qaeda terrorists from Syria and Jordan that the police had just deported.[41] It subsequently emerged that both Ganchi and Ismail were indeed in contact with these men, and had met them on several occasions in April 2004 shortly before their arrests.[42] They met at a mosque in Laudium, Pretoria, and a *madrasah* where Ismail attended Islamic education classes. And this was not their first contact with foreign Islamists. Three years prior to the events of 2004, Ismail had travelled to the United Kingdom where he met Islamists from London and Manchester.[43]

Worse was to come when SAPS intelligence officers confirmed that Ganchi and Ismail *had* targeted South Africa, thus contradicting Mr Mavimbela and the NIA. According to the police agents, they had been following the suspects and never doubted that they were targeting South Africa for terrorism purposes.[44] Yet the NIA's Mavimbela repeatedly denied that South Africa was being targeted by terrorists: 'In terms of the information we have as security services, we have got no information that any particular installation in South Africa is being targeted by al Qaeda, or any international terrorist organization.'[45] But according to Ronald Sandee, research director of the Nine/Eleven Finding Answers (NEFA) Foundation, in his testimony to the US Congress, upon returning to South Africa and being interrogated by South African officials, both Ganchi and Ismail admitted to targeting South Africa for terror attacks.[46] So why was Mavimbela so adamant that South Africa was not at risk?

More questions emerged. Had the SAPS known about the threat for over a year and a half[47] – they were actually following the suspects – and not tell the NIA about it? Certainly, on the face of it, the two security agencies – given their contrasting statements – were clearly not informing each other about their activities regarding the same suspects, despite the existence of a National Intelligence Coordinating Committee (NICOC) whose very existence suggests the sharing of intelligence between agencies. More importantly, why were Ganchi and Ismail allowed to fly from South Africa via Dubai to Pakistan on travel documents that were problematic at best? Ganchi and Ismail were again caught and detained in Guinea in December 2004 when they tried to cross the border into Sierra Leone. Here, Ganchi was using the alias Dr Mohammed Nazzal.[48] A few months later, on 7 March 2005, Ganchi and Ismail were again arrested, together with Muhsin Fadhi (aka Abu Sami from Kuwait) and Abu Ubaysah al-Turki (aka Ubaida Ubeyde from Turkey), when they tried to cross the border between Indonesia and East Timor.[49] These questions arose again in 2009 when Ganchi was detained by the Egyptian authorities en route to Gaza.[50]

Are Ganchi and Ismail guilty of the crimes that they have been accused of, or are they hapless travellers who were in the wrong place at the wrong time? Why are there contradictory statements coming from the security apparatus of the state? Is there a threat to South Africa or not? What accounts for these ambiguous responses despite the clarity evident in the country's anti-terror legislation?

The legacy of the anti-apartheid struggle

In this author's view, a major reason for this ambiguity relates to the historical legacy of an African National Congress (ANC) that fought the apartheid South African state and was labelled 'terrorist' by both Washington and London during the course of the anti-apartheid struggle. As such, many government officials and South African Muslim organizations repeat that rather stale mantra – 'One man's terrorist is another's freedom fighter.' Moreover, while in exile the ANC forged ties with several entities, including the Irish Republican Army (IRA) and the Palestinian Liberation Organization (PLO). These historical ties, and indeed ideology, have remained despite the transition of the ANC from liberation movement to government in South Africa following the first democratic election in 1994.

The ideological proximity of elements of the South African Government to terrorist entities is evident in a statement by former South African Deputy Minister of Foreign Affairs Fatima Hajaig. Addressing a meeting on 14 January 2009, she is alleged to have said: 'They [the Jews] control [America] no matter which government comes into power, whether Barack Obama or George Bush ... Their control of America, just like the control of most Western countries, is in the hands of Jewish money and when Jewish money controls their country then you can expect anything.'[51] The views allegedly expressed by Hajaig are no different from those expressed by various militant Islamist groups, who all speak of a Jewish conspiracy. The South African Jewish Board of Deputies decided to lodge a complaint of hate speech with the Human Rights Commission against Ms Hajaig. As its chairman, Zev Krengel, stated, 'The decision to lodge the complaint had not been taken lightly, but there had not been any realistic alternative. Not since the era of pro-Nazi Nationalist MPs more than half a century ago had such statements been made against Jews by a senior government official.'[52]

Despite Tehran reportedly being one of the leading sponsors of state terror, the South African Government has closely allied itself with Iran and its surrogates – Hizbullah and Hamas.[53] Tehran and Pretoria, for instance, established a Joint Bilateral Commission to expand political and economic relationships between the two countries. At the seventh South Africa–Iran Joint Bilateral Commission, former Foreign Minister Nkosazana Dlamini-Zuma spoke of 'the shared values between South Africa and the Islamic Republic of Iran, namely the promotion of democracy, justice, peace and prosperity'.[54] South Africa's proximity to the Iranian regime might well further complicate how it approaches Iranian-sponsored Islamist groups inside the country.

In June 2003, then Deputy Foreign Affairs Minister Aziz Pahad met with the chief of Hizbullah's Political Bureau, Mohammad Raad, in Beirut.[55] Following the meeting, the Foreign Ministry stated that a clear distinction must be made 'between terrorism and legitimate struggle for liberation'.[56] Was this a case of viewing Hizbullah through the ANC's own lens? Moreover, was Pretoria unaware of the five paramilitary Hizbullah training camps in South Africa?[57] Similarly, former Intelligence Minister Ronnie Kasrils invited Hamas leader Ismail Haniyeh to lead a delegation to South Africa.[58] These developments led Jonathan Schanzer in a prescient article to conclude that 'Overtures to Hamas and Hizbullah are indicative of Pretoria's utter indifference to the threat of radical Islamic ideologies and violence. The worst consequence of this blindness may be the creation of safe houses for terrorists in South Africa itself.'[59] Closely linked to the historical legacy of apartheid, and its pernicious influence on developing an effective counterterrorism strategy, is the issue of political correctness.

The eternal sin of political correctness

Political correctness characterizes the highest levels of South Africa's political establishment and undermines the fight against the scourge of terrorism. Ronnie Kasrils on one occasion stated, 'We guard against a rising international hysteria which serves to portray all Muslims as potential targets. The cry of "a terrorist in every Madrassah" echoes the "red under the bed" and "swart gevaar" [black danger] phobia of the Cold War and the apartheid era. We must never repeat such witch hunts in our country.'[60] This ideological blindness on the part of Kasrils refuses to recognize the qualitative difference between the armed struggle against apartheid and the current global jihadist scourge; indeed, it besmirches the noble struggle against the apartheid regime. The ANC engaged in a non-violent campaign against the apartheid state. When this was met with violent action on the part of the South African state and when the ANC was banned, thereby preventing legal avenues of redress from being explored, the armed struggle was embarked upon. Although there was the infamous Magoos Bar bombing, when a restaurant was targeted by the ANC's armed wing, attacks on civilians were not countenanced by the ANC leadership.[61] The idea that one targets innocent diners in a restaurant or passengers on a bus was anathema to the ANC. In this way, the ANC was able to maintain the moral high ground. Even more important is the limited goals of the ANC – a democratic, non-racial South Africa – compared with the ambitions of radical Islamists who seek to establish a global Muslim caliphate.[62]

The legacy of apartheid looms large over South African policymakers both domestically and internationally – and it should. But when policymakers examine everything through the lens of apartheid, they inevitably get it wrong, since other actors are motivated by other compulsions. As Anneli Botha has cogently argued, 'As a nascent democracy, South Africa is obsessed with protecting basic rights, rights that would be exploited by international terrorists working in tandem with local militants.'[63] Are we then surprised that, despite all the terrorist activity taking place on South African soil, so few individuals have been arrested for terrorism? What Pretoria seems to have forgotten is that these same terrorists are willing to deny the most fundamental of all rights – the right to life. Kurt Shillinger of the South African Institute for International Affairs (SAIIA) is also of the opinion that the reason why Pretoria has showed little desire to investigate its own Muslim community is because it does not want to alienate it.[64]

Internationally, South Africa's approach to issues of terrorism is also coloured by the ANC's own struggle against apartheid and the desire for political and economic equality. Thus, while commiserating with the US following 9/11, the South African Government urged Washington to adopt 'a longer-term response of isolating terrorists through international cooperation to eradicate poverty and underdevelopment'.[65] This was reiterated by former President Mbeki in his address to the United Nations General Assembly in 2003.[66] So, in the South African rendition, poverty breeds terrorism. International experience, however, undermines this assumption. Osama bin Laden is a Saudi multimillionaire. Bin Laden's successor and current al Qaeda chief, Ayman al-Zawahiri is a physician; Mohammed al-Atta, the leader of the 9/11 hijackers, was a German-trained architect and Umar Farouk Abdulmutallab, who tried to down an American airliner with explosives in his underwear, was the son of a prominent banker.[67] According to recent research on the subject, there is little to substantiate the notion that poverty leads to terrorism – indeed, if anything, global jihadis tend to represent the best and brightest of their societies who, if not necessarily wealthy, are at least middle class.[68]

Further, as Eric Rosand argues, 'Despite poverty being widespread, most of the world's poorest have not produced terrorist organizations, particularly not ones with an international scope. A Norwegian Institute of International Affairs panel of leading terrorism experts found there is only a weak and indirect relationship between poverty and terrorism.'[69] Other research has indicated that, far from using terror to attain certain political or economic objectives, Islamist terror aims only at threatening given social orders without having any feasible alternative. Indeed, this research has concluded that such 'terrorist activity is not motivated by a desire to reach any "constructive" goals, but much rather by a deep-seated psychological want to annihilate those who do not share the cultural worldview of the terrorist himself. In the case of Islamic terrorism, the mere existence of plural and secularist alternatives to a fundamentalist way of life is perceived to be unacceptable: the jihad as a conquest of the *dar al-harb*, the non-Muslim world, is a core motivation.'[70]

It is a sad truism that Pretoria knows neither its enemies nor their motivations – the ideological basis that instils hatred and violence towards the proverbial 'other'. How then can it ever hope to defeat terrorism within its borders?

Political correctness also breeds a false sense of security among South Africa's policymakers.

The danger of a false sense of security

There is some sense of naiveté among senior South African policymakers on the issue of terrorism. Responding to Ganchi and Ismail's arrest in Pakistan and the accusation that they were planning to attack targets in South Africa, Aziz Pahad stated: 'Anybody who has any sense would know that South Africa had taken consistently correct positions on issues like the Middle East and the war on Iraq, and there was no reason why anyone would want to attack it.'[71] From this perspective, then, South Africa is safe from terrorism because of its 'consistently correct' foreign policy positions vis-à-vis the Middle East. After all, South Africa is neither in Iraq nor in Afghanistan, and it is pro-Palestinian (whatever this means within the context of a pro-West Fatah vs a pro-Iran Hamas).

However, the urban terror campaign conducted by PAGAD in the Western Cape in the 1990s, as well as various other attempts to commit terror attacks since, suggests something different. PAGAD was established in December 1995 by Muslim groups, ostensibly to take on the scourge of drugs in the Western Cape.[72] However, its violent vigilante campaign against drug traffickers attracted the attention of the police authorities. This resulted in the organization targeting the state as well as various Western and Jewish interests and those institutions purported to promote 'immoral' behaviour. PAGAD's bombing campaign did not only target the US consulate in Cape Town or Western-associated restaurants like Planet Hollywood, but also synagogues, moderate Muslims, gay nightclubs and, very importantly, the organs of the South African state itself. In August 1998, there was an explosion outside the offices of the police special investigation task team, and in September of the same year the judge presiding over a case involving a PAGAD member was assassinated.[73]

The anti-secularist ideology of radical Islamism is another reason to doubt Mr Pahad's statement. During the 1990s similar structures to PAGAD, often with overlapping memberships, were established. One such structure was PAPAS, or the People against Prostitutes and Sodomites.[74] This points to the fact that radical Islamists are fundamentally intolerant of the liberal democratic and secular ethos of the South African Constitution. In his excellent book, *The War of Ideas: Jihadism against* Democracy, Walid Phares makes clear the radical Islamist antipathy towards liberal democracy values.[75] In this regard, it is important to note that while South Africa has been critical of US policies in relation to the Middle East, the country 'does display the general American preference for liberal democracy and individual freedom and remains part of the capitalist system that Bin Laden insists is preventing Islam from achieving its rightful place as the world's preeminent faith and religion'.[76] In other words, then, South Africa could be targeted on the basis of its secular ethos and its liberal democratic values, and not merely its foreign policy orientations.

Ambiguity in South Africa's counterterrorism response

There is a clear tension among South African policymakers when it comes to terrorism. On the one hand there is the demand of international law as represented by United Nations Security Council Resolution 1373 to take action against terrorists, which is reinforced by South African domestic legislation – The Protection of Constitutional Democracy against Terrorist and Related Activities Act. At the same time, because of the legacy of the anti-apartheid struggle, there is a certain ideological proximity between members in the ANC Government and terrorist movements – the notion that they are actually 'freedom fighters'. Thus, despite having the necessary legislation to take action against terrorists, the ANC Government lacks the political will to act. As a result, ambiguity has come to characterize South Africa's counterterrorism response.

This ambiguity arises from the gap between the dictates of the political correctness approach and a harsh reality that contradicts this. Various instances bear this out. Jackie Selebi, the former national police commissioner, informed the media that various al Qaeda operatives were planning to stage terror attacks during April 2004. A few months later, though, in August 2004, first government spokesman Joel Netshitenzhe, then former NIA Director-General Mavimbela and head of SAPS Crime Intelligence Ray Lalla denied that South Africa had been targeted by al Qaeda. However, they refused to provide further information, stating that 'operational security' precluded them from doing so.[77] This presents a quandary for those researching terrorism in South Africa. Do we listen to the national police commissioner or to the head of the SAPS Crime Intelligence Unit? Moreover, if South Africa was not targeted, what operational security considerations would prevent one from sharing this with the media?

Another example of this ambiguity among the country's policymakers was when former Intelligence Minister Ronnie Kasrils, in October 2004, denied media reports that South Africa was being used as a base for al Qaeda operations. However, in August 2005 he warned that al Qaeda was possibly trying to set up networks in southern Africa and that it would be easy for them to attack harbours.[78] So, does the 2005 statement from Mr Kasrils supersede the 2004 statement? Is al Qaeda using this region as a base for its operations?

Pretoria's ambiguous response to terrorism also extends into the international sphere. As mentioned earlier, in October 2006 during his meeting with the Indian prime minister, former President Mbeki spoke of the need for international cooperation in the area of counterterrorism. When such cooperation is needed from the South Africans, however, they balk. In January 2007, when South Africa was informed that the US intended to place two South Africans – the Dockrat cousins – on the UN Security Council's list of terror suspects, South Africa was vehemently opposed to this.[79] We have no reason for South Africa's opposition here unless we accept Kurt Shillinger's point, mentioned earlier, that Pretoria did not want to alienate its Muslim citizens. However, it should be noted that Muslims only constitute 1.5 per cent of the total population.[80] Electorally speaking, there will be little consequence should the ruling ANC adopt a tougher stance against terrorism. Needless to say, relations between Washington and Pretoria soured. These incidents raise the question of whether South Africa is prepared to 'walk the talk' in the global fight against terrorism. Put differently, is South Africa a credible partner in the fight against terrorism? On the available evidence, the answer has to be an emphatic 'no'.

Following the closure of the US embassy and consulates as well as the offices of USAID in September 2009 due to the al Shabaab threat, South Africa's then National Police Commissioner Bheki Cele said that the police were investigating the threat. However, he added that the police had not ruled out the possibility of a hoax. In the same statement he also said that police were pursuing some people and there would be arrests.[81] If the threat was a possible hoax, why were the police pursuing suspects for imminent arrest? Moreover, if the threat had been a hoax or 'not credible' as Cele subsequently asserted, why did it worry the South African Secret Service (SASS) enough to send agents to Kenya and Somalia to gather their own intelligence on al Shabaab?[82] This 'hoax' also prompted the NIA to conduct raids on a Somali organization in Johannesburg in November 2009.[83] Another consequence of this 'hoax' was a joint operation involving senior police officers, members of NIA and American agents. The operation resulted in the arrest of militants linked to extremists in Somalia and Mozambique and, ultimately, to al Qaeda lieutenants in Afghanistan and Pakistan.[84]

The ambiguity of the South African Government's responses sends confusing signals to the international community. In the process, South Africa loses credibility in the fight against extremism and terrorism. This ambiguity also emboldens terrorists to move to South Africa as a safe location from which to operate. In May 2013, for instance, it came to light that British-born Samantha Lewthwaite (the so-called 'White Widow'), who had strong links to both al Qaeda and al Shabaab, had spent two years in South Africa setting up a terror network that spanned the United Kingdom, South Africa and Pakistan.[85] It is also evident that such ambiguous policies produce much frustration within the country's intelligence apparatus – resulting in a high turnover of staff. In the process, the country's ability to secure its borders and protect its citizens is severely compromised.

Conclusion

South Africa confronts a very real terrorist threat. In the 1990s, the country experienced a wave of urban terrorism in the Western Cape. Since then there have been various attempts by Islamist militants to attack South African targets. In addition, South Africa continues to play host to various terrorist groups such as al Shabaab, Hamas and Hizbullah. This goes beyond the mere provision of safe houses where international terrorists can lie low: Hizbullah operates at least five paramilitary training camps. With the rise of Islamic State on the African continent, and according to the Institute for Security Studies, between 150 and 300 South Africans have been recruited into the 'caliphate', the threat has escalated.[86] Despite an excellent legal system taking a strong stance against terrorism, South Africa's counterterrorism strategy continues to be wracked by contradiction and general ambiguity.

A major reason for this ambiguity is the historical legacy of the anti-apartheid struggle, in which the ANC that now forms the South African Government was labelled terrorist. As such, Pretoria is loath to use this label to describe Islamist militants. As was mentioned earlier, when former South African Deputy Minister of Foreign Affairs Aziz Pahad met with Hizbullah, he stressed the distinction between terrorism and the struggle for liberation. If Hizbullah is indeed to be viewed as a group of liberation fighters by the South African Government, how are we to understand Hizbullah's attack on a synagogue in Argentina, its paramilitary camps in South Africa or its drug-trafficking and extortion rackets in West Africa?

From this legacy of apartheid stem the twin dangers of political correctness and a naïvely false sense of security. The latter emanates from Pretoria's 'consistently correct' foreign policy orientation, which it believes renders it immune to terrorist attack. This position is erroneous in the extreme, given the terrorist atrocities already committed on South African soil. All of this serves to undermine the effective implementation of counterterrorism legislation. While an argument could be made that since the late 1990s there has been no terrorist atrocity committed on South African soil, and that the country's seemingly ambiguous response is shielding it from such attacks, there were several attempts at terrorism in the country which were fortunately thwarted. Moreover, South Africa's ambiguous response to terrorism has resulted in it being used as an operational base to plan attacks elsewhere. This was the case of Haroon Rashid Aswat, a Briton, who exchanged a number of telephone calls with all four of London's 7 July 2005 bombers just before the London attacks, while Aswat was based in Johannesburg.[87]

The issue of South Africa as an operational base and a transit point and conduit for international terrorists to target other countries also emerged in the case of a Tunisian al Qaeda suspect, Ihsan Garnaoui, in 2004. Garnaoui was an explosives expert who trained in Afghanistan and was 'promoted' to being an al Qaeda trainer. He held several South African passports in different names (including in the names of Abram Shoman and Mallick Shoman) and travelled via South Africa to Europe, where he was accused of planning bombings on American and Jewish targets.[88] According to Ronald Sandee, most of Garnaoui's preparation for these attacks took place in South Africa, where he purchased sophisticated military-grade binoculars with an integrated digital camera, and diagrams and instructions for the assembly of detonators, as well as setting up networks in Berlin while still in South Africa.[89] It should be noted that both the international counterterrorism regime and South Africa's domestic counterterrorism legislation call upon the security services to prevent the operations of terrorism even when it is targeting a foreign country. In this sense, too, South Africa's counterterrorism regime must be assessed as a failure. To put it differently, terrorism is a global threat and to think of counterterrorism through the prism of narrow national self-interest (whether the host country is targeted), is extremely problematic. The recruitment of South African citizens into the ranks of Islamic State illustrates the connection between the global and the national very well. Whilst initially going to Raqqa, those trained also find their way back into the country, where they pose a threat to all South Africans.

In an effort to protect innocent lives from any fresh terrorist atrocity, Pretoria needs to jettison the ideological baggage of the past and understand that contemporary Islamist terrorism, with its nihilist violence and global ambitions, cannot be equated with the limited political goals of the anti-apartheid struggle. Moreover, Pretoria's political mandarins' historic antipathy towards the West for the initial support rendered to the apartheid state must also mature and understand that, given the existential nature of the threat posed by international terrorism, we all need to make common cause in the struggle against terrorist barbarism for the sake of our common humanity.

Notes

Valid URLs are included for online references wherever possible, but for some the URLs consulted are unfortunately no longer available and alternatives could not be found.

1 Hussein Solomon, 'Playing ostrich: Lessons learned from South Africa's response to terrorism,' *Africa Security Brief* 9 (January 2011): 1.
2 Hussein Solomon, *Jihad: A South African Perspective* (Bloemfontein, South Africa: Sun Media, 2013).
3 Solomon, 'Playing ostrich,' 1.
4 Angelique Serrao, 'Spy cables reveal SA's jihad camps,' *Independent Online*, 25 February 2015, available at: www.iol.co.za/news/politics/spy-cables- reveal-sas-jihad-camps-182316 (accessed 11 February 2016).
5 Anneli Botha, 'PAGAD: A case study of radical Islam in South Africa,' *Terrorism Monitor* 3:15 (2005): 10.
6 John Solomon, 'New report of terrorist camp in South Africa,' *Terrorism in Focus* 4:12 (2007): 6; De Wet Potgieter, *White Widow, Black Widow: Is al Qaeda Operating in South Africa?* (Johannesburg: Penguin, 2014).
7 US Department of State (USDS), *Country Reports on Terrorism 2014* (Washington, DC: USDS Bureau of Counterterrorism, 2015), available at: www.state.gov/documents/organization/239631.pdf (accessed 2 May 2016).
8 Author's interview with De Wet Potgieter, Bloemfontein, 10 January 2015. See also Solomon, *Jihad*.
9 UK Parliament, Select Committee on Foreign Affairs, 'Foreign Affairs – fifth report,' UK Parliament website,18 May 2004, available at: www.publications.parliament.uk/pa/cm200304/cmselect/cmfaff/117/11702.htm (accessed 3 September 2010).
10 Quoted in Privacy International, 'Terrorism profile: South Africa,' Privacy International website, 17 June 2004, available at: www.privacyinternational.org/article,shtml?%cmd%SD=x-347–66677 (accessed 19 March 2009), p. 1.
11 Martin Schonteich, 'South Africa's arsenal of terrorism legislation,' *African Security Review* 9:2 (2000): 40, available at: www.issafrica.org/pubs/ASR/9No2/Schonteich.html#Anchor-21093 (accessed 3 September 2010).
12 Solomon, *Jihad*, pp. 1–3.
13 Henri Boshoff and Martin Schonteich, 'South Africa's Operational and Legislative Responses to Terrorism,' in Jakkie Cilliers and Kathryn Sturman (eds), *Africa and Terrorism, Joining the Global Campaign*, ISS monograph 74 (Pretoria: Institute for Security Studies, 2002), pp. 18–35.
14 United Nations, 'Security Council unanimously adopts wide-ranging anti-terrorism resolution; calls for suppressing financing, improving international cooperation,' press release SC/7158, United Nations website, 28 September 2001, available at: www.un.org/News/Press/docs/2001/sc7158.doc.htm (accessed 20 August 2010).
15 UK Parliament, 'Foreign Affairs – fifth report.'
16 *Ibid.*, p. 2.
17 Quoted in Department of International Relations and Co-operation (DIRCO), *South African Intervention at the NEPAD Heads of State and Government Orientation Committee*, press statement (Kampala: DIRCO, 25 July 2010), p. 1.

18 Quoted in Paul Sperry, 'Homeland insecurity: US warns of al Qaeda from South Africa – inspectors on high alert for operatives using nation's passports,' *WorldNetDaily*, 6 August 2004, available at: www.wnd.com/?pageId=25969 (accessed 1 September 2010).

19 Quoted in Federal Research Division (FRD), Library of Congress, *Nations Hospitable to Organized Crime and Terrorism* (Washington, DC: FRD, 2003), pp. 23–4.

20 *SABC News*, 'State cuts deal with Muizenberg coup plot accused,' *SABC News*, 25 March 2008, available at: www.sabcnews.com/south_africa/crime1justice/0,2172,166418,00.html (accessed 6 May 2009).

21 *Independent Online*, 'Internet download leads to bust,' *Independent Online*, 23 March 2008, available at: www.iol.co.za/news/newsprint.php?art_id_=vn20080323115841846C64 (accessed 25 June 2008).

22 *Ibid.*

23 Legalbrief, 'Web site downloads lead to terror accusations,' Legalbrief website, 26 March 2008, available at: www.legalbrief.co.za/article.php?story=2008032608341632 (accessed 4 September 2010).

24 *Independent Online*, 'Internet download leads to bust.'

25 *Sunday Tribune*, 'Internet downloads lead to bust,' *Sunday Tribune*, 23 March 2008, p. 2.

26 Karen Breytenbach, 'Police to return "terror raid" material,' *Cape Times*, 26 March 2008, available at: www.iol.co.za/index.php?set_id=1&click_id=15&art_id=vn20080326052235418C855953 (accessed 31 August 2010).

27 Karen Breytenbach, 'Cape terror suspects fight case in court,' *Cape Times*, 25 March 2008, available at: www.iol.co.za/index.php?set_id=1&click_id=13&art_id=vn20080325054519104C525056 (accessed 31 August 2010).

28 Quoted in Breytenbach, 'Police to return "terror raid" material.'

29 Deon de Lange, 'Cape Terror suspects fight case in court,' *Beeld*, 28 July 2010, available at: www.iol.co.za/index.php?set_id=1&click_id=13&art_id=vn20080325054519104C525056 (accessed 31 August 2010).

30 Graeme Hosken, 'SA targeted by terrorists – police,' *Pretoria News*, 4 August 2004, available at: www.iol.co.za/index.php?sf=174&set_id=1&click_id=13&art_id=vn20040804052518353C413655 (accessed 3 September 2010).

31 Jawad Naeem and Graeme Hosken, 'Did SA pair confess to Pakistani officials?' *Star*, 4 August 2008 available at: www.iol.co.za/index.php?sf=174&set_id=1&click_id=3&art_id=vn20040804141036483C796053 (accessed 31 August 2010); Tisha Steyn, 'SA men "trained terrorists,"' News24 website, 26 July 2004, available at: www.news24.com/SouthAfrica/News/SA-men-trained-terrorists-20040726 (accessed 31 August 2010).

32 News24, 'Al Qaeda suspect co-operating,' News24 website, 29 July 2004, available at: www.news24.com/World/News/Al-Qaeda-suspect-co-operating-20040729 (accessed 31 August 2010).

33 Naeem and Hosken, 'Did SA pair confess.'

34 *Ibid.*

35 Steyn, 'SA men "trained terrorists."'

36 Andrew Meldrum, 'Terror link to South Africa after gun battle,' *Guardian*, 6 August 2004, available at: www.guardian.co.uk/world/2004/aug/06/pakistan.terrorism (accessed 4 September 2010).

37 Naeem and Hosken, 'Did SA pair confess.'

38 News24, 'SA men's fate unknown,' News24 website, 29 July 2004, available at: www.news24.com/World/News/SA-mens-fate-unknown-20040729 (accessed 4 September 2010).

39 Quoted in Deon de Lange, 'New twist in Al Qaeda arrests,' News24 website, 30 July 2004, available at: www.news24.com/SouthAfrica/News/New-twist-in-al-Qaeda-arrests-20040730 (accessed 4 September 2010).

40 Adriaan Basson, 'SA 2: Pakistan must decide,' News24 website, 23 August 2004, available at: www.news24.com/SouthAfrica/News/SA-2-Pakistan-must-decide-20040823 (accessed 4 September 2010); see also News24, 'NIA clear SA men in Pakistan,' News24 website, 21 August 2004, available at: www.news24.com/SouthAfrica/News/NIA-clears-SA-men-in-Pakistan-20040821 (accessed 4 September 2010).

41 Michael Schmidt, Kashiefa Akim and Noor Jehan Yoro Badat, 'SA pair accused of terrorism fly home,' *Star*, 18 December 2004, p. 1.

42 Hosken, 'SA targeted by terrorists.'

43 Jawad Naeem and Graeme Hosken, 'The hunt is on for al Qaeda recruiter,' *Cape Argus*, 4 August 2004.

44 Hosken, 'SA targeted by terrorists.'

45 Quoted in Moshoeshoe Monare, Graeme Hosken and SAPA, 'Government insists SA is not under threat,' *Mercury*, 5 August 2008, available at: www.iol.co.za/index.php?sf=116&set_id=1&click_id=13&art_id=vn20040805051704165C941309 (accessed 4 September 2010).

46 Ronald Sandee, 'Target South Africa,' presentation to US Congress, 26 May 2010, p. 4 (personal communication; text of presentation e-mailed to author 11 June 2011).

47 Naeem and Hosken, 'Hunt is on.'

48 Sandee, *Target South Africa*, p. 5.

49 *Ibid.*

50 News24, 'SA, Egypt in talks over doctor,' News24 website, 26 January 2009, available at: www.news24.com/NEWS24v2/components/Generic/News24v2_print_PopUp (accessed 26 January 2009).

51 *Independent Online*, 'Jews take minister to court,' *Independent Online*, 14 June 2009, available at: www.iol.co.za/general/news/newsprint.php?art_id-nw2009012814380093-C66 (accessed 15 June 2009).

52 Quoted, *ibid.*

53 Josh Lefkowitz, 'Terror's South African front,' In the National Interest website, 17 August 2005, available at: www.inthenationalinterest.com/Articles/Vol3Issue33/Vol3Issue33Lefkowitz.html (accessed 19 March 2008).

54 Quoted, *ibid.*, p. 3.

55 *Ibid.*

56 Quoted in J. Schanzer, 'Pretoria unguarded,' *Weekly Standard*, 12:35 (2007): 4, available at: www.weeklystandard.com/Content/Public/Articles/000/000/013/6771khfy.asp?pg=1 (accessed 20 March 2008).

57 Lefkowitz, 'Terror's South African front.'

58 Schanzer, 'Pretoria unguarded.'

59 *Ibid.*, p. 3.

60 Quoted in K. Shillinger, 'Al Qaeda in southern Africa,' *Armed Forces Journal*, 1 February 2006, available at: www.afji.com/2006/02/1813653 (accessed 8 June 2018).

61 Truth and Reconciliation Commission, 'Holding the ANC accountable,' in *The TRC Report*, vol. 6, sect. 5, ch. 3 (Cape Town: Government Communication and Information Services, Government of the Republic of South Africa, 2003), p. 649, available at: www.info.gov.za/otherdocs/2003/trc/5_3.pdf (accessed 5 May 2008).

62 Hussein Solomon, *Pakistan and the Legacy of Maulana Maududi*, occasional paper no. 9/2009 (London: International Institute for Islamic Studies, 2009), p. 2.

63 Botha, 'PAGAD,' 11.

64 News24, 'SA "a growing terrorist hideout,"' News24 website, 6 September 2005, available at: www.news24.com/SouthAfrica/News/SA-a-growing-terrorist-hideout-20050905 (accessed 20 March 2008).

65 Quoted in UK Parliament, 'Foreign Affairs – fifth report.'

66 South African Department of Foreign Affairs, 'Initiatives in the fight against global terrorism,' Department of Foreign Affairs website, 22 September 2003, available at: www.dfa.gov.za/doc/2003/ungao922.htm (accessed 24 June 2010).

67 Werner Swart, 'Terror Alert,' *Sunday Times*, 27 December 2009, p. 1.

68 Marc Sageman, *Understanding Terror Networks* (Philadelphia, PA: University of Pennsylvania Press, 2004).

69 Eric Rosand, 'The UN-led multilateral response to jihadist terrorism: Is a global counter-terrorism body needed?' *Journal of Conflict and Security Law* 11:3 (2007): 402.

70 Jan Schellenbach, 'Appeasing nihilists? Some economic thoughts on reducing terrorist activity,' *Public Choice* 129 (2006): 304.

71 Quoted in Solomon, 'Playing ostrich,' p. 4.

72 Solomon, *Jihad*, p. 85.

73 Sandee, *Target South Africa*, p. 2.

74 Botha, 'PAGAD,' 10.

75 Walid Phares, *The War of Ideas: Jihadism Against Democracy* (London: Palgrave Macmillan, 2007).

76 Andrew Holt, 'South Africa in the war on terror,' *Terrorism Monitor* 2:23 (2004): 1, available at: www.jamestown.org/terrorism/views/article_php?articleid=2368948&print this=1 (accessed 19 March 2008).

77 Hussein Solomon, *South Africa's Ambiguous Response to Terrorism*, CiPS e-briefing paper no. 55/2008 (Pretoria: Centre for International Political Studies, University of Pretoria, 2008), p. 2.

78 *Ibid.*

79 Schanzer, 'Pretoria unguarded,' p. 1; *Independent Online*, 'More SA names placed on terror list – Pahad,' *Independent Online*, 31 January 2007, available at: www.iol.co.za/index.php?set_id=1&click_id=13&art_id=qw1170276483482B236 (accessed 20 March 2008); M. Terdman, *Al Qaeda Inroads in Southern Africa*, Project for the Research of Islamist Movements (PRISM), *African Occasional Papers* 2:1 (2008): 3, available at: www.e-prism.org/images/PRISM_African_Papers_vol_2_no_1_Southern_Africa_March_08.pdf (accessed 25 March 2008).

80 Think Tank for the Research on Islam and Muslims in Africa (RIMA), 'Numbers and percentage of Muslims in African countries,', RIMA website, 2013, available at: https://muslimsinafrica.wordpress.com/numbers-and-percentage-of-muslims-in-africa (accessed 2 May 2016).

81 Peter Fabricius, Shaun Smillie, Gillian Gifford and Reuters, 'US still on terror threat alert in SA as buildings close,' *Pretoria News*, 23 September 2009, p. 1.

82 Adriaan Basson, 'Sizing up 2010 terror threat,' *Mail and Guardian*, 26:2 (2010): 6.

83 *Voice of the Cape*, 'Mixed responses to Somali militancy claim,' *Voice of the Cape*, 4 November 2009, available at: www.vocfm.co.za/index.php?section =newsandcategory=vocnews&article=49552 (accessed 5 November 2009).

84 Asian News International (ANI), 'Al Qaeda plot to attack 2010 football World Cup foiled in South Africa,' *Newstrack India*, 14 October 2009, available at: www.newstrackindia.com/newsdetails/128098 (accessed 28 October 2009).

85 Solomon, *Jihad*, p. 82.

86 Nivashni Nair, 'Driver's licence links "Islamic State fighter" to SA,' *Sunday Times*, 23 November 2015, available at: www.timeslive.co.za/thetimes/ 2015/11/23/Drivers-licence-links-Islamic-State-fighter-to-SA (accessed 11 February 2016).

87 Solomon, *Jihad*, pp. 38–9.

88 *USA Today*, 'Terrorists obtained South African passports,' *USA Today*, 24 July 2004, available at: www.usatoday.com/news/world/2004–07–27-sout h-africa-terrorists_x.htm (accessed 1 May 2016).

89 Sandee, *Target South Africa*, p. 6.

Conclusion

Michael J. Boyle

Rethinking terrorism and counterterrorism

As the case studies in this volume have illustrated, there is no single 'non-Western' approach to terrorism. What emerges from the case studies is quite the opposite: a wide diversity of conceptualizations of the threat that are not always wholly in sync with the depictions of the threat favoured by the United States and its allies. To be certain, there are points of agreement. All Western and non-Western countries agree that terrorism is a formidable challenge to the authority of the state and that it necessitates a serious response from the intelligence services and law enforcement. No state is in denial about the reality of terrorist violence; the vast majority of states concede that some kind of global collective action is needed to deal with the threat posed by groups like al Qaeda and the Islamic State. But the subtle differences in the way that each state has framed or described terrorism have clear implications for the policy responses that follow. For example, states that have framed terrorism as criminal activity tend not to accept calls for sweeping internal reform (such as improving good governance or rooting out corruption). They also tend to reject the typically American depiction of terrorism as an ideological struggle, casting counterterrorism instead as an incremental set of legal and intelligence steps rather than a comprehensive effort. By contrast, states that see terrorism as a mortal threat to the state's authority tend to favour aggressive military measures and to embrace sweeping legislation to address the threat. Finally, whether terrorism is seen as a unique threat or one of a related set of evils (for example, connected to separatism or nationalism) suggests quite a bit about whether the government will insist on handling the matter internally or seek out venues for international cooperation.

The different interpretations of 'terrorism' yielded by the case studies in this volume suggest that terrorism is a contested concept, though not necessarily an essentially contested one. These case studies do not suggest, as some scholars working within the critical terrorism studies (CTS) tradition argue, that actions labelled as 'terrorism' bear little in common and are grouped together for little more than political advantage.[1] Stronger constructivist versions of this argument within CTS suggest that what is considered terrorism is decided by a discursive struggle populated by actors (often governments) which have politically motivated reasons to deploy terms like 'terrorism' to describe their enemies and to mobilize state power against them.[2] At the root of this claim is an implication that the core concept of terrorism is so empty that it can be populated by virtually anything, provided that the offending action constitutes some sort of threat to the authority of the state. The findings of this volume do not go that far. The case studies certainly acknowledge that there is a clear discursive element to terrorism. For example, Oscar Palma's analysis of how the term 'narcoterrorism' was created and sustained in Colombia in order to mobilize domestic constituencies and stakeholders in the American government suggests that the labelling process for terrorism is crucially important. Other case studies on Brazil, Algeria, Lebanon, Iran, Egypt and South Africa in this book suggest either that the term 'terrorism' has been mobilized by the state for politically convenient reasons or that, conversely, it can sometimes be avoided based on the preferences of those in power. In this sense, this volume upholds a number of scholars' observation that there is an irreducibly subjective element to determining what does and does not count as terrorism.[3]

At the same time, the case studies here do not suggest that all things are discourse. Where this book parts company with CTS scholars is in the position that there is no fundamental core to the idea of terrorism and that it is 'essentially' contested. The case studies affirm that there is an essence to the concept of terrorism that travels across different cultural and political contexts. The underlying idea behind terrorism – that politically motivated and indiscriminate attacks against targets may be used to project fear on a wider population beyond the initial set of victims – is at the core of almost all Western and non-Western conceptions of terrorism.[4] There is a basic underlying agreement that terrorism is a unique subset of the broader category of political violence, marked by its indiscriminate nature and its broad communicative intent, even if there are disagreements on how it should be interpreted, described and responded to. In other words, this book confirms that terrorism is a contested concept, but it does not affirm the stronger claim that it is 'essentially' contested.

When that contestation occurs, it is clear from the studies in this volume that the process is deeply contextual and reflects in different combinations the dominant historical, political, cultural and religious factors present in that society. As the Introduction notes, these factors will be present in different proportion in each case, yet one or some combination of them will produce the dominant frame or interpretation for the threat of terrorism that will determine the government's response. For some countries, like Egypt and

Algeria, the history of violence within the state – specifically, the struggles for decolonization and the attending social fissures that came about afterwards – looms large and determines much about who is, and is not, considered a terrorist. For others, like Saudi Arabia, religion provides the overarching frame for understanding terrorism as a form of aberrant behaviour that produces disharmony and must be reconciled and rehabilitated, rather than defeated as Western discourse often suggests. For countries like Lebanon, contemporary politics – specifically, the state's long experience of terrorism and the role Hizbullah plays as power broker – plays a greater role in shaping its perspective on terrorism than does its historical experience of decolonization or diverse religious traditions. Finally, for countries like China and Japan, culture governs the interpretation of terrorist violence in a far more powerful way than the politics or history of the state. In each of these cases, one or more factors mattered more than the others in shaping the country's perspective on terrorism and the suitable responses.

What is clear is that the frame for terrorism and the responses to it are internally contested between stakeholders of different kinds, including governments, religious authorities, non-state actors and others. Yet this contestation is also not always symmetric. One of the key themes emerging from the case studies is that the negotiation over how to understand and interpret terrorism from within a society is not conducted by players with equal standing. As is the case with many Western states, the governments of non-Western states generally exert a stronger influence on who is called a 'terrorist' than other stakeholders in the society. Governments are always in a privileged position and can use their power to position their enemies as terrorists and therefore beyond the pale. This fact is particularly important here because many non-Western governments are dealing with an array of legitimate and illegitimate challengers to the state, such as secessionist groups, national minorities, insurgents, criminals and others, many of whom can be labelled instrumentally as terrorists. In each non-Western state, the way that the term 'terrorist' is applied in the bargaining process between the central government and its potential challengers on the periphery varies. Some states, like Pakistan, are selective in the way that they label some groups as enemies, but not do so for others that are useful to intelligence agencies like the Inter-Services Intelligence (ISI).[5] Others like India and Indonesia adopt counterinsurgency tactics to destroy a wide array of groups called 'terrorists' and to boost the power of the central government. The process of contestation – over who is a terrorist and who is not, and what consequences flow from that – is not a neutral one, but instead tends to tip the balance of power towards the government in decisive ways.

Given that terrorism is such a bitterly contested concept, it is hardly surprising that the responses to terrorism across Western and non-Western cases vary so widely. What is important to note from the case studies here is that the 'response' to terrorism in many non-Western states may be much broader than counterterrorism alone, especially if counterterrorism is narrowly defined as a securitized response to the threat.[6] Especially in the United States, counterterrorism is heavily securitized and cast in negative terms as any measure designed to prevent or disrupt acts of terrorism. Because it is so broadly defined, policymakers are often able to stretch counterterrorism as a concept to include anything that might, even potentially, stop a terrorist attack.[7] More generally, in the US the conceptualization of counterterrorism is negatively framed, with success being measured on the basis of the number of attacks prevented or otherwise disrupted. This negative goal – stopping terrorist attacks at whatever cost – is so ingrained that much of the counterterrorism literature argues that the only choice that governments face is between selecting a military or law-enforcement approach to this end.[8] Yet, as Martha Crenshaw has pointed out, few pay attention to the possible positive social benefits of counterterrorism, such as addressing long-standing ethnic or cultural grievances or providing new mechanisms for political inclusion for previously marginalized communities.[9] By contrast, many non-Western states conceive counterterrorism more broadly and positively than this. For example, as Ekaterina Stepanova argues, the Russian approach draws a distinction between anti-terrorism – generally, law-enforcement and intelligence services' responses to the terrorist threat – and counterterrorism, which involves a wide array of political, economic and social activities designed to end discontent among the marginalized. For Saudi Arabia, counterterrorism is partially about addressing aberrant interpretations of Islam and bringing what are considered wayward sons back into the fold.

These cases also affirm that counterterrorism is not a hermetically sealed concept. There is a leakage into it from other security approaches, such as counterinsurgency, which influence how it will be conducted and discussed. For example, many states – like India and Indonesia – adopt a blurring of counterinsurgency and counterterrorism and emphasize aggressive responses to violent challengers of all stripes for fear of encouraging secession and weakening the central government. Although there are important conceptual and practical differences between counterterrorism and counterinsurgency, these are essentially swept aside in cases where the violent challenges to the state are diffuse and overlapping.[10] For many states in the Middle East and Africa, such as Lebanon, Egypt and Nigeria, counterterrorism activities are also embedded in a wider set of negotiations with violent stakeholders over autonomy and their portion of power in central government. In cases like Iran and Nigeria, counterterrorism also overlaps with repression, particularly of ethnic minorities and dissidents, in ways that maximize state power. All of these cases suggest that considering counterterrorism in isolation, as a bounded and heavily securitized concept distinct from these other purposes, would be a serious mistake.

Findings

While there is no single non-Western response to terrorism and no single finding that applies to all cases, there are five major findings that emerge from a comparative analysis of the eighteen cases presented here. The first and most obvious is that most non-Western states conceptualize terrorism along a continuum with other non-violent threats to the authority of the state, including especially secession. In this way, they do not treat terrorism as a *sui generis* category or an exceptional threat, but rather as one of an array of ills that may afflict internal harmony within the state. For example, China depicts terrorism as one of the 'three evils', alongside separatism and religious extremism, that must be combated both at home and throughout Central Asia. This portrayal of the threat enables China to link any form of separatism in Xinjiang province as functionally equivalent to violence against the state. Along the same lines, Saudi Arabia's de-radicalization efforts have linked an inclination to terrorism with deviation from established religious practices and succumbing to unhealthy or distorted passions in one's personal life. Like China's cultural and political depiction of terrorism, this religious framing of the threat of terrorism enhances the legitimacy of the religious authorities and the state by positioning the rejection of terrorism as consistent with political and religious duties of good Muslims. In some rare cases, the cultural shadings of a country's understanding terrorism are designed to de-escalate the threat and allow the state greater leeway in responding in a nuanced way. For example, Japan's framing of terrorism emphasizes the criminal nature of the act and adopts a reactive, informal and communal response to dealing with it that minimizes the disruption to the harmony of its society.

Second, some non-Western governments import wholesale American or European definitions of terrorism and legal frameworks, but find that they cannot be easily applied to their own circumstances. In the post-9/11 era, African governments like Kenya, Nigeria and Uganda adopted the American definition of terrorism and constructed domestic legislation outlawing terrorism on that basis in order to secure generous American counterterrorism aid. But that was hardly the end of the story. Although it was deeply influenced by the American approach to terrorism and sought to emulate some of its laws, Nigeria struggled for years with various insurgencies by militant groups such as Boko Haram and failed to produce coherent counterterrorism legislation or policies that could deal with the complexity of the threat that it faced. Similarly, Kenya adhered closely to American conceptions of the threat, but found itself taking steps that deepened the tensions between the government and its minority communities. By contrast, Uganda adopted the American counterterrorism definition and approach but the Government of Yoweri Museveni ruthlessly exploited American sympathy and support to achieve greater standing in the competition for power in East Africa. For countries playing catch-up in developing counterterrorism legislation and practice, adopting the US approach is far from being a panacea.

Third, the politics of defining terrorism and regulating it in law is deeply influenced by the colonial legacy that the non-Western state has. Issues surrounding responding to terrorism are generally more polarizing in postcolonial states that have a strong legacy of opposing European imperialism. In Algeria, for example, the state itself was stained with violence throughout its colonial and postcolonial period, and interpretations of who was and was not a terrorist were filtered through this distorted political lens. In other cases, terrorism is the problem that does not speak its name. In Brazil, for example, the government was caught between the desire to criminalize terrorist activity and the political elite's unwillingness to admit that the country was itself a target for terrorist activity. The result of this denial of reality was that Brazil lagged in producing effective domestic legislation outlawing material support for terrorist activity. Similarly, the security services of South Africa were reluctant to admit that the country could be targeted by Islamic extremist forces because the African National Congress (ANC) had long adopted 'correct' positions on key issues like the Middle East peace process that they believed would insulate the country from the hatred of groups like al Qaeda and the Islamic State. The fact that some senior members of the ANC were once described as terrorists and a residual suspicion of Western motives from the apartheid era produced bureaucratic confusion and weak public messaging on the reality of the terrorist threat that South Africa faces. In a few cases, the infrastructure that non-Western countries operate with is drawn from a colonial legacy but successfully adapted to address contemporary counterterrorism threats. For example, Malaysia has drawn on decades of experience from the Malaysian emergency to produce legislation and police practice that enable a preventive approach to terrorism that has stopped a number of attacks. Similarly, Indonesia's security approach is 'postcolonial' in orientation, with its approach determined jointly by the legacy of state violence from Suharto and the Indonesian state's long-running efforts to quash local insurgencies.

Fourth, some non-Western governments have struggled to deal with terrorism because of a particularly diffuse security and intelligence establishment with multiple agencies clashing with each other for resources and influence in the counterterrorism policy space. This is hardly unusual or unique to non-Western states. But the degree of ethnic, religious and cultural antagonisms permeating the bureaucracies of many non-Western states can make developing a single counterterrorism policy particularly difficult. For example, as Rashmi Singh argues, India's counterterrorism infrastructure can be described as 'myopic and underdeveloped' because its activities are filtered through a political, ethnic, caste and sectarian lens. Similarly, Pakistan has lacked a cohesive narrative on terrorism because it faces such a diffuse range of threats from Kashmir, the Federally Administered Tribal Area (FATA) and other regions, but also because it has so many contending bureaucratic actors aligned to different political factions involved in shaping its counterterrorism response. Dealing with these diffuse security and intelligence establishments is particularly difficult in cases where the government is engaged in violent bargaining with non-state actors inside and outside its borders. In Egypt, the understanding of terrorism is negotiated by actors inside and outside the government, including key civil society actors (such as the Muslim Brotherhood) and external states like the United States. In Lebanon, terrorism has been recast or redefined to include or exclude actors opposed to the government. In all these cases, what counts as terrorism is negotiated politically between warring bureaucratic and political players that reflect the internal antagonisms within the society itself.

Fifth, for many non-Western states, the concept of terrorism is intricately tied to separatism and state violence. The degree to which a state faces a sustained insurgency from separatist or Islamic extremist forces often decisively shapes its worldview on terrorism. For example, Russia's perspective on terrorism is shaped by its battles with Islamic and ethnic separatists across the Caucuses. By contrast, Colombia's conception of terrorism has been deeply influenced by its battles against the FARC (Revolutionary Armed Forces of Colombia) guerrilla groups, as the spread of the term 'narcoterrorism' to describe its security problems shows. For both Algeria and Iran, the meaning of terrorism is connected to violence inflicted by the state. As George Joffé indicates, Algeria has a long history of violent extremism, as revolutionary and Islamist actors are caught in a mutual dialectic of violence with the state itself. By contrast, the Iranian Government exploits fears of terrorism from outside actors (like the United States), while employing state terror against its own citizens to suppress dissent.

Conclusion

In a world in which counterterrorism is globalized, international cooperation to confront diffuse and lethal terrorist threats has become more important than ever. In the future, it is likely that governments in this globalized environment will face hard bargaining over controversial issues like intelligence sharing and extradition. For those agreements to be viable and stable over the long run, this means that non-Western governments will need agreements which satisfy external stakeholders and domestic constituencies as well.[11] To make this happen, this book suggests that policymakers should do their best to understand the problem of terrorism as seen from 'inside' a community, rather than just simply assuming that American or European definitions of the threat are universal. But that is not all. It means paying attention to the stakeholders contesting the meaning of terrorism inside the society and understanding how the dynamics of negotiation among the government, non-state actors and key societal players for power and resources shapes the overall responses to terrorism in that case. It means shedding a narrow conception of counterterrorism and understanding that the 'responses' to terrorism may be framed in broader, more positive ways than merely prevention and disruption. Understanding how the non-Western world conceives terrorism, and offers a response to the threat that goes beyond the standard military and law-enforcement approaches, is a crucial first step towards achieving durable global counterterrorism cooperation in the future.

Notes

1 See particularly Richard Jackson, Marie Breen Smyth and Jeroen Gunning, *Critical Terrorism Studies: A New Research Agenda* (London: Routledge, 2009). For a critique, see John Horgan and Michael J. Boyle, 'A case against critical terrorism studies,' *Critical Studies on Terrorism* 1:1 (2008): 51–64.

2 Rainer Hülsse and Alexander Spencer, 'The metaphor of terror: Terrorism studies and the constructivist turn,' *Security Dialogue* 39:6 (2008): 571–92.

3 See particularly Bruce Hoffman, *Inside Terrorism* (New York: Columbia University Press, 2006); Louise Richardson, *What Terrorists Want* (London: John Wiley, 2007).

4 See particularly the review of definitions in Alex P. Schmid, *The Routledge Handbook of Terrorism Research* (London: Routledge, 2013).

5 See particularly Carlotta Gall, *The Wrong Enemy: America in Afghanistan 2001–2014* (New York: Houghton Mifflin Harcourt, 2014).

6 The literature on securitization is vast. See particularly Barry Buzan, Ole Waever and Jaap de Wilde, *Security: A New Framework for Analysis* (Boulder, CO: Lynne Reinner, 1998).

7 See particularly Giovanni Sartori, 'Concept misinformation in comparative politics,' *American Political Science Review* 64:4 (1970): 1033–53.

8 On counterterrorism, see Brigitte Nacos, *Terrorism and Counterterrorism* (London: Routledge, 2016); Laura K. Donohue, *The Cost of Counterterrorism: Power, Politics and Liberty* (Cambridge, UK: Cambridge University Press, 2008).

9 Martha Crenshaw, *The Consequences of Counterterrorism* (New York: Russell Sage, 2010), p. 6.

10 See particularly Michael J. Boyle, 'Do counterterrorism and counterinsurgency go together?' *International Affairs* 86:2 (2010): 333–53.

11 Michael J. Boyle, 'The war on terror in American grand strategy,' *International Affairs* 84:2 (2008): 191–209.